RUSSIAN PEASANTS AND SOVIET POWER

BY THE SAME AUTHOR

Le dernier combat de Lénine,
Paris, Les Editions de Minuit, 1967

The Great Debate: Russia in the twenties,
Englewood Cliffs, Prentice-Hall

RUSSIAN PEASANTS AND SOVIET POWER

A STUDY OF COLLECTIVIZATION

by M. Lewin
Senior Fellow, Russian Institute, Columbia University

TRANSLATED BY IRENE NOVE
WITH THE ASSISTANCE OF JOHN BIGGART

WITH A PREFACE BY
PROFESSOR ALEC NOVE

W · W · NORTON & COMPANY
New York · London

W. W. Norton & Company, Inc., 500 Fifth Avenue, New York, N.Y. 10110
W. W. Norton & Company Ltd., 37 Great Russell Street, London WC1B 3NU

TRANSLATION COPYRIGHT © 1968 BY GEORGE ALLEN & UNWIN LTD.

First published in the Norton Library 1975
by arrangement with Northwestern University Press

The French original
La Paysannerie et le Pouvoir Sovietique
first published in 1966 by Mouton

Books That Live
The Norton imprint on a book means that in the publisher's
estimation it is a book not for a single season but for the years.
W. W. Norton & Company, Inc.

Library of Congress Cataloging in Publication Data
Lewin, Moshe.
    Russian peasants and Soviet power.
    (The Norton Library)
    Translation of La paysannerie et la pouvoir sovietique, 1928-1930.
    Reprint of the ed. published by Northwestern University Press, Evanston, Ill.
    Includes bibliographical references.
    1. Agriculture and state—Russia. 2. Collective farms—Russia. I. Title.
HD1992.L413 1975   338.1'847   74-23401

ISBN 0-393-00752-9

Printed in the United States of America
4 5 6 7 8 9 0

PREFACE
by Alec Nove

Dr Lewin's book deals with a key period of Soviet history, with the events which led up to the decision to convert the peasants into collective farmers. This was the essential part of the 'revolution from above' which transformed the entire political, social and economic scene. In a sense it was more revolutionary than the Bolshevik revolution itself. In 1917 Lenin achieved power, landlords and capitalists were in due course expropriated, but for three quarters of the Russian people life went on in the old way. Indeed the traditional peasant communities were strengthened by the land seizures of the revolution, which affected not only landlords' land but also that of many of the better-off peasants. Could agriculture develop if it were based on smallholders? Could Soviet power survive if most villages, in which lived the majority of the citizens, were run by peasant communal institutions? How could all this be reconciled with the needs of economic development, of industrialization, of creating the material basis for military strength, under conditions of international isolation? Was there a grave political danger in the emergence of a commercially minded peasantry, producing for the market, employing their poorer neighbours and leasing their land?

These questions were indissolubly linked with factional struggles, and the men who argued about them were engaged in political battle. It is not particularly useful for us to debate the relative importance of political and economic factors in the process which led up to the events which are the subject of this book. This was 'political economy' *par excellence*, and both the objective issues and the struggle for power were realities, which interpenetrated each other.

Dr Lewin shows a rare depth of understanding of the complexities and contradictory nature of the problems of the twenties. We can learn from him how and why Stalin was led to consider the drastic solution which he finally decided to adopt, and that his decision was not due merely to arbitrary whim or vaulting ambition. But neither was it predestined, or inevitable. There were errors, illusions, incorrect price policies, the remnants of civil-war psychology among party officials, and the escalating logic of coercion once, apparently for emergency reasons, coercion was used. Dr Lewin devotes much space, very properly, to setting out the arguments of the principal opponent of Stalin's peasant policies, Bukharin, and he shows how Stalin paralysed his opponent by ingenious and ruthless political manoeuvering. Many of Stalin's own faction were opposed to some

7

of his extreme measures, such as mass deportations of so-called *kulaks* (i.e. better-off peasants), and they tried, in vain, to moderate his excesses. Stalin had to conceal his intentions, until the last minute, even from the bulk of the Party, which was why it was so ill-prepared for the task. Stalin had also to conceal what actually occurred, and in his lifetime official histories presented a basically false story. Dr Lewin has utilized many contemporary documents, and also some very useful publications which appeared in Russia in recent years. The result is that he has been able to present to us a real history of this vital period, a task which is still only very partially accomplished in the Soviet Union even today. The grim experience of collectivization cast a shadow over the Soviet villages and Soviet agriculture, as well as over the life of the entire country, which is still affecting the realities of life, and it is doubtless for this reason that Soviet historians are inhibited from a full and frank discussion of the events and problems which their country faced in those dramatic years.

If you want to know what really happened, and why, read Lewin.

CONTENTS

PREFACE   *page* 7

AUTHOR'S FOREWORD   11

INTRODUCTION   19

PART I   THE RÉGIME AND THE PEASANTRY AT THE CLOSE OF THE NEP PERIOD

1 *Features of Peasant Society*   21

2 *The Problem of Class Stratification Within the Peasantry* 41

3 *The Problem of Class Stratification Within the Peasantry (contd.)* 65

4 *The Establishment of the Soviet Régime in the Countryside* 81

5 *The Establishment of the Soviet Régime in the Countryside (contd.)* 107

6 *The Party and the 'Accursed' Problem*   132

7 *The Régime in Search of a Policy (1925–7)*   172

8 *The Ambiguous Nature of the Fifteenth Party Congress*   198

PART II   A TWO YEARS' INTERLUDE, 1928–9

9   *The Procurements Crisis of 1928*   214

10 *Stalin Changes Course*   250

11 *A Year of Drift—1928*   267

12 *The Last Opposition*   294

13 *The Five-Year Plan: Stalin Looks Ahead*   344

14 *The Crisis Continues*   383

15 *The Peasants Face an Unknown Future*   406

PART III   'THE GREAT TURN'

16 *The Signal for the Attack*   446

17 *Dekulakization*   482

Conclusion   514

Bibliography   521

Glossary   529

Index   535

In the work which follows, our purpose has been the study of the years 1928 and 1929, a particularly significant period in Soviet history which gave rise to the spectacular turn in Soviet policy often referred to as the 'second revolution'. A tremendous forward thrust in industrialization, coupled with mass collectivization of the peasantry—in itself an event without historical precedent—were the two principal factors which contributed to a radical change in structures, out of which there grew, in turn, the political and social régime of the USSR as we know it today. Despite its great importance, relatively little research has so far been conducted in this period. In the West, a number of valuable contributions have been made on the subject of industrialization, and the first Five-year Plan in particular, but no serious analysis of collectivization has yet been undertaken. What took place in those years was a revolutionary upheaval in the structures of a peasant society of some 25 million households, decided upon and carried through by the will of the government, an exploit such as no régime had ever before dreamed of attempting, and yet it is true to say that, to this day, it is still one of those events, or historical processes, about which much is said, but relatively little is known.

During the period from 1958 to 1965, and notably during the sixties, Soviet historians frankly admitted that they knew little about the 'great turn', and this realization on their part has afforded us a series of studies, based on material taken from the archives. Unfortunately, at the time at which we write, it would seem that this promising revival of interest among Soviet scholars in post-revolutionary history, and especially in recent agrarian history, has been discouraged for reasons connected with internal policy. We can only hope that this setback will prove to be temporary.

The present work comprises the first part of a longer project, which is intended to embrace a study of the social history of the USSR up to the year 1934, this being, in our view, one of the major formative periods in the evolution of Soviet society. What we propose to examine in the present context is the interlude between the 'grain crisis' of the winter of 1927–8, which heralded the general crisis in NEP, and the onset of intensive collectivization in the ruthless and wholesale form which it assumed during the winter of 1929–30. During this critical phase, the Party leadership, with Stalin at its head, had at all costs to find a new policy which would rescue the country from the impasse which it had reached. It was this desperate and dramatic search for a solution which was ultimately to lead

11

Stalin, once he had disarmed his Bukharinist rivals, to the 'personality cult'.

For a better understanding of the crisis in NEP, which gave rise to the shift in policy, we have thought it advisable to retrace our steps to the years 1925–7, particularly in order to study peasant society prior to collectivization in adequate perspective. This period is discussed in the first and introductory section of the book.

After having shown the manuscript to a number of friends and colleagues, I became aware that the readers' attention had been particularly drawn to the controversy between the Stalinists and the Bukharinists, although this comprises but one chapter of the book. Some of those who read my work while it was in preparation even went so far as to argue that I must have 'Bukharinist' sympathies. I am therefore prompted to add a few observations on this particular aspect of the subject.

I both understand and share the interest aroused by the struggle with the Right, and have my own views on the parts played by the protagonists. Nor have I made any secret of my personal prejudices or preferences, which are fairly evident from various comments I have made, and also, in some instances, from the general tone of the writing itself. However, I trust that the part played by my personal views has gone no further than this; essentially, my main concern has been to fulfil what, in my view, is the primary purpose of any work of historical research. I have endeavoured to grasp the broad general movement of the historical process in question, and to trace stage by stage the development of the social crisis which imposed a particular course of action on the individuals concerned. In order to reach a clearer understanding of the conflicting tendencies which divided the Party, I have first analysed the major contradictions inherent in the system, particularly the complexities of the relationship between the Soviet régime and the peasants. Once the essential facts of the situation have been safely isolated in this way, it is then possible to proceed to an assessment of the personalities and programmes involved in this confrontation without there being any danger that the picture will be distorted by undue reference to the personal prejudices of the author.

On the basis of the material here presented, some of my readers have reached the conclusion (which I do not share) that the solution envisaged and adopted by Stalin was, in fact, the only solution possible. I found this reaction very reassuring, for I had indeed been at pains not to lose sight of the fact that, in this work, we are dealing with the Stalin of 1928, who was still tentatively formulating his policy, and had no notion where it was to lead him.

On the other hand, although I may have shown Bukharin in a

somewhat sympathetic light, no attempt has been made to conceal his shortcomings, his lack of character and his weakness as a politician, a hysterical streak in his psychological make-up, and a number of other defects. Taken as a whole, this could scarcely be described as an idealized portrait of the man. The fact remains that the body of ideas which he advanced in the course of the struggle with Stalin, and which he defended vigorously but, in the final analysis, without greatness, is worthy both of attention and respect.

It is important, in the first place, to underline the difference between Bukharin's views at the time of NEP, when as principal spokesman for the majority he joined with Stalin in waging war on the Left, and the views which he later put forward at the time of his own struggle against Stalin during 1928-9. In the dialogues of the twenties, it was Preobrazhensky, the Left-wing's economic spokesman, who advanced the more accurate and the more reasoned long-term theories; in several important respects, the theories of Bukharin were only valid in the short-term. He allowed himself to be over-influenced by the success of the measures which the government had taken to overcome the 'scissors crisis' of 1923-4. This he used as an argument against Preobrazhensky's theories as a whole. Bukharin's opinions provided theoretical backing for the new measures introduced in 1925, which apparently gave NEP a further lease of life for another three years, but one need only reflect on the congratulations which Bukharin and Stalin bestowed on each other so wholeheartedly towards the end of 1927, when a grave crisis was already building up, to realize that the views held by the majority leaders at the time were not entirely free from illusion, while those expressed by Preobrazhensky occasionally had their share of prophetic truth. We have described the controversies of those years in the first part of the book.

When the crisis which Preobrazhensky had so clearly foreseen finally materialized, changed circumstances were to bring about a sudden and dramatic shift in the theoretical viewpoints and the political alignment of the different tendencies within the Party. Bukharin abruptly went into opposition against Stalin, and proceeded to the defence of a number of his 'classic' theories, advancing others which lent added weight to the general body of Bukharinist doctrine.

Stalin, for his part, appropriated a number of ideas from the Trotskyist canon, notably 'industrialism' and the assessment, in class terms, of the dangers to which the régime might fall victim; however, his intention was to carry out his policy entirely according to his own lights.

Seeing in all this the vindication of their own theories, the Left disintegrated, for their various leaders forsook Trotsky and rallied to Stalin in order to support him against the Bukharinists.

At this point, though not always aware that he was doing so, Bukharin came to accept certain ideas for which he had previously criticized the men of the Left. He now abandoned his earlier views on commodity circulation as being the primary source of accumulation; he recognized the need for draining an excessively high level of resources from the peasant sector in order to meet the needs of industry, and accepted the proposition that industrialization must go forward, not 'at a snail's pace' but at a greatly accelerated rate. But most significant of all was his support for the Left-wing viewpoint in the matter of the Party's internal organization, a question on which he had formerly deployed arguments of the most demagogic character against the Left. At the very moment when many of the Left Opposition were leaving prison to join Stalin in quelling the Right-wing, a sudden revelation as to Stalin's true nature converted Bukharin to what had been the Left's main thesis, on the need for democratization of the Party.

Looking back, one can now see the situation in all its absurdity: Bukharin, appalled by Stalin, whom he now saw as a 'dangerous Trotskyist', nevertheless adopting what were, essentially, the main planks in Trotsky's platform, i.e. acceleration of the rate of industrialization, a curb on the activities of the kulaks (though not, of course, the liquidation of NEP or of the kulaks) and, above all, the call for democratization of Party structures; and on the other hand Trotsky's supporters rallying to Stalin in an attempt to defend socialism against those 'champions of the kulaks' Bukharin, Rykov and Tomsky, whom they hated.

Before long, these men of the Right were to realize that Stalin was no 'Trotskyist danger' but something much worse, while the Left were to discover that the programme adopted by Stalin was beginning to look less and less like their own, and that the old distinctions between 'Left' and 'Right' were now out of date. By this time it was too late. The Bukharinists were already making their 'self-criticism', and proclaiming their adherence to the official line.

In our opinion, one powerful element in this drama of personal conflict, or rather this 'tragedy of errors', was the fact that, particularly in the economic context, the protagonists of the Right and the Left believed their respective theories to be contradictory, whereas in reality they were complementary, and had been so even while the dialogues of the twenties were in progress. A better understanding of Bukharin's 'pro-peasant' attitude would have enabled the Left to make a more valuable theoretical contribution in this domain. Similarly, Bukharin's ideas would have benefited from closer attention to the problems of industrialization; as it was, what Preobrazhensky had to say in this connection was of much greater significance. If those who subscribed to the theory of 'primitive socialist accumulation' had had the opportunity to express their general theory in terms of a concrete economic programme, they would have found a place for Bukharin's favourite arguments on the importance of the market mechanism, respect for the peasant, the importance of co-operation.

As for the requirement of Party democratization, this was an aim which, as we know, all the protagonists had formulated, but they had done so one *after* the other, having first opposed the faction which, in an earlier period, would have raised the banner of Party democracy. This is the logic—or possibly the irrationality—of factional struggles, and it created a situation in which different factions fought each other over various parts of what today clearly emerges as a single programme.

At the beginning of 1929, it seemed as if Bukharin, the leader of the last serious opposition to Stalin, had finally reached the point of reconciling these mutually conflicting elements, but by this time it was too late for him to make his voice heard. The views of his victorious rival were to prevail, irrespective of their validity from a scientific or any other point of view. From this time on, discussion of the actual merit of Bukharin's programme, and of the consequences which might have ensued had his policy not been rejected, ceases to fall within the context of strictly historical research, although of course it continues to afford fruitful grounds for speculation. None the less, at this stage, there are one or two brief points which should be made by way of clarification.

Discussion of the respective roles of Stalin, Trotsky and Bukharin —or indeed discussion of a similar kind which is bound to arise in the context of almost any work of historical research—involves the historian in adopting one or other of a number of characteristic standpoints. Some scholars, unhappy at the turn which events have in fact taken, indulge in speculation about what might have been, elaborating theories on the probable course of history if, for example, different policies had been adopted, or different individuals had been in the seat of power—an exercise which English writers who find this attitude irritating have sometimes dismissed as 'if history'. However, while claiming with some justification that idle conjecture has no place in the domain of historical research, the critics of 'if history' occasionally go to the other extreme, arguing that the historian should not even raise the question of an alternative, and thereby ruling out consideration of a potential pattern of events for which the necessary pre-conditions or forces did exist, but were not brought into play (for reasons which it is then the historian's duty to elucidate). It is as if they were mesmerized by the logic of events, by the lure of powerful personalities and conquerors in general. By refusing to examine the factors which were present in a given historical process, but were not allowed to operate, this particular school of thought also rules out a proper study of those who were defeated, and cuts itself off from an understanding of the true course of events. Are not these events, to some extent at least, the outcome of the struggle of various forces and interests for the adoption of an alternative policy, even if the alternative in question was in the end rejected?

To return to the case in point, it is perfectly permissible to argue that the line of development which culminated in the Stalinist régime was the only one possible in the Russia of the twenties, and that Stalin was the only individual who understood what had to be done. This is a view which is widely accepted, and seems indeed to be gaining in popularity, for the further we move away from the events, the greater seems to be the fascination exerted on historians by the personality of Stalin himself.

But unless they take a rigidly deterministic view of history, in which case the fact that events followed a particular pattern is of itself sufficient proof that no other pattern was possible, then historians who interpret Stalin's role in this light must be prepared to support their theory with proofs, as they would any other. In order to furnish such proof, they must examine the alternative courses of action which were proposed at the time, they must show what their weaknesses were, and how in the end they came to be rejected. It is just such alternatives that concern us in the present study, for in our view it is equally legitimate to argue from the opposite standpoint, and to demonstrate, where there are grounds for doing so, that there existed an alternative, which was a valid one but which, for certain reasons, was not adopted.

This is where certain pitfalls lie in wait for the historian who ventures too far in the realm of speculation, and he should beware, therefore, of overstepping the bounds of what is known about the history and the trends of the particular society under discussion, difficult though it sometimes is to draw a firm distinction between fact and conjecture. In a wider, less rigid context however, there is not only the possibility but the need for continued reflection on what did happen and what could have happened, the lessons to be learned from the past and the errors which might be avoided in similar circumstances, though such enquiries should be pursued outside the framework of historical research, and *on the basis of the information yielded by the latter*. Is not this, after all, one of the primary reasons for embarking on any study of history?

In conclusion, I should like to express my gratitude to my supervisor, Professor Roger Portal of the Sorbonne, whose expert guidance and invaluable help have been instrumental in enabling me to carry out the present study. I should also like to thank my teachers at the University of Tel-Aviv, particularly Dr Zvi Yaavetz and Dr Charles Bloch, who encouraged me to embark on this research.

My thanks are also due to Dr E. H. Carr (Cambridge), Professor M. Cherniavsky (Rochester), Professor R. Davies (Birmingham) and Professor A. Nove (Glasgow), who showed much forbearance with an ill-typed manuscript. I am indebted to them for detailed criticism and comment, both written and oral, prior to or following on the publication of the French edition of this book. Responsibility for the opinions expressed, and for any errors or shortcomings in the work is, of course, entirely mine.

TRANSLATOR'S NOTES

The system of transliteration adopted is broadly based on that used in the journal *Soviet Studies* of the University of Glasgow. Certain words which have almost passed into the English language, such as kulak or kolkhoz, for example, have been treated throughout as English words; the same principle has been adopted in the case of other words, such as bednyak, serednyak, batrak, etc., which may be less familiar to the English reader, but which occur with great frequency throughout the text. Other Russian terms are retained in their original form and italicized, an explanation being provided in the text, and in the Glossary.

INTRODUCTION

The collectivization of the peasants in the USSR constituted a social upheaval of a totally unprecedented nature. It was one of the most remarkable events of the present century and it has a history as long as that of Soviet power itself. The idea of a collectivized agriculture, much favoured by the leadership after the revolution, had been left in abeyance during the NEP period. Interest in the idea, and in the collective movement, revived at the time of the 'grain crisis' at the beginning of 1928. It was during this crisis that collectivization of the peasantry and the creation of a powerful kolkhoz and sovkhoz sector began to be taken seriously as a means of solving, at one and the same time, both the formidable problem of grain and the whole 'accursed problem' of relations between the Soviet authorities and the peasants.

In fact, the development of the various forms of producers' co-operatives, which began on a very modest scale, dates from this period, and for this reason the history of collectivization as carried out by Stalin's régime may properly be said to have begun at this time.

Moreover, it was the grain shortage during the winter and spring of 1928 which, by developing into a chronic social and economic crisis, impelled the majority of the Politbureau and especially their chief, Stalin, to a fresh evaluation of the role of kolkhozes. This time, round about autumn 1929, the Party leadership came to the abrupt conclusion that the kolkhozes were the only viable solution, and one that must therefore at all costs be implemented on a national scale, with the least possible delay. This was the 'great turning-point', the spectacular and dramatic change in policy which was decreed during November–December, 1929.

The régime then entered upon a trial of strength with the peasants, which was known as the period of 'mass collectivization', and which was to last for nearly four years. This was a veritable civil war, fought by both sides with unyielding obduracy. The peasants met the government's actions with what was mainly passive resistance, in the form of economic sabotage. The authorities retaliated with mass reprisals, which turned this period of Soviet history into a sombre drama in which an enormous number of people perished.

This trial of strength ended in victory for the authorities and was followed, from the summer of 1933 onward, by a period of calm. Collectivization was by no means complete, for over 30% of the peasants still hung on to their strip of land for a few more years.

19

but the fate of the individual farm had already been sealed, and Russia was irrevocably a 'collectivized Russia'.

The present work is a study of the period during which events drove the Communist Party leadership to embark upon mass collectivization. This is the main theme of the second part of the book. But for a better understanding of these events, it has been necessary to go back further, to the years 1925–7, and to examine the factors which led to the breakdown of NEP. This is the subject of the first part of the book. The third part is concerned with the 'turning-point' at the end of 1929 and the beginning of 1930.

Our research has been based on material drawn from the BDIC in Paris. The principal references have been taken from official documents and, in the main, from Soviet publications. The work being done by present-day Soviet economists and historians on unpublished material from the archives is proving to be an extremely important and increasingly fruitful source. Judging from their latest publications on the subject of collectivization, Soviet scholars are engaged in what is no doubt a painful reappraisal of ideas which have been accepted as dogma for the last thirty years concerning the policy followed by their government in relation to the peasants. This has been urged on them as a result of 'destalinization' on the one hand, and the weakness of kolkhoz agriculture on the other. Stalinist theories on collectivization, which were still the subject of unanimous approval as late as 1960, are now being challenged and refuted one after the other by Soviet scholars. Each new Soviet publication affords fresh criticism of the methods employed by the régime during the years from 1928 to 1933, and as such helps to shed new light on a period which, although relatively recent history, is still very little known.

PART 1

THE RÉGIME AND THE PEASANTRY AT THE CLOSE OF THE NEP PERIOD

Chapter 1

FEATURES OF PEASANT SOCIETY

1. *Cultural Level*

In 1928, the peasants constituted 80% of the Soviet population, and the proletariat were still a minority who, when faced with calamity, war or famine, could easily take root once more in the place from which they had sprung, in other words the village.

Thus, eleven or twelve years after the Revolution, Russia continued to be an agricultural country, and the bulk of its inhabitants were peasants, the *muzhiki*, as they had been familiarly known for generations. In the eyes of the world, the *muzhik* was the symbol of the backward, oppressed, uncultivated Russian masses. Despite the radical change effected by the revolution when it destroyed the old régime, in many respects the *muzhik* is as he was: but in the years of the Soviet régime, a change has begun to take place in the psychological make-up of the peasantry as a whole, in the general aspects of village structure, and above all in the nature of agricultural production.

Analysis of the character of the peasantry and the peasant is not an easy task. Literature abounds in descriptions, but these are liable to be both arbitrary and inconsistent.

The Russian intelligentsia has painted a picture of the peasant which is coloured by its own prejudices or disappointed hopes, and is therefore contradictory. Thus, in populist literature, the peasant appears as the salt of the earth, the ultimate repository of all the highest moral qualities; the village community was the embryo of a future socialist society which would even be able to assist the West to free itself from a 'decaying' régime.[1]

Towards the end on the nineteenth century, this attitude underwent a radical change. The populists regarded the peasant as 'good and thoughtful, a tireless seeker after truth and justice'. But Gorky, on the other hand, states: 'In my youth, I assiduously sought such a man in the villages of Russia, and nowhere did I find him.'[2]

On the contrary, in his view 'the fundamental obstacle in the way of Russian progress towards westernization and culture' was 'the deadweight of illiterate village life which stifles the town, the animal-like individualism of the peasantry, and the peasants' almost total lack of social consciousness'.[3]

There is a great deal of truth in this verdict, despite the obviously exaggerated terms in which it is expressed.

In Gorky's view, this situation was the result of a long history of oppression carried out in a very unusual natural setting. 'The endless plain with its huddled villages of thatched wooden houses has an insidious effect on man, exhausting him and emptying him of all desires.'[4]

The Russian peasant was the product of a life lived in incomparably difficult conditions. His total dependence on a natural environment which was both harsh and unpredictable, his spells of intense hard work alternating with periods of enforced idleness, and a life lived in villages far removed from any centre of civilization, all combined to produce a type that was both superstitious and mistrustful, unsure of himself except when treading the well-worn paths of tradition and already predisposed to submit to overmastering forces, whether these forces be supernatural, or the political forces of law and order, or simply the power of a richer neighbour.

So long as there was no change in the living conditions of the peasantry, superstition continued to be a very powerful force, particularly among the women.

A Soviet author describing life in a rural community round about 1927 reports that, when the hospital services of the *volost* were unsatisfactory, generally because of the inefficiency of the doctor who was working there, the local 'wise women' would immediately reappear, with cures that were accepted without question: thus, hens' droppings as a cure for pneumonia, human excrement for trachoma, powdered glass for intestinal ailments, onion seed vapour for the toothache, and of course all the traditional spells.[5]. . .

Religious belief was deeply rooted in the Russian peasant, but stemmed more from magic and paganism than from real religious faith. 'The Russian peasant lived in a world inhabited by evil spirits, rather than a world ruled over by God.'[6]

The peasants set great store by feast days, and ceremonies such as baptisms, weddings, and funerals, but gradually lost their respect for the village priest, and preferred to pick the one who would cost them least.[7] Although their church was stubbornly defended against any encroachment on the part of the authorities, this was often simply because the church was 'their property', and they were reluctant to see the authorities taking possession of it and demolishing it in order to use the bricks for other building work. . . .

Among the young, religious convictions became lukewarm, and some of the peasants, particularly among the local activists, began shamefacedly to conceal their attachment to certain religious rites or customs. But for the majority of the old people, and especially the women, religion was still a very powerful force, and there were even 'outbreaks of religious hysteria among kolkhoz women following on a number of divine manifestations', as a Communist Academy publication stated in 1930.[8]

Even today, the icon still hangs on the wall of a kolkhoz household, though it may be accompanied by pictures of Lenin and the present leaders. The persistence of this tradition is due to the fact that the Soviet régime had nothing to offer the peasants in its place, and above all to the fact that there has been little perceptible change in the cultural level of village life since about the end of the NEP period,

'It is too soon to abolish religion,' said one old peasant.

'A peasant's life is too full of hardship; livestock dying, the house going on fire, poverty. . . . Religion is your only solace: you tell yourself that only God knows what is good and what is bad, and that is some consolation. But if things were different, if someone made it up to you in full when something bad happened to you, then you would feel better, and you wouldn't need religion.'[9]

This matter-of-fact attitude reflects very clearly the precarious nature of the peasant's existence, and the way in which it colours his opinions and conditions his religious beliefs.

The cultural and educational level of the average NEP village was another major factor which influenced the psychological make-up of the peasant. The word *muzhik* had derogatory implications because the peasant was uncultured, or uncultivated. The people, the *muzhiki*, were *temnye*—dark, as the night is dark—a word which conveys the entire scope of the problem far more accurately than the word 'ignorant'.

'The Semi-Asiatic *bezkulturnost*',* as Lenin expressed it, was all too often, in the remoter regions, entirely Asiatic; it constituted a a terrible obstacle in the path of Soviet Russia, and Lenin longed for the day when the entire population would be able to read and write.[10] According to Lenin, Russia was embarking 'on what our enemies often describe as the hopeless task of establishing socialism in a

---

* *Bezkulturnost*—'lack of culture' is an inadequate translation. The word *kulturnost*, which occurs later, is used to denote 'having culture'.

country whose cultural level is not sufficiently high', but, as Lenin saw it, Russia was in fact at that moment on the brink of a 'cultural revolution'.

In some of his last articles (dictated in January 1923) he referred to this formidable task, and made it clear that in his view it dominated all else. A minimum of *gramotnost** would enable progress to be made in the economic field. By being able to read, the peasant would be able to make some improvements in his farm and his standard of living, and this would consequently afford him wider cultural opportunities; for where living standards and the level of culture were primitive, they would engender a self-perpetuating and mutually interacting condition of poverty and ignorance. Lenin therefore tried, by the use of NEP methods, to hasten the cultural revolution and to stimulate economic development by gradually improving the situation in both of these domains. A modicum of *kulturnost* in everyday life and in business dealings, a member of the collective who is also *kulturny* (the word has the same meaning in present-day colloquial Russian)—this was Lenin's prescription for setting Russia on the road to socialism.[11]

Unfortunately, as late as 1930, the hopes embodied in the 'testament', that is, the ideas put forward by Lenin in his last articles, were still very far from realization. The decision on compulsory education from the age of seven had been taken, at Lenin's instigation, in 1921. But this is what Bubnov, the commissar for Education, had to say on the subject at the Sixteenth Party Congress (June 16, 1930). He reported that, in the course of his travels, he had seen new factories going up everywhere, whereas such schools as existed were, by comparison, in a lamentable condition. The commissar protested to the Party Congress about the state of the schools in general. He then referred to a Party decision about compulsory education from the age of seven which had been taken in 1921, and a further decision on the same lines dating from 1930; 'How are we to explain the fact that, in a decision on education in 1930, we have been obliged to repeat what was said on the subject ten years previously?' Bubnov did not provide any answer, but added that, in this field, 'very little has been achieved in the last ten years'.[12]

Krupskaya unfailingly brought the subject up at all congresses and conferences. She usually painted an extremely grim picture of the state of cultural activity in the villages, and particularly underlined the shocking condition of the primary schools (those providing a four-year course of instruction) and the fact that they were so few in number.[13]

At the Fifth Congress of Soviets, in 1929, a great many of the

* *Gramotnost*—literacy, the ability to read and write.

peasant delegates complained that they were scarcely able to read, and could not cope with the great number of official forms. One delegate from Siberia reported that many villages had no school at all. Another said that the Nizhi Novgorod *oblast* had decided to provide elementary schooling (four years) for all its inhabitants, but that implementation of this decision was uncertain, because only 30% of the school buildings were usable, and 20% were completely derelict.

A woman delegate from the Novgorod *okrug* (Leningrad *oblast*) complained that the primary school was so inefficient that the pupils were not fit to go on to their secondary course (the fifth year of study).[14]

Kaganovich also deplored the lack of progress in combating illiteracy, and in 1930 stated that 'in this, the eleventh year since Lenin's decree on the wiping-out of illiteracy, we have still covered very little ground'.[15]

It should be added that, when this statement was made, the campaign for the so-called all-out collectivization of the peasants was in full swing.

At that time, there were 16 million illiterate in the sixteen to thirty-five age group, 30–40 million semi-literate in the same age group, and 5 million aged between twelve and sixteen were totally illiterate, not to mention those in the over thirty-five age group.[16] Thus, on the brink of collectivization, more than half of the peasants were illiterate, and in particular two-thirds of the female peasant population.[17]

2. *Peasant Society*

Traditionally, the social structure of the village was based on two very ancient institutions, which together dominated the life of each individual in it. The basic social unit was the *dvor*[18] (which might be translated as 'household'), in other words, 'the family and its farm'. These were often large peasant families, which still retained much of the patriarchal character they had had in the middle ages, ruled over by the father who, as head of the family and organizer of the farmwork, arbiter and final authority, was all-powerful. He was accustomed to a blind obedience which left no scope for individual initiative.[19] Any infraction of paternal discipline was severely punished, usually by physical cruelty in the shape of beatings of sometimes maniacal violence. This element of cruelty, which was a normal feature in the process of upbringing, was also a general feature of peasant life.

Gorky has many descriptions of the various forms which it took.[20] Women and children pitilessly beaten with sadistic delight, bloody fights with knife and hatchet, murder for vengeance and fire-raising— these were all commonplaces of village life. The writer exaggerates

25

the effect of the atrocities which took place during the Civil War, and tends to forget other, more sympathetic, manifestations of the human character. But generally speaking, life in the Soviet villages during the NEP period was still very crude, and hooliganism, bad language and brawling were extremely prevalent; as the judge of one rural *volost* remarked rather picturesquely, 'There has been increased activity in the punch-up sector.'[21]

Since the *dvor* was the basic social unit, modern democratic concepts such as the right to vote or any other civic rights were alien to village life. The Soviet régime tried to inculcate such concepts by accustoming the people to the idea of voting to elect their village soviets (*selsovety*). However, Soviet electoral procedure was such as to frustrate rather than encourage democratic habits. In fact, social life was centred on the *dvory*, for the heads of households continued to represent the other members of the family, and for the most part acted as they themselves thought best.

The second important social unit which governed the economic and social life of the peasant was the *mir*.[22] Once the populists, with their illusions about peasant socialism, had finally given way before liberal and Marxist thought and, above all, before capitalist economic development in Russia, the importance of the peasant community quickly declined, and it was regarded by many theorists as having definitely been superseded.

Oddly enough, however, there was a revival of the *mir* during and after the revolution. It was the *mir* which undertook the confiscation and redistribution of the estates of the landed gentry.[23] During the NEP period, it was an active village institution alongside which the *selsovet* was something of a Cinderella. Smirnov, the commissar for Agriculture, stated that in 1926, 90% of the peasantry belonged to the 'village societies' (*selskoe obshchestvo*, the juridical term for the peasant *mir*).[24] According to Larin, there were in the USSR some 350,000 of these village societies.[25] They settled all problems relating to land and agriculture and 'in practice controlled the economic life of the village'[26] for the community was in effect the landlord, and where necessary it undertook to share out the land in accordance with its own egalitarian principles. Despite certain changes wrought by the course of events or by Soviet legislation, a report published by the Communist Academy in 1928 stated that the village assembly which settled most of the questions which were of vital interest to the peasant 'was still the old *skhod*' of pre-revolution days,[27] which was still maintaining its own independent course alongside the Soviet institutions, because it was more deeply rooted in village life than the latter.[28]

We shall be reverting to this important point later. All that need be said at present is that the peasant was participating in a very primitive and very ancient form of democracy.[29] Some Soviet authorities looked upon the *mir* as a rudimentary kind of peasant socialism, which could be used as a basis for a wider socialist evolution; for others, it was simply a legacy from the past and an obstacle to progress.

In fact, Gorky's observations about the 'animal-like individualism' of the peasant were not the whole truth. The peasant belonged to a community which had rights of tenure over certain lands. The community owned communal grazings, forests and some enterprises; it also had some income. The peasants participated in the administration of the village economy, decisions being taken by the *khozyaeva* (heads of the *dvory*). The peasants, especially the poorer ones, even had a very strong attachment to the community, for it afforded them some degree of security, and only the better-off ones, and those who had a certain amount of initiative, had any desire to leave the *mir* and form a *khutor* or a *vyselok* independently of the *mir*.[30]

However, it would be equally misleading to over-emphasize the 'socialist' instincts of the peasants. Discussion of methods of handling the *mir* in relation to collectivization is another problem. But the peasant, although attached to his community, above all wanted to become a *khozyain*. The agrarian revolution which took place in October gave him land, it also gave him hope and incentive. He now wanted to 'make good', to better his lot, to hang on to his plot of land and to extricate himself from his poverty-stricken state. Formal problems of property mattered very little to him. Formally, the land might belong to the nation, or the community, or simply 'to God', and it might change hands, be reallocated, etc., but so far as he was concerned, the farm was indubitably *his* farm. This was the mainspring of his individualism and of the natural course which his economy and his aspirations followed, as a result of the revolution.

In the peasant's eyes, the revolution which had been carried out via the institutions of the *mir*, had only one purpose, and that was to give him a farm. So far as he was concerned, NEP was only a further stage in the progress towards the natural outcome of the agrarian revolution in October, which had been temporarily halted by the exigencies of the Civil War.

On the eve of collectivization, the feeling among the mass of the Soviet peasantry was rather that they had only just *begun* their journey along the right road, the road which they had been seeking.

As a *khozyain*, the peasant tended to gauge people and things, and his own conduct, according to his ideas of the good farmer. His prosperous neighbour might be hated as a grasping kulak who exploited others, but primarily he was envied and respected as a successful

27

farmer. This attitude was not at all in accordance with the aims of the Soviet régime, particularly as it represented a scale of values which left nothing but contempt for the *bednyak* (the poor peasant) at the bottom. Whatever the political and doctrinal views of the Soviet régime, there was no respect in the village for the poor peasant. He tended to be regarded as a good-for-nothing.

The *serednyak* (middle peasant) often said: 'how can we learn from the *bednota*, when they cannot even make their own *borshch*? Just think: are we idiots?'[31]

This was a perfectly natural reaction in a peasant whose ideas were practical and whose judgements were based on common sense. The peasant was primitive and hidebound, suspicious but shrewd in his own way; he was apt to size up men and matters by the same criterion that he used in his judgement of livestock. He had a deep mistrust, and sometimes hatred, for the town and everything that came from the town; those who sought to communicate with him, to earn his respect or to teach him would first of all have to make allowance for his way of life and his way of thought. Common sense had taught the peasant to accept as true only that which he could see and touch, not once but several times over, and with the greatest caution and prudence. Anyone who tried to teach him new ways might reach an understanding with him, but only if he had patience and compassion, and the necessary means to demonstrate his lesson in practical terms. What was needed was the qualities of a good teacher. . . .

3. *Living and Working Conditions*

In the entire country there was not a single peasant who had not been 'burned down' at least once. This really sinister fact was reported by *Pravda*.[32]

Every year 400,000 cottages went up in smoke, 'devoured by the red cockerel', as they said in the villages. It was very hard to recover from such a misfortune, especially if the livestock had also perished in the flames.

But an even more terrible hazard than fire was drought and frost, which constantly threatened the peasants' economic stability. In a vast agricultural country which was farmed by very primitive methods, economic existence, or rather existence itself, was dependent on the harvest. At least once in every three or four years the harvest failed, and there might also be two years of poor harvests as well. A good harvest scarcely made up for the losses suffered in the bad years. Given the farming methods used by the peasants, it was not to be expected that things would be any better, particularly in view of the unfavourable natural conditions governing Russian agriculture.

The peasants were virtually ignorant of multiple crop rotation, and the generally accepted method was that of the three-field system. Farming methods were those of the time of Peter the Great, or even more ancient.

The symbol of the backward and unproductive *muzhik* was the *sokha*, the wooden plough which was the peasant's main agricultural implement prior to the revolution. But as late as 1928 5·5 million peasant holdings[33] were still using this ancient implement, which was 'at least as old as the Pharaohs'.[34] Nor were the rest of their implements any more up-to-date. Of the area given over to summer grains, 10% was ploughed by the *sokha*, and three-fourths of it was sown by hand; 40% of the harvest was threshed with the flail, and almost half of it was reaped with sickle and scythe.[35]

The farms were often too small for it to be profitable to keep a horse (and consequently to buy a plough),[36] though there may be an element of artificiality in this particular calculation, in the sense that at least a quarter of the farms had no horse, although they would have liked one. It was not so very unusual to see 'a wretched wooden *sokha*, dating from the Flood, as you might say, often dragged along by a miserable yoke of lean oxen, or by the farmer, or even his wife . . .'.[37]

But there was another aspect of the situation, which was even worse. The lands belonging to a particular holding were not *zemleustroennye*, that is to say, they were not grouped together, but dispersed in single strips. This was the bane of the whole system. Speaking of it, Molotov declared at the Fifteenth Congress: 'The situation is intolerable.' He went on to say that no improvement in agriculture would be possible so long as a large number of peasants had to work their land in ten or twenty, or sometimes even a hundred separate strips. . . .[38]

A delegate from the Ryazan province added that in his region a fair number of farms had their land divided into fifty or sixty separate lots, and that, into the bargain, these were often separated one from the other by as much as fifteen, twenty or twenty-five versts. . . . What was needed to remedy this piecemeal cultivation was *zemleustroistvo*, that is, a rational re-allocation of the strips, but progress was slow. It was said in official circles that owing to lack of credits and specialists, improvements in this domain were only available to those who could pay for them.

In 1929, *Pravda* expressed alarm at the extent of this strip cultivation, which was fatal both for the peasant and for collectivization.[39] On this occasion, *Pravda* disclosed that in the RSFSR (with the exception of the autonomous republics) out of a total sown area of 257 million hectares, only 85 million hectares had been reallocated.[40]

Whatever the reasons put forward, the government's failure in this domain, 'in the year twelve of the Revolution' (*Pravda*) was a serious one. The peasant was literally at the mercy of adverse natural conditions, and often too at the mercy of a pitiless kulak. It was pointless to accuse the peasant of being *temny*, to hold him responsible for the weakness of agriculture; how could any farmer, literate or otherwise, cultivate scattered strips of land in a reasonable fashion, especially if he did not even possess a horse?

The lack of draught animals was another source of misery, and the cause of economic inefficiency in many peasant farms.[41]

Some 35% of the peasants were classified by the Ministry of Finance as bednyaks exempt from all taxes (in 1929). The term bednyak covered any peasant who cultivated up to two *desyatiny*,* had no horse or cow, and possessed so few implements that he could not work his land unless he hired tools, and a horse or an ox. About 30% of the peasants owned no draught animals,[42] and 50% of them had only one animal.

In certain large regions, the situation was even worse. In 1929, there were 5,300,000 farms in the Ukraine, but of those 2,100,000 had neither horse nor ox. Of the 520,000 holdings in the Tambov province (*guberniya*), 48% had no horse, 32% had no cow.[43] Of the 45–50% of serednyaks, about half were in the unenviable 'weakling' category (*malomoshchnye*),[44] who could not make ends meet, and were in constant danger of slipping back into the lower category. This section of the peasant population (the bednyaks, the *malomoshchnye* and over 3 million batraks) represented the 10–13 million people who, in European Russia alone, according to the calculations of *Narkonmzem*, were regarded as 'superfluous mouths'.[45] The degree of overpopulation was particularly serious in the Central Black Earth region,[46] in the Western province, in the Middle Volga, the Ukraine and Belorussia. Every years 5,000,000 adults went in search of gainful employment, because their tiny farms could not support them.

All too often, the Soviet village, cut off from the world as it was, often twenty or thirty kilometres away from the nearest centre, and with no decent road, presented a scene of indescribable poverty.

Even more eloquent than the overall figures, although they certainly speak for themselves, is the picture of the situation which is revealed in the complaints of the peasant delegates to the Fifth Congress of the Soviets; these are presented in unvarnished detail and with no eye to the approval of superior authorities. After one or two conventional phrases denouncing enemies of the people and praising the government, the delegates go on to speak of the troubles of their various regions. One peasant woman, an agricultural worker who is a

* *Desyatina*—measure of land = 2·7 acres.

member of her village soviet (in the Mariupol *okrug* in the Ukraine) reports that their village is situated very far away from the *raion*, which is itself at some distance from the *okrug*: 'that is why we are so isolated from medical services. If it's a rich peasant who is ill, he will go in his cart, but a bednyak might die before he can get to a doctor.' There was no drinking water in this village: 'We fetch water from twenty kilometres away. Here again, the better-off peasant can transport it on his horse, but the bednyak has to carry it on his back....'[47]

Another peasant woman from the Rykov *raion* (Leningrad *oblast*) reported that the entire *raion* consisted of bednyaks.[48] They bought their bread from outside the *raion*, since they did not grow enough to provide bread themselves, and economically they were impoverished. The credits granted to bednyaks and serednyaks were negligible. During the sowing season, they had only received 17% of the credits due to them. What could anyone do with such inadequate means? There was no question of increasing the amount of the local levy,* for the peasants were poor, there was nothing more to be got out of them. The nearest railway station was thirty-five kilometres away, and there was an extra fifty kopecks' charge on every pood of merchandise before it reached the consumer.[49] The peasant woman concluded with a humble request that funds be allocated to them for making 'a tractor road'.

Another delegate, this time a kolkhoz member, spoke for the peasants of the Nizhni Novgorod *okrug* (later Gorky), and said:

'It is my duty to report that in our *raion* the peasants are very badly off. In this, the twelfth year of the Soviet régime, the peasants are eating substitute bread (made with mountain spinach). In such conditions, the local Party officials are finding it hard to do any propaganda.'

The credit associations, went on the delegate, pay little attention to their needs: this year they promised seed grain, but in the end they allocated only 3·5 tons of oats (for the entire *raion*) and that was of poor quality. It is therefore very difficult 'to appeal to the masses' and to enlist the support of the bednyak, for the 'kulak and the *podkulachnik*[50] touch the most sensitive strings'.[51]

'The forgotten village' (*glukhaya derevnya*), the symbol of isolation and backwardness, was not a phenomenon peculiar to a few remote regions. The situation in the so-called 'national' republics of Central Asia or elsewhere, with their 90% illiteracy rate, was worse than in the Slav republics, but villages could be 'forgotten' as easily in the

* Local levy—taxes which were levied, in principle, by the village assemblies, and which were destined for local needs.

Moscow *oblast* as in the wastes of Siberia. The majority of the Russian peasantry lived in just such 'forgotten' corners.

Not even the briefest sketch of peasant life and customs would be complete without mention of another scourge of the peasantry, vodka. Vodka, which was made by the State, or the crude spirit which was distilled by the peasants themselves (*samogon,* 'moonshine') flowed like water in the countryside. Recourse to this particular panacea caused the peasants to sink even deeper into apathy and wretchedness. In the face of disaster, the peasant's most frequent reaction was *zapit*—to drink himself into oblivion. The Russian peasant was notoriously given to drowning his sorrows, or to celebrating some special occasion, by drinking until he ceased to behave like a human being at all; drinking bouts, with their frequent aftermath of violence and blood, provided most of the news items from the villages. To a certain extent, the natural common sense of the people acted as a safeguard against the dangers inherent in abuse of 'the demon drink', but often this could not prevail over a deep-seated psychological need which stemmed from the general conditions of life in Russia, and the use of vodka was just as widespread in the towns as it was in the countryside.

About 1924, the government, in the face of pressing economic needs, and also in the hope of partially alleviating the menace of *samogon,* had permitted the production and sale of vodka, which had been forbidden after the revolution. This soon brought protests from certain communists, for whom vodka was still the symbol of the degradation in which the people were wilfully maintained by the Tsarist régime.

This was not the only instance in which the Soviet régime had recourse to measures similar to those employed under the earlier régime. The fact remains that in the space of five years (1924–8) not only did vodka fail to oust *samogon,* but consumption of both rose considerably. Consumption of *samogon* in the countryside doubled (780 million litres in 1927–8), and in addition 300 million litres of vodka were consumed in the same year.[52]

4. *The Peasant and the Soviet Régime*

The peasant's attitude to the Soviet régime was never enthusiastic, except in the case of some of the bednyaks, and then only during certain periods. Their attitude was governed by the traditional mistrust of the Russian peasant for authority in all its manifestations. This mistrust was liable to disappear and to give way to a less strained relationship whenever the peasant was in a position to judge 'by results', to assess the actions of the authorities, the value of the promises that were made, and the practical nature of the assistance given. But even when relations were good, they were still liable to deteriorate at any given moment. No lasting state of mutual trust was established between the peasants and the Soviet authorities, or at least not up until the time covered by the present study.

Memories of the Civil War were still very much alive in the peasant consciousness, especially in those regions where the fighting had been worst.[53] Peasants had made up the bulk of the forces on both sides, but in the end, after much changing of sides and much wavering, the majority had given their active support, or had at least shown a 'benevolent neutrality', to 'the Reds'. The fact of this support, and of the changes in allegiance, had made a profound impression not only on the peasants, but on the authorities as well.

The Soviet régime was able to prevail, and to consolidate its power, by rallying the poorer peasants to its side at the necessary moment, and it was this sector of the peasantry which henceforth were assumed to be the most faithful allies of the new régime. This key factor in Soviet history played an important part in the process by which the theory of the unshakable nature of the alliance between the peasantry and the proletariat came to be deeply rooted in Party doctrine, and in the consciousness of many Party activists. But at the same time there were others, in whom memories of shifting peasant loyalties during the Civil War inspired rather different ideas. They were more conscious of the unreliability of peasant support, and were convinced that until there was a radical change in the relations between the towns and the countryside, the Soviet system would never be secure.

It is important to note that, despite all this, the peasantry had naturally no hankerings after the past. For the majority of the peasants, Tsarism and the *pomeshchiki* were gone for good. Their attitude to the new régime was governed by the new relationships which were being created, and the new problems which were arising. There were many things about their new masters which disconcerted the peasants, and with which they could not agree. The fact that the Bolsheviks had 'backed' the poor peasant (although this was often more of a formality than a fact) was both incomprehensible and unacceptable to the *khozyain* mentality. As for the poor peasant himself, even if he was not personally disappointed by the assistance which the authorities had given him, he did not seem to have overmuch respect for his condition or belief in his supposed importance. He, too, hoped to better himself and join the ranks of those who were more prosperous than he was. That is why 'he very often did not feel himself to be at all in command of the situation. Outside of the village assemblies, those to whom the bednyaks pay most attention are the better-off members of the community'[54] in other words the *khozy-aiskie muzhiki*, the prosperous peasants.

The peasant was keenly aware of the twists and turns which were so much a part of Soviet policy, and he deeply resented them. During the NEP period, he was exhorted to improve his farming methods, to practise a better system of crop-rotation, etc. The more energetic and enlightened elements responded wholeheartedly; but when they finally saw their efforts bearing fruit, and became a little more prosperous, it was only to find themselves qualifying as exploiters, and being deprived of their right to vote. This profoundly dismayed and discouraged many peasants who had no desire to oppose the authorities. Actions of this sort were beyond the comprehension of the peasant: 'You're better to stick to the three-field system[55] and not try too hard, because if you go in for multiple rotation, you'll find yourself branded as an "anti", and you'll end up with no vote.'[56] In such conditions, any political activity, even on behalf of the régime, was regarded as a pitfall.

Reactions from many of the peasants, who expressed themselves freely and frankly on this subject, closely reflected the above attitude: 'What use is politics to me?', or again, in response to exhortations from Party activists about an alliance with the poor in order to break the power of the kulaks in the villages:

'Who wants power? You can't get rich. They have you up on the carpet every time. They take your vote away from you. Get myself branded as an enemy? Not likely. I'd sooner let the farm go to the dogs. I'll do just so much, pay my taxes, keep a bit for myself, and that will be that.'[57]

There were too many unpredictable elements in the day-to-day relations between the peasants, the government and the communists. The effect of all the uncertainties and shifts in policy, and of the various manifestations of bureaucracy, was to engender a great deal of bitterness and interminable criticism, although this was not reflected in a more generalized outburst of indignation (it should be remembered that we are speaking now of the second phase of NEP, i.e. the period 1925–8). Soviet policy with regard to the peasant suffered from an inherent 'schizophrenia' which, at local level, took the form of innumerable infringements, by the authorities, of laws and rights which had, in fact, been accorded by the government itself. The authorities, who were always more inclined to browbeat the peasants than to explain things patiently to them, were constantly in breach of 'socialist legality'.

This was a source of never-ending discussion and complaints from the Party chiefs and activists. Marshal Budenny, who travelled widely, was keenly aware of the complaints of his peasant troops, and of the conditions in which they lived. In the Party assizes, he criticized the attitude of the authorities, who were too frequently given to the indiscriminate use of coercion in their dealings with the peasants, instead of trying to educate them. 'Forms of coercion', or 'bureaucratic methods', as he called them, were in his opinion hindering the growth of collectivization. What irritated him most of all was that such things had an adverse effect on the army's supply of good horses, who likewise 'did not respond well' to bureaucratic methods. 'We have too many of these methods,' said the Marshal.

'There are too many punitive measures, and too few attempts to activize the peasants themselves. This type of coercion must be stamped out as soon as possible, for it is bureaucracy at its worst, a show of violence and power directed at the peasants who, more often than not, cannot even understand what is wanted of them.'[58]

Molotov and Kalinin also spoke of 'the colossal number of blunders and abuses' for which 'we are responsible', which was why the peasants inveighed against the authorities and were 'violently critical' of them.[59]

Thus, the peasants did not keep quiet, they criticized and made representations. They had only too much cause to do so.

Pravda, in one of its many statements on the safeguarding of the rather elusive principle of socialist legality, indignantly reported that the peasants had been forced to lodge thousands of complaints with the *prokuratura*. In the Kaluga region alone, in six months, the *prokuror* had received 8,859 complaints about all sorts of injustices and persecution on the part of local authorities, and 81·8% (!) of these complaints had been found to be justified.[60]

The reason for this state of affairs lay not only in the fundamental characteristics of the Soviet régime, but also in the nature of the administrative structure, which left much to be desired. The fact remains that the peasant, who had learned from the bitter experience of centuries to be suspicious of all authority, still maintained a critical and sceptical attitude in his dealings with his new masters, with whom he was in varying degrees continually at odds.

The same was true in other spheres, particularly in respect of the laws and juridical structures of the new régime. The *Pravda* article, quoted above, angrily commented that many peasants treated Soviet laws as if nothing had changed since the days of the Tsarist régime. There were valid and well-founded reasons for this, but *Pravda* confined itself to a simple exhortation to 'consign to the dustbin of history all sayings about the laws which have come down to us through the centuries . . .'.

Here are some of those sayings which the newspaper found so 'irritating': 'The law', said the peasants, 'is just like the tiller of a boat, it points where you turn it.'[61] 'The law is a spider's web, the bumble-bee gets through, the fly is caught'; or again: 'What is the use of laws when the judges all know each other?'

Pravda's irritation is quite understandable. The peasant had not yet realized 'the basic difference between the laws of the old régime and Soviet laws'. But was this due to his lack of discernment?

The general attitude toward the Soviet authorities was not hostile,[62] it was above all profoundly passive. One Soviet writer, though not the only one, makes this point, albeit indirectly, when he says:

'The songs sung by the Cossacks at this period show no ill feeling either towards Denikin or the Soviet authorities, nor do they reflect any warm feelings for one or the other. They are deeply passive and politically neutral in a way which reflects the profound exhaustion of the masses after the imperialist and the civil war.'

'These masses,' the writer goes on, 'have adapted themselves to the Soviet régime.'[63]

This conclusion was true of the peasantry as a whole. They remained passive, took little part in Soviet life, not that their participation was very frequently sought, except at election times, if the numbers of electors taking part were not sufficiently large. . . . 'The population itself (in the villages) including batraks, bednyaks and serednyaks, live quite apart . . .', said Budenny in 1929. 'Nothing is done to make contact with them in their work, to provide guidance in the field of socialist construction.'[64]

The fact was that no one was leading the peasants towards socialism, and, as we have already said, their own inclinations lay in quite a different direction. The peasants identified the Soviet régime with NEP, and NEP with socialism. And so they accepted the régime, but without enthusiasm, for since the revolution they had not yet had sufficient opportunity to determine what real advantages it had to offer.

Not until 1925–6 did the peasants begin living above starvation level, for the first time since the revolution.[65] In the years that followed, a slight improvement began to take place, and the mass of the peasants had more to eat than they had had before the revolution.[66] However, the improvement was not a very marked one.

By 1927, the peasants were in possession of an extra 104 million hectares, in addition to the 210 million which had been in peasant hands prior to the revolution.[67] This land had to be apportioned among a population which was now much larger than had previously been the case, for in the last decade the 16 million pre-revolution holdings had grown by another 9 million. For lack of horses and implements, the majority of the bednyaks were unable to make full use of their land, and were obliged either to rent some of it to other farmers, or to hire horses and equipment, often at exorbitant rates.

Even among Party writers, the improvement in peasant living standards brought about by the agrarian revolution did not go wholly unquestioned. For example, Bolshakov, in a book for which Kalinin wrote the preface, gave a fairly detailed report of the gains and losses in income of the peasants of a particular *volost* during the revolution and in the years following the revolution up to 1926. His conclusion was that 'from the material point of view, the peasants lost nothing by the revolution'.[68] He did not, however, conclude that they had gained anything.

The revolution freed the peasant from the system of *barshchina* (service to the landowner), it gave him the status of an independent producer, and offered him renewed hope. However, it was neither past gains nor the doubtful improvements of the current situation which governed the nature of the relationship between the peasantry and the Soviet régime. A much more decisive part was to be played by certain new problems, of great urgency and complexity, which began to emerge.

In the course of its development, the Soviet régime had suffered from certain weaknesses and bottlenecks in its social and economic structures. These defects had once more come to the surface, this time in a more acute form than ever before, and they were again threatening to compromise the whole future of the régime.

There were two questions of overriding importance: one was the problem of the level of agricultural production, and the other that of the 'scissors' in prices for industrial products and agricultural products. The peasants reacted particularly strongly against a level of prices which very greatly penalized them.

In this context, any differences of attitude which might otherwise exist among the various strata of the peasantry tended to disappear, and therein lay an ever-present danger of deterioration in the relations between the régime and the peasantry as a whole. This fear of *razmychka*—'the rupture of the alliance'—was always uppermost in the minds of the Party leaders and theoreticians.

NOTES AND REFERENCES

1. N. Berdyaev, *The Origin of Russian Communism*. (London 1937), Ch. 1.
2. The quotations are from M. Gorky, *'Lénine' et 'Le Paysan Russe'*. (Paris, 1925), pp. 140–1.

3. *Russki Sovremennik* (1924), quoted by E. H. Carr, *A History of Soviet Russia: Socialism in One Country.* (London, 1958), Vol. 1, pp. 122–3.

4. M. Gorky, *op. cit.*, p. 110 (written in 1922).

5. Bolshakov, *Derevnya 1919–27.* (Moscow/Leningrad, 1927), pp. 294–5.

6. Nicholas Vakar, *The Taproot of Soviet Society.* (New York, 1961), p. 65.

7. Bolshakov, *op. cit.*, pp. 402–20, *passim.*

8. Ulashevich (ed.), *Zhenshchina v kolkhoze.* (Moscow, 1930), p. 65.

9. Bolshakov, *op. cit.*, p. 427.

10. e.g., V. I. Lenin, 'O kooperatsii', *Sochineniya* (4th edition), Vol. XXXIII, p. 430.

11. *ibid*, p. 435.

12. Speech by Bubnov, *16-ty S'ezd VKP(b)*, stenogramme, p. 185.

13. N. Krupskaya, *15-ty S'ezd VKP(b)*, stenogramme, pp. 1115–6.

14. *5-ty S'ezd Sovetov*, Bull. No. 3, p. 8; Bull. No. 4, pp. 16, 34; Bull. No. 16, p. 11.

15. *Kaganovich, Pravda*, January 21, 1930.

16. *Derevenski Kommunist*, October 20, 1929, No. 20.

17. Ulashevich, *op. cit.*, p. 58; *Bolshevik*, 1958, No. 11, p. 58.

18. A precise definition is given in R. Portal (ed.), *Le statut des paysans libérés de l'esclavage.* (Paris/The Hague 1963), p. 39.

19. For an analysis of the peasant family see Vakar, *op. cit.*, pp. 31–44.

20. Gorky, *op. cit.*, pp. 135–59.

21. Bolshakov, *op. cit.*, p. 316.

22. For a definition of the *mir* or 'community' see R. Portal, *op. cit.*, pp. 33–5, 37–8. The definition provided applies mainly to the pre-revolutionary period; after the revolution there were some changes.

23. Trotsky, *The History of the Russian Revolution* (London, 1932–3), Vol. III, Ch. 1, and L. E. Hubbard, *The Economics of Soviet Agriculture* (London, 1939), p. 74.

24. *Na Agrarnom Fronte* (hereafter referred to as *NAF*), 1926, No. 11–12—an account of a discussion at the Communist Academy.

25. *NAF*, 1927, No. 4, p. 41.

26. Rezunov, *Selskie sovety i zemelnye obshchestva.* (Moscow, 1928).

27. *ibid.*, pp. 6–7. *Skhod*—the assembly of heads of families which governed community affairs. For further information on the *mir* and the *skhod*, see Ch. 4.

28. The rural communities were to be abolished in the RSFSR by

a degree of July 30, 1930. See Kukushkin, *Rol selsovetov v sotsialis- ticheskom pereustroistve derevni*. (Moscow, 1962), pp. 99–100.

29. According to the Agrarian Code all members of the *dvor* aged eighteen and over were entitled to vote in the rural assembly. Tradition prevailed, however, and in practice only representatives of the *dvory* took part, and made decisions.

30. *Khutora and otruba* in 1927 accounted for only 3·5% of the land. 1% was in the hands of associations (*tovarishchestva*), 95% was cultivated by communities. See *Postroenie fundamenta sotsialisti- cheskoi ekonomiki v SSSR*, 1926–32 (Moscow, 1960), pp. 346–7.

31. *NAF*, 1928, No. 1, p. 93.

32. *Pravda*, May 18, 1929.

33. This figure is supplied by Yakovlev, *15-ty S'ezd, VKP(b)*, stenogramme, p. 1215.

34. The expression employed by Academician Vavilov.

35. Gaister, *Bolshevik*, 1930, No. 1–2, p. 34.

36. According to calculations made by Narkomzem; reported by Molotov, *15-ty S'ezd VKP(b)*, stenogramme, p. 1066.

37. Chakaya, referring to the Trans-Caucasus, *5-ty S'ezd Sovetov*, May 1929, Bull. 18, p. 8.

38. Molotov, *15-ty S'ezd VKP(b)*, stenogramme, pp. 1059, 1128.

39. *Pravda*, January 4, 1929. This is certainly the traditional *cherespolositsa, dalnozemelie, mnogopolositsa*.

40. By the use of vague terms, this state of affairs was glossed over; thus Molotov speaks of 'over half (the land) which has not been reallocated . . .', *ibid*.

41. On the difficulty of cultivating land because of the enormous amount of time wasted in moving from place to place, see Gomberg, *Zakony o zemle*. (Moscow, 1927), pp. 63–4.

42. Lyashchenko, *Istoriya narodnogo khozyaistva SSSR*. (Moscow, 1956, Vol. III. *Sotsializm*, p. 138.

43. Kosior provided these figures for the Ukraine in November 1929. He is quoted in *Voprosy Istorii KPSS*, 1962, No. 4, pp. 60–1. Figures for Tambov are provided by their delegate to the Fifteenth Party Congress. *15-ty S'ezd VKP(b)*, stenogramme, p. 1120.

44. Stalin, a speech delivered on February 19, 1933, *Sochineniya*, Vol. XIII, p. 246.

45. *NAF*, 1927, No. 4, p. 159.

46. *Tsentralnaya chernozemnaya oblast* of which the capital was Voronezh, and which also included Tambov, later to become a separate *oblast*.

47. *5-ty S'ezd Sovetov*, Bull. No. 3, p. 3.

48. *ibid*., Bull. No. 4, p. 18. *Bednyatskie raiony* were very numerous at this time.

49. In March 1931 a specialist informed the Sixth Congress of Soviets that in the Klinski *raion* of the Moscow *oblast* the average cost of delivering merchandise to the villages exceeded the cost of transporting the same merchandise from Odessa to England, or from Riga to America. *6-toi S'ezd Sovetov*, Bull. No. 20, pp. 26–7.

50. *Podkulachnik*—the kulak's hireling, the abetter of the kulak.

51. *5-ty S'ezd Sovetov*, Bull. No. 16, p. 4.

52. These figures are given by Larin, member of the anti-alcohol commission attached to the *TsIK*. *5-ty S'ezd Sovetov*, Bull. No. 19, pp. 23–4.

53. Very well described by Sholokhov in *Virgin Soil Upturned*, Vol. 1.

54. *NAF*, 1928, No. 1, p. 93.

55. It is only in translation that this sounds 'learned'; the peasant's expression is simply *trekhpolka*.

56. Bolshakov, *op. cit.*, p. 432.

57. *NAF*, 1928, No. 1, p. 93.

58. Speech by Budenny, *16-taya Konferentsiya VKP(b)*, stenogramme, p. 197. See also his speech in *5-ty S'ezd Sovetov*, Bull. No. 16, p. 6.

59. Molotov, *15-ty S'ezd VKP(b)*, stenogramme, p. 1065; Kalinin, *16-taya Konferentsiya VKP(b)*, stenogramme, p. 132.

60. *Pravda* editorial, February 2, 1929.

61. *Zakon kak dyshlo, kuda povernul tuda i vyshlo*. The others are: *Chto mne zakony, koli sudi znakomy*, and, *Zakon—pautina, shmel proskochit, mukha uvyaznet*.

62. The German specialist in problems of Soviet agriculture, Otto Schiller, who lived in the USSR during NEP, considers that this is true even of the kulaks. *Die Landwirtschaft des Sovietunion 1917–53* (Tubingen 1954), p. 19.

63. *NAF*, 1928, No. 1, p. 92.

64. Budenny, *5-ty S'ezd Sovetov*, Bull. No. 16, p. 6.

65. Vishnevsky of Gosplan in his introduction to a discussion at the Communist Academy, *NAF* 1926, No. 6.

66. Hubbard, *op. cit.*, p. 91. Vishnevsky, in the speech referred to in Note 65 declared that the peasant was consuming 15% more than before the war.

67. Carr, *A History of Soviet Russia; Socialism in One Country*, Vol. 1, p. 212.

68. Bolshakov, *op. cit.*, p. 100.

Chapter 2

THE PROBLEM OF CLASS
STRATIFICATION WITHIN
THE PEASANTRY

The peasantry, which had proved an indispensable ally during the October Days, and an unpredictable and troublesome support during the Civil War, continued to figure largely in the régime's concerns, a source of perpetual political and doctrinal anxiety.

During NEP, the divergence between the fundamental aspirations of the peasantry and those of the Soviet régime became more and more marked.

'The peasantry . . .', declared Trotsky, 'is the protoplasm out of which new classes emerged in the past, and are continuing to emerge in the present.'[1]

Lenin, in even more alarming terms, said that 'day by day, hour by hour, the peasantry is engendering capitalism . . .'.

By the middle of 1924, NEP had already proved itself by having got under way again an economy which had been wrecked by the Civil War. But this was not enough; great dangers continued to beset the régime. The resumption, modest as yet, of economic life following upon the recovery of agriculture, was accompanied by a rebirth of what the Party referred to as 'agrarian capitalism'.

Officially, the hiring of wage-labour by village entrepreneurs and the lease of agricultural land, were prohibited. But in fact no one could fail to notice that 'capitalist relationships', hence the use of wage-labour and the lease of land, had taken root in the countryside, that 'illegal capitalism'[2] was in process of developing, and that, as an inevitable consequence, a new stratification was forming within the peasantry, whose fortunes had undergone a marked levelling-out process during the revolution and the Civil War. The Left of the Party was alarmed by these disquieting signs, but the group in power was inclined to minimize the negative aspects of this trend, and to stress rather the practical and tangible gains of NEP. The Left wished—while continuing with NEP—to introduce a series of socialist measures (planning, industrialization, and perhaps a few steps in the direction of collectivization), and simultaneously to initiate action to limit the growth of the kulaks.

The group in power was ruled by a different logic: that of an increase in concessions to the peasantry.

At the beginning of 1925, then, NEP entered a second phase during which the restrictions impeding the free course of the private peasant economy were lifted. The hiring of wage-labour, and the lease of land were authorized [3] in order to 'liquidate the vestiges of war communism'.[4] As Premier Rykov explained to Party officials, administrative measures and repression would now no longer be allowed, even in dealing with kulaks; only economic measures would be permissible (in particular the use of fiscal policy, but also deprivation of the right to vote, although this was not an economic measure), together with a so-called positive policy, the aim of which would be to help the peasants.[5]

As early as May 1924, Zinovev was worried by the fact that 'something new has just begun. As a result of NEP, the countryside is undergoing a process of class stratification'. The régime had won support 'within the prosperous sector of the peasantry', which for Zinovev was a disquieting symptom. And yet Zinovev, who was soon to find himself dramatically opposed to the very policy which he was then advocating, declared that, instead of relentlessly bringing pressure to bear on the kulak, one must 'help the middle peasant, help the poor peasant'.[6]

The clearest and most optimistic description of this new phase of NEP was given by Bukharin in the famous watchword 'Get rich!'; this was apparently addressed to the peasantry as a whole, but it could have only one result.

'The beneficiaries of party and governmental favours were, on the whole, the enterprising and well-to-do peasants', notes E. H. Carr.[7] But these peasants were inevitably becoming kulaks.

From 1925 onwards, as a result of the inevitable interplay of market laws, and of factors peculiar to a primitive agricultural society, the process of stratification within the peasantry increased, and the Soviet régime was faced with a new class movement within the agricultural masses, a movement which ran counter to the régime's own objectives. A stratification similar to that of the pre-war period was beginning to emerge, and was causing widespread disillusion amongst the batraks and the bednyaks. Many of them had fought for the Soviet régime on the various fronts, or had requisitioned grain from the village exploiters, only to find that the government were now favouring these self-same property owners, and even the grasping kulaks themselves. The latter were meanwhile seizing control in the countryside, and beginning to support the poor man's Soviet régime.

This situation caused great anxiety among the leadership, and spread confusion among the activists. Opinions varied as to the extent to which these processes had taken root, and the dangers which might arise from them. This was a source of discord which caused some of the bitterest disputes within the Party. But even the optimistic Right-wing could not remain indifferent to the progress of the better-off strata in the villages, and their growing influence among the mass of the peasantry.

It was abundantly clear that the free dynamic of NEP was producing kulaks in the countryside, as well as Nepmen in the towns. Even the optimistic Bukharin, who foresaw the *vrastanie* (integration) of the kulaks under the socialist system, nevertheless looked on this class as an alien, and even a hostile one. If conditions unfavourable to the régime were to develop, there was the risk that a *smychka* (alliance) of hostile classes nurtured by NEP might combine against the Soviet government.

For this reason, it was of primary importance for the régime and its theoreticians to find out and to define as precisely as possible the degree of stratification, the extent of each stratum, and its economic strength.

However, the task was one of great complexity. The researchers and politicians worked within the context of certain basic concepts handed down to them by Lenin, that is, batrak, bednyak, serednyak and kulak. Definitions of these categories caused difficulty enough, but there were still further complications. Amongst the serednyaks, for example, distinctions were often made between the *malomoshchny* (weak), and the *zazhitochny* (better-off) or *krepki* (strong). Nor did the list end there. There was no question but that the poorer peasants were harshly exploited by the kulaks; the four basic categories undoubtedly existed, but these facts eluded definition and research because the interrelationships of peasant society at this time were blurred, and because the terms in which the Party sought to express these realities were inadequate.[8]

Two further obstacles prevented the Party's Marxist researchers from fully grasping the reality of the class situation in the countryside. The researcher was subject to the changing political line followed by the Party, and was also affected by the climate of the political struggles between opposing forces which were raging within the Party at this time. The risk of his being labelled a member of the opposition considerably distorted the course and conclusions of research.

Another handicap was the weakness of the Party cadres assigned to agriculture in general, and in particular to scientific research on the peasantry.

1. *Attempts at Classification and their Results*

The revolution, the agrarian reform, and the partial dekulakization movement of 1918 (the *kombedy*, or Committees of Poor Peasants movement) brought about a considerably greater degree of equality in peasant holdings. The kulaks seemed almost to have disappeared, whereas the bednyaks were receiving additional plots of land.

However, the trend towards a greater equality was only partial, at times indeed it was illusory. Although those without land, and those with too little, did receive additional holdings, when it came to the equipment which was necessary for the cultivation of the land, they either received too little, or none at all.[9] This situation created a veritable tangle of contradictions, which caused the re-emergence of the differences which had so recently been evened out.

A peasant who had no draught animals, or lacked sufficient agricultural implements to cultivate his land, had to hire them from a more fortunate neighbour, or else was forced to let part of his land for rent to a better-equipped *khozyain*, and then seek employment as a labourer under the same neighbour, or elsewhere.

According to one of the estimates made by the *TsSU* round about 1926, 28·2% of the farms in the RSFSR, 37·5% in the Ukraine, and 11·4% in Belorussia had recourse to the hiring of animals and implements in order to cultivate their land.[10] A situation in which a peasant had to borrow a horse or cart in order to work, usually at the cost of part of his crop, or was obliged to seek paid employment from other peasants, was in itself sufficient to give rise to economic inequalities, and to relationships which encouraged exploitation.

It must not be forgotten that where the countryside is poor, it takes little to create antagonistic social strata. Between the man who goes hungry, and the man who can satisfy his hunger, there is a world of difference, although, in economic terms, the difference may at times consist only of the few dozen extra poods of grain or potatoes possessed by the more fortunate peasant.

Luck had also something to do with these differences; a bad or a good year, a fire, an illness, or the number of workers in the family, personal qualities such as diligence, initiative, or cultural level (ability to read was in itself an enormously important factor) and sobriety, were all of prime importance to economic success. These qualities greatly favoured certain peasants who knew how to take advantage of NEP's already fairly well-developed market economy.

The peasant is at one and the same time producer and merchant. The Party theoreticians called him a 'small commodity producer'.[11]

The laws of the market, with its price fluctuations and its need for credit, small-scale mercantile production with its internal contradictions, the inequality of equipment and the reverses characteristic of a primitive level of agriculture—all of these factors contributed to the differentiation which resulted in the creation of social extremes within the peasantry: better-off peasants on the one hand, bednyaks and agricultural labourers (batraks) on the other.

It was not easy, however, to record or to analyse these facts. The degree of differentiation within the Soviet peasantry was not as yet very far advanced. Basically, the peasant masses were more or less homogeneous, and even those who claimed to discern amongst them the beginnings of social classes admitted that they were dealing only with the embryonic forms of a development which was still in its initial stages.

Poor or better-off, kulak or even (in a large number of cases) batrak, the peasant was first and foremost the owner of a farm. In this respect

'not only does almost every peasant work on his farm, but he himself or the members of his family also work outside of it: or again, he may take on workers, or hire the means of production from someone, or alternatively hire out his own means of production. He borrows or lends, for example, his seed-grain. In short, there are practically no cases where a peasant farm manages its production entirely independently. But very often it will nevertheless be managed, in substance, as an independent farm'.[12]

These remarks, made by a researcher specializing in the social structure of the peasantry, give a fair idea of the complexity of the problem.

The choice of criteria for classifying a peasant in a given group, and the working-out of research and statistical methods, represented an arduous undertaking. The simple-seeming category of batrak (agricultural wage-labourer) alone presented difficulties, since many batraks owned small farms,[13] sought employment by the day, and not for a season or a year, and for this very reason might only be bednyaks who also very frequently left (or sent a member of their family) to work as wage-labourers.

As for the bednyak, he was often defined as a husbandman, who sowed little, had no horse,[14] and who often went to work 'near by'. But according to Strumilin, the bednyak was the proprietor of a farm the revenus of which did not exceed that of a batrak, in other words eighty roubles per annum.[15]

There were still more definitions for this one category of bednyaks, who were looked upon as the mainstay of the Soviet régime in the countryside. It was difficult, too, to distinguish between the bednyaks and the neighbouring stratum of serednyaks, who were classified, from the doctrinal point of view, not as a 'support' but as an 'ally'. It was sometimes said that half of the sered-nyaks were 'weak' (*malomoshchnye*), for they did not sow enough, had very little equipment, and scarcely managed to make ends meet without additional work.[16] The difference between them and the bednyaks lay in the possession of a horse. But many peasants who had a horse were also classified as bednyaks.

It was difficult, moreover, to determine at what point a serednyak could be classified as 'strong', and especially at what point a 'strong' serednyak became a kulak; according to certain researchers a peasant, be he 'strong' or 'weak', who exploited no one was merely an 'allied' serednyak, whereas in their view the true kulak was ex-clusively the peasant who exploited wage-labour.

It would have been a simple matter if such had been the case. But in the first place, even a poor serednyak was very often an employer, and hired out means of production [17] and this, naturally, was even more true of the 'strong' serednyak. Moreover, a large number of kulaks, perhaps half of them, were classified as such according to other criteria than the hiring of labour, for they did not hire wage-labour.[18]

The criterion most frequently employed to determine the rural strata, that of a farm's sown area,[19] considerably distorted the pic-ture in favour of the better-off strata, for it greatly reduced the number of kulaks. In Soviet conditions in which the purchase of land was forbidden, and in which too large a farm attracted the attention of the authorities and tax-inspectors, and could result in deprivation of the right to vote, the economic activity of the peasant-entre-preneurs was directed instead towards the accumulation of power by commercial transactions, and the acquisition of implements, especially agricultural machinery.

Thus, a farm with a large sown area might belong to a large family of middle peasants, whereas a much smaller sown area might well, according to Soviet definitions, conceal a genuine kulak, who hired out agricultural machinery to peasants, stocked and resold grain, etc. He might, besides, sow much more than was apparent, on land rented from poor peasants, frequently on condition that the trans-action would not be registered.

The criterion based on number of livestock was no more reliable. Within certain limits it provided a clearer picture of the bednyak, but it left the researcher powerless in his attempt to define the other strata. In fact, a strong peasant, possessing some three cows and two horses, could very well be classified as a kulak, but he could just as easily be a 'good' serednyak, if he had a large family, did not hire labour, and was not involved to any great extent in trade.

Many departments concerned with the peasantry, notably the

Commissariat of Finance, the Central Statistical Administration, *Gosplan*, and probably the department of the Commissariat of Commerce responsible for State procurements, promoted or carried out sociological or statistical research. An important contribution was also to be made by the Republican Commissariats for Agriculture, especially those of the RSFSR and the Ukraine. Research and general studies were also carried out by the Agrarian Section (soon to be baptized the Agrarian Institute') of the Communist Academy, under the direction of a gifted researcher, Kritsman. Other sections of the Academy, notably the department of State and Law, were also involved.

Important research and surveys were carried out by the offices of the Commissariat of Inspection and by certain departments of the Central Committee; but despite the abundance of institutions dealing with the problem, the results obtained were meagre.

The Academy's Agrarian Section began to work out statistical tables combining data based on the value of means of production, including implements and livestock, with so-called 'direct social indices', such as the employment of labour, the hiring out of implements, and the renting of land. In 1928, Kritsman suggested to the Academy a very complicated but ingenious system embodying the results of the main indices which would, in his opinion, make it possible to differentiate between a 'petty bourgeois' farm, and a 'petty capitalist' or 'semi-capitalist' farm by determining in percentage terms the degree to which its economic contacts were those of an 'exploiting', 'exploited' or 'independent' farm.[20] Some of his listeners greeted all this rather sceptically as a sterile exercise in hair-splitting, but he told them: 'This is no easy task, given the multiplicity and complexity of the social relationships involved. But I am firmly convinced that it is a task which can be carried out. . . .'

He forgot, however, that he himself had declared, at the beginning of his exposé, that the calculations relating to this particular research were too crude, '. . . for our statistical materials are unfortunately ill-adapted to such comparatively subtle research, they are too rough for this purpose'.[21]

The weakness of the 'capitalist' factors in the peasant economy, which the author stressed several times in his speech, was another source of difficulties.

A first attempt at a census and presentation of a general account of the social stratification of the country as a whole was made in 1925 by the *TsSU*, within the context of the work of a commission instructed to estimate the availability of grain and fodder (*khlebofurazhny balans*). But these results were rejected by the Commissariat of Inspection, as was the sown area index which had been adopted.[22] Two years later, a special Commission was set up by *Sovnarkom* to study fiscal charges, and this included the leading specialists in the field, under the chairmanship of Frumkin, then Commissar of Finance.

They produced the following figures for the year 1925:

serednyaks	—	64·7%
bednyaks	—	24%
kulaks	—	6·9%, rising to 7·9% for 1926–7.[23]

Strumilin submitted another calculation for the year 1926–7, which took as its basic index the income of the farm. He based his findings on material published for tax purposes by the Commissariat of Finance. His results:

serednyaks	—	60·6%
bednyaks	—	30.3%
better-off	—	3%

His classification did not include the category of kulak. His calculations for 1927–8 gave an unexpected percentage of 45·9% bednyaks; he was obliged in view of this error to correct his calculations, and to submit another table giving, respectively, 56·8%, 37·9% and 4·8% for the better-off peasants.[24]

In 1928, an important new effort, undertaken under the auspices of the Agrarian Institute, was based on a census and detailed description of 700,000 households. Instead of the three groups which concerned the finance authorities,[25] this study distinguished four principal groups, worked out by means of combined indices, including:

1. Value of means of production.
2. Employment of labour.
3. The hiring and hiring out of means of production.
4. Non-agricultural income.

The results were then extended by extrapolation to 21 million households to give the following: proletariat 7·3%, semi-proletariat 18·5%, 'simple producers' (*prostye tovaroproizvoditeli*) 59·6%, 'petty-capitalists' 3·6%. This survey also showed that the percentage of this last category rose as high as 5% in contiguous agricultural regions only, but that in other regions the percentage varied between 1·9% and 3·5%.

One could quote a dozen more such studies, almost all of which give different results for each stratum, and which differ as much by the criteria adopted as by the classification itself.

We should also mention data published in the journal of *Gosplan* by two research workers (probably working in the Commissariat of

Finance) and based on *TsSU* material for 1926–7 but with approximate corrections for the year 1928–9.[26] They arrived at a figure of only 51% of serednyaks and 30·4% of bednyaks. There was no mention of the batraks who were probably included among the bednyaks. Moreover, 18·6% of the households, including 4·5% of kulaks and 14–15% 'better-off' were included in the *verkhushka* (upper stratum).

The existence of such a *verkhushka* as a separate category was disputed by other Party research workers, particularly Gaister, who stated very sensibly that the notion of *zazhitochny* was devoid of class content.[27] Now the Party leaders showed a predilection for the use of this extremely vague term *verkhushka*, which was taken at times to signify only the kulaks, at other times the kulaks and the better-off. When class tension and the political temperature mounted, it was the vaguest term which appeared most often in speeches and in the press, and the word kulak was then accompanied in many cases by the words: 'and the better-off' (*zazhitochnye*). For Stalin, these represented the 15% of households of which he was to speak in 1933 as belonging to the past.[28] Viewed in its historical context, this statement of Stalin's has a particularly sinister significance. . . .

For the moment, the difficulties of studying the stratification of the peasantry proved insurmountable, and in the end no valid and authoritative survey of this intractable problem was ever produced. The authorities took their own political decisions and acted accordingly, thus settling the question without waiting for an exact appraisal of the situation. . . .

At the Conference of Agrarian-Marxists (those dealing with the agrarian problem) which was held about the end of 1929, the small number of workers in this field met and took stock of the studies which had so far been carried out. As yet, they were neither adequate nor conclusive. But on the last day of this conference Stalin read a speech in which he spoke of the possibility of sending NEP 'to the devil'. In so doing, he was consigning every laborious incomplete survey, with its refinements, and its subtleties, to the same destination. . . .

We shall now examine our *dramatis personae*, in other words the batrak, the bednyak, the serednyak and the kulak, and try to arrive at an approximate estimate of the situation of each stratum, and of the problems which they presented to the Soviet régime.

2. *The Batrak*

Before the revolution, the batrak was to be found at the bottom of the social ladder. Towards the end of NEP, he was in the same position. According to doctrine, he was the associate of the urban proletariat in the exercise of the dictatorship; in reality the batraks constituted the poorest, most disinherited stratum of Soviet society in general, and of rural society in particular. The social definition of the batrak held that he was a proletarian, living solely from paid agricultural labour. We have seen that in practice the situation was always more complex. This explains the difficulty of determining the number of batraks. According to the figures submitted to the Conference of Agrarian-Marxists in December 1929, there were 2,760,000 batraks in 1927, but their numbers were constantly increasing. In 1929 they numbered 3,231,000. Of these, the number employed on a long-term basis was continually decreasing because of restrictions, and of the risk incurred by their employers of being classed as kulaks. On the other hand, the number of day-labourers, who were less protected by the law, was increasing. 20% of the number quoted above for 1927 were day-labourers, but in 1929 they were already 39%.[29]

We should first of all make it clear that the majority of batraks owned a plot of land. *Bolshevik* published an article which showed that in the entire country, in 1926, 63% of the batraks owned farms, and a third of these possessed arable land and animals, and still others had arable land alone. Some 35% no longer had any land,[30] but it is very likely that even they still aspired to possess some.

A small number of batraks was employed by the sovkhozes (160,000 in 1927), and a large number by the rural communities and the co-operatives. The communities employed mainly shepherds—851,000 shepherds in 1927, of whom 629,000 were employed by rural communities, and the remainder by individual peasants. The majority of batraks worked for individual peasants. It has been calculated that, in 1927, of all those registered as wage earners hired on a long-term basis (but for less than one year, the *srokovye*), 1,365,000 worked for individual peasants.[31] To these must be added a large number of day-labourers. But, and this is important, it was not necessarily the kulaks who employed wage labour. The employment of labour was widespread in the villages, and at times even a bednyak would be forced to employ a worker.

It is very difficult to obtain an exact idea of how the batraks were divided up. Lyashchenko reported that in the wheat producing regions of the RSFSR, 31.5% of all households employed wage labour.[32] It may be supposed that at times the serednyaks, too, employed *srokovye*, although mainly day-labourers, whereas the kulaks, while they employed day-labourers as well, employed most often on a long-term basis. In fact, the day-labourers evaded every census, for there was no shortage of batraks, and no one dreamt of declaring to the authorities hired labour of this kind. It is difficult, therefore, to determine how many batraks were employed by kulaks alone. Lyashchenko points out that only 51·1% of the rich hired wage labour, and provides an abundance of incomplete and relative figures, but no definite conclusions.

The fact is that the data were either lacking or unsuitable. The following, however, seems a reasonable hypothesis: if only half of the kulaks employed wage labour, and 1% only of all households employed more than one batrak (as Kritsman stated to the Communist Academy in 1928),[33] one would arrive at a figure of about one million batraks, on condition that one agreed on the percentage of kulaks, whether 3·24% as Lyashchenko would have it, or 3·9% as he claims in another page of his work, or, again, 5%, the figure accepted by the political authorities towards 1929. . . . Our estimate of the number of batraks working for kulaks is based on this last index which, as we shall see later, was never confirmed by research of any kind.

The working conditions of the batraks (even in a sovkhoz) were 'slave-like'. The *Platform* of the Left Opposition (September 1927) states as much[34] and there are ample official data as well as information published recently to confirm this opinion.

The batraks worked twelve to thirteen hours per day in summer, eleven hours in spring and autumn, and their earnings did not exceed the half of what was earned by a sovkhoz worker. In Siberia, where the inequality was greatest, they earned 2·5 times less than an industrial worker.[35] Part of this wage, moreover, was paid in kind. Sometimes employment even took the form of métayage or corvée (*izdolshchina*; *otrabotka*), especially in Central Asia, but elsewhere too. 'At every turn one encounters cases of the slave (*kabalny*) labour which lasts for several years, in the guise of education, fictitious marriage, pseudo-apprenticeship or blood relationship.[36]

It is worth mentioning that a fairly large percentage of batraks consisted of women, youths and children, and that more often than not they could neither read nor write.

Information furnished by the Soviet press of the period provides a fairly exact picture of the situation of the batraks in the Soviet village. Everything was against them. In embarking on the neo-NEP line, from 1925 onwards, the régime seemed to have made its choice.

'It is not a question now of preventing the better-off peasants from becoming richer', writes *Pravda* of March 20, 1925, 'but of getting the serednyaks to co-operate, and the batraks to unite.'

Of this, only the first part came about. Legislation for the protection of labour certainly existed, but was not enforced, because the

Inspectorate of Labour in the countryside had only a very small number of inspectors at its disposal. The authorities on the spot, including the peoples' tribunals, were inclined to be on the side of the more powerful.[37]

The Agricultural Workers' Trade Union (*Vserabotzemles*), even in the opinion of the Party's theoretical organ, did little to protect the batraks or to help them improve their lot according to their aims.[38] Of 3 million batraks, only a quarter were members of the Union, as Molotov regretfully noted in his speech to the Fifteenth Party Congress. He was probably exaggerating, for a publication of the Communist Academy in 1929 claimed that, of 3 million batraks, only 424,621 were organized. . . .[39]

In the same speech Molotov stated that only 14,000 batraks were Party members at the end of 1927. The situation was to change later, but very slowly. Data published by *Bolshevik* in 1929 show that in the Party's rural organizations the batrak sector was the least well-represented.[40] Certain officials would have nothing to do with them, on the grounds that 'they are all drunkards'. Others claimed, with reason, that it was impossible to recruit them into the Party because they were never free from their work. At times, at regional conferences, among the hundreds of delegates, hardly any batraks were to be found.

We know that the batrak aspired, like every other peasant, to become an independent farmer, to have more land, and more implements with which to cultivate it. He would perhaps have been prepared to join an agricultural collective, but no one invited him to join such a collective, the régime at that time not being in the least interested in collectivization. Nor did anyone think of providing the batraks with more land and implements.

The NEP economy needed the batraks, but the Soviet régime could not find the way to deal with their predicament. And so, for the moment, the batrak continued to figure as the pariah of the society which had emerged from the October Revolution, and to wait for his share in the fruits of that revolution. Meanwhile, where was no domain of Soviet life in which the gulf between doctrine and reality was more blatantly obvious, and more compromising for the socialist idea. . . .

Consequently this state of affairs weighed heavily on the revolutionary conscience of many activists.

3. *The Bednyak*

The bednyak, the batrak's closest neighbour on the social ladder, figured in the Party's political vocabulary as the 'social support' of the Party in the countryside, together with the batraks.

We have seen that, for Larin, the bednyak was primarily a peasant without a horse. Official estimates of the 'horseless' oscillate around 30%. We are dealing in any case with a peasant whose income from his farm is clearly insufficient to support his family, even in a fertile agricultural region. This forces him to seek his means of subsistence in supplementary work, and primarily in agricultural wage labour.

Another criterion, aiming at greater precision, attempted to define the bednyak in terms of a certain relationship between the lack of means of production, and the surplus of labour resulting from this.

Proceeding from this definition, one group of researchers distinguished between the bednyaks of the so-called 'proletarian' farms and those of the so-called 'semi-proletarian' farms. The first category included those farmers who sold their labour-power for more than fifty days per year. The second category comprised those who sold their labour-power for twenty to fifty days per year, or hired draught animals for more than twenty days, or implements for over ten days per year.[41]

If the first were estimated, *grosso modo* at 3 million, and contained some 10 million souls, the others, the bednyaks proper numbered 6 or 7 millions.[42]

According to Strumilin, the standard of living of the bednyak was scarcely superior to that of the batrak. For him, a bednyak differed from an unemployed peasant only in that he was not registered at the unemployment exchange, and that he possessed a plot of land which entitled him to be considered a farmer.[43]

According to another author, the bednyak's situation was useful to the country's economy, since they represented a labour force which could be preserved for the future of industrialization, without dispersing or degenerating. In fact, the notorious (and disastrous) overpopulation of the Russian countryside (calculated variously to be in the region of 8–10 or more million workers) did relate mainly to this stratum.

Although the facts and figures quoted above may give an adequate idea of the poverty of the bednyak and the pressure he was capable of creating in the political and economic life of the country, they do not sum up the whole problem. The role of this stratum in the complex interplay of social forces is better understood when one remembers that this 'poor devil' was nevertheless a wheat producer and that his contribution to the State's all-too-modest grain balance could not be ignored. He controlled a certain percentage of the sown area (no figures are available), he was a seller of grain and a purchaser of manufactured products. The bednyak's share of marketable grain is not indicated. It was small, but counted nevertheless.

Gaister, who has emphasized these points, even tried to calculate the contribution of the bednyaks to the peasants' grain reserves. According to him, the first two categories (proletarians and semi-proletarians) must have held, in 1927, 22·2% of the reserves in the Ukraine, 19·7% in the Northern Caucasus, 10·5% in the Urals. 32·1% and 17·2% respectively of the peasantry's purchases of manufactured goods in these last two grain producing regions, were said to have appertained to these categories.[44]

On the one hand then, because of their poverty and destitution, the poor were ready to accept the slogans of the Party, and to collaborate with it in introducing the socialist changes preached by the Soviet régime, provided they be given the necessary material assistance. On the other hand, being producers and buyers, they were treated as such by the authorities. During the many clashes between the régime and the peasantry over the *zagotovki* (grain procurements), and over the prices policy in general, the poor reacted in exactly the same way as the other producers. In this respect they considered themselves peasants like the others, and were treated as such by the procurement agencies and the Politburo. The difficulties and ambiguities of the relationship between the government, and that part of the peasantry considered to be the basic link of the *smychka* are already apparent in this context.

After the proclamation of the pro-kulak phase of NEP, there was a flood of reassuring decisions aimed at calming the fears of the poor and the idealistic activists. At a plenary session of the Central Committee of the Party in 1925, Molotov announced a series of measures to be taken to organize the *bednota*, to help them economically, enlist them in the co-operative movement, and strengthen their role in the selsovets and other village institutions.[45]

The Party, the Agricultural Workers' Trade Union and the Soviet organizations, were called upon to undertake the task of aiding the poor, batraks or bednyaks, who were the Party's staunchest support amongst the peasantry. There was even a lengthy discussion of the need for various forms of collective organization and for activating the peasants' mutual aid committees (*KKOV*).[46] There was no shortage of Party and *TsIK* decrees and circulars on these matters. We shall see what the practical outcome was.

It is significant that the same session approved the decision of the Party in the Ukraine to reorganize its 'Poor Peasants' Committees' (*Komnezamy*), which had been recognized as official organizations since the time of the great *Kombedy* movement in 1918, and to transform them into voluntary organizations.[47] Naturally, this was tantamount to abolishing them. The reason for this reform is clear; it was important not to embitter relations with the more enterprising peasants, who were expected to provide an appreciable increase in agricultural production.

And yet the Party has maintained all along, and still maintains today, that massive aid was constantly being given to the bednyaks to enable them to produce more, to climb the social ladder, and to become serednyaks. According to this particular argument, a continual *oserednyachivanie* (levelling process) was taking place during the NEP period, bringing about an uninterrupted improvement in the conditions of the poor.

At the same time the Party admitted, with a degree of emphasis which varied according to the bitterness of the internal struggle and the line adopted by the Politburo, that a fairly rigorous process of stratification was taking place in the countryside, and had in fact gathered momentum in the last years of NEP. This assumed the exact reverse of the preceding argument, because the process must necessarily have resulted in the disintegration of the middle stratum, by creating a rich 'bourgeois' minority at the one extreme, and an increasingly numerous *bednota* at the other.

In an attempt to reconcile the two theories, it was suggested that, in Soviet conditions, this process of differentiation was of a special kind. Faced with the rise of a better-off, exploiting class from amongst the serednyaks, the Soviet government, by its unfailing vigilance, had reinforced the latter in even greater proportion, adding to their ranks by the promotion of numerous bednyaks.[48] To say the least, this theory has never been satisfactorily proved.

In further support of the argument, Molotov adduced the results of work which had been carried out by a commission of experts; but he criticized this same commission for having concluded, from its findings, that the number of serednyaks had tended to become stabilized. He also criticized it for having underestimated the number of bednyaks. About thirty pages further on, Molotov announced that, from now on, 35% of peasant households would be exempt from the agricultural tax as being bednyaks. Until then, only 27% had enjoyed such exemption. Again quoting the same source, we find Molotov, two years after his decrees on the organization of the bednyaks, noting the failure of that undertaking, and describing the work among the poor as 'scandalously' (*bezobrazno*) neglected, particularly 'these last few years'.[49]

One very reliable economist, Lyashchenko, in a volume published posthumously in 1956, assembled data and statistical tables in support of the official argument, but his figures prove very little. He himself admitted that, in fact, 'we have no statistical data, however incomplete or approximate, on the evolution of class structure in the Soviet village over any given period of years'.[50] This is an important admission, when one comes to assess the extent of the Party's knowledge of the social structure of the peasantry.

In fact, during the NEP period, one could say that there were opposing forces at work within the peasantry, or at least that there was a movement in two different directions: on the one hand there was the embourgeoisement of certain of the serednyaks, who were becoming kulaks, while, on the other hand, certain bednyaks were rising to the rank of serednyaks, provided they had been able to acquire a horse and a plough.

'The revival of agriculture during the NEP period created an illusion of general advancement'—thus one of the Party's own writers. 'But this was by no means a one-way process. The creation of capitalist elements was accompanied by the ousting of another village sector, that of the weaker farms, from the number of economically independent units.' [51]

Certain serednyaks, according to this author, and to numerous other sources, had therefore lost their footing, and were slipping back down the social ladder. Many bednyak farms disappeared completely, while other bednyaks became batraks, and others still went off to find work in the towns, or to add to the already numerous ranks of the unemployed.[52]

The situation was thus very much more complex than the official explanation suggested. But in the absence of data, it is not easy to give an exact account of the changes which were taking place. At all events, as we have seen, the official arguments were questioned by certain Party experts who were in no way involved in any kind of opposition. It could be said that there had been some increase in the number of peasants possessing sown land, but this improvement was by no means universal, and in certain regions a reverse tendency was in evidence; there was probably also a decrease in the number of households without productive livestock, but here again there was no definite trend. According to Lyashchenko, in the RSFSR the number of these households without livestock had decreased between 1924–6, from 31% to 30%.[53] These figures were obtained by sample-survey, and the author himself seems to admit tacitly that they prove nothing. This trend seemed to be more marked in the productive regions of the Russian republic, but in other instances there was even evidence of a reverse tendency.

Thus, the theory of the 'constant improvement in the condition of the bednyak', and of the 'special nature of the differentiation' applied to the increase in the number of serednyaks, is one which we cannot accept, although it is still put forward today by some Soviet authors. The available evidence does not support it. Indeed, the opposite hypothesis is more readily defensible: many serednyaks were becoming poorer, and turning into bednyaks. If the numbers of serednyaks were not decreasing, it is because they were being reinforced by frequent divisions of households whose members, while formally continuing to be classified as serednyaks, were in fact becoming poorer as a result of these divisions. Many bednyak farms were disappearing, but others came to replace them from the ranks of the serednyaks. The general impression is rather one of an increase in the category of bednyaks, and a slight decrease in that of the serednyaks.

According to another official theory, it was held that the assistance given by the régime to the bednyaks, and the successful organization of batrak-bednyak groups, helped to win over the serednyak to the side of the proletariat, thus isolating the kulak.[54] This kind of argument is repeated *ad nauseam*, but is likewise without substance. An adequate impression of the situation of the bednyaks during the final years of NEP can be obtained from a study of the official sources. Following investigations by the Commissariat of Inspection, *Pravda* of April 7, 1928, noted 'a disgraceful disparity between the amount of energy expended in raising funds for the relief of the poor, and the use of these funds in practice'. But the sum gathered at the cost of so much 'energy' was, for the RSFSR, 20 million roubles, and the editors knew perfectly well that, even if used properly, this sum was absurdly low.

In the course of 1928, a whole series of resolutions were adopted, including one important *Sovnarkom* decree on relief for poor peasants.[55] Henceforth 40% of all credits granted to the peasants were to be made available, on favourable terms, to the bednyaks. When the decree was promulgated, one author, who probably worked in this field, published an important article, in which he insisted, as *Pravda* had in the above-mentioned issue, that these decrees had so far had very little practical result. The sum allocated under the new decree would increase the amount of the special credit fund for the poor to 80 million roubles, but this was still very inadequate in relation to their needs.[56]

This special fund was set up in 1926, to remedy the flagrant injustice suffered by the poor peasants under the co-operative movement's distribution of credits, but it was never to prove very effective. The poor took very little part in the co-operative movement, whereas the better-off were strongly represented in it, and occupied a position of control, a situation which was, moreover, entirely in keeping with the spirit of NEP. The co-operatives dealt with the sale of agricultural products, and the purchase of means of production, etc. The peasant who produced little or nothing at all had little place in the co-operative movement. The credit co-operatives naturally preferred the better-off client, and were wary of the bednyak who had not sufficient means to guarantee repayment of his loan. Thus, according to Lyashchenko, only 5·8% to 18·7% of the lower strata benefited from any kind of credit, whereas in the 'petty-capitalist' category 36·1% of households received loans, and much larger ones than the poor.[57] Ignat spoke of this state of affairs as 'an inadmissible distortion of the Party's class line'. On reading the details one can understand his indignation.

The bednyak who needed, essentially, a long-term loan, received only a short-term one, and then only if he offered guarantees, even if he was a member of the co-operative. Those who were not obtained credit even less frequently. The sums loaned were too small: 30–40 roubles for the purchase of a horse, which cost 150, and sometimes (in Belorussia) 25 roubles for construction work, etc. The loans were therefore of no use. They were spent mostly on food (if not on drink), and the fact that they were difficult to recover made the banks even more reluctant to grant credits to the poor.

The above-mentioned special credit funds for the poor, which were administered by the co-operatives, made little impact. Data assembled by the *RKI*, the Finance Inspectorate and by Party offices reveal that all too often these sums failed to reach those for whom they were intended, and were directed instead towards more reliable recipients, particularly the kulaks. The amounts in fact received by the bednyak were, as before, inadequate, and the terms on which they were granted were unfavourable. The hard facts of village life defeated the intentions of the decrees, especially if the latter were not followed up by energetic measures, or rather by the radical reforms which were in fact necessary.

Here is a striking example:

'The bednyak Belov received a loan of 25 roubles from the (credit) association of Lyudnikova, *guberniya* of Bryansk. However [as he was not a member of this co-operative association—M.L.], an initial deduction of 5 roubles 50 kopecks was made for membership and share contribution (*vstupitelny i paevoi vznos*). It was then discovered that Belov had paid 2 roubles to a 'kind-hearted' neighbour for signing his guarantee (such cases were frequent), and in this way a third of the loan went up in smoke as soon as it had been received'.[58]

It is obvious, says the author, that such a loan will not be repaid when due, and will not have helped the bednyak, since it will probably have been 'eaten up'.

The Belovs must surely have been wondering what kind of régime this was, which had promised them so much, but which in practice helped only the most powerful *khozyain*, while the poor continued to live in the greatest distress.

In the political and propaganda context, the bednyak was represented as the faithful mainstay of the régime, the sole representative, together with the batrak, of the dictatorship of the proletariat in the countryside. It was in fact easy for the bednyak to join the Party, he was often chosen as candidate for the local selsovet, and for other posts, especially during periods when relations between the régime and the mass of the peasantry were strained. But economically, in respects of credits and supplies, which were his most immediate concern, the bednyak was the victim of discrimination. It was the other strata who were on top, and who occupied, in practice, a privileged social position in the village, while the bednyak had to be content with a few more or less intangible benefits. This divergence between the realities of the social and economic situation, and the arguments of the political theorists, reflected the fundamental divergence between the position and the objectives of the NEP peasantry, and the objectives of the Soviet régime. Such political consolation prizes as the Party could offer the bednyaks, in the shape of slogans and the few measures designed to organize them in groups with the batraks (the *batratsko-bednyatskie gruppy*) were little more than empty words.

At the end of 1929, two years after the régime's 'turn to the left', during which the bednyak should have been in an increasingly favoured position, there were, in the RSFSR, only 12 thousand organized groups attached to the selsovets, containing in all 139 thousand (!) bednyaks.[59] In three-quarters of the *selsovetsy* there were no groups at all of this kind. Such was the situation even after a considerable amount of agitation and innumerable circulars and editorials, and despite the fact that a special department had been set up in the Central Committee to deal mainly with the political organization of the bednyaks.

The bednyaks, discouraged and disillusioned, did not conceal their discontentment. Ignat, whom we have already quoted, reports that the authorities and the Party cells only turned to the bednyaks when their support was indispensable, especially before elections. Thereafter they were ignored. Speaking of their 'discontent and disappointment', the author quotes as typical the words of a bednyak during a regional conference held by the Orel *Gubkom*:

'The Party cell and the *volkom* call us together only when they are anxious to obtain the largest possible number of votes for their candidates. But afterwards no one takes any interest in us, and nothing is done for us. In fact, we wish to register a protest with the *prokuror* about this attitude towards work with the *bednota*.'

'So far,' the author concludes, 'poor peasants' groups do not seem to be much in evidence in the countryside.'[60]

The remarkable failure of the régime and the Party in this sector of village life will be better understood when one comes to analyse the extent to which the Soviet régime had in fact established itself in the countryside. For the moment, it should be noted that fundamentally the bednyak quoted above, while expressing his disappointment, still had a deeply pro-Soviet attitude. He and his friends wished to complain to the *prokuror* that the official line was not being followed. But there were other reactions, too, of a much more hostile nature.

NOTES AND REFERENCES

1. Trotsky, *op. cit.* (see Ch. 1, Note 23), Vol. I.

2. For example, Kritsman, 'K voprosu o klassovom rassloenii sovetskoi derevni', *NAF*, 1925, No. 2, pp. 50–7.

3. See the resolutions of the Fourteenth Party Congress of April 1925, and in particular those of the Central Committee of April 30, 1925, in *KPSS v rezolyutsiyakh*, Vol. II, pp. 116–26. For a brief outline of this policy see R. Daniels, *The Conscience of the Revolution.* (Cambridge, Mass., 1960), pp. 257–9.

4. Rykov, quoting the resolutions of the Fourteenth Conference, in his 'Osnovnie voprosy nashei politiki v derevne', *NAF*, 1925, No. 10, p. 13.

5. *ibid.*, pp. 8, 13–14.

6. Carr, *A History of Soviet Russia; The Interregnum.* (London, 1954), p. 47 gives this quotation from the Thirteenth Party Congress, stenogramme, pp. 100–2.

7. Carr, *A History of Soviet Russia; Socialism in One Country*, Part I, p. 98.

8. *ibid.*, p. 93.

9. Described by Kritsman, *op. cit.*, by Vermenichev in his contribution to a discussion at the Communist Academy, *NAF*, 1928, No. 5, and by Trifonov, *'Ocherki klassovoi borby v gody NEPa, 1927–37'* (Moscow, 1960), pp. 182–3.

10. Vermenichev, *NAF*, 1928, No. 5, p. 138.

11. *Melkotovarny proizvoditel.*

12. Kritsman, *NAF*, 1928, No. 4, p. 142; an article entitled 'Criteria for the study of the class structure in the countryside' (a discussion held at the Communist Academy in January 1928).

13. Libkind, 'Sotsialno-ekonomicheskaya geografiya krestyan-skogo khozyaistva', *NAF*, 1929, No. 2–3, p. 57.

14. Larin, *Sotsialnaya struktura* SSSR *i sudby agrarnogo per-enaseleniya*. (Moscow/Leningrad, 1928), quoted by Libkind, *op. cit.*, p. 58.

15. *Planovoe Khozyaistvo*, 1929, No. 8, p. 54.

16. Stalin, *Sochineniya*, Vol. XIII, p. 246.

17. Gaister, *NAF*, 1927, No. 11–12, p. 20. Lyashchenko, *op. cit.* (see Ch. 1, Note 42), Vol. III, p. 138 reports that in the cereal producing regions of the RSFSR 34–37% of peasants with 0·1 to three desyatins of sown land employed wage labour. The problem is complex enough as it is; however, it should be added that a serednyak or a kulak would most often go in person to carry out a job on the bednyak's land, taking with him his own horse and imple-ments. In this way he appeared to be a day-labourer employed by the bednyak.

18. According to Lyashchenko, *op. cit.*, Vol. III, p. 138, in the wheat-growing zone 44·3% of all wage-labour in 1926 was employed by households sowing more than twenty-five desyatins. But 31·5% of all households in this zone also employed labour. On pp. 238–9 the author states that 51·1% of all kulaks in the country, estimated at 3·24% of all peasant households, employed wage-labour.

19. A survey carried out by the *TsSU* in 1925 was criticized by Yakovlev of the Commissariat of Inspection for employing this criterion. See Gaister's speech to the Conference of Agrarian Marx-ists, *NAF*, 1930, No. 1, pp. 92–3.

20. This system was explained to the Communist Academy by Kritsman. *NAF*, 1928, No. 4. The contents of this discussion are contained in Nos. 4, 5, 6, of this journal.

21. *NAF*, 1928, No. 4, pp. 115, 140.

22. According to Gaister, *NAF*, 1930, No. 1, pp. 92–5, and other sources.

23. The criteria adopted were sown area and number of draught animals, and for the *verkhushka*, long-term employment of wage-labour. Molotov's speech to the Fifteenth Party Congress was based upon these figures. *15-ty S'ezd VKP(b)*, stenogramme, pp. 1053–7.

24. For Strumilin's rather fruitless effort see his article 'Rassloenie sovetskoi derevni', *Planovoe Khozyaistvo*, 1929, No. 8.

25. Gaister, who supervised this work, proposed as many as five groups: proletariat, semi-proletariat, serednyaks, entrepreneurs, and a group of semi-capitalists and petty capitalists. See his article 'Sootnosheniya klassov i grupp v derevne', *NAF*, 1927, No. 10, p. 25. Since, according to his estimate, the two upper strata con-stituted 15·5% in the Ukraine, 23·6% in the North Caucasus, and

24·7% in the Urals, his results were used by the Left Opposition. This forced him to retract in another article, 'Rassloenie derevni i oppozitsiya', *NAF*, No. 11–12, in which the figures for the same groups nevertheless remain very high. The suitability of the category 'entrepreneur' was questioned on all sides and it was therefore abandoned by its authors.

26. Averbukh and Bryukhanov, *Planovoe Khozyaistvo*, 1929, No. 11, pp. 91–2.

27. Gaister, *NAF*, 1927, No. 11–12, p. 20.

28. Stalin, speech to the Congress of Kolkhoz Shock Workers, *Sochineniya*, Vol. XIII, p. 246.

29. Gaister, *NAF*, 1930, No. 1, pp. 96–7. Note that there is a difference of about one million persons between the figures of the *TsSU* and those of the Agricultural Workers' Trade Union.

30. Spektor, 'Profsoyuzy i rabota v derevne', *Bolshevik*, 1928, No. 8, p. 74. Larin gives the figure of 1,300,000 for those without land. 'Chastny kapital v selskom khozyaistve', *NAF*, 1927, No. 4, p. 40.

31. In a 1928 *TsU* publication quoted by A. Levin, *NAF*, 1929, No. 10 (bibliographical index).

32. Lyashchenko, *op. cit.*, Vol. III, p. 130.

33. *NAF*, 1928, No. 4, p. 117. In 1926 Kritsman estimated that the *total* of peasants employed one and a half million batraks. *NAF*, 1927, No. 2, p. 10. The *TsSU*'s figure of 1,100,00 batraks and shepherds in 1926 is quoted by Larin, *NAF*, 1927, No. 4, p. 41. However, Larin questions the *TsSU* figure and insists that in 1926 2·5 million batraks and shepherds were in the employ of private peasants.

34. *Les Bolcheviks contre Staline*, 1923–8. (Paris, 1957), p. 95.

35. Trifonov, *op. cit.* (see Note 9), p. 180.

36. N. Vizen, an article on the problem of batraks' wages, *NAF*, 1929, No. 7, p. 123.

37. e.g. Koshelev, 'Batratskie zabastovki', *NAF*, 1929, No. 10, p. 86. Koshelev states that the tribunals frequently protected kulaks, passed verdicts in their favour, and 'undermined the willingness of the batraks to prosecute their employers'. This was taking place not only in 1927, but as late as October 1929!

38. Spektor, *op. cit.*, p. 76. There is an abundance of evidence to support this: e.g. the official data of the Commissariat of Inspection on the application of the law concerning the protection of agricultural wage-labour are quoted by Pleshkov in *NAF*, 1927, No. 11 (bibliographical index).

39. Molotov, *15-ty S'ezd VKP(b)*, stenogramme, p. 1093; An-

garov, *Klassovaya borba v sovetskoi derevni.* (Moscow, 1929), pp. 41–2.

40. Vareikis, 'Korennie voprosy raboty sredi batrachestva', *Bolshevik*, 1929, No. 2, p. 90.

41. Gaister, *NAF*, 1927, No. 10, pp. 27–8.

42. Ignat, 'Khozyaistvennaya pomoshch derevenskoi bednote', *NAF*, 1928, No. 10, p. 93.

43. Strumilin, *op. cit.*, p. 56.

44. Volf, 'Problemy rekonstruktsii selskogo khozyaistva', *Planovoe Khozyaistvo*, 1929, No. 2, pp. 100–1; Gaister, *NAF*, 1927, No. 10, pp. 33, 36. Gaister admits that these are very rough estimates; they are to be taken only as an order of magnitude.

45. Summarized in an article by Milyutin, *NAF*, 1925, No. 9.

46. The importance of these *krestkomy*, with their local and central organization, budgets, Congresses, etc., should not be overstressed. The poor quality of their work was condemned in a Party resolution of September 6, 1929. See the collection of documents *Kollektivizatsiya selskogo khozyaistva.* (Moscow, 1957), doc. No. 53. See also Bolshakov, *op. cit.* (see Ch. 1, Note 5), pp. 148–51.

47. The same decision was applied to Kazakhstan, Yakutsk, etc., where, as in the Ukraine, the *kombedy* still existed.

48. Thesis of the Central Committee for the Fifteenth Congress, *KPSS v rezolyutsiyakh*, Vol. II, p. 417.

49. Molotov, *15-ty S'ezd VKP(b)*, stenogramme, pp. 1053, 1082. The final quotation from Molotov is on p. 1093. The figure 27% is from *Kollektivizatsiya selskogo khozyaistva*, doc. No. 16, p. 75.

50. Lyashchenko, *op. cit.*, Vol. III, p. 240. However he himself provides many relevant data on collectivization in pp. 136–9, and 238–42.

51. Larin, 'Chastny kapital v selskom khozyaistve, *NAF*, 1927, No. 4, p. 38.

52. Larin in the article mentioned above estimates that the unemployed in the towns numbered two millions, of whom the majority were peasants. Most of the new arrivals in industry were also peasants.

53. Lyashchenko, *op. cit.*, Vol. III, p. 138.

54. See, for example, Trifonov, *op. cit.*, pp. 181–2.

55. *Kollektivizatsiya selskogo khozyaistva*, doc. No. 13, pp. 68–71.

56. Ignat, *op. cit* (see Note 42), pp. 63–86 deals with aid to the *bednota*.

57. Lyashchenko, *op. cit.*, Vol. III, p. 239. Other data from Ignat, *op. cit.*

58. Ignat, *op. cit.*, p. 68.

59. Kukushkin, *op. cit.* (see Ch. I, Note 28), p. 43. There existed other groups, attached to the agricultural co-operative organization, and the *raiispolkomy*, but no figures are available for these. The figure given refers to the end of 1929. At the beginning of 1927, the period which concerns us here, the bednyaks were undoubtedly very poorly organized.

60. Ignat, *op. cit.*, p. 79.

Chapter 3

THE PROBLEM OF CLASS STRATIFICATION WITHIN THE PEASANTRY (cont.)

1. *The Serednyaks*

The serednyaks made up the greater part of the peasantry. Defined in terms of Party propaganda as the 'central figures in agriculture', they were poor tenants of small farms, very weak agricultural producers, and in many cases illiterate, or almost so. It was in this light that they saw themselves, rather than as impressive figures. Nevertheless, they were in fact at the very heart of the social and economic life of the country, and as such they proved a perpetual source of trouble to the régime and its theoreticians.

The Party had great difficulty in defining the exact social function of the serednyak in the accepted Marxist terms. Lenin, for example, never made it clear whether he looked upon the peasantry as a 'stratum' or a 'class'.[1] On occasion he even used both terms in the same sentence, when referring exclusively to the serednyak. 'When we consider a stratum such as the middle peasants,' he said, 'it would appear that this is the kind of class which vacillates.' Referring to the peasant in general, he goes on

'He is partly a property owner, partly a worker. He does not exploit other workers. For years, he had to defend his position against the greatest odds. He suffered exploitation at the hands of the *pomeshchiki* and the capitalists. He put up with everything. Nevertheless, he is a property owner. For this reason, the problem of our attitude towards this vacillating class is one of enormous difficulty.'[2]

Leaving aside a certain vagueness in terminology, which reflects the complex nature of the question, Lenin clearly and repeatedly stated that he was well aware of the difficult task which confronted the Soviet régime, both from the political and the doctrinal point of view, in dealing with the deceptively simple *muzhik*.

Theoreticians of the thirties, who were given to over-simplification, and had neither the talent nor the intellectual stature of their master, nor indeed the opportunity to express themselves freely, were frequently driven almost to despair in their efforts to classify this 'amorphous mass' of the peasantry; they even went so far as to identify four distinct classes: the 'proletariat', the 'semi-proletariat' the 'serednyak' and the 'rural bourgeoisie'.[3] But by the same dubious process of reasoning, these four classes could equally have been said to exist within the serednyak stratum itself; for it is not true to say that the serednyak did not exploit. Indeed Lenin himself, in another article, stated that the serednyak hired labour fairly often, and that, while he was a worker, he was also at the same time a 'shark' and a 'speculator'.

We have already mentioned the categories of *malomoshchny* and *zazhitochny* which Soviet writers frequently discerned among the serednyaks. The profusion of subtle gradations and distinctions within the serednyak layer greatly clouded the issue, and made it extremely difficult for politicians to form a balanced judgement. The peasant who was at one and the same time an agricultural producer and a 'shark and speculator', the worker who frequently employed hired labour, the 'ally' whose main dream was to become a kulak, certainly presented a problem, particularly because, as many bolsheviks asserted, he had two sides to his nature, being both a proletarian and a capitalist.

If the peasant (middle or otherwise) vacillated, it was because he was all too often confronted by alternatives which baffled him, especially if he were illiterate. Faced with similar alternatives, intellectuals and proletarians were at times even more hesitant. It was not the peasant who had a split personality (as suggested by a terminology which was itself excessively divorced from reality), but rather the Party, which repeatedly wavered and shifted in its policy towards the serednyak, adopting first one line and then another, while each change in policy was usually accompanied by deviations and excesses, the brunt of which was borne by the peasant in general, and the middle peasant in particular.

The Party, and especially the local 'activist-executive', always found it much easier to deal in extremes—to put its faith in one group, and distrust another; but when obliged simultaneously to trust and distrust the same social group, as doctrine prescribed in almost so many words, it lost its assurance. The activist, constantly urged by his superiors to follow lines of conduct which seemed to him to be contradictory, dispensed favours or retribution according to his own lights, only to find himself accused of excesses and deviations from a line which was itself, by definition, assumed to be entirely correct.

There are plenty of examples of such shifts in Party policy. The results of the departure by the Plenum of October 1924 from the 'administrative' and pro-bednyak line, and of subsequent measures further implementing NEP, have been described by Khataevich, who had access to Central Committee source material.[4] The activist could make nothing of the sudden *volte face*, and felt he had been betrayed.

Despite the new decisions of 1925, the bednyaks were completely neglected. The serednyaks and the kulaks were gaining control of the *selsovety*. . . .

Sensing that it was losing ground in the countryside, the Party applied the brake, and issued new instructions in order to remedy the situation during the electoral campaign of 1926–7. The results, as described in a collection of articles edited by Pashukanis, were as follows: [5] The bednyaks were being forced into the *selsovety* by all possible means, and the serednyaks were being thrust aside. The right to vote was being withdrawn indiscriminately, and thousands of complaints from unjustly treated serednyaks were pouring into the electoral committees. These injustices, it was claimed, would be rectified later, as far as possible. 'But certain persons, particularly the middle peasants,' the same source stated, 'are beginning to feel that the Party and the Soviet régime are deliberately excluding them from direct participation in the government and control of the state.'

In order to calm the fears of 'these persons', a series of measures were adopted by the Plenum of February 1927, while at the same time deviationists were accused of having aided the kulaks, and of having, by their neglect of the serednyaks, and their exclusive support of bednyak candidates, jeopardized the dictatorship of the proletariat. Contributors to Pashukanis's book provide the following explanation:

'There was a flagrant lack of comprehension of the Party's directive concerning reinforcement of the organization of the bednyaks and batraks. It had been forgotten that this "reinforcement" presupposed the simultaneous growth and strengthening of links between the block of the *bednota* and the serednyaks—the basic mass of the peasantry in the countryside.' [6]

While continuing to fulminate against the men on the spot in this way, the men at the top at no time gave any clear indication as to how 'the two extremes', which to the activist seemed so far apart, should be reconciled. Bewildered, the men on the spot continued to turn first one way, then the other. . . . [7]

These fluctuations in the Party line were to increase during 1928, with consequences which were much more serious than those which had ensued during the period 1924–7. During 1928, the line was to change several times in response to the vicissitudes of the internal struggle with the Right. But the fluctuations of that year were mild compared with those which occurred between the end of 1929 and the beginning of 1930, and which had such widespread repercussions.

The serednyak was always the one who was chiefly involved in these switches in Party policy. In 1927, the number of serednyak households was estimated by the tax authorities at 14·3 millions. Together with the bednyaks, they harvested 85% of the grain (gross yield) and provided three-quarters of the marketable grain.[8]

In so far as the harvests from 1925 onwards allowed of any reserves being built up, these were naturally for the most part in the hands of the serednyaks. In this sense, the serednyak was undoubtedly the central figure in agricultural production. All the stresses and strains which arose in the economic life of the country stemmed from the inadequacy of his contribution to agricultural production, and the resultant clashes inevitably resolved themselves into a confrontation between the serednyaks and the authorities.

The serednyak naturally occupied a special place in Party doctrine, but the doctrinal view of the realities of the situation was apt, like a photographic negative, to get things the wrong way round. As we have seen, alongside the concept of the serednyaks as a homogeneous stratum, there was another view, held by certain economists and some of the Party leadership, who claimed that the *zazhitochny* formed a distinct category within the serednyak stratum.[9] Estimates of the size of this category varied between 10% and 15%. There are very few estimates of the economic strength of the *zazhitochnye* alone.

In statistical exercises and statements of social policy, the *zazhitochnye* were often grouped with the kulak. Both, it was claimed, had accumulated a certain sown area, a certain number of implements and a certain amount of marketable grain (40% according to one source). They were depicted as rich peasants, at the opposite extreme of the social scale from the batraks and the bednyaks. Consequently, a considerable number of serednyaks (some two and a half million households) could at any given moment be removed from the serednyak category, and find themselves figuring, not as 'allies', but as 'class enemies'. As may readily be imagined, the very vagueness of what constituted *zazhitochny* represented a real threat to the serednyaks, especially when accompanied by other ill-defined terms such as *krepki serednyak, khozyaistvenny muzhik, bogaty serednyak.** There were unlimited opportunities for arbitrarily so defining any serednyak, thereby including him in the kulak stratum.

In his speech to the Fifteenth Congress, Molotov berated the opposition for having demanded an individual levy on the upper 10% of the peasants, and argued that this would be an 'anti-serednyak' measure, since the 10%, consisting of the richest peasants, in addition to genuine kulaks, inevitably included ordinary serednyaks.[10] Evidently he refused to accept *zazhitochny* as a social category. But as E. H. Carr has shown: 'It was no longer true that class analysis

* Strong serednyak, efficient peasant, and rich serednyak, respectively.

determined policy. Policy determined what form of class analysis was appropriate to the given situation.'[11]

Soon after, during 1928, when the political situation had changed, the terms which were used were to become increasingly obscure. This is a clear indication that the attitude towards the serednyak was changing, although political propaganda continued to direct its attacks exclusively against the rich peasants in the villages. This was the precise purpose served by the imprecise term *zazhitochny*.

At this point, something should be said about the concept of the 'alliance' or the 'bloc' of the proletariat and the peasantry (*smychka* in Russian). This was a key weapon in the strategic armoury of Leninism, though it could not be described as a set formula, designed to fit every situation.

In the first place, even when Lenin was alive, the expression 'alliance with the peasantry' changed its meaning several times. After the initial stage of the *smychka* with the peasantry as a whole against the *pomeshchiki*, the emphasis, as times changed, shifted to the struggle being waged against the kulaks on behalf of the bednyaks, the serednyaks having been neutralized. During the Civil War, however, what was required of the serednyak was no longer 'neutrality' but 'alliance'. This formula remained valid for strategic purposes during the NEP period. As class stratification became more marked during the twenties, the leaders continued to make use of the *smychka* formula, always quoting from some text or other by Lenin, but with the emphasis which best suited current political concepts.

Everyone agreed on the necessity for 'seeking the support of the bednyak, having the serednyak as an ally, and combating the kulak'. But this 'threefold' formula can scarcely be said to have borne any relation to the realities of NEP, either during its apogée in 1925–6, or during its eclipse from the end of 1927 onwards. During the NEP period the bednyak who, as we have already noted, had been the object of all manner of political misfortunes (especially during elections), was socially the most under-privileged individual. The serednyak enjoyed certain concessions, but the one who derived most benefit from the situation was the comfortably-off peasant, or the peasant who was in process of becoming so.

During and after the crisis at the beginning of 1928, the bednyak's stock rose steadily, although this did not bring about any real improvement in his position. From this time on, the kulaks were increasingly restricted and resisted; but many of the restrictions aimed at the kulak continued to hit hardest at the serednyak. During and after the 'neo-NEP' period, Stalin often repeated the alliance formula, which was regarded as a supreme example of the Party's political wisdom, and its guide in the day-to-day conduct of affairs.

69

Its aim was the 'threefold' task (*triedinaya zadacha*) of winning the support of the poor peasants in order to combat the rich, while at the same time seeking alliance with the middle peasants.

There was, however, a continuous divergence between Party propaganda and the policy which was actually pursued, for the choice of a policy with regard to the peasantry was by no means a simple one. Any aid granted to the batraks, and any serious steps taken to protect them, were liable to damage the interests of the serednyaks (to whom, as we know, hired labour was important) and this greatly impaired the chances of an increase in production by the 'strong' sector. Concessions made to the bednyak, and the organization of bednyak groups, irritated the others, who felt such measures to be discriminatory, and inconsistent with the slogans of the alliance. Moreover, though the granting of aid to the peasants was essential for the government's prestige, and its standing in the countryside, such aid, modest though it was, was economically unproductive, since the bednyak simply ate a little better, without increasing his supplies to the market! [12] Whenever it was at all beneficial, it enabled the bednyak to realize his dream of becoming a serednyak, with the result that he ceased, doctrinally speaking, to serve as the mainstay of the alliance.

Large-scale aid for the serednyaks (tax concessions, credits, agronomic assistance, etc.) was indispensable if their political goodwill was to be secured, but the economic value of such aid was debatable, and in any case it required much time and patience, and was liable, in the end, to produce undesirable results.

The prosperous serednyak also underwent a change in social character, and became a kulak. For him, of course, the change was not a disagreeable one, but many activists considered this policy to be fatal, since its only result was to create an increasing number of enemies. The Party became more and more aware that the customary forms of aid being granted to the serednyak were producing the very opposite results from those intended by the régime. Many Leninists were of the opinion that the effect of strengthening the serednyak sector as such was simply to create more kulaks, thereby weakening the peasantry's loyalty to the collective ideal. Kalinin clearly said as much: 'Reinforcement of the middle strata, by complicating the task of organizing the peasants, makes it much more difficult to guide them towards collectivization.' [13]

The third aspect of the 'threefold task'—that is, the struggle against the kulaks—was likewise fraught with difficulties and contradictions, as we shall see.

The above brief summary of the problems and inconsistencies inherent in this situation reveals it to have been one requiring flexibility, patience and foresight; what was needed was a policy which had both breadth and perspective. It is also clear that sooner or later it would be necessary to introduce large-scale measures, and to make radical and far-reaching structural changes. The success of such a policy may be gauged not only by the extent to which the necessary measures can be planned and set in train, but also by the time factor, in the sense that action should be taken sooner rather than later. Further on, we shall be examining the nature and the scope of the measures which were in fact devised, and the manner in which they were implemented.

Meanwhile it should be noted that:

(1) *The alliance formula at this stage gave no clear indication of the policy which should be followed, or of the real attitude of the régime.*

(2) *Treatment of the serednyak, who was in principle the indispensable 'ally' of the formula, was in fact inconsistent: he was alternately favoured, subject to pressure, or merely tolerated.*

The Right were prepared to seek a policy based on the concept of a genuine alliance, which they firmly believed to be practicable. The Left were more sceptical, especially with regard to the comfortably-off peasants. However, they could foresee a number of difficulties, and had no intention of opening hostilities against the peasantry.

Within the Party, yet another opinion had for some time been gathering weight. This opinion, to which Stalin himself later subscribed, was that the midddle peasant was not only a source of trouble to the régime, but was in fact the origin of all their difficulties, the real stumbling-block.

Many activists were agreed that the peasant was a stumbling-block, but some of them were increasingly coming to regard him as an enemy who must be resisted. The more those of this persuasion emphasized the watchword of alliance with the serednyak, the more pronounced, in practice, grew their hostility towards him.

2. *The Kulak*

The effect of inadequate statistics and ill-defined socio-political terms on the Party's understanding of the social structure of the peasantry may also be observed in its attempts to define the kulak. In this context, bearing in mind the tragic fate of the kulak stratum, the vagueness of the terms employed was to have particularly dangerous and sinister consequences.

Estimates of the number or proportion of kulaks in the population differ. There are plenty of inflated figures, and even some of the more realistic ones vary to the extent of being at least double others.

Larin estimated the proportion of the 'strictly capitalist' group, which constantly hired labour, at about 2% of all households (or 450,000 families) at the beginning of 1927.[14] During the Fifteenth Party Congress at the end of that year Molotov, while insisting that it was 'an almost impossible task' to give an exact estimate of the number of kulaks, nevertheless gives a figure of 3·7% which, for 'an impossible task' is rather too precise.[15] One year later, at the November Plenum of the Central Committee, Stalin was to speak of the number of kulaks as amounting to 5% of the peasantry.[16] Had they become more numerous during the year, or was the 'increase' due to a change in criteria?

The percentage given by Stalin was at all events widely disputed. At the same time *Gosplan*, in its calculations for the Five-Year Plan, had adopted a figure of 3·9%, without however entering into any discussion about it.[17] *Narkomzem*, too, had reached a different conclusion. In its 'control figures' for 1928–9 it quotes 3·8% for Russia, and 4·2% for the Union.[18] Estimates in other Party circles also varied.

At a time when Stalin was adding 1·3% to the percentage of kulaks quoted by Molotov (it must be borne in mind that each percentage represents some 250,000 families, or about 1,250,000 souls . . .) it was stated in an official report submitted to the Conference of Agrarian Marxists that the number of kulaks had diminished during 1928, as a result of the anti-kulak policy.[19] The speaker was not perhaps aware that a few days earlier a special committee appointed by the Politburo to make detailed preparations for dekulakization, and composed mainly of *oblast* secretaries and heads of agricultural departments, had estimated members of kulak families at about 5–6 millions.[20]

The inconsistencies which were apparent in the statistics were, however, merely symptomatic of deeper and more fundamental contradictions. During the same Congress at which Molotov had given the proportion of kulaks as 3·7%, Milyutin, an agrarian expert, enquired: 'What is a kulak? So far, there has been no clear, concise definition of the kulak's role in the process of stratification which is now taking place'.[21]

Molotov, in his estimate of the rural bourgeoisie, seems to include farmers who exploited labour, and who leased additional land. Milyutin does not take the lease of land into account, but suggests as criteria for the definition of the kulak the employment of labour, or exploitation by commercial transactions (money lending, or the hiring-out of agricultural equipment).[22]

Kritsman and his colleagues of the Agrarian Institute of the Communist Academy believed that the basic form of 'capitalist exploitation in the countryside', which more than any other encouraged the growth of agrarian capitalist elements, was the hiring-out of implements and draught animals.[23] According to one who shared this view, the economic strength of the kulak 'at present finds direct expression in the hiring-out of agricultural equipment'. Anyone familiar with the real conditions 'knows perfectly well that the village kulák cannot be traced directly. [i.e. by direct reference to statistics of the exploitation of wage-labour.—M.L.] He cannot be identified by straightforward means, nor is it possible to determine whether or not he is a capitalist'.[24]

Kritsman's definition, too, was vigorously challenged both outside the Party and by communist research workers. One who totally rejected it as a valid criterion was Sukhanov, the non-communist Marxist, and former Left-Menshevik, whose criticisms based on Marxist ideas were a source of constant irritation to the agrarians of the Party.

In his view, the practice of hiring out animals and equipment, although fairly widespread, was only a transitory phase.[25] Once the peasant had gained an economic foothold, and acquired an animal and some implements, he would suddenly break loose from these so-called relationships of capitalist exploitation. The hiring-out of animals or equipment was not a sign of 'agrarian capitalism', as Kritsman maintained, but an 'antagonistic relationship', like the relationship between buyer and seller, which was not necessarily a class relationship. In Sukhanov's view, there was only one criterion of class relationship (and hence of agrarian capitalism), and that was the hiring of wage-labour by a rich farmer.

Dubrovsky, another agrarian research worker, and a Party member, was also violently opposed to the view that the hiring out of implements should be regarded as the main criterion of agrarian capitalism. In his opinion, what was involved was a straightforward relationship between peasants, which had nothing to do with exploitation or capitalism. He too considered that the determining factor was the purchase and sale of labour power, and the ownership of means of production extensive enough to qualify as capital.[26]

The capital criteria used by the specialists of the Commissariat of Agriculture (RSFSR), in arriving at the estimates already quoted, would appear to have been similar to those suggested by Dubrovsky. In their kulak category, a figure of 2·1% was given for farms hiring labour systematically (the criterion being the hiring of labour for more than fifty days of the year); an additional 1·3% represented farms involved in agriculture but which also possessed 'enterprises of the entrepreneurial type', and 0·8% was given for other farms which owned enterprises of this kind, but did not take part in agricultural production.[27] Two criteria had therefore been employed: the hiring of labour for a period in excess of a given number of days, and 'enterprises', such as mills, creameries, hulling mills, etc., where-ever these were operated by 'motor power'.[28] It was not until June 1929, by which time the Right had been virtually eliminated, and a new policy was already in train, that the *Sovnarkom* accepted the hiring-out of agricultural equipment as the criterion for including a farm in the kulak category.[29]

Both inside and outside of Party circles there was yet another, quite different view of the kulak question. According to Bazarov, the eminent non-communist Marxist economist, the kulak was primarily a usurer, who continued to flourish in Soviet conditions, and amassed resources which enabled him to indulge in widespread speculation, his activities often being furthered by errors in government policy.[30]

As late as 1926, this view was shared by Smirnov, the Commissar for Agriculture of the RSFSR, who distinguished, on the one hand, between the exploiting kulak or *miroed* (devourer of the *mir*) of the pre-revolutionary type, who according to him, and contrary to Bazarov's belief, had almost ceased to exist in the Soviet context, and the *krepkoe trudovoe khozyaistvo* where the farm was diligently managed, and where the lease of an additional plot, and even the employment of labour, were not symptomatic of capitalism.[31]

The source of his ideas is fairly obvious. An important pamphlet by Bukharin, published in 1925, reprinted several times thereafter, and regarded as authoritative at the time, reveals that the principal Party theoretician of this period distinguished two categories, one being the 'better-off innkeeper, the village usurer, the kulak', the other the *krepki khozyain* who employs several batraks, reaps the benefit of their labours, and reduces them to a state of dependence; the latter individual, in his opinion, was obviously not a kulak.[32] Bukharin did not repeat this view some three years later, but it is probable that he continued to think in this way.

The foregoing ideas are quoted simply as examples of the body of opinion on this problem; many more could be given. When one attempts to obtain even a rough idea of the true situation, one realizes that the farms which could, according to Soviet definitions, be classified as kulak were in fact fairly small.[32] Only a proportion of those peasants whom the authorities classed as kulaks were in the habit of employing labour. In 1927, 41% of these rented land in addition to the legal allotment (*trudovoi nadel*) to which Soviet law and custom entitled them. 41·5% of them hired out implements. [34] Some were involved in additional activities, such as trade, money-lending, the lending of grain, etc. Such peasants could acquire considerable economic power.

Some reports noted the existence of exceedingly well-off peasants who owned large tracts of land, and many horses and cows, and who permanently employed three or four workers, and a score of day-labourers. The peasants nicknamed them 'the new *pomeshchiki*'. Such cases were rare, however, and were looked upon as 'scandals', or 'nests of corruption' (*gnoiniki*), the result of collusion between the local authorities and the entrepreneurs.[35]

The average kulak (or rather the average farm amongst those classified by the authorities as kulak) had little in common with these. Only a minority of them owned three to four cows and two to three horses (and it should be remembered that this minority had first of all to be classified as kulak in other respects, since three to four cows could be found on a farm which in no other sense gave any sign of being kulak). Those of them who employed wage-labour employed, in the majority of cases, only one batrak. According to Kritsman, only 1% of farms employed more than one paid worker.[36] According to the tax authorities, 2·5% of the *verkhushka* of kulaks had an annual income exceeding 700 roubles.[37] The remainder had less. Strumilin, who considered the proportion of kulaks to be no greater than 3–4%, estimated that the kulak's average earnings were five times greater than those of a bednyak, amounting to about 400 roubles of taxable income, while he paid twenty times more in tax per household, and thirty more per head.[38]

All things considered, the dimensions of the so-called *kulatskoe* farm were modest. It was, moreover, difficult to identify the kulak, since the signs by which he was to be recognized were widespread among the serednyaks. It would be a mistake, however, to consider that the social and economic importance of the kulaks may be measured in terms of the modest size of their farms. Nor is the case of the average Western European farm analogous. The position of the kulaks in relation to their neighbours was one of some strength and considerable influence. Most of them could read and write, and they were strenuous workers, more generously endowed with initiative than their fellows. Their ability to save some reserves of grain enabled them to await the most propitious moment—the spring—when there was a general rise in grain prices, and then to sell on the market, or to their poorer neighbours. There was nothing unusual in such behaviour, since every serednyak did the same whenever he could. Even a poor peasant, if by chance he happened to find himself with more grain than usual, would try to sell it at the best price possible.

The same kulak also lent money, grain and implements, and on fairly stiff terms. He might also contrive to increase his sown area by leasing land in addition to his own legal allocation (*nadel*) or by a variety of other devices.[39] There were many ways in which rural conditions favoured the concealment of income from the authorities, either with the connivance of the officials themselves (although neighbours would know and could denounce the offender if they wished), or by camouflaging one's activities amid innumerable transactions of the same type taking place between neighbours.

It is difficult to arrive at a reliable estimate of the resources accumulated by the kulak stratum. One source claims that by about 1927 they controlled 6% of the sown area, 8% of crops, and 20% of marketable grain.[40] But according to another writer, they controlled 12·9% of the sown area, and a third source 'specifies' that this amounted to 15 million hectares.[41] The facts as given either fail to tally, or at times completely contradict each other. Logically these kulaks should have had more implements and agricultural machinery than the other peasants. A Soviet writer has stated recently that 16% of all the forces of production were in their hands. This may well have been the case, but it is difficult to tell whom this author had in mind, for he sometimes refers to 'the kulaks', and at other times speaks of 'the kulaks and the *zazhitochnye*'.[42] We cannot therefore accept unreservedly either these figures, or the figures for the reserves the kulaks were alleged to have held, or the frequently quoted figure of 20% for the marketable grain they were supposed to have had in their possession. But whether this last figure is correct or has been exaggerated, the economic presence of this stratum could not be ignored. Its social, and, in the event, its political influence was potentially greater than its economic importance, and this was just what the more determinedly anti-kulak faction among the Soviet leaders feared.

Despite what was often alleged in propaganda statements, the kulak, under Soviet conditions, was not a man who was hated by the peasants. Their anger might be aroused by certain extreme cases, in particular those kulaks who engaged mainly in speculation and money-lending, and did not themselves work, but these were not typical. The typical kulak was primarily a worker, and for this reason he was looked upon by the villagers as a peasant like the rest of them.[43] He was prosperous, and envied, but respected too. The poor might have mixed feelings on the subject, especially if painful memories of the pre-revolutionary and Civil War periods were involved. Nevertheless, the political influence of the kulaks was increasing more rapidly than their numbers. A witness of note, Kalinin, has explained why.[44]

The role of the kulak, he says, is not entirely a negative one. The problem would have been much simpler if such had been the case. 'He also has a positive part to play in the rural economy.' In practice, the kulak 'rescues the bednyak from his difficulties in time of distress' by granting him a loan. What Kalinin said, in effect, was that the bednyak often felt that the government only promised to lend at a favourable rate of interest, and then in fact gave nothing, whereas Tikhon Ivanovitch would indeed advance a loan in springtime, even if in the autumn one had to pay through the nose. Likewise, when the kulak killed a cow, the bednyak could always buy a pound of meat.

However, these practical considerations, though they throw an interesting light on Kalinin's understanding of rural problems, are not the whole truth. The root of the matter lies elsewhere. The Soviet kulaks were only an enlarged version of the serednyaks; they were still very far from constituting an entirely different class.

The difference between the activities of the kulak and those of his neighbours was a quantitative and not a qualitative one. The same may be said of his basic interests. The serednyak suffered as much as his richer neighbour from the gap which existed between industrial and agricultural prices, and which penalized the peasantry as a whole. The *zagotovki* (state procurements), effected at prices which were too low, smacked of exploitation, and were harmful to their interests in the same way. The serednyaks were unanimous in demanding an increase in grain prices, and greater market freedom. In this respect the better-off peasant, whether kulak or not, could act as a leader to the others, for their interests were identical.

Official spokesmen avoided any public admission of this fact. When, however, from 1928 onwards, they began to claim that the kulak was withholding bread, preferring to sell to private retailers rather than to the State, they knew perfectly well that they were also referring to the serednyak, who held most of the commercial grain supplies (together with the bednyaks they were said to control 80%). *For propaganda purposes the kulak was singled out as the scapegoat but behind him lay the serednyak, who was the real obstacle. The entire attack upon the kulak was bound also to affect the mass of middle peasants who, not only because they represented millions of households scattered over a wide area, but also by reason of their very weakness as producers, constituted a formidable obstacle indeed.*

The true significance of the increasingly frequent references to 'the kulak and the *zazhitochny*' by the leaders of the Stalinist faction, and most of all by their leader-in-chief, thus becomes clear. The *zazhitochny* was unquestionably as much a serednyak as his neighbours, if a little better off. The leaders who spoke of 'the kulak and the *zazhitochny*' in the same breath, thus equating them as a single social category, thereby discredited their own theories and the entire Party theoretical apparatus whose purpose was to arrive at a definition of the rural 'capitalist' stratum. If a peasant who was merely 'better-off' was to be equated with the kulaks, it made nonsense of the concepts then current within the Party; one might as well say that the entire peasantry consisted of capitalists (and as we shall see, there was in fact such a theory) or else admit that, in the Soviet context, the concept of 'rural capitalism' was a highly questionable one.

We now know that, during the NEP period, the kulak was a hard-working peasant, who sometimes (though not always) employed one or, more rarely, two paid workers, and owned a few agricultural machines which he would hire out to his neighbours. He cannot therefore be defined as either a 'capitalist' or a 'semi-capitalist'. The term 'petty-capitalist', then in current use, scarcely sheds any further light on the matter.

In the politico-social context, and given the way in which circumstances developed from 1928 onward, the fusion of 'kulak' with 'better-off peasant' did make sense. In terms of economic interests and attitude towards the régime, the two categories were as one. Sociologists might find grounds for differentiating between them. For the Stalinist politician, no difference existed at all.

NOTES AND REFERENCES

1. Carr, *A History of Soviet Russia: Socialism in One Country*, Part 1, pp. 94–5.

2. *8-oi S'ezd VKP(b)*, stenogramme, p. 300, quoted by Stalin, *Sochineniya*, Vol. XI, p. 106.

3. Vermenichev in his outline of doctrine, *Bolshevik*, 1930, No. 9, p. 34.

4. Khataevich, *NAF*, 1925, No. 5–6, pp. 198–212.

5. Pashukanis (ed.), *15 let sovetskogo stroitelstva* (Moscow, 1932), pp. 453–4.

6. Both quotations, *ibid.*, p. 454.

7. In *Pravda* December 25, 1928, Meshcheryakov writes: it is difficult to say which error was more widespread, negligence in work with the poor (more common at the local administrative level), or 'simplifications' in dealing with the serednyaks (more widespread at *guberniya* level). Reported by Angarov, *op. cit.* (see Ch. 2, Note 39), p. 64.

8. Stalin, *Sochineniya*, Vol. XII, p. 85, and Trifonov, *op. cit.* (see Ch. 2, Footnote 9), p. 185.

9. Gaister, however, maintained that the concept of *zazhitochny* was devoid of class content, that most serednyaks employed wage labour, hired out implements, etc. *NAF*, 1927, No. 11–12, p. 20.

10. Molotov, *15-ty S'ezd VKP(b)*, stenogramme, p. 1092.

11. Carr, *op. cit.* Part 1, p. 99.

12. Many Party members were of this opinion. See Ignat *NAF*, 1928, No. 10, p. 64.

13. Speech by Kalinin to the *TsIK SSSR, Pravda* December 14, 1928.

14. Larin, *NAF*, 1927, No. 4, p. 43. The figure applies to Russia, Belorussia, and the Ukraine.

15. Molotov, *15-ty S'ezd VKP(b)*, stenogramme, pp. 1055–6.

16. Stalin, *Sochineniya*, Vol. XI, p. 265.

17. Volf, head of the agricultural section of *Gosplan*, in an official *Gosplan* report, mentions 10% of better-off peasants, including 3·9% kulaks. *Planovoe Khozyaistvo*, 1929, No. 2, pp. 100–1

18. Quoted by Rykov, *Bolshevik*, 1929, No. 2, p. 74.

19. Speech by Gaister, *NAF*, 1930, No. 1, p. 99.

20. From Soviet archives, referred to in *Voprosy Istorii KPSS*, 1962, No. 4, p. 68. It is not clear here whether 'members of families' includes kulak heads of families. A wealth of detail concerning these commissions of the Politburo is to be found in the same review, 1964, No. 1, pp. 32–43.

21. Milyutin, *15-ty S'ezd VKP(b)*, stenogramme, p. 1191. Note that Strumilin made the same point a year and a half later, in connection with the problem of the class structure of the peasantry as a whole. He writes, 'No authoritative solution has even been found yet to the fundamental problem of criteria by which the kulak may be distinguished from the serednyak, and the serednyak from the bednyak.' *Planovoe Khozyaistvo*, 1929, No. 8, p. 49.

22. Molotov, and Milyutin, *15-ty S'ezd VKP(b)*, stenogramme, p. 1056.

23. Kritsman, *ibid.*, p. 1197 and in his many articles, previously quoted, in *NAF*.

24. Naumov's contribution to a discussion of the ideas of Kritsman, *NAF*, 1928, No. 6–7, p. 189.

25. Sukhanov, in a discussion at the Communist Academy. *NAF*, 1928, No. 6–7, pp. 178–83. Sukhanov, known for his voluminous *Zapiski o revolyutsii*, a chronicle of the Russian revolution, was a student of agrarian problems during the Soviet period. He was among the accused during the trial of the Mensheviks in 1931.

26. See Dubrovsky's contribution to the same discussion, *NAF*, 1928, No. 5, p. 133 *passim*. He is the author of a number of studies on agrarian problems.

27. Rykov, *Bolshevik*, 1929, No. 2, p. 74.

28. The 'entrepreneur type' is defined in *Sobranie Zakonov i Ras-*

poryazhenii (hereafter referred to as *SZ*), Part 1, 1929, No. 12, par. 103, p. 29.

29. *SZ*, Part 1, 1929, No. 34, par. 301.

30. Bazarov, *Planovoe Khozyaistvo*, 1928, No. 2, p. 43, quoted by Veisberg in *Planovoe Khozyaistvo*, 1930, No. 1, p. 36.

31. A pamphlet by Smirnov, *Na pomoshch krestyanskomu khozyaistvu* (Moscow/Leningrad, 1926), pp. 39–40, quoted by Sulkovsky, *NAF*, 1930, No. 9, pp. 20–1.

32. Bukharin, *Put k sotsializmu i raboche-krestyanski blok* (Moscow/Leningrad, 1926), p. 13.

33. In the opinion of Larin, a notorious 'kulakophobe', the majority of kulak farms were small (*melkie*). *NAF*, 1927, No. 4, p. 44. All research workers agreed on this point.

34. Figures from *Postroenie fundamenta sotsialisticheskoi ekonomiki v SSSR 1926–1932*, p. 272.

35. Larin, *op. cit.* (see Note 33); Koshelov, 'Batratskie zabastovki', *NAF*, 1929, No. 10. Antselovich mentions the *gnoiniki* in *NAF* 1930, No. 3, p. 19; Trifonov, *op. cit.* (see Ch. 2, Note 9), p. 183.

36. Kritsman, *NAF*, 1928, No. 4, p. 116.

37. *Postroenie fundamenta sotsialisticheskoi ekonomiki v SSSR 1926–1932*, p. 271.

38. Strumilin, *Planovoe Khozyaistvo*, 1929, No. 8, p. 57.

39. See a study by Kubanin, 'Klassy v borbe za zemlyu v sovetskoi derevne', *NAF*, 1929, No. 11–12.

40. Gaister, *NAF*, 1930, No. 6, pp. iii–iv. This is impossible if Nemchinov's statement, quoted by Stalin in 1928, that the kulak sold 20% of his harvest, is correct; for the kulak to provide 20% of the country's marketable grain from 8% of the country's entire harvest, 30% of his crop would have had to be marketable, and not 20%.

41. Konyukhov, *KPSS v borbe s khlebnymi zatrudneniyami v strane 1928–1929* (Moscow, 1960), p. 201; *SZ*, Part I, 1928, No. 6, p. 120. The first figure refers to *zernovye*, but the second would give more than 13% of the entire sown area, and not only of the area under wheat.

42. Trifonov, *op. cit.*, pp. 182–3.

43. The Soviet kulak is an unimpressive figure by comparison with the kulak of the Stolypin period. Larin claimed that three-quarters of Soviet kulaks had been kulaks before the war. However, Katsenelenbogen, in an article which is none the less violently anti-kulak in tone, believes that Larin was exaggerating. *Bolshevik*, 1929, No. 12.

44. Kalinin, *op. cit* (see Note 13).

Chapter 4

THE ESTABLISHMENT OF
THE SOVIET RÉGIME
IN THE COUNTRYSIDE

1. *The 'Selsovet'*

At the outset of its existence the *selsovet*, which was the basic
element in the structure of government, had a difficult passage in the
Soviet villages. No sooner had it been set up than it found itself in
competition with another organization which had also been created
by the régime, that is, the 'Poor peasants' committees' (*kombedy*).
During the upheavals of the Civil War, the *selsovet* was not very
popular with the peasants. After the Civil War, the number of
peasants taking part in the elections was still small, although it
showed a very gradual increase from 22·3% in 1922 to 47·5% in
1925–6 (the percentage was the same for the next elections); but
this was still not far in excess of the minimum of 35% which had
been fixed by law as the requirement for valid elections. However,
there were many villages in which no more than 10 to 15% of the
peasants would turn out to vote.[1] Their lack of interest in this particular Soviet institution is readily understood when one considers
the functions of the *selsovet* and the methods by which it was
elected. In its capacity as the 'rural arm of the dictatorship of the
proletariat', the *selsovet* was controlled by the authorities, and its
membership was decided upon by the Party in the *volost*, in consultation with the local Party cell, if there was one. Officially, the
elections were controlled by electoral committees (*izbirkomy*) but
the composition of these committees was in fact determined by the
authorities themselves. The Party chose the candidates, making
great efforts to ensure a favourable 'class representation' (according
to whatever happened to be the current Party line). The Party
manned the *selsovet* with batraks and bednyaks, or even with
workers sent out from the towns to strengthen 'the dictatorship of
the proletariat' in the villages. We learn from Soviet sources that
the work of the *selsovety* was carried on without support from the
mass of the peasantry. The chairman took all the decisions, sometimes with the help of the secretary, general meetings were seldom
convened, or, when called, were poorly attended. In particular,
writers deplored the fact that Party organizations had taken the

place of Soviet organizations and that the Party was imposing its own candidates.[2]

In any case, as another author tells us, their function was purely nominal (until the adoption of the new Party line, of which we shall shortly be speaking) for the *selsovety* were nothing more than 'executive bodies carrying out tasks delegated to them by the various administrative and juridical organizations (the issuing of summonses, help in the work of tax-collection, etc.)[3]

In fact this latter duty was the *selsovet*'s basic function, the execution of which was accompanied by all sorts of abuses and forms of coercion on the part of its officials, a fact which was constantly condemned by the Central Committee. It can readily be understood, therefore, that the population looked upon the *selsovet* primarily as an organization for exacting things from them, without giving anything in return—a state of affairs which never commended itself to the peasant. By the end of 1924 the Party leaders, seriously alarmed at the extent to which relations with the peasantry had deteriorated, owing 'to the vestiges of war communism', as had been explained in the decisions of April 1925, announced their 'new line', which was to widen the scope of NEP. '. . . we have begun to realize', said Kalinin at this point,

'that the organizations responsible for implementation [of the policies of the régime] are tending to atrophy, to become fossilized . . . they are to a certain extent undergoing a process of bureaucratization, and this is being reflected in a loss of the people's confidence in us, if I may so express it.[4]

The watchword of those days 'Look to the countryside' was partly intended to remedy the Party's ignorance of the realities of village life. There were set up rural committees, which were attached to the Party committees in the *gubernii* and the *uezdiy*. The Central Committee recruited 3,000 persons who were sent to 3,000 of the 9,000 *volosti* in the country to conduct an enquiry into rural problems at local level.[5] There was a flood of reports, but no visible improvement in the work of the *selsovety* as a result of this sudden burst of energy. Basically, the position remained the same, despite the government's effort. The second phase of NEP brought the *selsovety* no significant increase either in their legal attributes or their financial status (the *selsovet* had no budget). The chairman was so poorly paid (his salary was sometimes a ridiculously low sixteen to twenty roubles per month) that he often deserted his post. The resulting turnover in these officials (three to four chairmen in a year) precluded any possibility of the *selsovet*'s being able to function efficiently.[6] The bednyak, who was the Party's favourite candidate for this post, frequently could not afford to fill it, and it often fell to the more comfortably-off peasant.[7]

Lack of financial resources was one of the main reasons for the *selsovet*'s failure to play any significant part, or indeed, as sometimes happened, any part at all, in the various activities which concerned the population (road-building, education, public health). What was even more important was that the *selsovet*, through lack of means as much as through lack of power, played no part in anything relating to agriculture, such as *zemleustroistvo*, the improvement of farming methods, co-operation, etc. All these activities were in other hands. This is the reason why, more than three years after the call to 'Look to the countryside', and to 'rehabilitate the *selsovety*', the local state apparatus was still weak, badly organized and partly or wholly unfitted for its task, and why 'local life went on regardless of it'[8] The problems were to come up again, with even greater urgency, when these underpowered organizations, further weakened by opposing pressures from the village and the authorities, suddenly found themselves facing the colossal task of all-out collectivization.

The predicament of the *selsovety*, and the various pressures to which they were subjected, provide a valuable illustration of the forces which were at work in the Soviet village. Soviet sources furnish a sufficient insight into the curious contradictions of *selsovet* activities.[9] These sometimes took the form of an authoritarian handling of affairs, by means of orders and reprimands (*okrikom*)—known at that time as *administrirovanie*. This happened every time that the activists of the *selsovet* and the local Party cell, overwhelmed by orders from higher up which they had not the strength or the local backing to carry out, tried to implement the desired policy by having recourse to administrative pressure, and therefore to violent methods. This was immediately followed by the eviction[10] or the silencing of the serednyak, which in turn gave rise to animosity between the serednyak and the authorities (that is, the local authorities), and if relations became too embittered, the central authorities would react by accusing the local authorities of deviationism. None the less, the threat of renewed violence was one which could always be held over the peasant's head.

At the same time, alongside these tendencies, or operating in successive waves, there were other processes at work in the local state apparatus, processes which were to be described during the next policy shift as 'degeneration' (*vyrozhdenie*) and 'coalescence' (*srashchivanie*). The Party, showing less vigilance than in 1925, particularly because it was anxious not to antagonize the mass of the peasantry, allowed the elections of 1926–7 to take place in a freer atmosphere, with less supervision. The result was immediately noticeable: the villages showed a tendency to oust the poor peasants who, unless vigorously prodded by the Party, were not very active on their own account. Of those elected, the poor peasants who were exempt from tax (27% of households at that time) represented only 16.1%. (In 1929, there was to be a spectacular reversal of this trend, with 28·7 to 37·8% of bednyaks elected, although this figure was subsequently held to be inadequate). In the RSFSR, only 5% of those elected were batraks and workers. Party members comprised only 7·7% of those elected (plus a certain percentage of *Komsomol* members) but 10% of the chairmen of *selsovety*.[11] In these conditions, the serednyaks were the dominant element, and this automatically left a wide sphere of influence to the better-off among their number, and even to those who were known to be kulaks. The latter were deprived of the right to vote, but this measure had not proved very effective.[12] In such a situation, the preponderance of serednyaks amounted to a renewal in the influence of the better-off strata of the peasantry.

As soon as they began to introduce unpopular measures, the authorities would not fail to observe that the *selsovety*, as well as the *raion* organizations,[13] were opposed to these measures, 'were forming a bloc with the kulaks' (or in other words were joining them) and were in process of 'degenerating' (*pererozhdennye*). From the point of view of the individual, too, the transition of the bednyak activist who was worthy of the Party's confidence, or might even be a Party member, 'from a favourable class position to a hostile one' was one which took place with astonishing ease, for as soon as this kind of activist had improved his material circumstances he became a serednyak, and soon began to 'slip'[14] into a new set of political attitudes which were more in keeping with his improved condition.

This was a constant, though almost imperceptible process, and it had a markedly weakening effect on the ranks of Party members and supporters. Later on, when we come to analyze the Party cells, we shall see this process at work more clearly: for the moment, it need only be said that this erosion of the ranks of their supporters (or those whom they had counted upon as their supporters) was the source of much anxiety and loss of confidence among the Party leaders and the activists. Lenin's recurrent image of communism as an island in the petit-bourgeois ocean, under constant threat of being submerged or eaten away or otherwise destroyed, was one which haunted the Party activists.

There were other, even more disturbing aspects of the situation in which the *selsovety* found themselves in the countryside, and these did nothing to lessen such fears.

2. The 'Mir'

Parallel with the 'soviet' aspects of its history, the peasantry continued after the revolution to pursue a course of development which had been peculiar to it for generations. The *mir* is a striking example of this. It was generally agreed that this particular peasant institution had been well and truly on the decline long before the war. On the eve of revolution, in forty-seven *gubernii* of European Russia, fewer than 50% of the peasants were still members of the *mir* (the village community).[15] Eight million households held their land as private property, while 7·4 million holdings were still communally owned. The decay of this relic of the ancient peasant community was hastened by the increasing degree of social stratification within the peasantry. However, at the time of the revolution, the *mir* took on a miraculous new lease of life. The miracle can be explained by the fact that the agrarian reform, which freed the peasants from the bonds of feudalism, also evened out the differences among them to a very considerable degree. Having got rid of the *pomeshchiki* and some of the kulaks, the peasants reverted to the old egalitarian relationships of the *mir*, and by the same token to the institution itself. Once more the *mir* became representative of the great majority of the peasantry. By about 1927 95·5% of the holdings were in 'communal ownership', and only 3·5% were farmed as *khutora* and *otruba* with a further 1% as co-operatives (*tovarishchestva*).[16]

Ample evidence of the existence and the prevalence of the communal form of land tenure is afforded by the agrarian code of 1922, which deals with it in great detail. The Party, however, appeared to take little account of this factor, and of its possible implications. A lively discussion about this problem arose among the experts and scholars in 1926, in connection with two draft statutes on land tenure and the reallocation of holdings (*zemleustroistvo*).[17] But during 1927, and particularly in 1928, the problem came under discussion in the press among the senior officials of the *TsIK* and the Party.

During 1926 and 1927 the *RKI* (the Workers' and Peasants' Inspection) conducted some enquiries on the *mir*, and produced findings which were both surprising and disquieting, and at least focused the Party's attention on the problem. Attitudes varied considerably as to the role of the village society under Soviet conditions, and the policy which should be adopted towards it. But the facts revealed by the *RKI* investigators and the researches of the Communist Academy were not disputed: between 1922 and 1927 the village society, by virtue of the general improvement in the economy, had grown considerably in strength, its budget had increased and, despite the efforts of the authorities to encourage the *selsovety*, it was the *mir* which continued to be 'the sole organization in charge of the economic life of the village'.[18]

Under the agrarian code, the *mir* was recognized as a 'legal entity' (*yuridicheskoe litso*) and was authorized to buy and to sell, to sue and be sued, to apply for credits against bills of exchange, to undertake work connected with improvements or reorganization, and also to acquire machines and to organize co-operatives and various enterprises.[19] The village society often owned a variety of enterprises, such as mills, hulling-mills, cheese-making establishments, forges, from which it derived an income. It also had a further source of income from land, forests, gardens and other pieces of communally-owned property, and from the allocation of ground for markets and other commercial undertakings. Its importance lay primarily in the fact that the village society managed the land, some of which was shared out among the households, while the rest (grazings, forests, reserves, etc.) was communally exploited. The society was responsible to the State for the good management of the land, and for ensuring that there was no waste, or impoverishment of the soil.

It will be seen, therefore, that in practice the principle of nationalization of the land took the form of communal management by the village society, which was not required to pay any rent either for the land or for any other rights. In practice, and in the eyes of the peasant, the land belonged to everybody or to the *mir* (*mirskoe*), or 'to God', and therefore to the man who worked it—what he never said was that the land belonged to the State.[20] In the mind of the town-dweller, nationalization was equated with State ownership, but to the peasant it was something different, a concept which was more archaic in one sense, but at the same time nearer to certain modern socialist ideas.

In law, the village society was free to opt for whichever form of tenure best suited it. Soviet law recognized three such forms:

1. the co-operative form (*tovarishcheskoe*), which at this time was the least common (affecting 1 to 2% of holdings) and which involved collective ownership and cultivation of the land;

2. the various forms of private ownership (*uchastkovoe*) in which the holdings were grouped together and allocated to the various households without any fresh reallocation: the *khutora* and the *otruba* came under this heading;

3. the form known as 'communal' (*obshchinnoe*) which was the most widespread (the figures have been given above). Its main feature was that the land was subject to further reallocation, on a fair shares principle, if the composition of the households changed to such an extent as to endanger this principle.[21]

By law, the *mir* was bound in the event of a majority vote to carry out a general or partial reallocation of the land, but not more than once in every three rotation cycles (i.e. every nine years), and after the decision had been ratified by the *volost* authorities. It could also increase or reduce the allocations of land to certain families, but not more than once in every cycle, and only at the beginning of the cycle. The *mir* decided the total amount of land to be allocated to each family on a fair shares basis (an equal quantity per head or per worker) but the land thus allocated to each household was made up of several strips, or sometimes a considerable number of strips, which might be widely separated, or mixed up with those of other families. Pastures were allocated in a similar manner.

The prospect that their land might subsequently be reallocated discouraged the peasants from making any investment in it, and considerably hampered efforts to improve farming methods. In 1926, the Commissariat for Agriculture, disturbed by this development, decided that peasants whose holdings had been particularly well farmed should receive compensation, in so far as this was possible, if they had to change strips in the event of a fresh redistribution of land.[22] But it was a long time before this measure yielded any results.

The *mir* had numerous areas of responsibility, and its duties were many and complex: it was responsible for determining the most efficient use of land in the context of *zemleustroistvo*, and for deciding on methods of crop rotation; it organized the communal use of grazings and forests, and, as previously stated, undertook the fair distribution and reallocation of strips; it was also responsible for the enrolment of new members, or for dealing with withdrawals of members who were retaining the land allocated to them, and for the election of officials. As the foregoing list will show, it played an extremely important part in village life. It had other functions too, over and above those strictly pertaining to agricultural problems.

Decisions were taken by a majority vote of those members present at the assembly (*skhod*). The members were all those who belonged to households (*dvory*) and who were over the age of eighteen. Those of the villagers who had no farm (batraks, smiths and other artisans, officials, teachers) did not have the right to vote. Assemblies were probably called fairly frequently, and in some regions very frequently. According to Rezunov, for example, in twenty districts in the Tula province there had been 19,242 assemblies during 1925–6. This is confirmed by other information from the same source.[23] The apparently small attendance at the *skhody* is explained by the fact that it was not citizens who voted, but heads of households. The Code allows for this by stating that a quorum should consist, not of a percentage of citizens, but of half of the representatives of *dvory*.[24]

In accordance with the most time-honoured tradition, the *skhod* consisted of bearded men.[25] Women and young people only rarely took part. It was the duty of the *skhod* to elect officials who were responsible for representing the village society and managing its affairs.

The legal status of the *mir* was not very clearly defined, and reflected the fact which Kosior had noted in his report to the Fifteenth Party Congress, that the *mir* was a village organization which played an 'extremely vital' role, and to which 'not enough attention has so far been paid by us'.[26]

'Not enough attention' was a common enough euphemism, in official parlance, for describing negligence and a variety of shortcomings. In this instance, however, it might more accurately be described as a lack of foresight on the part of the authorities during the final years of NEP, rather than simple negligence.

Communist authors were not agreed over their interpretation of the role of the *mir* in the context of Soviet legislation. Some (like Zdanovich) held that such an institution came within the province of public law (*publichnopravovy*), others (Rezunov, for example) held that it came under the heading of private law. Sukhanov, however, pointed out with some justification [27] that it had elements both of a private and a public institution. The attitudes of the authors towards the *mir* were reflected in the opinions expressed about its juridical status.

As we have seen, the *mir* had very wide-reaching powers and responsibilities in all matters concerning the land, and, in practice, those who cultivated it. However, the agrarian code defined the village society as a voluntary institution.[28] It was administered by its elected representatives. But when, as very frequently happened, the *mir* and the *selsovet* found themselves operating alongside each other, it was the *selsovet* which was supposed to carry out the decisions of the *skhod*. The *skhod* decided whether new members should be admitted, but it could not expel a household. It could deprive a household of land, but only for a limited period, and the State could force it to admit a new member if it was considered that the *mir* had sufficient reserves of land at its disposal. In principle, a peasant could not leave the society and keep his land without the agreement of the *skhod*, but in this respect there were certain important exceptions: a group of fifteen members who wished to form a collective had the right to leave, and the society was bound to allocate to the fifteen members the land to which they were entitled. Peasants who wished to leave the society and set up in *khutora* or *otruba* could do so even without the permission of the *skhod* if their group consisted of a fifth of the members of the society.[29]

The dubious legal standing of the *mir*, and the contradictions and defects which were apparent in its structure, were also, as we have said, the result of a lack of foresight in Soviet policy during the NEP period. This same factor was to be responsible for the way in which the authorities reacted at the time of the big turn in policy, to what was an authentic manifestation of rural democracy, and to the facts which demonstrated the extent of its influence.

It will readily be understood that the village society, which decided so many problems of importance to the peasants, had a great advantage over the *selsovet*, an unpopular organization whose administrative role was a restrictive one, a body which had no standing as a 'legal entity', unlike the village societies, and which, above all, had no funds: only 3 to 6% of the *selsovety* had a budget.

In an effort to improve the standing of the selsovet, the Russian *VTsIK–SNK* gave orders, in 1927, that thenceforth the agrarian assembly (*zemelny skhod*) should deal only with problems relating to land management and other matters which were fundamentally the concern of the society, while the *selsovet* would be responsible for calling village meetings (*selski skhod*) to deal with general questions, municipal and cultural matters, etc.[30] Those who had not the right to vote, and who, on the other hand, were members of the *mir* and had the right to take part in its activities, were to be excluded from the village meetings. On the other hand, batraks, officials and members of the proletariat, who did not belong to the *mir*, were to take part in the citizens' village meetings.

This decree reflected a lack of understanding of the realities of village life. All sources confirm [31] that these so-called general meetings were in most cases straightforward *skhody* of the village society, and consequently attended and controlled by the *khozyaeva*, and not by the citizens, and that the batraks did not take part in them, whereas the kulaks, who had been deprived of their voting rights in the *selsovet* elections, continued to take part. In addition, these *skhody* discussed all the financial affairs of the community, and also other social and economic questions, such as the building of roads, schools, etc.

Since the *mir* had the power to impose local levies (which the *selsovet* did not have) and had also other sources of income, it had considerable funds at its disposal, as much as 100 million roubles, according to some sources. It assumed financial responsibility for the *selsovet*, and often paid its officials. General meetings and meetings of the presidium of the *selsovet* were relatively infrequent, and did not give overmuch attention to the general body of problems affecting the villages, whereas the very frequent *skhody* covered practically every aspect of the peasant's daily life.

In such circumstances, the *selsovety* were overshadowed and virtually assimilated by the village societies, and we can now see the force of the frequent statements by officials like Kosior, whom we quoted earlier on, to the effect that 'by satisfying the economic and purely cultural needs of the village, the village society is in practice taking over control of the rural economy'.[32]

This 'discovery' revealed the weakness of the *selsovet* which, instead of leading the village, was itself dominated by the autonomous *mir*, the successor of the ancient *obshchina* which had so often been condemned as obsolete. This led certain of the Party officials to conclude that the mass of the peasantry were evading the influence of the Soviet authorities, and coming under the control of the kulaks, and that eleven years after the revolution kulak domination was still on the increase.

'The question is not only a financial one,' wrote *Izvestiya* in May 1928—'it is also a political one.' In a report submitted to the *Sovnarkom* of the RSFSR on March 20, 1928, the Commissariat of Inspection reported that

'a situation has developed in which there is reduplication of work between the *selsovet* and the village society, so that there is now a *dual authority* in the villages, particularly because the *mir*, by virtue of its material advantages, is supplanting the *selsovet* and is playing a decisive role in the economic and administrative affairs of the village'.[33]

Similarly, Molotov expressed the view that, until the village societies had been brought to heel by the *selsovety*, it could never be said that the watchword 'all power to the soviets' had become a reality in the USSR. He accordingly launched a campaign to strengthen the *selsovety* and to bring the village societies under their control; but, he added, when summing up the discussion on agricultural questions at the Fifteenth Party Congress, 'the campaign should be energetic, but not drastic, and we should not act hastily or peremptorily'.[34]

The important enactment on the principles of land tenure which was promulgated on December 5, 1928 [35] apparently allowed the village society to retain its powers in matters relating to land management, but laid down that its most important decisions should be subject to confirmation by the *selsovet* (with right of appeal to the *ispolkom* of the next highest soviet). In addition, it was stated that all inhabitants of a village who had the right to vote should henceforth be admitted to the village society, while those with no voting rights must be excluded from membership. The above provisions effectively brought the *skhod* under the control of the *selsovet*, but the question of the part which the village society could play in the future drive towards collectivization was still unsettled. The same law laid down that the *mir* could take decisions in matters affecting co-operation and collectivization in its village, and it was this measure which proved to be the most controversial issue in the discussions on the *mir* which went on among the experts and senior officials of the Party and the government throughout 1926.

Some held that the *mir* was a decaying institution, which was hampering economic development by preventing the more progressive elements in the villages from introducing improvements in farming methods. It was therefore regarded as a reactionary body, particularly because it was said to be controlled by the kulaks. Those who held such views came to the conclusion that the *mir* should simply be abolished.

But there were those who defended the village society, even within the ranks of the Party. Some of its more lukewarm supporters felt that it would be enough to ensure that the *selsovet* gained the upper hand, without prejudice to the future of the *mir*, but there were others who made out a positive case for the *mir*, on the grounds that communal organizations could represent a force for socialism.

There was truth in the allegation that the communal system of land ownership acted as a brake on development, involving as it did reallocations of holdings, the cultivation of scattered strips, and methods of crop rotation which had to be decided upon by a majority vote. The majority who decided such matters in the *skhod* reflected the general level of village conservatism. With the departure of the better elements either to the *khutora* or to other forms of holding, the *skhody* lost their most enterprising members, who in their turn showed an increasing preference for private ownership and management of their land. Was it therefore expedient to encourage this trend, which ran counter to the whole idea of collectivization, in other words to the direction in which the authorities believed the future of the villages to lie?

The other allegation that the *skhody* were controlled by the kulaks was more open to question, and was in fact challenged on occasion by some communist writers. Molotov may have regarded the *skhod* as the final refuge of the kulaks[36] but we find a much more balanced picture in a paper published by the Communist Academy, which set forth the official conclusions at the end of the Fifteenth Party Congress.[37] The data available to the Academy clearly proves, as one would expect, that there was a preponderance of serednyaks in the *skhody*, that there was, on occasion, some influence on the part of the better-off peasants, and also, though less frequently, on the part of the poor peasants, when they were organized. There were also indications of what was described as 'purely serednyak' influences. Despite the view sometimes held that it was mainly the kulaks who were interested in preserving the village societies, because it was they who were in control, a survey carried out in the Rybinsk region showed that the great majority of the better-off peasants preferred the *khutor* and the *otrub*, and that a similar percentage of bednyaks (roughly 75% remained loyal to the village society.[38] Among the serednyaks opinions were more divided, but even so 55% of them preferred the older institution.

The danger of kulak domination was obviously exaggerated, even bearing in mind the situation with regard to the bednyak organizations, the Party and the *selsovety*, and despite all the other evidence of the slowness of growth of the Soviet régime in the countryside. Those who supported the *mir* questioned the allegation of kulak domination, and counter-attacked by stressing 'the possibility of using the communal form of land-ownership to further the building of socialism in the villages . . .'. The same author also stated categorically that the dissolution of the village society would amount to an act of aggression against the serednyak, and that the idea of using the *selsovety* to effect the move of the peasantry to a collectivized form of agriculture 'would only be putting the administrative machine into reverse.'[39]

It is significant that nearly three years went by before the above-mentioned law (i.e. the law on land-ownership) was promulgated. In 1926 two draft laws were drawn up, one by a drafting commission attached to the Union *SNK*, and the other by the government of the RSFSR, in effect by the Russian *Narkomzem*. The two different drafts were referred by the government to the Communist Academy, which was subsequently to submit its conclusions to the *Sovnarkom*.[40]

The most important point of variance between the two drafts was the definition of the 'principal land-holder'.[41] According to the commission's draft, the principal land-holder was held throughout to be the *dvor* and, secondly, the co-operatives, while the village society, which represented some 90% of the peasants, was for all practical purposes eliminated. For in terms of this draft the village society could be a land-holder provided that it became a producers' co-operative; but at this stage no one envisaged any such possibility. Smirnov, the Russian *Narkomzem*, insisted that the village society must be recognized as the principal land-holder—which it was, in effect—though certain changes would have to be made in its structure. He wished it to become an organization of which membership would be obligatory, and which would include the batraks,[42] etc. The rival draft, which pinned its faith on the *dvor* and saw no future in the *mir*, treated the latter, on the other hand, as a voluntary organization, and regarded as members only those who possessed *dvory.*

In the end, the Academy expressed its preference for the *Narkomzem*'s draft. During the discussion, the most vigorous support for the village society came from the non-communist Sukhanov, who urged that it should be reshaped and merged with the *selsovet* to form an organization which would be recognized by the law as the basic cell of the Soviet régime in the countryside.[43] He particularly stressed this argument because of the possibility that the village society could become a socialist institution. He made out an eloquent case for the *mir*'s socialist potentialities, at the same time criticizing both drafts for failing in practice to incorporate any measures designed to encourage socialist structures in the villages. Many communists shared his views. Bauman, for example, during a regional Party conference at Moscow in 1927, stated that 91% of the holdings in the Moscow region were communally owned, and that this form of ownership was much more favourable for collectivization than either the *khutor* or the *otrub*.[44]

In the Five-year Plan which was officially adopted in May 1929, a very important role was assigned to the village society. Since the greater part of the grain procurements at the end of the first Five-year Plan would still be coming from private farms, they would have to be acquired under contracts exchanged between the State and the co-operative sector or, in effect, the village societies. In *Gosplan*'s view, this kind of contract would even encourage the village societies to turn increasingly to co-operative forms of production, and to develop into collectives.[45] But *Gosplan*, which was planning five years ahead, was unaware of what was to happen before a year had elapsed.

And so we are left with a paradoxical situation, in which the village organization which stood for all the collectivist aspects of village life, and which had been rooted in the village for centuries, was given no part whatsoever to play in the collectivization of the peasantry. And this was done in the face of constant criticism and complaints from those in power about the individualism of the peasant who would not give up his strip of land.

The *mir* was to perish in the holocaust of collectivization,[46] seemingly vanquished by the *selsovety,* but it was not even the *selsovet* which proved to be the essential factor in collectivization.

3. Co-operation

In the Party's view, co-operation (the co-operative movement) together with industrialization, was the road which would lead the peasantry to socialism, the way to an improved standard of living for the masses and an increase in agricultural production. This belief, allowing for certain variations in emphasis, was held by all sectors of opinion within the Party, and it was a legacy from Lenin, his final injunction, which had expressed the hope that co-operation would indeed be the vital link in the chain which, in the hands of the Party, would lead to the socialist goal. However, this idea of Lenin's was still something new at the time, for as late as August 1922 the Party was still subscribing to another view of Lenin's which regarded co-operation as 'co-operative capitalism', which was no doubt useful in the short term, but was an aspect of 'State capitalism'.[47] However, in two short notes which were dictated in January 1923, and entitled 'On co-operation', the ailing leader radically changed his standpoint, and declared: 'essentially, all that we need is that the Russian people should co-operate deeply and widely within the framework of NEP . . .'. According to Lenin, the aim was to set up a régime of 'civilized co-operators' which, 'given socialist ownership of the means of production, and the victory of the proletariat over the bourgeoisie, would in fact amount to a socialist régime.[48]

This testament, however, raised a number of questions, and left some of them without a clear answer, which inevitably gave rise to dispute. It is interesting to note that collectivization, as a specific problem and procedure, is not once mentioned. The emphasis was clearly on the commercial functions of co-operation, for Lenin stressed several times the need for acquiring the aptitudes of a 'sensible and literate trader (*torgash*)' and for engaging in trade 'in the European manner', as opposed to the 'asiatic' forms of trade which had up till then been customary. To achieve this end, Russia would have to pass through a period during which she would undergo a 'real cultural revolution'.[49] It should be noted that in the whole of this crucial article there is nothing which could be interpreted as justifying even the smallest degree of violence. Moreover, when Bukharin and his supporters were to argue later on that it was the commercial aspects of co-operation which Lenin regarded as the essential ones, they were justified in their contention.

During the years 1925–7, up until the Fifteenth Party Congress, at which point a certain change took place in their ideas, the Right (or rather the future Right) followed Lenin's articles to the letter; they advocated broadly-based co-operation in the commercial sector, and a 'civilizing' drive, 'using NEP methods', as being the direct road to socialism, while leaving until a later stage of development the question of introducing co-operation into the production sector.[50] But Bukharin's opponent Preobrazhensky likewise observed the spirit, if not the letter, of Lenin's article when he said that in Lenin's view (despite strong indications to the contrary) not every co-operative enterprise, even under Soviet conditions, was necessarily a socialist enterprise. Only those co-operatives which were collectivizing production could properly be defined as socialist. Such an undertaking assumed the existence of a powerful industrial sector, since the organization of agricultural production on a collective basis would be unthinkable without modern equipment.[51]

This then was the heart of the great debate, which we shall be discussing at a later stage, but which in the present context need concern us only in respect of timing and the rhythms of development. For Bukharin and Preobrazhensky, as well as Stalin and Molotov, were all agreed that co-operation was the only solution for the countryside, and that this should be preceded by a stage of 'traditional' co-operation. According to the then current theories, the first stage of co-operation should consist of accustoming the peasant to collaborate with his neighbours, initially in matters of credit and buying and selling, the next stage being the setting up of enterprises for the processing of agricultural products, and the final one the gradual introduction of co-operation into the various branches of agricultural production itself. The natural conclusion of this gradual and complex process would be the collectivization of the whole of agricultural production.

Nowadays it is still claimed in the USSR, though with lessening conviction, that this is the way in which things actually happened, although it is admitted that the Soviet authorities were obliged to hasten the natural process of development, but no more than that, since in any event conditions were more or less ripe for this particular transition to socialism in the countryside. Thus, it is claimed, everything went according to the provisions of what is described as 'Lenin's plan for co-operation'. As we shall see, this interpretation is not borne out by the facts.

During the period of 'war communism', the co-operative movement was simply an offshoot of the Commissariat of Supply, in other words it was mainly a governmental organization, to which producers and consumers were obliged to belong. With the advent of NEP, and especially after 1925, the co-operative movement regained its voluntary status, in principle at least, and acquired its own administrative bodies. From the doctrinal point of view, the Party supported the co-operative movement wholeheartedly; materially, its support, though less unqualified was still an imtortant factor.

About 1928-9, the co-operative movement, after making a certain amount of headway, began to show signs of extreme complexity and cumbersomeness in its structures.[52] The consumers' co-operatives, which we need not dwell upon in the present context,

RUSSIAN PEASANTS AND SOVIET POWER

were controlled by the *Tsentrosoyuz* through its intermediate organizations, the final outlet being the *lavka*, the village shop which dealt in consumers' goods. Its role and its social function were fairly limited, and the members of the co-operative had virtually no say in the management of the *lavka*, since membership itself was little more than a formality. This sector of the co-operative movement had some nine million members, but its shops were too few in number,[53] they were poorly supplied and badly managed, so that the peasants were too frequently obliged to fall back on the private trader, who was more competent and better supplied. Despite the government's efforts to oust it, and to put state and co-operative trading organizations in its place, retail trade, whether legal or illegal, continued to provide a foothold for private enterprise during the final years of NEP, and even later.

In all cases where writers and official documents mention the co-operative movement as the road to socialism and collectivization, what is meant is *agricultural co-operation*, in other words that aspect of co-operation which embraced activities relating to the production and the sale of agricultural products, and to the supply of the means of production, and similarly to the credit associations which financed those activities.

During the period 1921–7, the *Selskosoyuz*, which was the organization in charge of the co-operative movement after 1921, was split into sixteen 'centres'. The seventeenth was created in 1927, to administer the kolkhoz sector of the movement. These 'centres' were specialist departments in charge of the various branches of production, such as grain (*Khlebotsentr*), livestock products (*Zhivotnovodsoyuz*), flax (*Lnotsentr*), etc. They were headed (after 1927) by the *Soyuz Soyuzov*, which had no commercial functions, and no executive powers, but was responsible for general administration. The *Selskosoyuz* itself, in company with a number of other bodies, became the centre responsible for supplies of the means of production for the movement as a whole. But these were the 'centres' of the Russian republic; the other republics had their own central organizations. A 'Union Council for the Agricultural Co-operatives' was set up in 1928, to administer the movement as a whole, and to deal with its doctrinal problems: this council was to be superseded two years later when its activities were taken over by the *Soyuz Soyuzov*, which had become an all-Union organization, but was itself to be abolished a year later. . . .

At *oblast* and *raion* level, there was a tendency for the central organization to increase the number of their local 'centres', and by about 1930 this had resulted in a proliferation of interconnected organizations. A survey carried out in 477 *raiony* of the RSFSR revealed the existence of 1,500 'entirely useless' local organizations.[54] Round about the same time Yakovlev, the Commissar for Agriculture, stated that, despite the plethora of administrative bodies, there was virtually no one to lead the co-operative and kolkhoz movement. The Central Black Earth Region, for example, was divided into 170 administrative *raiony* but had 500 local co-operative offices (*soyuzy*) in these *raiony*, twenty-eight in the *okrugi*, eleven in the *oblasti*, and, in certain *raiony*, some five or eight different so-called 'specialist' *soyuzy*. '. . . As a result . . . there is a muddle (*putanitsa*), too much red tape, a waste of public resources. . . .' This administrative apparatus was visibly developing according to Parkinson's law, and naturally at very high cost. The author quoted above was shocked by the fact that the administration of the agricultural co-operative sector was costing some 450 million roubles per annum, although during all the years of its existence the movement had never acquired more than 100 million roubles in assets, and its debts were far in excess of this figure.[55]

The base of this administrative pyramid consisted of the local associations, which varied very widely in type, according to the region and the kind of activity in question. There were some forty to fifty types of association, including, for example, general co-operatives concerned with a number of different crops; co-operatives which specialized in one particular crop (potatoes, sugar beet, milk, eggs, hemp, flax, tobacco, vegetables) and which acted primarily as selling organizations; various kinds of processing co-operatives (dairies, mills); a multitude of 'simple co-operatives' concerned with the production of one single product, or the purchase of machinery for communal use, or with raising selected seeds, or with land improvement, etc.); there were also various types of kolkhozes and, lastly, the credit associations. The latter were located mainly in the *raion*, and had an average membership of between 2,500 and 2,700, including individual members and collective members (co-operative associations). They disbursed the bulk of the credits allocated for agriculture. Because of the important nature of this function, and particularly in view of the amount of public funds involved in rural credits, and the limited private resources at the disposal of the co-operative movement (members' contributions, deposits, profits), the credit associations were more in the nature of a government organ controlled by the Agricultural Bank, although within this framework the co-operative 'centres' still had a certain amount of influence.

The net effect of these arrangements was simply to complicate still further the already complicated machinery of the co-operative movement, both at headquarters and at local level. In practice the credit association was a universal organization, which often engaged in activities which were strictly the responsibility of other sectors (purchases and sales, enterprises), and which at the same time was overwhelmed by a vast number of operations which it carried out on behalf of the co-operative movement or the government (such as the financing of procurements contracts, or sowing).[56] This left it little time for its proper function of disbursing credits to the peasants, and ensuring that these funds were productively used and paid back. Like all other Soviet organizations, the credit association was swamped by the flood of forms which had to be filled up, and reports which had to be submitted to numerous superior authorities, such as the agricultural bank, the headquarters of the co-operative movement, *Gosplan*, the *oblispolkom*, etc. And yet, despite its tendency to bureaucratization and to top-heaviness, the co-operative movement was making headway. It enlisted more peasants and continued to break fresh ground. By 1929, the movement comprised some 90 to 100,000 local associations, with a membership said to be in the region of 11 to 12 million. Its turnover was increasing, and so also was its contribution to the supply of agricultural raw materials and to food supplies.

In the Party's view, the function of the co-operative movement was to ensure an improvement in agricultural production, to help the peasants to cultivate their land more efficiently, and to assist the poor peasants to move up the social scale in the villages, or at least to better their lot by forming producers' associations. To some extent, it did all of these things, but the results were unimpressive.

It played a decisive part in the acquisition of industrial crops and livestock products, but had little effect in respect of grain, being responsible for only 30% of the total State procurements (*zagotovki*). In this, the most important sector of agricultural production, the co-operative movement's record was in general very poor, a fact which was deplored by Kaminsky, the chairman of the *Soyuz Soyuzov*, at the Fifteenth Party Congress.[57] At that time, the *Khlebotsentr* had fewer than one million households in its local associations.[58] At the beginning of 1928, and throughout that year there was a slight increase in activity, and in the number of grain co-operatives, but this did not bring about any very marked change in the situation. Support for the movement was still much greater among the producers of potatoes, beet and cotton.

The entire movement had only 3,000 agronomists (of whom some, if not most, were concerned with administration rather than field work) and this was an infinitesimal number given the vast extent of the Russian agricultural plain. The task of the many different 'stations' set up by the co-operative movement (about 20,000) was to help the peasants with such activities as grain-cleaning, the hiring of agricultural machinery, or selective livestock-breeding, but they were too small and too few in number to achieve any noticeable improvement. On the subject of agricultural co-operation in general, Stalin told the Fifteenth Party Congress that 'terribly little' had been done in this field,[59] and the same statement was made repeatedly during 1928 by Party leaders and officials of the co-operative movement, and in many official documents.[60] In fact, as Kaminsky stated in January 1929, during a conference of heads of the Land administration (*Zemorgany*) *the backwardness of the co-operative sector was one of the basic causes of the fall-off in agricultural production.*[61] *This was fundamentally a grave admission, and an indictment of Party policy.*

In 1929, the co-operative movement embraced only one third of the agricultural population (households). The figures given vary between 30 and 40% of all households. According to *Gosplan*, 37·5% of households belonged to the co-operative sector, and it set its target for 1933 at 85%.[62] Bearing in mind what was to be the course of events from the end of 1929 onward, it is important to remember that '*up until very recent times, the greater part of the rural population remained outside the co-operative movement, even for the purposes of trade . . .'.*[63]

Given that those organized in the co-operative movement had joined it only relatively recently, and despite the fact that the quality of the organizational work left much to be desired, it is particularly interesting to see in what measure rural co-operation, which was to pave the way for collectivization in the countryside, was developing in a direction consistent with official doctrine. There is agreement among reliable sources that the co-operative movement mainly served the interests of the better-off peasants.[64] By comparison, the poor peasants had very little part in the co-operatives, although a certain amount of assistance was given them by the State, as we said earlier on in connection with the bednyaks. It was the middle peasants and especially the better-off among them who were most conscious of the advantages of co-operation. These strata were therefore the best organized, and inevitably they and the kulaks wielded greater influence and occupied a dominant position in the local co-operative associations. At this stage, therefore, the movement which, according to doctrine, was to be a major factor in leading the peasants towards socialism was mainly of benefit to the *khozyaeva*, and helped the private farmer to improve his individual holding. *The only possible result of this was further to reinforce the general trend towards individual farming which had been a feature of village life during the* NEP *period. The Party was unable to alter the course of this development.*

This conclusion is borne out by analysis of the achievements of the co-operative movement in the field of production, and more particularly in the collectivization of production. One of the ways of assisting the process of collectivization was by means of co-operative processing enterprises. Results, however, show that activity in this particular sector was practically nil: there were 16,000 'enterprises' by the end of 1927, all of which were very small, and some of which had been described by Molotov as *khlam* (trash).[65] According to one expert, they played no part in collectivization.[66]

The peasant learned much more about collective work through contact with the thousands of so-called 'simple' (*prostye*) associations which were formed for communal activity on certain sectors of production. Such associations, as we mentioned earlier on, might be set up for the communal purchase of a tractor, or some other item of agricultural equipment, or they might be *tovarish-chestva* engaged in communal sowing or tilling of the land, or in draining some marshy area; and there were many other such associations which undeniably played a valuable role as 'collectivizing' forces. During 1928 and 1929, associations of this kind made a certain amount of headway; there were some 30 to 40 thousand of them at that period, comprising some hundreds of thousands of peasants. However, they were so small that it was decided to fix a legal minimum membership of ten; otherwise, it was often found that, alongside the genuine co-operatives, there were too many simple 'family co-operatives',[67] which banded together for the purchase of equipment, or as a cover for commercial activities, and then reaped the benefit of the concessions which were made to the co-operatives.

None the less, whether they ranked as genuine co-operatives or not, these 'simple' associations were an authentic peasant institution, a manifestation of local, independent peasant initiative. The surprising thing is that the co-operative movement and its organizations had virtually nothing to do with these very small associations, which were for the most part 'wild', in that they existed outside the co-operative movement proper.[68] The same was true of the *kommuna*, the *artel* and the *toz*, with which we shall be dealing later. At best, they were affiliated to a credit association. Otherwise, these 'simple' associations operated at their own expense, for they had not been set up by the co-operative movement, which had neither the organizational nor the financial means, nor indeed the desire, to deal with structures of this kind.

These facts were officially stated in respect of the years 1927–9. At the end of 1927, Milyutin said that, under existing conditions, co-operative structures were not adapted for dealing directly with the processes of production in the countryside.[69] A year and a half later, the chairman of the Council for Agricultural Co-operation explained the shortcomings of the kolkhoz movement as being due to the fact that it had not been based on the co-operative movement. Likewise, another leader of the co-operative and kolkhoz movement told the 'Kolkhoz Council' that up till then the kolkhozes had developed without any relation to the co-operative movement.[70] It was not until the middle of 1929, he maintained, that the situation had taken a different turn. We shall be able to examine the truth of his allegation at a later stage.

It was unquestionably in the 'wild' associations, or in other words the 'simple associations' and many of the kolkhozes, that the people's co-operative activities found their most authentic expression. Despite the liberalizing measures of the NEP period, the official co-operative movement had never become a genuinely autonomous movement representing the activities of the peasantry as a whole. On the contrary, its organs had tended to develop along the lines of administrative bodies, and to become more and more an adjunct of the State administrative apparatus. The Central Committee and the government decided what its tasks should be, organized and reorganized its structures at will, and appointed its leaders. These self-same Party-appointed officials did in fact complain on numerous occasions, as we shall see, about the Commissariat for Trade which was responsible for grain procurements, and which laid down laws and issued orders to the co-operative organizations as it would have done in the case of its own departments.

In fact the co-operative movement was developing more and more into an appendage of the government procurement organizations, and by 1928 this was what it had become. This trend was already being discussed in an official document from the Central Committee even before the Fifteenth Party Congress.[71] Soviet society was being brought within the orbit of State control, and the co-operative movement proved no exception to this general rule. Inevitably, the growth of co-operative and collectivist ideas among the rural population was bound to suffer in the process.

Irrespective of the turn which events took in the future, it can be said that at the end of the NEP period Lenin's dream of the 'civilized trader' was still a long way from realization. At that time, the great majority of the peasantry had still never belonged to any form of co-operative association, apart from their own skhod (a point which should be stressed). As for that sector who already formed part of the co-operative movement, no clear socialist line of action had as yet been laid down for them to follow. The co-operative movement was mainly of value to the better-off peasants, and still had very little to offer to the poor. Moreover, the theory advanced in party doctrine and propaganda that co-operation would automatically give rise to the collective (*kolkhoz*) phase of development was purely hypothetical, and was not supported by the facts, either up until the middle of 1929 or later. The same theory and the same hopes were to be expressed by other socialist countries at a much later date, though of course these latter-day experiments have not as yet reached a conclusive stage.[72]

Notes and References

1. Figures from Pashukanis, *op. cit.*, (see Ch. 1, Note 5); p. 433.
2. *ibid*, p. 423.
3. Zdanovich, 'Selsovety i zemobshchestva', *Bolshevik*, 1928, No. 6, p. 46.
4. Kalinin, quoted in Pashukanis, *op. cit.*, p. 423.
5. Khataevich, 'Litsom k derevne', *NAF*, 1925, No. 5–6.
6. Angarov, *op. cit.*, (see Ch. 2, Note 39); p. 75. On p. 76 the author quotes a member of the *TsIK* as having the described the local administration as a 'breeding-ground for neurotics'.
7. Kukushkin, *op. cit.*, (see Ch. 1, Note 28), p. 42. There was also a considerable turnover among other officials, such as secretaries, heads of sections, etc.
8. Zdanovich; *op. cit., loc. cit.*
9. Angarov; *op. cit.*, pp. 75–81. Note the innumerable occasions on which the Party took action to curb *administrirovanie* on the one hand, and *vyrozhdenie* on the other.
10. In Soviet political jargon, there was a rich variety of expressions for describing the State's relations with its '*serednyak* ally', e.g. *zazhimat*; *ottesnit*; *otteret*, etc.
11. Figures for the RSFSR are taken from Konyukhov, *op. cit.* (see Ch. 3, Note 41); p. 32, and have been supplemented by data taken from Kukushkin, *op. cit.*, p. 36. In 1929 30·6% of all chairmen of *selsovety* were Party members, and 7·3% members of the *Komsomol*.
12. In 1926 1·2% of individuals in the countryside were without the right to vote; this figure greatly increased towards 1927 when 3·5% or 2,110,650 persons were without the vote. In 1929 the pro-

portion of *lishentsy* (individuals deprived of the right to vote) was 4·1%. These figures are taken from Pashukanis, *op. cit.*, p. 431.

13. In 1927 this would apply to the *volosti*. The new administrative division was introduced in 1929, when the *raion, okrug*, and *oblast* replaced the former *volost, uezd, okrug*, and *guberniya*. In 1930 the *okrug* too was abolished.

14. Angarov, *op. cit.*, p. 76. The expressions in quotation marks are translations of terms current in the political vocabulary of the time.

15. Zdanovich, *op. cit.*, p. 40. We shall not dwell here on the subtle distinctions between the *mir, obshchina*, and *zemobshchestvo*. See R. Portal, *op. cit.* (see Ch. 1, Note 18), pp. 33–4, 37. It should however be pointed out that the peasants called the institution *mir*, whereas the authorities, according to the Agrarian Code, tended to use the expression *zemelnoe obshchestvo*.

16. *Postroenie fundementa sotsialisticheskoi ekonomiki v SSSR 1926–32*, pp. 346–7; Carr, *A History of Soviet Russia; Socialism in One Country*, Vol. 1, pp. 214–15, gives the following figures: in 1927, of the 233 million desyatins of peasant land in the RSFSR, 222 million were in the tenure of communities, two million in the tenure of *khutora*, and six million in that of *otruba*.

17. This discussion was published in *NAF*, 1926, No. 5–6, 7–8, 9, 10, 10–12.

18. Rezunov, *op. cit.* (see Ch. 1, Note 26), pp. 6–7. Angarov, *op.cit.*, p. 79, reaches the same conclusion, although with greater reservations.

19. Gomberg, *op. cit.* (see Ch. 1, Note 41, pp. 117–18. For details on the *obshchina* as a form of proprietary tenure see *ibid*, p. 35, passim.

20. Kritsman, 'Novy etap,' *NAF*, 1927, No. 2.

21. Gomberg, *op cit.*, p. 35, passim.

22. *ibid*, p. 39.

23. Rezunov, *op. cit.*, pp. 33–4.

24. Gomberg, *op. cit.*, p. 39.

25. *Boroda* (beard); a term frequently employed to refer to the 'head of the *dvor*'. When used by officials, however, it becomes a contemptuous term for the peasant in general.

26. *15-ty S'ezd, VKP(b)*, stenogramme, p. 97. Stanislas Kosior was at this time an alternate member of the Politburo, and a secretary of the Central Committee of the Party.

27. Sukhanov, during a discussion at the Communist Academy, *NAF*, 1926, No. 11–12, p. 101.

28. Gomberg, *op. cit.*, p. 36.

29. *ibid*, p. 58.

30. Rezunov, *op. cit.*, p. 23.

31. Zdanovich, *op. cit.*, p. 49; Rezunov, *op. cit.*, p. 37 *passim*; Molotov, *15-ty S'ezd VKP(b)*, stenogramme, p. 1086; Kukushkin, *op. cit.*, pp. 14–15.

32. Rezunov, *op. cit.*, p. 20; Enukidze, *15-ty S'ezd VKP(b)*, stenogramme, p. 1111.

33. Kiselev, *Izvestiya*, May 20, 1928, quoted by Rezunov, *op. cit.*, p. 22.

34. Molotov, *15-ty S'ezd VKP(b)*, stenogramme, pp. 1086, 1232.

35. *Obshchie nachala zemlepolzovaniya i zemleustroistva*, par. 47–51, in *Kollektivizatsiya selskogo khozyaistva*, doc. No. 20, pp. 105–6.

36. Molotov, *15-ty S'ezd VKP(b)*, stenogramme, p. 1086, and the contribution of Kubanin to the discussion at the Communist Academy, *NAF*, 1926, No. 11–12.

37. Rezunov, *op. cit.*, pp. 36–40.

38. *NAF*, 1927, No. 1, p. 137.

39. Zdanovich, *op. cit.*, pp. 44, 47. See also Gilinsky, *15-ty S'ezd VKP(b)*, stenogramme, p. 1130.

40. Discussion at the Communist Academy (see Note 27). The findings of the Communist Academy, presented on January 15, 1927, to *Sovnarkom* are contained in *NAF*, 1927, No. 1, p. 104.

41. The RSFSR and Belorussia further objected that the draft law of *Sovnarkom* was too detailed, and encroached upon the rights of the Republics and of their *Narkomzemy*. This point too was disputed, although less so than the one we have mentioned.

42. Speech by Smirnov to a gathering of peasant members of *VTsIK*, *NAF*, 1926, No. 11–12.

43. Sukhanov, discussion at the Communist Academy (see Note 27). Sukhanov's idea was that as a result of such a merger the *selsovet* would become the mouthpiece of the democratic community.

44. Zdanovich, *op. cit.*, p. 44.

45. Volf, *Planovoe Khozyaistvo*, 1929, No. 2, p. 111.

46. Decree of *VTsIK-SNK* RSFSR quoted by Kukushkin, *op. cit.*, pp. 99–100, according to whom the community should cease to exist in a region which had been 75% collectivised.

47. Carr, *A History of Soviet Russia: Socialism in One Country*, Vol. 1, pp. 276–7.

48. Lenin, 'O kooperatsii', *Sochineniya*, Vol. XXXIII, pp. 430–1.

49. *ibid.*, pp. 430, 435.

50. Kukharin, *op. cit.* (see Ch. 3, Note 32), pp. 32–8, 47.

51. Preobrazhensky, *Novaya Ekonomika* (Moscow, 1926), p. 209.

52. For details concerning the co-operative organizations see *Soviet Union Year Book* (London, 1930); Lyashchenko, *op. cit.* (see Ch. 1, Note 42), Vol. III, p. 144; Ratner, *Agricultural Cooperation in the Soviet Union* (London, 1929).

53. Lyashchenko, *op. cit.*, Vol. III, p. 250. In 1927 there were 26,272 'consumers' associations', i.e., rural shops. However, the RSFSR alone had over 50,000 *selsovety* (70,000 was the figure for the country as a whole) and something like 150,000 villages.

54. Lvov, *Pravda*, July 30, 1930; Yakovlev, *16-ty S'ezd VKP(b)*, stenogramme, p.643.

55. Lvov, *ibid.*

56. Sevruk, article on 'credit co-operation', *NAF*, 1929, No. 6; Ratner, *op. cit.*, p. 7.

57. Kaminsky, *15-ty S'ezd VKP(b)*, stenogramme, p. 1219. Kaminsky was one of the leaders of the co-operative movement and was soon to become chairman of the *Kolkhoztsentr*.

58. Ratner, *op. cit.*, p. 46 states that in 1927–8 *Khlebotsentr* was responsible for 2,000 co-operatives, embracing 950,000 households.

59. Stalin, report to the Fifteenth Congress, *15-ty S'ezd VKP(b)*, stenogramme, p. 57.

60. e.g. the Central Committee, in a letter published on the occasion of the founding of the rural Party bureaux, states that agricultural co-operation was still 'extremely weak'. The letter is in *Kollektivizatsiya selskogo khozyaistva*, doc. 6, the quotation on p. 53.

61. Kaminsky, *Pravda*, January 11, 1929. It was Kaminsky who called for a 'real' co-operative movement as opposed to the 'formal' one which existed purely for statistical purposes.

62. Veisberg, *Planovoe Khozyaistvo*, 1929 No. 3, p. 101. Ratner claims that 20% of the figure of 11–12 million members is due to double accounting. One should therefore reckon only 8–9 million households as belonging to co-operative associations.

63. Kritsman, 'O reshayushchem etape kollektivizatsii', *NAF* 1930, No. 5. Emphasis supplied.

64. Kraev, 'Pyatiletni plan razvitii selskokhozyaistvennoi kooperatsii,' *NAF*, 1929, No. 5; Carr, *A History of Soviet Russia; Socialism in One Country*, Vol. 1, pp. 281–2.

65. Molotov, *15-ty S'ezd VKP(b)*, stenogramme, p. 1070.

66. Vladimirsky, *16-taya Konferentsiya VKP(b)*, April 1929, stenogramme, p. 114.

67. Ratner, *op. cit.*, p. 57; Kalinin, *5-ty S'ezd Sovetov*, stenogramme, Bull. No. 15, pp. 26–8; Libkind, *NAF*, 1927, No. 8–9, p. 63 *passim*.

68. Molotov claimed that these associations comprised 1 million households (which for that period seems an exaggerated figure) but

that only 6% of these belonged to the co-operative movement. *15-ty S'ezd VKP(b)*, stenogramme, p. 1074.

69. Milyutin, *15-ty S'ezd VKP(b)*, stenogramme, p. 1189.

70. Vladimirsky, *16-taya Konferentsiya VKP(b)*, p. 114; Kaminsky, *Pravda*, June 20, 1929. For an affirmation that the co-operative organization was not adopted to the needs of the kolkhozes, and was doing nothing for them, see also Grigorev, 'Kollektivizatsiya sovetskoi derevni,' *Bolshevik*, 1928, No. 7.

71. *KPSS v rezolyutsiyakh*, Vol. II, p. 423.

72. We refer here to Poland, and especially to Yugoslavia. See Kardel, *Les problèmes de la politique socialiste dans les campagnes* (Paris, 1960).

Chapter 5

THE ESTABLISHMENT OF
THE SOVIET RÉGIME
IN THE COUNTRYSIDE (contd.)

1. *The Kolkhozes*

A brief sketch of the history and the state of the kolkhozes up to the end of 1927 provides a striking example of the short-sightedness of Soviet policy during the NEP period. The régime's policy in the countryside during the Civil War reflected the general current of Utopianism which prevailed within the Party. Collectivist organizations in the rural areas, such as the *kommuna*, the *artel* and the *toz* (and particularly the first-mentioned of these, in line with the prevailing illusions of the period) received a vigorous stimulus which was followed up by administrative measures based on the methods of 'war communism'. 'Policy was directed towards straightforward socialist ownership of the land,' as Lyashchenko wrote. 'In practice,' he adds, 'this encouraged a sudden and sometimes completely artificial increase in co-operative organizations, which often concealed a purely individual enterprise.'[1]

In the end, however, this enthusiasm for collectivization came to almost nothing.[2] A decline set in at the beginning of the NEP period, and most of the communes went the way of a great many other illusions of that time. The workers who had formed the nucleus of the *kommuny* and *arteli* left the villages and went back to the factories. During the respite afforded by NEP, the peasants who had taken refuge in the communes as a means of saving their property from being requisitioned were able to emerge and go back to their individual farms.[3]

The new policy which was directed towards ensuring, at all costs, an increase in agricultural production by the peasants, was 'imperfectly understood' by the local authorities, who set about purging and liquidating a great many collective farms with the same zeal that they had shown in creating them. Special *troiki* were sometimes set up for this purpose. Once the collective farm had been cleansed of anti-Soviet elements, and if it survived this operation, the services of the State enterprises which had previously assisted it were also withdrawn.[4]

In 1923, there was an appreciable drop in the number of collective organizations, which had not in any case been very high; the decrease was particularly marked in the case of the *kommuna*, and less so in respect of the *artel*; on the other hand, the *tozy* continued to increase in number and in proportion to the total. There was also a rapid growth of 'simple producers' associations', which were not kolkhozes in the strict sense of the term, since there was only a minimal degree of communal work and ownership. This trend toward a growing number of simple associations, particularly *tozy*, relative to the number of *kommuny* and *arteli*, continued to be an increasingly noteworthy feature of the kolkhoz movement up until the end of 1929.

Thus, the collectivist movement did not go under. It remained in existence, through a variety of ups and downs, as an expression of the collectivist tendencies which were always present, to a greater or lesser extent, within the peasantry, but particularly as a response to the desperate situation of the *bednota*. The bednyaks were constantly on the look-out for ways and means of improving their condition, and many of them were prepared to try the collectivist solution, especially as the land which was allocated to the kolkhozes came from the State reserve. Up till 1927, the movement consisted of bednyaks, and collective farms were set up on publicly owned land, on former landed estates which had belonged to the nobility, or other land belonging to the State.

In about 1924–5, the movement showed some recovery; the number of collective farms increased, though this was mainly due to the fact that further land had become available as a result of the liquidation of a fair number of sovkhozes at this time.[5] By 1927, there was no more free land and this source, which had supplied the kolkhoz movement, therefore dried up.[6] The years 1926 and 1927 brought a fresh crisis, and a decrease in the number of collective farms. There is said to have been some subsequent improvement in conditions within the kolkhozes, but all writers on this subject are agreed that during the whole of the preceding period, the kolkhozes were engaged in a struggle for survival.[7]

It is impossible to arrive at an exact figure for the number of kolkhozes in existence at the end of 1927. It is not even easy to discern accurately what was being done about them. The information provided by different departments varies, as is shown by a survey carried out by the Commissariat of Inspection. The following table gives various estimates for the number of kolkhozes, the sources being the *Kolkhoztsentr*, the *Narkomzem* and *Narkomfin*.[8]

	Kolkhoztsentr	*NKZ (em)*	*NKF (in)*
1924	12,005	9,718	8,641
1925	15,974	12,609	9,277
1926	11,851	12,099	8,023

Apart altogether from the general poverty of statistical material and the lack of specialist organizations for dealing with the kolkhozes, the task of carrying out a proper statistical survey of the kolkhozes was further complicated by the difficulty of classifying and distinguishing between the various types of kolkhoz organization. The *kommuny* were comparatively easy to identify, but the other forms were much less so, for the differences were not very clearly defined. The organizers of a particular association would often register it as an *artel*, whereas it was really only a *toz*, or vice versa, Not infrequently, the authorities would describe as kolkhozes bodies which were actually 'simple associations', such as, for example, a *mashinnoe tovarishchestvo* (an association for the communal purchase of a piece of machinery or a tractor).

It is easy to see how serious discrepancies in the statistics could arise. In addition, new associations were constantly springing up while others disappeared, and the statistics never kept pace with the changes. The *RKI* experts observed that the figures put forward included many 'dead souls', and concluded that the kolkhoz sector had become smaller. The following estimate, compiled from various sources,[9] is suggested for the end of 1927: there were 18,000 kolkhozes in the country as a whole, of which 6,000 were in the Ukraine, and there were also some 26,000 to 30,000 so-called 'simple' associations—of which over 5,000 were in the Ukraine—for the purchase of machines and tractors. The population of the kolkhozes numbered some 950,000 to 980,000 'mouths', of which one-third were in the Ukraine. There were said to be 1,000,000 households in 'simple' associations, although this figure seems exaggerated. It should be made clear that the great majority of these households (700,000) belonged to 'land-improvement associations', and that they had therefore virtually nothing of the character of genuine collectives. From this point of view, a much more important element was the associations which existed for the purchase of a tractor, or some other item of agricultural machinery (a mere 100,000 households) with, in addition, some tens of thousands of households belonging to associations for livestock-raising or sowing. Despite the faith which some Party activists and officials placed in associations of this kind, they cannot be classified as kolkhozes; all too frequently even the *tozy* could scarcely qualify as genuine kolkhozes.

The proportions of the various types of association which together made up the kolkhoz movement were subject to constant change. About 1921, the *kommuny* represented about 20%, and the *tozy* 15%; the greater part of the movement was made up of associations known as *arteli*. But round about 1927, during the NEP period, the proportion of *kommuny* fell to 8.5%, while that of the *tozy* rose to 40.2% (by 1929 it was 60.2%).[10]

No clear-cut distinctions ever existed among these three forms of association. In terms of their constitution, they were defined differently in different republics and even *oblasti*, so that what ranked as an *artel* in one place might be rated as a *kommuna* or a *toz* elsewhere.[11] The definitions of *toz* and *artel* were particularly vague, and the two were frequently confused. The *kommuna*, which had obtained the most favoured treatment during the period of 'war communism', was for long regarded as the 'highest' form, the one which had advanced furthest along the road to socialism in the countryside. In the *kommuna*, not only the land and the means of work were collectivized, but also housing and consumption.[12] The *kommuna* worked on egalitarian principles of distribution; families left their cottages and lived in rooms allocated to them in communal living quarters; everyone ate in a communal refectory; in principle, the children were brought up and educated by the *kommuna*, and lived in schools or nurseries under the care of persons appointed by the *kommuna*. There were individual variations in the details of organization as between one *kommuna* and another, and the above principles were implemented according to the means and the abilities of the *kommuna* in question.

One significant point which should be made is that this form of association was preferred by the poorer peasants, for they were less reluctant than the others to share their possessions with the community, since they had so few possessions in any case, and particularly since the *kommuna* was obliged, by definition, to feed them once they had joined it. The whole conception of socialism or communism during the Civil War period was based on this primitive form of communism, which was the direct reflection, not of an advanced degree of culture or technical evolution, but of extreme poverty.[13] When the 'communism of poverty' failed, other concepts were put in its place.

In the *artel*, collectivization did not extend to housing or consumption. Family life retained its private character, as it had before. Land was held in common, except for a small strip attached to the house, and the size of this strip varied according to the decisions taken by the local authorities. In principle, all important implements, and draught animals, and occasionally either all or some of the cows, were communally owned.

The amount of goods contributed to the *artel* by a household was often taken into account in the sharing-out of income, and the household received a bonus in proportion to its 'investment'; is some cases, the amount of goods thus invested by each family formed the main basis on which distribution of the *artel*'s income was decided. This kind of arrangement appealed to certain middle or even better-off peasants, for it was sometimes to their advantage to form an association of this kind themselves, in that they could then go on living much the same way as before. This was one of the reasons for the existence of 'false kolkhozes'.

In the *toz*[14] either all or part of the land was held in common ownership, and communally divided. In the majority of cases, income was distributed in accordance with the size of each peasant's holding. It was rare for livestock and the majority of the farm implements to be collectivized, but the heaviest and most expensive machines, such as tractors or steam threshers, which the individual farmer could not afford, were owned communally. In this type of association there was considerable variation in the degree of collectivization and the amount of the property held in common. This form was more in keeping with the peasant mentality, and appealed to the middle and the better-off strata more readily than the other types of association. But according to some views, the whole collective movement was based on the bednyaks, who made up 70% of its strength.

However, the problem of the various forms of collectivization is best approached by analysis of the evidence on the degree of communal ownership of property, and thus on the degree of 'socialization' which existed in the associations in question. In the *kommuny*, which were the minority group within the movement, socialization of horses, cows, land and machines was almost total.[15] In the other forms of collectivization, the situation was different and there was wide variation in the degree of socialization. In the *arteli* and especially in the *tozy*, the majority of the horses (80% and 92% respectively) and the cows (73% and 94%) and a large part of the equipment (half in the case of the *arteli*, and the greater part in the case of the *tozy*) remained private property (except for the more complicated items of machinery).[16]

It was clear that the members of the kolkhozes were still very far from being convinced that the form of association which they had chosen was the best one, and all the groundwork was yet to be done, before they could be induced to form a genuine collective farm, even one with the status of a *toz*.

All the kolkhozes represented very small agricultural enterprises. The average *kommuna* had more members and more land, whereas the *tozy* often consisted of only a few families. The average kolkhoz might have about fifty mouths to feed (that is, a dozen or so families) and fifty desyatins of crops, five or six horses, and seven cows. According to the information on the Ukraine, the average *kommuna* consisted of about thirty-three members, the *artel* averaged only eighteen members (48·5 souls) and the *toz* twelve members.[17] In the opinion of many observers, the scale of these operations, particularly in the case of the *toz*, was much too small to demonstrate the advantages of large-scale cultivation and, therefore, to attract the mass of the peasantry. It was suggested that the size of such associations would have to be increased, as a matter of urgency.

However, at this point, around the year 1928, the size of the kolkhozes was in fact continuing to decrease. Their economic situation was often far from healthy. The authorities and the experts were all agreed that, until 1927, the kolkhozes had done nothing but 'eat up' the funds allocated to them by the government. At this stage in the development of the kolkhozes, according to Kulikov, the material circumstances of kolkhoz members differed very little from those of the private peasants, and sometimes did not go beyond what was regarded as 'the minimum subsistence level for a member of a collective farm'.[18] But in maintaining this 'minimum subsistence' the entire gross revenue of the kolkhoz was swallowed up in food, and there was nothing left over for development of the collective farm, and for kolkhoz funds.[19] The most important factor in this situation was low labour productivity. Another contributory factor was the instability of the kolkhozes, whose numbers fluctuated to an extent that was described by officials and experts as being both abnormal and alarming. There were times when as many as a third of the kolkhozes which had recently been formed disappeared almost as soon as they had been set up, leaving no lasting trace behind them except in the statistics.

In most of the kolkhozes (apart from the *kommuny*) there was very little socialization of property, so that the peasants who belonged to them went on farming their own holdings more or less as before. Such a situation favoured the growth of a great number of 'false collective farms', which were either deliberately set up as such, or became 'false' through a process of degeneration. Some of the better-off peasants were often tempted to set up a little 'collective', which provided a convenient screen for their activities as individual farmers, and enabled them to enjoy certain privileges and concessions, until such times as they were able to return to private farming without the camouflage. According to the observers, many such cases had been discovered. The *RKI* reported that in 1926–7 some 20% of the kolkhozes in the North Caucasus were 'false'.[20] In the Smolensk province the authorities liquidated 30% of the kolkhozes, in the Urals 42% were dissolved (in two years), and in Samara 52%.

Other authors, on examining this problem reported that out of 700 kolkhozes registered in the province of Ulyanovsk, 250 were actually in existence, and the others had been liquidated at various times, because in the majority of cases they had only been set up for the sake of the credits, which were then shared out among the individual farms.[21] The findings of one survey were that in some provinces there were as many as 22–60% of 'false' kolkhozes. But the same authors also admitted that the authorities had very often been unduly drastic, and swept away genuine kolkhozes composed of bednyaks, although these were reasonably 'healthy', or could at least have been 'cleaned up'. Yakovlev also was of the opinion that this particular danger had been exaggerated, and that not more than 10% of kolkhozes were false.[22] And indeed it was hardly likely that the better-off peasants, or kulaks, during what were relatively good years for them, should go to the trouble of organizing false collectives as a screen for farming activities which they could in fact carry on in the normal manner. It was a fairly frequent occurrence for them to join together, thus qualifying for credits and concessions, and then to break up again within a short space of time, but there is little evidence to suggest that, except in rare instances, this was the result of a calculated manoeuvre; in any event, even if the element of calculation were present, the setting up of false kolkhozes during this period could equally involve serednyaks and even poorer peasants.

Although the collective farms had been set up with the best intentions, the danger of degeneration was real enough, but it lay much more in the difficulties which arose over their subsequent development, in that the members did not know how to set about managing a complex undertaking. In associations of this kind, where the organization was poor and the element of collectivization very small, the peasants continued to hold on to their private farms; the kolkhoz body was easily infected by any number of harmful 'germs'. There was, for example, the over-frequent use of paid workers, which sometimes became a regular practice; or again, the hiring of machines to the villagers at rates which brought a very high return; sometimes the principles which were adopted in relation to the internal organization of the kolkhoz and the distribution of its income were such that before long there were more inequalities after the setting-up of the collective than there had been before.

In those cases where distribution of the kolkhoz income was governed by the amount of each family's 'investment', or the number of implements or livestock which they contributed to the communal effort, it was not long before the bednyaks were being exploited by the stronger elements. In such conditions, the better-off peasants sometimes paid a neighbour to take over their share of the work in the fields belonging to the collective. For the same reasons, they sometimes hired a batrak from outside the kolkhoz. The press often reported such cases. In this way, there was a combination of circumstances which could lead to the kolkhoz's becoming a mere label. When this happened, the funds and the credits which it received were simply shared out among its members. In such instances, a purge was clearly called for, but remedial action of this kind needed careful handling. In practice, however, this was rarely possible, for neither the local authorities, nor indeed the central authorities, had specialists who were competent to deal with anything as complicated as kolkhoz organization. This is why the authorities either tolerated 'degenerate' bodies of the strangest kinds, or else set about a wholesale purge, without discrimination or guiding principles.[23]

During the second phase of NEP, the government's attitude towards the kolkhozes was one of total neglect. Since the régime at this time were concentrating exclusively on broadening the basis of NEP, their policy took no account whatever of the kolkhozes. However, by about 1925 there was a growing feeling among many of the Party activists that a new era was opening in the country's development. So far, the achievement of NEP had been to set on its feet an economy disrupted by a world war and, more particularly, by civil war. Agricultural production was at last beginning to approach pre-war level, but industry was still marking time. The Left were particularly conscious of the gap between the two, and feared that lack of growth in the industrial sector might endanger agriculture and jeopardize the socialist aims of the régime. The feeling that a new situation called for a new policy was to a large extent responsible for the resurgence of the internal struggle within the Party, which now raged more fiercely than ever.

The Party leadership introduced a series of measures, aimed mainly at ensuring a higher rate of agricultural production and at coming to terms with the peasants, by offering a greater degree of freedom to the better-off private farmers. Having openly committed themselves in this direction, the Bukharin-Stalin coalition left themselves with no alternative position on which to fall back if need be. This is why there was no response to those who pressed for greater emphasis on the development of the kolkhoz movement at this time. In January 1925 Lyashchenko, who was already a well-known economist at the time, stressed that although it was of overriding importance for the country to expand its economy by the use of NEP methods, some attention must be given to encouraging the collectivist sector, extending more positive aid to the poorer peasants and devising a policy of *zemleustroistvo*, 'by taking some elementary steps towards socialization, and making adequate preparations, including drawing on State budgetary resources'.[24]

Two other authors argued in effect that the co-operative sector, which at that time was engaged only in selling and procurement

114

operations, would not provide a solution to all the problems.[25] Since the enormous bednyak stratum had very little to sell, co-operation in this sense would have nothing to offer them. So far as the bednyak was concerned, they maintained that the only solution was communal production. But more often than not the existing kolkhozes were left to their fate (*bezprizornye*). The Commissariat for Agriculture had no 'centre' and no department which was responsible for the kolkhozes.[26]

There were many appeals similar to the one mentioned above, and many similar complaints about neglect on the part of the authorities. At the conference of kolkhoz members, which was held at Moscow in February 1925, a number of speakers called attention not only to the failure of the local soviets and local Party organizations to assist the kolkhozes, but also to instances in which they had displayed a negative attitude towards the kolkhozes, or had even actively hindered them.[27] The kolkhozes received no agronomic assistance, no attempt was made to reallocate land on a rational basis, thus rendering it impossible to introduce a proper system of crop rotation, the attitude both of the authorities and of the co-operative sector was one of neglect: this was the burden of the complaints made by kolkhoz officials and members, and it summed up the situation in which the collective movement found itself. . . .

Descriptions in the press provide a fair number of illustrations of the treatment meted out to the collective farms by the local authorities. One of the biggest and oldest associations, situated in the Tula province, was from its inception subjected to an interminable series of obstacles and attacks. This attitude apparently arose from the fact that the chairman of the association was a former member of the Social-Revolutionary party. Molotov himself had to intervene to remedy the situation. Later on, the same association was accused by the local authorities of being 'kulak', because it had adopted a system of remuneration based on the amount of work done, and not on the number of 'mouths', which was the accepted practice at that time. Once again, it needed high-level intervention (by the *Narkomzem* in this instance) to save the association from the unpleasant consequences of this charge.[28] But high-level intervention of this kind was exceptional, and did nothing to extricate the kolkhozes as a whole from the morass of difficulties in which they were floundering. The Party leadership were well aware of the position of the collective farms. Molotov, and others too, visited the kolkhozes from time to time, and realized how precarious their situation was. Thus, in 1925, after having visited several collective farms, Molotov declared that 'living conditions were extremely poor; in one of the collectives, for example, the members were living in small, evil-smelling rooms (and this in what had been the fine house of a nobleman)'.

The author who quoted these words of Molotov's two years later declared that since Molotov's visit in 1925 things had not changed much.[29]

The delegates at the kolkhoz conference at the beginning of 1925, which we have already mentioned, were well aware of the reasons for this state of affairs. The following is the answer which Bukharin, chief government spokesman at the conference, made to the complaints and demands of the kolkhoz members and the officials working in the collective sector: 'We cannot approach collectivization from the production end, we must begin at the other end. The main approach is through co-operation . . . the collective farms are not the main line, or the highway which will lead the peasants to socialism.'[30]

Despite protests from the Ukrainian delegates, the resolutions adopted by the conference, as E. H. Carr says, reflected Bukharin's views; it was not surprising that the conference rejected the need to provide the collective movement with independent centres and organizations, instead of attaching it to the agricultural co-operative organizations. In an important political statement which was published some months later, Bukharin shifted his ground slightly, by declaring that the poor peasants, being 'in a desperate pass' and having nothing to sell, 'must inevitably gravitate towards different forms of collective (*kolkhozy*) in the strictest sense of the term'.[31] However, he apparently did not feel himself bound to go very far in drawing practical conclusions from this statement, for he went on to say, in the same text, that since individualistic attitudes were too deeply ingrained and of too long standing, and since this affected the poor peasants just as much as the others 'it was scarcely to be supposed that the collective movement could absorb the entire mass of the rural *bednota*.[32] In his view, the 'sovereign remedy' for the problems of the poor was to be found within the general framework of the co-operative movement.

Later on, Bukharin was to come under ceaseless fire on account of these statements, but at the present stage it was the enfeebled kolkhoz movement which paid the price of a policy which still had several years to run.

Two years later, in a memorandum submitted to the *Sovnarkom* (on the two draft measures of land legislation which were then being debated) the Communist Academy criticized both drafts, and indeed all previous agrarian legislation, on the grounds that no provision had been made for 'clauses designed to offer even the slightest encouragement in respect of joint working of the land'.[33] The agrarian codes of Belorussia and the Ukraine—the memorandum went on to say—contained certain clauses of this kind, but they were not explicit enough. This was why many of the kolkhozes did not even have sufficient lands distributed on a rational enough basis to enable them to manage their farms properly; the memorandum concluded with the suggestion that clear provisions relating to the rights and facilities which should be granted to the collective farms should be embodied in the enactments.[34]

The first decree of all-Union significance relating to the kolkhoz movements was published on March 16, 1927.[35]

This document, issued by the *TsIK* and the *Sovnarkom*, reaffirmed the Bukharinist theory that the principal solution for the peasantry lay in the general co-operative movement, and that the collective movement would have to solve its problems within the context of co-operation. Collectivism was confirmed as being the most important way of assisting the bednyak, but it was stated that, since the land belonging to the former landed estates was no longer available, the development of the kolkhozes would henceforth be dependent on the activity of the masses and on State aid. The decree further stated that, of all the possible forms of collective association, the simpler ones were also those which were more accessible to the peasants, and more susceptible of development. Special attention should be paid to them, and it was to them that the bednyaks must initially be recruited. The local authorities were warned about false kolkhozes—although the text did not go into details on this question—and the *TsSU* were also called upon to carry out constant surveys on the collective farms.

There follow several recommendations on organizational measures which should be introduced; the kolkhoz General Council was to set up parallel centres in the republics, and these would continue to be part of the co-operative organization, while special departments, or 'kolkhoz bureaux', were to be set up to deal with kolkhoz problems within the framework of the regional co-operative organization, in those regions where there was a greater concentration of collective associations.

However, the amount of practical assistance for the kolkhoz movement envisaged in terms of the above decree was very small. It was decided to reduce by 25% the amount of the agricultural tax per head, but this was of little importance, since the poor peasants who were the main candidates for kolkhoz membership paid very few taxes, and would soon be exempt from tax altogether. Another measure proposed the return to the kolkhozes, without compensation, of small enterprises which they had up till then held on lease from the government. The decree also gave an undertaking to the kolkhozes that measures for *zemleustroistvo* would be carried out until the end of the year at the government's expense, and that a long-term credit fund would be set up for them, from funds made available by the government and the agricultural bank. The sum contributed for this purpose was to be five million roubles, which was ridiculously small. Credits promised to the kolkhozes in the RSFSR for 1927 were to be 13·7 million (the total for the country as a whole being 18 million).[36]

In all, this first government decree on the Kolkhoz movement did not reflect any change in attitude towards the kolkhozes, and made no substantial contribution to the collective movement in the countryside. There is reason to believe that even the modest sums promised under the decree did not reach the recipients. Indeed, it was clear from many articles in the press, and from the *RKI* surveys, that, limited though they were, the government's proposals for assisting the kolkhozes were not implemented in any sector. There was still no *zemleustroistvo*, and no one to take charge of the kolkhozes, and above all there was a great deal of confusion in the matter of credits. The funds which had been allocated to the kolkhozes were not utilized: the existing kolkhozes were already heavily in debt, while the setting up of new kolkhozes was beyond the means which had been made available to the credit associations for this purpose.[37]

As one author pointed out,

'the lack of any precise directive on the question of who is responsible for the organization of the kolkhozes, the delay in setting up kolkhoz departments, the failure on the part of anyone at all to take steps to organize kolkhoz services—all of these factors have been responsible for the inefficient use of the credits allocated to the kolkhozes'.[38]

Other authors, and also the *RKI*, pointed out that the credits reaching the kolkhozes were by no means available on the favourable terms which had been envisaged by the decree. The rate of interest paid by the kolkhozes was high, the repayment periods were always too short, and there was no supervision of the way in which the credits were used. The result was that the kolkhozes, instead of benefiting from the credits, fell deeper and deeper into debt. There were frequent instances of kolkhoz property being seized and auctioned off by the authorities, because the kolkhozes in question had been unable to discharge debts incurred by the purchase of a tractor. The loans granted to them for this purpose had to be paid back after two harvests, and this was too short a period for them to be able to finance purchases of heavy equipment.[39]

The recital of these, and similar, shortcomings could be continued *ad infinitum. The surprising thing is that this movement, which received little assistance and no guidance at all, did in fact survive, and went on clinging to its existence.* The greater part of the bednyaks who belonged to the collective were illiterate. It is not surprising that they were incapable of drawing up proper production plans, and correctly organizing their activities; one can scarcely wonder at their inability to keep accounts, though this was essential, or their failure to cope with problems as complicated as, for example, the method of distributing kolkhoz revenues. This they did as best they could, and the methods they invented were sometimes quite ingenious,[40] but for the most part they fell back on peasant tradition, which was still very much alive, particularly among the bednyaks, and adopted an egalitarian system of sharing out income on the basis of 'mouths'. Who was to teach them how to cope with their problems? The few available agronomists hardly knew themselves. *Pravda* itself stated, with regret, that even in the Moscow *oblast* the assistance they gave could be of no practical value. What was happening in other places? The agricultural schools and institutes were supposed to be responsible for supplying equipment, handbooks and above all specialists, but 'in our area, unfortunately, none of the agricultural institutes in the RSFSR have so far provided any courses on the collectivization of agriculture'.[41]

The vast wealth of experience provided by thousands of collective associations of many different types was almost entirely disregarded, and was virtually lost to those who were destined to need it in the years to come.

2. The Rural Communists

The history of the Party cells in the countryside reflects a very curious combination of factors and influences which are all traceable to contradictions inherent in the Soviet régime and its uneasy relationship with the peasantry. After 1928, when the tension built up by procurements and collectivization had increasingly brought home to the Party the insecurity of its position in the villages, greater attention was paid to the Party cells in the countryside. Surveys were carried out by the *TsSU* and also by the recently created rural office of the Central Committee, and certain other bodies, and these afforded the Party leaders a closer insight into a sector of the Party whose activities had up till then attracted little notice. The purge carried out towards the end of 1929 also served to focus attention on the rural cadres. The picture which emerged was such as to cause serious anxiety, and to call for action to remedy the situation.

At this time, only one-tenth of the communists who were members of the rural organizations had already been Party members in 1917, or before that date. The number of peasants joining the Party during the Civil War period was not very high, and represented one sixth of overall Party strength.[42] A great many of these members (between 1917 and 1921) were not peasants, but workers living in rural areas.

During the first few years of NEP (1922–3), according to the afore-mentioned author, 'only an infinitesimal number of communists in the villages' rejoined the ranks of the Party, a fact which bore witness to the unpopularity of the Soviet régime in the countryside during the difficult years which followed the great famine.

Thus, in September 1924, there were in all only 13,558 of these village Party cells, comprising 152,993 members and candidates (as against 521,108 in the towns). A typical cell at this time was made up of about four or six members, distributed over three or four villages which might be ten or fifteen versts apart.[43] At this time, the prevailing conviction, not only among the peasants but within the cell itself, was

'that one need only be a member of the Party cell in order to make requisitions, or arrests, or to confiscate whatever one will without any special authorization from the appropriate authority. . . . It was diffi-cult to tell where the Party cell ended, and the tribunal, or the police, or the land commission, etc., began.'[44]

Given this situation, which before long met with strong criticism from the Party, it is easy to understand why the peasants distrusted the cells, and showed little interest in them, and why recruitment to the Party was so poor at this period. Following on the concessions which were made to the peasants in the subsequent period, relations between the peasantry and the Soviet authorities did, for a time, become more normal and more regular. The Party took as its watch-word 'Look to the Countryside', and established closer contact with the villages. The local soviets and the co-operatives gained a stronger foothold, and the peasants, coming to terms with the realities of everyday life and the activities of the authorities with whom they had to deal, accepted recruitment into the Party more readily, and even on occasion found it to their interest to do so. From then on there was a steady increase in membership, and there were 217,400 members (17,500 cells) by 1927; in the following year the number was 299,000, and in 1929 there were 333,300, distributed over 23,300 cells.[45] Occasionally, some of the cells were fictitious, as Yaroslavsky ironically remarked;[46] they only figured in reports, in which they even had some remarkable achievements to their credit. . . .

The main body of recruitment to the Party in the countryside took place, therefore, between the years 1925–9. These were latter-day communists, whose membership was no longer dictated to any great extent by socialist ideals or ideological considerations. In addition, the Party had, at best, only one cell to roughly every three *selsovety*, and this proportion was not only too small, but scattered over too wide an area.[47] This weakness was to be felt very acutely during the trials of strength which took place between the régime and the peasantry as from 1928, particularly since the social composition and the innate tendencies of the rural communist sector served to aggravate it still further. In the first place, contrary to the officially-held theory, the number of 'proletarian elements' in the rural Party was very small indeed. Molotov made a statement to this effect at the plenum in November 1928, and another author stated that batraks and agricultural workers comprised only 5% of the Party strength.[48] The leader of the agricultural workers' Union was alarmed by these facts. He quoted, as an example, the situation in the cotton plantations in Uzbekistan, where over 100,000 batraks were employed. Of these, only 696, including 18 women, had joined the Party. In the Ukraine, there were 200,000 batrak women and 100,000 women agricultural workers working in the sovkhozes, and of these only 84 were Party members. The same facts were noted two years later by officials of the local Party organizations, in the countryside.[49] During the years 1929–30, there was to be some improvement in the position, but only after an intensive recruitment campaign had been undertaken under pressure from the Central Committee; the situation as it existed in the period prior to this date simply reflected the realities of life in the Soviet countryside.

The problem of the social composition of the Party membership was by no means an easy one to tackle, either for the Party experts or the research workers. The results of surveys varied according to whether the criteria adopted were those of social origin, or actual occupation at the time of the survey. On the basis of the first of these criteria, results for the Party as a whole, at the beginning of 1929, showed 62% of workers, 21% of peasants, 5·6% officials, and 10·3% others.[50] But the three senior Party officials who quoted these figures admitted that they gave a false picture of the social composition of the Party. Estimates based on the actual occupation of members at the time of the survey showed 42·3% of factory workers, 2% of batraks and agricultural workers, 12·8% of peasants, and 42·9% officials and others.[51] 12·8%, in other words, 123,828 peasants who were members of the Party, depended on agriculture for their livelihood, but at this time the rural Party cells had 333,000 members. An overwhelming majority of these, therefore, were not peasant farmers. Batraks and workers (i.e. workers who were employed in the sovkhozes, in forestry work, and in enterprises situated in the rural areas or in the towns, but who lived in the villages) still only made up roughly 20% of the total, even after the intensive recruitment drive which had been carried out among these same elements in 1928, in order to 'improve the social composition' of the Party.

Most of the cells consisted of officials. One source gives the proportion of officials as something over 50%, another puts it at 37·58%,[52] but the latter figure includes only those officials who owned a farm (or who belonged to a family which owned a farm, and remained economically part of that family). If one adds to this figure the number of officials who had no direct connection with any agricultural occupation, then the two estimates tally.

Like the other social and administrative institutions which operated in the countryside, the Party cells, which were few in number and scattered over a vast rural population, were influenced by their environment. However, these influences gave rise, within the Party, to tendencies whose consequences were even more complex and far-reaching than in other contexts.

The Party recruited its leading officials for the *selsovety* and the village or *raion* co-operative organizations from the ranks of the rural membership, and these posts, especially in the co-operatives, represented a certain source of influence and of income, the latter being partly direct, in the form of wages, and partly indirect, in the sense that the communists enjoyed certain facilities in the matter of supplies and credits and other concessions. In this way, a bednyak who belonged to the Party, and who was appointed to an administrative post, became an employee.

Such positions were sought after, even by the 'strong' serednyak. The better-off peasants, if in doubt about putting themselves up before the Party as candidates, for fear of not being admitted, would send another member of the family who 'passed muster' more readily than the head of the *dvor*.

The fact that membership of the Party could bring with it additional income, or other advantages, immediately set in motion a process with which we are already familiar, and brought about a change in the social condition of the peasant, with the improvement in his opportunities, small though this might be.[53] The poor began to turn into serednyaks, and the serednyaks rose higher in the social scale, a process which was described in the Party at this time as *obrastanie* ('going to seed'), or, more strongly, as *pererozhdenie* (degeneration).

Surveys carried out by the *TsSU* on behalf of the Central Committee, or undertaken directly by the Central Committee itself, showed that there was a smaller percentage of the economically weak elements in the Party than in the rural population as a whole, and also that the better-off categories were increasingly strongly represented.[54]

Among the peasants who belonged to the Party there were to be found representatives of all the social strata in the villages, but, paradoxically, with this difference, that thanks to the Party, 'economic advancement' took place much more rapidly than it did outside the Party.

The peasant-communists tended to employ more paid help than the other peasants, often because they were busy with their official duties, but many did so simply in order to enrich themselves.[55] Whatever their motives for employing labour, the results were more or less the same. The communist who had become a 'strong' serednyak began to give more and more time to his farm, and either neglected or gave up his Party activities altogether, and from the Party's point of view the net effect was the same as if he had become a kulak.

The result of this process was twofold: on the one hand, it produced *obrastanie*, but on the other hand it also gave rise to *zasorennost*, infiltration by 'alien elements', and to *razlozhenie* (decomposition) and *srashchivanie* (coalescence);[56] this rich variety of terminology was used to designate the various phases of a single process which was the outcome of the 'corrosive and corrupting' influence (yet more terms which were applied to this particular phenomenon) of a petty-bourgeois environment and a market economy upon the Party.

Thus, we have the economic advancement of the peasant who grows more comfortably-off and turns into an entrepreneur, a similar tendency in the case of the official who was still connected with a farm, the influences which each exerted upon the other by reason of the many contacts and interests which they had in common, and the solidarity, both at local and at raion *level, of officials and indeed entire administrations with the upper stratum of the rural population. Such was the process in which the members of the Party in the countryside found themselves involved.*

A resolution adopted by the Party at the end of 1928 was to describe these tendencies in the following terms:

'the proportion of proletarian elements in the composition of the rural organizations (of the Party) is still infinitesimal, and the number of kolkhoz cadres is negligible. Moreover, in certain instances, these organizations contain a considerable number of better-off peasants and near-kulak elements, which are degenerate and totally alien to the working class'.[57]

About the end of 1929, when the Party began a major purge, it was the rural cells, the weakest links in the Party chain, which were the main object of attack: over 15% of the members were purged, a great many of them being classified as 'alien elements'.[58]

However, as we have seen, it was often the very fact of Party membership which helped to create these 'alien elements'. Many poor peasants who had belonged to the Party in the heroic days of the

Civil War, or later, either left it of their own free will, or were purged as 'alien'. This was an effect of the 'spontaneous' element in rural society and the rural economy which the Party had only very partially succeeded in eradicating, both from its own rural organizations and from the co-operative and kolkhoz sectors.

It is hard to say how things might have turned out if the rural Party organs had been set up and administered with greater efficiency. In this, as in many other sectors, it cannot be argued that a more intensive effort would have been impossible. But it would have required, firstly, a policy which was more clearly defined, and better suited to the nature of rural life, and secondly, different methods of leadership. As it was, the Party at this stage had for long been a 'bureaucratic machine',[59] an administrative apparatus which was geared to relaying orders from the summit, while the lower echelons carried them out without necessarily understanding them.

This kind of Party, which was so very different from the idealistic, dedicated 'advance guard' who had wrought the revolution, had no idea of education, in the strict sense of the word. The only thing it understood was propaganda and orders. One delegate to the Sixteenth Party Congress and the only one to voice such sentiments, declared that, in a Party which already had nearly two million members, only 'the minutest fraction' were 'stalwarts' with a proper ideological grounding.[60]

No one denied that this was so. But what proportion of this 'minute fraction' found their way to the villages?

During the periods when attention was suddenly focused in this direction, the only measures taken with regard to the communists were either purges, or large-scale campaigns for the recruitment of new members. Once the members had been recruited, however, nothing was done to provide any basic training for them. Yaroslavsky, who was a member of the 'Collegium' of the Party Control Commission confirms the fact that members, and candidates in particular, were given virtually no political education.[61] Many of the members, he said, had hoped that, once inside the Party, they would receive some attention, but it had turned out that even less interest was taken in them when they were in the Party than before they had joined. Other leaders complained frequently about the 'lack of culture, and the bureaucratic nature of the co-operative and Party organizations' . . . in the villages.[62]

This was a serious handicap, and one which was to some extent a legacy from the past, but nothing worthwhile had been done to raise the level of education among the rural communists; the leaders who complained of this situation were undoubtedly partly to blame for it themselves.

If the local cadres were weak, so also were the upper echelons of the Party structure. As one responsible communist said, 'Fundamentally, the same defects which are apparent in the rural cells are repeated, in many instances, at *raion* level and upwards, by the Party Committees in their administration of economic, co-operative and soviet organizations.'[63] There was a long list of such defects, and many authors called attention to it. Essentially, the trouble was that the small Party cells in the villages were undermined by the social influences which we have been describing, they lacked proper guidance and were ill-prepared for their task, and were therefore incapable of fulfilling the role of leadership which was theirs by definition; hence the frequent criticism that life in the villages 'went on regardless of them', as was also the case with the *selsovety*.

With only a precarious foothold in the countryside, and constantly under pressure of orders from above, the local Party cells were obliged to resort to 'campaign tactics' (*kampaneishchina*) which meant that their operations were characterized by successive bursts of activity directed towards some specific end, alternating with periods of complete calm and inaction.[64]

The strong tendency towards *administrirovanie* which was a feature of the Party was even more marked in its rural organization,[65] which was isolated from the masses and their problems, and had no idea how to fulfil its multifarious functions other than by administrative pressure.

In general, the Party member did not stand out from his fellows either in respect of political training or conduct, and since, by virtue of his position as the representative of the régime, he was more in the public eye than the others, his authority was still further weakened. Naturally, some communists were able to win the respect of their neighbours thanks to their efficiency and conscientiousness, and their high moral qualities. The peasants reacted positively to examples of this kind, and were not slow to show their appreciation of such persons, but these cases were relatively rare. Moreover, any energetic and dedicated Party activist, especially if he was a good administrator, was soon recruited to the upper echelons, which were always short of cadres.

For the rest, the image of the Party official was that of the *nachalnik*, the big or the little 'boss' who had to be obeyed. This was the way the village saw them, and underlying this attitude there was a fundamental indifference which, at times, turned to disrespect or hostility.[66] The reasons for this were not political; more often than not they stemmed from the fact that the officials in question were not only inefficient at their work, but were frequently corrupt and time-serving as well, and given to lying and stealing. Naturally, the Party realized that a situation of this kind in no way served their interests and they incessantly inveighed against the growing number of *gnoiniki*, against degeneration in the Party, and against the various fraudulent and other criminal acts committed by Party members[67] whose official positions afforded them a wider opportunity for abuses of this kind than was otherwise the case.

Of the 15·4% of members of rural cells who were purged during 1929–30 (not counting those who were removed by the processes of the law) 9·2% were expelled for criminal offences, such as bribery and corruption, embezzlement and fraud, 6·4% for refusing to join collective farms, 2·2% for concealment of bread supplies (from the procurement officials), etc., and only a very small percentage—0·8% —for bureaucratic abuses. . . .[68] These all too frequent occurrences were not calculated to enhance the Party image in the eyes of the peasantry. The peasants, moreover, had enough experience to be critical of other shortcomings as well as those of a criminal nature. They reacted against cases of inertia and mismanagement, and all the other weaknesses in the communist organization. They were unequivocal in their criticism of the Party cells, and their disapproval found expression in the many songs known as *chastushki*, a mordant and typically peasant commentary on the problems of the day.[69]

All too often, the Party cells proved to be totally incompetent. There are cases on record where they put up as candidates for the *selsovet*, or for kolkhoz management, 'a former *uryadnik*, a former prostitute or a former bandit'—the latter instance being quoted by Bauman during a Party conference at Moscow, when it caused some amusement; but another writer mentioned similar cases, in which the local Party had nominated some drunkard or liar for office, as being an everyday occurrence.[70]

The foregoing outline of the position with regard to the *selsovety*, the co-operative movement, the kolkhozes and the rural Party cells, serves to give some idea of the extent to which the Soviet régime had been able to establish itself in the countryside.[71] At this period, the rural sector was undoubtedly the weakest and most vulnerable point in the Soviet system.

In this sector the greatest dangers lay in wait for the régime, and it was in this sector that the boldest policies, and the most unremitting efforts, were called for. And yet this was the very sector in which the fewest forces were deployed, and to which the Party gave least attention. The Party was fundamentally an urban one, and it failed to learn, from its experience during the NEP period, how to come to terms with the countryside, how to devise more suitable instruments of administration, and how to formulate an original policy which would combine to serve the aims of socialism and the specific character and needs of the peasantry.

NOTES AND REFERENCES

1. Lyashchenko, *NAF*, 1925, No. 1, pp. 25–6.
2. Carr, *A History of Soviet Russia: The Bolshevik Revolution* (London, 1950), Vol. II, p. 156.
3. Volodkovich and Kulikov, *NAF*, 1927, No. 1, p. 55. For further information on the communes see R. Wresson, *The Soviet Communes* (New Brunswick, 1963), and Yakovtsevsky, *Agrarnye otnosheniya v SSSR v period stroitelstva sotsializma* (Moscow, 1954), pp. 273–93, and particularly pp. 283–9.
4. *ibid.*
5. Grigorev, 'Kollektivizatsiya sovetskoi derevni', *Bolshevik*, 1928, No. 7, p. 38.
6. *ibid.*
7. A decree of *TsIK-Sovnarkom* of March 16, 1927, mentions a 'crisis during the first years of NEP' in the kolkhoz movement. *Istoriya kolkhoznogo prava* (Moscow, 1959), Vol. I, p. 94; Kulikov, *NAF*, 1927, No. 1, p. 79.
8. *NAF*, 1927, No. 5, pp. 111.
9. These figures are taken from the control figures for 1927–8 given by Kulikov in *NAF* 1928, No. 3, p. 81, and from Tsylko, *NAF*, 1928, No. 9, p. 5; Terletsky, 'Kollektivnoe zemledelie na Ukraine', *NAF*, 1928, No. 3; Molotov, *15-ty S'ezd VKP(b)*, stenogramme, p. 1075.
10. For 1929 see *Postroenie fundamenta sotsialisticheskoi ekonomiki v SSSR, 1926–32*, p. 345; *NAF*, 1927, No. 11–12, p. 81.
11. Bumper, 'Dalneishie vekhi kolkhoznogo dvizheniya', *Bolshevik*, 1929, No. 1, pp. 43–4; Terletsky, *Pravda*, June 18, 1929.
12. Yakovlev, *16-ty S'ezd VKP(b)*, stenogramme, pp. 595–6; Wresson, op. cit.
13. The Israeli Kibbutzim, which could be defined as 'communes', were also set up in time of distress, and were forced by hardship to adopt the principle of communal consumption. Many kibbutzim have since become flourishing enterprises—some are even rich—and the communist principle as regards consumption is being less widely applied; in some cases it has been abolished.
14. *Tovarishchestvo po obshchestvennoi obrabotki zemli*. The word kolkhoz refers to one or other of these three forms.
15. Yakovlev states, however, that in the communes 87% of horses were collectively owned. If in 13% of the communes the

horses remained privately owned how could these organizations be called communes?

16. Round figures. Yakovlev, *NAF*, 1927, No. 4; Kulikov, *NAF*, 1927, No. 11–12, p. 88.

17. Kulikov, *ibid*, p. 82. For the Ukraine, Terletsky, *NAF*, 1927, No. 3. Other estimates give even smaller dimensions.

18. Kulikov, *ibid*, p. 81. Kulikov's description is cautiously worded; the middle peasant was better off in this respect than the *kolkhoznik*. See also Yakovlev, *op. cit.*, p. 5.

19. Yakoviev, *ibid*, p. 9. At this time Yakovlev was deputy-Commissar of Inspection; at the end of 1929 he became Commissar of Agriculture.

20. *NAF*, 1927, No. 5, p. 117.

21. Volodkovich and Kulikov, *NAF*, 1927, No. 2, pp. 31–6. The first part of this article is contained in the previous issue.

22. Yakovlev, *op. cit.*

23. In 1927 the Commissariat of Inspection (*RKI* in Russian) adopted a number of principles whereby the 'true' was to be distinguished from the 'false'. The application of these principles, however, demanded a great deal of experience, and a great deal of common sense. Indications of the 'false' were: wages higher than authorized by the law; attempt by a private farm to pass for a kolkhoz; refusal by the kolkhoz to remain 'open'; exploitation within the kolkhoz; diversion of materials belonging to the State in such a manner as to benefit the private peasant. Such practices could be traced in any kolkhoz or commune; this did not necessarily mean, however, that they were mere façades, concealing private agriculture.

24. Lyashchenko, *NAF*, 1925, No. 1, p. 28.

25. AB and Larin, 'Kooperatsiya i kollektivizatsiya', *NAF*, 1925, No. 1, pp. 78–80.

26. *ibid*, p. 78.

27. Terletsky, 'K itogam vsesoyuznogo soveshchaniya kolkhoznikov', *NAF*, 1925, No. 4, pp. 34–40.

28. The Krasivo-Mechenskoe Tovarishchestvo, founded in the spring of 1921. The facts which follow are reported in *NAF*, 1927, No. 1.

29. *ibid*. Molotov, who visited several kolkhozes at this time, visited this one in January 1925.

30. Quoted by Carr, *A History of Soviet Russia: Socialism in One Country*, Vol. 1, p. 21.

31. Bukharin, *op. cit.* (see Ch. 3, Note 32), p. 47.

32. *ibid*.

33. Resolution of the Presidium of the Communist Academy, January 15, 1927, *NAF*, 1927, No. 1, p. 103.

34. *ibid*, pp. 100–3.

35. *Istoriya kolkhoznogo prava*, Vol. 1, pp. 94–8.

36. This figure is given by Yakovlev, *op. cit.* (see Note 16), p. 14, and *Pravda*, May 24, 1928.

37. This was widely reported. See Kulikov, *NAF*, 1927, No. 11–12; Kindeev, *NAF*, 1928, No. 5 (an article based upon *RKI* material); *Pravda*, April 1, 1928.

38. Ignat, *NAF*, 1928, No. 10, p. 72.

39. Yakovlev, *op. cit.* (see Note 16), p. 15.

40. This problem will be discussed later.

41. *Pravda*, April 1, 1928.

42. Yaroslavsky, 'O kommunistakh v derevne', *Pravda*, August 25, 1929.

43. Khataevich, 'Partiya v derevne', *NAF*, 1925, No. 2, p. 107. The *versta* was equal to 1·06 km.

44. *ibid*, p. 110. In 1927 the author became a candidate member of the *TsK*; in 1930 he became a member. As *kraikom* secretary of the Middle Volga he was to be responsible for the collectivization of the region.

45. The figures are from Konyukhov, *op. cit.* (see Ch. 3, Note 41), Kukushkin, *op. cit.* (see Ch. 1, Note 28), gives slightly different figures.

46. Yaroslavsky, *Bolshevik*, 1929, No. 20, p. 15.

47. In the Ukraine, where there were 25 million rural inhabitants, there were only 3,000 party cells, and 25,000 party members employed in agriculture. See *KPSS v Rezolyutsiyakh*, Vol. I, pp. 661–2.

48. For the resolutions of this session see *KPSS v Rezolyutsiyakh*, Vol. II, pp. 546–7. Note that 'agricultural workers', as opposed to 'batraks', refers to wage-earners regularly employed in sovkhozes and other state agencies.

49. Antselovich, *15-ty S'ezd VKP(b)*, stenogramme, p. 1138; *Derevenski Kommunist* 1929, No. 18, p. 3.

50. Yezhov, Mekhlis, Pospelov, *Bolshevik*, 1929, No. 16, p. 56.

51. *ibid*. The total membership, including candidates, on January 1, 1929, was 1,436,160.

52. *Derevenski Kommunist*, 1929, No. 18, p. 3; Gaister and Levin 'O sostave derevenskikh partiinykh yacheek', *Bolshevik*, 1929, No. 9–10.

53. This state of affairs has been widely reported in articles and official documents, e.g. Gaister and Levin, *op. cit.*; Ignat, *NAF*, 1928. No. 10; Paikin, *Bolshevik* 1929, No. 17—on the state of the Party in Belorussia.

54. Gaister and Levin, *op. cit.*, p. 76; Ignat, op. cit. In some *gubernii* this trend was particularly marked; Gaister and Levin give Smolensk as one example.

55. Ignat, *op. cit.*, pp. 81–2; Gaister and Levin, *op. cit.*, p. 80.

56. *Derevenski Kommunist*, 1929, No. 18, pp. 3–4. A translation of these terms is given in the glossary.

57. Resolution of the November 1928 session of the Central Committee, based on a report by Molotov, *KPSS v Rezolyutsiyakh*, Vol. 2, pp. 546–7. See also an identical resolution of the November 1929 session, *ibid*, pp. 661–2. The resolution refers to rural cells in the Ukraine. However, in a document of this kind such a statement would apply to the whole country. Konyukhov, *op. cit.* (see Ch. 3, Note 41), p. 10, reports that in 1929 27% of peasant members of the Party had farms economically on a par with the *zazhitochny*, and 8% owned farms in the kulak category.

58. *Bolshevik*, editorial, 1929, No. 18, p. 6.

59. Noted as early as 1923 by Trotsky, in a letter of October 8, 1923, addressed to the Central Committee. The letter is mentioned in a footnote in *Sotsialisticheski Vestnik*, 1924, No. 2, p. 5. Bukharin, belatedly, made similar bitter comments at the beginning of 1929. *Sotsialisticheski Vestnik*, 1929, No. 9, p. 11.

60. Kubely, the Leningrad delegate to the Sixteenth Party Congress. *16-ty S'ezd VKP(b)*, stenogramme, p. 341.

61. Yaroslavsky, *op. cit.* (see Note 46), p. 15. Konyukhov, *op. cit.*, p. 14, claims that in 1927 the majority of peasant members of the Party had received no political education, but that later many courses providing such education were made available.

62. Molotov, *15-ty S'ezd VKP(b)*, stenogramme, p. 1081.

63. Ignat, *op. cit.*, p. 81.

64. Konyukhov, *op. cit.*, p. 10. The 'campaign' method was a characteristic *modus operandi* of the Soviet State and Party apparatus, at least at this period. The bureaucratic machine, being unsuited to, or ill-prepared for its task, can only be galvanized into action by a directive from above whenever action, and in particular urgent action, is required; however it is incapable of functioning in a systematic fashion. The root cause of this lies not at the lower levels of the administrative apparatus, but in the pyramidal structure of the administration and in the methods it employs.

65. Angarov, *op. cit.* (see Ch. 2, Note 39), pp. 81–8.

66. Bolshakov, *op. cit.* (see Ch. 1, Note 5), pp. 325–9.

67. e.g. the decision of the Sixteenth Party Conference, 1929, relating to the purge. *16-taya Konferentsiya VKP(b)*, stenogramme, pp. 605–8.

68. *Bolshevik*, 1929, No. 18, editorial; Konyukhov, *op. cit.*, p. 11,

arguing on the basis of incomplete data for 1929, claims that 65·8% of those purged in the villages were elements whose degeneration was due to *obrastanie* or speculation.

69. Bolshakov, *op. cit.*, has a chapter on the *chastushki*, which often reflect political attitudes.

70. Bauman, *Pravda*, March 7, 1929; Vareikis, *NAF*, 1929, No. 8, pp. 70–1. Bauman was the Moscow Party secretary and head of the department for rural affairs of the Central Committee. Vareikis, a member of the Central Committee, was also Party Secretary of the Central Black Earth Region.

71. We have not discussed the *Komsomol*, but to a great extent the same tendencies and problems would have emerged in this context as well.

Chapter 6

THE PARTY AND THE
'ACCURSED' PROBLEM

The Russian Revolution had broken out in a backward, and basically peasant country, in which the term 'peasant' was synonymous with misery and ignorance. Intellectuals, Russian and foreign alike, thought of the *muzhiki* as the cornerstone of the most reactionary régime in Europe. In their minds, the *muzhiki* were associated with servitude of the most abject kind, and symbolized the misfortunes of the Russian people. But history, once again, had proved the theoreticians wrong. A socialist, proletarian revolution had succeeded in Russia, the country which was least prepared for it, and its success was in part due to these very *muzhiki*.

In Marxist terminology, the particular combination of circumstances which had proved so propitious for the outcome of the October epic was described as 'a proletarian revolution flanked by a peasant war'. Now this was the crux of future problems which were to beset those whom the revolution had brought to power. Was the October Revolution so unique, the Bolsheviks would frequently ask, that it could be regarded, without reservation, as a single social revolution which was socialist in character?

In the sense that any historical event is unrepeatable, the revolution was certainly unique. But implicit in the Marxist formula, which described the simultaneous occurrence of a proletarian and a peasant revolution, there already lay the suggestion of another possible approach to the question, and another possible answer. Did the two great currents, whose convergence had enabled the Bolsheviks to seize power, really form part of a single stream? Or was it merely that two streams, temporarily following the same course, had happened to converge but were destined to diverge again, once their common primary objectives had been attained? This was the heart of the problem.

The 'bloc', or 'alliance of the proletariat and the peasantry', held firm, despite some rather troubled interludes, as long as the common enemies, the Tsar and the *pomeshchiki*, continued to threaten. But now that these had been defeated, and relegated to the past, had not the two allies, or one of them at least, achieved all that they desired?

The proletariat had reached out for control of government, for control of the factories, and the towns in general. All this they had won, and for this reason the seizure of power was described by the theoreticians as a 'proletarian revolution'. The peasants acquiesced, for they too had attained their ends. The old order of the landed proprietors and the Tsarist political system had been swept away, and the peasants had been given the land they coveted, or rather they had simply and unceremoniously taken it.

However, a revolution may be defined as socialist only if it brings forth a socialist régime. No doubt the proletarian partner in the alliance was, by its very nature, disposed to pursue a socialist objective, but what prospect lay before the peasants, now that they had obtained the land they required? The next stage of development dictated by their social condition and their interests had nothing in common with socialist ideals.

This self-evident truth had already given Lenin himself some cause to hesitate over the timeliness of calling his achievement a 'socialist' revolution, but he had perforce overcome his scruples when the village poor, the famous *kombedy*, backed up by detachments of the proletariat who had come from the towns to requisition grain, took the offensive against the kulaks, and deprived them of surplus land, agricultural equipment, and part of their livestock. This was the famous 'first dekulakization', which according to Lenin signified that the socialist revolution was being carried into the countryside, since the *kombedy* were striking this time not against feudal landowners, but against 'rural capitalists'.[1]

However, certain Bolshevik theoreticians questioned the validity of this interpretation. Kritsman, a leading agrarian expert who was in charge of the agricultural section of the Communist Academy, held the view that the second series of events which had taken place in the countryside, although undoubtedly anti-capitalist, was in no way socialist. The village poor had not seized the kulaks' land in order to place it under common ownership and organize farms on socialist lines. They had done so in order to achieve their ambition of becoming serednyaks like the rest. Therefore their revolution was not socialist at all, merely petty bourgeois.[2]

Thus, Kritsman had clearly perceived the dual nature of the October Revolution. In itself, this was fairly self-evident, and although his interpretation was not in agreement with Lenin's, no one was shocked by it, and for years no one dreamt of looking upon it as heresey. It must have been widely held, at the time, that Lenin himself would not have persisted in his view, for his decision to introduce NEP had in fact been a result of his frank appraisal of the situation, and his parting, however reluctantly, with the illusions of 'war communism'. NEP was certainly the first consequence of the incompatibility which existed between the aims of the former allies, and during the years of NEP the divergence was to become increasingly marked.

The state sector, which was steadily developing in the direction of centralization and planning, and emerging as a more or less coherent whole, was coming into conflict with other sectors of the economy, and in particular with the peasantry. At the same time these other sectors, within the framework of NEP, were following just as normal a course of development. Bukharin was to quote a widely-held view of the stages through which Soviet policy had passed. Essentially, this was to the effect that 'we began by collaborating in the villages with the batraks and the poor against the nobility and the kulaks. Then we switched to alliance with the middle peasant by granting him NEP. Now (in the summer of 1925), we are about to give the strong peasants and the kulaks the green light.'[3]

Bukharin realized that his listeners were perturbed by this development, and he did his utmost to reassure them, but the view he had quoted, and indeed criticized, was in fact a correct reflection of the general trend of events. There was nothing surprising in this to anyone who had realized that NEP was, by its very nature, destined to be a battle-ground between two opposing forces, and that this was a direct result of the special nature of the Russian Revolution.

There was general agreement that NEP had been a necessary development. But how long should it last, and where would it lead? Everything depended on the relationship between the régime and the peasants, or rather on the peasants themselves. The peasant problem was a major source of anxiety, a riddle on whose solution the entire fate of the régime depended. It lay at the heart of the dilemma which now confronted the very men who had made the October Revolution, and it was round this problem that the discussions and the heartbreaks, the personal conflicts, and the whole drama and tragedy of the Soviet régime, ultimately revolved.

As we have seen, the essence of the problem was as follows: Were the post-revolutionary tendencies of the proletariat and the peasantry compatible? Could they be reconciled and directed towards a common socialist goal? If so, how could this be brought about in the context of Soviet society?

The solutions to this problem varied according to individual appraisals of the likely course of future developments, and of the political line which should be followed. Naturally, no one dared to assert openly that there was a basic incompatibility between the two elements, but the more sceptical were convinced that without a worldwide revolution the Russian Revolution would always be in danger, and that in any case, without help from outside, it would be impossible to build a socialist society.

Others believed that, sooner or later, there was bound to be a critical confrontation between the two main classes, but that even in the absence of a European revolution it might still be possible to survive such a crisis. At all events, the situation was a dangerous one, for if the country were to advance towards socialism, the natural tendencies of the peasantry would somehow have to be checked and redirected towards the desired goal. This would be a complex and painful process, mainly because the peasants themselves would have to bear the cost. Would they be willing to do so?

The Left had vague hopes of being able to find a way out, but never stated explicitly how this was to be done. While they knew what they wanted, they never had the opportunity of proving whether they were capable of avoiding disaster, or recourse to disastrous methods, which in a sense amounted to the same thing. At all events, by the end of 1925, the Left were convinced that the crisis implicit in a 'NEP-type' régime had finally overtaken Russia. The problem could only be solved by increasing the pace of socialist change and thereby, paradoxically, aggravating the original crisis. Trotsky and Preobrazhensky were persuaded that only in this way could disaster be averted. The danger would have to be met head on, and the sooner the better.

Such ideas horrified a man like Bukharin, who was one of the principal architects of the 'neo-NEP' policy, and the leading theoretician in this context. At this time, Bukharin held quite different views on the nature of the situation and the policy which should be adapted.

The Views of Bukharin 1925–6

Although Bukharin frequently followed the then current fashion, and referred to the relationship between town and country as the 'accursed' problem, the term was, for him, no more than a figure of speech. In his opinion, there was nothing 'accursed' about this relationship, and accordingly the theory and the political programme which he advanced, as well as his view of future developments, followed logically from his own premises. His entire theoretical model was based on the following two hypotheses:

(a) Power is in the hands of the proletariat, by virtue of its role as a guiding and creative force in the shaping of policy;
(b) An alliance between the proletariat and the peasantry is the foremost aim of government policy, and the fundamental principle of socialist strategy.

The first of these constituted a safeguard against those ever-present tendencies which were a potential danger to the régime. The second indicated the path which would lead Russia slowly but surely out of her backward state and on to socialism.[4]

Bukharin's main requirement, therefore, was that the alliance with the peasantry should be safeguarded, thereby ensuring the survival and success of the régime. In this context, it would seem that the principle of the alliance was for him sacrosanct.

'Provided the alliance is safeguarded . . .'; the phrase was constantly cropping up, with fresh arguments to support it. It was clear that protecting the alliance was no simple task. The peasant, as a small property owner, was ever open to bourgeois influences. He lacked political experience, and the proletarian sense of solidarity. Consequently, the peasant was divided in his loyalties between the proletarian and the bourgeois; in the latter, he saw his own natural ideal, a figure whom he could therefore respect.[5]

The second difficulty with the alliance was a consequence of the first. The peasantry was as much in need of socialism as the other strata, but lacked comprehension of this objective fact. The proletariat, on the other hand, being anxious to ensure progress towards socialism, found it necessary to arrogate to itself one of the fundamental privileges of the alliance, namely, exclusive political power. However, when one party to an alliance treats with the other on terms which from the outset are so markedly unequal, a conflict is bound to arise. At the same time, discrimination in this way was unavoidable, and the difficulty simply had to be overcome. Bukharin had not overlooked the drawbacks and the contradictions inherent in this situation, and he had certain solutions to put forward.

In his opinion, the importance and the usefulness of NEP lay in the fact that it provided an essential meeting-point for the interests of both state-controlled industry and the private peasant landowners. In this context, the *smychka* was effected through the operation of the market. It had been a mistake during the period of war communism, Bukharin explained, to think that a direct transition to socialism could be achieved while by-passing the market economy phase. Socialism could in fact be attained by exploiting the laws of the market economy, since it was possible to ensure that, in the normal course of development, the market economy would destroy itself.[6]

This concept of development, and of the way in which an agricultural country might be guided towards socialism, is very characteristic of Bukharin. Essentially, his views may be summarized as follows: the peasant, reacting under NEP conditions to the constant pressure of self-interest and benevolent state guidance, would increase the size of his tiny and unprofitable farm, and extend the range of his economic activities. For the peasant masses, there was only one path towards expansion on this scale, and that lay through co-operation. By means of collective purchasing, and the organization of sales and credit, the peasant would consolidate his holding, learn new methods of cultivation, and practice co-operation in an increasing number of sectors of economic activity (for example, in cheese and butter-making establishments, and other such food processing industries). In all this, Bukharin stressed the role of the State, whose policy would be based on the granting of aid.

As the peasant's standard of living improved, an important dual process would begin to operate. The peasant economy would gradually become collectivized, and at the same time it would move closer to the State sector, join with industry, and finally become integrated with the economy of the towns to form a single, planned, industrio-co-operative economy.[7] This was Bukharin's concept of socialism. By the time it came about, the peasantry, initially more backward, would have changed in character, and become an integral part of the proletariat. The privileges of the proletariat would cease to be exclusive, and the dictatorship of the proletariat would come to an end.[8]

If this goal were to be attained, steps must be taken to ensure that socialist industry functioned efficiently, and in such a way as to satisfy as effectively as possible the needs of its most important customer, which was the village.[9] (In Bukharin's view, it was axiomatic that socialist industry, by virtue of its inherent superiority, would develop more rapidly than the other sectors of the economy.) In addition, there should be no element of coercion in the administrative methods employed by the government. Since co-operation was to be the medium of socialist education for the peasantry, it must become an institution which they would accept, and cherish. It was imperative that two principles be observed: all peasants should be eligible for membership, but membership should be voluntary. The Party would secure the influence it required over the membership uniquely by means of persuasion, and by seeking the support of the bednyaks.

Class problems, and the class struggle, did not, apparently, loom very large on these untroubled horizons. Certainly Bukharin expected the class struggle to continue, but he believed that it would change its character in response to the political, and particularly the economic, pressures exerted by the government. The proletarian régime hoped for peace between the classes, and worked for this end.[10] It would permit certain bourgeois strata to take part in the economic life of the country, and this would be of use to the State, since funds could be raised for the state sector as a result of the stimulatory effect of such participation on market exchanges. This activity would, however, be strictly controlled, and any attempt to break the truce would be ruthlessly suppressed.

Basically, therefore, the form which the State's offensive would take would be that of exploiting, restricting, and ultimately eliminating the bourgeoisie through the medium of economic competition in the market. By competing in this way, the State would demonstrate its superiority, and convince the peasants of its ability to function more efficiently, and to produce better goods at lower cost, etc.

The idea that socialism should prove itself by first of all demonstrating its potentialities, if not its overwhelming superiority, in the economic sphere, was one which greatly appealed to Bukharin. Later on, he was to state specifically that the socialism in which he believed would inevitably prevail by virtue of its economic superiority, but that the victory would owe nothing to those zealous 'administrators' who were bent on imposing on the peasants socialist forms whose 'superiority' had not yet been demonstrated in practice. Such an approach, in his view, could only lead to disaster.

The régime should, therefore, strive to demonstrate the superiority of socialism in the economic sphere, and victory achieved in this sphere (i.e. in the market) would be striking proof of the socialist character of the new structures. . . . That socialist forms are not superior *a priori*, but must first be shown to be so, is a sound precept, as certain socialist countries, Yugoslavia in particular, have come to understand.

According to Bukharin, the social development of the villages would follow a different course from that of the towns. Only for a minority of bednyaks would the kolkhoz be the best means of improving conditions. Deeply ingrained traditions and the habits of centuries would prevent the majority from accepting the kolkhoz in this light.[11] With the help of State aid, however, they would gradually be able to develop their own farms, until it became possible for them to join the co-operative movement as a whole.

Moreover, they would have their own co-operative organizations, whereas the majority of such organizations would be in the hands of the serednyaks, who constituted the 'central figures in village life'. These two adjacent, or intermingling currents would reach their socialist destination via co-operation whenever industry was in a position to provide sufficient electricity to enable them to collectivize their agricultural activities by themselves.

Bukharin said nothing of the form, kolkhoz or otherwise, which this collectivization was to take, but in any case it represented the most distant prospect in his scheme of things.

As to the kulaks, they too would be entitled to separate co-operative organizations. It was unlikely, in Bukharin's opinion, that the

138

kulaks would progress more rapidly than the industrial sector or the other strata, and their future would therefore be determined more by the general movement of the economy. In his view, the social and economic structure of society during the dictatorship of the proletariat was such that the kulaks' co-operative organizations would, from the outset, be contained within a framework determined by the government. Thus, they would be encircled by State banks and a state industrial sector. The great co-operative enterprises managed by the other rural strata would compete against them with increasing effectiveness. The kulak organizations would therefore have no choice but to serve the State, and to become, like the other strata, an integral part of the whole economy,[12] although they would always remain, like the capitalist concessions, an 'alien element'.

At this juncture, Bukharin plainly contradicts himself, for he also explains that in the villages, as in the towns, the co-operative enterprises of the 'non-exploiting' peasantry would defeat the rural capitalist enterprises, and eliminate them from the market.[13] '*Elimination*' and '*integration*' are not quite the same thing. However, this inconsistency does not greatly alter the general pattern of the policy advocated by Bukharin.

A policy based on Bukharin's strategic approach would ensure steady though naturally very slow progress towards socialism. Progress 'at a snail's pace' was the expression used by Bukharin, and it was to earn him a great deal of obloquy at a later stage. He does not seem to have been unduly worried by the prospect of possible international complications. He considered that as long as the revolution had not triumphed in Europe, a socialist country had no definite guarantee that the old order would not be restored at bayonet point by a foreign power. But he believed in preparing for any such contingency by ensuring the internal stability of the régime, and winning the support of the peasantry, rather than by seeking salvation in a spectacular build-up of the industrial base, and in an arms race.

His attitude might well be summed up in the statement that the country would be no better defended by a well-armed, but hostile, peasantry, than it would be by a peasantry which was less well-armed, but willing to defend the régime. In the light of subsequent developments, it will be seen that at this stage Bukharin was guilty of over-optimism. This particular flaw in his reasoning was to lead to others. Constantly preoccupied as he was with the interests of the peasantry, Bukharin could conceive of only one possible chain of events. As a result, his outlook became dangerously one-sided. In his anxiety to preserve the alliance at all costs, and to avoid harming the peasantry in any way, he made it a *sine qua non* of the success of the socialist experiment that nothing should ever be undertaken which the majority of the peasants had not first understood and accepted. Thus, he made everything depend upon one single factor, and this was the strategic weakness of his theory. Moreover, while such an attitude only too easily found acceptance amongst the bourgeois strata in the country, it was unpalatable to the membership of a revolutionary Party. This was, in addition, a tactical weakness.

In his pamphlet, Bukharin states: '. . . the task of the working class, and the task of urban industry, is to develop production in such a way as to satisfy the needs of the rural population fully and cheaply.'[14] Thus, in this context, industry was viewed exclusively in its relation to the peasantry, who were regarded as its most important customer, and indeed its sole *raison d'être*. According to Bukharin, industry would draw its resources from straightforward commercial exchanges with the peasants. In view of the stress which he laid on securing the agreement and the understanding of the peasantry for all measures undertaken by the régime, he would clearly have rejected any suggestion that, in order to speed up industrial accumulation, these exchanges might possibly, or even necessarily, be effected on terms detrimental to the interests of the peasants. He described any approach of this kind as 'foolish'.[15] However, he was later obliged to accept, albeit reluctantly, the need for such a policy, and this in itself is evidence of the weakness of his arguments during the period from 1925 to 1926.

Bukharin must be given credit for having clearly emphasized the need for the State sector to develop more rapidly than the others. Indeed, he went so far as to make this a precondition for the success of his policy as a whole. But his writings give little indication of the way in which an adequate rate of industrial development was to be achieved. He is clearly relying upon the capacity for spontaneous growth inherent in a socialist industry which is, by definition, superior to all the other sectors of the economy, but this in turn contradicts his own theory that such superiority must first of all be established and demonstrated in practice.

Bukharin believed in slow progress, and continuous development. He foresaw a great many upheavals, and a sudden resurgence of the class struggle in its old forms, that is to say, violent conflict, and bitter resistance. But these outbreaks would be a purely transitory phenomenon, resulting mainly from the poor quality of Soviet administrations in the localities concerned.[16] Bukharin was aware of the problem created by the relationship between industrial and agricultural prices, and admitted that in this sector, 'there exists a direct contradiction between the interests of the working class and and those of the peasants.' [17]

His solution, however, is surprisingly vague and ineffectual: the two sectors of industry and agriculture, he argues, are interdependent. Moreover, if the growth of the national income were assured, both sectors would see their share in it increase. . . .[18] He was unaware of any fundamental factors which might give rise to crises. At this point, his theory fails completely to measure up to the more ominous developments which others saw as inevitable, and which called for advance preparation if they were to be dealt with adequately. What was required in this context was a more realistic view of industrialization, which in turn would have led the theoretician to adjust his outlook, and would have forced him to accept the fact that, in Soviet conditions, industry, especially in the initial stages, would have to make a considerable leap forward.

Given the backwardness of the agricultural sector and the fact that it occupied so large a place in the national economy as a whole, Russian industry was too weak to be able to assert its influence and its economic supremacy from the outset, and thus to provide the necessary safeguard for the survival of the régime.

Slow development would not of itself have led to disaster, but even leaving aside the external threats to the régime, and the frequently exaggerated fears which they aroused within the Party, there was a danger that the régime might collapse, if the process of development were excessively prolonged. Without a sufficiently broad base, industry would have been incapable of providing the impetus required even for the slow development of co-operation, or the gradual socialization of the peasantry. It would have been unable to ensure a rise in the living standards of the towns sufficient to maintain the faith of the masses in the socialist character of the régime. Nor could it have contributed to an increase in agricultural output, which was no less essential to the proper functioning of the system.

A more penetrating analysis along these lines would reveal the existence of two problems related, firstly, to the rate of industrial development, and, secondly, to the indispensable core of heavy industry. These two problems were, in fact, tackled lucidly, and with irrefutable logic, by Preobrazhensky. Bukharin fiercely opposed Preobrazhensky's aguments, but during 1926 there were signs of his having realized that the rate of industrial growth would have to be accelerated, and that the peasants would inevitably have to bear a large part of the cost; this he was forced to admit explicitly in 1927. In 1926, therefore, the most far-sighted could see that what lay ahead was a vigorous pursuit of industrialization, and with it a complicated political situation involving a more or less long-term period of strained relations with the peasants. Programmes and solutions would have to be prepared in order to meet such a situation. Although Bukharin set his mind to this problem later than the Left, his theoretical contribution was to prove a remarkable one. From the political point of view, however, it came too late.

2. The Left

The ideas of the Left at this time differed fundamentally from those of Bukharin. There was greater realism in the Left's approach, and a greater understanding of the 'explosive' elements latent in the Russian situation. By contrast with Bukharin's 'faith in co-operation',[19] the principal spokesmen of the Left, whether from the oppositions of 1923 or 1926, accepted the conclusions forced upon them by the backwardness of the Russian economy, and declared that the key to the essential problems lay in rapid industrialization.

In the spring of 1923, Trotsky had advanced this theory at the Twelfth Party Congress, though it was little understood by his audience at the time. He had suggested that the economic difficulties and the threat to the alliance with the peasantry were the result of the 'scissors' represented by the high prices of industrial goods, and the excessively low prices of agricultural products (these being lower than pre-war). The fact that conditions of exchange between the peasantry and the towns operated to the disadvantage of the former could not but create a source of constant difficulty.[20] The root cause of this disastrous imbalance was the weakness and backwardness of industry. Trotsky considered it imperative that the basis of any action should be the slow but unremitting encouragement of the forces of socialism. At the same time, the methods employed should remain within the framework of NEP and should, so far as the peasants were concerned, be those of a market economy. This should nevertheless go hand in hand with a speed-up in the rate of industrialization, and within the state sector there should be increasing emphasis on central planning. It is interesting to follow Trotsky's efforts, from 1920 onwards, on behalf of industry and planning, and particularly his advocacy of priority for heavy industry. It is also interesting to follow the course of his discussions on these subjects with Lenin, who at that time found his ideas, and especially the prospect of full-scale planning, premature, not to say ill-advised.[21]

Trotsky nevertheless succeeded in persuading his ailing leader to agree in principle to his 'pro-planning' line,[22] and also to accept his diagnosis of the real source of the plague of bureaucracy which was infecting the State. According to Trotsky, this was the Party Secretariat, directed by Stalin.[23] In the belief that he would, before long, be able to enlist Lenin's support for his ideas (which support never materialized, since Lenin's death intervened), Trotsky therefore avoided all tactical skirmishing during the Twelfth Party Congress, the first to be held without Lenin. Instead, he confined himself to setting forth his theories and envisaging the pattern of future developments as he saw them.

In particular, he stated:

'Our new economic policy was introduced with serious intent, and for an extended period, but it was not intended to last for ever. We have introduced the "new" policy in order to transcend it, according to its own rules and methods. Ultimately, we shall extend the planning principle to the entire market, and by so doing we shall absorb and eliminate it. In other words, our successes based on the new economic policy automatically bring us nearer to the point where it will be liquidated, and replaced by a "newer" economic policy, which will in effect be a socialist policy. [24]

Trotsky's speech to the Twelfth Party Congress is remarkable for the way in which it anticipated future developments, and it was the source from which the Left opposition were later to draw the arguments and hypotheses which they advanced in support of the economic policy which they advocated. Trotsky was soon to develop his arguments in a series of articles, the publication of which, in a collection entitled 'The New Course', triggered off a concerted attack by the Triumvirate in power.* For a long time, he had been the target of a skilful campaign of criticism and calumny, aimed at proving that he was anti-*muzhik*, and therefore hostile to the alliance with the peasantry. In an article published in *Pravda* of December 6, 1923,[25] Trotsky defended himself against rumours 'spread by the great landowners, the capitalists and their minions.' . . . Quoting Lenin in his defence, he outlined his own concept of the *smychka*. This was no matter for 'idle talk' over a so-called principle with which his enemies were obsessed, and which they were now treating as an article of faith. The problem was a practical one, and any solution would require to be based on a practical appraisal of the circumstances.

Some means would have to be found of 'adapting industry to the peasant market', or even, on a broader basis, of 'adapting the Soviet State to the needs and potentialities of the peasantry'.[26] If the peasant needed matches, soap and paraffin, then a cheap supply of these must be provided. But the *smychka* would remain viable and meaningful only in so far as the proletarian character of the State,

* i.e. Stalin, Zinovev, Kamenev.

and the socialist character of industry, were preserved. In Trotsky's view, this was, of course, still the fundamental principle, and good relations with the peasantry were merely a means to this end. Moreover, Trotsky was convinced that it was through industry that an influence could be exerted, either directly or indirectly, on agriculture. For this reason, it followed that if industry were to adapt itself to the needs of the peasantry, the peasantry must reciprocate, by adapting itself to the needs of industry. In subordinating the interests of the peasantry to those of the State, there would however be no question of overstraining the potentialities of the peasants, but rather of extending them.

Industry was still the key to the problem. Without industry, there would be nothing for the peasants, no fertilizers, no implements. A good newspaper should be published for the peasants, but even this would be impossible without industry. The needs of the *smychka* made it imperative that the 'scissors' be reduced, but this too could only be achieved by reducing production costs and increasing labour productivity, and in accordance with Trotsky's second assumption, nothing would be accomplished in this sphere without proper planning. 'We can, and we must continue to improve our understanding of the fundamental elements in the economy, and try to anticipate the future interrelationships of these elements in production and in the market. There must be proper co-ordination, both in qualitative and in quantitative terms, of all these elements among the various sectors of the economy, and industry as a whole must be adapted to the needs of the rural economy. This is the real way to go about consolidating the *smychka*.' [27] The only way to the desired objective, therefore, lay through a 'rationally organized industrial sector, which would be administered according to a pre-determined plan' and which would be 'profitable'.

The foregoing arguments bear some superficial resemblance to those of Bukharin, but Trotsky places quite a different emphasis on the needs of industry, and consequently makes greater demands on the peasantry. His attitude differs fundamentally from that of Bukharin, who at this time seemed to consider it of overriding importance that the State should unilaterally adapt itself to the needs of the peasants. From these initial differences in viewpoint, it followed that the attitudes of the two men diverged in other important respects.

Far from relaxing in their efforts to speed up industrialization, the Left pursued their campaign with increasing vigour after 1925, and particularly in 1926,[28] the year in which Trotsky returned, after a brief respite, to the political struggle, and in which the 'united opposition' with Zinovev and Kamenev was born. The basic stand of the new opposition remained unchanged, since in its eyes the conditions already existed (for Trotsky they had even existed as early as 1922) for 'the launching of a socialist offensive, slowly, but without any further retreats'.[29]

At this time, the Left gave repeated warnings of the crises which were liable to overtake the economy, and the régime in general, as a result of the backwardness of industry. As we have already seen, they had been emphasizing the danger of the 'scissors' as far back as 1923. In a pamphlet which was circulated secretly in 1926, Trotsky expressly stated 'the *smychka* is at present jeopardized by the backwardness of industry on the one hand, and by the growth of the kulak stratum on the other'.[30] In another text, dating from the same period,[31] he pointed out that the problem of class stratification 'then only in its initial stages' was also becoming more acute, and for the same reason. However, 'provided it was properly managed, the growth of industry would forestall the process of class differentiation within the peasantry, and nullify its effects'. In even more urgent and more specific terms, Preobrazhensky had predicted that, without a minimum of investment in industry, 'under-production, which has been serious enough in 1925 and 1926, will become critical', and that the régime would be bedevilled by 'certain inescapable facts, such as an increasing shortage of industrial goods (*tovarny golod*), and increasing accumulation by private individuals. These would constitute a threat to the existence of the entire system. . . .'[32]

Trotsky was by no means unaware of the risks of rapid industrialization, but he foresaw that other, and even graver, dangers might arise if this were not done and for this reason he recommended that the appropriate action be taken as soon as possible.

How, then, were these increased investments to be financed? He fully realized the complex nature of the problem, since he had frankly described the difficult stage through which the Soviet régime would have to pass as 'the stage of primitive socialist accumulation'. This was a term he had used towards the end of 1922, and also in his speech to the Twelfth Party Congress. He knew that industry would have to derive profits from exchanges with the peasantry, and that the peasantry would therefore have to be taxed. He seems to have believed, however, that the greater part of the effort would come not from the peasants but from the proletariat.

Trotsky was a romantic, steadfast in the heroic traditions of the Civil War; he had faith in the proletariat, and its willingness to make sacrifices if called upon by the Party to do so. By this time, however, such faith was already a little outdated.

'There may be times,' he told the Twelfth Congress,' when the

State fails to pay you a full wage, or only pays half, and you, the workers, will give your State credit, out of your own pocket.' [33]

He did not count on this kind of support from the peasants, but hoped that the workers would willingly act in this way 'for their State'. This was the democratic, or rather the 'proletarian democratic' aspect of Trotsky's political personality, which was common to the entire Left. The proletariat would respond as long as they felt themselves to be in control both in the State and in the Party. But the State at this time was falling victim to the growth of bureaucracy, with its ever-increasing ramifications, and the Party too was losing the solidarity it had known in the days when it had consisted of men who were free to express and to fight for their opinions within its ranks. Now it was turning into a 'fossilized' body in the control of a 'secretarial machine'.

The Left's presentation of industrialization policy was indissolubly linked with its concept of proletarian democracy, which should first and foremost exist within the Party itself: and yet, precisely within the Party, democracy was on the point of being stamped out for good. It is as well to emphasize the views of these men who had helped to bring the Soviet State into being, since events were in fact moving in a diametrically opposite direction. Certainly their democratic aspirations must be viewed with some scepticism, in that they were constantly being voiced too late, when the leaders in question had already lost power, and had themselves participated in anti-democratic and even totalitarian practices.

While the criticism is surely a valid one, it can however be said, in this context, that there was never any question of the sincerity of a man like Lenin, or of his anxiety to combat bureaucratic tendencies. The same may be said of Trotsky, Zinovev, Kamenev and Bukharin, despite the lack of foresight which led them to wage an unbelievably bitter struggle against their future allies, and to ally themselves with their future executioners.

The determination of men like Trotsky, Rakovsky and others to revive proletarian and democratic traditions within the Party of Lenin was firmly rooted in their socialist background, and in their very European view of socialism. Would it have been possible to carry out the industrialization of Russia without recourse to totalitarian methods? Once in power, and rid of Stalin, could these men have managed Russian affairs differently, or would the inexorable realities of life in a backward country have driven them to act as their rival did? This is a far-reaching question, whose implications do not lie wholly within the province of historical research. It can however be said that where leaders are concerned, qualities such as breadth of vision, moral integrity, intelligence and level of culture are just as important as other historical factors, and may, in certain circumstances, play an even more decisive role. Time and again, as history has shown, there have been statesmen who have weakly yielded to external pressures, who have been guilty of opportunism, who have betrayed their principles. But this is not always necessarily so. Fortunately, there have been, and there will continue to be, other cases, which are such as to restore one's faith in the possibility that politics can be honest, bold and incorruptible.

Except at a later date, when he was in exile outside of Russia, Trotsky probably never conceived of Soviet democracy as being anything other than a single party democracy, supported by a united proletariat. Although they rarely admitted it, other members of the Left had, however, examined the possibility of some more broadly-based political framework, which would permit the existence of other parties. For example, Zinovev, when he went into opposition about 1925, though still firmly convinced that his return to power was imminent, is said to have reflected frequently upon the problem of democracy, and to have been 'in the process of reconsidering his support for iron-hard Bolshevik discipline as the guiding principle of a State Party'.[34]

Ruth Fischer, who claims to have had lengthy discussions with Zinovev at this period, reports that he was convinced that 'unless communist thought and action can become fully diversified, we are lost'. He was therefore thinking in terms of the admission of the Mensheviks, and of a peasant party, to the soviets. There would seem little reason to discount these statements, particularly in view of the campaign which Zinovev and Kamenev waged against Lenin in 1917 for the admission of other parties to the soviets and to the government.

The repeated demands of the Left that the poor peasants be organized (some even called for the setting-up of an autonomous organization at national level) also offered some hope of political self-expression for that sector of the peasantry.

Above all, it is clear that despite the charge of being anti-*muzhik* which was levelled at them by their enemies, and by Bukharin in particular, over a considerable period, the Left had as little thought as Bukharin himself of using force to change the way of life and socio-economic structure of the peasantry. This emerges clearly from an analysis of the Left's ideas on collectivization.

The Left believed that the peasant and his private plot, and even the kulak, would continue to exist for a very long time to come.[35] According to Trotsky, the use of force as a means of changing peasant structures was unthinkable, but he was undoubtedly sceptical about the extent to which other methods could be relied upon to bring about any radical change in the character of the peasantry in the short term. This being so, he ruled out any possibility of constructing a socialist society without the aid of a successful revolution in at least one other industrial country in Europe. He was, of course, prepared to limit the growth of the kulaks by means of State intervention, but what he had in mind was primarily the use of economic and fiscal measures.[36] A forced loan of 150 million poods of grain from 10% of the richest peasants was the most sweeping administrative measure that the Left ever called for.[37]

On the problem of social structures in the countryside, the attitudes of the two principal rivals, Bukharin on the Right and Trotsky on the Left, were not fundamentally very different, despite the initial divergence of viewpoints, and the mutual suspicion and recriminations which accompanied it. Bukharin, believing as he did that it was possible to construct socialism in one country, also believed that the peasants could be persuaded to follow the path of socialism. He neither saw nor accepted the need for imposing anything upon the peasantry, beyond the principle of the pre-eminence of the proletariat in the Soviet State. Trotsky, on the other hand, rejected the possibility of 'socialism in one country', and therefore he too declared himself anxious to remain on the best possible terms with the peasants. No structural changes should be forced upon them, nor should they be subjected to pressure. (There was, particularly towards 1928, a difference of emphasis, but it was purely a matter of emphasis, and it applied only to the kulak problem. ....)[38]

At this point, we come to Bukharin's main argument, and the basic point at issue between him and Trotsky, namely the question of *primitive socialist accumulation*. The term, as we have seen, had been used by Trotsky[39] and round it Preobrazhensky had built an entire doctrine; it seems to have created an unbridgeable gulf between the two rivals. Because of its historical associations, and its potentially disastrous implications, a man like Bukharin was horrified by its use, especially as Preobrazhensky interpreted it much more rigidly and narrowly than Trotsky. Preobrazhensky in fact considered the term 'NEP', which was widely employed to describe the then current period of Soviet history, as being inappropriate, in that it failed to express a fundamental aspect of the Soviet economy. The essential feature of this economy was that it comprised two different sectors, state and private, which were governed by different internal laws, and were in a state of conflict, each being bent on the total destruction of the other.[40]

In this struggle, the socialist sector enjoyed two important advantages. The first was the identification of the nationalized sector with State power. The second was that the socialist sector could present a united front in the face of an opponent whose forces were scattered, each enterprise having to wage its own individual struggle.[41] Any socialist enterprise, considered in isolation, is weaker than almost any capitalist enterprise. This may be explained by the more general rule that in the initial period of development in a backward country, or even in a country at a more advanced stage of its development, socialism is not immediately able to demonstrate its superiority over the private or capitalist sector, even when the State intervenes to maintain the latter in a position of inferiority by discriminating against it. Preobrazhensky several times emphasized this weakness of the socialist sector,[42] pointing out that initially the worker must of necessity be worse off, and that the requirements of the accumulation process would lead to a delay in the introduction of true socialist relationships. The concept of 'socialist accumulation' must not, therefore, be confused with that of 'primitive (or initial) socialist accumulation', which refers to the stage during which the socialist sector wages a life or death struggle in order to establish a broader base as rapidly as possible.

'Socialist accumulation in the strict sense of the term, that is to say accumulation founded on a socialist technical-economic base which is already in possession of all its characteristic features and *the advantages appertaining to it* can only commence after the Soviet economy has passed through the stage of primitive accumulation.'[43]

For Preobrazhensky, this then was a law, which would eventually assert itself after a period of difficulties and crises. Failure to grasp the fact that it was a law was not only a *'theoretical error, an indication of a reactionary and hardened attitude, it was also a real danger, in that it threatened the very existence of the collective economy which we are struggling to create'.*[44]

Preobrazhensky gave repeated warnings to the effect that this law must be strictly observed, if dangerous economic and political crises were to be avoided.[45] The first requirement was overall planning, for which suitable conditions had long existed; but planning was being developed in a haphazard fashion, with no sense that this was another factor which was unavoidable in the long term. 'The transition to planning of this order is inevitable. Now that we have nationalized industry and transport, we cannot prevent it, *it is not in our power to do so.*'[46]

Only by foresight on the part of the planners would it be possible to ensure satisfaction of overall economic requirements; failure to take the necessary action in 1926 could only lay up trouble for 1930. A good plan would be one which would correctly apply the growth law proper to a socialist economy, by seeking to ensure that industrial production would increase from year to year. Growth in the socialist sector must be relatively greater than that of the private sector, and within the socialist sector, at each stage, there must be a regular redistribution of productive forces, if the proper proportions required for an expanded socialist production were to be maintained.[47]

Preobrazhensky considered it self-evident that the more backward the country, the greater must be the accumulation, if the minimum of investment necessary for the efficient functioning of the socialist sector were to be obtained. In the case of Russia, the relative weakness of the socialist sector called for a rapid rate of development, and the highest possible level of accumulation. The period through which the country was at present passing should not, therefore, be referred to as 'NEP', but as the period of 'primitive socialist accumulation'.

Preobrazhensky then goes on to formulate the essential elements of his theory, and its consequences, with a degree of logic and intellectual honesty which is admirable. The sources of this primary accumulation, which would last as long as the socialist sector was unable to stand firmly on its own feet, would be more limited than had been the case during the capitalist period of initial accumulation, for Russia had no colonies on which to draw. On the other hand, Russia, unlike the capitalist countries, would be able to draw certain resources from its own capitalist sector. But the main source, as during the period of capitalist accumulation, would be the petty bourgeois sector, and there would be no alternative but to draw 'very freely' upon this source. The idea that a socialist economy might be developed without tapping the resources of the petty bourgeois and, above all, of the peasantry 'can only be described as a reactionary petty bourgeois day-dream'.[48]

In his earlier writings, Preobrazhensky had had no hesitation in describing the peasantry as an 'internal colony' of the socialist sector. In his book, he suppressed certain expressions such as 'colony', but refused to suppress the term 'exploitation'.[49] The proletariat would also be called upon to make its contribution to the accumulation process, and this would take the form of 'freely-accepted restrictions', for the proletariat were in a position to comprehend the necessity underlying such action. This, as Preobrazhensky argued in reply to Bukharin's attacks, was why he had not spoken of any exploitation of the peasantry by the proletariat, for there could be no such exploitation.[50] On the other hand, the relationship between the socialist sector as a whole, and the petty bourgeois sector, could well be described in this way.

The means by which the resources of the private sector would be transferred to the socialist sector, that is to say the *perekachka* (pumping action), are analysed in detail in the book, and cover taxation, the acquisition of income from the monopoly of external trade, credits, loans, etc. The most important source was to be that of 'non-equivalent exchanges'[51] which would result from manipulation of the prices for industrial goods. Preobrazhensky maintains that equivalent exchanges between town and country are not a feature of the capitalist system nor did they form part of the Tsarist régime. The immediate task was to take from the pre-socialist sector even more than had been taken from it under the Tsars.

Preobrazhensky's analysis was remarkable for the way in which it foresaw the actual course which events were to take in the very near future; it was, at the same time, accompanied by a number of reservations inspired by the author's anxiety not to be misunderstood. When two years later Stalin gave the first indications of what his policy on the problem of primitive accumulation was to be, Preobrazhensky, who was by that time in exile, interpreted Stalin's action as being a striking vindication of his own theories, and for a time rallied to the Stalinist line. Previously, however, in a text circulated among deportees of the Left opposition, he had declared that Stalin was merely the blind agent of historical necessity, carrying out uncomprehendingly, and therefore badly, those tasks which were being forced upon him.[52]

If a correct policy had been adopted much sooner, as the Left had demanded, the situation would have been less grave.[53] The crisis he had foreseen had now arrived, and at such a time leisurely action was a luxury one could not afford. But even during this difficult period the measures advocated by Preobrazhensky were purely economic,[54] whereas the special measures adopted by Stalin, affecting as they did the middle peasants and the bednyaks, appeared to him to be dangerous. In his book, which was published in 1926, he gives some indication of the way in which he thought the problem should be tackled. He emphatically denied that there was any need for the peasants to be plundered. The *perekachka* should be aimed only at a part of the surplus product (*pribavochny produkt*) and 'only within the limits of what is economically possible, technically feasible, and rational'.[55]

In a reply to Bukharin which figures in the appendix to the same book, he even claims to have shown that if the *perekachka* increased, it would strike at income which had itself increased by a relatively greater degree. According to him, the agronomists believed that, with intensive methods of cultivation, incomes in the countryside could be tripled. If this were so, it would simply be a matter of imposing higher taxes on an economy which had become more profitable.[56]

Preobrazhensky defends himself against Bukharin's accusation that he wanted 'to kill the goose that laid the golden eggs'. After all, he had explained at length in his book that taxation through the price mechanism, which he considered to be the principal means of obtaining resources for industry,[57] must be accompanied by a stable price situation, or even a lowering of the general level of prices. This could have been of major importance, both politically and economically, since it would have made possible a greater volume of exchange, which in its turn would have contributed to the accumulation process and simultaneously benefited the peasantry. But was this not asking the impossible?

Preobrazhensky, as a socialist who had faith in planning, and faith in the highly developed political consciousness of the proletariat, believed that a solution could be found. A well-managed industrial complex would ensure increasing labour productivity and decreasing costs. The lowering of prices would then be entirely feasible, while large profit margins could still be maintained. He was at pains to point out that the *perekachka* policy, no matter how it was implemented, would not adversely affect the village poor, who were exempt from tax, and whose purchases of industrial goods were on a very small scale.[58]

Irrespective of his aspirations, or his intentions, Preobrazhensky was well aware that the period of primary accumulation would be one of tension, and that it would be productive of crisis and danger. For this reason, he hoped that his country would 'pass through this stage, as quickly as possible, and rapidly reach a point where the socialist system will deploy all its natural advantages over capitalism . . . For the socialist state, this is a matter of life and death.' [59]

However, this stage might well last about twenty years. What lay ahead, therefore, was a lengthy struggle between 'two different types of economy', the outcome of which would be the 'adaptation of inferior forms to superior ones'.[60]

In Bukharin's view, this approach to the problem amounted to revision of the Leninist theory of the *smychka*.[61] He was convinced that a twenty-year period under such conditions would lead to a breakdown of the *smychka*, with all the terrible consequences for the Soviet régime that this implied. Preobrazhensky's 'monstrous' comparison with 'primitive capitalist accumulation', and his use of terms such as 'colony', 'exploitation' and *pozhiranie* all confirmed him in his belief that such an approach could only lead to disaster.[62]

Bukharin's fear of the Left was genuine. He fiercely denounced the arguments of Preobrazhensky and his colleagues, who were interested only in 'extracting the maximum amount possible', determined not to 'spend a single kopeck on co-operative nonsense', and bent on 'opening fire on the villages'.

Preobrazhensky replied in measured terms. Bukharin's attacks, he explained, were concerned with the political aspects of the problem, which he had not touched upon at all. Instead, he had confined himself to a strictly scientific analysis of the actual conditions, and had followed through to their logical conclusions the trends which he had observed. In subsequent volumes of his work, he promised to provide an analysis of industry, agriculture, and the problems of the *smychka*, and to outline a suitable policy. If Bukharin had been less impatient, Preobrazhensky went on, he would eventually have realized that he, Preobrazhensky, had no intention of drawing the political conclusions which had been attributed to him.[63] Theoretical research provides the basis for the formulation of an 'optimum policy', but real policy 'diverges from this optimum'. Therefore, Preobrazhensky argued, until his work was completed it was unjust to accuse him of advocating the kind of sinister developments of which Marx had spoken in connection with the era of capitalist accumulation.

But Preobrazhensky never wrote the promised works. He and his colleagues were soon to become embroiled in the most bitter internal struggle which the Party had ever known. In his reply to Bukharin, however, he not only demonstrated that he was perfectly aware of economic realities, and of the requirements for an economically and politically viable prices policy, he also gave his rival a sharp lesson in Leninist theory on the subject of the alliance with the peasantry. His interpretation of the *smychka* was as follows: Since the peasants wavered, everything should be done to prevent them from going over to the capitalists. This was imperative, from the point of view of military requirements in the event of war, and also in view of the needs of agriculture and industry. This was why the Party programme advocated persuasion and concessions, although 'solely as means calculated to bring about socialist change'.[64]

Quoting Lenin in his defence, Preobrazhensky agreed with Bukharin that if concessions were not made to the peasantry, this might lead to the collapse of the proletariat. But the danger of collapse might be even greater if the proletariat lost sight of the purpose behind these concessions, which was socialist change, in the course of which an inferior form of production, represented by the peasantry, 'would be ousted and give way to a higher form'.

Preobrazhensky then went on to develop the theme of his book, on the way in which the 'threefold task' of accumulation, increased wages and lower prices might be fulfilled through increased industrial productivity. In his view, this was 'the real meaning of the alliance between the proletariat and the peasantry in the most important sector of the economy'. This was the way to satisfy the needs of the peasants and to develop agriculture, thereby bringing about the conditions in which it would be possible to achieve coexistence (*uzhitsya*) with the peasants.

As we have said, the main point at issue between Bukharin and Preobrazhensky was the question of primitive accumulation. In the course of the next two years, however, Bukharin's ideas were to undergo a considerable change. He came to understand the importance of industrialization, and to accept the fact that the peasant must inevitably bear the cost of accumulation. His opponents had no intention of robbing the peasants, or of totally disregarding their interests, despite the harsh terms in which Preobrazhensky had spoken. Bukharin came to accept the need for 'taking' from the peasant, although this must be done with the greatest caution; Preobrazhensky was convinced that while it was necessary to 'take a great deal', there were nevertheless many factors for which allowance must be made. These were

'the relatively *slow* rate of accumulation of a peasant farm, and the relatively slow growth of the peasant's purchasing power; the problem of balanced industrial development; the size of the harvest in a given year; the possible volume of exports; the world market price of grain; the prices of exports, etc.' [65]

If Preobrazhensky was prepared to take all of these factors into account, then the disagreement between him and Bukharin was no longer one of principle, but one of practical policy. Unfortunately, the factional struggle blinded the opposing sides to the possibility of agreement. Both sides were to wake up too late to the realization that they had failed to recognize their true adversary.

The margin of disagreement between Left and Right over the question of peasant co-operation and collectivization was also fairly small, and was to become even smaller in the course of the next two years.

The Left did not look upon collectivization as a major issue.[66] In 1922, Preobrazhensky made, as it were, a prophetic utterance, in the shape of a lecture supposed to be given by a historian to an audience of workers in the year 1970; in it, he maintained that the peasant economy would function mainly by means of long term credit. This would bring about the collapse of private agriculture, but above all it would lead to a mass movement by the younger generation into the new lands, where some would establish individual settlements of the traditional type, while others would set up sovkhozes and collective farms. The State, which would by this time have become wealthy, would make this possible by supplying them with machines, building materials, etc. However, this would take place only in the peripheral regions of the State. Preobrazhensky's Utopia does not go any further on this subject.

At a later date, the writings of the Left, although they did not go into detail, were to become more explicit about the prospects for collectivization in the villages. In 1925, Trotsky was to speak of 'the gradual transition to collective agriculture' which would only become practicable after the creation of an adequate technical base.[67] In 1926, one of the suggestions which he made to the Central Committee was that more attention be paid to collectivization with particular reference to the bednyaks.[68]

Like Trotsky, Preobrazhensky believed that agricultural cooperation (co-op. *proizvodstvennaya*) was 'theoretically possible', and 'in practice inevitable', but only if the socialist base were developed sufficiently quickly. He had been criticized by Bukharin and Motylev for having failed, in his book, to discuss co-operation, either in general terms, or in relation to agricultural production, and for having thereby neglected Lenin's 'plan for co-operation'. In reply, he explained that he agreed entirely with Lenin's article 'On Co-operation', but that Lenin had said nothing in that article about collectives. Lenin was no Utopian, nor did Preobrazhensky seek to be so labelled.

In Preobrazhensky's view it was unlikely that proletarian forms of agricultural production, that is sovkhozes, would play an important part in the foreseeable future. The predominant form of socialization of the land would, of course, be 'co-operative agricultural production by the peasantry'. On the other hand, 'no one knows at present, nor can one know, what course socialization will follow, what forms it will take, or what types of co-operation will ultimately be adopted'.

Co-operation in the spheres of consumption and exchange, including the granting of long-term credits, was not the only road towards collective exploitation of the land. Although Lenin in his last articles had not mentioned other possibilities, Preobrazhensky considered he was accurately following Lenin's line of reasoning on this subject in saying that electrification, and the introduction of tractors, were likewise indispensable. Transformations on this scale would cost milliards of roubles, and there was still only one means of financing them. Intensive development of the socialist industrial sector was a pre-condition for the rapid growth of co-operation among the peasants.

Preobrazhensky then went on to make the pertinent comment that the proliferation of socialist forms of agricultural production would at first make exchange conditions even less advantageous for that part of the peasantry which continued to operate independently.[69]

The Left had therefore no intention of precipitating collectivization in the countryside. They had no overall plan for collectivization, and before undertaking such a task they wished to be sure of the necessary resources, both in technical and other respects. Nor were the Left committed to any particular form of change; they expected that private farming would continue to be the dominant form in the countryside for a long time to come. However, in the context of practical policy, the Left increasingly urged, from 1926 onwards, that serious steps be taken to further the setting-up of collectives, particularly within the framework of aid to poor peasants. The watchword of collectivization, which it was believed had originated elsewhere, had already received considerable attention in the *Platform of the Left* in September 1927. The *Platform* was soon to provide ideas for the official line, although with some difference in the proposed methods of implementation.

The *Platform* was the last great document to come from the Left.[70] Although its members at this time still belonged to the Party, their expulsion was only a few months off. The document had been prepared secretly and in haste by Party officials who had recently been relieved of their posts, and cut off from their sources of information.[71] As a whole, it suffers from many inconsistencies and certain specific defects, but it nevertheless provides a realistic picture of the social situation inside Russia, and also indicts the vacillating policies which were meeting with failure in the international sphere (in China, and in England) and undermining the position of socialism at home.

The régime is consistently referred to as a 'workers' state', but one which shows 'bureaucratic deformations'. 'The privileged and disproportionately large administrative apparatus absorbing a very large share of the surplus value . . .' Meanwhile, 'no progress is being made in increasing the strength of the working class, or improving their lot'.[72] In the factories, the managements were all-powerful. The trades unions had failed to fulfil their basic task of defending working-class interests. 'Never before have the working class and the trades unions been so isolated from the management of industry as they are at this moment.'[73]

The *Platform* called for the democratization of the trades unions and the soviets, and especially of the Party, for it was within the Party that the growth of bureaucracy and the stifling of working class interests were at their most serious.[74] The document analysed the various trends within the Party, revealing the existence of a Right-wing faction, and of a 'centre faction' consisting of Stalin, Molotov and Kirov (it erroneously included Uglanov); it predicted that the feud between these two elements, which were temporarily united in their hatred of the Left, would become increasingly embittered once the Left had been eliminated.

In retrospect, the economic proposals put forward by the Left appear very moderate indeed, and they doubtless reflect the electoral considerations of a group which was being subjected to violent and slanderous attacks. This is particularly evident in the demands which are made on behalf of the workers. But on the whole, the *Platform* does define those limits beyond which the advocates of sinister 'primitive accumulation' had no intention of proceeding.

The chapter on industrialization, which was edited by Trotsky, called for a rate of industrialization which, it was claimed, would provide the solution to the current pressing problems, though it was emphasized that this could only be achieved at the cost of 'an unprecedented strain on our means and resources'. An analysis of possible sources of investment speaks of 500 to 1,000 million roubles per annum to be granted to industry by 1931, while the bourgeoisie and the kulaks were to pay higher taxes, in the region of 150–200 million. In addition, 10% of the more prosperous peasants were to contribute to a compulsory loan of 150 million poods of grain. The document estimated that this stratum possessed reserves of 800–900 million poods.[75]

In the same chapter, the *Platform* claimed that industrialization would be impossible 'without a decisive improvement in the productive forces of agriculture, and an increase in its commercial capacities'.[76] This was preceded by a repetition of the traditional Leftist argument that it was the backwardness of industry which hindered the progress of agriculture. The authors themselves doubtless realized the difficulty of achieving both of these objectives simultaneously, particularly during a period of primitive accumulation, but they hoped that in practice solutions would gradually be found, given a rational economic policy, and adherence to a Leninist class line.

About this time, the Left were beginning to have hopes that collectivization might prove more practicable than they had previously thought possible. In the chapter on agriculture (edited by Zinovev and Kamenev) an attempt was therefore made to repair some of the obvious weaknesses in the opposition's agricultural policy.[77] In fact, up till this time, the opposition spokesmen had tended to wait for the positive results of industrialization to manifest themselves, and to let rural affairs slide, their main concern being that the kulaks should not gather too much strength. Bukharin, as we have seen, had an immediate programme and a set of proposals to make to the peasants, whereas the Left had been rather passive in the matter of working out a programme of social development for the country-side. There was a danger that a theoretical weakness of this order might well degenerate into political negligence should the Left ever come to power.

While constantly on their guard against the dangers implicit in any significant strengthening of the kulak sector, the Left had continued to show a great deal of understanding of bednyak problems, but had little to offer the serednyaks. The Left were exclusively pre-occupied by industrialization, which they regarded as the only way of 'providing for all the needs of the peasantry', and they therefore failed to pay sufficient attention to practical agrarian problems and policies, and to the search for original methods and structures which might lead to the creation of an authentically peasant socialist movement.

In this sense, the *Platform* was an attempt to make up for the Left's earlier shortcomings in the matter of programmes (Bukharin's attacks no doubt contributed to this heightened awareness) firstly, by reviving the old theme of the batraks and the *bednota*; secondly, by harking back to another equally old question which was now presented in a new light, namely the need to link 'Lenin's plan for co-operation' with his plan for electrification, a synthesis which 'certain people' had tended to overlook.[78] At this point, the text took up Bukharin's ideas on co-operation, minus the reservations previously expressed by Preobrazhensky, and also discussed, on a much broader basis than any official pronouncement had so far done, *'the task of transforming small-scale agricultural production into large-scale collective production, a transformation which must affect the entire co-operative effort'.*[79]

More resources should be allocated to the kolkhozes and the sovkhozes, since the development of these forms would henceforth be the main objective of socialist construction in the countryside. Collectivization now figures in the text as a policy devised not only for the benefit of the bednyak, but also of the middle peasant, who would 'little by little' be guided along this path by means of State aid, the granting of credits, a rational prices policy and the positive results of co-operative activity.

*   *   *

The foregoing is but a brief summary of the ideas which were current among the Left and the Right up until 1927. They are the first important reflections to have been made on the formidable problem of industrializing a backward country, and as such they merit close attention. We have indicated some of the defects and inconsistencies from which they suffered, but at the same time it must be borne in mind that to this day no universally acceptable theory, or coherent set of measures for solving this type of problem has yet been advanced.[80]

We have also seen that the Left, and later the Right, attached great importance in all their plans and aspirations, to the direct democratic appeal to the proletariat, and to the initiative (*samodeyatelnost*) of the peasants. In this respect, the Left addressed themselves primarily to the poor, the Right to the other strata as well. It should also be noted that both oppositions laid great stress on the need for a rational economic policy, a sphere in which Bukharin's contribution was soon to become increasingly noteworthy.

These men were not themselves given the opportunity of putting their theories on industrialization (including the industrialization of agriculture) into practice. Had they been given a chance to do so, the history of their country would have, or might well have, taken a different course.

3. *Stalin*

Since his accession to power, a power which Lenin in his 'testament' had described as immense (*neobyatny*), Stalin seemed to be primarily concerned with strengthening his position and setting up, within the Party, an administrative structure which would serve him as a bastion against all attacks.[81] He was more anxious than most of his old Bolshevik comrades to secure for himself all the levers of personal power, and more skilful than the others who, like Zinovev, shared his taste and his capacity for bureaucratic organization.

During the twenties, and up until the elimination of the Left, Stalin's most significant theoretical contribution had been the theory of 'socialism in one country', which he had put to good use, and never more so than in his power struggle with successive oppositions. Indeed, it is characteristic of Stalin that he should have used this doctrine as a weapon in the struggle for power, rather than as a 'guide for action', which was what the doctrine claimed to be. Since his main objective was victory over possible rivals, Stalin wasted little time over questions of doctrinal consistency; in fact the history of his rule bears witness rather to his anxiety to eliminate any who might make an issue of inconsistencies in this field.

In any case, the theory of 'socialism in one country', as a systematic doctrine, was strictly speaking the work of Bukharin.[82] It was to become 'Stalinist' mainly because of the manner in which it was applied, thanks to Stalin's acute awareness of the state of mind of Party cadres, and his constant appeals to irrational factors.

In May 1924, Stalin in common with Trotsky and all the others, was still speaking the language of Lenin, the language of 'permanent revolution'.

'The final victory of socialism and the organization of socialist production will never be brought about by the efforts of one single country, least of all an agrarian country like Russia. If this end is to be attained, the efforts of several developed countries will be indispensable.' [83]

In December 1924, however, in an article entitled *'The October Revolution and the tactics of the Russian Communists'*, Stalin completely reversed his position. This about-turn was presented simply as a correction of his previous view, the implication being that no serious self-criticism was called for.

Stalin now distinguished between two types of contradiction: external contradictions in the country's relationships with the capitalist world, and internal contradictions in the relationship between the proletariat and the peasantry. He wished his earlier view to be taken as meaning that, while there was a risk of intervention by hostile forces capable of restoring the former régime, the victory of socialism in one country could not be regarded as assured. But leaving aside this danger, the second type of contradiction, which was the contradiction in relationships with the peasantry, could be overcome, and would not constitute an obstacle to the building of socialism in one country. 'Together with the peasants, we can and we shall build socialism, under the leadership of the working class.' [84] But if, as Stalin himself had said,[85] the peasantry, by their very nature, were not socialist, how could they participate in the building of socialism, rather than obstruct it? Stalin's answer was a twofold one.

Firstly, he declared that everything would work out for the best, because the Russian peasants were unlike any others, although no evidence was offered in support of this claim. The peasants had come through three revolutions with the proletariat, who had given them both land and liberty.

'Traditionally, the Soviet peasants have always valued the political friendship and the *political* collaboration of the proletariat; they owe their liberty to this friendship and collaboration, and they cannot but be exceptionally well-disposed towards economic collaboration with the proletariat.' [86]

These compliments were doubtless inspired by polemical considerations, in the sense that they would contrast favourably with the opinions of the anti-*muzhik* opposition, which 'underestimated the peasantry'. The second part of Stalin's argument, however, demonstrated the need for some factor which would prove more reliable than the peasantry's supposed 'habit' of collaborating with the proletariat.

The peasant economy, he claims, is a small market (*melkotovarny*) economy, which stands 'at the crossroads between capitalism and socialism', and is capable of taking either direction. This lack of independence, according to Stalin, is a result

'of the piecemeal nature of peasant farming, with its inadequate organization, its dependence on the towns, on industry, on the credit system, and the nature of the government in power, and, finally, it is a reflection of the universally accepted fact that, both in the material and the cultural sphere, the village follows, and must follow, the town.' [87]

Stalin made no effort to substantiate these arguments, beyond offering as proof of their validity a quotation from Lenin, who in 1915 had discussed the possibility of creating socialism in one country. Stalin was quite undeterred by the fact that Lenin had, in this context, been referring to a developed country.[88]

Whatever the theoretical validity of Stalin's arguments, it should be emphasized that the above quotation undoubtedly reflects his genuine view of the peasantry; he was convinced that the peasants as a class could be guided in the direction desired by the government. The dependence of the peasantry on the towns, their lack of organization, the fragmentation of their economy, were all factors which were to influence Stalin in his future decisions. For the moment, however, the second part of his doctrine, comprising a programme of practical measures for the countryside, was borrowed in its entirety from Bukharin, and particularly from Bukharin's theory of co-operation.

According to Stalin, the peasantry would follow '*en masse* the path of co-operation, backed by the State, which will provide credit on favourable terms'. He fully accepted the Bukharinist theory of co-operation as an activity controlled primarily by means of credit. He also subscribed to Bukharin's views on what the stages of future development should be. The peasantry should be encouraged to participate in the building of socialism 'by the gradual application of socialist principles in agriculture, firstly in the marketing of produce, and subsequently in the production sector'.[89]

At a later date, nothing was to remain of this vision of more or less slow and laborious development, from the initial phase of 'co-operative marketing of produce' to the later stage of 'co-operative production'. For the moment, however, Stalin had no alternative to propose.

There are two points of particular interest in the arguments which Stalin was putting forward at the beginning of 1926, when his struggle with the 'new opposition' of Zinovev and Kamenev was at its height. Stalin repeatedly subjected his opponents to vigorous criticism for their 'lack of faith in the victory of socialist construction'.[90] 'Lack of faith' in this context meant lack of faith in the *possibility* of leading the peasants towards the construction of socialism in Russia, and lack of faith in the *capacity* of the proletariat, who occupied the commanding position, to lead them.[91]

The tendency to regard acceptance of the 'theory of socialism in one country' as an act of faith, thus dispensing with the need for proof, was to become more and more marked. Within a few years, it had become a cult, and the doctrine which was one of the basic elements of the cult had become dogma, which demanded unquestioning belief.

The other point which was characteristic of Stalin was his interpretation of Lenin in general. In an article written in memory of Lenin, Zinovev had maintained that 'the fundamental problem of Bolshevism, of Leninism . . . relates to the role of the peasantry'. Stalin, however, wished to figure as the defender of Leninism against all who might seek to detract from its 'universal applicability'. His reply was presented as a supreme truth, and a profession of faith. 'Leninism is the Marxism of the era of imperialist wars and of world revolution which began in a predominantly peasant country'. He then went on to quote his own 1924 formula: 'The fundamental problem of Leninism, its point of departure, is not the peasant question . . . the problem of the peasant as ally of the proletariat during its struggle for power is merely a secondary issue'.[92] The basic problem, Stalin insisted, was the dictatorship of the proletariat.

There is much that is typical of Stalin's personal approach in the excessively universalist (as opposed to the more narrowly Russian) interpretation which is given to the theories of the late revered leader, and also in this second assertion that possession of power was the fundamental issue of Leninism, and should take precedence over all others. As for the other parts of Lenin's doctrine, these were of little importance to him.[93]

Power he unquestionably had, by the time that NEP had entered upon its second phase, but the policy followed at this stage was the policy of Bukharin and Rykov. Indeed, with the exception of those distinctive features which we have mentioned, it is difficult to detect any outstandingly different or individual element in Stalin's views at this stage.

There is still no indication, at this point, that he was thinking of collectivization in any sense as a practical proposition. There is no trace of the word *kolkhoz* in his writings before the Fifteenth Congress; only the very general term *tovarishchestvo* (association) is to be found. In a very lengthy report on the problem which he made to delegations of foreign workers two months before the Fifteenth Party Congress, or 'Congress of Collectivization' as it was to be called, Stalin stated: 'We wish to introduce collectivism in the agricultural sector gradually, using economic, financial, cultural and political measures to this end';[94] he was here referring to progressive stages of co-operation, in the sense in which he had already envisaged them. In any case, the *tovarishchestva* were intended exclusively for the poor, and realization of the collectivist ideal was not, apparently, regarded as a short-term possibility, since it would require 'enormous financial resources, which the State does not yet possess', and which would only accumulate 'over a period of time'.[95] Thus, collectivization, which was later to become indissolubly linked with the name of Stalin, was not the outcome of long premeditation in the doctrinal sense.

Nor was rapid industrialization originally a Stalinist policy. On the contrary, Stalin was known, during the NEP period, as an opponent of the Left-wing 'super-industrializers'. His opposition to the *Dneprostroi* project is sufficient indication of his almost total commitment at this time to the pro-*muzhik* line, which he followed partly out of conviction, and partly out of anxiety to enlist Bukharin's support against Trotsky.[96]

This project, to which Trotsky attached great importance, was debated in the Central Committee in April 1926. Stalin opposed it in the following terms:

'*Dneprostroi* would have to be financed with our own resources, and would cost a great deal—some hundreds of millions. We must beware of acting like the peasant who acquired some extra cash and, instead of repairing his plough or improving his farm, bought himself a gramophone and was ruined. Are we justified in ignoring the resolutions of the Fourteenth Congress, which stated that our plans must be in keeping with our resources? Clearly, comrade Trotsky has not taken these decisions into account'.[97]

This statement has never been officially admitted, but even if its authenticity were in doubt, the general content of Stalin's policy and his public statements provides ample evidence of his lack of enthusiasm for an all-out programme of industrialization. At the end of 1926, during the Fifteenth Party Conference we find him pledging his support for industrialization only in so far as it would result in an immediate rise in the workers' standard of living. The arguments with which he prepared to meet the opposition at the Conference contain a statement to the effect that industrialization would only be feasible 'if it were based upon a progressive improvement in the material condition of the peasantry'.[98] At the same time, he declared that he was anxious to avoid any extreme measures, and that no disparity must be allowed to develop between industry and agriculture, between industry and the available means of accumulation.[99]

His concern for the peasants is reflected in his criticisms of those 'dangerous elements' who regard the peasantry as a subject for exploitation. 'It is not the function of the peasantry to serve as a subject for exploitation or a colony for the proletariat.' Then follow the standard recommendations which were being made at this time: caution should be exercised in the choice of price and fiscal policies, the régime should concentrate on accumulating reserves, and on creating favourable conditions for the operation of the peasant market, which was the mainstay of industry, and so on.[100]

Having adopted this political line, Stalin then went on to defend those who advocated it. His defence of Bukharin in particular verges on the dramatic. At the Fourteenth Party Congress, while the Zinovev faction had insisted that the Party could not accept the idea of a 'duce' (*vozhd*) and criticized Bukharin's pro-kulak line, Stalin figured as the champion of collective leadership, who was anxious to protect the reputation of the leaders.

'It is impossible,' he exclaimed, 'to direct the Party without Rykov, without Kalinin, Tomsky, Molotov and Bukharin. . . .' In subsequent editions of this speech, the names of all but Kalinin and Molotov were to be omitted, but this was at a later stage, when circumstances had changed. For the moment, Stalin denounced the opposition's attacks on Bukharin in even more forceful terms. '"Why must this unbridled calumny of Bukharin continue?', he demanded. 'They are out for comrade Bukharin's blood. . . . Is it Bukharin's blood you are after? You shall not have it." (Applause.)'[101]

The political line which was adopted at this time, and subsequently followed, was one which had been worked out by Bukharin and Rykov, and Stalin was entirely in agreement with it. None the less, in the intricate by-play of set formulas and public declarations he manoeuvred with great care, and avoided openly committing himself to any applications of the policy which might have been constructed as deviations from the orthodox Leninist line. Stalin was primarily a tactician, and his chief concern was for his own ideological alibi. This left him free to pursue the internal struggle within the Party, and in this art he was a past master.

Without taking any radically different stand, he was careful to dissociate himself from the honest but misguided watchword of Bukharin, who had urged the peasants to 'get rich!'[102] He poured scorn on the opposition's demands for industrialization at the Fourteenth Congress, while at the same time supporting the cause of an independent Russia which would be able to produce its own equipment.[103] This Congress was in fact to proclaim the end of the stage of 'economic rehabilitation' and the beginning of the period of 'reconstruction'. However, translated into practical terms, the analyses and the proposals which followed this announcement were limited to a very narrow range of objectives and they 'amounted to nothing more than a diluted and incomplete version of the policy which Bukharin and Rykov had advocated'.[104] It was Bukharin and Rykov who had to shoulder the responsibility for studying and finding solutions to the many economic and political problems, sometimes of the most intractable nature, which confronted the country.

Deutscher has described Stalin's policy at this time as 'an exercise in evasion'. In his view, Stalin at this stage of his career emerges as a man of compromise who, although by nature not at all inclined to conciliation and appeasement, contrived to reassure the Party activists by avoiding extremes.[105]

As for those who were Stalin's opponents at the time, their view of his policy differs little, in essence, from that of the present-day scholars whom we have quoted. In 1927, the *Platform of the Left* described his policy as consisting of 'short zigzags to the left, followed by long zigzags to the right'.[106]

Stalin's character was naturally well known to the other leaders, not only from personal experience, but also from a text in which Lenin had attributed to him a number of shortcomings which are disconcerting to say the least. In a letter addressed to the Thirteenth Party Congress, Lenin recommended that Stalin be dismissed from office on the grounds that he was coarse, and intolerant, lacking in loyalty and in politeness towards other comrades, and unpredictable. . . .[107]

In a society and a Party which had only recently emerged from the trials of a terrible civil war, it was natural enough that the General Secretary's uncouth habits, which in any case were known only to a relatively small circle, should pass unnoticed or at least be tolerated. Lenin himself had been tolerant long enough, and it was only on his death bed that he had realized the danger of leaving such vast power in the hands of a man who had so many faults. The other leaders, blinded by the factional struggles in which they were involved, thought themselves more than a match for Stalin, and believed that they would be able to handle him when the time came, because of his lack-lustre personality, his unobtrusiveness, and his mediocre qualities as a theoretician, another aspect of his character which had not been mentioned by Lenin. On the other hand, Stalin's skill as a back-stage intriguer, which was also well known to them, aroused no anxiety, and was indeed considered by his associates as a useful quality.

Curiously, as in the case of Lenin himself, the politicians who were associated with Stalin discovered the blessings of democracy too late, when Stalin was becoming more dangerous than they had thought. In April 1926, Zinovev and Kamenev, who had been co-members of the Triumvirate against Trotsky, confided to the latter, after a sensational switch in allegiance, that 'Stalin is not interested in ideas. It is power alone which attracts him. He is cunning and cruel'.[108]

Two years later Bukharin in his turn revealed to Kamenev, whom he had helped to overthrow, some even more alarming truths about Stalin. In fear and trembling, Bukharin spoke of 'this Genghis Khan who will destroy us all . . .'.[109] And so, in the end, Lenin's 'testament' fell into the hands of the last person to whom he would have wished to bequeath it. Yet this was the source from which Stalin, after his own fashion, had drawn his inspiration.

Lenin had warned the Party against two dangers. The first, a short-term eventuality, was that of a split in the Party caused by rivalry between Trotsky and Stalin. Stalin was able to avoid this by eliminating Trotsky. The second, and even graver danger, was the risk of a split with the peasantry. Stalin faced up to this danger, and found the way to overcome it by eliminating the possibility of any eventual break. But the methods adopted by this unwanted heir were very different from those envisaged by his master.

NOTES AND REFERENCES

1. Lenin, speech to the Sixth Congress of Soviets. *Sochineniya* (5th edition), XXXVII, pp. 141–4.

2. Kritsman outlined his ideas in a series of articles which appeared in 1925 in *NAF*, beginning in No. 2 of that year under the title 'K voprosu o klassovom rassloyenii sovremennoi derevni'. When, in 1930, these ideas came under attack, he continued to defend them. See Livyant's article, 'V osnovnom voprose revolyutsii nuzhna yasnost' in *NAF*, 1930, No. 4, and Kritsman's reply, *ibid*, pp. 96–114.

3. We are here summarizing an attitude described by Bukharii on p. 60 of *Put k sotzializmu i raboche-krestyanski blok*; he wa: opposed not so much to the substance of this interpretation as tc the manner in which it was presented.

4. This summary of Bukharin's position in 1925–6 is based upon the pamphlet mentioned above. (See Note 3.)

5. *ibid*, pp. 12–13.

6. *ibid*, p. 64.

7. *ibid*, p. 49.

8. *ibid*, p. 72.

9. *ibid*, p. 98.

10. *ibid*, p. 52.

11. *ibid*, p. 47.

12. *ibid*, p. 49.

13. *ibid*, p. 65.

14. *ibid*, p. 26.

15. *ibid*, p. 44.

16. *ibid*, p. 53.

17. *ibid*, p. 40.

18. *ibid*, p. 44.

19. The expression was used by Preobrazhensky in his reply tc Motylev in *Novaya Ekonomika*, p. 261.

20. On Trotsky's views at the time of the Twelfth Congress, see Deutscher, *The Prophet Unarmed*, pp. 98–103, and Carr, *A History of Soviet Russia; The Bolshevik Revolution*, Vol. II, pp. 381–2.

21. Described by Carr, *op. cit.*, pp. 370–81.

22. See 'the testament' in Lenin, 'O pridanii zakonodatelnykh funktsii Gosplanu', *Sochineniya* (4th edition), Vol. XXXVI, pp. 548–51.

23. Deutscher, *op. cit.*, pp. 65–74, 88–92.

24. Twelfth Congress, quoted by Carr, *A History of Soviet Russia; The Interregnum*, p. 23.

25. This article was reissued in 1924 in Trotsky's *Novy Kurs*. The version to which we refer is contained in *Les Bolcheviks contre Staline*, pp. 75–81.

26. *ibid*, p. 77.

27. *ibid*, p. 79.

28. Carr, *A History of Soviet Russia; Socialism in One Country*, Vol. I, pp. 354–5.

29. Trotsky's letter to the Comintern in 1928 is contained in *The Third International After Lenin*. (New York, 1936), under the heading 'What Now?'.

30. *ibid*, p. 270. Trotsky here quotes himself.

31. The Preface, written in November 1925, for his pamphlet

Towards Socialism or Capitalism (1926), quoted by Carr, *A History of Soviet Russia; Socialism in One Country*, Vol. I, p. 355.

32. Preobrazhensky, *op. cit.* (see Ch. 4, Note 51), pp. 30, 40.

33. Quoted by Carr, *A History of Soviet Russia; The Interregnum*, p. 25.

34. Ruth Fischer, *Stalin and German Communism*. (London, 1948), pp. 545–6.

35. This is the line taken by Preobrazhensky, for example, *op. cit.*, pp. 111 and 261.

36. On his insistence, at the Plenum of the Central Committee of April 6–9, 1926, that a more progressive agricultural tax be levied, see Deutscher, *op. cit.* (see Note 20), pp. 276–7 and Carr, *A History of Soviet Russia; Socialism in One Country*, Vol. I, p. 355.

37. The *Platform* of 1927, in *Les Bolcheviks contre Staline*, p. 112. One pood is equal to 16·38 kilogrammes, or 36 pounds.

38. This also shows that the debate between the champions of 'permanent revolution' and those of 'socialism in one country', which is often supposed to have been the root cause of these differences, was not so crucial after all. The supporters of either theory might disagree among themselves as to the policy which should be pursued, while in practice the two opposing camps still arrived at a common programme.

39. The term originated with V. M. Smirnov, an economist working with *Gosplan* and a member of the 'workers' opposition'.

40. Preobrazhensky, *Novaya Ekonomika*, pp. 37, 231. The main chapter of this book, which was published in 1926, appeared separately in 1924 in *Vestnik Kommunisticheskoi Akademii*. It is without question the best work ever written on the economic problems of the Soviet Union at this time.

41. *ibid*, pp. 107–8.

42. *ibid*, pp. 45–6, 58, 91, 104–5.

43. *ibid*, p. 55. (Emphasis in the original.)

44. *ibid*, p. 41.

45. *ibid*, pp. 30, 40.

46. *ibid*, pp. 39–40. (Emphasis supplied.)

47. *ibid*, p. 39.

48. *ibid*, pp. 63–4.

49. *ibid*, p. 88.

50. *ibid*, p. 215.

51. *ibid*, p. 88.

52. *Levy Kurs v derevne i perspektivy* is contained in the Trotsky Archives at Harvard.

53. A summary of the ideas contained in *Novaya Ekonomika* is provided by Deutscher, *op. cit.* (see Note 20), pp. 415–26.

54. Erlich, *The Soviet Industrialization Debate*, 1924–8 (Harvard 1960), p. 170.

55. Preobrazhensky, *op. cit.*, pp. 109, 116.

56. *ibid*, pp. 241–3.

57. *ibid*, p. 88.

58. *ibid*, p. 88.

59. *ibid*, p. 63. (Emphasis supplied.)

60. *ibid*, p. 231.

61. Bukharin attacked Preobrazhensky in *Pravda* of December 12, 1924. Preobrazhensky replied early in 1925 in *Vestnik Kommunisticheskoi Akademii*. His reply is contained in an appendix to *Novaya Ekonomika*, pp. 210–55.

62. Devour, swallow up. Preobrazhensky used to say that superior forms 'swallowed up' inferior ones; in his book, however, he spoke only of 'exploitation'.

63. Preobrazhensky, *op. cit.*, pp. 210–13.

64. *ibid*, p. 234; following quotation, p. 235.

65. *ibid*, p. 238.

66. Preobrazhensky, *Ot Nepa k sotsializmu.* (Moscow, 1922), pp. 106–7.

67. Trotsky, Preface to the English edition of *Towards Socialism or Capitalism*, quoted by Carr, *A History of Soviet Russia; Socialism in One Country*, Vol. I, p. 355.

68. Deutscher, *op. cit.*, p. 277.

69. Preobrazhensky, replying to Motylev, in *Novaya Ekonomika*, p. 261.

70. The cyclostyled text of the *Platforma bolshevikov-lenintsev k 15-omu s'ezdu partii*, signed by thirteen members of the Central Committee and the Central Control Commission is in the B.D.I.C. A French translation, from which the last pages have been omitted without this being indicated, is contained in *Les Bolcheviks contre Staline*.

71. V. Serge, *Memoirs of a Revolutionary.* (London, 1963), (pp. 242–3 of the French edition).

72. The *Platform* in *Les Bolcheviks contre Staline*, p. 94.

73. *ibid*, p. 97.

74. *ibid*, pp. 119–26.

75. According to the decisions of the Plenary session of December 1930 of the Central Committee, investments in industry (in both new and existing installations) were to reach 7,740 million roubles.

76. The *Platform* in *Les Bolcheviks contre Staline*, p. 107.

77. Serge, *op. cit.*, gives details of the editors of these chapters.

78. The *Platform* in *Les Bolcheviks contre Staline*, p. 101.

79. *ibid*, p. 108. (Emphasis supplied.)

80. The American economist Erlich has examined the theories of those who took part in this debate, and has paid tribute to the high level of the ideas which they advanced.

81. Notes dictated by Lenin on December 25, 1922, *Sochineniya* (4th edition), Vol. XXXVI, p. 544.

82. See Bukharin, *op. cit.* (see Ch. 3, Note 32), pp. 101–6. The body of Bukharin's ideas, as elaborated, notably, in this pamphlet, constitutes a complete theory on the construction of socialism in one country. See also his article 'O kharaktere nashei revolyutsii i o vozmozhnosti pobedonosnogo sotsialisticheskogo stroitelstva v SSR', *Bolshevik*, 1926, No. 19–20, pp. 28–59.

83. Quoted by Stalin himself in his pamphlet 'Ob osnovakh Leninizma', *Sochineniya*, Vol. VIII, p. 61.

84. *ibid*, p. 64.

85. *ibid*, pp. 79–80.

86. *ibid*, p. 76. (Emphasis in the original.)

87. *ibid*, p. 78.

88. Daniels, *op. cit.* (see Ch. 2, Note 3), p. 25. The quotation is from Lenin 'O lozunge Soedinennykh Shtatov Evropy', *Sochineniya* (2nd edition), Vol. XVIII, pp. 352–3.

89. Stalin, *op. cit.* (see Note 84), p. 77.

90. *ibid*, p. 75.

91. *ibid*, pp. 75–6. (Emphasis in the original.)

92. Stalin, *Sochineniya*, Vol. VIII, pp. 14, 15–16.

93. We shall not attempt to decide which of the two more accurately interpreted Lenin; in the Party both were regarded as very poor theoreticians.

94. Stalin, *Sochineniya*, Vol. X, pp. 221–6. The quotation is from p. 221.

95. *ibid*, p. 225.

96. On this pro-*muzhik* line, and on Stalin's centrism, see Deutscher, *op. cit.* (see Note 20), p. 245.

97. Trotsky confirms this, in a text found in the Trotsky archives at Harvard. The quotation is taken here from Erlich, *op. cit.*, p. 94, and the end of the quotation from Carr, *A History of Soviet Russia; Socialism in One Country*, Vol. I, p. 355.

98. Deutscher; *op. cit.*, p. 298; Stalin, *Sochineniya*, Vol. VIII, p. 223.

99. Stalin, *Sochineniya*, Vol. VIII, pp. 131–2. For his remarks against the 'dangerous individuals', see *ibid*, p. 142.

100. Stalin, *Sochineniya*, Vol. VII, p. 29.

101. *14-ty S'ezd VKP(b)*, *stenogramme*, pp. 504–8. Quoted by Daniels, *op. cit.* (see Ch. 11, Note 3), pp. 268–9. The references to the 'blood of Bukharin' were later to be suppressed.

102. Erlich, *op. cit.*, pp. 90–1; Deutscher, Stalin. (London, 1949), the chapter 'The Great Change'.

103. *14-ty S'ezd VKP(b)*, *stenogramme*, pp. 2–28.

104. This is the opinion of Erlich, *op. cit.*, p. 95.

105. Deutscher, *Stalin*, 'The Great Change', passim.

106. The *Platform* in *Les Bolcheviks contre Staline*, p. 93.

107. The letter was dictated by Lenin between December 23 and 31, 1922. The remarks concerning Stalin are contained in an appendix to the letter of December 24, written on January 4, 1923. Lenin, *Sochineniya* (4th edition), pp. 545–6.

108. Deutscher, *The Prophet Unarmed*, p. 263.

109. In a conversation between Bukharin and Kamenev in *Sotsialisticheski Vestnik*, 1929, No. 9, p. 10.

Chapter 7

THE RÉGIME IN SEARCH
OF A POLICY (1925–7)

1. *Agricultural Production at a Standstill*

With the disappearance of the landowners and the wealthy farmers, the peasantry's hopes were at last realized, and they entered upon a phase of *oserednyachivanie* (levelling), which had been clearly foreseen by Lenin, and which was to transform them into a mass of small agricultural producers of more or less equal economic condition. This equalization, or levelling-out process, was something which reflected the fundamentally egalitarian aspirations of the peasantry, and which particularly commended itself to the poor peasant's idea of social justice. However, this situation did not last. With the advent of NEP, it gave rise to two important developments, the results of which were to become obvious by 1928, and which were to involve the régime in very serious difficulties.

There were two growing dangers, one which stemmed from the agrarian revolution itself, and the other which was engendered by NEP.

Initially, the benefits of NEP were clear for all to see. There was a sustained improvement in agricultural production, the most important sector of all; livestock production was also looking up. By about 1926, overall agricultural production had already reached pre-war level, and there were in fact more cattle than before. There had been a spectacular rise in grain production: the average harvest for the years 1922–5 had been 57·7 million tons, whereas for the years 1926–9 it was 73·5 million tons.[1]

At this point, however, grain production began to mark time, and even to show signs of decreasing. Although overall production (in value) had reached the pre-war level, this was not so in the case of grain, on which the country depended for its existence. In 1926–7, the sown area (all grains) was 92% of the pre-war figure; there was a slight increase in the following year (94·61%), and this again dropped in 1928–9 to 92·2%.[2]

What was even more serious was that the traditional grain-producing regions, which provided the bulk of the marketable grain, had not returned to their former level of production, and the shortfall was even more marked in those regions than over the country as a whole. (It should be borne in mind that, in normal conditions, the Ukraine and the North Caucasus alone provided half of the total marketable grain).[3] In the North Caucasus, in 1928, 88% of the former sown area had been sown, but the grain harvest was only 62% of the former total. The sown area figures for the Lower Volga, the Crimea and Bashkiria were 80·5%, 71·5% and 68·5% respectively of the pre-war totals, but the shortfall in production was even greater in these regions.[4] Over the country as a whole, grain production was 76·6 million tons in 1925–6, 73·1 million tons in 1926–7, 73·3 million tons in 1927–8 and 71·7 million tons in 1928–9, as compared with 81·6 million tons in 1913.[5]

It should be noted that at this period, Soviet statistics, and particularly those relating to agriculture, were honest enough as far as they went, but they were not sufficiently accurate. Bolshakov[6] describes how the men on the spot, deluged with innumerable forms and interminable demands for information from their superiors, coped with the situation as best they could: 'We cannot understand half of the questions', the officials of the *VIKi* complained, 'we just put down the first thing that comes into our heads . . .'.[7]

Another author, in an article entitled 'Statistical Sixes and Sevens' showed how the Central Statistical Office, Gosplan, the Commissariat of Inspection, and the statistical departments of the co-operative movement, were producing widely conflicting figures on identical problems, sometimes on matters of the greatest importance, such as procurements, sown areas, or the five-year plans.[8] Matters were to become more serious later on, when the uncertainties of rule of thumb methods were aggravated by conscious attempts at falsification by the authorities themselves.

After an impressive start, the production of livestock also began to mark time; there was a falling-off in the rate of growth, and finally, by the autumn of 1928, a downward trend set in which was not to be arrested for many years. By that autumn, there were already fewer head of livestock than there had been the previous autumn.[9] The peasants began killing off and selling their beasts on a very large scale, a phenomenon for which there are always serious economic reasons.

Volf, who was head of the agricultural division of Gosplan, made the pessimistic forecast, 'As far as any increase in the number of livestock is concerned, the outlook for the year 1928–9 is not promising.'[10] He summed up the prospects for agriculture rather guardedly: 'At all events, indications over the past year and a half are of a certain downward trend in agriculture.' He went on to say, that this was not attributable to the reverses which agriculture had undoubtedly suffered, but to more deep-seated causes.

If such a statement had been made by a member of the Right, he would have been anathematized, as had been the case with Frumkin, who said the same thing but in much more forceful terms.

In fact, the situation was much more dangerous than the cautious wording suggested. The population was increasing, the towns were growing, every year brought 500,000 new peasant households. There were 14 million additional mouths to feed, and agricultural production was not even at pre-war level. In 1914, grain production per head of the population had been 584 kg. In 1928-9, it was only 484.4 kg.[11] and the gap was widening all the time. . . .

One reliable economist [12] described the development of agricultural production as chaotic, and pointed out that in those sectors which had initially been expanding there was either a positive downward trend, or a slackening off in the rate of growth; he produced the following table: (value of production by sector, in 1926-7 prices)

	Grain	Industrial crops	Livestock
1926-7	+8	-14	+8
1927-8	-8	+19	+3
1928-9	-1	+6	-3

Thus, in addition to a drop in production of grain, and the beginning of a decisive decline in livestock, there was a slowing-down in industrial crops as well.[13] The unfortunate Frumkin's findings were fully vindicated,[14] but by the time the above information was published, in June 1930, Frumkin was no longer in a position to take the credit for them.

It should also be noted that, in the case of bread grains, in other words wheat and rye, the drop in production continued to be more accentuated than that for grain production as a whole. Later on we shall be examining the reasons for the reduction in this sector, and for the marked preference which the peasants showed for other crops.

Certain studies which appeared after the death of Stalin have furnished a great deal of detailed information, which sheds further light on the situation. In 1928, the sown area for industrial crops was 91% greater than in 1913, but this, as our source points out, was mainly accounted for by the increase in the cultivation of sunflower.[15] Yields per hectare were lower than in the pre-war period, the sugar-beet and flax harvests were smaller than they had been prior to 1914, and the amounts of raw cotton harvested were scarcely any higher.

The figures show, therefore, that agricultural production was smaller than it had been pre-war, even in the case of certain industrial crops, and that a dangerous slowing down in the growth of livestock production had soon developed into a definite downward trend.[16]

Obviously, this weakness in agriculture spelled great dangers ahead for the Soviet régime, both economically and politically: it meant shortages of raw materials for industry, particularly the textile industry, a threat to supplies of livestock products and, even more serious, the danger of a shortage of bread.

A backward agricultural country, impoverished by war and over-dependent on the current harvest, could be brought to the very brink of disaster by even a minor climatic failure, such as could overtake it at any time. The country was under constant threat of famine, and, if famine should break out, the régime would find itself disarmed and powerless. The régime's very existence was at stake, and it had every reason to seek a solution to this unhappy situation. There was, however, no ready-made solution.

A clearer idea of the position may be obtained if one looks at these problems in the light of the *zagotovki* and the market production.

2. *The Problem of the Market Production*

Before the war, half of the grain production had come from the big private estates, and the kulak farms. The remainder of the peasantry accounted for only 50% of grain production. Even more important, from the point of view of the country's economy, was the fact that the *pomeshchiki* and the kulaks together produced over 71% of the grain which was available for the market, this being also the bulk of the supplies available for export.[17]

After the revolution, there was a radical change in this situation, and the consequences which ensued were both unpredictable and disastrous for the country as a whole. The big estates, and some of the land belonging to the former kulaks, passed into the hands of the peasants; but by 1928, the number of peasant households was no longer 16 million, but some 25–26 million.

Despite the fact that the revolution had brought them more land, the enormous increase in the peasant population led to a large-scale subdivision of peasant holdings. The bulk of the holdings were now very small. By 1928, even the kulak had become, essentially, a small farmer who was economically far weaker than his pre-war counterpart.

The very low productivity of agriculture is readily understood when one considers the lack of proper implements, which we discussed in Chapter 1, and the fact that the peasants had virtually no chemical fertilizers (the quantity of organic fertilizers was always inadequate, because of the weakness of livestock production in Russia). At the same time, the peasant who had formerly produced

50% of the grain, and consumed 60% of that, was now producing 85% (without the kulaks) but was consuming 80% of what he produced.[18] The effect of these changes on *tovarnost* was such as to place the régime in an impossible position. Before the war, 26% of agricultural production had gone to the market. By 1928-7, the proportion had been reduced by twice as much, and this from a total production which was itself much smaller. *In that year, State procurements had amounted to 630 million poods of marketable grain, whereas the pre-war figure had been 1,300·6 million poods.*[19]

By eating the greater part of his grain harvest (which was raised in small quantities) the peasant was unwittingly putting the régime, as it were, in a noose. And the noose was tightening, for the situation was going from bad to worse. From the State's point of view, the proportion available for the market (the *tovarnost*) was only 13·3%; but the outlook for the Soviet régime was even gloomier, when one considers how these availabilities were distributed among the various strata of the peasantry.

The bulk of the marketable production, amounting to about 80%, came naturally from the bednyaks and the serednyaks; but the kulaks, who represented some 3–5% of the total of peasant households, were responsible for the other 20%. Their farms were economically more productive than the others, and they were able to sell 20% of their harvest (34% pre-war), whereas the rest of the peasantry were selling only 11·2% These figures may be open to question,* but they are indicative of the general trend.

The fact that the kulak accounted for a large proportion of the production of marketable grain, as we have noted above, was one that weighed very heavily in the minds of a large section of the Party. During the NEP period, the numbers of kulaks had been constantly on the increase, and they were regarded as 'class enemy No. 1'. In a period of scarcity, with market production at the low ebb which it had reached, the kulak was in a position to speculate on the grain market, thereby jeopardizing the interests of the régime.

---

* The figure of 13·3% for *tovarnost* in the year 1926–7 takes only State grain procurements into account, so to this extent it may give an unduly sombre picture of the situation. The peasants sold more than that, and some present-day Soviet scholars put the figure for *tovarnost* at 20·7%, which is not so very far off the pre-war figure of 26% (see *Istoryia sovetskogo krestyanstva i kolkhoznogo stroitelstva v SSSR*, p. 258). This does not lessen the gravity of the situation to any marked extent, though it does suggest a rather different interpretation. Less blame would attach to the backwardness of the private producer, whereas a greater responsibility would lie with the Soviet authorities for having failed to get more grain from the peasants by the use of economic methods.

Whether the danger was real or imagined is a problem which we shall be examining at a later stage; none the less, this is how the situation appeared to many Party members, and they regarded it as a grave danger.

The peasants were eating more, the numbers of livestock were greater than before and they too required more food, harvests were small, and all of these factors combined to produce a situation in which the peasantry tended to hoard as much as possible. At the same time, some 50 million poods of grain went into the making of *samogon* every year.[20]

The smallness of the market availabilities of grain had a disastrous effect on the country's economy, by virtually ruining the traditional export trade in grain. In the past, Russia had exported 11.4 million tons of grain annually;[21] *the amount of grain at the State's disposal had now gone down in a proportion of 2:1 and exports had gone down in a proportion of 20:1!* By about 1928, after two years in which there had been a very slight recovery in exports, the export of grain had practically ceased. The population were short of bread, and their numbers were constantly increasing. Since the annual rate of growth of the population was between 2 and 3%, an extra 4 million tons of grain was needed to feed them. In these circumstances, there was no grain for export, and it became difficult to find the resources which were urgently needed for industrialization.

Consequently, every year the Soviet régime was faced with a task which had not existed in Tsarist times. The *zagotovki* (that is, State purchases of agricultural produce from the peasants) became an operation of the utmost importance, one which presented considerable organizational and economic complexities, and which was, moreover, extremely difficult to handle from the political angle. Everything depended on the success of the *zagotovki* and the methods used to carry them out; it was the *zagotovki* which determined the nature of the relations between the régime and the peasantry, the availability of food for the towns, and the possibility of making progress with plans for industrialization. *The very existence of the régime was at stake during this campaign. Inevitably, the Soviet authorities found that the* zagotovki *dominated all other considerations, and they were obliged to strain every nerve merely in order to survive.*

During the second phase of NEP, the problem had not yet assumed quite such a dramatic form, but every year brought fresh grounds for anxiety. This is readily understandable, when one considers the following figures for the *zagotovki,* provided by the Commissar who was responsible for them [22]:

1926–7	10·6 million tons
1927–8	10·1 million tons
1928–9	9·45 million tons

The above figures are the totals for all grains. The totals for food grains alone show a much sharper drop: viz, 8·30, 8·05 and 6·20 million tons respectively!

Thus, there was a consistent and alarming drop in the procurement figures. But by this time, the crisis in NEP and in the régime, which had set in towards the end of 1927, was already well under way. The battle was on, and it was a battle for grain, in which the Soviet régime was impelled to launch a positive onslaught. This, at all events, is how Stalin saw the problem, and the statement which he made on this issue was in fact entitled 'On the grain front'.[23] And on the grain front, things were going badly. . . .

3. The Effects of Spontaneous 'Bukharinism'

Within the Party there was feverish activity, as the various factions strove to extend their influence or to promote their respective policies; this internal struggle went on against a background of social and economic realities which took their course, and which promised still further complications.

The bitterness of the internal struggle, particularly during the years 1926–7, is explained primarily by what was at stake, in other words, control of the Party and of the country; but it also arose from the fact that behind the conflict there lay the constant threat that at any moment the régime might find itself unable to feed the people. The government had no grain reserves,[24] a situation which was grave enough for any government in an agricultural country, but which was worse in the case of Soviet Russia, where the régime was beset by fears of capitalist encirclement from without, and peasant disaffection from within. Even the forces of nature were to be feared, for the climate was yet another imponderable; a bad year could leave the country on the brink of famine, while a good harvest brought its own social problems, by encouraging the middlemen, the speculators and the kulaks who were hostile to the régime.

The Soviet régime, whose 'command points' were mainly situated in the towns, had not succeeded in establishing itself firmly in the rural areas; it did not know how to handle them, either from the social angle, or from the point of view of production. Its 'strongholds' in the villages were still very weak, and in addition the economic policy of the central government, being both incoherent and inconsistent, merely served to make matters worse. Absorbed as they were by the internal conflict within the Party, the leaders

178

had little time to spare even for the most urgent problems. Stalin, as we have seen, was more concerned with making sure of his own support inside the Party than with working out a policy. This was left to Bukharin, but Bukharin's theories were not backed by such measures as would have been necessary to ensure their proper implementation in practice. The local administrations and the peasants practised a sort of 'home-made' Bukharinism, as they understood it, and the central authorities seemed to have faith in their recipe. All these factors were combining to produce a crisis which would in the end have to be met with vigorous measures, but under the most unfavourable conditions.[25]

We have already discussed the essential elements in the agricultural situation: the sown areas which, by about 1926-7, were showing no further expansion, the harvests of those same years, which either showed no increase or were actually decreasing (with a particularly marked drop in wheat and rye), and the raw materials shortages in cotton, wool and leather, which meant that Russia, an agricultural country, was in fact having to import these items.[26] Such imports could no longer be financed by the traditional exports of grain.[27]

Although they still would not admit it, the government's chief hope of remedying the situation depended on the 'strong' peasant, or indeed the kulak. They also believed that the co-operative movement could help to raise the level and the quality of production, by co-ordinating the efforts of the ever-increasing number of middle and poor peasants. Small and backward though they were, the farms belonging to the middle peasants had a productive potential which was not being fully utilized, because of the primitive level at which cultivation was being carried on. The official spokesmen frequently and quite rightly made the point that, with a minimal amount of agro-technical improvements hitherto unknown to the peasants (for example, selected seeds, better farm implements, more fertilizers, autumn ploughing and above all multiple crop rotation) yields could easily be increased and there would be a marked improvement in harvests.[28] The authorities introduced the idea of the *agrominimum*, with this end in view, and action was taken throughout the country to see that the peasants had some elementary knowledge of farming techniques.

It was also decided to complete the reallocation of strips as quickly as possible, for until this was done the above improvements could have little effect. However, the authorities failed to implement these measures vigorously enough, or on a sufficiently large scale, and *zemleustroistvo* continued to mark time. Progress with the *agrominimum* in the countryside was even slower. By the end of

1927, 8·5% of the peasants in the RSFSR had made some improve-ments; the corresponding figure for the Ukraine was only 5·8%. It was only the better-off elements among the peasantry who adopted the new ways, and even then the results obtained were not out-standing. The position was the same with those peasant farmers who were Party members; of this group, the numbers who adopted any of the proposed improvements totalled 16% in Russia, and 14% in the Ukraine, a proportion which was similar to that noted among the better-off strata of the peasantry.[29]

Two years later, the results were still no better. During the spring sowing of 1929, only 8·3% of the sown areas were sown with selected seeds. In addition, the population were buying very few farm implements, even of the simplest kind, for they had not the money to pay the excessively high deposits required by the State or co-operative stores.[30] In this sector at least there was a state of 'relative overproduction', for the stores were overflowing with implements. . . .

As with many other projects for agricultural aid, the major decisions and the decrees relating to these problems remained mainly on paper.[31] The relatively small sums voted at this period for the co-operative movement and for rural credits were partly swal-lowed up by the local administrations, and for the rest found their way into the hands of a minority of the better-off peasants.[32] The amount allocated for aid in this way was in any case negligible, compared with what was actually needed, and the régime's efforts fell far short of what was called for in the circumstances.

Nor was it apparent how the peasants were to be taught to im-prove yields. In 1927, there were only 18,500 agronomists,[33] a mere drop in the ocean as far as the countryside was concerned. The local administrations in the rural areas were ill-adapted to serve the needs of agricultural production and an agricultural society. The agricultural experts and the members of the Politburo were only too well aware of this: '. . . the weakness of the local Party and co-operative organizations, and their inability to respond to the need to rehabilitate agriculture, and to mobilize the mass of middle and poor peasants to this end' [34] were no secret. Whatever action the local authorities were called upon to take, the manner in which it was implemented was always the same; initial delaying tactics were followed by a burst of activity aimed at executing the given orders, there was incompetence and lack of understanding, and a tendency on the part of the 'men on the spot' to repair their own errors by putting administrative pressure on the peasants. The same pattern was apparent when it came to the essentially complex task of providing basic instruction in the rudiments of agronomy for peasants who were frequently illiterate.

We have already discussed the slowness, not to say the failure, of the campaign against illiteracy. In this domain, also, the methods used were all too often those of the notorious *goloe administrirovanie*, in other words barefaced coercion. The effects of this we already know.[35] Since its inception, the Soviet régime had alternated between the only two courses known to it—*samotek* or drift, and shock tactics, with all the concomitants of violence that the latter implied.

Members of the Politburo who often spoke of the incompetence of the local authorities were inclined to blame the men on the spot for the 'colossal number of blunders and the inefficiency'[36] which had poisoned relations with the peasantry, among other things in the matter of price policy; but these failures were in fact attributable to the men at the top.

In 1927, Kalinin noted bitterly[37] that work in the villages was utterly neglected (*zabroshenny*). His subsequent criticisms on the same theme reveal what had for long been a significant feature of the workings of Soviet administration and Soviet policy in the countryside: press and propaganda statements laid great stress on co-operation, and played down problems such as taxation. But in the villages, the situation was reversed. The efforts of the local organizations were geared mainly to the task of tax collection, and very little was done to promote co-operation.[38]

It was understandable that the local authorities, who received little practical guidance from Moscow, should function along the usual bureaucratic lines and concentrate on routine administrative tasks such as taxation, or population statistics or police matters, without seeking or indeed being able to involve themselves more deeply in questions which in fact required clear directives from the centre.

However, the centre itself seemed to be acting more or less in the same way: it dealt with its day-to-day problems as best it could, and did little to forestall or to check harmful tendencies, and to foster those elements in the situation which could have been of positive advantage. It was clear that the centre had no long-term policy. Nothing was done to encourage the so-called 'State co-operative' sector, which could have provided a social basis and an assured source for agricultural production, and by 1926–7 this sector was in fact on the decline. As one Soviet writer says: ". . . Unlike our industrial sector, the State co-operative sector [i.e. in agriculture.— M.L.] far from showing a more rapid growth than the private sector, in the main stagnated and sometimes even declined.'[39]

At the Fifteenth Party Congress, Stalin stated that 'we have achieved terribly little' in the field of co-operative production.[40] As late as 1927, official decisions and reports show very little concern with what was happening in these sectors. Sometimes, major policy decisions on the economy would contain no more than a few conventional phrases about the kolkhozes and the sovkhozes.[41] The funds allocated to this sector are a direct reflection of the amount of attention paid to them: 32·4 million roubles for the sovkhozes (which were still struggling and permanently in debt) and 18 million roubles for the kolkhozes in 1927.[42]

As an instance of the lack of interest shown in collectivization in the USSR during the NEP period, one present-day author quotes a young woman who had graduated from the 'Timiryazev' Agricultural Academy, and who said at the beginning of 1928: 'During my course of study, I heard the word collectivization mentioned perhaps twice.' [43]

While the régime's strongholds in the countryside were undermanned, the agricultural co-operative sector, making up roughly only one third of the total households, and the other elements in the villages, remained outside the régime's sphere of influence, and were developing along lines which would inevitably prove dangerous.

A Soviet survey of rural conditions in the Saratov province in 1927, which was published in 1929, stressed the lack of impact which Soviet economic policy had had in this region: 'Our researches, covering the year 1926–7, reveal that, in that part of the Saratov province which was under study, the effect of the *direct* intervention of State economic policy on the class stratification of the Soviet village is very limited.'

The author went on to state that 'the kulaks' were impervious to the influence of measures taken by the government to protect the batraks, and that they were profiting much more than the other peasants from the reserves of land held by the State. Their incomes were very little affected by taxation and 'the bulk of the credits furnished by the State find their way into the hands of the village capitalists'.[44]

It is not surprising that socio-economic policy had so little impact on the problem of class differentiation in the villages, and this failure was soon to be officially admitted by Stalin.[45] But it must not be assumed that the rural economy was unaffected by economic policy, or that it failed to react to it. On the contrary, it has been shown that the peasant was very sensitive to government action, particularly on prices and reserves, and reacted immediately to such measures. This emerges very clearly when one looks at Soviet price policy. In this domain, the régime had no idea where it was going, the decisions it took lacked coherence and served only to disrupt agricultural production.

At the Fifteenth Party Congress, Molotov spoke of scandals in prices policy, for which 'someone' was to blame. At the same Congress, Kaminsky referred to the 'fluctuations and uncertainties in the prices for agricultural production which have been a feature of our attempts at price regulation during the past two years . . .'.[46] As an example of the incoherencies in price policy, he instanced the fact that, between 1925 and 1927, the authorities had, on no fewer than five occasions (!) announced changes in the prices for flax, varying from slight increases to a sharp decrease. The peasants did not take long to react: they sowed less flax, and increased production of woven cloth for domestic use.[47] A further example is provided by the policy on grain prices. These were consistently kept at a low level compared with prices for other crops, and for livestock products [48] and the peasant, deprived of any incentive to produce grain crops, went over to industrial crops whenever this was possible. These incessant changes in policy, which operated in an arbitrary manner, sometimes occurring in the middle of the season, disrupted agricultural production at every turn, and had a particularly damaging effect on grain production. The response to price fluctuations was rapidly reflected in sowings, and production varied, therefore, from year to year. In 1926, following on changes in prices, there was a reduction in sowings of industrial crops, and an increase in the areas turned over to grain, and to livestock production. The following year, prices again changed, and this time there was a drop in the grain sowings, and an increase in industrial crops. The year 1928 brought still more changes in prices, the result being a drop in livestock production, a slight increase in the sowing of grain, and a marked increase in the cultivation of industrial crops. However, in 1929 procurements of industrial crops were not successful, because these had been offset by a rise in the price for grain.[49] The same pattern is apparent in the indices of production.[50] Molotov was justified, therefore, when he spoke of 'colossal blunders'.[51]

Not surprisingly, the effect of this policy was further to aggravate the existing weakness of the *tovarnost* (marketable production) which was already a source of such anxiety. Officially, there was a tendency to attribute this weakness solely to the piecemeal nature of agricultural production, but as Kaminsky very shrewdly observed at the Congress 'the instability in the *tovarnost* . . . is very greatly influenced by price policy'.[52] Certain other writers were also of the same opinion.[53] Many authors drew attention to one important factor which partly explains the drop in the production of grain, and also in the proportion of marketed produce and the level of reserves. They pointed out that prices paid for procurements by the government did not even cover the costs of production. As Strumilin observed—'Earlier prices did not even guarantee the necessary minimum of profitability for agricultural produce.' [He was referring to prices up to the middle of 1928.—M.L.] [54]

In such circumstances, a further decline in the proportion of marketed produce was inevitable. And yet there was still more marketable grain than the government could lay its hands on. Some 57–71% of the available supplies reached the government by way of procurements, the rest passed through the hands of the private middlemen. Indeed, as compared with industrial crops, where the position was much better, the 'uneconomic' prices paid by the government, and the inevitable rise in grain prices on the private market, meant that the role of the private trader was further strengthened, and by 1928–9 the proportion contributed to the *zagotovki* by this sector had risen to 23%, as against 14% in 1926–7. [55]

In economic terms, this leakage of grain on to the free market was completely understandable. Another factor which continued to be of major importance was the 'scissors' between the prices paid by the State to the producer, and the retail prices for industrial products. [56] The need to finance industry was one of the causes of the low prices paid to the peasants, but this in itself in no way explained the 'blunders'. At all events, the effect of the poor prices paid by the government for its grain was further intensified by the extremely high prices for industrial products, which hit hardest at the large stratum of poor and middle peasants; and lastly, there was the famine of industrial products, the *tovarny golod*, an expressive term which brought to mind the other kind of famine which was so dreaded in the Russian countryside. All these factors inevitably played a part in the declining *tovarnost*, by encouraging the peasants to keep their grain for themselves and their animals.

These were the essential facts of production, and of social and economic policy in the countryside, underlying the hidden forces which for several years had been operating underground—as the *Platform* said [57]—until they suddenly and dramatically came to the surface. The *Platform* was referring in this context to the general social crisis, but the description might equally apply to the economic crisis which developed with apparent suddenness at the beginning of 1928, but which had in fact been building up for several years.

Under pressure from the price relationships, the peasants were producing and selling more raw materials and livestock products, but much less grain and feeding-stuffs. Despite the drop in sales of these important products, there was a marked increase in peasant incomes. Between January 1927 and January 1928, for example, peasant incomes from the sale of grain went down by 100 million roubles whereas their earnings from sales of other products doubled.[58] It has also been calculated that the rise in peasant incomes owed something, in addition, to increased State expenditure on industrialization, since many peasants were in the habit of taking temporary work in the towns, in forestry or elsewhere, particularly in the winter months (indeed, some member of the household was always going off to the town).

The peasants found themselves with greatly increased purchasing power, but with fewer goods on which to spend their money. Goods were dear, and often scarce and of very poor quality. By the middle of 1928, after the government had made an effort to improve the supply of consumers' goods to the villages, it was calculated by the departments concerned that the shortfall in supplies, as compared with demand, was 14% in the case of cotton cloth, 34% for wool cloth, 40% for iron ware (for agricultural needs), 53% for sunflower oil, and 25% for sugar. . . .[59]

The peasants had sufficient money to pay their taxes, and little incentive to produce grain for the market; they preferred to build up their stocks of grain and feeding-stuffs. Kulaks, serednyaks and even bednyaks [60] all found it to their advantage to hoard their grain, and whenever they could do so they waited for prices to rise, or for an opportunity to sell to private traders. Consequently, there was a rise in grain prices on the free market and, above all, a partial breakdown in the supply chain between country and town. The peasant, who could 'revert with astonishing ease to the primitive forms of economy' [61] was dissociating himself from the State sector, at least so far as grain was concerned; he was no longer willing to sell to the State, was less responsive to economic incentives, and had less interest in the improvement of his farm. In particular, the better-off peasant, who was a producer and a supplier of some importance, and who had been counted upon to remedy the situation, in fact became hostile to the idea of trading with the State, and set about accumulating grain (which he was better able to do than the rest of the peasantry) in order to sell it to the private trader (*chastnik*) or sometimes simply 'in order to teach the communists a lesson'.

This breakdown virtually assumed the proportions of a total disruption of the country's economic existence. In addition to the shortage of industrial products facing the peasants, the towns and the agricultural regions which were not grain producers were faced with a shortage of grain. This was the prelude to the 'procurement crisis' which overtook the country at the beginning of 1928, and to

185

a food crisis which was to last for several years; it also foreshadowed the dreaded razmychka, *the break with the peasantry, fear of which had been an important factor in Soviet policy from the very beginning.*

Stalin was full of confidence. At the end of October 1927, he stressed the virtues of his policy in the Central Committee, claiming that it had led to

'the pacification of the villages, and improvement in relations with the broad mass of the peasantry, and the creation of conditions in which the *bednota* could be organized as an independent political force, the kulaks would be isolated, and the millions of individual peasant strips could gradually make the transition to State and co-operative forms of production.'

This was all due, Stalin claimed, to the policy adopted by the Four-teenth Party Congress, which had wisely refused to heed the ill-conceived recommendations of the opposition, whose policy was 'in essence, one of re-enacting the Civil War in the countryside'.[62] This was, indeed, more or less what was to happen two months later, though not, of course, as a result of the policy allegedly put forward by the opposition. Stalin was, naturally, making a political speech, and obviously tended to exaggerate the positive results of his policy, but in fact he had virtually no suspicion of what was about to happen. Until October, there was a deceptive air of success about the course of the procurements campaign, but in October a downward trend set in, and by November this had become disastrous.[63]

The country was on the verge of a crisis, the opposition were sounding the alarm, but the General Secretary's reaction was one of blissful and, for the most part, perfectly genuine optimism. His opponents said that he and his supporters were leading the country in the dark. They were not far wrong.[64]

4. *The Shadow of Dual Power* (Dvoevlastie)

The various factions within the Party all realized, with varying degrees of anxiety, that acceptance of NEP left the way clear for capitalist forces which would prove hostile to the régime. There was an element of the sorcerer's apprentice in the use of capitalism as a means of consolidating Soviet power, and although this had been a fundamental tenet of Lenin's policy, and was for some ten years to prove a salutary experience for the régime, there were many who felt that it was playing with fire, and that NEP, unless properly controlled, might well prove fatal for the revolution in the long run. Apart from the opposition on the left-wing of the Party, who constantly urged that 'a gradual socialist offensive' should be re-opened 'within the framework of NEP' before it was too late, it would seem that Lenin himself was already aware of the long-term vulnerability of NEP, for he admitted that the downfall of the Soviet régime could be brought about by a failure of the alliance between the proletariat and the peasantry. 'But,' he said, 'I hope that this day will never come,' and, in order not to sow the seeds of doubt, he added: 'it would be a very unlikely event.' [65]

But Lenin, already ailing, and reflecting upon the situation of the 'machine' which travels 'in a totally different direction from that imagined by the man at the steering-wheel . . .' [66] left to the delegates at the forthcoming Party Congress the fruit of his reflections and his misgivings about the 'distant future'.

NEP in fact offered ample scope for the development of a capitalist sector controlling numerous enterprises, which were for the most part small or medium-scale in size, and which functioned in the towns, mainly in branches of the consumer goods industry; in addition, an improvement in the circumstances of some of the better-off peasants had produced a fair number of kulaks, who wielded real power in the countryside. The strength of this private sector lay mainly in the part which they played in trade, especially in retail trade, not only in the towns but even more so in the villages. There were two factors which consistently favoured the private trader; one was the inadequacy of the state and co-operative trading organs, and the other, even more important, was the shortage of manufactured goods and, later, the shortage of food which soon followed in the wake of the procurements crisis.

Official estimates put the private sector's share in retail trade at something between one quarter and one third.[67] But in the rural areas, during the same year, almost half of the products reaching the peasants—and probably more—were provided by private traders, allowing for the fact that consumers' co-operatives accounted for only 52% of households, according to the official figures, which were still optimistic.[68]

According to the information given by Stalin and Molotov at the Fifteenth Party Congress, the private sector in 1926–7 was responsible for 5·1% of wholesale trade, 32·6% of retail trade, and for a very large share, some 23% in fact, of industrial production. The private trader also played a very important part in grain procurements, his share of the total being sometimes as much as one quarter, and in addition his influence often extended beyond those activities covered by the official figures. One paper from the Central Committee claimed that the private sector was growing (though it was said that this was by reference to overall figures only, and that its share of the total, in comparison with that of the state sector, was in fact decreasing). In the textile and leather industries, new millionaires were emerging.[69]

Nevertheless, the official statistics do not give a complete picture of the strength and the true role of the private sector. The co-operative and industrial organizations also suffered from the shortages, and they too were imbued with the 'NEP spirit'; for this reason, they frequently collaborated with the 'Nepmen', and always encouraged speculation, particularly at times of crisis in the supply situation, even if they did not indulge in it on their own account. Such transactions naturally did not appear in the statistics.

As a result of its role in branches of the economy which, in terms of economic policy, were regarded as being of secondary importance only, but which took on key significance in conditions of scarcity, the private sector acquired considerable influence, and sufficient 'purchasing power' to corrupt not only individual officials but entire administrations.

The Left, alarmed at the growth of these forces, violently denounced the Party leadership who had encouraged 'the Nepmen, the kulaks and the bureaucrats', thus inviting 'pressure from hostile elements'.[70] Meanwhile, the proletariat, who were by definition in the seat of power, were steadily losing ground, their standard of living had not improved, and their socialist consciousness was being increasingly blunted.

During the NEP period, the influence exerted on large sections of the Soviet state apparatus, and of the Party itself, by the 'Nepman and the kulak', and by the intellectual (whether 'bourgeois' by origin or inclination, or simply non-socialist) was a very real one. It was a source of anxiety and misgiving to the Party activists, particularly as it was accompanied by a widespread bureaucratization of both State [71] and Party, and a growing tendency for power to be concentrated in the factory administration, while the unions were silenced and the workers lapsed into indifference. At the same time, the Party was undergoing a change, and power was being wielded by the men at the summit of the administrative pyramid, who stifled all opposition and individual initiative. The Left had made a penetrating analysis of these tendencies, and it did everything in its power to combat them, but even the Left did not fully comprehend that what was taking shape in the USSR was a new political régime, which would later be seen as totalitarian in character.

The struggle with the opposition drove the Politburo to harden its attitude, and to strengthen its system of controls and administrative organs until they became a dominant feature of the situation; what emerged was one of the most powerful and all-pervasive bureaucratic machines of modern times. Those revolutionaries who still clung to their ideals and their illusions regarded it, at the time, as a 'bureaucratic deviation' in a State which was still described as a 'workers' State'. However, two elements in this workers' State were increasingly coming to the fore: '(1) a privileged class of administrators whose numbers had grown out of all proportion, and were absorbing a very large part of the surplus value; and (2) a growing bourgeoisie which, thanks to its trading activities and the existing price disparities, was acquiring part of the surplus value generated by State industry.' [72]

The most remarkable document on the changing character of the State which had been born in October 1917, on a wave of enthusiasm and Utopian dreams of social equality, is undoubtedly Rakovsky's *Letter to Valentinov*.[73] Rakovsky writes with disillusioned clarity, drawing frequent parallels with the policy and the downfall of the Jacobins; he begins by outlining the very facts about which the Left had been expressing alarm for several years; firstly, there was 'the terrible decline in the militant spirit of the toiling masses, and their growing indifference to the fate of the dictatorship of the proletariat and the Soviet State'.[74] And again: 'The working class and the Party are no longer what they were ten years ago; I am not exaggerating when I say that the activist of 1917 would find nothing in common with his 1928 counterpart.'[75]

In fact, since the seizure of power, processes had been at work which, in one sense, suggested a parallel with the French Revolution. A political reaction which had set in before Thermidor 'was characterized by the fact that power began to be vested in an increasingly smaller number of citizens. Little by little, . . . the mass of the people were excluded from the government of the country'.[76]

The same sociological process had been at work in Russia, in that the class which had seized power had handed over the functions of government to a few of its members; it was difficult to see how this process could be reversed, although Rakovsky believed that this might still be possible. 'This is how bureaucracies are born.' [77] Once this small group had become the executive organ of power, it was influenced by a number of factors which combined to produce the 'occupational hazard of power', whereby the bureaucracy increasingly became a class apart, isolated from the masses, enormously privileged and enjoying a standard of living such that its members were soon being described as 'satraps', and the 'new aristocracy'. Under the influence of the new division of functions, and of the 'car-harem syndrome' [78] the working class split up, and the new privileged clique of bureaucrats, avid in the exercise of its power and its privileges, frequently became a prey to corruption itself, and a source of corruption in others.

So far, says Rakovsky, 'not enough has been said about the part played by the bureaucracies of the soviets, the Party and the Soviet State' [bureaucracies reinforced by deserters from other classes, and by their influence.—M.L.] [79]

As in France at the time of the Revolution, the factors which contributed towards the rise of a class of bureaucrats cut off from the people were not only the material advantages enjoyed by those in control, but also the silencing of the left-wing opposition, and the gradual replacement of the principle of election by the principle of nomination.[80]

Rakovsky saw that the country had already gone some way in this direction, and that the trend could only be reversed by a radical change in methods of administration. The Party leadership ought to have done their duty, which was 'to preserve the Party and the working class from the corrupting influence of privilege and favouritism and the tolerance of abuses, which are the dangers inherent in power . . .' and to preserve them, likewise, from the effects of NEP, and to set up a new administration. Thus, Rakovsky foresaw and condemned the evils of the 'cult of personality', with a perspicacity which was amply demonstrated thirty years later. 'It must be fully and frankly admitted, for all to hear, that the Party apparatus has not fulfilled this task. Faced with the dual obligation of preservation and education, it has proved itself to be utterly incompetent, it is bankrupt, and insolvent'. And he goes on to say pessimistically, 'I am convinced that the present bureaucracies of the Party and the Soviets will continue, with the same degree of success, to feed their festering sores. . . .' [81]

The activists on the Left feared that, the more the régime became bureaucratized, the more the administration would be cut off from the masses, and the more susceptible it would be to the influence of the new NEP bourgeoisie. In this sense, 'Thermidor' was already knocking at the door. The fears of the Left are readily explained in terms of the atmosphere prevailing during the latter stages of NEP, particularly in 1928, when the country was the scene of endless cases of corruption, in which senior officials in the soviet and Party administrations, frequently at *oblast* level, were found to be involved with the business men. The rank and file of the Party knew what was happening, but were too frightened to do anything but hold their tongues.[82] At this point, the Left did not foresee exactly how the Soviet régime would develop, or what form the Soviet 'Thermidor' would take. Trotsky, writing from his exile in Alma Ata in 1928, had only a presentiment, though it showed insight. He said— 'The idea of a bureaucratic superman is at the root of the present usurpation of power (in isolated instances); it is also unconsciously paving the way for a possible usurpation on a widespread and systematic scale.' [83]

However, the Left had no intention of creating panic by exaggerating these dangers. Their aim was simply to keep a watchful eye on forces harmful to the régime, and, above all, to pursue a consciously socialist policy designed not to eliminate these forces but to keep them in check. NEP was still indispensable, and so therefore were the Nepmen and the kulaks. 'These forces cannot be eliminated either by administrative measures or by straightforward economic pressure.' Such forces would persist; what was needed was a 'clear policy' and a policy of industrialization which would prevent them from realizing the dualism of power which they sought.[84]

The ideas of the Left, the weaknesses and dangers to which they drew attention, are not only important in themselves, as being the ideas of a defeated group which should, in the interests of historical accuracy, be taken into account. There is more to it than that; some of these ideas were, before many months had elapsed, to become part of the official body of opinion [85] and to be embraced by Stalin himself.

Indeed, Stalin came to regard these dangers in an even graver light than the Left had done. With the procurement crisis of 1928, and the process of 'naturalization' which was visibly developing in the peasant economy, events already foreshadowed the dreaded *smychka* between the peasantry and the increasingly powerful forces of the 'Nepman, the kulak and the bureaucrat' (the expression which, since Trotsky's exile, the leadership had itself adopted).

Thus, the régime found itself up against unforeseen difficulties, and the leadership wasted time. They failed to make provision for the future by taking measures which would have eased the transition to a further stage in development.[86]

The Left deserves the credit for having protested at the lack of foresight shown by the leadership. The result of these shortcomings was that NEP ran into a crisis; as one observer put it, NEP was 'foundering',[87] and the leaders were caught unawares. Opinions were divided as to the nature of the situation and the measures which should be taken to deal with it; neither the exiled Left, nor those of the Right-wing who were still in power, wished to make an end of NEP. The Left was in favour of industrialization while retaining a market economy, and believed that a 'mixed economy' of this type could still be made to work. Bukharin held that the crisis could be cured by the use of purely 'NEP' measures. But Stalin, who held the real reins of power, had a different view of the situation. In his estimation, the dangers of *dvoevlastie* were more real than they had appeared to the Left, who had certainly drawn attention to them long before he had, but in terms which suggested that the threat, although it existed, could easily be averted. Stalin soon ceased to believe that the indirect and complex methods of NEP could provide a workable solution to the problem of controlling a multitude of small farms. In his view, the *muzhik* was simply the raw material for a never-ending series of recruits to the anti-Soviet alliance of Nepmen, kulaks, intellectuals and corrupt bureaucrats. Consequently, a new policy must be found, one which was in keeping with his own personality, and the nature of his régime. The method which was finally adopted involved the use of 'sweeping measures', and the strengthening of the most important lever of political power which the régime had, namely bureaucracy and the bureaucratic apparatus.

Before very long, it was resolved that the existing structures must at all costs be changed. It took some time, however, before the appropriate means of implementing this decision were found.

Notes and References

1. *Postroenie fundamenta sotsialisticheskoi ekonomiki v SSSR 1926–32*, pp. 258–9.

2. Rykov, *16-taya Konferentsiya VKP(b)*, stenogramme, pp. 10–11. These figures were, in any case, over-optimistic. At the Plenum of November 1928 the sown area was said to be 90·1% of what it had been before the war. The percentages for the harvest and marketable grain were only 80% and 56% of pre-war, respectively. See *KPSS v Rezolyutsiyakh*, Vol. II, p. 527.

3. Konyukhov, *op. cit.* (see Ch. 3, Note 41), pp. 11–12. Kurbatov in *NAF*, 1929, No. 5, gives the following figures: North Caucasus—63·7%; Lower Volga—92·9%; Ukraine—83·3% Urals —94·1%; Kazakhstan—82·8% (compared with pre-war). The only exception was Siberia, where the sown area was 16·7% greater than before the war.

4. Konyukhov, *op. cit.*, p. 59.

5. Quoted from Zaleski, *Planification de la croissance et fluctuations économiques en URSS*. (Paris, 1962), p. 350.

6. Bolshakov, *op. cit.* (see Ch. 1, Note 5), pp. 8–9.

7. *Otvechat iz potolka*, a Russian expression meaning 'to answer anything at all'.

8. *NAF*, 1928, No. 1, pp. 153–5.

9. Kurbatov, *NAF*, 1929, No. 5.

10. Volf, *Planovoe Khozyaistvo*, 1929, No. 2, p. 99. The following quotation is from p. 100.

11. According to the Central Archives of the Party. Quoted by Konyukhov, *op. cit.*, p. 43.

12. Kritsman, chief editor of *Na Agrarnom Fronte* (and soon to be dismissed). *NAF*, 1930, No. 6, p. 8.

13. Until this time, there had been a spectacular increase in the production of industrial crops. It was thanks to this improvement, together with the progress made in livestock-breeding, that the so-called period of 'recovery' could be said to have been completed. Overall agricultural production had indeed regained its pre-war level, but this was not true in the case of sown areas, or the grain harvest.

14. On Frumkin, member of the Central Committee, and his opinions, see Ch. 12.

15. *Postroenie fundamenta . . .* (see Note 1) pp. 258–9. It was claimed that grain yields were slightly higher than pre-war (though the authors suggest that the increase was still not sufficiently marked).

16. The number of draught animals never regained the earlier level. The increase was mainly in the number of cows. For every 100 cows in 1923 there were 114·3 in 1928–9, but for every 100 horses in 1923, only 90·1 in 1928–9. There were also more pigs and small livestock than before the war. See Kurbatov, *NAF*, 1929, No. 5. The shortage of horses made it difficult to increase the sown areas.

17. These are Nemchinov's figures, quoted by Stalin in *Sochineniya*, Vol. XI, pp. 82, 83, 85.

18. For the last figure, see Hubbard, *op. cit.* (see Ch. 1, Note 23), p. 112. We should add that, at the Plenum of November 1928 there was said to have been a reduction in sown areas over the preceding two years. See *KPSS v Rezolyutsiyakh*, Vol. II, p. 528.

19. Stalin, *Sochineniya*, Vol. XI, p. 85; *Istoriya narodnogo khozyaistva SSSR* (Moscow, 1960), p. 527.

20. Konyukhov, *op. cit.*, p. 72.

21. Lvov, *NAF*, 1928, No. 9.

22. Mikoyan was the Commissar for Trade. The figures are from his article in *Bolshevik*, 1929, No. 15, p. 16. It should be noted that different sources give different figures, which lend themselves to varying interpretations. Those given refer to 'centralized' procurements; the total is increased slightly if the 'decentralized' procurements, i.e. those made by government agencies but destined for local consumption, are added.

23. Stalin, *Sochineniya*, Vol. XI, p. 82 passim: a speech made in May 1928.

24. Stalin, in a speech delivered to the Plenum of July 1928 stated that the country did not possess the reserves which would be essential in the event of war or famine (the speech was not published at

the time). *Sochineniya*, Vol. XI, pp. 173, 176–7. Bukharin in his 'Notes of an Economist' in *Pravda* September 30, 1928, declared that there were no reserves of any kind, either in the form of currency, gold, merchandise or grain.

25. Mudrik, 'K voprosu o prirode sovremennykh rynochnykh zatrudnenii', *Bolshevik*, 1929, No. 7, p. 10, and Konyukhov, *op. cit.*, p. 49.

26. According to Kalinin 550,000 large hides and 16,000 tons of wool had been imported in 1927, and in 1928 1,400,000 hides and the same quantity of wool. *5-ty S'ezd Sovetov*, stenogramme, Bull. No. 15, pp. 1–2.

27. Exports reached a level of almost two million tons in 1925–6 and in 1926–7. In 1927–8 344,000 tons of wheat were exported. (!) These figures are from Hubbard, *op. cit.*, p. 90. Pre-war exports exceeded eleven million tons.

28. This was widely discussed, for example by Yakovlev in *Pravda*, October 28, 1928, and by Stalin, Kalinin and Molotov. In 1928 a special decree of the *TsIK* expressed the hope that the fertility of the soil could be increased by 35% in five years thanks to such 'small improvements'. *Kollektivizatsiya selskogo khozyaistva*, December 15, 1928, doc. No. 19.

29. An article by Gaister and Levin, *Bolshevik*, 1928, No. 9–10, p. 84.

30. Kurbatov, *NAF*, 1929, No. 5, p. 87.

31. Lyashchenko, in *Istoriya narodnogo khozyaistva*, Vol. III, p. 237, states that these elementary improvements are 'still far from widespread'.

32. Many Soviet sources confirm that it was the richest peasants, and not the masses, who derived most benefit from credits. Lyashchenko, *op. cit.*, p. 39; Sulkovsky, *NAF*, December 1930, p. 82.

33. Lyashchenko, *op. cit.*, p. 249.

34. Quoted by Tsylko, *NAF*, 1929, No. 8, p. 7. Tsylko was shortly to be appointed deputy-Commissar for Agriculture.

35. There is an abundance of examples and texts to illustrate this, e.g. Tsylko, *NAF*, 1929, No. 8, p. 8.

36. Molotov, *15-ty S'ezd VKP(b)*, stenogramme, pp. 1063, 1095.

37. Kalinin, *ibid*, p. 1102.

38. Kalinin, *16-taya Konferentsiya VKP(b)*, stenogramme, p. 57.

39. Kritsman, *NAF*, 1930, No. 6, p. 13. For these figures see p. 15.

40. Stalin, *15-ty S'ezd VKP(b)*, stenogramme, p. 57.

41. See, for example, the theses prepared by Kalinin for the Fourth Congress of Soviets (quoted by Yakovlev, *NAF*, 1927, No.

4); the decisions adopted by this Congress were in the 'classic' NEP spirit. See *Istoriya kolkhoznogo prava*, doc. No. 73.

42. Kurbatov, *NAF*, 1929, No. 5, p. 76. These investments are called *kapitalnoe vlozhenie*.

43. Borisov, *Podgotovka proizvodstvennykh kadrov selskogo khozyaistva SSSR v rekonstruktivny period*. (Moscow/Leningrad, 1960), p. 238.

44. Sulkovsky. The quotation from his book is in *NAF*, December 1930, p. 182. The book itself, which we have not been able to trace, contained a preface by Kritsman and was probably published by the Communist Academy.

45. Stalin, report to the *15-ty S'ezd VKP(b)*, stenogramme, pp. 50–60.

46. Kaminsky, *ibid*, p. 1217.

47. *ibid*.

48. Konyukhov; *op. cit.*, p. 60 gives the price indices. Grain prices fell from 111 in 1925–6 to 89 in 1926–7, whereas the prices of industrial crops rose from 116 to 146 and the prices of livestock products from 166 to 178. Yakovtsevsky, *op. cit.* (see Ch. 5, Note 3), p. 176 gives the following grain prices in roubles per pood: 1913—0·79; 1923–4—1·05; 1925–6—1·04; 1926–7—0·92. The price given by Hubbard is not, therefore, per quintal. (See Note 54 below.)

49. Kritsman, *NAF*, 1929, No. 6, p. 8. Also Mikoyan, *15-ty S'ezd VKP(b)*, stenogramme, pp. 977–8; Kurbatov, *NAF*, 1929, No. 5, p. 84.

50. While not exclusively responsible for these fluctuations, prices policy was nevertheless the main contributory factor.

51. *15-ty S'ezd VKP(b)*, stenogramme, p. 1005.

52. Kaminsky, *ibid*, p. 1217.

53. Konyukhov, *op. cit.*, p. 43.

54. Strumilin, *Planovoe Khozyaistvo*, 1929, No. 3; Lyashchenko, *op. cit.*, p. 244; Hubbard, *op. cit.*, gives the price paid by the government for rye in 1927 as 4·41 roubles per quintal, whereas the cost was 4·73.

55. Lyashchenko, *op. cit.*, pp, 244, 257, 258.

56. Economists of the Left estimated that the peasant was obtaining 125% of pre-war grain prices for his produce, whereas he was paying 220% of pre-war prices for manufactured goods. Thus it would appear that in 1926–7 the peasantry were mulcted to the tune of one billion roubles. See the *Platform*, in *Les Bolcheviks contre Staline*, p. 90.

57. *ibid*, p. 89.

58. This income was 369·7 millions for grain at the beginning of

1927 and 272·5 millions in early 1928, whereas for raw materials and livestock products it was 419 millions in January 1928 compared with 273 millions the previous year. *TsSU* figures are given by Milyutin in an article on procurements in *NAF*, 1928, No. 9. See also an article on the same subject by Lvov in *NAF*, 1928, No. 9, pp. 56–8.

59. Lvov, *ibid*. Lvov was a specialist working in the Commissariat of Trade. See also Mikoyan, *15-ty S'ezd VKP(b)*, stenogramme, p. 976.

60. Lvov, *ibid*, *passim*, and Hubbard, *op. cit.*, pp. 97–8.

61. Kaminsky, *15-ty S'ezd VKP(b)*, stenogramme, p. 1217.

62. Stalin, speech delivered on October 25, 1927, *Sochineniya*, Vol. X, pp. 196–7.

63. Mikoyan, *15-ty S'ezd VKP(b)*, stenogramme, p. 976.

64. The *Platform* in *Les Bolcheviks contre Staline*, p. 91.

65. Lenin's 'testament', dictated on December 25, 1922. *Sochineniya*, Vol. XXXIII, p. 250.

66. Lenin, speech to the *11-ty S'ezd VKP(b)*, *Sochineniya*, Vol. XXXIII, p. 250.

67. Lyashchenko, *op. cit.*, p. 259.

68. Trifonov, *op. cit.* (see Ch. 2, Note 9), pp. 131–8.

69. Stalin, *15-ty S'ezd VKP(b)*, stenogramme, pp. 52–3, 57, 60; Molotov, *ibid*, p. 1064; *KPSS v Rezolyutsiyakh*, Vol. II, pp. 3, 27.

70. The first part of the *Platform* in *Les Bolcheviks contre Staline*. The quotation is on p. 88.

71. Trotsky's letter to the Comintern Congress is contained in *The Third International after Lenin* (see Ch. 6, Note 29), p. 243. He writes:

'The most general, the most striking, and at the same time the most dangerous feature of the last five years has been the gradual and ever more rapid *growth* of *bureaucratization* and the arbitrary procedures which are associated with it, not only in the *VKP(b)* but also throughout the entire Comintern.'

This was written in exile in Alma-Ata in 1928.

72. *ibid*, p. 94.

73. This letter by Rakovsky, entitled 'The occupational hazards of power' is contained in *Les Bolcheviks contre Staline*, pp. 151–63.

74. *ibid*, p. 151.

75. *ibid*, p. 157.

76. *ibid*, p. 154.

77. *ibid*, p. 154.

78. An expression coined by the journalist Sosnovsky, referring

to the role of the automobile and of women in the creation of the new privileged class, and of its mentality.

79. Rakovsky, *op. cit.*, p. 159.

80. *ibid*, p. 155.

81. *ibid*, p. 162.

82. The press commented frequently on these *gnoiniki* and on the scandals reported in Smolensk, Artemovsk, Chita, Vladimirsk and Khersonsk. See also Trotsky, 'What now?', in *The Third International After Lenin* (see Ch. 6, Note 29), pp. 302–3.

83. Trotsky, *ibid*, p. 307.

84. The *Platform* in *Les Bolcheviks contre Staline*, pp. 88–90.

85. Editorial in *Pravda*, February 15, 1928.

86. Daniels, *op. cit.* (see Ch. 2, Note 3); p. 495.

87. Yugov, *Narodnoe Khozyaistvo Sovetskoi Rossii.* (Berlin, 1928), quoted by the author in his *Pyatiletka.* (Berlin, 1932), p. 132.

Chapter 8

THE AMBIGUOUS NATURE OF
THE FIFTEENTH PARTY CONGRESS

The Fifteenth Party Congress took place in December 1927, two years after the previous Congress. This was the first time in the history of the Party that such a delay had occurred, for the Party statutes laid down that Congress should meet every year.[1] It was also one of the first Congresses in which the discussions and decisions became a mere façade, in the sense that the real decisions were either taken elsewhere, were already in process of being implemented, or were still to be reached.

This Congress was later described as having been an epoch-making one, particularly in the domain of collectivization. The handbook *Istoriya KPSS* edited in 1962 says that this Congress 'went down in Party history as the *Congress of the collectivization* of agriculture and of the socialist offensive on all fronts'.[2] In fact, the Congress was less sure of its role than has been suggested. The greater part of its efforts and its discussions was taken up with the ritual liquidation of an opposition which had, for all practical purposes, already been eliminated some time previously. The leadership had poured most of its time and energy into the bitter factional struggle that had raged over the past two years, and this was reflected in the extreme and curiously disproportionate nature of the voting, which suggested that the opposition had been very weak; it was said that there were only 4,000 votes for the opposition, as against 724,000 for the majority.[3]

However, political feelings still ran so high that most of these decisions were dictated not so much by consideration of the real issues as by the desire to condemn the shortcomings of the opposition, and to endorse the views of the leadership.

This reaction might at first sight appear excessive, were it not for two important factors. The Party leadership were engaged in executing a manoeuvre which, despite the fact that the Congress was well-disciplined and the opposition had been completely silenced, was nevertheless a fairly complex one. This consisted of appropriating the essential elements in the opposition's programme, and presenting them as having been part of the leadership's own policy for a long time. In the second place, the Politburo, though well aware of the necessity of producing a new policy which would meet the country's urgent needs, still had nothing to offer but general formulae, and

198

these, moreover, were very differently interpreted by the different wings of the Central Committee and the Politburo, which had hitherto stood together against the Left, as well as by the rank and file activists.

The Congress had already been adjourned, in order to enable the Central Committee and the Central Supervisory Commission[4] to carry out the expulsion of Trotsky and Zinovev from the Party, so that they would not be present at the Congress. The texts which were to be ratified by Congress had been hurriedly prepared, the purpose being to have ready a document which would act as a counterpoise to the opposition's *Platform*,[5] and to present it to the country at least a month before the Congress, so as not to lose the confidence and support of the masses.

So long as any trace of an organized opposition survived, even if only in prison or exile, some attempt was still made to observe the formalities of democratic procedure within the Party, for there were many activists who had not yet forgotten the days of Lenin. But the documents which were produced in this instance bore all the marks of hasty improvization.

The theses which were prepared by the Central Committee in October for the Fifteenth Congress[6] embodied 'directives for the preparation of the Five-year Plan' and an outline of the policy to be pursued in the countryside. They stressed, firstly, the renewed prospects for a socialist offensive which had recently opened up. In this, the leadership were strongly influenced by their desire to counter the attacks of the Left, who had spoken up vigorously about the danger of a new 'Thermidor', and had accused them of 'encouraging the excessive growth of those elements who are trying to influence the development of our country along capitalist lines', 'weakening the position of the working class', and countenancing 'a workers' state with bureaucratic deviations'.[7] Since the leadership were extremely sensitive to accusations of this kind, every effort was made in the official documents to prove the contrary. Stress was now laid on the liquidation of capitalist elements in the villages and in the towns, and on the reinforcement of socialist 'strongholds'.[8] It was suggested that the foundation for these efforts had been laid by the régime's previous policy, the success of which had brought about a new situation, in which the socialist sector of the national economy would not only decide what the general direction of development should be, but would also put a check on private capital, and stimulate the agricultural producers by gradually transforming the character of their economy. It was also claimed that 'the ranks of the working class had grown, its contacts with the masses had increased, and the dictatorship of the proletariat had been further strengthened'.[9]

The anti-kulak and anti-Nepman slogans which recurred again and again in these directives, and in the speeches at the Party Congress, were presented as 'a continuing but *more* systematic and *more* intensified policy for the limitation of the kulak and the *chastnik*',[10] in order to underline the fact that the basic policy would remain the same, the only change being in the methods of implementing it. This is one example of the lack of coherence apparent in these documents, the authors of which were constantly torn between the desire to figure as the creators of a new major policy, and the need to pass off their previous policy as having been a consistently socialist one.[11]

Another factor which also contributed to the lack of coherence was the desire on the part of the leadership to avoid any clash with Right-wing minority opinions or susceptibilities, thus preserving the compromise which had enabled them to offer a united front to the Left opposition. Some vagueness was already apparent on the point mentioned above, with regard to the struggle against the capitalist elements. Opinions on this issue differed very considerably from group to group within the Party. Whereas the texts had spoken of *limitation*, the term used by Stalin and Molotov at the Congress had been a very different one, namely *liquidation*.[12] It had not been thought that the latter policy would be practicable, in the absence of the forces necessary to carry it out, but Molotov suggested that these forces were already available. A policy of limitation and a policy of liquidation were, of course, two very different things.

At this stage, it seemed as though a choice were being made, whereby the *chastnik* (the private entrepreneur) would merely be eased out as the state and co-operative sectors gradually improved.[13] But no such reservation was made in the text dealing with work in the countryside, although in this instance there was no mention of any sort of liquidation, but only of *increased limitation*. What is more, one passage stated that, despite the policy of limitation, the total of capitalists in the towns and villages would still continue to increase.[14]

Thus, the real import of these slogans varied according to the spokesman concerned. It was obvious that there were two schools of thought, both of them using more or less the same language, but whereas one was thinking in terms of *bringing pressure to bear* on the capitalist elements, *in order to suppress them*, the other aimed at *limiting and stripping* them, but allowing them to survive.

There was some ambiguity, too, on the question of the socialist offensive. The speeches had called uncompromisingly for the liquidation of capitalist elements, because 'the country was advancing rapidly towards socialism', but the resolutions spoke merely of a 'more rigorous attempt to oust them by economic measures'.[15]

An examination of the other subjects discussed at the Congress reveals the same contradictions: certain far-reaching recommendations are made, but when it comes to practical application, these are scaled down in tone and content.

An interesting illustration of this persistent ambiguity is provided by the directives on the Five-year Plan for industry and agriculture. From the economic point of view, the content of these directives was unimportant. The only reason for their appearance was that the planning organs[16] had so far been unable to produce a satisfactory draft. Five or six versions of the plan had already been prepared, but Rykov stated that all of them showed appreciable defects; they were 'statistical in character' and detached from economic realities, nor had the regional aspects of the plan been adequately worked out.[17]

This was why the only draft submitted to the delegates was that of the *VSNKh*, which was to serve purely as an example, while the Congress confined itself to recording, in its resolutions, the objectives which had been achieved, and those which were still to be implemented, the latter coming more or less within the category of pious hopes, since they represented the sum total of desirable objectives. Speaking of the decisions taken at the Fifteenth Congress, a present-day Polish economist has observed: '. . . in so far as politics is the art of choosing, these decisions cannot be regarded as a proper statement of policy intentions. They represented a call to launch an offensive, without the necessary decisions about the call-up of reserves, or about probable losses.'[18]

However, there were very clear indications of a desire to minimize the losses, and to bring about the changes as painlessly as possible. The documents in question contained so many injunctions about the need for caution, and so many warnings against excesses in the policy of industrialization, or over-zealous implementation of the changes planned for the countryside, that it may reasonably be assumed that they emanated mainly from the Right. The planners were enjoined not to lock up too much capital in long-term construction programmes, or projects which would not yield a fairly rapid return in terms of production; they were called upon to ensure that a proper balance was maintained between the production of heavy and light industry, between the costs of production and the total wages bill, and between the needs of the home and the export market, etc.[19] The accent was on heavy industry, which had become the 'centre of gravity' of industrialization, but it must not be forgotten that the rapid development of light industry could itself be beneficial to heavy industry. . . .[20]

Needless to say the entire plan, according to these resolutions, was only conceivable on the basis of an accompanying rise in wages and in peasant living standards; it was constantly stressed that such conditions were an essential prerequisite in any socialist policy of industrialization, despite the fact that the Left had been accused of demagogy and ignorance of the laws of economics when they put forward the same suggestions.[21]

This concern for the maintenance of economic equilibrium became the Right's main theme in the months that followed, and it had its counterpart in the adoption, by the future Bukharinists, of a pro-industrialization line, and acceptance of the need for a more radical policy in the countryside.[22] At this stage, they were prepared to put greater pressure on the kulak, and to take steps to intensify collectivization.

Rykov, whose function it was to report to Congress on the Five-year Plan, gave ample proof of this change in attitude. He accepted the principle of priority for industry and industrialization in the choice of main objectives in the country's economic policy, and he was also in agreement with the principle of priority for heavy industry, and the urgent need for development in this sector, even at the cost of sacrificing the income from light industry; he denounced men like Sokolnikov, who were unwilling to give priority to industry, and particularly to heavy industry.[23] At this point, Rykov accepted the proposition that priority for heavy industry would mean that 'for some time to come, we will have to make sacrifices. There is no other way out'.[24] Consequently he was obliged, however reluctantly, to agree to the *perekachka* of the resources of the peasantry for the benefit of heavy industry, an economic fact which had for long been dismissed as nonsense. Rykov now admitted that 'some degree of *perekatchka* (though naturally within certain limitations) is both inevitable and admissible, but only at the present stage in the country's economic development, and until such times as industry has achieved an adequate level of growth. . .'.[25] It should be noted that this was, in substance, little different from what Preobrazhensky had said.

However, so far as Rykov and his supporters were concerned, there was no question of carrying these principles to extremes. There was a continuing need for prudence and economic calculation in implementing the aims of industrialization, and planners and politicians must bear in mind the necessity of preserving the 'market equilibrium'. Several times in his report Rykov emphasized the gravity of the issues at stake, and the extent of the pitfalls lying in wait for the unwary. 'If the country's economic affairs are not run with great enough efficiency, these dangers, and certain other factors, may combine to upset the balance of the national economy, and give rise either to immediate and localized economic disorders, or to more general economic ills.' Later on, he disclosed that what was really weighing on his mind was the danger of a 'general crisis'.[26]

For Rykov, the vital question was accumulation, or rather one particular aspect of the problem: What burden were the peasants to bear in this connection? He knew that, by overstepping the mark here, the régime might well provoke a grave crisis. But whom did he suspect of wishing to advocate exactions on such a scale?

It is clear that Rykov's warnings were intended not for the opposition, who had already been handed over to the *GPU*, with Rykov's own approval, but for his own associates in the Central Committee and the Politburo; in fact, he was afraid that they might go even further than the now exiled Left. He must already have had some indication of this in his contacts with Stalin and Molotov within the Politburo.

Rykov and his supporters could see no future for the régime other than in the context of NEP, with its free market and its market economy, and with the continuing, though more carefully restricted, participation of the private sector of Nepmen, middlemen and kulaks. In his view, this was the only way in which the transition of the economy to a further phase in its development could be effected without, as he stressed, too many shocks or crises.

Many people believed that, given the state of the country as it then was, there were only two possible solutions, and that the choice lay between NEP, and a policy of violence against the peasantry, which would inevitably engender a social upheaval, the consequences of which would be unforeseeable. Rykov's choice was clear and unequivocal, but he had grounds for believing that Stalin and Molotov had other plans in mind.

The speeches of the two leaders were overloud in their criticisms of the private sector; Molotov was still proclaiming his faith in NEP, but his statements were highly ambiguous. He described NEP as a policy of 'concessions made to the middle peasant', which would continue as long as the latter preferred his private plot. He affirmed that this 'was, is and will continue to be our policy, for as long as small peasant producers exist'.[27] To all appearances, this was the light in which NEP was usually presented, for care was taken not to admit that the concessions involved the capitalist elements as well as the serednyaks. But in the case of Molotov, when he attacked a speech of Trotsky's in 1925, in which Trotsky had described these concessions for what they were, there were indications that his interpretation went beyond the simple need for care in the choice of terms.

Molotov, inveighing against Trotsky, says:

'Anyone who cannot see the difference between the concessions which, within certain limitations, we have made to the small peasant producer . . . and a policy of encouraging rural development by the use of 'capitalist methods', that is, methods which Marx so strikingly described as draining the life-blood from the peasant's heart and the brain-matter from his head, does not know the first thing about Marxism, and is in fact joining the ranks of the bourgeois ideologists'.[28]

For those who knew how to read the signs, the effect of such 'reinterpretations', coupled with certain other opinions about the kulaks, which we shall be discussing later, was somewhat disquieting. Moreover, rumours about the coming demise of NEP must have been circulating among the specialists outside the Party. In his memoirs, Volsky (Valentinov) tells of a meeting which he had, prior to the Fifteenth Congress, with Rykov whom he knew well.

'. . . Speaking in vague, rather general terms, I said I had heard rumours that NEP was soon to be abolished, and I asked him if the rumours were true. Rykov flared up, and, banging his fist on the table, he shouted: "It's all nonsense, a lot of idle talk from people who don't realize that if they want an end of NEP heads will have to roll first, mine included, and I'm not the sort of person to stand for that." '[29]

The uncertainties about the fate of NEP reveal the extent to which the various factions within the leadership differed in the interpetation which they placed on the watchwords of this Congress. The most striking example of this relates to the slogan about 'the offensive against the kulak'. It was neither Stalin nor Molotov but Bukharin who first used this particular watchword, at the regional conference of Moscow Trades Unions. He even spoke of a 'forced offensive against the kulak, and against capitalist elements in general'.[30] This was, evidently, a tactical move designed to forestall the others and to make it easier for him to interpret the slogan in his own way. The Left opposition congratulated themselves, declaring that this change of attitude on the part of Bukharin was due to the pressure they had exerted,[31] but Kalinin, speaking for Bukharin, made clear to the delegates, who were no doubt perplexed by this watchword, what Bukharin's view actually was, and how it coincided with his own. There was no question whatsoever of using the methods of 'war communism', for 'have we any reason to expect that . . . by applying administrative pressure, by expropriating the kulak elements, we will really and truly succeed in overcoming the kulaks?'.[32] No violent expropriation was to be permitted (a point which Kalinin underlined several times), because, so long as the peasant economy was based on separate holdings, more kulaks would continue to emerge. The offensive would require 'a new, and more complex, approach' in order to curb the kulak's 'exploiting tendencies' and to keep the growing numbers of kulaks within bounds, but this must still be accomplished by 'methods which we have worked out in the context of NEP'.[33]

These explanations served to allay misgivings in the appropriate quarters. Did they, however, bear any relation to the views of those who held the real reins of power?

Stalin, too, began by making reassuring statements. After referring to the growth of kulak and capitalist elements over the last few years, a point which, when it was made by the Left, the leadership always denied, he went on to say: '. . . They are mistaken, those comrades who think that we can and should get rid of the kulak, by using administrative pressure, or handing them over to the *GPU*. There's nothing cut and dried about it . . . the kulak must be dealt with by economic methods, and on the basis of socialist legality.' However, he was not as forthright as Kalinin in his condemnation of violence. On the contrary, he said: 'This does not, of course, exclude the possibility of administrative measures being used against the kulak. But such measures must not take the place of economic measures.'[34]

Molotov's statements provide an even more striking illustration of the different interpretations which were put on this widely used slogan. He too spoke of measures 'to restrict the growth of capitalist elements', but reminded his listeners that the task was one of 'completely overcoming and liquidating' these elements, and that this task was 'none other than the task of building socialism'.[35] Judging from his remarks it was clear that Molotov felt the time for such a solution was ripening, particularly as he now had an entirely new explanation of the 'basic weakness' of the rural economy, which must surely have come as a surprise to the Congress.

It was nothing new for the leadership to attribute the fundamental weaknesses in the rural economy to the piecemeal nature of cultivation, the lack of machinery and the low cultural level. But Molotov now produced a new diagnosis. 'Essentially, the problem of growth in the village economy comes down to this, that the better-off peasants are now enjoying the advantages of having a larger farm, and that is why they are *economically getting the upper hand* over the poor and middle peasants.' And he added: 'the basic mass of serednyaks and bednyaks cannot compete with those larger farms, and they are in a well-nigh impossible position, for every day sees their economic subjection'. This, he said, was the 'fundamental weakness of the villages'.[36] Molotov was not unduly perturbed by the fact that this argument destroyed the whole basis of the case which he had carefully built up at the same Congress, and which was intended to demonstrate that, under Soviet conditions, the lot of the poor and middle peasants was improving, and that inequalities of income were to a certain extent evened out under the Soviet system, and had in this sense a special character.[37]

The above arguments were unconvincing enough; he was now blatantly contradicting himself in advancing the further argument that the 'basic weakness' of the countryside was the unfair competition between the better-off peasants and the others.

What then were the solutions? The first, and as yet unspoken one, was to consist of intensifying the class struggle in the countryside, and using methods to deal with the better-off peasants and the kulaks which were very different from those envisaged by Kalinin. The other solution, which was explicitly stated, was to be an increase in the speed of collectivization, which would remedy the weaknesses of an agricultural economy based on individual farming.

At this Congress, therefore, the subject of collectivization unquestionably assumed a much greater importance than had ever been the case at any previous Party Congress. It was now discussed as a matter which had reached the operational stage.

'We must, as a matter of prime importance, and within the framework of continuing co-operation, direct our efforts to the gradual transformation of individual peasant holdings into large-scale farming enterprises (that is, communal cultivation of the land based on intensified agriculture and increased mechanization) by using every means to foster the growth of socialist agriculture in its early stages'.[38]

The above resolution was adopted following on the report submitted by the Central Committee, and it was repeated and further developed in other drafts submitted to the Congress, particularly in the resolution relating to the overall Five-year Plan, and in the resolution concerning the work to be done in the rural areas. But at this stage there was no suggestion of resorting to extreme measures.

Some of the speakers believed that this marked a turning-point in policy; but Molotov, who was the principal spokesman on agricultural questions, spoke simply of a 'turning-point in the attention'[39] of the Party and of public opinion, which was now focused on the creation of large-scale collectivized agriculture. There is no question but that Molotov, and Stalin, were both sincere in their insistence that this would be a very gradual process, which would be based on modern techniques, and would take place 'slowly but surely, not as a result of pressure, but of example and conviction. . . . There is no other way'.[40]

Stalin no longer believed that there was any future for agriculture within the framework of NEP methods, because of the impossibility of controlling and planning the petty bourgeois element in the peasant economy. But at this stage he thought that the ideal State, in which the villages could be manipulated with the same degree of ease as the state sectors, was still a long way off. His spokesman Molotov declared: 'it will take a good many years to make the transition from individual farming to socialized collective farming,' and 'individual farming will continue to flourish for years and years to come. . . .'[41] This was a genuine conviction. The Politburo's aim was a very modest one, namely to '*strengthen the influence* and to foster the growth of socialist elements in the countryside . . .' and no more. [our italics—M.L.]

According to Molotov, the Party had learned during the NEP period how to use all the necessary patience in its dealings with the peasants, a point which was of particular importance in the task of building socialism. This was why Molotov also repeatedly called for prudence and moderation. There was to be nothing hasty or precipitate in the relations of the Party or the Soviet authorities with the middle peasants.[42]

However, even if the Party wished to bring about a significant increase in the pace of collectivization—and no one believed that this was possible—none of the specialists or institutes at the time were able to give any indication of how this might be done. Stalin at this stage[43] was putting faith in the activities of the Machine Tractor Stations, which were still relatively few in number, although a new version had recently made its appearance in the Ukraine, at the Shevchenko sovkhoz. This station hired out tractors under contract to the villagers whose holdings were then farmed communally. But at the period in question, this was still an isolated instance; Molotov did not even remember it. He tended rather to stress, mistakenly, that the kolkhozes would not be set up by a direct process, as had previously been the case, but that they would evolve gradually from the totality of existing forms of the co-operative movement. He emphasized that, in this context, 'we must keep both feet on the ground'.[44]

Molotov hoped that the system of *kontraktatsiya*,* which up till then had been confined to industrial crops, and to co-operative enterprises engaged in the process of agricultural products, could be used as an aid to collectivization. He was also encouraged by the

* *Kontraktatsiya*—the signing of contracts in spring between the procurement organizations and the peasant producers. These contracts related to the future supply of agricultural produce to the State, at a pre-determined price, and to the seed, machinery, fertilizers, etc., to be supplied by the State. See Chapter 15.

rapid growth in the 'simple producers' co-operatives', in which he saw the real solution to mass collectivization, although the element of communal work in these organizations was as yet limited.[45]

In the resolutions which were adopted by the Congress no distinction was made between the different forms of collective. The authorities were called upon to 'give a large measure of support to all dynamic forms of *producers'* co-operatives', and likewise to the sovkhozes,[46] to which more attention was to be paid in future.

The resolutions promised more credits for the kolkhozes, but did not specify the scale on which these were to be granted, or how they were to be financed. Stalin said vaguely: 'I believe that these funds will now be forthcoming,' but Molotov gave the impression that it might be possible to '. . . get the peasant's "little kopeck" and make it do the work of co-operation'.[47] Thus, the régime were still without concrete proposals at this stage, and there was no department with special responsibility for collectivization.

The Congress decided to set up the *Soyuz Soyuzov* for agricultural co-operation, and for some time to come this body was to have central responsibility for all branches of the co-operative movement. Congress also made provision for the setting up of 'rural departments' under the Central Committee and the regional Party committees, but collectivization was not regarded as being their primary task.[48]

It is certain that the subject of collectivization was brought up simply for the sake of raising the matter, and in order to steal a march on the opposition, whose submissions had laid great stress on it. It had to be shown, for one thing, that the opposition were guilty of having failed to recognize the seeds of socialism in the countryside, whereas the leadership had been fully alive to them.[49]

But in the context of the factional struggle being waged within the Party, this desire to outdo the opposition had a curious influence on the actual course of political developments, for the leadership, while eliminating their opponents, were constantly taking over large sections of the opposition programme. The same thing happened in the case of collectivization.

During the NEP period, the delegate to Congress had become accustomed to a considerable amount of divergence between the socialist content of the resolutions formulated by the Congress, and the realities of his daily routine, as exemplified by the fairly matter-of-fact nature of the flood of official papers which reached him through the usual departmental channels. This being so, the delegates to the Fifteenth Congress saw nothing unusual in the decisions which were taken, and failed to attribute any real significance to them.

Behind the scenes, there was cynical comment about the new 'turning-point' which was being announced yet again.[50] The leadership must have been irritated by this show of scepticism, for they were anxious to avoid any suggestion that, apart from violent denunciation of the opposition, they had nothing new to say. This may explain the last-minute appearance of an amendment to the Central Committee's previous decisions on collectivization, which was introduced *only a few minutes before the Congress was closed;* henceforth, it was stated, 'the task of amalgamating and transforming small individual peasant holdings into large-scale collective farms is to be regarded as the Party's *overriding task* in the countryside'.[51] During the discussions which took place at the Congress, not one speaker had raised the problem in such terms.

But the new amendment caused no raised eyebrows; Yakovlev, who was reading it, was hard put to it to retain the attention of the delegates, who by this time were getting up and hurrying out of the Congress hall.

On the face of it, the delegates were quite right, for the new formula did not alter the fact that what had been put before them was not a coherent programme, but a series of *ad hoc* proposals. But in another sense, they were wrong. Something new had emerged from this Congress, though only in the matter of intentions as yet. Rykov, making the closing speech before an already restless audience, gave a hint of these intentions when he emphasizd that 'in this Congress, *we have made a start on implementation of a full-scale programme of socialist construction*'. And again: '*for the first time, the problem has emerged as a concrete task relating to the building of socialism in the countryside, on the basis of collectivization and the socialization of the peasant economy*'.[52]

But beyond these declared intentions, which were moreover differently interpreted by the two opposing factions, neither one side nor the other had as yet any concrete proposals to offer. A further year and a half was to elapse before the Five-year Plan was ready. Projects for agriculture and the rural areas were more than a little vague. No one knew where the *kopeechka* (little kopeck) was to come from all the changes that were planned, nor indeed who was to carry out these changes.[53] One well-informed delegate (Krzhizhanovsky, the chairman of *Gosplan*) summed up the situation thus: 'We have left our old familiar shores. Of course, the new land is not yet in sight. The world has never known planning on such a scale as ours'.[54]

The delegates had spent seventeen days in conference, and they were in a hurry to get back to the many complex problems which awaited them, and on which this Congress had given no guidance. They left without being unduly preoccupied by what had been said about the basic policy choices, and concerned themselves only with what appeared to them to be more or less clear-cut decisions: more pressure was to be put on the capitalist elements, and they would be taxed more heavily, while 35% of poor peasants would be totally exempt from taxation as from the coming year; the kulaks would get fewer machines and virtually no credits, but apart from a few restrictions the hiring of land to them, even by the State, would go on. More would be done for the batraks and the bednyaks, the Party having just set up a special body for this purpose (the 'rural departments').[55]

Such matters were more or less assured, whereas the decisions promising further assistance for the kolkhozes and sovkhozes, more tractors and machinery, and more cultural services in the villages etc., were greeted with scepticism.

Meanwhile, in the interim before the appearance of the great Five-year Plan, the local Party secretaries needed guidance on the day-to-day conduct of affairs in their areas. Promises had been made in this domain as well: there would be an effort to bring down the prices of industrial goods, while agricultural prices would remain unchanged.

The latter decision[56] is evidence of the extent to which the Congress had failed to make a realistic assessment of the problems of the countryside. Practically no one said anything about immediate difficulties, and about what was happening on the food front.[57] Mikoyan, as Commissar for Trade, was the only one to speak up about the bad news which was coming in from the rural areas, where the figures for the *zagotovki* had fallen below danger level.[58]

Chairman of the Council Rykov was aware of these facts, as were all the other members of the Politburo, and this lent added weight and conviction to his repeated appeals for caution, if a crisis were to be averted. But the crisis, as he must have known, was already virtually upon them.

NOTES AND REFERENCES

1. The next Congress was to meet six months later than had been agreed at the Fifteenth Congress, but the Seventeenth met four years after the Sixteenth, and the Eighteenth five years after the Seventeenth.

2. *Istoriya KPSS.* (Moscow, 1962), p. 417.

3. *KPSS v Rezolyutsiyakh*, Vol. II, p. 432.

4. Plenary session of the Central Committee and of the Central Control Commission, October 24–26, 1927. See the resolutions of this session in *KPSS v Rezolyutsiyakh*, Vol. II.

5. Anything could be imputed to the *Platform* since it had never

been legally published. The Party had no knowledge of it; nor probably had the majority of delegates to the Congress.

6. Apart from certain minor changes, the theses had been embodied almost word for word in the resolutions of the Congress. At the last moment, however, an important passage concerning kolkhoz construction was added.

7. The *Platform* in *Les Bolcheviks contre Staline*, pp. 91, 94.

8. Stalin in his report to the Fifteenth Party Congress, *15-ty S'ezd VKP(b)*, stenogramme, p. 53.

9. *KPSS v Rezolyutsiyakh*, Vol. II, p. 397.

10. *ibid*, p. 400 *passim*. (Emphasis supplied.)

11. Molotov declared to Congress that the problem of a 'resolute offensive' no longer arose, since the latter was already underway, stenogramme, p. 1078. Yakovlev (p. 1211) disagreed with those delegates who refused to recognize that the Congress, as Molotov had pointed out (p. 1063) represented a turning point. Rykov declared that 'we have undertaken a wide-ranging programme of socialist construction', which, as far as the countryside was concerned, had been placed on the agenda 'for the first time'.

12. Stalin, *ibid*, p. 53; Molotov, *ibid*, p. 1062.

13. *KPSS v Rezolyutsiyakh*, Vol. II, pp. 406–7.

14. *ibid*, p. 399.

15. Stalin at the Fifteenth Party Congress, *15-ty S'ezd VKP(b)*, stenogramme, p. 52, and the resolution based on the report of the Central Committee in *KPSS v Rezolyutsiyakh*, Vol. II, p. 437.

16. 'Organs', since *Gosplan* was up against powerful competition from *VSNKh*, which was producing its own draft five-year plans, and doing its utmost to have them accepted.

17. Rykov's speech on the plan, *15-ty S'ezd VKP(b)*, stenogramme, p. 769.

18. Bobrovsky, *op. cit.* (see Chapter 7, Note 87), pp. 48–9.

19. *KPSS v Rezolyutsiyakh*, Vol. II, pp. 399–404.

20. *ibid*, p. 399.

21. This was explained away by arguing that the Left had proposed a *maximum* increase in both simultaneously, whereas the 'correct policy' was aimed only at an *optimum* increase in investments and in the standard of living. There were many examples of this kind of deviousness.

22. The American economist Erlich, in *The Soviet Industrialization Debate*, pp. 84–5, has very correctly pointed this out.

23. Rykov defended his principles in a speech which wound up the discussion on the Five-year Plan. *15-ty S'ezd VKP(b)*, stenogramme, pp. 1040–1. For Sokolnikov's opposing views see *ibid*, pp. 1005–12.

24. Rykov's speech, *ibid*, p. 774.

25. *ibid*, p. 772.

26. *ibid*, pp. 771, 774–5.

27. Molotov's report, *ibid*, p. 1058.

28. *ibid*, p. 1052. Trotsky said in 1925 that as long as there was a shortage of the technical resources needed in the villages, the only possible alternative to 'war communism' was a policy of 'allowing the village to develop its forces of production, by the use of capitalist methods if necessary'. This was a correct presentation of the reasoning behind NEP.

29. Volsky's memoirs are in the Russian archives, University of Columbia, Vol. III, p. 2. The quotation here is taken from Abramovich, *The Soviet Revolution*. (London, 1962), p. 329. Volsky also gives an account of this episode in *Sotsialisticheski Vestnik*, April 1961, p. 70.

30. See Kalinin, *15-ty S'ezd VKP(b)*, stenogramme, pp. 1097–99. Bukharin wrote in *Pravda*, November 4, 1927, 'Now we are in a position to increase pressure on our main enemy, the kulak'. Quoted by Erlich, *op. cit.*, p. 86.

31. Bakayev, *15-ty S'ezd VKP(b)*, stenogramme, pp. 336–7.

32. *15-ty S'ezd VKP(b)*, stenogramme, p. 1098.

33. *ibid*, p. 1098.

34. Speech by Stalin, *ibid*, p. 60.

35. Molotov, *ibid*, pp. 1061–2.

36. Molotov, *ibid*, pp. 1066–7. (Emphasis in the original.)

37. *ibid*, pp. 1052–3.

38. Resolution based upon the report of the Central Committee, *KPSS v Rezolyutsiyakh*, Vol. II, p. 437.

39. Speech by Molotov, *15-ty S'ezd VKP(b)*, stenogramme, p. 1063.

40. Stalin, *ibid*, p. 56.

41. Molotov, *ibid*, p. 1057.

42. Molotov, *ibid*, p. 1078.

43. Stalin, *ibid*, p. 57–8.

44. Molotov, *ibid*, pp. 1072, 1079.

45. Molotov, *ibid*, p. 1073.

46. *KPSS v Rezolyutsiyakh*, Vol. II, pp. 460–2. We shall not go into the question of the sovkhozes at this stage. Molotov claimed at the Congress that they had now become profitable, and should be turned into model enterprises. Of these two propositions, the first was untrue, the second was not realized.

47. Stalin, *15-ty S'ezd VKP(b)*, stenogramme, p. 57, and Molotov, p. 1236.

48. In *KPSS v Rezolyutsiyakh*, Vol. II, p. 488, it was explained

that it would be the task of the new departments to call conferences of the bednyaks. The task of collectivization was not highlighted.

49. Molotov, *15-ty S'ezd VKP(b)*, stenogramme, pp. 1088–90.

50. Yakovlev, *ibid*, p. 1211. The well-informed Strumilin had no hesitation in contradicting Motylev in his article 'O tempakh nashego razvitiya', *Planovoe Khozyaistvo* 1929, No. 1, pp. 111–2; he claimed that the decisions of the Fifteenth Congress 'contained nothing absolutely new or unexpected, nothing which had not already appeared in a series of decisions by the Party Congresses, and in other directives'.

51. *15-ty S'ezd VKP(b)*, stenogramme, pp. 1268–9.

52. Rykov, closing speech, *15-ty S'ezd VKP(b)*, p. 1272.

53. The sum allocated for the purposes of collectivization in 1927–28—65 million roubles—will provide some indication of the modest level of both plans and achievements in this domain.

54. Krzhizhanovsky, chairman of Gosplan, *15-ty S'ezd VKP(b)*, stenogramme, p. 792.

55. The decisions relating to the practical steps to be taken are in *KPSS v Rezolyutsiyakh*, Vol. II, pp. 425–9. On the rural departments see Molotov's speech to the Fifteenth Party Congress, *15-ty S'ezd VKP(b)*, stenogramme, p. 1250.

56. On cereal prices see the appropriate resolutions in *KPSS v Rezolyutsiyakh*, Vol. II, and Molotov's speech to the Fifteenth Party Congress, *15-ty S'ezd VKP(b)*, stenogramme, p. 1064.

57. Rykov's closing speech in the discussion of the Five-year Plan. *15-ty S'ezd VKP(b)*, stenogramme, p. 1037.

58. Mikoyan, *ibid*, p. 975–8.

PART 2

A TWO YEARS' INTERLUDE (1928–9)

Chapter 9

THE PROCUREMENTS CRISIS OF 1928

1. *The Emergency Measures*

No sooner had they returned from the Congress than the delegates were faced with problems which before long proved to be far graver than any which had beset them during the NEP period. This was, in fact, a major crisis, the prelude to a series of events which were of crucial importance for Soviet society.

By January 1927, the procurements for the economic year 1926–7 had yielded 428 million poods of grain. Since the State's minimum requirement for maintaining supplies at a safe level was in the region of 500 million poods, the work of procurement went on, but the results were reassuring, and augured well for the success of the current economic year. However, during the last two months of 1927, the procurements for 1927–8 suddenly began to show a downward trend which caused considerable alarm.

At the Congress, Rykov spoke of '. . . the existence of a number of unhealthy symptoms' which had developed in the national economy. He was referring primarily to a situation in which increased purchasing power on the part of the public was accompanied by a great dearth of manufactured goods, but he also had in mind certain other signs of economic instability. The country was short of consumers' goods and flour. The effects had already been felt in the towns during the year, and matters had been further aggravated by a war scare, which had caused a run on the shops and markets.[1] The rumours had begun to circulate in the spring, and had only died down just before the Congress met. The effect of this sudden 'demand explosion', to use the current phrase, had been to dissipate the stocks of manufactured goods which the State had been keeping in reserve against the coming procurements.[2] Another particularly disquieting development which the Head of the Government mentioned was the disparity in prices for the various crops, although it was not at this stage possible to predict what the extent of the coming difficulties would be.

The Central Committee at this point confined itself to issuing the usual directives. By the second half of December, its instructions had become more urgent [3] but they had little effect.

The reports from the Commissariat of Trade, which was responsible for the procurements campaign, filled the Politburo with alarm, but had so far failed to make the same impression on the local Party officials. From their experience of previous procurements campaigns, the 'men on the spot' had already become accustomed to the idea that the grain would come 'by itself', by a process of *samotek*, as a subsequent letter from the Central Committee had put it. Even the threat of failure did not alarm them as it did the Central Committee. As it was, everyone still remembered the failure of the 1925 procurements, after a good harvest that had given the government hopes of being able to purchase grain on an unprecedented scale. In that year, the *muzhik*, moved by his own needs and his own economic calculations, had dealt a crippling blow to the government's plans for increasing exports, importing industrial equipment and speeding up industrialization. Everything had had to be postponed. The rise in prices which followed the low procurements had meant that grain exports ceased to be profitable, and exports had in any case to be stopped in order to meet the increasing needs of the home market.[4]

However, the failure had stopped short of catastrophe. The local authorities remembered what the outcome had been: there had been a marked scaling-down of investment plans, and the Central Committee had decided that, in the event of a recurrence of similar difficulties, the loss would be offset by increased imports of raw materials for light industry or even, in the last resort, by imports of manufactured goods.[5]

In any case, it had been possible to provide for the needs of the towns, and to ensure supplies for the army by switching the government's entire resources of grain to the home market, and also by buying on the free market, where there was plenty of grain, although at much higher prices.

Memories of this earlier crisis may explain the lack of vigilance on the part of the local authorities, who were moreover incapable of devising any solutions other than those usually applied during the NEP period. In the event of such solutions proving ineffective, the only course left open to the local cadres was to await further instructions.

But the Central Committee were no longer living in 1925. In the intervening years, there had been significant changes within the régime and the Party, and within the peasantry as well, though of course the extent of the changes in the latter instance was a matter for dispute among the Party leaders. A sizeable proportion of the leadership believed that the time had come for further radical changes. For two years the speed of industrialization had been increasing, and it was likely that the pace would be further accelerated, but meanwhile the situation with regard to the peasantry was developing in a way which gave greater grounds for anxiety and mistrust than had hitherto been the case.

Consequently, when it became clear, at the end of December, that the procurements had yielded only 300 million poods of grain, and that bad weather and impassable roads would hold up the work of procurement for several weeks to come, the leadership felt that disaster was threatening. They might have to face discontent among the troops, and among the workers who were short of food, with the added prospect of a drop in wages and a rise in prices, the inevitable failure to supply bread to the regions producing industrial crops, the collapse of all their economic plans,[6] in short a situation which imperilled the very existence of the régime. Some months later, an official document stated that what had only narrowly been averted was the danger 'of a nation-wide general economic crisis'.[7]

As we shall see, the Politburo had every reason, after the event, for wishing to present the crisis (which they hoped they had overcome) in as sombre as light as possible; the fact remains that the situation had been a difficult one.

In January 1928, reports expressing alarm began to come in from various *obkomy*, particularly in Central Asia, where it was said the cotton-growers were short of food supplies. Uzbekistan, which should have received 3·8 million poods of grain in January, had only had 40% of that amount. The Uzbek Party Central Committee feared that the plan for increasing the cotton sowings would not be carried out unless grain was immediately forthcoming, since the peasants were likely to give up planting cotton and go over to food crops. There was every reason to suppose that the flax and beet producers in other regions would react in the same way.

The authorities of the Abidzhan *okrug* reported that by the March 15th they should have received 1,301,000 poods of grain, whereas they had only had 277,000. The members of the Samarkand *okrug* Committee wrote to the Central Committee that bread and seed were both beginning to be in short supply. The peasants were living on substitutes, and selling their draught animals to buy bread and seed from private traders.[8]

The leadership had been taken unawares by the extent of the crisis, a fact which Rykov himself admitted [9] although he had paid more heed to the bad news from the countryside than the other Party chiefs. In December, Molotov was still of the opinion that the difficulties were purely temporary, and that they arose from the fact that 'the peasant is teaching us a lesson, as he so often does (as, for example, in the present procurements campaign)' . . . by reacting against the countless 'follies' of the local officials.[10]

Feeling that they were in an impossible position, the Politburo, at Stalin's personal instigation, embarked upon a large-scale operation of a type that recalled the time of the Civil War. On January 6th, the local soviets received a directive which Stalin himself described as being 'absolutely exceptional both in tenor and content',[11] and which threatened the officials concerned with the direst consequences if they did not succeed in effecting an improvement in the procurements campaign.

In February 1928, Stalin was still feeling the need to offer excuses for this peremptory tone, which was soon to become characteristic of the Politburo in its official dealings. At this stage, he had not yet taken over complete control of affairs. It had been announced that the procurements campaign was to be regarded as a 'front', and consequently the methods employed were of a military nature: mobilization of Party cadres, emergency measures, 30,000 Party activists drafted as envoys to those regions which were of the greatest importance for the *zagotovki*. By order of the Central Committee, each of the local committees set up 'emergency committees of three for grain' (*troiki*), which were to be in charge of the offensive. The form which these took was one which was well known to the 'chekists' in times of emergency.

All the Party representatives were armed with full powers to countermand any orders given by the local authorities, and to take measures which were in keeping with the spirit of the Central Committee's directives. The members of the Central Committee and the Politburo themselves joined in the task. Andreev, Zhdanov, Shvernik, Mikoyan, Kosior, Postyshev, all left for the Ukraine, the North Caucasus, the Volga regions and particularly Siberia, in order to direct operations. (At the moment, contemporary Soviet sources mention only those leaders who were of the Stalinist faction.) The purpose of these operations was two-fold, in that it involved not only supervision of the work of mobilizing supplies from the peasants, but also a task of equal importance, namely the purging of those local organizations which were either refractory or unco-operative, or were simply incapable of taking action along the lines required by the Central Committee, who were no longer interested in the use of NEP methods.

This time, it was Siberia which was regarded as the country's richest source of grain, for the harvest had been good, and it was a region which, not being accustomed to trading in grain, had plenty to spare, and sold very little of it. And it was Siberia that Stalin had singled out as his personal battle-ground, in order to instruct the cadres in 'the art of Bolshevik politics', and to teach them a proper 'class attitude'.

In Siberia, Stalin met the *kraikom*, and also had discussions with several of the *okrug* committees, and with meetings of activists. None of his speeches were published at the time [12] for he had addressed his audiences in very abusive terms, virtually accusing them of sabotage and of links with the kulaks. He had told them— 'Although there is a surplus here, your men are not really concerned with helping the country to surmount the grain crisis.'

The local officials still had no fears about speaking up before the General Secretary, and when they made no secret of their grounds for pessimism, he rounded on them: 'Are you afraid of upsetting your friends the kulaks?' It was argued that the quantities of grain demanded by the Centre were excessive,[13] but the General Secretary retorted that the kulaks in Siberia had huge reserves, amounting to about 50–60 thousand poods per farm (a figure which the officials thought was probably unreliable) and that they were waiting for prices to rise before selling, whereas the poor and the middle peasants had already sold their surplus.

Stalin had no hesitation in improvising arguments to suit his immediate purpose, no matter how over-simplified they were. He had no means of knowing how large the kulaks' surplus reserves of grain were. He was well aware, and moreover he said so himself, that the largest source of unsold grain in Siberia, as in the other regions, was in the hands of the middle peasants.[14] What really mattered, however, was inducing the local authorities to implement the emergency measures, the key to which was article 107 of the penal code, which the cadres were reluctant to enforce.

This article had been introduced by the *VTsIK* in 1926 as an anti-speculation measure. It provided for prison sentences of three or even five years, with confiscation of property, for persons found guilty of causing a deliberate rise 'in the price of goods by repurchase or receiving of such goods, or by failure to offer the said goods for sale on the market'.[15]

This article was aimed at speculators, and not at the peasants, nor had it been used against the peasants the previous year. In the view of those officials who were concerned with administering the law, there were plenty of legal arguments, as well as political ones, against applying it to the peasants. Stalin's blunt retort was that the judges and prokurors who were opposing its use were only doing so because they had allied themselves with the kulaks. He gave orders that the judges be purged forthwith.[16]

There were objections and criticisms from all sides, but once again Stalin made no attempt to counter these with logical arguments.

'You say that the use of article 107 against the kulak is an emergency measure, that it will not produce any positive results, that it will worsen the country's situation ... but use of this provision has given excellent results in other *krai* and *oblasti*, it has enabled us to rally the toiling mass of the peasantry to the support of the Soviet régime, and has improved the position in the villages.' [17]

He did not specify what the 'excellent results' were, or which regions had produced them.

A kulak who refused to sell his surplus grain at State prices was, therefore, to be treated as a speculator, and the surplus was to be confiscated; however, 25% of the grain thus confiscated was to be handed back to the bednyaks either at reduced prices or on long-term credit, as had been the case at the time of the *kombedy* in 1918. It was essential to the success of the operation that it should be presented as an aspect of the class struggle. According to Stalin, this was the only way to enlist support from some of the poorer elements, and to be sure of crushing any opposition. His tactics were to present the crisis as a 'strike of the kulaks'. This enabled him to use coercive measures not only against the kulaks, but also against the majority of the peasants and against those elements within the Party who had doubts about the operation. In fact, the danger of being labelled as an 'ally of the kulaks' was such that no communist could afford to incur it. Moreover the argument was sufficient to convince many of the Party activists, and to inspire them to act without mercy.

Memories of the Civil War were still fresh. The terrible struggle for survival and the passions it had aroused, the climate of hatred and blind devotion to the cause—these were things which neither the Party nor the country had yet forgotten. By re-creating this climate, the Politburo were releasing powerful forces which would enable them to exercise greater control over the cadres, and guide their efforts towards the difficult tasks which had to be accomplished. The atmosphere of emergency was one which was calculated to inspire devotion, and the leadership did not hesitate to build it up for this purpose. The slogan about the 'strike of the kulaks' fitted well into the pattern. Later on, the atmosphere of the Civil War period was to become all-pervading, although there were certain clearly-defined changes and developments. At this earlier stage, however, what emerged was simply a repetition of the earlier pattern.

* * *

At the beginning of the year, the State announced that there were to be contributions to a 'loan for the development of the agricultural economy'.[18]

Firstly, the *TsIK* and the *Sovnarkom* of the RSFSR promulgated a law relating to 'local levies' in the countryside.[19] All villages were empowered, by decision of the village society, as represented by a quorum of half the citizens, to make a compulsory levy on the entire village, including those persons who had no voting rights. The income derived from this tax was to be used for local needs. Payment of the levy was spread out over the various households according to the same provisions as those governing payment of ordinary taxes, and cases of non-payment were to be dealt with by the *selsovety* through the usual administrative channels.[20]

At the same time, the fiscal authorities undertook the task of speeding up payment of taxes, and recovering arrears by what the Plenum of April 1928 described as 'rigorous disciplinary action'; it was admitted by the Plenum that this mulcting of the peasants was part of the emergency measures.[21]

In addition to all this, the co-operative organizations also launched a drive for payment of share contributions and membership dues which, needless to say, in the circumstances could hardly be regarded as voluntary. Consequently, State revenue for the third quarter of the year 1927–8 was 15.5 times greater than in the first quarter.[22]

A special effort was also made through the normal trade channels to increase the supply of manufactured goods to the grain-producing regions, in order to provide the peasants with an added incentive for selling their grain. However, because of the general shortage of consumers' goods, the authorities could only do this by 'stripping the towns'[23] and the regions which were not grain producers, and diverting from them any goods which were likely to appeal to the peasant with grain to sell.

As a result of these emergency tactics, eleven of the grain-producing regions received more goods than the rest of the country, but this method of extracting the maximum amount of grain did not on the whole prove very efficacious. Much more positive results were obtained from direct pressure on the peasants.

Armed with emergency powers, spurred on by urgent directives from the Centre and from the Party emissaries on the spot, and terrified by the purge and by the threat of being classified as 'degenerate elements who are unaware of the class situation in the countryside' and who are unwilling 'to quarrel with the kulaks',[24] the local authorities set about their task as best they could. It was not an easy one. The bulk of the grain which was to be seized was in the hands of the middle peasants; in principle, article 107 and the other penal measures applied only to the kulaks, whereas the financial measures were of general application. How were the local officials to take 'from the kulaks' grain which was mainly in the hands of the other peasants?

Everything depended on the way in which the majority of the local officials interpreted their instructions. Some preferred to take them literally, and to apply article 107 to the kulaks, but not to put any pressure on the serednyaks. However, at the end of several *pyatidnevki* (progress reports were published every five days) they still had not obtained any grain, thus rendering themselves liable to be purged. It was not long, therefore, before most of the cadres realized the exact import of the directives: at all costs, the grain must be got. This meant taking it wherever it could be found. If no one said in so many words that pressure must be put on the serednyaks, the Centre made it clear to the cadres that the 'dictatorship of the proletariat must speak to the peasant in its deep bass voice'.[25]

However, both the kulaks and the other peasants had good reason to hang on to their grain, for prices were too low, and goods too dear and, above all, too scarce. No matter what stratum the peasants belonged to, they were all demanding a better price for their grain. As one present-day Soviet writer has said: 'The serednyak, like any other small farmer, wanted the best price for his grain, and that was why he was holding it back for a time. . . .'[26] In fact, he was holding it back as long as he could, and longer than he had ever done before.

Mikoyan, as Commissar for Trade, was in practice in charge of the special department responsible for the *zagotovki*, and he also states: 'The real bulk of the grain surplus was owned by the serednyaks, who were often in no hurry to sell, if the appropriate quantities of consumers' goods which they needed to buy were not available, or if they were not pressed by the need to discharge debts owing to the State or to the co-operative movement.'[27]

On February 2nd the *krai* Party Office of the North Caucasus, which was a key region in the procurements campaign, sent the following circular to the *obkomy* and the *okruzhkomy*:

'While continuing to drain the surplus grain from kulak households, and employing whatever means are necessary to encourage them to sell their surplus to the State, we must bear in mind that the main bulk of the grain reserves is, nevertheless, in the hands of the middle peasants. For this reason, the February procurements will be made mainly at the expense of the mass of serednyaks in the villages, that is to say they will be amassed in small quantities.'[28]

In the North Caucasus, where Andreev was probably already in charge of operations, it could not be said that the authorities showed any undue tenderness for the feelings of the kulaks. And yet the above circular, which was intended only for senior officials at *oblast* and *okrug* level, suggests that the *krai* authorities had little hope of finding much more grain in the hands of the kulaks, for it was the serednyaks who held on to their grain longer than the other peasants. How were they to be induced to part with it, if the Politburo obstinately refused to raise prices, and described any attempt to do so as 'enemy pressure'?[29] Two months later, official documents and the press were to furnish a fairly accurate picture of the methods which were used to bring the peasants to heel.

When the Party spoke of 'the battle for grain', the term was not entirely figurative; in fact, the overall picture of events in the regions affected by the procurements very often assumed the lineaments of a real battle.

The local authorities were under the command of the *troiki*, and at all levels were subject to supervision by the Party secretaries. The Politburo had made it quite clear to the latter that in this operation their careers were at stake. Since one of the reasons officially put forward for the crisis was the inefficiency of the procurement organizations, the work of procurement which had previously been the sole responsibility of these organizations was placed under the direct supervision of the Party. In the first place, there were too many of these organizations [30] and they had been indulging in 'cutthroat competition' (Stalin) for the peasants' grain, thus contributing to a rise in prices.[31] Steps had been taken to reorganize them, while the procurements campaign was in full swing, but no improvements in this direction could be expected before the coming year. In the meantime, the Party assumed direct responsibility for the task, and was unable thenceforth to relinquish it.

The local soviets, and the local Party cells, received instructions to provide a given quantity of grain within a stated time. According to one present-day Soviet author: 'the *selsovety* and the local Party cells, with the assistance of activists from among the bednyaks and serednyaks, disclosed the stocks of grain held by *each peasant* [our italics.—M.L.] and particularly by the kulaks and the better-off peasants. . . .' They then submitted to the village society the total quantities which were to be contributed by each household. The various kulaks were bound, by a majority decision of the village society, to sell a given quantity of grain to the State. If a kulak refused to abide by this decision, he was subjected to pressure from the village by being socially ostracized, having his name published in the local newspaper, being refused goods at the co-operative store or being excluded from the co-operative movement.[32]

The same author, however, gives a factual description of the way in which the procurements were carried out in the Poltava *stanitsa* of the Kuban *okrug* (North Caucasus); this is rather less euphemistic in tone than the general description quoted above:

'After consulting with the chairmen of the local co-operative on the steps which should be taken to increase the procurements, the *selsovet* decided to make a thorough investigation (*prosmotret*) of the situation of each of the citizens of the *stanitsa*, in order to arrive at an approximate estimate of the amount of surplus grain in his possession; it was further decided to inform each householder of this figure, and to suggest that he supply the requisite quantity of grain, on the assurance that he would have every right to receive manufactured goods.' [33]

Upon completing their investigation—though there is no indication as to how this was carried out—the officials of the local soviet reckoned the amount of the 'surpluses', decided what quantities were to be procured, and informed the peasants accordingly. Armed with these 'control figures', the members of the *selsovet* went to the peasants who were thought to have a surplus of grain, and handed them a summons to appear before the *selsovet*, where 'the Soviet régime's policy with regard to procurements was explained to them'. The author states that 500 persons were summoned in this way, but that no results were forthcoming. At a special meeting of *stansovet*, members were instructed to hand over their own surplus within one day (a thing which up till then had not been done) and to ensure that thereafter a further 500 poods per day would be mobilized from the sectors of the village for which they were severally responsible. Those members who failed to carry out instructions were severely reprimanded, and four members were expelled from the soviet.

At the end of January, it was reported at a meeting of the village society that many citizens were still concealing their surplus grain. The meeting called upon 'all *khleboroby* (corn-growers)', and on 'all the workers of the *stanitsa*' without exception to give up their grain. In order to encourage them to do so, the authorities made public the names of those who had been found with hidden stocks. Some were immediately expelled from the *mir* and from the co-operative (a severe punishment in the latter instance, since the offenders were thereby debarred from being able to purchase manufactured goods); others were threatened with the same penalties, and the rest were reprimanded.

Despite all this, only 63% of the January plan was fulfilled, and in the case of February only 28% (though some of the failure in this instance was attributed to bad weather); meanwhile, the correspondent of the local newspaper was reporting that there was no shortage of grain, particularly where the serednyaks were concerned. It was not until March that the monthly procurements plan was approximately fulfilled; the document does not indicate how this was achieved.

The author from whom the foregoing examples are quoted has chosen to describe a case in which the procurements operation took place in a relatively calm fashion, but even here the element of pressure can be detected fairly clearly. There is hardly any mention of the kulaks, or even of article 107, probably because the people concerned were the reluctant majority of the villagers, and the kulaks had either been dealt with separately, or would be later on.

However, even in such relatively straightforward cases as the one quoted, it should be borne in mind that there were additional sources of tension, since, apart from the work of procurement, there were other tasks in hand at the same time. We quote once more from the same author.

For example, by April 1st, the *krai* had raised 101% of the agricultural tax, 100% of the social insurance, 94% of the local levy, and also a large part of the 'peasant loan', for the year.[34] As regards the *stanitsa* mentioned above, the author says nothing about the way in which these operations were carried out, but it is clear that the resistance and the unco-operative attitude of the peasants had to be overcome, and we know from other sources what methods were employed to this end.

His testimony is borne out in substance, if not in general tone, by that of the oppositionist Sosnovsky, who was exiled to Siberia, in all probability to Barnaul, and who based his observations on the local Party newspaper. He wrote: 'They fell on him [i.e. the peasant.—M.L.] with a concerted ferocity seldom seen since the days of 1918–19, and there were fifteen different campaigns all going at the same time, all of which could be summed up in one word: *Daesh!* (Give!).' Sosnovsky then quotes the local paper: '*Daesh* grain, taxes (before they are due), insurance and social contributions, the loan, the local levy, the sowing fund—(and it seems that that is not all).'[35] As Sosnovsky observes, even if all this had been done circumspectly, the peasant would still have taken fright. It might have been possible to win him over, but there was no one to do so, because the apparatus 'either echoed the kulaks *sotto voce* (or out loud), or else went headlong like a hound let off the leash'.

The local authorities, anxious not to leave the peasant with many alternatives, or to see him led into 'temptation' by more profitable transactions, forbade all private individuals to buy from the peasants, and also restricted the amount of grain which might be ground in the mills to the minimum quantities judged necessary for the peasant's own private consumption.[36] To some extent this amounted to controlling peasant consumption. Naturally, as long as the markets remained open, they provided an outlet for considerable quantities of grain, so the markets were mostly closed. The free market for bread ceased to exist. In cases where the market retained a token existence, the militia intimidated the peasants by carrying out spot checks on the numbers of people selling in the markets; they demanded licences from the peasants which normally only the professional traders possessed (this was reported by Mikoyan [37]) and the militia and officials of the local offices of the Commissariat of Trade fixed prices and forced the peasants to sell exclusively to the State procurement organizations.[38] The militia very often extended their search to the roads, confiscating any grain which they found on the peasants without undue concern either for its destination or its provenance. In such circumstances, it mattered little to the arm of the law whether the peasants in question were bednyaks or serednyaks.[39]

In a secret letter to members of the Politburo on June 26th, Stalin placed the entire responsibility for the closing of the markets on the local authorities. Since the Party had never ordered such steps to be taken, he said, 'the Centre had forthwith instructed the local authorities to re-open the markets immediately, and to put an end to such deviations.'[40]

According to Stalin, this order had been given on May 26th, 1928. The Politburo had therefore taken some time to act, although well aware of what had been going on since February; it had no doubt withheld its hand on purpose, before finally calling a halt to the closing of the markets. However, Stalin's countermeasures cannot have been particularly forceful—they were certainly never made public—because they had no effect, and the markets remained closed. It was not until June 30th that Mikoyan, through the medium of *Pravda*, publicly appealed to the local authorities to forbid the closing of the markets, the fixing of prices, and other abuses which 'were in flagrant contradiction of our policy, and could not be tolerated'.[41]

Faced, on the one hand, with the undisguised hostility of the peasants, no matter what their social condition, and with intense and unremitting pressure from the Centre on the other hand, the local authorities resorted to ever-increasing controls; they organized illegal house-to-house searches, and confiscated grain in a manner which the Party, after the event, described as having been 'illegal'; all this was done without reference to any clause, or any form of judicial procedure.[42]

In order to stop traffic in grain among the villages, the militia set up road-blocks, while the methods employed for taking the grain came more and more to resemble the *prodrazverstka* (surplus appropriation system)[43] which the peasants had so hated during the Civil War. An arbitrary assessment was made of the amount of grain to be supplied by each household; this was followed by house-search, confiscation, and acts of brutality on the part of local officials. Finding himself once more faced with Civil War methods, the peasant had no need of propaganda from any quarter to make him take fright, and believe rumours, or even spread them himself, about the Bolsheviks re-introducing confiscation, and about the end of NEP.[44]

In addition, the measures which were being introduced to damp down purchasing power, such as the local levy, the loan, the speed-up in the recovery of income tax arrears and other payments, themselves offered vast scope for the arbitrary action of which the authorities were constantly guilty. Whether or not they had been formally sanctioned by the village societies[45] these payments were obtained by putting pressure on the peasants, and by subjecting them to a great many troublesome procedures which seemed to them to border on the fraudulent, and were indeed so, from the legal point of view. Later, the press and Stalin himself were to list some of these procedures, such as, for example, the straightforward *razverstka* of the loan or the 'local levy' by the authorities; payment for grain which had been supplied by vouchers instead of in cash; the use of these same vouchers to reimburse part of the value of postal orders which were often sent to the peasants by members of their families working in the towns; making purchase of certain goods which were said to be in short supply conditional upon possession of these vouchers, and so on. Inevitably, this incessant arbitrary behaviour raised a storm of protest and bitterness, and was the source of deep unrest among the peasants.[46]

The fate of the bednyaks in all these upheavals was not an enviable one. Like the rest, they were obliged to hand over their surplus grain, and there is plenty of evidence from Soviet sources that they too had grain confiscated, and were subjected to various forms of extortion.[47]

The authorities were trying to organize the bednyaks, and sought to enlist their support, through the poor peasants' organizations, against the rich peasants with large reserves of grain, but the bednyaks were first called upon to set an example by handing over whatever they had,[48] failing which they suffered endless abuses.

At this time, as we have already seen, the bednyak and batrak organizations were virtually non-existent. According to a present-day Soviet writer, it was only about the middle of February, when the thousands of activists who had been mobilized for the campaign began to arrive in the villages, that it finally became possible to take effective steps to use the *bednota* as a weapon against the better-off peasants in the procurements operation. It was not until then, he states, that the *bednota* 'went over to the offensive'.[49]

However, since the batrak-bednyak groups were still relatively few in number, their 'offensives' cannot have been very frequent.[50] It is likely that the inducement of a loan of 25% of the grain confiscated from the kulaks enabled the local officials and the Party cells to recruit some of the poor peasants to help in the work of procuring grain and searching for hidden stocks. But in the spring, precisely at the moment when they needed help from the bednyaks, the authorities stopped helping them. The government had no grain to give or lend them, and so the *bednota* went over to the enemy. As Bauman observed in *Bolshevik*, 'the bednyak proved a valuable support during this winter's procurement campaign, but we failed to provide him with grain at a fixed price in the spring and summer, he frequently did not have enough to eat, and so he too has gone cap in hand to the kulak'.[51] Mikoyan also spoke of the bednyaks' 'wavering', which he put down to the influence of the kulaks, but he also admitted that this influence had been greatly strengthened by the 'administrative methods' employed by the local authorities.[52]

The treatment meted out to the kulaks was, naturally, of a special order, and it followed the lines which Stalin personally had laid down. As he liked to remind the activists, one must not 'be afraid of upsetting our friends the kulaks'. In a circular to Party committees, in which the word kulak was repeatedly coupled with 'the better-off', he wrote: 'The strata of kulaks and better-off peasants in the villages must be made to bear an even higher rate of taxation, and must be subjected to increasing pressure for the recovery of debts and other payments.'[53] Efforts must be made to ensure that the better-off strata paid a greater proportion of the 'local levy', and that they bought more bonds. The famous article 107 was to be invoked against those who were hoarding large quantities of grain—the figure he quoted was any amount in excess of 2,000 poods—'but in no circumstances are the serednyak elements in the villages to be affected by this measure'.[54]

The kulaks, if not the rest of the *zazhitochnye*, were bound to supply the quotas of grain fixed for them by the local authorities. Failure to do so within the stated time was followed by a positive flood of reprisals: fines, house-searches, confiscations and summonses to appear before tribunals which imposed heavy prison sentences, confiscation of grain, and other penalties laid down under article 107. This was followed 'automatically' by expulsion from the *mir* and the co-operative organization. In less severe cases, the offender was boycotted by the co-operative, which meant that, until he had discharged his obligations, he was debarred from buying goods.[55]

Committees of poor peasants, summoned by the local cells or the Party representatives from the towns, took the decision to 'mobilize' from the kulaks and other better-off peasants[56] implements and draught animals which the committees considered the kulaks did not need for their agricultural work.

The Ukrainian *TsIK* made a special law providing for the confiscation of land which was 'illegally' held by the kulaks. According to *Pravda*, some kulaks had gained possession of 100–120 hectares in this way.[57] The *TsIK* envisaged taking back 50,000 hectares from the kulaks, and restoring them to the village societies. In the space of two months 30,000 hectares were recovered from 6,214 individuals under the above provisions.[58]

This was something not far removed from straightforward dekulakization. In towns and villages, the rumours spread that these dreaded measures were already being enforced in various places. Even if this were true in a few isolated instances only, the news would still have travelled far and fast enough. Given the atmosphere of tension and anxiety in which they had been living over the past few months, the peasants were alert to the slightest sign of danger. The Party denied the rumours, and put them down to enemy propaganda, but in a secret letter, which was not published at the time,[59] Stalin admitted to the Politburo that there had in fact been instances of dekulakization.

Could matters have been allowed to rest there? Would it have been possible to confine these measures exclusively to the kulaks? The answer is that the punitive and coercive tactics which the authorities were employing to extract grain from a better-off element among the peasants could not be confined to one clear-cut social stratum. In villages where the dividing lines between the social strata were anything but clear-cut, the 'pure' kulak and the 'pure' *zazhitochny* were rare phenomena, whereas grain had no class connotations, whether it was concealed by a serednyak or any other peasant. *The overriding duty of the local authorities was to bring the procurements operation to a satisfactory conclusion. Since the grain was mainly in the hands of the mass of serednyaks, everything was done to extract it from this quarter.*

Thus, it was the serednyaks who felt the full force of a blow which, according to the Politburo, was aimed exclusively at the speculators and those who were hoarding grain on a massive scale. In July, Bauman, writing in *Bolshevik*, confirmed what was a foreseeable development: 'In a number of regions, clause 107 was used not only against the kulaks, but equally against the serednyaks.' And again: 'In several areas, we have been guilty of excesses in the use of administrative measures against the serednyaks.' [60]

The same thing happened in the case of another measure which had been intended as a weapon against the kulaks, namely the 'individual levy', in which the tax assessment was made, not in accordance with the normal criteria, but on the basis of individual enquiry into the circumstances of the person concerned. Before long, this practice was restricted exclusively to 3% of the 'richest kulaks', but it too affected many of the serednyaks. [61]

One can hardly escape the conclusion that the emergency measures were a method of 'handling' the population, particularly the peasants in the grain-producing regions. The effect of these measures was to imbue the entire apparatus with a spirit of combativeness, which was fed easily enough by the ever-present tensions inherent in the uneasy relationship between the Soviet régime and the peasantry, and also by the propensity of local officialdom for acting as *derzhimordy* (the term formerly used for the Tsarist police who were noted for their brutality). Bukharin had already protested against this use of violence, and Astrov also added his protest in an article in *Pravda* in July 1928. He spoke of countless instances of violence, culled from the local newspapers, and quoted some of the worst examples. He mentioned cases in which the local agent responsible for procurements had called a meeting of the village society, and proceeded to address it with his revolver prominently displayed on the table in front of him. Another agent had expounded the principles of the Soviet régime to the peasants in the following terms: 'their hands at your throat and their knees on your chest.' [62]

These examples provide a fair illustration of the treatment meted out to the peasants during this procurements campaign. The villages, especially those in the grain-producing regions, lived through a reign of terror, characterized by arbitrary procedures, extortion, injustice, and arrests at every turn—'excessive arrests', as Stalin later described them[63]—and it was not long before the peasants began to fight back, in so far as they were able to do so.

While the countryside was living through the grave events which marked the 'battle for grain', and which in fact signified the end of an epoch, and the beginning of a new, and very ominous one, the towns too were the scene of acute anxiety, which deepened as the news continued to pour in from the rural areas. Since the autumn, the shortage of supplies had become noticeable: the towns were short of milk, butter and bread,[64] which did nothing to lessen people's fears. Changes were made in the administration of the Russian Commissariat for Agriculture, and although this was done discreetly it could not go unnoticed either by the specialists and the intellectuals, or by Party circles. In fact, the very moderate A. P. Smirnov was replaced in February by Party Secretary Kubyak; Smirnov's assistants Svidersky and Teodorovich also went with him to other posts. Informed observers were in no doubt that these three senior officials had been demoted. They were all three wholehearted supporters of the 'classic' NEP model, devotees of the *obshchina*, but also of the *khutor* and of private agriculture, who had been relatively unmoved by the supposed threat from the kulaks.[65]

There were plenty of other factors which helped to build up the atmosphere of uncertainty engendered by the countless 'fantastic rumours' which *Pravda* denounced,[66] rumours about the end of NEP, about the return of the *prodrazverstki* and the dekulakization measures, and the threat of famine. Everywhere, it was rumoured that the régime was in difficulties, and that a serious crisis had developed in the relations between the régime and the peasants. In the upper reaches of the Party, and in many circles outside the Party, the fateful words *razmychka* and 'peasants' strike' were gaining widespread currency.[67] In the most informed circles, there were whispers of 'angry words' which were supposed to have passed between Rykov and Stalin after the latter's return from his tour of Siberia.[68] Rykov, with the help of Tomsky and Kalinin, was said to have succeeded in curbing the General Secretary's lust for battle, and limiting the scope of certain purges which he had been minded to undertake.

During the month of January and the first half of February, at a time when the procurements campaign with all its excesses was already raging in the countryside, not one word was said in the press about what was happening. The words 'kulak', 'emergency measures' and 'article 107' never figured in the newspapers. The only evidence was the progress reports on the *zagotovki* from the Commissariat of Trade which were published every five days, and which gave news of ever-increasing deliveries of grain, on a scale which was absolutely unprecedented for the time of year.[69] In the months from January to March, a total of 273 million poods was collected, more than in the corresponding period for the previous year. It was in fact claimed, at the April session of the Central Committee, that in nine months of procurements slightly more grain had been mobilized than in the same period of the previous year.[70] However, in this instance there was no mention of the fact that the methods employed to procure the grain were very different from those used earlier. In other respects, too, this current campaign differed widely from earlier ones.

The government were perfectly well aware of what was going on, as Stalin's February letter to the Party leadership amply demonstrates,[71] and they seemed to have misgivings about the consequences of such severe measures in view of the onset of the sowing season. It was suggested that Mikoyan's department were worried by a visible tendency on the part of the peasants to cut down their sown areas. In particular, the better-off peasants had made no secret of their intention to do so, since they had no incentive to amass surpluses which caused them so much trouble. Some of them were no doubt actively encouraging the other peasants to cut down their sowings, and their propaganda often fell on willing ears. *Pravda* reported that this trend was widespread throughout the peasantry, and urged the Party to take steps to combat it.[72] It was obvious that such a tendency would gravely endanger future harvests, and have a disastrous effect on procurements.

There must have been a powerful current of opinion in the Party in favour of redressing the balance, and placating the peasants. Mikoyan was the first to sound the alarm. For the first time in the columns of *Pravda*, he admitted that the current campaign had been a difficult one, and that it had involved the use of 'administrative pressure', including, in particular, 'road-blocking parties' and other arbitrary procedures on the part of the militia, which he described as *'harmful, unlawful and inadmissible'* (the latter words being underlined in the text).[73] He issued a warning about 'the recurrence of the anti-serednyak deviation', for which he tried to blame the Left, and, while justifying the use of article 107 (which up till then *Pravda* had never once mentioned) he attempted, at the same time, to reassure the public by pointing out that 'it would be unrealistic to suppose that we are now bent on destroying the kulak. The kulak will still be with us, his numbers may still increase, and go on increasing for years to come . . .'.

However, this departure on Mikoyan's part cannot have had the Politburo's wholehearted support. The continuation of his article,

231

which was supposed to appear the following day, never did appear. The General Secretary himself resumed control of the operation, so as to be able to conduct it on his own lines. He had doubtless decided that it was too soon as yet to call a halt to the methods which were being used in the countryside. By mid-February, the campaign was just beginning to yield some promising results. The rate of progress during the first few days of February had been lively, and there was a danger that the local organizations, who had achieved this progress under strong pressure from above, and at the cost of purges and administrative changes undertaken on the spot, might be thrown off balance by a public retraction of policy at this stage. So far as Stalin was concerned, there could be no question of compromising a policy which he had advocated, and which he was preparing to present as being a sound one. But since some measure of revision was called for, he preferred not to leave such a delicate task to a third party.

On February 13th a letter, signed by Stalin, went out from the Party to the officials concerned; Stalin no doubt thought it more expedient, at this stage, to use the Party rather than public channels. The letter set forth the new policy as being simply a continuation of the previous line. In it, Stalin explained the origins of the crisis, which was primarily due to the fact that '. . . the village expands, and grows richer, but essentially it is the kulak who has grown in stature and in riches'.[74] Stalin admitted that it was not the kulak who was the main source of surplus grain, but held that he was, primarily, a powerful political influence. 'He is an economic power in the village . . .' and, by virtue of his contacts with speculators in the towns 'he can set the pace, where the price of grain is concerned, with the serednyak following on behind'.[75] Such a statement, coming from Stalin himself, was something new. It amounted to an admission that, in opposition to the Party and under its very nose, another force had arisen which was capable of leading the peasants. The activists who still remembered the deadly war they had waged against the Left, for having uttered such heresies, must have thought they were dreaming.

But Stalin had no wish to figure as a neo-Trotskyist. He had enough skill, and above all enough influence, to be able to present matters in a different light. 'In a number of regions, there have been deviations from the Party line, owing to incorrect interpretation of the Party's watchword: "rely on the *bednota*, make a lasting alliance with the serednyak, and never for one moment relax the struggle against the kulaks".' It was apparently the first and the last terms of this 'threefold' injunction which had not been properly implemented. According to Stalin, the local authorities had reached an understanding with the serednyaks, but the organization of the bednyaks was defective, and the struggle against the kulak was being neglected. The earlier policy was therefore said to have been deviationist, and it was essential

'to put an end to the deviations which have arisen in our practical work in the villages, by laying greater emphasis in the future on the task of combatting the kulak danger, and by obliging our local Party organizations to continue to develop [here he is quoting the Fifteenth Congress.—M.L.] their offensive against the kulak'.[76]

This was not, according to Stalin, a change of policy, but simply a matter of correcting the existing line for deviations which had arisen 'in practice', in other words, deviations for which the local authorities were to blame.

At the same time, the men on the spot were also made to shoulder a large part of the responsibility for many other shortcomings, such as the delay in making preparations for the procurements campaign, the inefficiency of the local agencies whose task it was to carry out procurements, the failure to restrict purchasing power in the countryside, and the slowness in making supplies of goods available in the villages. However, Stalin gallantly admitted that the Central Committee had also been at fault to some extent.

Nevertheless, the context of his letter tended to suggest the very reverse. The 'deviations' were presented as being the cause of the crisis, and these deviations were said to have sprung up inside the various local Party organizations and also outside the Party. Within the local organizations 'there have recently emerged certain elements which are alien to the Party and blind to the class position in the villages. They do not understand the basis of our class policy, and are attempting to carry out their tasks while refraining from offending against anyone in the village, continuing to live at peace with the kulak, and in general retaining popularity among "their own sort" in the countryside.' He demanded that all such 'degenerate elements' be purged from the Party organs, the village soviets and the co-operative organizations.[77]

The letter endorsed the emergency measures, with the proviso that there should be an increase in the amount of fiscal and other pressure exerted on the better-off peasants, and particularly on the kulaks, but that 'in no circumstances should these measures be allowed to harm the mass of middle peasants'.[78]

There was no explanation as to how the grain was in fact to be taken from them without 'harming' them, particularly as the measures for extracting payments were intended in any case to apply just as much to the serednyaks as to the others. Stalin even demanded that there should be an end of the *prodrazverstka*, and other illegal forms of pressure which had been used, and which he condemned as 'abuses' (*peregiby*). This was part of the camouflage by which the new policy was to be presented as a continuation of the old, and it was accompanied by a placatory manoeuvre which fulfilled the threefold purpose of disarming the critics and the opposition, finding an excuse to blame the men on the spot for the *peregiby*, and guarding against the danger of a reduction in future sowings.

With this design in mind, Stalin announced in his letter that the emergency measures had, for the most part, been introduced only for the current procurements period,[79] and that the many payments, which he listed, did not form part of these emergency measures and had nothing to do with the Party line. This was characteristic of Stalin's tactics. His policy was always presented as an ideal one— the *general line*, as he called it—which could not be compromised by excesses on the part of ignorant officials. All errors were deviations from this ideal line, and as such attributable to the men on the spot. This technique is the prerogative of the autocrat who is firmly in control, and it is one which Stalin perfected during the procurements campaign at the beginning of 1928. In April, when he was under attack for having brought a reign of terror and violence to the villages, his answer was that the critics could not see the merits of the line which was being followed. 'By behaving in this way, they are closing their eyes to the essential realities of the situation, and concentrating on the particular and the irrelevant', for the excesses in question were merely deviations 'which were not in any way attributable to the policy adopted by the Party.'[80]

This was the method constantly used by Stalin and the Central Committee to explain away all injustices and failures. It enabled them, on occasion, to use the greatest frankness in acknowledging any number of grave errors on the part of the régime, while providing them with perfect cover: all these abuses were deviations, and responsibility for them lay with the local authorities.[81]

It was during the crucial year of 1928 that the leadership finally perfected the technique of drawing a distinction between 'line' and 'deviation', and presenting a change in policy, on occasion, as a continuation of an existing policy. A feature of these tactics was the use of frankness as a smoke-screen for the régime's own deficiencies and misdeeds, and it has resulted in the survival of a certain number of texts such as, for example, the indictment drawn up by the Central Committee in April against the abuses and excesses to which the peasants had been subjected. This document lists, and denounces, the following activities: '. . . confiscation of grain surpluses (without judicial reference to article 107), the ban on buying or selling in rural areas, or the banning of the "free" market in general; the use of house searches in order to uncover hidden reserves of grain; the use of road blocks; the obligatory allocation of bonds as payment for the grain, and in respect of sales to the peasants of goods said to be "in short supply"; the issuing of bonds or other vouchers as part-payment for postal orders; the use of administrative pressure against the serednyak: the introduction of barter, etc. . . .'[82]

In this document, which dates from April, the Central Committee were calling for a stop to practices which, it will be remembered, Stalin had already forbidden in January. As we shall see, they were again forbidden in July, and again they continued to occur.

The truth was that NEP, *in its 'classic' form, was virtually dead.* However, any such suggestion was treated by Stalin, as we have seen in the letter previously quoted, as 'counter-revolutionary nonsense'. For two more years, he was to go on insisting that 'NEP is the basis of our economic policy, and will continue as such for long in our history'.[83]

Before the letter addressed to the Party Secretaries had reached them, they learned the substance of it from *Pravda* on February 15th. The document in question was a key one, for it already contained, in outline, the essence of Stalin's future *modus operandi*, and the decision to publish part of it must have represented a change in tactics on Stalin's part.

The public were unaware that the unsigned editorial, headed 'First results of the procurements campaign, and the tasks facing the Party', had been written by Stalin, but informed observers could hardly fail to note the significance of allegations about the kulak who was influencing the serednyak, the mention of an offensive, and of 'degenerate elements', etc. The informed minority was very small at this time,[84] but they were all agreed that these indications portended 'a left turn' in policy, though no one could yet say how long it would last, or on what scale it would be.

In the issue of *Pravda* which published Stalin's anonymous editorial, banner-headlines with the words 'Kulak grain speculators' also heralded a violent campaign against the kulaks, who for weeks past had never even been mentioned in the newspaper. February 15th 1928 marked a beginning; from this day on, and for years to come, the kulak theme was never absent from its pages, and it even continued to recur for some time after the kulaks had vanished from the Soviet scene.

2. *The Return to* Prodrazverstka

About the beginning of April, the Party cadres, under pressure of events, must have begun to feel the need for reassurance, and for some clarification on future policy. The Plenum of the Central Committee and the Central Control Commission, which met from April 6th to 11th, and which was mainly concerned with two major problems, namely, grain and the *Shakhty* affair,[85] did its best to reassure those who needed reassuring, and to satisfy everybody, without in fact departing from the basic principles of the new policy in the countryside.

Mikoyan, the spokesman on agricultural questions, submitted an analysis of the crisis based, somewhat incoherently, on a number of diverse and often contradictory factors.[86] It was suggested that the crisis had arisen, in the first place, from a 'sudden upset in the equilibrium of the market' while the 'growing disparities . . . between the purchasing power of the peasants and the supply of goods' were due to the increase in incomes in the villages 'particularly in the incomes of the better-off strata and the kulaks'.[87] The government had failed to act quickly enough in introducing fiscal measures to limit this spending power; nor was it able to increase the supply of goods. A faulty price policy had further contributed towards a growing disincentive on the part of the peasants to sell their grain, so that they now preferred to increase their reserves, and their own private consumption.

Logically, in this context, the crisis could have been averted 'assuming that steps had been taken in time to achieve a proper equilibrium in the basic elements of the economy, and to eradicate weaknesses in our economic apparatus and in the Party'.[88] Was this NEP-like, very Bukharinist argument intended as a gesture towards the future Right or, rather, towards the prevailing current of opinion at that time among the *Tsekisty* (members of the Central Committee)? Would it have been possible, at this stage, to find a solution to urgent problems, and to avert crisis, by seeking to establish a proper balance between supply and demand, mainly by the use of financial and fiscal measures? If this had been so, it would have been possible to ensure the survival of NEP without any significant change in its character.

There were repeated declarations to the effect that 'NEP is the road on which the Party's feet are firmly set', but the Plenum gave no clear answer to the above questions. Indeed, in the decision subsequently taken by the Plenum, another explanation for the current difficulties was advanced, the argument being different from the one put forward in Mikoyan's text.[89] In this instance, the difficulties were said to have arisen from the stresses and strains of rapid industrialization, and from the nature of the internal and the international situation, as well as from faults in planning. This was a different interpretation, which was soon to be accepted as the only official one. Whereas the first line of argument assumed the continuance of the general framework of NEP, and laid the blame mainly on weaknesses in the government's policy, the alternative hypothesis freed the goverment of any responsibility for the crisis, which was thereby attributed to external factors and to the needs of an inevitable industrialization. In this context, the leadership emerged blameless, and such errors as had been committed were the fault of local officials who had deviated from the Party line.

In this text the kulaks figured only as a secondary factor in the situation, mainly in the sense that they exploited its defects and difficulties, and the lack of economic equilibrium. This must have been a reflection of what was, at the time, the majority view among the members of the Central Committee.

However, on this question Stalin persistently followed a different line. In his public speech at Moscow after the meeting, he developed the argument that the latest crisis 'represented, within the framework of NEP, the first serious intervention by capitalist elements in the countryside against the Soviet régime . . . over the question of procurements'.[90]

This, as Trotsky was to point out later, 'was tantamount to representing the grain crisis as having been inspired exclusively by kulak hostility . . . to the socialist State, that is, by political motives of a general nature'.[91] Trotsky could scarcely be accused of any desire to defend the kulaks, and yet he firmly dismissed any such interpretation. Nor was any suggestion to this effect made at the Central Committee meeting.

This was not the only instance in which Stalin's attitude differed from that of the majority of the Central Committee and the Party at the Plenum. The situation was to change later, but for the moment an explanation had to be offered for the nature and scope of the emergency measures, and the significance of the watchword about 'the offensive against the kulaks'. This the resolution set out to do, incoherently and at some length.[92]

The Central Committee promised to wage this offensive entirely within the context of NEP, using fiscal and legislative methods, and basing its policy with regard to credits and the supply of machinery on class principles. Essentially, the offensive would be based on increased aid for the co-operative sector, and various forms of 'State intervention and planning in respect of the market and small-scale peasant production'.

What then was the position with regard to the 'emergency measures'? The Plenum listed a number of 'deviations' which could not be blamed on the emergency policy, and which were described as being virtually 'steps on the slippery slope towards *prodrazverstka*'. This 'degeneration' was formally denounced on the grounds that it had, according to the Plenum, injured the serednyaks, and 'threatened to produce negative results . . . over a long period'.[93] The emergency measures themselves would ultimately have to be superseded, but only 'as and when the difficulties with regard to procurements were overcome.'

Thus, there was no undertaking from the Plenum that these measures would simply be discontinued. Indeed, Stalin made it clear, in his speech after the Plenum, that they would be intensified, if the abnormal conditions persisted.[94]

Despite these reservations, however, the general atmosphere was conciliatory. The Plenum declared that a major crisis had been averted; some days earlier, Stalin had already announced that the country was emerging from its difficulties. Did he believe this? His Moscow speech contained a curious reference in praise of the emergency measures which, according to him, had produced 'beneficial and really significant results', for the kulak had been forced to retreat, the Party was united, and the majority of the peasants had sided with the régime, so that the kulak was isolated.[95]

If the situation was so favourable, why was the threat of exceptional measures still held over the peasants? The events of the weeks that followed were to provide the answer. The 'beneficial results' of the emergency measures, and the encouraging procurement figures reported by the April Plenum, had to stand the stern test of reality after the Plenum was over.

Partly, the trouble was attributable to climatic reverses. In the spring, the peasants and the authorities became aware that the winter wheat in the Ukraine and the North Caucasus had largely been destroyed. Dismayed by these losses and by the poor prospects for the coming harvests, the peasants had decided to use the respite offered by the lateness of the spring and to take the precautions which they felt to be necessary. They knew that, in the event of famine, no help would be forthcoming. In the regions which were affected, seed was needed for fresh sowing; they also had to guard against a possible shortage of fodder, and to make provision for feeding themselves. In view of all these circumstances, they stopped such sales as they could still have agreed to during the spring and at the beginning of summer.[96]

The State, for their part, committed errors of judgement and errors of an economic nature, whose only effect was to increase requirements in a situation in which availabilities were curtailed. The departments responsible grossly overestimated the amount of reserves which the peasants were supposed to be holding,[97] possibly as a result of a false impression given by the Central Committee and Stalin, who had repeatedly stated that the villages were growing ever more prosperous. 'There is a great deal of grain in the country, but the *zagotovki* are falling,'[98] he said in April. These pronouncements tended to allay the fear of famine, and to quiet the scruples of the activists who were responsible for procurements. When things were presented in this light, the suggestion underlying the words 'Plenty of grain, but . . .' was that the main cause of the trouble was obstructionism on the part of the *muzhik*. This being so, the best way out of the difficulties was to make a show of firmness.

However, the State was suddenly called upon to help the peasants of the Ukraine and the North Caucasus with the resowing of their fields. It had little to give. The emergency measures, which had led to the closing of the markets, had forced the State to assume responsibility for supplying many regions which otherwise could have provided their own supplies. This, and a number of other hidden factors, including possibly a degree of over-optimism, had involved the State in an excessive expenditure of large quantities of grain just at the time when the procurements position no longer warranted it.[99] As it happened, after the improvement in January–March, when the figure had reached 275 million poods, deliveries for the period April–June had scarcely exceeded 100 million poods, at a time when large quantities of grain were still needed in order to ensure the minimum essential reserves.

The government reacted by returning to the type of measures which it had used the previous winter. After the Plenum, some relaxation had been permitted the local organizations, but these were once more alerted. The pressure now put upon them by the Centre exceeded anything they had experienced during the winter. *Pravda* of April 26th exhorted them 'under no circumstances to slacken the offensive against the kulak and better-off strata who are systematically sabotaging our procurement plans, and encouraging the mass of the peasantry to do likewise'. The officials concerned were called upon to achieve 'unconditional fulfilment of the plans'. This could only mean one thing: the local officials were obliged to fall back upon the previous methods, but on a very much greater scale. All this took place barely a week or so after Stalin's public statement (on April 13th) that 'the crisis had been averted'.[100]

Once again, the government had reverted to the use of 'emergency measures', and all the concomitant 'deviations' without which the 'Party line' could not have produced any results. Again, the official documents reported, after the event as usual, the use of a whole range of methods associated with *prodrazverstka*.[101] But this time, the whole tenor of the official explanations suggested a very tolerant and indulgent view of the activists' tendencies towards 'over-zealousness'.

239

'The fact that the Ukraine and the North Caucasus are no longer functioning as grain-supplying regions, because of their winter losses, has meant that a considerably greater degree of pressure has been put on other regions this summer (May-June). In view of the need for vigorous action in this field, in view also of their great responsibilities and the demands being made on them by the Centre, the local authorities have been impelled to adopt certain measures, such as house-to-house searches, confiscations, and the closing of markets, etc.'[702]

The 'anti-serednyak' nature of these measures was now more freely admitted than had been the case in the winter. And indeed, the situation was far more serious than in the previous quarter. For example, the official gazette published a statement by the *Sovnarkom*, signed by Rykov, which said: 'The emergency measures which have been adopted during the procurements campaign have in a number of regions affected not only the kulaks but also a wider sector of the peasantry.' [103] (It will be noted that Rykov is not speaking of 'deviations' but of the emergency measures *per se*.) Local excesses in respect of 'the *zagotovki*, the local levy, loan contributions, etc.' were represented, in this context, as being merely incidental to the main action.

It is clear, moreover, that without conducting house-to-house searches, the detachments of *zagotoviteli* (procurement agents) could not have found any grain, for the peasants had no more 'marketable stocks', as Mikoyan's officials put it. In other words, they had nothing to sell. This being so, their grain-stores had to be searched, and the contents either taken, or shared with the peasants. In the words of the experts, this was known as 'tapping the serednyak's safety margin'.

Stalin and Bauman publicly admitted that this was indeed the case, but according to Stalin the government had been obliged to take this step.[104]

In the agricultural regions, and throughout the country as a whole, this requisitioning of the 'safety margin' created an enormous amount of tension. The government took steps to ensure supplies for the towns, but the measures in question were dictated by the acuteness of the immediate shortage. The sale of bread was controlled and restricted in most regions, in order to discourage speculation, among other things. This did not prevent the speculators, however, from getting hold of large stocks. In the towns, long queues appeared at the shops, owing to the restricted and uncertain nature of the supplies. Ration cards for bread were introduced in the Urals, and in several 'consumer' regions.[105]

The political situation was becoming increasingly critical. Stalin himself admitted in July 'that repeated recourse to emergency powers and arbitrary administrative action' had 'aggravated the political situation throughout the country and constituted a threat to the *smychka*'.[106]

The peasants retaliated with every means that lay in their power, and one unfailingly effective political weapon was to make their complaints known to their sons who were serving in the army. In the eyes of the peasant, a son in the army was, in a way, a link with authority. The army was consequently swamped by a flood of letters from the countryside, complaining of the wrongs which the peasants were suffering at the hands of the local authorities. There was every likelihood of hostile reactions from the soldiers, most of whom were peasants, and it was not long before such reactions were to make themselves felt [107]

Rumours of the most alarming kind began to spread among the population; it was said that there would be famine, that war and the fall of the Soviet régime were imminent. Violence or the threat of violence against the Party activists became an everyday occurrence. From Kherson, Melitopol, Semipalatinsk and other regions came reports of fires, the looting of food from shops and warehouses, civil disorder and attempts to prevent the authorities from taking grain from the agricultural regions. Public discontent in the towns and villages found its expression in riots and demonstrations against the authorities, particularly in the provinces of Leningrad, Ivanovo-Voznesensk, Nizhni-Novgorod (later Gorky), Tula, Yaroslav, and others.[108] There was trouble, too, in the North Caucasus and in other regions. In the towns, the authorities and the *GPU* noted a great deal of discontent among the workers, especially the new arrivals who still maintained close contact with their families in the countryside; this ill-feeling broke out in a number of demonstrations.

So widespread was the unrest that the Central Committee were forced to admit publicly that the situation was grave. The July Plenum confirmed that there was 'unrest among certain sectors of the peasantry, which has found its outlet in demonstrations against the arbitrary way in which the authorities have acted in several regions'.[109]

In his deep distress and uncertainty, the peasant was turning his back on the Soviet régime, and this was happening irrespective of any consideration of class stratification; so far as the authorities were concerned, therefore, he was 'going over to the kulaks'. Bauman, who was then Moscow Party Secretary and head of the Central Committee's agricultural department, stated that 'the serednyak has turned against us and sided with the kulaks', and this was true also of the bednyak, who had helped the authorities during the winter, and now had to turn to the kulak, because the State had no bread for him at the time when he most sorely needed it.

Bauman's appraisal of the situation was as follows: 'And so, during the recent period, certain political and social changes have taken place in the villages which are not to our advantage, but to that of the kulak. The kulak has reinforced his rearguard, he has allied himself with the *bednota*.' In this context, the threat to the *smychka*, and 'to some extent the weakening of our support in the countryside —that is, the *bednota* . . .'[110] were fully recognized.

The authorities were obliged to retract. A gesture of appeasement was made in the propaganda statements, which repeatedly explained that the emergency measures were merely accidental, and that only the Trotskyists had ever aimed at establishing them as a recognized procedure,[111] but apart from all this, the measures themselves were suspended after the July meeting.

So far as Stalin was concerned, it is true to say that the restriction was only a partial one, for article 107 had in no sense been rescinded, and could be reintroduced at any time, but the press assured the public that emergency measures would play no part in the coming procurements campaign which had just opened.[112]

In addition, the July Plenum decided to increase the prices paid for grain to the producer, a step which up till then had been represented as a 'kulak demand'.[113] One further step was taken, much to the humiliation of the Politburo; in June, Russia, a country renowned as an exporter of grain, bought grain abroad, thus causing a sensation on the world grain market and in political circles. In the period from June to August 1928, 250,000 tons were imported, a small quantity but sufficient to indicate the seriousness of the situation, and the problems facing the State until the next harvest was due.[114]

According to Bauman, these concessions, and hopes for a good harvest which the press did its best to encourage, 'went some way towards relieving anxiety among the peasants'. And indeed, the situation did undergo some improvement, as a result of the optimism engendered by favourable prospects for the coming harvest, and also as a result of the cessation of the emergency measures, which meant that the peasants could look forward to a year of procurements carried out under normal conditions. So, for the time being, disaster had been averted. But in terms of the economy, the overall results for the year were negative, both in respect of grain reserves, and of the régime's relations with the peasants. The same was true in several other sectors.

Despite the régime's vigorous offensive, and its use of violence, the amount of its grain reserves was smaller than in the previous year. The plan was not fulfilled. Moreover, the total figure was misleading, in the sense that a large proportion consisted of secondary crops, such as oil-yielding seeds, for example, whereas the proportion of those grains which were of primary importance, that is wheat, oats and barley, was less than it had been in the previous year (except in the case of rye).[115] The enormous effort which had gone into the procurements campaign, and which had proved so damaging from the political point of view, because of the profound mistrust, and indeed hostility, which it had engendered among the peasants, had not even ensured the necessary minimum of grain reserves.

Thus, the State was still in a precarious position, owing to its lack of reserves of grain and agricultural raw materials, while the peasants were also deprived of a sizeable proportion of their small stocks of grain.

As we shall see, the events of this year were to have important repercussions on the course of agriculture in the year that followed. Policy decisions in this field met with little success, for they were always taken too late, and thereby lost their effectiveness. Thus, the increase in the prices paid for grain to the producers, and the decision to import grain, were measures which were first strongly opposed, and then subsequently adopted. According to those politicians and experts who had vainly pressed for them at the time, the crisis might have been avoided, or might at least have been less severe, if the decision to raise prices and to buy grain abroad had been taken in time. This would have given the State room to manoeuvre on the market, and would thus have enabled them to convince the peasants that it was to their advantage to sell, and that they had nothing to gain by withholding their grain. Stalin himself admitted in February that such measures might well prove effective, but he argued that the country did not have sufficient reserves of currency for the purpose.[116]

However, in July, when it was too late, those reserves were found.

The net effect of the 'emergency measures', as Bukharin expressed it at the Plenum,[117] was an economic result of doubtful validity, and a definite worsening of the situation in the social and political field.

Looking back on an agricultural year that had been so beset with difficulties of an economic, social and political order, the observers and the experts were unanimous in their view that things were still in the balance, and that unless some coherent policy were worked out, the prospect for the coming year was one of renewed crisis.

The Politburo and Stalin in particular, were abundantly aware of this fact. The battle over the zagotovki *led them to draw certain conclusions, whose import was soon to become clear. Their experience impelled them to a reappraisal of past methods and future prospects, and obliged them to formulate a new policy.*

It is for this reason that the events of the period from January to June 1928 played a crucial part in shaping the future of the Soviet Union.

NOTES AND REFERENCES

1. According to Rykov, *15-ty S'ezd VKP(b)*, stenogramme, p. 761. On the effect of rumours of an imminent outbreak of war in creating a run on supplies in the shops, see *ibid,* pp. 762–3. Mikoyan also mentioned this.

2. Rykov, *ibid,* p. 762.

3. Stalin, *Sochineniya,* Vol. XI, p. 11.

4. On the procurements campaign of 1925 see Rykov, *NAF,* 1925, No. 10. This is his speech on the situation on the 'grain front'. See also the resolutions of the Plenary session of April 1926 of the Central Committee in *KPSS v Rezolyutsiyakh,* Vol. II, p. 262–4.

5. The Plenum of April 1926, *KPSS v. Rezolyutsiyakh,* Vol. II, p. 264.

6. See Stalin's letter of February 13, 1928, to the Party organizations in *Sochineniya,* Vol. XI, p. 11.

7. Resolutions of the Plenum of April 1928, *KPSS v Rezolyutsiyakh,* Vol. II, p. 492.

8. These data, taken from the Central Archives of the Party, are given by Konyukhov, *op. cit.* (see Ch. 3, Note 41), p. 66.

9. Speech in *Pravda,* March 11, 1928. See also Daniels, *op. cit.* (see Ch. 2, Note 3), p. 326.

10. Molotov, *15-ty S'ezd VKP(b)*, stenogramme, p. 1065.

11. Stalin, letter from the Central Committee of February 13, 1928, *Sochineniya,* Vol. XI, p. 11.

12. Twenty years later these speeches were published in *Sochineniya,* Vol. XI, pp. 1–19, oddly enough in the form of a 'summary'.

13. *Ibid,* pp. 2–4.

14. 'The kulak, admittedly, cannot be regarded as the principal stock-holder of grain. . . .' In the resolutions of the Plenum of April 1928 it is also stated that '. . . the greater part of the grain is not in his [the kulak's] hands . . .' Stalin, *Sochineniya,* Vol. XI, p. 12.

15. According to Konyukhov, *op. cit.,* pp. 98–9; Trifonov, *op. cit.* (see Ch. 2, Note 9), p. 198.

16. Stalin, *Sochineniya,* Vol. XI, p. 4.

17. *ibid.*

18. Konyukhov, *op. cit.*, p. 98.

19. See *Pravda*, January 8, 1928.

20. The sum of the local levy was fixed at 35% of the total of agricultural tax paid by the village. As we shall see, this was simply another form of taxation.

21. The resolutions of the Plenum of April 1928 of the Central Committee officially admitted that the shortening of the time allowed for payment of loan and local levy contributions, and 'the stringent provisions enforced with regard to the time allowed for payment', were emergency measures. See *KPSS v Rezolyutsiyakh*, Vol. II, pp. 494–6, and Stalin, *Sochineniya*, Vol. XI, p. 14.

22. Konyukhov, *op. cit.*, p. 93.

23. Resolutions of the Plenum of April 1928 *KPSS v Rezolyutsiyakh*, Vol. II, pp. 494–6.

24. *ibid*, p. 495.

25. This phrase is reported by Bauman in 'Uroki khlebzagotovok', *Bolshevik*, 1928, No. 13–14.

26. Konyukhov, *op. cit.*, p. 138. He goes on '. . . but he had no wish to harm the Soviet régime which had done so much for him.'

27. Mikoyan, *Pravda*, February 10, 1928.

28. This letter, taken from the Central Archives of the Party, is quoted by Konyukhov, *op. cit.*, p. 152.

29. In April the Central Committee was still speaking of the 'stability of grain prices' and resisting pressure from the villages, and from certain of the cadres, to increase the price paid for grain to producers. *KPSS v Rezolyutsiyakh*, Vol. II, p. 494.

30. These organizations were: *Khlebotsentr, Khleboprodukt, Tsentrosoyuz*, and a number of republican or *krai* organizations, such as: *Vuk, Selkhozgospodar, Ukrkhleb* (all of which were in the Ukraine), *Kavkhleb* (North Caucasus), etc. See *Pravda*, February 15, 1928.

31. Stalin, letter of February 13, 1928, *Sochineniya*, Vol. XI, p. 12, and at every Plenum, on the work of the procurement agencies. See also the article by Lvov, in *NAF*, 1928, No. 9.

32. Konyukhov, *op. cit.*, p. 149.

33. Material taken from the Central Archives of the October Revolution, by Konyukhov, *op. cit.*, pp. 140–3.

34. *ibid*, p. 153.

35. Sosnovsky, a letter of 1928 in *Byulleten Oppozitsii*, 1929, No. 3–4, pp. 16–20. Sosnovsky was a journalist well known for his articles in *Pravda* before he became active in support of the Left opposition. He quotes here the Barnaul Party journal, *Na Leninskom Puti*, 1928, No. 4, which, in an article by Nussinov, a senior official, protests against 'wildly excessive bureaucratic methods'.

36. Konyukhov, *op. cit.*, pp. 88–94.

37. Mikoyan, *Pravda*, February 12, 1928.

38. Reported by Mikoyan, *Pravda*, June 30, 1928.

39. Astrov (still editor of *Pravda* at this time), *Pravda*, July 3, 1928.

40. Stalin, *Sochineniya*, Vol. XI, p. 125. This letter was published for the first time after the war.

41. An appeal signed by Mikoyan, *Pravda*, June 30, 1928.

42. This was widely noted in the resolutions of the Plenum of April 1928. *KPSS v Rezolyutsiyakh*, Vol. II, pp. 495–6; July, Plenum, *ibid*, pp. 516–7.

43. Stalin confirms the use of methods of *prodrazverstka* in his letter of February 13, 1928, *Sochineniya*, Vol. XI, p. 18. This letter was kept secret at the time. The April Plenum also mentioned 'the gradual acceptance in practice of *prodrazverstka*'. *KPSS v Rezolyutsiyakh*, Vol. II, p. 496.

44. Panic, and rumours about the resumption of *prodrazverstka* are reported by Trifonov, who, however, accuses the kulaks of spreading them. Trifonov, *op. cit.*, p. 197.

45. The local authorities had little difficulty in obtaining the consent of the rural assemblies, since no one took steps to see that the quorum was properly constituted, or that the other rules of assembly were duly observed.

46. Stalin, *Sochineniya*, Vol. XI, p. 18; *KPSS v Rezolyutsiyakh*, Vol. II, p. 494.

47. Astrov, *Pravda*, July 3, 1928.

48. A letter by Sosnovsky, *Byulleten Oppozitsii*, 1929, No. 3–4, pp. 16–20.

49. Konyukhov, *op. cit.*, p. 20.

50. This is the opinion of *Sosnovsky* (see Note 48). However the weakness of the organizations of the *bednota* is also widely attested by official sources. See Stalin, *Sochineniya*, Vol. XI, p. 13. Mikoyan in *Pravda*, February 12, 1928, stated that work with the bednyaks was 'frequently very poor'.

51. Bauman, *op. cit.* (see Note 25), p. 74.

52. Mikoyan, *Pravda*, February 12, 1928.

53. Stalin, *Sochineniya*, Vol. XI, p. 18.

54. *ibid*.

55. Konyukhov, *op. cit.*, p. 21.

56. Konyukhov, *op. cit.*, pp. 20–1. The author states that the kulaks and the better-off peasants were involved. He does not regard this in any sense as a deviation.

57. *Pravda*, March 21, 1928.

58. Konyukhov, *op. cit.*, p. 93–4. A simple arithmetical calcula-

tion will show that the seizure of land by individuals classified here as kulaks had been insignificant.

59. Stalin, *Sochineniya*, Vol. XI, p. 124. See also Belov, *The History of A Soviet Collective Farm*. (London 1956),pp. 5–6.

60. Bauman, *op. cit.*, pp. 45–6.

61. This failure to discriminate between serednyaks and kulaks occurred not only during the procurements, but in the course of implementation of every other measure (deprivation of the right to vote, individual levy, imposition of loans, credit policy, etc.) as is admitted in official sources, which also reveal that this took place on a vast scale. See Angorov, *op. cit.* (see Ch. 2, Note 39), p. 64; Kalinin, *Pravda*, September 23, 1928 and the editorial of the issue of September 25, 1928.

62. Astrov, *Pravda*, July 3, 1929.

63. Stalin, *Sochineniya*, Vol. XI, p. 17.

64. On the food shortage see Ciliga, *Au Pays du Grand Mensonge*. (Paris, 1950), p. 34.

65. *Pravda* announced the replacement of Smirnov by Kubyak in its 'circular' on February 17, 1928. On March 23rd the paper announced in the same way the transfer of Svidersky to the post of Commissar of Education. On Teodorovich see *Pravda*, March 2, 1928.

66. *Pravda* editorial, January 26, 1928.

67. Ciliga, *op. cit.*, pp. 34–5 and numerous documents of the Right.

68. Daniels, *op. cit.*, p. 325, based upon Smilga, *Platforma Pravogo Kryla VKP(b)* in the Trotsky Archives in Harvard.

69. Generally the procurements improved towards the end of the year, then tailed off subsequently.

70. Stalin, speech delivered in Leningrad, July 13, 1928, *Sochineniya*, Vol. XI, pp. 204–5.

71. For this letter see Stalin, *Sochineniya*, Vol. XI, pp. 10–19.

72. *Pravda*, editorial of February 14, 1928.

73. Mikoyan, *Pravda*, February 12, 1928.

74. Stalin, *Sochineniya*, Vol. XI, pp. 10–19.

75. *ibid*, p. 12.

76. *ibid*, pp. 13–15.

77. *ibid*, pp. 13–16.

78. *ibid*, p. 18.

79. *ibid*, p. 15.

80. Stalin, speech to the Moscow Party Organization, *Sochineniya*, Vol. XI, p. 48–9.

81. Invariably it is stated that only 'certain officials', 'here and there', 'sometimes', 'in certain places' committed errors.

82. *KPSS v Rezolyutsiyakh*, Vol. II, p. 496. Later we shall explain the decisive part played by the Right (at this time still very influential), in this indictment.

83. Stalin, *Sochineniya*, Vol. XI, p. 15.

84. Trotsky's letter of July 12, 1928 in *The Third International After Lenin* (see Ch. 6, Note 29), pp. 273–6; Ciliga, *op. cit.*, pp. 34–5.

85. At the beginning of 1928 the *GPU* arrested dozens of the leading engineers in charge of the Donbas coal mines. In a sensational trial in Moscow, from May 18th to July 5th, 1928, they were accused of having set up (with help from abroad), an organization for sabotage. Of the forty-three accused, eleven were condemned to death, of whom five were executed.

86. See the resolution of the Plenum, based upon Mikoyan's report in *KPSS v Rezolyutsiyakh*, Vol. II, pp. 492–500.

87. *ibid*, pp. 492–3.

88. *ibid*, p. 494.

89. *ibid*, p. 497.

90. Stalin, *Sochineniya*, Vol. XI, p. 45.

91. Trotsky, *The Revolution Betrayed*. (London 1937), p. 30 of the French edition.

92. *KPSS v Rezolyutsiyakh*, Vol. II, pp. 496–7.

93. *ibid*, p. 496.

94. Stalin, *Sochineniya*, Vol. XI, p. 46.

95. *ibid*, pp. 46–50.

96. See Lvov, *NAF*, 1928, No. 9, pp. 56–8; Konyukhov, *op. cit.*, pp. 158–9.

97. Kurbatov, *NAF*, No. 9, 1929, p. 73 provides a statistical table which summarises the errors committed by the *TsSU* in calculating the *khlebo-furazhny balans*.

98. Stalin, speech delivered on April 13, 1928, *Sochineniya*, Vol. XI, p. 39.

99. Konyukhov, *op. cit.*, and Stalin in his speech of July 13, 1928, *Sochineniya*, Vol. XI, pp. 205–6.

100. Stalin, speech of April 13, 1928, *Sochineniya*, Vol. XI, p. 48.

101. Bauman, *op. cit.*, Konyukhov, *op. cit.*, p. 113; Stalin, *Sochineniya*, Vol. XI, p. 206.

102. Bauman, *op. cit.*, pp. 45–6; *KPSS v Rezolyutsiyakh*, Vol. II, p. 515. (The July Plenum.)

103. *Sbornik Zakonov*, June 30, 1928, No. 44, Part I, par. 400, p. 823.

104. Bauman, *op. cit.*, p. 46; Stalin, *Sochineniya*, Vol. XI, pp. 205–6.

105. According to the Party's Central Archives, cited by Kon-

yukhov, *op. cit.*, pp. 159–60. See also *KPSS v Rezolyutsiyakh*, Vol. II, p. 515.

106. Stalin, *Sochineniya*, Vol. XI, p. 206.

107. Daniels, *op. cit.*, pp. 331–2. Daniels quotes the minutes of the July session, found in the Trotsky Archives.

108. Information taken from the Party Archives by Konyukhov, *op. cit.*, pp. 158–9.

109. *KPSS v Rezolyutsiyakh*, Vol. II, p. 515; Daniels, *op. cit.*, p. 328, quotes the minutes found in the Trotsky Archives.

110. Bauman, *op. cit.*, pp. 46–7.

111. Bauman, *op. cit.*, p. 48; *KPSS v Rezolyutsiyakh*, Vol. II, p. 515 call for action against those who were insinuating that there was a tendency to transform the temporary emergency measures into a 'permanent line'.

112. e.g. *Pravda*, editorial of August 14, 1928.

113. *KPSS v Rezolyutsiyakh*, Vol. II, p. 516: the resolutions of the session.

114. See *Sbornik Zakonov*, July 8, 1928, No. 13. This figure is given by Mikoyan in *Bolshevik*, 1928, No. 15, p. 16.

115. According to Mikoyan, *Bolshevik*, 1928, No. 15, p. 16, the 'centralized' procurements amounted to 10·1 million metric tons in 1927–8 (the quantity for the previous year had been 10·6 million). On the composition of the quantities obtained, see Lvov, *NAF*, 1928, No. 9, pp. 56–60.

116. For a criticism of the government and an opinion on some possible ways of avoiding the crisis see Lvov, *NAF*, 1928, No. 9, See also Stalin, *Sochineniya*, Vol. XI, p. 11. Later, in April 1929, Stalin was to provide a different explanation.

117. Speech to the Plenum of July 1928, quoted by Daniels, *op. cit.*, p. 331.

Chapter 10

STALIN CHANGES COURSE

The grain crisis and the social and political upheavals which followed it proved to be the key factors in the sequence of events in which the Soviet government was now caught up, and in which it was to find itself committed to policies which went far beyond anything that even its most determined leaders would have wished.

The first 'left turn', which occurred in the winter of 1928, took place not as a result of any premeditated policy, but under pressure of circumstances. Initially, there was probably general agreement among the leadership that urgent measures were called for, but it soon became apparent that there was some divergence of opinion as to the extent of the change in policy, and the methods by which it should be implemented. Faced with the sudden exigencies of a situation in which the country was short of food for the towns and the army, the leadership put forward a variety of proposals for dealing with the crisis, and these differed according to the ideas and temperament, the background and character, of the individuals in question. Since it was on Stalin that the fate of the country was ultimately to depend, it is clearly important to chart the course of Stalin's ideas and actions at this time.

There can be no doubt that the grain crisis, and the offensive against the peasants, in which Stalin played an active and leading role, were of capital importance in shaping his new line of thought. His ideas, conditioned as they were by the pressure of events which were driving the country from crisis to crisis, bear all the traces of the troubles which marked the first half of 1928. It was during this period that he first came forward with his personal appraisal of the country's position and of the methods which should be adopted to deal with it, together with his real views on the peasantry and his firm decision to effect a radical change in policy in the face of a situation which was steadily going from bad to worse; these views were presented in texts which in some cases were made public at the time, while others were kept secret.

He was well aware of the position. The two successive waves of emergency measures, which had been introduced in order to extract from the peasants the necessary minimum of grain which the State required, had highlighted the fact that the country was producing too little, and that, even when there was no shortage, the task of taking the grain was one of enormous difficulty. Stalin was painfully conscious of the extent to which the régime was dependent on the good will of the *muzhik*. In January, he had told the Siberian Party officials,[1] 'Our industry must not be dependent on the whims of the kulaks,' and he had gone on to say that 'as long as there are kulaks, they will continue to sabotage the procurements'.

However, as Stalin very well knew, the trouble could not be attributed exclusively to the kulaks. The bulk of the grain supplies were in the hands of the rest of the peasants, a fact which had repeatedly been stated; the only difference was that the kulak was rather more obstinate, and being materially better off, was in a better position to withhold his supplies until such time as prices had risen. In any case, he was rich only in a very relative sense. While the grain was being confiscated during the *zagotovki*, the total amount taken, on two occasions, from the kulaks, including no doubt numerous other peasants who were described as kulaks, was 150 million poods of grain.[2] Even assuming that the kulaks had been able to conceal as much, or more again, the above figure serves to reduce the fabled 'kulak hoards' to something nearer their true proportion, and likewise to give a more accurate picture of the kulak's powers of resistance.

Despite the tone of the propaganda statements at the time, and despite the efforts of the leadership to avoid any pronouncement which might be construed as anti-serednyak, the real nature of Stalin's intentions is clear. His attitude is partly revealed by a letter which was written in February 1926, and which was not made public at the time. Stalin was replying to three Party members who, he said, had been 'shocked' by the fact that he 'regarded the peasantry as a rather unstable, and not as reliable an ally as the proletariat in advanced capitalist countries'. He went on to remind his three correspondents of some of the basic facts about the behaviour of the peasants during the Civil War. 'The peasants frequently wavered in their allegiance, sometimes siding with the workers, and sometimes with the generals! And what about all those who served as volunteers in the armies of Denikin and Kolchak?'[3]

Stalin's mistrust of the peasants as allies grew even deeper in 1928, and his policy towards them was conditioned by this mistrust. Addressing the students in Moscow in the month of May, he incautiously, though quite sincerely, observed that 'the contradictions which exist between the working class and the peasantry, in the context of the alliance between workers and peasants will . . . gradually be eliminated, and the need for emergency measures during the procurements will disappear . . .'.[4] Here was the connection between the peasantry as a whole and the emergency measures, expressed in the most unequivocal terms. On this occasion, he reminded his listeners that the alliance had only three aims, namely to consolidate the position of the working class, to confirm the working class in its leading role, and to eliminate classes and the class society. Anyone who thought that the alliance should have further objectives, said Stalin, should be regarded as a Menshevik, an 'SR', and not a Marxist.

This remark was aimed at political opponents of whose existence his audience were still unaware. But they may well have wondered what were the rights of the other party to the alliance, in a situation in which the objectives had been formulated exclusively from the point of view of the 'working class'. His youthful listeners must certainly have had some misgivings on this score, for Stalin embarked on a laborious explanation aimed at proving that the *smychka* formula had no inherent contradictions, and was a model of clarity. However, he only succeeded in complicating the issue still further by quoting a remark of Lenin's to the effect that 'the peasantry were a class apart', and that they were 'the last remaining capitalist class'.[5]

Leaving aside the question of the extent to which such an allegation was justified, the important point is that this was Stalin's genuine view of the peasantry. *According to him, the peasants were a class— the last remaining capitalist class—whose characteristic feature was that it constantly engendered from within itself . . . a capitalist class.*

In this context, the question of coherence has little relevance: the essential fact which must be grasped is that when Stalin and those of his immediate circle publicly stated that 'we cannot be dependent on the kulaks', what they were in fact thinking was 'we cannot be dependent on the *muzhik*'!

According to one document whose authenticity is unquestioned[6] Molotov had said at the July session that 'the serednyak has grown more powerful, and that is why he is at loggerheads' [with us]. In fact, it was the serednyak who was the real problem, and this was why Stalin frequently stressed the fact that if the serednyak, or the peasant in general, was to be kept within the limits of the role laid down for him by the régime—that is, the role of ally—he would require to be hedged around by certain safety measures. Essentially, these were as follows: '. . . the alliance with the serednyak can be made safe provided that we undertake a determined offensive against the kulaks and consolidate our efforts with the *bednota*; in the absence of these conditions, the serednyak may look to the kulak as a guiding force'.[7] Pressure must therefore be brought to bear on the middle peasant from all sides, otherwise it would be impossible to guide him towards what Stalin considered to be the régime's most important task, that of assisting the peasantry to reorganize their farms 'on a new technical basis. . .'.[8]

In this context, he quoted Lenin, but added a remark of his own which was not entirely in keeping with the spirit of Lenin's testament: 'There is no point in coaxing the peasant, and taking such an approach as a model of what our relations with him should be. Soft words will not get us very far. . . .'

'No soft words' was intended as a jibe at the Bukharinists and their theories; it was also meant to convey his own opinion of the old, classic NEP methods, and to make it clear that he no longer had any faith in them as a means of extricating the country from the predicament in which it now found itself.

So far, the methods adopted by Stalin had been scarcely more effective, though he could hardly have been accused of 'softness'. The emergency measures had produced relatively little grain, and their only result had been a further worsening of the prospects for agriculture. There had again been a decrease in sowings in 1928, despite efforts to prevent this. Some writers openly affirmed that the emergency measures were partly responsible for the crisis, which had been aggravated by the loss of the winter grain in the Ukraine.[9]

There was a further reduction in the sowings of winter grain at the end of 1928. The experts attached to *Gosplan* and other institutes noted a falling-off in the hitherto favourable rate of progress in livestock holdings. In 1928, for the first time, there was a drop in the number of livestock, because the peasants were selling a great many of their animals.[10]

Once again, this was due partly to natural causes, and partly to social factors. During the summer, there had been a recurrence of the unfavourable conditions in the Ukraine and the North Caucasus, and the harvest in these regions in 1928 was bad. Over the country as a whole, the yield of wheat and rye was smaller than in the preceding year. These disasters were speedily reflected in the numbers of livestock, since the peasants sold off their animals in order to buy seed grain, or because they were short of fodder. The negative role of the authorities in all this was clearly underlined by an expert of the Commissariat of Trade, who listed, as being partly responsible for the fall in livestock production, '. . . the fiscal *peregiby*, individual levies and, to some extent, the tendency for the better-off strata of the peasantry to avoid inclusion in categories which would place them in a disadvantageous class position in the villages'.[11] Thus, the country was facing the prospect of a shortage of livestock products, in addition to the already existing grain shortage.

Against a background of shortage, and additional stresses and strains connected with the industrialization effort, the Soviet economy began, during the course of this year, to show signs of economic crisis. At the session in October 1928, some of these symptoms were listed as follows:

'The grain problem, the acute shortage of metals and building materials, the general dearth of manufactured goods and the problem of reserves, the drop in export trade occasioned by the lack of grain for export, and the resulting drop in imports, and lastly the problem of consolidating the currency'.[12]

The slowness of industrial development also laid a great burden on the economy, and was giving rise to increasing social pressures. Trotsky, writing from exile in Alma Ata, analysed the situation in a letter which he sent to the Comintern Congress in July 1928. This letter was never made available for discussion at any meeting, and the country remained unaware of its contents. Stalin, naturally, read every word written by his rival, whose existence still represented a threat to his own position. The influence exerted on him by certain of Trotsky's ideas, or at least the resemblance between the two in matters of diagnosis, is clearly discernible.[13]

Trotsky had written in his letter 'The retarded rate of industrial growth has given rise to a wholly unacceptable scissors movement in prices. . . .' This was an old theme of Trotsky's, but this time the effects of the 'scissors' were much more far-reaching.

'The immense advantages which accrued to the peasantry as a result of the agrarian revolution of October are now being eaten away by the prices of manufactured goods. This is destroying the *smychka* by driving vast numbers in the various strata of village life to join forces with the kulak, whose watchword is free trade at home and abroad.'[14]

This weakness was causing an adverse movement in public opinion, which would be dangerous for any régime, but was particularly so in the case of a revolutionary régime. The mass of the population had taken part in the revolution in a spirit of unbounded optimism, but the slow rate of progress towards any improvement in their living standards would inevitably lead to 'a loss of faith in the ability of the Soviet government to bring about any radical transformation of society within the foreseeable future'.[15]

Having stressed, at considerable length, the 'menace of dual power', that is, the potential danger to the Soviet régime which might arise from a coalition of hostile social forces made up of Nepmen, kulaks, and petty bourgeois in the towns, with growing support from large sections of the bureaucracy and the Party, Trotsky issued the following warning. The régime must not wait for these hostile forces to attack, 'we must forestall them by taking the offensive ourselves . . .'. For Trotsky, there was no going back, and he therefore judged, correctly, that Stalin's left turn was not a temporary manoeuvre; on the other hand he believed, wrongly this time, that the moment of victory for his faction was drawing near.

His proposals for carrying out the offensive were that the 'centre-right line' should be dropped in favour of the 'Leninist line', that is the line suggested by the *Platform*.[16] It should however be noted that in August Trotsky had already criticized the manner in which Stalin had carried out his 'left turn', and had pointed out that it was important to examine not only what Stalin was doing, but also the way in which he was doing it.[17]

Stalin was in agreement with Trotsky's reading of the situation. He was now convinced that, unless there was a radical change in policy, and unless the solutions which he proposed were put into effect, 'the return of capitalism would be inevitable'.[18] The dilemma, as he expressed it at the time, was one of *kto kogo* (who [is to defeat] whom), and this reflected his profound conviction that the only way out lay in a general offensive, though at this stage he still did not think of it as being waged simultaneously 'on all fronts'. A wide range of peasants would still be left in peace with their plots of land, and even given whatever assistance was possible. The repeated statements which he made to this effect in the course of the year also reflected a sincerely held belief.[19] When such sentiments were voiced by a man like Rykov, they arose from his conviction that something could still be done to achieve progress in agriculture within the framework of the private sector. On the other hand, as far as Stalin was concerned, the private sector was nothing but a source of trouble. He was simply hoping to bypass the peasantry until such times as he was able to put his new plan into effect.

This plan had been conceived amid the stresses and strains of the *zagotovki*. Stalin felt that it was not enough to appear before the Siberian activists whip in hand, and that it was incumbent on him to offer them some more constructive long-term programme, and some reassurance for the future. This he did towards the end of January and the beginning of February, when he outlined, for the benefit of his Siberian listeners, his two principal solutions, namely the sovkhozes and kolkhozes.

According to Stalin, the fundamental objective was to set up, in the villages, strongholds similar to the 'strategic positions' which the régime held in the towns. In his view, there was little justification for the belief, widely publicized by the Party in its theory and propaganda, that rural co-operation under Soviet conditions would automatically be 'socialist' in form. Experience had shown that local co-operative organizations tended merely to become strongholds for the better-off peasants. Stalin now advocated the large-scale creation of kolkhozes and sovkhozes 'with all the resources and means at our command'; only these organizations would have the right to rank as socialist. Their main function would be to provide the government with large quantities of grain, which would make them independent of the private sector, and even enable them to exert a guiding influence on the latter.

'For this reason,' said Stalin, 'we must ensure that, during the course of the next three or four years, the kolkhozes and sovkhozes are in a position to supply the State with at least a third of the necessary minimum. Even this would be enough to undermine the influence of the kulaks . . .',[20] and it would provide the State with the minimum supplies required for feeding the workers and the army, as well as building up the reserves of grain which were so sorely needed. While supplying the régime with the minimum necessary to safeguard its own interests, the kolkhozes and sovkhozes would, at the same time, be contributing to 'the victory of socialist construction in the countryside'.

Stalin knew that the promise of bread alone was not enough, and that it was important to present the Party cadres with an objective, in the shape of ideas which would revive their flagging hopes and imbue them with renewed vigour, while illuminating the splendid prospects opened up by the new policy of which he was the architect. From this time on, every step taken by the régime was to be linked with the idea of socialism and measured in quantitative terms, thus, so many per cent of the peasants collectivized, so many per cent of the national income represented by the State sector, and so on. With the help of these figures, it would be possible to announce, at a given moment, that the socialist régime, of which generations of revolutionaries had dreamed, was well and truly established.

In this context, Stalin introduced the Siberian cadres to a theory which they had not hitherto encountered, and which was to become a sort of watchword for the years to come. This went as follows. Up till this time, the Soviet régime had been based on two unequal factors, namely 'a unified, socialized industry, and small-scale cultivation of the land based on the individual peasant holding, and, therefore, on private ownership of the means of production'. 'Can the Soviet régime go on existing on the basis of two such conflicting factors? No, it can not'.[21]

Here was a categorical statement which dispensed with the need for reasoned argument, and it reflects Stalin's anxiety to ensure that the Soviet régime should be established upon 'a single, stable base', thus giving the State the same control over agriculture that it already exercised over industry. This hypothesis could be presented to the activists as a socialist one. However, even at this stage, some of his opponents had already dismissed it as the dream of a 'super-bureaucrat', who was only interested in creating an easily manipulated piece of social machinery whose every cog would be controlled from a decision-making centre.

However, the theoretical aspects of this particular doctrine were another matter; Stalin, under pressure from immediate difficulties, was concerned with the *tovarnost*, which was a matter of overriding importance. In May, he spoke to the communist students about his faith in large-scale agricultural enterprises, emphasizing their superiority over other forms.[22] The idea of ever-larger enterprises was subsequently to become a myth, until belief in them became an article of faith. There was even a tendency to use their size as a criterion in demonstrating the superiority of socialism over capitalism.[23] This exaggerated over-emphasis on large-scale forms was to have a very damaging influence on the Soviet régime, and its effects are still being felt to this day.

At the period of which we are speaking, it had been discovered that the kolkhozes and sovkhozes were able to supply almost half of their production to the market, that is to say four times more than the average peasant farm. From the outset, Stalin was aware that these state or co-operative organizations might be as unwilling as the rest of the peasants to supply the State with grain, if the prices paid by the State were unacceptable to them. As we shall see, he had at his disposal sufficient evidence to convince him beforehand that prices would in fact be regarded as unfavourable, and for this reason the campaign of 'socialist construction in the countryside', as exemplified by the creation of the kolkhozes, was accompanied by a search for a *modus operandi* which would ensure that the State obtained the desired proportion of production, regardless of the opinions of the producers.

Addressing the same audience of young Party intellectuals, Stalin put the problem with brutal frankness. 'We must,' he said, 'devise a procedure whereby the kolkhozes will turn over their entire marketable production of grain to the state and co-operative organizations under threat of withdrawal of State subsidies and credits.'[24] [He had at this time no inkling of the difficulties he was to encounter later on with the state sovkhozes.—M.L.]

The concrete results which Stalin was hoping to achieve in three or four years time included, for a start, a contribution of some 100 million poods of grain from the sovkhozes, though those of his colleagues in the Politburo who still had a say in the matter had suggested to him that the time involved was likely to be nearer four to five years. It was believed that the sovkhozes offered the best prospects for a speedy improvement in the situation in the short term. These hopes were to prove illusory, but for the moment it was the sovkhozes which received the largest allocation of resources. Both the former kolkhozes and the new ones were expected to make an equivalent contribution.

By use of yet another method, namely the contract method (though this was regarded as being the least reliable) it was hoped to extract an additional 50–100 million poods of grain. This total of 250–300 million poods of grain, which would be secured by the rural agencies of the State, was regarded as a minimum 'which would be more or less sufficient to ensure the State freedom to manoeuvre either at home or abroad'.[25] Stalin also expressed the hope that supplies of this order would enable the régime to surmount the annual procurements crisis without having recourse to emergency measures.

The above objectives were, in themselves, ambitious enough, but it must be remembered that, at the same time, the government were also aiming at an immense amount of investment in industry. Here too the targets which had been set were expressed in exclusively quantitative indices related to the level of investment.[26]

An essential prerequisite of the changes which were envisaged for the rural sector was the existence of a powerful industrial sector, particularly in the field of heavy industry, which would create the conditions for a new *smychka*. Under the earlier policy, the *smychka* had been 'based on textiles'; Stalin's programme, as put forward in July, presented the *smychka* in a new guise, as one 'based on metal', which would be related not merely to consumption and exchange relationships, but to the actual process of production itself.

How were these operations to be financed? This intractable problem had already been analysed with great frankness by Preobrazhensky, and Stalin's solution followed closely along the lines suggested by the latter. In a speech at the July session, which was not published until twenty years later, Stalin revealed to the Central Committee members certain 'most unpleasant truths', indeed he presented them as a vindication of his policy. He confronted them with the fact that the Soviet régime had only two sources of accumulation open to it, namely the working class and the peasants. Out of consideration for his audience, Stalin said nothing about the contribution which the proletariat should be called upon to make, but the role of the peasantry was highlighted in the most unequivocal terms. As Stalin put it, the peasants were not only subject to direct taxation by the State in the usual way, but in addition were '*paying too much* for manufactured goods, whose prices were relatively high, and, secondly, were *losing* on the prices paid for agricultural produce. . . . This is a form of "tribute", or super-tax, which we are forced to levy on them temporarily, if we are to maintain and also to increase the present rate of industrial development . . .'.[27] He declared that, at the present stage, the country could not do without this 'tribute', and that it would be 'several years' before they could afford to waive it.[28]

This frank admission carried with it the prospect of increasing social tension during the four or five years which would be required to pave the way for the ultimate elimination of the contradictions of the *smychka*. The breach between town and country, which had already widened alarmingly after the events of the winter, was to become wider still, as valuable resources were increasingly drawn off from the countryside in order to finance industrial investment. It was obvious that the country was doomed to a period of increasing shortages and a heightening of the class struggle, and was facing a highly explosive situation. What was to be done to ward off the worst effects of the storm and bring the country safely through a perilous passage?

The answers which Stalin found to these questions were, to a large extent, a reflection of his experiences during the *zagotovki*. As he saw it, the régime must be prepared to take whatever steps were deemed essential. Since he was now determined to meet the situation head on, regardless of the cost, the first requirement for success was to wield sufficient power.

Bukharin, at this juncture, had become aware of those aspects of Stalin's personality which appeared to him to have sinister implications; he summed up Stalin's attitude, essentially, in the following way. Since taxes would increase, to the accompaniment of growing popular resentment, a firm line would be called for; should any difficulties arise, there would be no hesitation in falling back on the emergency measures.[29]

Stalin denied any such allegation, but nevertheless let it be understood that these measures were capable of producing results, and must not be rejected out of hand; this he did with all the more assurance in that he felt his position within the Central Committee had been strengthened. It was clear, from the above statements, that the use of coercive measures would not be definitively abandoned until such times as the country had emerged from its difficulties. When addressing the Central Committee in July, he confirmed that the possibility of such measures could not be ruled out. 'The use of emergency measures must be looked at from the dialectical point of view, since everything depends on the given conditions at a given time and place'.[30] At this time, he was still claiming that the emergency measures would not have been introduced if the exchequer had had currency of the order of 100–150 millions with which to import grain. But one year later, he was sufficiently confident of his position to be able to assert that the emergency measures had been the result of a deliberate policy, which was not dictated by shortage of currency (Rykov, who had pressed for grain to be imported, was well enough informed to know that the necessary resources could have been mobilized) but purely by considerations of expediency.[31]

Stalin clearly preferred the use of force to the slower and more complex procedures of economic policy. It is of course arguable that his subsequent assertions were an attempt to rationalize, in retrospect, the use of methods which were the outcome of sudden panic. The fact remains that from this time on such methods continued to find favour.

A terror-stricken Bukharin, in conversation with Kamenev, had prophesied in July: 'He (Stalin) will have to drown the uprisings in blood'.[32] Stalin was prepared to do so, if necessary, but he was also perfecting other methods, which reflected his tactical skill, and the keen perception which he brought to bear on the choice of ways and means to keep him in power. He contrived to create, throughout the country as a whole, among the activists, and within the Party in particular, a social and intellectual atmosphere in which any kind of resistance was impossible, and in which any attack on his political line was doomed to failure, not only because it could be put down by police action, but because such opposition was construed as a morally reprehensible act, which automatically attracted a charge of heresy, and identified the critic with the enemy and all his works. These methods reached their final apotheosis in the Stalin cult, that combination of police repression and semi-magical, quasi-religious orthodoxy which had come to fruition during the period of the 'left turn'.

The principal device used in the rural areas to create the kind of social climate in which the peasants would prove most amenable to the wishes of the authorities was the exaggerated emphasis placed on the kulac menace, and the fomentation of the class struggle to a degree of intensity which it would not have reached, without official encouragement. These were methods which had already been adequately tested during the procurements campaign.

Experience had shown that any attack directed against the kulaks could always be extended, with the minimum of effort, to cover vast numbers of other peasants; this could either be done directly by 'erroneously' branding them as kulaks, (in which case the local authorities could subsequently be used as scapegoats), or else they could be threatened with the label of *podkulachniki*. In this way, the authorities had a ready-made bogy, suitably blackened and blown up out of all proportion, with which the peasants could be terrified into submission whenever this was thought advisable.

This was a technique which was henceforth to work with unfailing efficacity, particularly because it proved acceptable to Party members who were alive to arguments of a class nature. Similarly, it commended itself to a certain section of public opinion abroad, among socialists, or liberals, who saw no reason to question the need for extremely stringent measures against the kulaks who were standing in the way of socialism and progress for the mass of the *muzhiki*.

There was one other important function which the anti-kulak measures were designed to fulfil, even if they were more or less confined to a narrow category (and as we have seen this was not possible, because of the additional factor of the *zazhitochnye*). Their effect was to block the serednyak by preventing him from realizing his dream of becoming a kulak, and inducing him to accept the idea of the kolkhoz. Stalin presented a slightly distorted view of this process in April, when he said: 'If the serednyak is prevented from rising higher and becoming a kulak, and cannot reasonably be expected to come down in the social scale, then we must hold out to him the prospect of being able to improve his own economic condition by collaborating in the creation of the kolkhozes'.[33]

Read the other way round, this 'proposition' clearly illustrates the point we have been trying to make: the serednyak was to be denied the prospect of becoming a kulak, in order that he should accept a different prospect. As a result of a formidable campaign, in which the kulak was subjected to increasing restrictions and persecution, the serednyak found himself cut off from the future as he saw and preferred it, and realized that he might well suffer a similar fate, should he attempt to defy the authorities.

This was an extremely effective way of bringing pressure to bear on the broad mass of the peasantry, and it had the additional result of sowing the seeds of dissension among their ranks, since the poor peasants, and indeed many of those who were slightly less poor, had no direct incentive to defend the most prosperous elements in the villages.

In the meanwhile, Stalin had taken advantage of another event in order to provide himself with a weapon for keeping the towns in submission. The event in question was the hunt for saboteurs. In the villages, the kulak could be blamed for all misfortunes, but in the towns it was impossible to assign the same role to the Nepman. He had no direct access either to major industrial undertakings or to important State organizations, and could not therefore conveniently serve as a scapegoat. This part was to be played, much more significantly, by the non-communist intellectuals, large numbers of whom were involved, at that time, in industry and in the ministries, as well as in the universities.

The trial of the *Shakhty* engineers, who had been arrested by the *OGPU* at the beginning of the year, gave Stalin the opportunity to work out a number of devices which were to prove particularly effective in muzzling the non-Party cadres, and were later to be used to silence the Party itself.

As for the truth of the accusations made against the engineers during the show trial, which went on in Moscow for over two months) from May 18 to July 5, 1928), this is a matter which cannot be discussed within the context of the present work. What is important is the use which Stalin made of the event, and the lessons which he learned from it. These were entirely unrelated to the problem of the engineers' guilt, even if in fact they had committed the crimes of which they were accused.[34]

In his speech at Moscow in April, in the section dealing with the *Shakhty* affair, Stalin drew the following conclusions: the communists were not sufficiently well-versed in the technical aspects of the enterprises of which they were in charge; the young communist specialists were inexperienced, and had not received adequate training for their job from the technical institutes concerned; no effective check was made in economic and other organizations to ensure that the various decisions were properly implemented. Among the measures envisaged for overcoming this weakness, it was suggested that there should be constant on-the-spot checks by administrators from the Centre, and an increase in the practice of appointing workers to posts in factory management, etc. . . .[35]

One may ask whether it was necessary to conduct a trial of 'saboteurs' in order to arrive at conclusions of the above order, which relate to elementary aspects of administrative procedure. At all events, the method was to become a common one, and it consisted of linking changes in policy, or personnel, or the introduction of a major campaign, with some alleged démarche by forces hostile to the régime. This device enabled the authorities to give 'political point' to the action they had taken, and to make it appear in the desired light.[36]

But there was much more to it than that. In the case of the *Shakhty* affair (which had not yet come to trial, although the Politburo were said to have proof of the allegations), Stalin announced that it was evidence of a major manoeuvre devised along new lines, and directed against the USSR by the forces of capitalism. . . . 'The point at issue is one of economic intervention in our industrial affairs by western European capitalist organizations who are hostile to the Soviet Union'.[37] The exaggerated nature of the allegation is readily understood when one bears in mind the use which was subsequently to be made of it. Stalin went on to say that, after their efforts at military intervention had failed, 'the forces of international capital', that is, the aforementioned 'capitalist organizations', had changed their tactics. 'Now they are engaged in an attempt to undermine our economic position by economic intervention of a kind which, although invisible or not always immediately detectable, is none the less equally dangerous, and consists of fomenting all sorts of crises in various sectors of industry, thereby paving the way for future armed intervention'.[38]

Stalin's desire to be constantly forearmed with a readymade explanation for 'all sorts of crises' could not have been more clearly expressed. The suggestion of capitalist 'cunning' as being the principal motivating force behind these crises, was sufficiently plausible to serve as a direct and logical link with future shortcomings, errors, opposition, or even simple criticism directed at the régime.

Sabotage, as Stalin had emphasized, was invisible, not readily detectable. . . . It could therefore be detected anywhere, at any given time. Thus, by misuse of Marxist class theory, there was developed a system of interpretation and apologetics whereby any opposition, whether real or imagined, could be traced directly, without the need for further proof, to the machinations of spies in the pay of 'the forces of international capitalism' which, in this context, were purely mythical. 'It all hangs together,' as Stalin had said, speaking of the engineers' trial, 'there is no question of its being accidental'.[39]

Some months later, a new factor came into play, and was in turn used to provide further justification for these manoeuvres, and to give added power to the weapon with which future coercive measures were to be enacted. The factor in question was the famous theory, now discredited in the USSR, about the intensification of the class struggle which was to accompany the growing power of socialism in the country. According to this interpretation, the more the class enemy was defeated and eliminated, the greater the power of socialism would become, and the greater would be the danger represented by the class enemy. The argument was put forward with just that element of rationality which lends verisimilitude to concepts of this kind. Stalin explained that the forward march of socialism would leave in its wake the ruined hopes of thousands of merchants, small-scale and medium-scale capitalists, and a section of the kulak population. 'Is it to be expected that these individuals will accept their downfall in silence, without seeking to organize some form of resistance? Of course not!'[40] There was a certain logic in his argument, since it might be supposed that any such group of people would try to resist, given their extreme discontent. But the thread of logic runs out at this point, and we find instead a totally unsupported generalization. 'As we march forward, resistance from these capitalist elements will steadily increase, and the class struggle will grow more and more bitter, while the Soviet régime, with steadily mounting strength, pursues a policy aimed at encircling the hostile forces. . . .'[41] Bukharin, who was regarded by Lenin as the best theoretician in the Party, dismissed this theory as 'ignorant nonsense'.[42]

However, the scientific basis for these theories was of relatively little importance, when the main consideration was to devise a weapon for political domination, whose efficacy would not be measured in terms of its intellectual content. When one comes to consider Stalin's writings and his actions, one has the impression that his thoughts were turned primarily to the hidden springs of power. The theories and the practical policies which he was to adopt in later years were merely a further development of the experiences and, so to speak, the inspiration vouchsafed him in 1928.

Stalin and the Politburo were preparing for a leap into the unknown, and the best way to ensure a safe landing seemed to be the existence of a powerful authority, preferably with Stalin himself firmly in control.

In the meantime, while preparing to meet the dangers that lay ahead, Stalin set about reducing the Party to a state of docility, a task which was still a long way from having been accomplished. Given the steadily worsening state of affairs within the country, and above all the explosive nature of the peasant situation, there were still too many elements in the Party who might combine to obtain a majority vote in the Central Committee and overthrow Stalin.

Although exiled, Trotsky and his supporters were not forgotten and their standing was still fairly high among the activists, a good few of whom were in fact secret Trotskyists, or had not entirely forsworn their former allegiance. There must have been many communists in the upper Party echelons who were well aware of the 'Trotskyist' content of the new line, and failed to understand why it was necessary to continue the campaign of denigration against Trotsky, instead of putting him in power.[43] As Deutscher has explained,[44] Stalin fully understood that for every exiled Trotskyist there were two 'capitulators' within the Party who were still Trotskyists at heart, and two more who were 'two faced' (dvurushniki) and whose sympathies also lay with Trotsky.

In addition, the Politburo itself was soon to be the scene of a battle against the new opposition from the Right. This year found Stalin strenuously engaged in eliminating opposition from within the Party, and removing potential rivals who might threaten his power. The most important of these rivals, Trotsky himself, was finally expelled from the USSR at the beginning of 1929, and thus ceased to be a force in Soviet politics. The man who might have acted as a rallying point for all Stalin's opponents had been put out of harm's way. At about the same time, the Right opposition was also virtually eliminated, and Stalin was left with a clear field in which to pursue his personal policies unopposed. By November, he had already issued his watchword 'catch up and overtake' (*dognat i peregnat*), calling upon the Party and the people to mobilize their forces for the urgent task of industrialization.[45] Six months later, the famous Five-year plan had been adopted.

Before discussing the Soviet 'great leap forward', we must examine the policy which was pursued in the intervening months, and try to follow the course of the struggle against the Right, for while the Right continued to function as a political force, Stalin's hands were tied.

NOTES AND REFERENCES

1. Stalin, *Sochineniya*, Vol. XI, pp. 4–5.

2. This figure is given by Trifonov, *op. cit.* (see Ch. 2, Note 9), p. 200. It will be recalled that the Left had suggested mobilizing this quantity as a compulsory loan. For this reason the figure was not made public at the time.

3. Stalin, *Sochineniya*, Vol. VIII, p. 93.

4. Stalin, *Sochineniya*, Vol. XI, p. 95.

5. Stalin, *Sochineniya*, Vol. XI, pp. 95–6. It should be borne in mind that Lenin is not at all clear on this point.

6. Sokolnikov to Kamenev in *Sotsialisticheski Vestnik*, May 1929, No. 9, p. 9.

7. Stalin, *Sochineniya*, Vol. XI, pp. 96–7, 106.

8. *ibid.*

9. Tsylko, *NAF*, 1928, No. 9, p. 8; Stalin, *Sochineniya*, Vol. XI, p. 261 (The November Plenum); Vishnevsky, *NAF*, 1928, No. 10, pp. 87–92; Volf, *Planovoe Khozyaistvo* 1929, No. 2, p. 100.

10. Kurbatov, *NAF*, 1929, No. 5; Vishnevsky, in *NAF*, 1928, No. 10, pp. 87–92 discusses these poor prospects; Volf, *Planovoe Khozyaistvo*, 1929, No. 2, p. 99.

11. Lvov, in *NAF* 1929, No. 1, describes the first part of the procurements campaign of 1928–9.

12. Resolution of the Plenum of November 1928 in *KPSS v Rezolyutsiyakh*, Vol. II, p. 527.

13. According to Deutscher, Stalin read Trotsky attentively, and was impressed by his analyses. In the opinion of Deutscher, Trotsky was unquestionably the father of Stalin's new line. See *The Prophet Unarmed*, p. 466.

14. Trotsky, 'What Now?', in *The Third International After Lenin*, pp. 294–5.

15. Trotsky, *op. cit.*, p. 295.

16. Trotsky, *op. cit.*, pp. 296–7.

17. See Deutscher, *The Prophet Unarmed*, pp. 446–7.

18. See his speech to the Plenum of November 1928, *Sochineniya*, Vol. XI, pp. 254–5.

19. See, for example, his letter to the Politburo of June 20, 1928, in which he declared that the private sector would remain 'the centre of gravity', but that this was no longer enough. *Sochineniya*, Vol. XI, p. 123.

20. Stalin, *Sochineniya*, Vol. XI, p. 6.

21. *ibid*.

22. *ibid*, p. 84.

23. This theme appears as early as July 1928 in Stalin's speech to the July Plenum; thereafter he introduced it frequently.

24. Stalin, *Sochineniya*, Vol. XI, pp. 88–9.

25. *ibid*, pp. 90–2 contain the whole plan. The quotation is from p. 92.

26. *ibid*, pp. 257–8 (The November Plenum). 1,320 millions in 1927–8, 1,650 millions in 1928–9.

27. Stalin, 'Ob industrializatsii i khlebnoi probleme', *Sochineniya*, Vol. XI, p. 159. (Emphasis in the original.)

28. *ibid*, p. 160.

29. *Sotsialisticheski Vestnik*, March 1929, No. 6, p. 11.

30. Stalin, *Sochineniya*, Vol. XI, p. 175. In April 1929 the emergency measures were officially and openly sanctioned as being legitimate and permanent. See Stalin's speech to the April 1929 Plenum, *Bolshevik*, 1929, No. 23–4, p. 34, and *Sochineniya*, Vol. XII.

31. Stalin, *Sochineniya*, Vol. XI, pp. 173, *Bolshevik*, 1929, No. 23–4, p. 183, and in particular Vol. XII, p. 94. This part of the speech remained secret at the time.

32. Conversation between Bukharin and Kamenev, *Sotsialisticheski Vestnik*, May 1929, No. 9, p. 10.

33. Stalin, *Sochineniya*, Vol. XI, p. 41.

34. Stalin, *Sochineniya*, Vol. XI, pp. 53–63, in his speech in Moscow, after the April Plenum.

35. *ibid*, pp. 58–63.

36. The Russian expression is *politicheski zaotrit*.

37. Stalin, *Sochineniya*, Vol. XI, p. 53.

38. *ibid*, p. 54.

39. *ibid*, p. 54.

40. *ibid*, p. 170.

41. *ibid*, p. 171.

42. Bukharin to Kamenev, *Sotsialisticheski Vestnik*, March 1929, No. 6, p. 10.

43. According to Deutscher, *The Prophet Unarmed*, pp. 455–7.

44. *ibid*. For Stalin's tactics, see pp. 409–10.

45. *KPSS v Rezolyutsiyakh*, p. 526.

Chapter 11

A YEAR OF DRIFT—1928

At this time, the attention of the leadership was taken up with a number of new ideas which were beginning to form in their minds, and with the internal struggle, to which they continued to devote the greater part of their energies. Meanwhile the government, lacking any overall view of the situation, and with no clear idea of long-term prospects, failed to formulate a coherent economic policy, and instead took measures of a partial and provisional nature, devised in response to immediate problems.

One disastrous consequence which followed rapidly on the winter's clash with the peasantry was that the peasants had reduced their sown areas to an extent which imperilled the forthcoming harvest. The government therefore made all possible haste to introduce a number of preventive measures. However, sowing was an activity which, up till now, had been entirely in the hands of the peasants, and the authorities, lacking previous experience, had no idea how a sowing campaign should be conducted. *In addition to the labours of administration, the régime were now saddled with the new and formidable task of ensuring that millions of households would sow a given number of hectares.* For the first time, sowing had become a matter for propaganda and pressure, a campaign involving the mobilization of *selsovety* and *raiispolkomy*, and the participation of Party organizations.[1]

Henceforth, the government itself would have to undertake the task of organizing sowing. In due course, it would acquire responsibility for every other aspect of the agricultural cycle as well. Confronted by this additional burden, the authorities were understandably anxious to devise methods of control and cultivation which would most effectively ensure that the peasants carried out instructions. The Council of Commissars issued a special decree relative to the measures which were to be taken to increase the spring sowing, and the Presidium of the *TsIK* made a solemn appeal to the peasants to increase their sown areas.[2]

The *selsovety* responded as best they could to the urgent demands of their superiors, and improvised methods for arresting the decline in sowing. Some had recourse to the methods previously used during the procurements campaign, inviting the peasants to the office of the *selsovet*, and making them sign an undertaking to sow on the required area. It would appear that this practice was later prohibited, owing to the discontent it aroused amongst the peasants. In other instances, the village society would be asked to give its agreement to the sowing plan, or alternatively the peasants would be visited in order to find out what their intentions were. Another method, also badly received in the villages, was to require a better-off peasant to help a poorer neighbour increase his sown area by lending seed and implements. The bednyaks' Mutual Aid Committee offered a very dubious guarantee of repayment by the bednyak in question.[3]

In order to assist the peasants with their sowing the State supplied seed, credits, implements and even tractors; but in the spring of 1928 its resources were few. The arrival of tractors in the villages certainly created a sensation, but they arrived late, in insufficient numbers (only 20% of the number ordered), and achieved little. No drivers had been trained. The engines, brand new, broke down and were straightaway in need of repair.[4]

During this campaign, an important new method was tried. The *kontraktatsiya* or contract system, as it was called, had been employed since 1927 in connection with industrial crops. Since the State was virtually the sole purchaser of these crops, the results obtained had been both speedy and satisfactory. As a possible means of encouraging the peasants to sow more, it was now suggested that *kontraktatsiya* be extended to the purchase of cereal crops.

The contract, signed by the representatives of a State or co-operative organization and a group of peasants, was originally intended to contain clauses of advantage to both contracting parties. The State (or the co-operative) undertook to make payments on future sales, to lend seed grain and to facilitate the purchase of equipment. The peasants who signed would also be entitled to agronomic aid. The contract could be with an entire peasant community, or with associations specially set up for this purpose.

For their part, the farmers were to introduce improved methods of husbandry, to sow on a stipulated area, and in particular to supply the State with an agreed minimum of grain at fixed prices which were subject to increase according to quality and date of delivery. This minimum could be as much as 200% of the sum advanced.[5]

Here was an idea that had interesting possibilities. Had it been patiently worked out over a number of years, it might well have proved an effective means of enabling the State to intervene in agricultural production in a manner which was both profitable and, at the same time, acceptable to the peasants. The potential advantages of this method aroused great hopes among the heads of the various agricultural administrations. At one time, the Politburo came near to holding the view that *kontraktatsiya* was a major breakthrough which would permit the State to apply proper planning methods to the agricultural sector, thus making it possible to administer a branch of the economy which had hitherto resisted all such interference. It was also believed that the contract system would serve as an excellent lever for the introduction of collectivization.

As yet, it was far from being any such thing. *The State itself was the first to break the newly signed contracts. Kontraktatsiya* was too late in being introduced, and there was no time to explain the various clauses to the peasants concerned. The manner in which it was carried out was chaotic, since it involved the ill-co-ordinated efforts of a host of different organizations.[6] Credits allocated for *kontraktatsiya* arrived too late, and were too small. These sums were then distributed haphazardly, and their effect was lost. In some cases they could not be recovered.[7]

In such conditions, the clauses relating to improvements which were to be introduced during the sowing campaign became largely meaningless. An enquiry carried out in the Stalingrad region revealed that in some *raiony* there had been a certain increase in sown areas, but that 'the effect of *kontraktatsiya* in improving agriculture had been negligible'.[8]

During the subsequent procurements, the results achieved by the contracts system varied according to the manner in which the campaign had been organized. Grain deliveries, however, were no better in areas covered by contracts (7·5 million ha.) than in those which were not, for the very low prices prompted everyone, kolkhozes and sovkhozes included, to sell on the free market instead. According to Lvov, 'the contract measures have so far amounted to no more than a simple purchasing procedure'.[9]

Nevertheless, the Politburo did not despair, believing that the errors born of inexperience could be rectified the following year. A special commission for *kontraktatsiya* was set up under the Politburo to study the problem and suggest possible solutions.[10] Another commission attached to the Central Committee was already at work on the kolkhoz question, and a parallel committee had been set up under the *Soyuz Soyuzov*.[11]

The kolkhoz movement, after years of stagnation and decline, made notable progress during the months March–May 1928. It was reported that the number of kolkhozes in the country had almost doubled, increasing from 14,000 at the end of 1927 to 23,000 by about the beginning of May 1928. At the same time, the number of simple producers' associations had risen from 26,000 to 45,000.

During this period, there were 376,000 households participating in the kolkhoz movement. This was a modest figure, but there were instances in the North Caucasus, and in the Volga regions, of entire villages adopting one or another form of collectivization in order to cultivate their land in common.[12]

According to the *Khlebotsentr*, at least some of this movement was a direct result of *kontraktatsiya* which, it was claimed, had given rise in Russia and the Ukraine to the formation of some 6,000 kolkhozes, a large number of 'associations for the acquisition of machines', and thousands of associations of a new type—'grain associations' (*zernovye tovarishchestva*).[13] Other sources insisted, however, that these claims were exaggerated; the *Khlebotsentr* had already been under fire for its poor performance in the domain of collectivization.[14]

Whatever the true figures may have been, the development certainly presented a number of interesting features. The newly formed kolkhozes, and the *tozy* in particular, were very small. Those consisting of twenty to twenty-five households were considered large. The majority were only dwarf-enterprises, and at times no larger than a fair-sized private farm.[15] Many were unstable organizations which disbanded whenever they encountered the slightest obstacle; frequently they were little more than 'transit-points' with a rapid turnover of arrivals and departures. Towards the end of the year *Bolshevik* spoke of 'catastrophic disintegration' within the kolkhoz movement. In the North Caucasus 80% of former members had quit. 'It is high time,' wrote Bumper 'to put a stop to the practice of using the kolkhoz as a sort of inn where people enjoy a temporary advantage before returning to the more routine and more taxing forms of everyday life.'[16]

In *Pravda*, Yakovlev likewise drew attention to these disquieting features.[17] It is interesting to note that he favoured the *toz*, rather than the other kolkhoz forms. His preference merely confirmed the existing trend; at the time the *toz* was largely predominant in the kolkhoz movement, accounting for 65·9% of collectives, 26·3% of which were *arteli*, and 7·8% *kommuny*.[18]

This upsurge in the kolkhoz movement had developed during the spring, in the wake of the *zagotovki*, and of the first sowing campaign to have been conducted by shock tactics. In this respect it resembled many other events of the period, which was one of feverish activity. An immense organizational effort was being made in the villages, in an attempt to deal simultaneously with the procurements, the receipt of various kinds of payments, the sowing campaign and *kontraktatsiya*. The peasants were already overwhelmed beneath the flood of administrative orders. However, the authorities, making the most of the opportunity, had also begun to organize kolkhozes. Occasionally there were instances of excessive administrative zeal.

Astrov, quoting Bukharin, wrote in *Pravda*:

'Some people have an extremely primitive understanding of what is involved in the strengthening of the collective sector, and as a result collectives were organized almost on the principle of a *razverstka* [allocation of tasks according to a pre-arranged pattern]. There is evidence that when funds were received, they were poured into pseudo-kolkhozes. Anyone at all would be recruited, and even petty kulaks found their way in.' [19]

However at this juncture the element of force was still of marginal importance only. During this period, the poor often found themselves in a desperate plight. It had always been difficult to obtain food in the spring, but this year the better-off peasants, to whom the bednyaks usually turned for aid, retaliated against the special measures by refusing to lend grain or seed, horses or implements. They also stopped renting land from the poor peasants, thus depriving them of a source of income.[20]

Although the State at this time had no grain to give the bednyaks, it nevertheless offered certain advantages to those who agreed to join the kolkhozes. Some 60–65 million roubles, or double the previous year's figures, were allocated to the kolkhozes, most of which went on the purchase of livestock.[21] Occasionally, a tractor and other implements were supplied, and free *zemleustroistvo* was also promised.

The Commissariat of Finance granted the *kolkhozniki* sizeable tax rebates, amounting to as much as 60% on occasion.[22] Aid for the poor, credits for *kontraktatsiya*, and other forms of assistance were also provided. *The entire sum was insufficient to finance the construction of large kolkhoz enterprises on any appreciable scale (60 million roubles was the cost of building a single factory) but it was large enough to attract thousands of underprivileged bednyaks, for whom it represented a ray of hope, a chance to try their luck. In this sense, it may be said that the kolkhozes which appeared that spring owed their existence to a spontaneous movement on the part of the bednota. This movement soon acquired such proportions that local soviets and Party organizations were caught off guard.*[23]

Some of the new kolkhoz members took the newspaper articles and the speeches very seriously, and were prepared to give their enthusiastic support. At the same time, there was no lack of comment from all sides: 'We agree that collectivization is the only solution, but you (the authorities) will have to tell us how to go about it, for we have neither examples nor instruction manuals to guide us.' Others again said, 'All right then, give us a tractor, we'll see to the organization.'[24]

Tsylko complained not only of the absence of a coherent policy, but of the tremendous amount of confusion which reigned in the organization of collectivization. The co-operative organs were supposed, by definition, to be responsible for the organization of the collectives, but they had not as yet formulated any plans; in the article which we have already mentioned, Yakovlev called upon them to draw up plans immediately, and gave them one month, until the opening of the conference on the kolkhoz movement, to do so.

In a letter to the chairmen of *ispolkomy*, Kubyak the Commissar for Agriculture urged them to take the administration of the movement in hand, since his local agrarian departments (*zemotdely*) were incapable of doing so, and the co-operative movement's organizations for kolkhozes had been so recently set up that they were as yet unequal to the task.[25]

In the spring of 1928, the Soviet government were not sufficiently organized to be able to assimilate the relatively small but spontaneous movement of peasants[26] who had followed the course which was incessantly being urged upon them by all the propaganda organs, and shown their willingness to try the new experiment.

A great many of the kolkhozes and other associations, whose exact status in this context was relatively unimportant, were not responsible to any administrative body. These were the so-called 'wild' or free-wheeling organizations which belonged neither to the co-operative movement, nor to any kind of kolkhoz organization, except possibly a credit organization, if credit had been granted them.

Even for the limited movement which had taken place, the funds allocated were inadequate; 70% of both old and new kolkhozes had no tractors, and just over half were without a single agricultural machine. Despite the numerous decisions which had been taken by the State and the Party, the majority were without *zemleustroistvo*.[27] Many officials of the co-operative and kolkhoz movements warned the Party that if this state of affairs were allowed to continue, there was a danger that the entire kolkhoz image would be damaged in the eyes of the peasants. A leading co-operative official, who was also a member of the Central Committee, wrote that if new machinery were not supplied, and kolkhoz members had to make do with whatever miserable equipment they possessed, if indeed they possessed any at all, then 'instead of the communal organization of a large collective enterprise, we shall simply have endless trouble, and nothing good will come of it'.[28]

Everyone at this time, including the Politburo, held the same view. In this, they were merely following the lines of Marxist doctrine and the writings of Lenin. No one dreamed of forcing the movement artificially to a degree which would be inconsistent with available material and technical resources. The more sceptical were prepared, at this stage, to accept a moderate rate of progress, whereas the optimists, counting on the results of industrialization, believed that a more impressive development was possible. Both of these viewpoints still found support within the Central Committee and the Politburo. But even the optimists, insofar as they hoped for immediate and tangible results, were looking mainly to a rapid build-up in the sovkhoz sector, for it was to the sovkhozes that the largest share of up-to-date technical equipment would be channelled. No one at this stage was thinking in terms of a large-scale kolkhoz movement in the near future. Most writers were of the opinion that the principal threats to the stability of the kolkhozes, and to their standing with the population, were firstly the imbalance between the growth of the movement and its requirements in tractors and other types of equipment, and secondly the failure to organize production efficiently.

There were a small minority who were even more acutely aware of another weakness, which was the low level of culture and education in the kolkhozes. This was, in fact, the most neglected sector of kolkhoz administration. The kolkhozes had neither schools, hospitals nor newspapers. These services, in so far as they existed at all in the countryside, were far from adequate, and were intended only to meet the needs of the private or uncollectivized sector of the population. It was significant that a region like the North Caucasus, which comprised 34.8% of all Russian kolkhozes and was in the forefront of the kolkhoz movement in the RSFSR, and which was in fact to make even greater progress in the next few years, was culturally and educationally one of the most backward regions in the Republic.[29]

In such conditions, there was a danger that the kolkhozes, instead of serving as an example to the rural population, would become squalid backwaters where ignorance and disease went unchecked. There was nothing in their way of life or their habits which distinguished them from their surroundings, and some intensive effort in this sphere was urgently required. One minor anecdote will perhaps serve to illustrate the problem. In a commune (*kommuna*) in the Stalingrad region, where it had been the custom for all the members to eat from the same dish, someone suggested that separate plates might be provided. The idea was greeted with a wave of derision. 'There's a fuss-pot for you! What does it matter as long as we have our cabbage soup? The common dish is good enough for us!' [30] (Nevertheless it would seem that the suggestion was eventually taken up.) But what was to happen when these peasants had to fulfil a production plan and learn to keep accounts, or drive the tractor, or use fertilizers, or carry out even more complex tasks? How would tractors and threshing-machines fare in the hands of semi-illiterate individuals?

Many of the leadership at this time had begun to regard the tractor almost as if it were endowed with supernatural properties, which would solve all their difficulties for them. In this, they were guilty of a rather too superficial interpretation of Marx's theory concerning the leading role which would be played by the forces of production. The entire Stalinist approach to the building of socialism was later to be based on just such an over-simplified view.

Not only were the kolkhozes in urgent need of cultural services; they were totally lacking in trained personnel who were capable of undertaking the work of management and of organizing production. Moreover, there were still too few administrative bodies dealing with the kolkhoz movement. The government had only recently decided to set up an independent network of kolkhoz unions and departments parallel to organizations of the co-operative movement, and under the general supervision of the *Kolkhoztsentr*, which had been in existence since 1927. These administrations were gradually created during 1928.[31] They attempted to recruit agronomists whose services would be exclusively at the disposal of the kolkhozes. Towards the end of the year it became apparent that there were fifty kolkhozes and sixty associations of other types, for every one agronomist in this category. Thus, few kolkhozes had the chance of ever seeing an agronomist, let alone of consulting one, even during a lightning visit. The agrarian departments (*zemotdely*) of the Republican Commissariat of Agriculture were scarcely better off.[32]

A great many of the new associations, whatever their statute, *artel*, *toz* or even *kommuna* on occasion, were collective enterprises in name only. In practice a large proportion of their land, if not all of it, continued to be privately cultivated. The small degree of socialization was due principally to lack of means of production, and to inexperience and the inability to organize properly. In half the *arteli*, the majority of the *tozy*, and sometimes even in the *kommuny*, private exploitation of the land continued to flourish. It was quite possible to use the kolkhoz label simply as a device for diverting a share of the social funds to the private sector.[33]

The departments concerned, and the experts who wrote about these matters, were all aware of the dangers inherent in this situation. The remedy seemed to them to lie in the supply of heavy equipment, and also in the training of personnel. The Central Committee itself felt obliged to take the initiative in training staff of intermediate rank. Three hundred and fifty candidates were recruited for a one-year course, at the end of which they were to work in co-operative organizations, or as instructors and kolkhoz chairmen.[34] But this was a mere drop in the ocean. Were plans for the expansion of the kolkhoz movement in the near future really on so modest a scale?

According to the control figures prepared by *Gosplan* towards the end of the year, the targets proposed for 1929 were indeed very moderate; there was to be a 17% increase in the number of kolkhozes in the coming year, or 38,000 as opposed to 32,506 in 1927–8. On the other hand, it was intended that the kolkhozes should increase in size, and improve in quality; it was hoped, for example, to extend the area of collectivized land by 60%. It was also anticipated that by the end of 1929 the kolkhozes would be supplying 4·1% of the marketable production of grain.[35]

Clearly, *Gosplan* had opted for moderation. Believing that quality was more important than quantity, they had resisted the pressure that was being applied from various quarters to force the pace. For the majority of *Gosplan*'s specialists, the chief concern continued to be the private agricultural sector. We shall see later what their views were on kolkhoz prospects over the next five years.

At this point, the main consideration was assistance for the private peasants. Repeated promises were made to this effect during the Central Committee session in October 1928. The Committee even went so far as to criticize local authorities for not having done enough to raise the level of private farms.[36]

However, towards the end of the year those who were in favour of assisting the private sector began to realize that the Politburo had other ideas. During the Plenum of the Central Committee in November 1928, at which the control figures for the following year were ratified, Commissar Kubyak complained of the reduction in aid to private agriculture. Stalin contrived to give the impression that this was not the case.[37] However the relevant figures, which were published at a later date, reveal a very marked drop in the credits and investments allocated to the private sector, both relatively and absolutely from 1929, and relatively as early as 1928.[38] For a long time to come, the role and future prospects of private agriculture, and the degree to which it should be subsidized, were matters which gave rise to considerable controversy among the Party leadership and the administrative departments concerned.

Even the Stalinist majority in the Central Committee were divided on this particular issue.

At the end of the year, the *TsIK* issued a lengthy decree containing a detailed programme for increasing yields by 35% during the quinquennium.[39] The authors of the decree stressed their continued reliance on the private sector, and their anxiety that this sector should be provided with a concrete programme and a basis for confidence in the future. The *TsIK* hoped to achieve this increase in yields primarily by the introduction of such simple improvements in farming methods as would be within the peasants' grasp. These included the use of cleaned seed, hoeing, an attack on weeds, etc. This plan for a 35% increase in soil fertility was regarded by a number of experts as being extremely unrealistic, but it was forced upon *Gosplan* as the basis for its Five-year Plan for agriculture. In the event, this project proved no more than a pious hope, and the entire decree was ultimately pigeon-holed.

One reason for this, *inter alia*, was that those who were really in control in the Politburo were coming to, or had already reached the conclusion that investment in bednyak farms paid no dividends in increased production, Nor did they see any point in assisting the seredynaks, since this would merely encourage their pro-kulak tendencies and make it more difficult to collectivize them.[40] Instead, they now preferred to invest in the 'simple producers' associations', the kolkhozes and the sovkhozes.[41]

An analysis of the credits which were actually allocated reveals that the Politburo had begun to act upon this conviction. The sovkhozes, which had scarcely made any progress during the year, now received priority treatment. In April the Politburo decided to set up huge sovkhozes, or 'grain factories', on large unoccupied areas of land in Russia and the Ukraine; it was intended that these enterprises, while helping to ease the grain shortage in the short term, should also serve as industrial centres for the processing of agricultural products from the peasantry in the surrounding areas; it was also thought that they would fulfil the same purpose as the Shevchenko sovkhoz in the region of Odessa, by providing an effective means of furthering the process of collectivization.[42]

A Politburo Committee, consisting of Mikoyan, Kubyak, Kviring, Latsis, Yakovlev and Bauman, under the chairmanship of Kalinin (none of whom, of course, were men of the Right) discussed the matter, and decided to build a number of sovkhozes which would be capable of producing 100 million poods of grain in four to five years. Committees for aid to the sovkhozes were set up under Party organizations in the localities concerned. In August, the aforementioned Committee was designated 'Committee of the *TsIK*, for the promotion of sovkhoz construction'. Among other things, this committee even proposed that the construction of large state farms be entrusted to foreign entrepreneurs.[43] At about this time, a special organization known as *Zernostrest*, and directed by the able Kalmanovich (co-opted from *RKI*) was set up to manage these future factories. The importance of this body was underlined by the fact that it was given the status of an autonomous organization, directly responsible to *STO*.[44]

Thus the aim was to create State-run 'proletarian strongholds' in the countryside where, it was hoped, they would influence and impress the peasantry. Past experience in the sovkhoz sector, however, was not of a kind to encourage high hopes. The sovkhozes, administered by *Gosselsindikat*, which had been in existence since 1922, were in a lamentable state. They were short of personnel and equipment, encumbered with debts and neglected by the State; worst of all, their workers lived in poverty-stricken conditions, a fact which could not but damage the sovkhoz image so far as the peasants were concerned.[45]

Initially, it had been intended that *Gosselsindikat* should draw up plans for the expansion of the new sovkhozes, but *Gosselsindikat*'s inefficiency was such that the Politburo chose instead to entrust the task to a new body. When in 1929 it was decided to rehabilitate the older, ailing sovkhozes, *Gosselsindikat* was abolished and replaced by a new administration which was provided with large sums of money, considerable supplies of equipment and reserves of personnel, some of whom it was even intended to send abroad to study the management of large-scale agricultural enterprises.[46]

Meanwhile, nothing had got beyond the stage of planning and intentions. During the course of 1928, the government's economic policy lacked coherence, and was not conceived as part of an overall plan. Since earlier plans and figures were now out of date, the only available framework for new plans was that of the control figures for the following year. There was no five-year perspective to guide the planners, since the Five-year Plan was not yet in existence. The *Sovnarkom* found itself obliged to draft a provisional decree, which would at least provide a budgetary framework for the year; this it did, in the form of a decision of March 2, 1928,[47] relating to measures to be taken with regard to agriculture during the year 1927–8.

Only six months now remained before the end of the economic year which had begun on October 1st. Apart from an appraisal of the situation based on earlier Party decisions, and an enumeration of desiderata, the document had little to suggest that was of any relevance to the current year. Its most interesting sections, such as the project for rural industrial co-operatives, merely took the form of instructions to *Gosplan* to work out the appropriate plans for the future.

During the year, the government reacted to the dictates of the moment, wrestling with current problems as and when they arose. The greater part of their energies were expended on projects for the future, with particular reference to the coming year. Meanwhile the prevailing atmosphere was one of uncertainty and the interplay of opposing forces; to this was added an element of ambivalence, arising from the fact that while the departments concerned were engaged in drawing up one set of plans, the Politburo was busy on others, and frequently altered its aims and objectives without necessarily admitting that it had done so.

The Politburo had in fact begun to take the initiative in an increasing number of fields. It now tended to anticipate the government on every issue, and it would appear that this was particularly so in the case of agriculture. It was responsible for a commission dealing with the allocation of credits to the kolkhozes (there was a parallel commission attached to the *Soyuz Soyuzov*), and also for a commission on *kontraktatsiya*, and for another which dealt with the sovkhozes. Curiously enough, it was the Politburo which was instructed by the October 1928 Plenum to devise measures for increasing the sown area in the Ukraine, where for several years agricultural production had been steadily falling. One reason for this concentration of decision-making in the hands of the Politburo was that the two senior administrative organs concerned, that is the Commissariats of Agriculture and Trade respectively, disagreed with each other on matters of departmental responsibility, and on questions of policy and methodology, and could only be made to agree by the Politburo.

The above commissions which were attached to the Politburo also acted, to some extent, as 'shadow organizations' to the government departments directed by Rykov. At this time, despite the purges which had been mainly directed at 'bourgeois' specialists,[48] these departments were still full of 'sceptics', Right-wing sympathizers and liberals who opposed the initiatives of the Secretariat of the Central Committee. Bukharin, Rykov and Tomsky could now be confronted with *faits accomplis*, and various matters could be taken out of their hands to rest securely with the Secretariat.

There is no doubt that during this period there were, in effect, two Politburos, just as there had been at the time of the struggle with the Left. On the one hand, there was the Plenum of the Politburo, and on the other the Stalinist enclave, who discussed each problem among themselves before deciding whether it should be brought before the Plenum. For some time, there existed within the Politburo a group of waverers, who were probably more inclined towards Bukharin's views, but who were either afraid of the General Secretary or could not conceive of anyone who was capable of replacing him.[49]

Thus, the Politburo itself was divided during 1928, and it was not until the end of the year that it was finally taken in hand by Stalin and his supporters. However, Stalin and Molotov did control the Secretariat, which was responsible for practical matters.[50] The fact that Stalin's own position was not yet sufficiently secure helps to explain why he had to deploy all his tactical skill in order to demolish the Right. This is a point to which we shall be returning later.

At the end of the year, Stalin himself admitted that practically nothing had been achieved, and he called upon the Party 'at long last . . . to devise practical measures for the improvement of grain production . . . and of the kolkhozes and sovkhozes'.[51]

While the country, and the agricultural sector in particular, drifted from one expedient to the next, the organizations whose duty it was to work out coherent long-term plans, that is *Gosplan*, *VSNKh*, the *Sovnarkom* and the Politburo itself, to name the most important, failed to find a programme which was acceptable to them all, owing to differences in outlook which could not be reconciled. *Gosplan*, which still numbered among its ranks a great many men of prudence and intellectual integrity, was constantly being challenged by the industrial planners of the *VSNKh*. The latter, under the leadership of Kuibyshev, who was an enthusiastic industrializer, strove continuously to outdo *Gosplan* by submitting ever more extreme variants of the Five-year Plan, based on increasingly bold assumptions of future economic growth. *Gosplan* struck back at the 'builders of ice-palaces,' at those who were attempting to 'bite off more than they could chew' (both of which criticisms were quoted by Kuibyshev himself) and put forward more moderate proposals. When, however, in August 1928 *Gosplan* produced a draft Five-year Plan, including a section on agriculture, the Polituburo rejected it, on the grounds that it 'had not fully evaluated our resources'.[52] This was a phrase which the Politburo used frequently at the time, to indicate that it was not satisfied with the rate of growth proposed.

The same criticism was made of the *VSNKh*, who had prepared at least six different drafts during 1928; all of these had been rejected.[53] Eventually one of these versions was adopted, but only as a basis for the 1928–9 industrial control figures, which were ratified by the Plenum of November 1928.

There followed a whole succession of proposals and counter-proposals until *Gosplan*, in response to intense pressure by the Politburo, and at extremely short notice, succeeded in producing a draft which was agreed at the Party Conference in April 1929. As we shall see, the history of these drafts for the first Five-year Plan did not end there. Meanwhile, it is worth bearing in mind that the control figures for the year 1928–9, the first year of the Five-year Plan, which were adopted in November 1928, could scarcely have belonged to any true five-year perspective, since at this time the Five-year Plan was not yet in existence. When the Five-year Plan was finally announced as such, it was in reality only a four-year plan which provided a framework for the figures of the 1929–30 annual plan.[54]

Our description of the government's actions in 1928 would not be complete without a brief mention of the offensive which was carried on against the private sector in the towns.

Throughout the year, concerted action was taken against Nepmen, industrialists, traders and speculators, the principal weapon being a punitive rate of taxation. When the private enterpreneurs had been ruined, and could no longer pay their taxes, legal proceedings were instituted against them. Some were prosecuted for running 'false co-operatives', a practice which was very common in the private sector at this time. These prosecutions were accompanied by sanctions, and many private traders were eliminated in this way. The number of private industrial and artisanal enterprises fell sharply during the year, and the share of the private trader in retail trade fell to 24·8%.[55]

This attack on the private sector naturally affected the artisans as well, irrespective of whether they belonged to co-operatives or not; the charge most frequently brought against them was that of 'pseudo-co-operation'. Some senior officials were convinced that 80% of artisans' *arteli* were 'phoney'. Within a short time the artisan sector began to decline, and finally went the same way as the private trader.

In July 1928, Stalin observed that '. . . in the onward march towards socialism we are eliminating, perhaps even without being aware of it, thousands of capitalists, in the shape of small and medium-scale industrialists'. This was also true of 'thousands and thousands of small and medium-scale traders'.[56]

According to Stalin, this was an indication of the country's progress towards socialism. But the State had at present nothing to take the place of artisanal production and the private commercial network. The influence of Bukharin had led the Fifteenth Party Congress to speak of small-scale industry and the artisan sector as factors which could serve to alleviate 'the famine of manufactured goods'. Now, only a short time after these decisions had been taken, the State was eliminating both factors, without having made adequate provision for a state network to take their place.[57] The structures which the government had hastily devised as a substitute for the private sector were cumbersome and inefficient, and served only to add to the confusion which was already apparent in the supply system. *The dual reign of shortage and speculation now began: it was destined to last for a long time, and to cost the country untold losses.*

The struggle against the kulaks was carried on with the help of a number of legislative and other measures, whose effect was to impoverish many of the better-off peasants. The methods which had the most serious repercussions were those employed during the *zagotovki*, when the peasants were obliged by means of special measures, or others which were less harsh but no less effective, to hand over their grain to the authorities in the quantities specified. From 1928 onwards, the financial pressure which was already being exerted in the form of loans, local levies and advance payment of taxes was further intensified by the addition of an 'individual levy', aimed specifically at the richest peasants. While the majority of the peasants were taxed at standard rates, a special enquiry was conducted by tax officials in order to determine the total income of better-off peasants. Particular attention was paid to income deriving from trade and enterprises, etc., which was to be taxed at a higher rate.

The Commissariat of Finance tried in vain to provide their officials with a definition of the kulak, and to identify for their benefit what kinds of income 'did not derive from labour' (*netrudovye*); the results of the 'individual levy' clearly showed that there was much confusion over this problem at local level. By law, 3% of the richest peasants were subject to this tax. The Commissariat's own figures showed that in the RSFSR the tax was in fact collected from just over half this number.[58] The kulaks knew how to take cover, often with the connivance of others, and in any case the village kulak did not always fit the official definition of him. In his article in *Bolshevik*, Bumper admitted that the categories of 'better-off kulak, rich kulak, less well-off kulak', as employed by the authorities responsible for this policy, were purely notional and had little validity.

In consequence, some local officials could find no kulaks at all, or were unable to find them in sufficient numbers, while others found kulaks at every turn. According to Bumper, there was not a single village which had not been searched for kulaks. In other words, whenever it was absolutely necessary, the 'richest kulaks' could always be found even if, as often happened in many of the poorer villages, none existed at all. In some places, 10–12% of the villagers were affected by this form of arbitrary taxation.[59]

Bolshevik expressed alarm at the situation. 'The system of the individual levy is being badly applied. There have been a great many blunders, abuses and deviations.'[60]

Indeed, there was no end to the excesses and the abuses to which this policy gave rise. The local authorities received instructions from their superiors relating to the number of peasants who were to be taxed 'individually'. If the local officials failed to find a suitable number of candidates, down came the order forthwith: *dovyyavit*— 'Seek out the rest!'[61] From the very beginning, there had been reports of cases in which peasants had been named at random, when no kulaks could be found. Since trading was classified as a source of income 'not deriving from labour', peasants who sold bottles of milk or a few glasses of sunflower seed at railway stations were included in the category of those liable to the individual levy. In the North Caucasus, tax was levied on agricultural income which had been classified as exempt under a law intended to encourage certain branches of agriculture. In other areas, farms with an annual income of 130 or 180 roubles were treated as kulak farms. The fact that a man had well-kept livestock or well-cultivated land, that he had a good cart or employed a nurse, or that there might be some professional source of income in the household (in cases where there was a doctor or a teacher in the family) or again the fact that he might, at some time in the past, have employed wage-labour, were all interpreted by the 'ill-trained and overworked' tax officials as indications of kulak status. In Siberia, some peasants were subject to the individual levy because they 'had not wished to contribute to the loan', or because 'this one's a trouble-maker, he's always complaining'. There were countless such cases.

From the very outset, this form of arbitrary taxation gave rise to a flood of complaints, appeals and protests. The Central Committee had to intervene in order to put a stop to the many abuses. Upon enquiry, when the records had been checked, half of those who had been taxed in this way were recognized as being serednyaks.

Nevertheless, according to the incomplete information available, some 0·7% of Russian peasant taxpayers paid almost 7%, and in some *gubernii* as much as 11%, of the entire agricultural tax. In the Ukraine, after injustices had been rectified, the 1·1% who finally paid this individual levy contributed 12·5% of the total sum gathered. Over the country as a whole, 1·2% of the peasants paid 50–60 million roubles, or at least 15% of the total.[62] To this sum must be added at least as much again, in the shape of local levy and loan contributions, which the better-off peasants were compelled to make in proportion to their agricultural tax payments.

During the course of the year, in addition to the *zagotovki* and to the fiscal measures which had been adopted, the government took a whole series of steps which were either directly or indirectly anti-kulak in intention. Viewed as a whole, these reveal a trend in government policy which was to find expression in the 'general principles of the possession and distribution of land', a legislative text which was adopted by the session of the *TsIK* on December 15, 1928.[63] The purpose of this document was to replace the now obsolete agrarian code of 1922, and to provide a framework for agrarian legislation in the Republics. Work on it had begun in 1925, but had been held up time and again by disputes on matters of agricultural policy. Its completion had also been greatly delayed by opposition from the Republics to what they considered an encroachment on their rights, since they had previously been solely responsible for agrarian legislation. This document had therefore had a long history, and despite the fact that it was to have virtually no future, it none the less reflected the general attitude of the régime in the period towards the end of 1928.

This set of proposals differed from all the earlier drafts in that it recommended favoured treatment for the various forms of rural collectivization, in the shape of concessions and priority in the allocation of credits, machines, fertilizers and the best land, plus free *zemleustroistvo* and tax reductions. The creation of *khutora* and *otruba* was strongly opposed, and the authorities were given the right to prohibit the setting-up of *khutora* in cases where it could be shown that this would 'contribute to the reinforcement and expansion of the kulak stratum'.[64]

However, the attitude to collectivization as reflected in these recommendations was that this was a movement primarily intended for the 'broad mass of economically weak peasants' (*malomoshchnye*).[65] Whatever may have been stated on matters of general principle, no one at the end of 1928 seriously considered that the mass of serednyaks should embark upon collectivization, and the document did not suggest any such course.

The activities of the better-off peasants were to be restricted in a number of ways. It was not forbidden to lease land to this stratum, but any such arrangement was not to last for more than six years, and the authorities were given the right to restrict or prohibit the lease of land altogether. In order to comply with the law, the lease of land had to be registered with the *selsovet*, which was also to supervise the terms of the agreement. Sub-letting was punishable by imprisonment.[66]

Agricultural wage-labour now came under stricter supervision by the labour inspectorate and the *selsovet*. Kulaks who employed labour were obliged to comply with the provisions of the labour laws, whereas the employment of 'auxiliary labour' by the rest of the peasants was covered by other special regulations which were less scrupulous in their protection of wage-labour.

These measures in themselves provided ample scope for harassing the kulaks and restricting their activities. A further provision in the text empowered the authorities, in effect, to confiscate land at will; they were authorized to 'reallocate' land whenever 'the need to combat the kulaks' made this necessary.[67]

Although these measures were officially intended for use in promoting the class struggle 'against the kulaks', every one of them was in fact a double-edged weapon, since it constituted a permanent threat to the other peasants. The authorities could prevent a peasant from renting his land, thereby depriving him of a source of income. They could also make life difficult for him if he chose to employ a batrak. Given a little ill-will, or even simply a lack of understanding, the dividing-line between 'exploitation' and 'auxiliary labour' could easily be blurred.[68]

In view of the priority given to collective associations in the allocation of land, the clause relating to 'reallocation' opened the door to a variety of punitive measures, not excluding the possibility of outright confiscation of land, with no redress whatever.

All of these measures which were officially devised as 'anti-kulak' instruments were potentially 'anti-serednyak' in their side-effects. This emerges clearly from the provisions relating to the statute/constitution of the village societies, as outlined in the text. Henceforth, those peasants who had no vote were not to be permitted to vote in the *skhod*, whereas wage-labourers who had no *dvor*, but were inhabitants of the village, were to become members as of right. Furthermore, decisions taken by the *skhod* could be quashed by the *selsovet* whenever the latter deemed them contrary to the laws or policy of the Soviet régime.[69] In this way the *skhod*, a peasant institution in which the serednyaks were largely predominant, was brought under the control of an organ of State power, which the Party had deliberately 'bednyakized' and which it could manipulate at will.

During the electoral campaign, or rather the campaign for the 'renewal of the soviets' at the beginning of 1929, the régime's effort to consolidate its position in the countryside was reflected in increased official activism among the bednyaks; numerous assemblies of poor peasants were convened, and bednyak groups were organized. These measures aroused a great deal of antagonism among the other strata of the peasantry.

As for the serednyaks, no matter how well disposed they were towards the régime, no matter how seriously they took their obligations to it. there was not one who did not feel bitterly disappointed at the turn which events were taking, since it seemed as though the serednyaks were being rejected.

At an election meeting in a village in the Vladimir *guberniya*, one serednyak had the following observations to make: 'Citizens, the Party might at least organize us in serednyak groups; they seem to think we aren't human beings at all. The kulaks organize themselves, the Party organizes the bednyaks, but as for us, we've been forgotten.'[70]

In his innocence, the serednyak complained of having been 'forgotten', but what was in fact taking place at this time was a process of *ottesnenie*, or eviction. Strict control was exercised over the membership of the *selsovety*, and it was clear that the serednyack element was being ousted. Those right-wing members of *Pravda*'s editorial staff who had not yet been purged protested about the *obednyachivanie* or 'bednyakization' of the *selsovety*.[71] There were also protests from the Communist Academy, which reported similar instances of serednyak eviction in a number of regions. The practice was most noticeable in the grain-growing areas. The percentage of bednyaks represented in the electoral committees and also in the *selsovety* was often far in excess of the proportion of bednyaks in the population as a whole, there being a corresponding decline in the number of serednyaks so represented. In the Don *okrug*, the proportion of serednyaks in the *selsovety* fell from 43·4% (in 1927) to 40·9%; in Mariyupol from 40·9% to 27·8%; in Kherson *okrug* from 31·8% to 29·3%.

In the above regions, and in others, the corresponding proportion of bednyaks rose to 50% or more. In the North Caucasus, where relations with the peasantry were particularly strained, the composition of electoral committees was as follows: 61·5% bednyaks, 37·4% serednyaks, 0·5% better-off peasants. But these percentages refer to peasant members only, of whom there were 3,372, out of a total of 6,368 members, for the electoral committees, whose function it was to prepare for elections to the *selsovety*, consisted of 23·9% of officials, 6·1% of workers, and 9·1% of batraks.[72]

This then was the régime's reaction to the deterioration in relations with the mass of the peasantry. The authorities had deliberately brought about a recrudescence of the class struggle, thereby adding to the already existing pressures in the countryside.

In a speech delivered before a relatively small audience, Kaganovich said quite openly that 'The serednyak is sometimes influenced by the kulak and expresses his dissatisfaction. . . .'[73] But Kaganovich, of all people, must have known that this had very little to do with the kulak. On his own admission, the serednyak had been hit 'by rather heavy taxation, and by our inability at the present time to offer him prices for his grain which are commensurate with the prices of manufactured goods'. He added that 'we have penalized them' in the process of taking action against the kulaks.[74]

This was not all. 'Concessions to the serednyaks', he went on, 'are possible, and at times necessary, but we shall never be able to make concessions of a kind which might undermine the foundations of our industry. . . .' Consequently, since the concession of which he was speaking carried this risk, it followed that 'certain difficulties in our relations with the serednyaks are unavoidable . . .' but 'these difficulties can be overcome'. He did not, however, explain how this was to be done.[75]

By the autumn and winter of 1928, implementation of the Stalinist version of the *smychka* had begun. Stalin's formula was as follows: all possible aid was to be given to the bednyaks, and war was to be waged on the kulaks in order to achieve mastery over the serednyaks. This interpretation of Party policy with regard to the peasants was to enable Stalin to fulfil certain objectives which he regarded as being of overriding importance.

At the present stage, however, application of this threefold formula was having the most serious repercussions on the country's economy. Aid for the poor peasants, which was in any case limited, had no effect in improving the State's grain reserves. The leadership had no illusions on this score, and such assistance, at least in its then existing form, was soon discontinued, for it was of advantage only to the individual bednyak, and then only to a very limited extent.

The offensive against the kulaks, and the harmful effects which it had on the serednyaks, served only to weaken the peasant economy, particularly by restricting the activities of the better-off peasants. The latter had already cut down their spring sowings, and were to repeat the process in the autumn. Other peasants followed suit, how many it is difficult to say.

In agricultural production, the contribution of the kulaks and the better-off strata in general had declined. They were also disposing of some of their livestock, and there were reports of *samoraskulachivanie*, or 'auto-dekulakization', when kulaks had either reduced their farms to minimal proportions, or sold them off completely. The latter practice was not yet common, but was to become more so as time went on.

The authorities reported that the 1928 grain harvest was poorer than that of the previous year, and put this down to bad results in the Ukraine and the North Caucasus, but there is no doubt that the twists and turns of agricultural policy were also partly to blame.

The sowing campaign in the autumn of 1928 was a failure; instead of the hoped-for increase in sown areas, it was officially admitted that there had been a drop of 4·5%.[76] In this case, natural hazards were even less to blame, whereas social factors had clearly played an important part. These same factors were fully operative during the régime's next time of trial, the procurements campaign of 1928-9, which was marked by the greatest difficulties from the very outset. The authorities firmly denied having had recourse to special measures, and in so far as the first part of the campaign was concerned, this was perfectly true; but in September, *Pravda* spoke of a 'recurrence of various forms of coercion during the procurements'.[77]

In October deliveries took a turn for the better, but in November and December there was a further falling-off. In December, *Pravda* criticized the local procurements agencies for their 'laxity' and 'passivity', while at the same time expressing indignation at the 'scandalous way in which the men on the spot have maltreated serednyaks and bednyaks who have been honestly delivering their grain through co-operative organizations'. These acts, the newspaper alleged, were the result of kulak influence.[78]

An increase in prices to producers, by decree of the session of July 1928, proved to be totally ineffectual. The increase, which came too late, was more than offset by the enormous increase in free market prices. The difference between State prices and free market prices was now 300%, and as much as 400% in the Ukraine and the Central Black Earth Region, although less in Siberia and Kazakhstan, where the harvest had been better.[79]

Despite the measures which had been adopted, mainly during the second half of the campaign (from the end of the winter of 1928 until the spring of 1929), the State failed to fulfil its procurements plan, although this had been markedly scaled down by comparison with that of the preceding year. The total delivery was considerably lower than in 1928, but the decline in stocks of bread-grains was of disastrous proportions. According to the official figures, the reduction was of the order of 25%.[80]

In 1928, the population had had to queue at the shops for supplies which had been steadily shrinking since the spring. It now seemed that 1929 would be another difficult year. *Pravda* carried cautious admissions to this effect, and made a number of reassuring promises, but the people had no need of newspapers to tell them that what lay ahead was a hard winter and a hungry spring.

By December, the authorities had begun to introduce food rationing, and this was to be progressively extended as time went on.[81] Stalin had been right, therefore, when he said in November that 'the most urgent problem facing us at present is agriculture, and grain in particular; we must learn how to reconstruct our agricultural sector on the basis of new techniques'.[82]

The situation was now highly dangerous, and in Stalin's opinion the time for half-measures was past. What was needed was drastic action. As he saw it, the only solution open to the régime was to modernize agriculture, as he had said in his speech, and to go over from small to large-scale farming. In his eyes, a radical change of this order would have the additional merit of establishing socialism once and for all. On the other hand, if the Party deviated from the path he had marked out for them, they could expect the worst, for 'a return to capitalism might prove unavoidable'.[83]

However, the reconstruction of agriculture was conditional upon the existence of a powerful industrial sector. In 1928, Soviet industry was too weak for such an undertaking. All in all, it was still too weak to provide a sufficiently stable base for a régime which had been described as 'the most progressive in the world'.

Viewed in this light, the task assumed even more formidable proportions, and an even greater degree of urgency. Stalin saw industrialization in terms of a crash-programme, a race against time in which speed and rate of growth were of the essence. 'Catch up with, and overtake, the advanced technical development of the capitalist countries' became the new watchword. The issue was one of dramatic simplicity: 'We shall either succeed, or go under.'[84]

It was now for the authorities to determine, through the medium of the Five-year Plan, what the speed and duration of the race would be.

NOTES AND REFERENCES

1. Kviring, *NAF*, 1928, No. 6–7, pp. 34–47. Kviring was Deputy-Chairman of *Gosplan*.

2. See the collection of documents *Kollektivizatsiya selskogo khozyaistva*, footnote to p. 30, and *Sobranie Zakonov*, 1928, No. 14, par. 1119.

3. According to Kviring, *op. cit.*

4. *ibid*.

5. See 'Kontraktatsiya posevov zernovykh', a decision of *SNK*, in *Kollektivizatsiya selskogo khozyaistva*, doc. No. 11, pp. 65–7.

6. Kviring, *op. cit.*

7. From the results of an enquiry carried out in the rural districts of the Stalingrad *guberniya* on behalf of the Central Committee in Stalingradskaya derevnya posle 15-togo S'ezda, *NAF*, 1928, No. 11, pp. 131–2.

8. *ibid*, p. 131.

9. The figure, obtained from the Central Archives of the October Revolution, is given by Konyukhov, *op cit.* (see Ch. 3, Note 41),

p. 185. On the results of the procurements campaign see Lvov, *NAF*, 1929, No. 1.

10. Konyukhov, *op. cit.*, pp. 184–5.

11. Speech by Yakovlev, *Pravda*, April 1 and 2, 1929.

12. Tsylko, *NAF*, 1928, No. 9, p. 5.

13. Konyukhov, quoting the Central Archives of the October Revolution, in *op. cit.*, p. 187; *Postroenie fundamenta sotsialisticheskoi ekonomiki v SSSR 1926–32*, p. 382.

14. Lvov, *op. cit.* (see Note 9), p. 9, disputed the figures of the *Khlebotsentr.*

15. Tsylko, *op. cit.* (see Note 12); p. 8, and Yakovlev in *Pravda*, April 2, 1928. According to data published early in 1929, over half of the kolkhozes consisted of less than ten families. Sefler, *NAF*, 1929, No. 1. Many *arteli* and *tozy* consisted of from five to ten families. Gaister, *Dostizheniya i trudnosti kolkhoznogo stroitelstva* (Moscow 1929). Towards the end of the year a kolkhoz consisted of, on the average, 13·7 households, or fewer than in 1927, had a sown area of 44·5 hectares, and possessed five or six horses and seven head of cattle. Kulikov, *NAF*, 1928, No. 12, p. 25.

16. Bumper, *Bolshevik*, 1928, No. 20, p. 78.

17. Yakovlev, *op. cit.* (see Note 11). By the end of the year it was known that a quarter of the kolkhozes had broken up. See a speech by Vlasov delivered as part of a discussion at the Communist Academy in Gaister, *op. cit.*

18. Tsylko, *op. cit.*, p. 7.

19. Astrov, *Pravda* July 3, 1928. Sosnovsky, in *Byulleten Oppozitsii*, 1929, No. 3–4 provides further evidence of this.

20. Tsylko, *op. cit.*, p. 6.

21. This figure is given in *KPSS v Rezolyutsiyakh*, Vol. II, p. 498; it represents a very small sum. Milyutin, in *NAF*, 1928, No. 12, p. 10, states that it was less than the cost of a single factory.

22. *Istoriya kolkhoznogo prava* (see Ch. 5, Note 7), doc. No. 37, pp. 111–2.

23. Kuzmin, *Pravda* April 28, 1928; Gaister, *NAF*, 1928, No. 12.

24. Kantor, *Pravda* March 10, 1928, and the article 'Stalingradskaya derevnya posle 15-togo S'ezda,' *NAF* 1928, No. 11, p. 137. The words *organizatsiya* and *kolkhoz* were synonymous for many peasants.

25. Kubyak, *Pravda*, March 10, 1928.

26. 'Spontaneous' in this context refers not to a deliberate movement with socialist aims, but merely to a willingness on the part of the peasants to join the kolkhozes on the condition that they be supplied with what one Soviet commentator has described as 'the invigorating beverage of credit'. In the article 'Stalinskaya

derevnya . . .' (see Note 7) the same commentator writes that 'in this respect it would be sheer utopianism to consider that collectivist consciousness or realization of the advantages of socialist exploitation of the land are acting as motivating forces'.

27. Tsylko, *NAF*, 1928, No. 9, pp. 10–13; Gaister, *op. cit.* (see Note 15), p. 25.

28. Tsylko; *op. cit.*, p. 4. The same ideas are to be found in an article by Bumper, *op. cit.* (see Note 16), pp. 76–7.

29. The figure is given by Gaister, *NAF* 1929, No. 10. For details concerning the degree to which the North Caucasus lagged behind the rest of the RSFSR, and data on illiteracy, the number of schoolchildren, etc., see *16-taya Konferentsiya VKP(b)*, stenogramme (Moscow 1962), p. 795, note 144.

30. Aggeev, *NAF*, 1928, No. 11, p. 142; Tsylko, *op. cit.*

31. *Kollektivizatsiya selskogo khozyaistva*, doc. No. 4, a decision of the Central Committee of March 26, 1928.

32. Data provided by Kulikov, *NAF* 1928, No. 12, p. 29. The brochure mentioned in Note 15 is an expanded version of an article by Gaister contained in the same issue: See also Tsylko, *NAF* 1928, No. 9, p. 16.

33. On this problem see Gaister, *op. cit.* (see Note 15), p. 26; Aggeev, *NAF* 1928, No. 11 (Stalingrad); Kotov, *NAF* 1929, No. 4 (Middle Volga); Bumper, *Bolshevik*, 1928, No. 20, pp. 76–7; Kulakov, *NAF*, 1928, No. 12, pp. 30–2.

34. *Kollektivizatsiya selskogo khozyyaistva*, doc. No. 4, a decision of the Central Committee of March 26, 1928.

35. Reported by Kulikov, *NAF*, 1928, No. 12, pp. 20–2.

36. *KPSS v Rezolyutsiyakh*, Vol. II, p. 531.

37. Stalin, *Sochineniya*, Vol. XI, p. 268.

38. In *Postroenie fundamenta sotsialisticheskoi ekonomiki*, published as recently as 1960, it is stated, on p. 496, that in 1926–7 the kolkhozes received 8% of all agricultural credits, and 53·6% in 1929–30. Thus during the same period the credits allocated to private agriculture fell from 55·9% to 5·4%.

39. A decision of the *TsIK* of December 15th, in *Kollektivizatsiya selskogo khozyaistva*, doc. No. 19, pp. 89–96.

40. Kalinin, in a speech to the *TsIK* expressed the opinion that the aid being given to the serednyaks was leading them away from collectivization; he did not, however, use this as an argument for stopping aid to the serednyaks. *Pravda*, December 14, 1928.

41. See the decree of *Sovnarkom* of March 2, 1928, *Kollektivizatsiya selskogo khozyaistva*, doc. No. 3, p. 35.

42. Session of July 1928. *KPSS v Rezolyutsiyakh*, Vol. II, pp. 517–18.

43. Pravda July 27, 1928; *Sobranie Zakonov*, October 12, 1928, No. 52, part two; *KPSS v Rezolyutsiyakh*, Vol. II, p. 518.

44. '*16-taya Konferentsiya*', stenogramme (Moscow, 1962), p. 793, Note 129.

45. On the state of these sovkhozes and their achievements see Antselovich, *15-ty S'ezd VKP(b)*, stenogramme, p. 1137; a special decision of Sovnarkom of April 25, 1929, in *Kollektivizatsiya selskogo khozyaistva*, doc. No. 33, pp. 130–40; in *Istoriya kolkhoznogo prava*, doc. No. 81, p. 114, it is revealed that the *RKI* (*Raboche-Krestyanskaya Inspektsiya*) had taken cognizance of the fact that the decisions taken earlier concerning the sovkhozes (on March 16, 1927) had not been implemented.

46. Decision of *Sovnarkom* of April 25, 1929, *Kollektivizatsiya selskogo khozyaistva*, doc. No. 33, in particular p. 141.

47. *Kollektivizatsiya selskogo khozyaistva*, doc. No. 3, pp. 30–41.

48. The changes which took place in *Narkomzem* have been noted above. At the same time Milyutin replaced Osinsky at the head of the *TsSU*. (See *Pravda*, March 8 and 24, 1928). Specialists such as Kondratev, Oganovsky, Yurovsky and Makarov, and the Marxists Sukhanov and Bazarov, who had played a leading role in the Commissariats of Finance and Agriculture and in *Gosplan*, were dismissed from these organizations. See Jasny, *Soviet Industrialisation* (Chicago 1961), pp. 52–3, and Daniels, *op. cit.* (see Ch. 2, Note 3), p. 359.

49. See Bukharin to Kamenev, *Sotsialisticheski Vestnik*, 1929, No. 6, No. 9. Bukharin mentions meetings of 'the seven' (probably the trio plus Stalin, Molotov, Kalinin, and Voroshilov), 'the five' (these four plus, perhaps, the candidate member Kaganovich), and of the 'troika', that is Bukharin, Rykov, and Tomsky.

50. Uglanov had been a member of the Secretariat elected after the Fifteenth Party Congress, but must have been excluded when the divergence of views became apparent.

51. Stalin, *Sochineniya*, Vol. XI, p. 203.

52. Daniels, *op. cit.*, p. 350, quoting Gladkov, *Planovoe Khozyaistvo* 1935, No. 4, pp. 126–30.

53. '*16-taya Konferentsiya*', stenogramme (Moscow 1962), p. 787, Note 97.

54. Zaleski, *op. cit.* (see Ch. 7, Note 5), p. 83.

55. According to Trifonov, *op. cit.* (see Ch. 2, Note 9), pp. 120–38, and Lyashchenko, *op. cit.* (see Ch. 1, Note 42), Vol. III, p. 259.

56. Stalin, *Sochineniya*, Vol. XI, p. 170.

57. Nove, *The Soviet Economy* (London 1961), p. 305; Trifonov, *op. cit.*, pp. 126–31; Erlich, *op. cit.* (see Ch. 6, Note 54), pp. 84–5.

58. *Bolshevik*, 1928, No. 2, p. 64.

59. Stalin, *Sochineniya*, Vol. XI, pp. 264–5.

60. *Bolshevik*, 1928, No. 2, p. 65.

61. *ibid, loc. cit. dovyyavit*: 'seek out the rest'. The information which follows is from pp. 65–7.

62. *ibid*, pp. 70–3.

63. 'Obshchie nachala zemlepolzovaniya i zemleustroistva', *Kollektivizatsiya selskogo khozyaistva*, doc. No. 20. The preliminary draft, prepared by Milyutin, is in *NAF*, 1928, No. 4. The commission responsible for drawing up the earlier draft of 1926 was dissolved.

64. *Kollektivizatsiya selskogo khozyaistva*, Ch. 5, pp. 101–2. Other measures are listed elsewhere in the text. The *khutor* and *otrub* are dealt with on p. 99.

65. *ibid*, p. 101.

66. *ibid*, p. 104; *Code Pénal*, (Paris 1935), par. 87/a, pp. 69–70: *Kollektivizatsiya selskogo khozyaistva*, doc. No. 10.

67. *Kollektivizatsiya selskogo khozyaistva*, doc. No. 20, par. 14, p. 99.

68. Frumkin stated in June that 'the outlawing of the kulaks has given rise to the perpetration of illegal acts against the peasantry as a whole'. Quoted by Stalin, *Sochineniya*, Vol. XI, p. 123.

69. *Kollektivizatsiya selskogo khozyaistva*, doc. No. 20, par. 47–51, pp. 105–6.

70. Angarov, *op. cit.* (see Ch. 2, Note 39), p. 45. Bauman, less naïve than this peasant, also speaks of 'neglect of the serednyak', although, of course, only 'here and there'.

71. *Pravda*, December 25, 1928, and March 5, 1929 (Kiselev).

72. Angarov, *op. cit.*, p. 47. All figures are from Angarov.

73. Kaganovich, *Bolshevik*, 1928, No. 19, p. 20.

74. *ibid*, pp. 20–6.

75. *ibid*, p. 20.

76. Kurbatov, *NAF*, 1929, No. 5; '*16-taya Konferentsiya*', stenogramme (Moscow, 1962), p. 11.

77. *Pravda*, editorial, September 5, 1928.

78. *Pravda*, editorial, December 2, 1928.

79. Lvov, *NAF* 1929, No. 1.

80. Mikoyan, in 'Novaya khlebozagotovitelnaya kampaniya i zadachi partii', *Bolshevik*, 1929, No. 15, p. 16, gives the following figures: in 1927–8 8·05 million metric tons of food grain, in 1928–9, 6·20 million metric tons. Andreev stated at the session of April 1929 that in the Ukraine and the North Caucasus 243 million poods less than the previous year had been collected. His speech, taken

from the Central Archives of the Party is quoted in '*16-taya Konferentsiya*', stenogramme (Moscow 1962), p. 772, Note 12.

81. Mendelson, *Planovoe Khozyaistvo*, 1929, No. 5, p. 61.
82. Stalin, *Sochineniya*, Vol. XI, p. 45.
83. *ibid*, pp. 254–5.
84. *ibid*, p.248.

Chapter 12

THE LAST OPPOSITION

1. *The 'Danger from the Right'*

The Party majority which had fought the Left opposition was far from homogeneous in character. In 1926, according to Trotsky, there had been three tendencies within the Central Committee: a pro-peasant tendency represented by Rykov, Tomsky's syndicalist group, and the supporters of the Party 'apparatus' led by Stalin.[1]

Towards the end of 1927 the Left, in its *Platform*, had revealed the existence of a 'Right' and a 'Centre' tendency, had identified the supporters of both fairly accurately, and predicted that once their common enemy had been eliminated, a split between the two was inevitable.[2] Our analysis of the Fifteenth Party Congress has also shown that, despite the appearance of common terminology and unanimous resolutions, there were in fact two opposing tendencies at work.

Soon, what Trotsky had predicted came to pass. The unity of the Politburo split during the very first crisis. Before they had finished celebrating their victory over the Left, the Party leadership were again divided and found themselves once more at each other's throats in an atmosphere that was heavy with hatred and intrigue.

The new opposition, which was to be the last of any importance, differed from the Left opposition in that it did not believe that the controversy should be carried on in full view of the Party. This time, however fierce the struggle, it was to be kept within the confines of the Politburo or, on occasion, the Central Committee. Only when the fight was over did the public learn of its existence, when the victor, having vanquished and silenced his opponents, denounced them before the entire country.

The historian Daniels, in a remarkable chapter on the Right opposition, observes that 'the history of the Right opposition affords the singular spectacle of a political group's being defeated first, and attacked afterwards'.[3]

The Right themselves were partly to blame, for they resolved in advance to stick to the rules, and to avoid bringing their differences out into the open. These tactics, instead of affording them greater protection as they had hoped, merely delivered them into the hands of an opponent who was more skilled in organizational warfare than they were, and who finally outmanoeuvred them.

The struggle took the form of a series of palace intrigues, but what was at stake was of capital importance to the nation, for it involved the choice between two kinds of programme, or two opposing views of the way in which the country should progress towards socialism. The fundamental point at issue was the 'accursed' peasant problem, that is, the problem of deciding how a backward and predominantly peasant society should be industrialized.

Inevitably, the differences between these two currents of opinion came to the surface when force of circumstance, and Stalin's swift and vigorous tactics with the Politburo, resulted in the government's decision to adopt 'emergency measures' in the countryside. These measures created havoc in the rural areas, and had immediate repercussions in the upper echelons of the Party, where the methods and possible aims of Stalin and his associates engendered a distrust which was soon to turn to hostility.

The first to react were Rykov, who represented the majority opinion of the government apparatus, and Kalinin, who spoke for those members of the *TsIK* who were in close touch with rural affairs, and were very much alive to the many signs of unrest which were apparent in all parts of the country.

These two leaders, themselves of peasant origin, had long been known for their pro-peasant attitude, and their intimate knowledge of the countryside. Tomsky had already joined forces with them. When Stalin returned from his tour of Siberia, he was more than ever convinced of the efficacy of his strong-arm methods, and he determined to carry out wholesale purges in Siberia and other regions in order to overcome resistance to these same methods within the Party organization. He thereupon came up against the opposition of the aforementioned members of the Politburo, and it would appear that to some extent they succeeded in restraining him. One source reports that the Politburo was the scene of 'some very heated exchanges' between Stalin and Rykov.[4]

Stalin was not the kind of man to take such criticism lying down. His first action against those who opposed the emergency measures was to carry out a purge in the Commissariat of Agriculture, in the guise of a simple organizational reshuffle. Other purges were to follow, though these attracted less attention at the time, since they had been carried out discreetly so as to avoid providing the Politburo with a *casus belli*. The most important element in Stalin's long-term strategy was the launching of a campaign against a 'deviation' whose existence he now revealed to the Party and, some days later, to the country as a whole. However, at this point no names were mentioned, and only the local authorities came in for criticism.

In a letter to local officials written on January 13th, or over a week after his return from Siberia (by which time the altercation with

Rykov may already have taken place) Stalin mentioned as one of the causes for the deterioration of work in the countryside the recent appearance, in Party and other administrative organizations, of 'elements alien to the Party, who are not alive to the class problem in the countryside, who do not understand the bases of our class policy, and who are endeavouring to conduct affairs in the rural areas without offending anyone, in the hope of living in peace with the kulak and, in general, remaining popular with "their" strata in the villages'.[5]

During the months which followed, this theme was gradually built up, and used as the *leitmotiv* for propaganda attacks on a deviationist trend which, in the initial stages of the campaign, was presented as something which had developed at local level, far from the centre. The leadership accordingly joined in deploring this tendency, in the form in which it was defined, though there were undertones in their criticisms which were apparent only to those few who were 'in the know'.

By March, it was being rumoured among high-ranking officials that there were differences of opinion between Stalin and Rykov, though as yet the nature of the split was unknown. In their dealings with Stalin, these same officials noted an unexpected and rather disquieting easiness and flexibility, instead of the stubbornness and intransigence which more usually characterized his behaviour.[6]

The Plenum of the Central Committee which met at the beginning of April was no doubt fairly uneventful. On the other hand, many delegates, particularly those from the provinces, were disturbed by the negative effects of the coercive measures which had been enforced in the villages, and majority opinion at this time was probably not very favourable to Stalin.[7]

Nor had Stalin yet taken over control of the Politburo. Its members, at this stage, had no clearly defined policy in view. Analysis of the resolutions which were adopted at this session suggests that every phrase must have been closely argued in the Politburo, and it is clear that the various currents of opinion did their utmost to ensure that the essential points in their respective theses were adequately reflected in the final resolutions of the session.

On this occasion Stalin found it necessary to carry out a full-scale retreat, and he agreed that the resolutions should embody the main points of the Bukharinist arguments on the role of a flexible prices policy and the importance of market relations, a very moderate interpretation of the concept of the 'offensive against the kulaks', and a formal denunciation of all abuses, etc. He took care, however, to include his own personal view on the kulak's part in the difficulties which had arisen during the *zagotovki*, and to stress that introduction of the emergency measures had been unavoidable. He also stated, in very ambiguous terms, that these measures would soon be revoked, but only 'as and when the difficulties are overcome'.[8]

Stalin also succeeded in obtaining approval for the government's policy on wheat prices, in ensuring that the purge of administrative organs would continue, and in introducing two separate clauses denouncing 'degenerate' elements within the Party who 'ignore the class position in the countryside, and are incapable of forcing the kulaks to beat a rapid retreat'.[9]

The Central Committee was not apprised of the differences of opinion within the Politburo, and was presented with a unanimous resolution. That these differences existed may be clearly seen from the reports on the results of the Plenum which were, according to the usual practice, submitted to Party activists in the large towns.

In Moscow, Stalin congratulated himself on what he considered to have been a fruitful session. There had been no 'internal disputes', and all decisions had been reached unanimously 'without factional attacks or demagogy'.[10] Having said this, he went on to elaborate his own personal theories, which we have already discussed in the preceding chapter. He was particularly lavish in his praise of the emergency measures which, he claimed, had made it possible to overcome the crisis, and which would be employed again if circumstances demanded.[11] Without mentioning any names, he launched into an attack on those who disapproved of his policy. The argument he used was crude but effective. Anyone who aimed to please both the poor and the rich was 'not a Marxist but a fool (durak)'.[12]

With growing anxiety Stalin's critics, and Bukharin in particular (who would seem to have joined forces with Rykov by March at the latest) realized that the line he and his associates were pursuing was becoming increasingly dangerous.[13] From the theoretical point of view, they were given a thoroughly satisfactory explanation of the situation, and of the need 'to achieve equilibrium in the various sectors of the national economy'. However, theorizing could do little to dispel their fears. It seemed that the policy which was to be implemented would be a repetition of that of the previous spring, or even worse.

Bukharin reported to the Leningrad Party on the conclusions reached by the Plenum. He began his speech with a dutiful recital of the criticisms which had been levelled against 'the conservative element' in the Party, which understood neither the unprecedented nature of the situation, nor the 'necessity for a forced offensive against the kulak'. Having 'lost its sense of class awareness' this element 'sought no quarrel with the kulak'.

At this point, however, Bukharin struck a different, much more personal note, which had been entirely absent from the resolutions of the Plenum.

'On the other hand,' he went on,

'we have also observed a tendency to omit certain indispensable stages of development. This is reflected, for example, in the failure of certain people to appreciate the conditional nature of the emergency measures, which they seem to regard as more or less normal. Similarly, there is a tendency to deny that the growth of the individual farm is important, and a tendency to place excessive emphasis on the use of administrative methods. Certain sound principles which should constantly be borne in mind, for example those concerning the middle peasantry, seem at times to be forgotten.'[14]

This allusion, which could have been taken as a criticism of the Trotskyists, was in fact part of a covert attack on Stalin. At this stage, Bukharin dared go no further.

By June, there was mounting criticism of Stalin's policy, and an increasing determination to oppose him. Few data are available on this particular period, but the Trotsky archives (quoted by Daniels) provide some important clues.[15] It would appear that at this time Uglanov, the Moscow Party Secretary, addressing a small audience of one of his Moscow organizations, severely criticized Stalin's erroneous policies, which he claimed were based on inadequate statistical data. At the same time Slepkov, another of Bukharin's supporters, attacked Kirov in Leningrad. Dissatisfaction spread to many of the proconsul's subordinates. Tomsky, head of the Trades Union movement, was preparing for battle, and did not hesitate to confer with Pyatakov, a Trotskyist who had very recently 'capitulated'. At the beginning of the month Bukharin referred to Stalin in private as a 'carrier' of Trotskyism,[16] but by the end of the month he must have realized that 'the Trotskyist danger' constituted much less of a threat than Stalin himself, and that the latter would have to be deposed if the country were to be saved from disaster.

When, at the beginning of summer, compulsory procurements were resumed, relations with the peasantry became strained to a degree which was unprecedented since the introduction of NEP, while relations between the protagonists in the Politburo likewise entered upon a new phase of tension, more acute than anything which had been experienced since the downfall of the Trotskyists.

Personal feelings ran so high that by June Bukharin was no longer on speaking terms with Stalin. Both in the private and the political context, the break was complete. Bukharin, Rykov, Tomsky and Uglanov, a candidate member of the Politburo as well as the Moscow

Party Secretary, met in order to agree on their next move. Their rivals did the same.

The two sides now entered upon a struggle for the support of such relatively uncommitted members of the Politburo as Kalinin, Voroshilov and Andreev who, according to Bukharin, were 'with us', but recoiled before the prospect of deposing Stalin.

Meanwhile, the only individual to launch a direct attack on the Politburo was a second-rank political personality, the deputy Commissar of Finance, Frumkin. In a letter of July 15, 1928, addressed to the members of the Politburo, he spoke of the offensive which the capitalist world was mounting against the USSR.[17] However, Frumkin argued that the principal danger lay, not in the strength of the enemy forces, but in the 'political and economic depletion of our own forces',[18] thereby implying that the alleged danger of attack from outside, which was used for propaganda purposes whenever the authorities thought fit, was in reality less serious than the danger arising from the implementation of ill-judged policies at home. In his view, these policies had induced among the majority of poor peasants and serednyaks 'an anti-Soviet frame of mind, which is spreading to the working-class centres'.[19] He went on to criticize the policy which had been adopted after the Fifteenth Congress, describing this 'new political approach with regard to the countryside' as 'pernicious', in that it had led to a deterioration in the country's economic situation. 'The outlawing of the kulak,' he alleged, 'has led to the perpetration of illegal acts (*bezzakoniya*) against the entire peasantry'.[20]

Frumkin condemned *razkulachivanie* as a wholly unjustified method of combating the kulak, and recommended a return to the decisions of the Fourteenth and Fifteenth Congresses, and the adoption of a series of practical measures, including an increase in grain prices, the re-opening of the markets, the resumption of the normal functions of the grain market and, of course, an immediate end to all emergency measures.

His letter also contained a statement which reflected the general viewpoint of a great many high-ranking officials at the time.

'Whatever criticisms may be levelled at me, I am bound to assert that in the present situation, given the low level of agricultural production, every million poods [of grain], whichever group supplies it, reinforces the dictatorship of the proletariat, and contributes to industrialization, whereas every million poods lost weakens us.'[21]

The Politburo decided to circulate Frumkin's letter to the members of the Central Committee, and to follow it up with a reply on behalf of the entire Politburo membership, but Stalin bypassed this decision, and sent a personal reply.[22] He confined his criticisms to a few details in Frumkin's letter, the main accusation being that Frumkin wanted to see the kulaks reinstated in their political rights.[23] On the other points which Frumkin had made, Stalin gave ground by admitting that acts of dekulakization had taken place, and claiming that instructions had already been given to re-open the markets, and that the decision to increase procurement prices had already been taken some time ago. . . .

Bukharin, Rykov and Tomsky took Stalin to task for having dared to override a Politburo decision, but the only satisfaction they obtained was a mild reprimand for the General Secretary, which took the form of an admission by the Politburo that his reply had been incomplete.[24]

Stalin therefore emerged unscathed, by judiciously conceding almost every point and forestalling criticism from his opponents in the Politburo. This was made all the easier for him since the majority of the Politburo were still unresolved as to the fundamental aspects of the problems facing them, and were not prepared to dissociate themselves from Stalin's unilateral action. In Bukharin's opinion, Stalin was behaving as though the Politburo were a mere appendage of the General Secretariat, but the others did not see the matter in this light. It is likely that, in order to avoid being accused of acting in a manner which was inconsistent with the principles of collective leadership, Stalin did, on occasion, consult or make a show of consulting with the other members of the Politburo, though not with the three, or with Uglanov. No doubt he had other ways of influencing the Politburo as well, and dissuading them from attacking him. Even the outspoken Frumkin refrained from attacking Stalin personally, and blamed only Molotov and Kubyak for the excesses which had occurred.

Stalin was a master of tactics and, what is more important, a past-master in the art of manipulating the Party apparatus. He accordingly played his cards with the greatest skill. He had the knack of avoiding any engagement on unfavourable ground, and so he took care at all costs not to provoke a general discussion, whether in public or within the confines of the Central Committee, but used the attack on a minor personality like Frumkin to discredit ideas which he knew were those of the Bukharinists, but which the latter had not yet found the courage to call their own.

Stalin also manoeuvred his opponents into attacking in circumstances which would make them appear as schismatics and deviationists. To this end he spread rumours about his imminent reconciliation with the Left. There seems little doubt that he was considering such a step, not merely as a means of provoking Bukharin, but as a possible move which must be taken seriously into account. The same rumours also served to divide and weaken the ranks of the Trotskyists and to recruit some of their members, while at the same time further isolating Trotsky himself.[25]

Doctrinal considerations played no part in these tactics, the sole purpose of which was to strengthen Stalin's personal power. The discovery of this side of Stalin's character made a deep impression on Bukharin, and put him on his guard. 'He is an unprincipled intriguer,' he exclaimed in horror, 'who puts his desire for power before all else. He will change his theories at a moment's notice in order to get rid of someone.'[26]

Before the July session, the break between the two was final. The first major clash between them occurred during the preliminaries for this session.[27] Bukharin at this point was insisting that Stalin should open a general discussion of overall policy, but Stalin persistently evaded the issue. After several exchanges between the two, and after Bukharin had sent two letters to the Politburo, the matter was placed before the 'Seven'.[28]

According to Bukharin 'There was a terrible scene. He began to shout at me. I quoted his remarks about the Himalayas.[29] He shouted "You're lying! You made all this up in order to turn the members of the Politburo against me!" '[30] At a subsequent meeting Bukharin read a long statement, consisting of his draft theses for the July session. He took care not to let the documents out of his hands. ('He cannot be trusted with a single bit of paper.') Molotov, who was unskilled in such matters, reacted immediately by alleging that Bukharin's draft was an 'anti-Party document', but Stalin used the same tactics as he had done in the case of Frumkin's letter. Only this time he went much further, by announcing that he was prepared to agree 'nine-tenths' of Bukharin's theses.

His draft having been accepted as a basis for discussion, Bukharin set about revising it in preparation for the Plenum. Once again, his opponents stole a march on him; without warning, 'the others' tabled a resolution 'which they stole from my declaration'. Now that Stalin had given way on most of Bukharin's criticisms, the general discussion which Bukharin had insisted upon never materialized, and the Politburo could be sure once more of presenting a united front to the Central Committee. The three could see no alternative to this, and had to be content with a few amendments.

Before the session opened on July 4th an odd duel was fought out in the columns of *Pravda*. This habit of using the press as an instrument in the strategy of indirect attack was to persist for some considerable time. Astrov, the editor of *Pravda* and a supporter of Bukharin, published an article expressing the strongest disapproval of acts of violence which had been committed against the peasants, with a fair amount of evidence in support of his statements. He also quoted freely from Bukharin's criticisms of those elements within the Party who tended to place undue emphasis on the use of administrative methods, and believed it possible to omit certain necessary stages in the process of development. (These views of Bukharin's have already been mentioned in the preceding pages.)

However, the General Secretary was not to be outdone. The same issue also carried a letter written by Stalin three weeks previously, and which he had now hastily released as a counterblast to Astrov's article. Lest *Pravda*'s complaints about the ill-treatment of the serednyaks should have led any of the readers to feel undue sympathy for them, Stalin countered with his own interpretation of the *smychka*, which was that the hesitant serednyak would never prove a trustworthy ally 'unless the kulak is resolutely opposed, and a sustained effort is directed at increasing activity among the *bednota*'. We have already discussed this particular view of the *smychka*.

Although there was no general discussion of overall Party policy at this session, there was a confrontation between the two opposing tendencies over the emergency measures, and the question of 'tribute'. The majority of the speakers were restrained in manner, and the Right likewise observed a proper decorum. None the less, there were frequent heated exchanges.

The liveliest part of the debate centred on the grain problem and the procurements, and lasted from July 9th to the 11th.[31] Kalinin's report on the sovkhozes, Molotov's report on the kolkhozes, and Mikoyan's statement on the progress of the *zagotovki*, were all moderate in tone. Mikoyan's speech, which provided the basis for the unanimously adopted resolution, was a compromise statement which, as we have seen, had been agreed in advance by the Politburo.

After Mikoyan had spoken, Osinsky, Andreev, Stetsky and Sokolnikov all pressed for more concessions to the serednyaks. Uglanov and Rykov warned the authorities about the danger of allowing the emergency measures to become a feature of regular policy, and drew attention to the widespread discontent in the country.

The Stalinists, however, stood firm in their insistence on what they considered to be the key points at issue. Kaganovich, who only a little time before would have been unwilling to commit himself, now spoke out in favour of the emergency measures, on the grounds that it was not enough simply to rely on manipulation of the price mechanism.[32] Rykov counter-attacked and, according to Sokolnikov, 'made mincemeat of him'. He was hardly to be taken in by the crude, and now well-worn Stalinist distinction between the 'Party line' and the 'excesses' committed in implementing it.

'There is a whole series of abuses,' he declared, 'which are an organic part of the body of procurement measures which we introduced in January.' He then added, 'in essence, Kaganovich's speech amounts to a defence of the emergency measures as a policy which is applicable at all times and in all circumstances'.[33]

On July 9th, Stalin himself delivered a lengthy speech, which was not published at the time.[34] The main burden of his discourse, with which we are already familiar, related to the following items: 'surtax' or tribute which it was necessary to levy on the peasantry as an essential pre-condition of industrialization; the class struggle, which must increase in intensity with the growth of socialism; the emergency measures, which he defended as a legitimate instrument of policy; and the need for strong leadership, with the leaders exempted from self-criticism.[35]

Bukharin spoke on the following day, after Stalin. In the interval, the Secretariat lobbied intensively in order to win over those members of the Central Committee who were opposed to the 'tribute' and in favour of a change in price policy which would be more advantageous to the peasants. Since the Leningrad delegation were probably the most hostile in their attitude towards the tribute, they were given the most intensive 'working over'. Bukharin must already have begun to suspect that majority opinion, which he had at first thought to be behind him, was now shifting in favour of the Secretariat. His address to the Plenum was repeatedly interrupted by Voroshilov's attempts to discredit his arguments. Yet at the beginning of the session, Voroshilov had been one of those on whom Bukharin was counting.

Bukharin ascribed the gravity of the situation to the fact that forces hostile to the régime were still strongly entrenched. 'The slightest hesitation within the ranks of the Party over the question (the peasant question) will have disproportionately serious political repercussions.'[36]

The grain crisis, he claimed, was symptomatic of the country's fundamental weakness—a lack of reserves of any sort. In such conditions, it was impossible to advance simultaneously on the three fronts of industry, agriculture and consumption. 'Let's have your universal remedy, then!' interjected Voroshilov. Bukharin replied with the utmost gravity, 'I have no universal remedy to offer you, and I beg you not to make jokes at my expense.'

He went on to criticize Stalin for implying that industrialization must inevitably threaten the *smychka*. He also denied that there was any justification for the view that price regulation was a 'capitalist' device. On the contrary, he said, it afforded a means of exercising a decisive influence on the economy. Faulty planning and a defective prices policy had been responsible for the recent crisis, which in turn had led to the adoption of measures which were likely to end in a return to the system of 'war communism'.

From the economic point of view, these measures were of doubtful validity, and in the political sense their effect was harmful. At all' costs an attempt must be made to preserve good relations with the serednyaks, and to enable them to improve their condition. The offensive against the kulaks could be allowed to continue, but the only form which it should take should be exploitation of their productive capacity through the medium of taxation. The kulak was harmless so long as the serednyak did not join forces with him. 'Under no circumstances can we afford to jeopardize the alliance with the peasantry.'

Towards the end of his speech Bukharin turned his attention to a matter with which he was to deal more fully later on. He uttered a serious warning about excessive centralization of the State administration, which tended to stifle initiative and encourage irresponsibility.[37]

In the meantime, to the astonishment of the Right, the Leningrad delegation had dissociated themselves from a speech made by one of their members, Stetsky, who had criticized the tribute. Sick at heart, Bukharin 'retired from the field without firing a single shot', as Sokolnikov put it.

Molotov was now sufficiently emboldened to launch an attack on *Pravda*, which, thanks mainly to Astrov, was still in the hands of the Bukharinists.[38] In *Pravda* of July 7th, Astrov had appended a critical note to an article in which it was claimed that the agricultural sector had been making progress, largely due to the decisions of the Fifteenth Party Congress. In his note, Astrov had politely put the enthusiastic author in his place, pointing out that there was little justification for over-stressing these successes, least of all where the procurements were concerned. 'Success of this order', he argued, 'would have contributed towards a further reinforcement of the alliance between the proletariat and the mass of the peasantry. However, this is not borne out by the countless letters which the editors have received, and which may be supposed to provide an adequate reflection of popular opinion.' The editors also took the author of the article to task for suggesting that the emergency measures were consistent with the decisions of the Fifteenth Party Congress, and should therefore be recognized as a contributory factor in the alleged upward trend in agriculture; the editors categorically denied that there had, in fact, been any such improvement.

The Secretariat were no longer prepared to tolerate this amount of 'editorial licence' on the part of *Pravda*; hence Molotov's broadside against its editors. Molotov furnished his own explanation of the current difficulties. The cause of the crisis, he maintained, was the serednyak. Sokolnikov quotes him as saying, '*The serednyaks have gathered strength, this is why they are at loggerheads*' [with the régime. Our italics.—M.L.].

Tomsky's counter-attack on Molotov, although moderate in tone, was not lacking in bite. Sokolnikov summarizes what he had to say as follows: 'If Molotov was right, what solutions would be open to us? You want NEP without Nepmen, without kulaks and without making any concessions to anyone. But such a policy could not possibly succeed.'[39] Tomsky accordingly pressed for greater consideration and more genuine concessions for the serednyaks.

By this time, the Secretariat's manoeuvres had proved successful, and Stalin's support among the *Tsekisty* (members of the Central Committee) had been further strengthened and confirmed. Most of the speakers who had demanded a price policy which would be more favourable to the peasants (*vosstanovitelnye tseny*) now withdrew from this position.[40] The principle of tribute (*dan*), which was of great importance for Stalin, was agreed by the majority of the *Tsekisty*. The latter withdrew their objections without being unduly concerned over the exact definition of a term which was so vague that it covered a whole range of possible methods by which resources could be drained from the rural sector, varying from procedures which might be marginally inconvenient for the peasants, to ruthless and systematic exploitation on a vast scale.

The average Central Committee member, according to Bukharin, grasped neither the extent, nor the implications, of this conflict of views. However, neither Bukharin nor his colleagues did anything to enlighten them. In any case, the members of the Central Committee, *apparatchiki* for the most part, were more concerned with questions relating to the balance of power within the Party apparatus than with political or ideological differences.

The leader of the Leningrad delegation, Komarov, who had decided not to support the statement made by Stetsky (who was still a Bukharinist) later went out of his way to apologize to Bukharin in private.[41] He may well have been threatened, or had pressure put on him, by the Secretariat, and no doubt this is the excuse which he offered.

Once his position had been secured, Stalin's attitude hardened. His next speech took place on July 11th. Roused by the battle which, unbeknown to the majority of the *Tsekisty*, was being fought behind the scenes, he turned on Tomsky. Part of his speech is quoted by Sokolnikov.

'. . . I was astounded by Tomsky's speech. He seems to think we have no option but to make concessions to the peasants. This is a defeatist attitude which betrays a lack of faith in socialist construction. What if the serednyaks went so far as to insist on concessions over the monopoly of foreign trade, or demanded a *krestyanski soyuz* (peasants' union)?[42] Would we have to give in over these too? This is defeatism. Our strength lies in the sovkhozes and the kolkhozes, and in our efforts to activize the *bednota*.'[43]

Sokolnikov adds a description of Stalin as he was making this speech: 'Swarthy, sour, wrathful and vindictive. A forbidding sight. We now realized that Stalin too was on the offensive, as well as Bukharin. What struck us most was his coarseness.'[44]

Stalin went on to attack those delegates 'who had not even referred to the kolkhozes and sovhozes'. This was now his favourite theme, and indeed it had received little mention from the Bukharinists. However, the less attention they paid to kolkhozes and sovkhozes, the more Stalin stressed their significance as an effective means of establishing socialist strongholds in the countryside *immediately*....[45]

Stalin had been contemplating this solution since the beginning of the year. He presented it for the first time during this session as a universal remedy, the very cornerstone of his counter-plan. For the benefit of those who remained sceptical about the possible success of giant agricultural enterprises in the USSR or elsewhere, he quoted the example of the huge, prosperous farm of over 39,000 hectares owned by the American Campbell, in Montana. He claimed that the USSR, and the USSR alone, had all the necessary pre-conditions for the creation of even larger farms, these conditions being the nationalization of the land, the absence of rent of any kind, the absence of the profit motive, and large-scale State aid.[46]

Stalin's audience was familiar with the proposition that the dictatorship of the proletariat was in all ways superior to other forms of government, and they were accustomed to taking this superiority for granted. The fact that Stalin's arguments were derived from strictly ideological hypotheses, and in no way provided the economic evidence which would have been necessary to support his claims for the collective forms under discussion, could well have escaped his listeners. But for a realist like Rykov, or an economist like Bukharin, the viability of the kolkhozes and sovkhozes had been demonstrated neither by experience nor by economic calculation. To rely exclusively on their success was to risk everything in a venture that was doomed to failure. However, the Right were outvoted. Whatever views they may have expressed in private, Kalinin, Voroshilov and Ordzhonikidze, on whose support Bukharin and Rykov had been counting, went over to the side of the General Secretary who, according to Bukharin, held them 'by mysterious threads'.[47]

Bukharin and his colleagues were now convinced that Stalin was leading the country to disaster. They knew that he was determined to take the grain from the peasants, undeterred by the prospect that this might provoke civil war. The Central Committee must therefore be warned at all costs, and persuaded to depose Stalin. There was no time to be lost, for Stalin meanwhile was preparing to ambush his rivals, and 'cut their throats'.

Warning the Central Committee was no easy task. Whatever their views of Stalin as a person, hardened Bolsheviks and *apparatchiki* who were accustomed to the use of summary methods were not likely to be alarmed by his attitude to the kulaks, and his remarks about those who refused to take a tough line with them, or by his enthusiasm for emergency measures. It would be even more difficult to convince them that he was aiming to use the emergency measures as the basis for a system of wholesale coercion. Accurate as the Bukharinists' prediction proved to be, it was based on mere intuition, and it was difficult to prove. There was only one way of opposing Stalin, and that was to attack his entire policy fearlessly and in public. Bukharin contemplated such a move, but Stalin did everything to forestall it. It was for this reason that he had given ground by agreeing to end the emergency measures and to increase the grain prices. As we shall see, he feared a public trial of strength.

Unfortunately, the three also feared this. They were afraid of civil war, afraid of splitting the Party, in short afraid to act. Bukharin knew that a direct confrontation would immediately arouse the most extreme animosity. He tried to foresee what would happen if he were to attack Stalin. 'We will say—"Here is the man who has reduced the country to ruin and famine", and he will say—"Here are the champions of the kulaks and the Nepmen."'[48]

What the three feared most of all was the charge of splitting the Party. They were themselves largely responsible for having made a fetish of Party solidarity during the conflict with the Left. Now they were hoist with their own petard.

Kamenev notes that at this time Bukharin was like a man with his back to the wall, and indeed some of his remarks reveal the most profound despair.

'Sometimes I say to Yefim [his secretary] "Are we not in a hopeless situation? If the country is doomed, we are doomed with it. If the country survives, then Stalin will execute a smart about-turn, and we shall still be doomed. How can you fight a man like this? As for this Genghis Khan atmosphere in the Central Committee. . . .".'[49]

The plan for launching a general attack on Stalin was therefore postponed. Bukharin admitted that this was perhaps due to cowardice on his part. Be that as it may, the three decided to await a more propitious moment for their offensive. In the meantime, Bukharin decided to publish a series of articles in *Pravda*, in an attempt to inform the Party, and the country, of the situation. He also considered whether it might be wise for the three to tender their resignations, thus avoiding responsibility for a disastrous policy. When Stalin's failure had become apparent, they would then be in a position to take appropriate action. The three did, in fact, adopt this tactic, with what results we shall see later.

In order to forestall any move on Stalin's part to crush them by making a pact with the Trotskyists, the three now decided to strike first. On July 11th, Bukharin and Sokolnikov burst in on Kamenev without warning, and proposed an alliance against Stalin. Bukharin knew that the Left had been expecting overtures from Stalin rather than from the Right, whom they looked upon as their worst enemies. Accordingly, he made up his mind to enlighten the Left as to the true nature of Stalin and his projects. 'Our differences with Stalin,' he declared to an astonished Kamenev, 'are much greater than our differences with you.'[50]

This was a moment of truth. Trotsky, in exile in Alma-Ata, was also in favour of a change in tactics. He agreed to a conditional alliance with the Right, with a view to restoring the principle of democratic leadership within the Party, and calling another Congress. However, Trotsky's supporters, although in exile, were still full of the fighting spirit, and his suggestion met with vigorous opposition from them.[51] They saw no reason for an alliance with the Right, whom they detested, when Stalin was about to adopt their own line—or so at least they thought at the time. Anxious to avoid dissent within his own camp, Trotsky did not press the matter; nor did the Right. Although Bukharin and Kamenev continued to meet, the old antagonism and mistrust were too deeply rooted for such an alliance to take place.

Thus, the behaviour of the Bukharinists after the Plenum was influenced by their desire to postpone a major confrontation and to avoid laying themselves open to the charge of causing a split in the Party. Nevertheless in their speeches they continued to develop their favourite arguments, taking the opportunity to criticize as and when it arose. They believed that by forcing Stalin to deny persistent rumours of dissent within the Politburo—which Stalin readily agreed to do—they would succeed in retaining some freedom of action, while continuing to harass the Stalinists. This was a blunder. In the press and in their speeches, both sides pursued the strategy of indirect attack with the appropriate weapons of allusion and insinuation; only those in the inner circles of the Party could have told what was going on.

In his report on the results of the Plenum, Stalin began by repeating those clauses in the resolutions which had been inserted purely as a concession to the Bukharinists. He then admitted the gravity of the events which had taken place during the second phase of the procurements campaign, but immediately went on to justify the use of coercive methods, and categorically denied the existence of a *razmychka* (split with the peasantry). This was a crucial point of difference with the opposition. The Right were convinced, although they did not publicly say so, that the peasantry had already turned its back on the Soviet régime. Frumkin was no doubt expressing his own personal opinion when he assured the Plenum that the fatal *razmychka* had already developed; none the less, he had put into words what the rest of the opposition were thinking.[52] An admission that this was so would have been tantamount to outright condemnation of the Politburo's policy, so Stalin vigorously denied the allegation, and retorted that those who put forward such opinions lacked firmness of purpose and self-control.

Rykov, in his own way, was no less aggressive. In his report to the Moscow Party,[53] he too began with a dutiful recital of the principles embodied in the general resolutions—that is, the offensive against the kulaks, and the *perechachka*—but denounced those who saw no need for moderation in the implementation of these policies. In connection with the offensive against the kulaks, he rejected any suggestion that this should be extended to include dekulakization. Rykov also made a plea on behalf of the small peasant farms, and openly insisted that the kolkhozes were still not sufficiently advanced to serve as an example to the peasants. He made a firm promise to put an end to the anti-seredynak abuses, of which he gave numerous alarming examples. Several lengthy sections of the resolutions of the Plenum justified him in speaking in this way.

According to one writer, Rykov went so far as to assert that if the emergency measures were reintroduced 'it would be the end of NEP . . . the army would certainly revolt. It was Voroshilov who told me so.'[54] It is possible that Rykov did make such a remark, but more likely that he did so before a more restricted audience. The source in question is clearly mistaken as to the occasion on which this statement was made. A member of the Politburo would weigh his words carefully in an official report to the Moscow Party organization. But even leaving aside a possible remark which was not meant for the record, the official text of the speech reveals a barely disguised criticism of Stalin's analysis of the origins of the grain crisis.[55]

In seeking to identify the fundamental causes of the crisis, Stalin tended to stress objective factors, laying particular emphasis on the fragmented nature of peasant agriculture. Rykov, on the other hand, stressed the part played by government policy.

'Could these objective factors [fragmentation, private ownership of the farms. . . . M.L.] not have been modified in the course of the last three, five or ten years, and would they not have appeared in a different light if government policy, while continuing to observe the principle of priority for the rapid development of industry, had paid more attention to the interests of agriculture, and to the interests of the grain-growing sector in particular?'

As a counter-argument, he quoted the decision to construct the sovkhozes, which were now being hailed as the answer to all the country's problems, though in Rykov's opinion they were far from fulfilling any such hope. 'Why,' he asked, 'was this decision not taken a year ago?'[56]

Only those in the inner councils of the government administration were able to appreciate the finer points of the duel which was being fought out between the two opposing sides. There were some who even believed that it would be Rykov's views which would prevail.[57]

In fact, the tactics of the Right, which consisted of sniping at the Stalinists in private while concealing the split from the Party and the public, could not have suited Stalin better. As we have said, he was not yet ready for a public confrontation.[58] In the ranks of the local administration, there were many officials, even at *oblast* level, who either had doubts about the advisability of using coercive methods, or openly expressed their disapproval; so much was apparent from the many letters of protest which reached the Central Committee.[59] The central government administration, headed by Rykov, was opposed to coercion, and certain of the Army leaders, and even the heads of *OGPU*, had reservations about the matter.[60] Stalin had not yet achieved the degree of mastery over the Central Committee which he felt was necessary to him.

Given a highly explosive political situation, the danger so far as Stalin was concerned was that a publicly acknowledged split in the Central Committee and the Politburo might bring about a reconciliation among the different elements of the opposition. The possibility that, in a moment of crisis, the Right and the Left might form an alliance in order to save the country and the Party, and to depose Stalin himself, was one that still had to be taken into consideration. In these circumstances, the Right-wing's anxiety to maintain secrecy about the split in the Politburo merely made it easier for Stalin to encompass their downfall.

At the end of July, Stalin embarked on an elaborate manoeuvre which was intended to pave the way for the final destruction of the Right. On the one hand, he continued to co-operate in preserving the façade of unity within the Politburo, and took care not to make any kind of accusation about the three leaders in public. However, at the same time he was carefully preparing public opinion and, more important still, the Party, for news of a Right-wing deviation. At first, the whole idea was presented in impersonal, almost abstract terms, but gradually it was transformed into something much more sinister, by means of a propaganda campaign of increasing violence.

The Right, suspecting nothing, even joined in the campaign against the 'danger from the Right', and on occasion found themselves drafting Party documents on the evils of the Right-wing deviation....

While this was going on, Stalin was also taking steps to weaken the influence of the Right in the Party and other branches of the administration. When the time was ripe, he planned to take the initiative, and to strike first within the Central Committee and then in public. Meanwhile, since the Comintern Congress was taking place in Moscow during July and August, he turned the occasion to advantage by forcing Bukharin himself to make a statement about Right-wing deviationism in the foreign communist parties. Bukharin was therefore the first person to inform a Russian audience, in Moscow, that since the Trotskyists had been defeated the danger from the Right now represented the most serious threat to communism. He did not indicate, however, that any such danger existed within the country itself.[61]

Because of his scruples about engaging in open warfare, Bukharin now found himself in a position in which he was acting against his own interests. Since he himself was convinced of the staying-power of capitalism, he rejected Stalin's new ultra-left line in the Comintern, and would have preferred an alliance between communists and social democrats in order to combat the fascist danger.[62] Far-sighted though this view was, Bukharin unfortunately kept it to himself, and as long as it remained a purely private opinion, it could serve no useful purpose.

Stalin, meanwhile, was making steady progress. In its editorial of September 15th, *Pravda* called upon its readers to carry on the struggle against the Trotskyists, but also made reference to certain other elements who were 'reluctant to quarrel with the kulak', and accordingly drew attention to the need to wage war 'on both fronts'. There was still no mention of the 'Right' as such. Three days later, however, another *Pravda* editorial revealed the existence of a 'fundamentally Right-wing attitude' not only in the Comintern but also within the *VKP* (*b*). This was the first time there had been a specific reference to 'the danger from the Right' in Russia itself. Gradually another idea was introduced, that of a 'conciliatory attitude' with regard to the danger from the Right. This was the necessary prelude to an attack on those communist activists who could not be accused outright of acting as spokesmen of the hostile classes.

In the domain of economic policy, Bukharin now launched an attack on the Central Committee, by publishing in *Pravda* of September 30th an article of great importance entitled *Zametki Ekonomista* (An Economist's Notes); but although this article contained what amounted to an alternative programme for the construction of a socialist economy, its political impact was negligible. Neither the public nor the Party activists had ever seen, let alone understood, the Stalinists' programme; in fact no such document existed. Consequently, they were unable to appreciate the importance of the issues involved. Stalin did his best to ensure that the article passed unnoticed. There was no direct rejoinder to it, and at the November session of the Central Committee, in the course of his reply to Frumkin, Stalin pretended that he had nothing against Bukharin's article.[63] In fact, the publication of this article triggered off a series of powerful blows at the Right. During October the Bukharinist strongholds in Moscow, which had been held by Uglanov's efforts, were demolished without difficulty.

The second bastion of the Right, the Trades Union organization led by Tomsky, was shaken to its foundations and virtually destroyed two months later[64] with the appointment of Stalin's *politruki* (political officers), a move which was made with scant regard for the rules. Tomsky's position as leader of the unions was soon to be taken over by Kaganovich and Shvernik. Other *politruki* were appointed to the editorial board of *Pravda* in order to curb Bukharin's activities there.[65]

While these developments were taking place, Stalin was systematically instilling fear of a 'danger from the Right' in the popular mind. The first official document to deal with this matter appeared at the time when action was being taken again Uglanov's supporters: it was entitled: 'An appeal to the Moscow Organization of the *VKP(b)*,[66] and referred to the need for fighting 'on both fronts', against the Trotskyists and the Right. The Moscow leaders themselves were not accused of deviationism at this stage, but they were criticized for their lack of firmness and their conciliatory attitude towards deviationist tendencies. Stalin chose this moment to make a personal statement in Moscow about the Right-wing danger, which he dwelt on in a particularly ominous manner, linking it by implication with social democracy and the forces of capitalism: '. . . the victory of the Right-wing deviation in our Party would be an indication that preparations are being made to create the conditions which are required for the restoration of capitalism in our country'.[67]

He suggested that this 'heretical' tendency within the Party 'had not yet crystallized, and was possibly still unconscious'.[68] Nevertheless, there was a tendency to 'deviate from the Party line in the direction of bourgeois ideology', and 'perhaps a subconscious desire to adapt our socialist aims to the tastes and needs of the Soviet bourgeoisie'.[69]

According to Stalin, the so-called deviationists were in effect guilty of recommending a slowing-down in the rate of industrialization, and of underestimating the importance of the kolkhozes and sovkhozes. Their attitude was due to panic in the face of the difficulties which were an essential part of 'our development'. Here, too, he speeded up the process by demonstrating that the danger from the Right was now more tangible than the danger from the Left, 'owing to the strengthening of the petty-bourgeois element following on last year's procurements crisis', and also owing to the fact that 'certain sections of the Party are not as alive to this danger as we are'.[70] These arguments were now taken up by *Pravda*, which henceforth referred to the effort to combat the Right-wing danger as *'our most important task in the period ahead'*.[71] Having drawn attention to the danger that Right-wing deviation might lead to the restoration of capitalism (he had to stress the point in view of the apparent scepticism of his audience) Stalin went on to present the government's policy as being aimed at the construction of socialism in the immediate future, and to suggest that the most serious single obstacle to achievement of this glorious objective was the danger from the Right.

Here we have an example of Stalin's skill as a tactician. He had conjured up a situation in which the Party was in grave danger from a terrible enemy who must at all costs be challenged. The Party activists were easily convinced, and prepared to give battle. From all sides they demanded that the enemies be named. However, Stalin was not yet ready to do so. 'We are not concerned with individuals,' he said; it was a question of ideological tendencies, one of which was overtly opportunist in character, while the other was conciliatory in its attitude towards deviation, and therefore equally to be condemned.[72] During this phase of the operation, both the 'danger' and the 'tendencies' were described more or less in the abstract, and there was no attempt to identify any specific Right-wing group, the implication being that at this stage the Right-wing deviation was only just beginning to assume a more tangible form.

'Neither the Right nor the Left have any adherents or sympathizers in the Politburo,' Stalin solemnly informed the Moscow Party members.

'This must be stated categorically. Enemies of the Party, and all manner of disaffected elements, have been spreading rumours to the effect that there exists, within the Politburo of our Party, a Right-wing opposition, or a group who adopt a conciliatory attitude with regard to such opposition. It is time these rumours were quashed.'[73]

In November these ideas were further enlarged upon. The Plenum of the Central Committee publicly announced that the pressure of petty-bourgeois *stikhiya* had brought to the surface 'a Right-wing deviation of an overtly opportunist nature, which found its expression in the tendency to press for a slower rate of growth, and to arrest the forward march of socialist construction'. Other features of this deviation, it was alleged, included a tendency to underestimate the potential role of the kolkhozes and sovkhozes and to neglect the class struggle, particularly with regard to the kulaks, as well as underestimating the danger of war, and failing to appreciate the need for action to curb bureaucratic practices.[74] This marked a new stage in the operation, in which the campaign by insinuation was followed by an attempt to discredit the opposition's programme in advance, without identifying its authors.

A slight recrudescence of Trotskyist activity in the urban centres now forced Stalin to 'telescope' the two deviationist tendencies. The Trotskyist deviation was also denounced for 'concealing its Right-wing, semi-Menshevik nature behind Left-wing phraseology'.[75] If it could now be said that the Left were merely the Right in disguise, then it could openly be asserted that the 'principal danger' came from the Right. There is little point in discussing the validity of Stalin's attempt to argue that the Right and the Left were one and the same thing. In practice, both threatened him in the same way, a fact which he understood better than the others who were involved.

This move enabled Stalin to fulfil several purposes at once. In the first place he had silenced Bukharin and his supporters, and prevented them from publicizing their disagreement until he was ready for them to do so. In the second place, he was now in a better position to exaggerate the extent of the 'danger from the Right'. If the personalities concerned had been named before the public had been worked up into a suitable state of alarm, the manoeuvre might have failed. No one at this point could have seen Bukharin or the Premier (Rykov) in the role of enemies of the State. Once the scene had been properly set, however, Stalin had only to bring on his actors and the dénouement would be swift and final.[76]

We have seen that, in addition to the 'principal danger', Stalin had identified another secondary source of danger, in the shape of the 'sympathizers'. As a further refinement, this group was subsequently joined by the 'sympathizers with the sympathizers'. This provided Stalin with a suitable stick with which to beat any Party members who might be inclined to minimize the danger from the Right, or to deny that it existed. It also enabled him to attribute guilt by intention, without the need to furnish proof. Intentions could easily be imputed to anyone at all, for the 'carrier' of a conciliatory attitude, like the carrier of a germ, might be unaware of the harm he was doing, and might unsuspectingly be furthering the cause of the class enemies.

Myth-making is an art which requires patience, skill and time. It was one of Stalin's most valuable weapons, and one which he had to some extent perfected during the conflict with the Left. It took him almost a year and a half to build up his myth of a 'danger from the Right', which was to play such an important part as an instrument of domination and terror during the 'second revolution'. By November, the anti-Right campaign was at its height, and the press were inflaming public feeling to white heat over an enemy who had not yet been identified, though oblique references to various persons were gradually beginning to emerge. Bukharin and his associates felt that they were being broken without being named, and that the noose was tightening round their necks.

At the beginning of November, by which time control of the Moscow Party organization had been lost, and the press campaign against the Right was in full swing, Bukharin tried to retaliate. He returned post haste from Kislovodsk where he had been taking a cure, in order to prevent Stalin from 'twisting Rykov round his little finger' over the theses on the control figures for 1928–9. He was late in arriving at Moscow (the *OGPU* having succeeded in delaying his departure by plane) but although the Politburo had already discussed the theses, he demanded another meeting. Stalin and Molotov refused, and accused him of obstructing the collective work of the Politburo. However, they agreed to include certain amendments in the prepared theses.[77]

The three now met to consider the situation. They decided to press on with their attack, and presented Stalin with a list of seven (or possibly eleven) points. The exact contents of this document are still not known, but their demands would seem to have included the dismissal of several Stalinists (notably Krumin, of *Pravda*); a press campaign against the 'baseless rumours' concerning a split in the Politburo, a criticism of the system of arbitrary taxation and a general review of the country's situation.[78] The demands took the form of an ultimatum. Stalin announced that he was prepared to agree to them, and a committee consisting of Bukharin, Rykov, Stalin, Molotov and Ordzhonikidze was appointed to study the proposals, but Stalin went back on his word and failed to call a meeting.

Meanwhile the Plenum was already sitting, having begun its session on November 16th, and the Bukharinists, who were by now exasperated at the delay, demanded that a meeting of the committee be held. The meeting eventually did take place, but Stalin now refused to hear of the proposals in question. Bukharin described his reaction: 'I flew into a rage, swore at him, and rushed out of the room.' In the corridor, he handed to a member of the Central Committee a letter of resignation which had been prepared in advance and signed by himself and Tomsky. Rykov later reported that after Stalin had read the letter, he was prepared to withdraw, and his hands had trembled as he asked them to reconsider their resignations.[79]

As it happened, Stalin judged that the time was not yet ripe. If these resignations had been made public, they would have had the effect of highlighting Bukharin's disapproval of an unpopular policy, and of shifting the entire responsibility for it on to Stalin himself. It was already obvious that the latest procurements campaign was running into difficulties, and that the population would have an exceedingly hard time in the months ahead. Consequently, Stalin could not afford to let men of such standing as Bukharin and his associates go, without first ensuring that their reputations were sufficiently compromised in the eyes of the public by their having been associated with the new policy.

The Bukharinists had insisted that action be taken to put a stop to the rumours of a 'supposed divergence of views', thinking that this would afford them some protection against the incessant 'working over' (*prorabotka*) to which they were being subjected, either directly or by implication. To this naïve demand Stalin acceded gracefully, and made other minor concessions as well.

At the Plenum, he again singled out Frumkin as an outstanding example of Right-wing deviation. In a further letter to the Politburo,[80] Frumkin had asserted that there was now a recession in the agricultural sector. He had repeated the arguments put forward in his previous letter, and proposed that investments be scaled down from the level fixed by the *VSNKh* and the Politburo. His letter contained *inter alia* the following observation: 'Athough we must continue to oppose the kulaks' tyrannous (*kabalnaya*) exploitation of their neighbours, we must not obstruct production on their farms'.[81] Stalin's wrath was therefore directed at Frumkin, while Bukharin emerged unscathed, and his *Zametki* were mentioned in reasonably favourable terms.[82] Apparently it was not the moment for the Notes to be identified with the opinions of a man like Frumkin.

Stalin made a further concession to the Right, by stating that, at this stage, no 'bureaucratic action' should be taken against them (in other words, the members of the Right were not to be dismissed from their posts) and they should be opposed purely on ideological grounds, for as yet the deviationists were still subject to Party discipline, had not formed a factional group and in all probability would never do so.[83]

In this speech, Stalin expanded his ideas on the need for a vigorous leap forward, and quoted in support of his argument Lenin's own words 'either forge full steam ahead or perish'.[84] This was the essence of the programme which Bukharin so greatly feared. Yet Stalin's few concessions to the Right, plus a fresh statement on the absence of any split within the Politburo, sufficed to make Bukharin and Tomsky withdrew their resignations. Once again, Bukharin, Tomsky and Rykov found themselves associated with a unanimous decision of the Central Committee endorsing a policy which they believed to be disastrous.

From this time on, the conflict with the Right began to follow a consistent pattern which revealed that, the more Stalin broadened the base of his indirect attacks in the public forum, the more the Right found themselves in the position of agreeing to confine their direct attacks to the absurdly restricted private forum of the Politburo, or of the joint sessions of the Politburo and the Central Control Commission. And yet, the more the area of discussion narrowed, to the point of stifling the Right and its conceptions, the more breadth these conceptions acquired, until eventually they formed the basis of an alternative communist programme to that proposed by the Stalinists.

For a while, Stalin stood by the concessions he had made to the Right. As late as December 19th, he was informing the Presidium of the Executive of the Communist International that a distinction should be made between the Right-wing members of foreign communist parties and those of the Russian Party. The Right in the *VKP(b)* had not yet formed a faction, and had never infringed Party discipline. But despite a statement to this effect published in *Bolshevik*, a *prorabotka* campaign of insinuations, planted questions and whispered propaganda began in the closed sessions of the local Party organizations.[85] The names of the opposing leaders were leaked, and became known to the activists. This concerted action by the Secretariat resulted in what one of the three described as their 'organizational encirclement', and in what was soon to become 'civil death'.[86]

The three's only remaining weapons were the articles Bukharin was still able to publish in *Pravda* (he published several important ones in January) and the threat of resignation which, though still potentially effective, would not remain so for long. The three had already consented to withdraw their resignations in November when Tomsky, infuriated by the surreptitious and unconstitutional introduction of a *politruk* from the Politburo into the Trades Union leadership, had tendered his resignation a second time. It is not clear whether this was still his position during the turbulent events of the end of January 1929.[87]

In their capacity as members of the Government and of the Politburo, the three continued to participate in day to day affairs, opposing some moves, criticizing or expressing doubts over others, occasionally acting on their own initiative. However, such action as they took tended to be inhibited by their constant fear of being accused of 'disrupting Party Unity'.

2. The Upheaval of January-February 1929

Meanwhile the Party machine went about its business in the usual manner. An important event now took place: Stalin decided to send Trotsky into exile abroad. He had several reasons for doing this. By exiling Trotsky he was removing a rival from the scene at a time of serious social unrest. Furthermore, since Trotsky could be expected to criticize the régime from abroad, it would be possible to accuse him of 'collaborating with the capitalists'. The ever-present threat of a pact between the Trotskyists and the Bukharinists would be removed, and, finally, the main points of Trotsky's programme, and his supporters, could be taken over without Trotsky himself having to be recognized as victor.[88] This move provides a further illustration of Stalin's growing mastery of tactics.

Stalin weighed up the pros and cons with great care. The case he put forward to the Politburo for Trotsky's deportation came up for discussion in the period from December to January. Bukharin, Rykov and Tomsky put up a fierce resistance; Bukharin, it seems, shouted and wept during the meeting, but the majority voted in favour of Stalin's proposal. On January 20th, guards surrounded Trotsky's house in Alma-Ata and informed him that he was to be deported.[89] This was another heavy blow for the Right, since it meant that Stalin's grip on the Party was further tightened. They began to feel that their days were numbered.

However on January 20th, the same day on which the order for Trotsky's deportation had been given, the Right acquired a new ally in the person of Krupskaya, whose voice, though timid, could still command some attention. Owing to Stalin's influence, she had for long been virtually excluded from the political scene, and had been devoting her energies to her work on education. She now published an article in *Pravda* entitled 'Lenin and Kolkhoz Construction'.[90] Lenin's widow had good reason to distrust Stalin's methods on personal as well as on ideological grounds. She was on friendly terms with Bukharin, who had dedicated a most cordial article to her on the occasion of her sixtieth birthday.[91] Like Bukharin, she must have had grave doubts about Stalin's projects for the collectivization of the peasants.

Her article began with a brief outline of what Lenin had said and written on this subject. While acknowledging that Lenin had been aware of the importance of co-operation and large-scale farming as factors in the task of socialist construction, she laid particular emphasis on the problem of methods. She spoke at length of the views Engels had expressed in his famous article in *Neue Zeit* in 1894. Engels had stressed that under socialism, the peasant would not be expropriated, but helped to move towards co-operative methods of cultivation, or even to form communes; he would, however, be encouraged to do so purely by example, and all the necessary patience must be used in the process. Lenin had never quoted this article before the revolution, although he had done so afterwards, but Krupskaya was at pains to point out that he had often spoken about it. This remark was no doubt intended for all those who might seek to use Lenin's omissions as a pretext for ignoring what Engels had said. Several times, Krupskaya quoted and underlined Lenin's warnings. He had said, for example, '. . . it was madness to imagine that collective farming of this kind [which he had previously recommended —M.L.] could be decided and dictated from above.' He had also said that 'there could be no greater folly than to imagine that coercion can play any part in economic relations with the middle peasant'.

In view of the circumstances in which she was writing, Krupskaya's choice of quotations could have left no doubt in the minds of those Party members who knew what was going on. She further reminded her readers that 'the reconstruction of the very foundations of agriculture is a long-term affair. Such sweeping changes in agriculture cannot be imposed "from above"'. As an illustration of Lenin's understanding of the peasant mentality, she quoted another of his ideas. In the peasant's mind, Lenin had said, large farms were equated with the hated feudal domains and the *barshchina* (service to the land-owner). The first thing to do, therefore, was to provide the peasant with tractors and qualified drivers. Then, and only then, would he be won over and say—'I am for the *Kommuniya!*'[92]

It was as if the old leader had risen from his tomb to join in the dispute, and were speaking with the voice of his widow. Krupskaya's knowledge of his views was unrivalled, but her arguments fell on deaf ears. Lenin now belonged to the past, and his heirs were content to make use of his memory and his theories in the way which best suited them.[93]

As we have seen, Krupskaya's article appeared on the day of Trotsky's exile abroad. Trotsky's supporters chose this moment to cause a sensation, by secretly circulating a pamphlet entitled 'To the Party Conferences. The Party is being led blindfold towards disaster'. This document contained a record of the conversations between Bukharin, Sokolnikov and Kamenev, which Kamenev had preserved for use by Zinovev,[94] and in due course it came to the notice of the Politburo. (It may be that Stalin knew of these conversations beforehand, since Bukharin was under observation by the secret police.) The Politburo was at this moment preparing its theses on the Five-year Plan, the grain problem and a number of other questions which were on the agenda for the forthcoming Party Conference. The incident was exploited by both sides in the most violent clash that had taken place since the beginning of the conflict with the Right.

Bukharin had been preparing for this clash, though in doing so he had been motivated by his own sense of political integrity and his desire to prove equal to the occasion, rather than by any hope of victory. For some weeks he had been publishing articles, and had also given much thought to the preparation of a *Platform* which he was proposing to submit to the Politburo. This time he had determined not to be put off by any consideration of the consequences which might ensue from his putting forward a set of proposals in direct opposition to the Politburo's line. 'What else could one do?', he enquired of Pyatakov, who had been trying to persuade him that since Stalin had the majority behind him, a challenge to his authority could not but end badly.[95]

During the stormy sessions of the Politburo and the Presidium of the Control Commission, the three went further than they had ever done before with their criticisms and counter-proposals. At the session of January 30th, 1929, Bukharin read the thirty pages of his *Platform*, and all three spoke in support of their joint programme. There was an acrimonious discussion which went on for the next three days, at the end of which a further declaration was signed by the three. This was read at the session of February 9th.[96]

The above texts, which were known to members of the Central Committee at the time, are now in the Party archives in Moscow. At present, their contents can only be partially reconstructed from quotations and resumés made by opponents of the three.

Bukharin and his associates did not deny that the conversations with Kamenev had taken place, nor did they deny the authenticity of the Trotskyist pamphlet.[97] They argued that they had been obliged to seek some solution to the problems with which the leadership had confronted not only them, but the entire country.

'Problems of great seriousness are not even discussed,' Bukharin declared. 'The entire country is deeply concerned about the grain problem, and the problem of food supplies. Yet the Conferences of the proletarian Party in power remain silent. The whole country feels that all is not well with the peasantry. Yet our Party conferences say nothing . . . instead we have a flood of resolutions about deviations, always couched in the same terms. Instead, we have rumours by the thousand, and gossip about the members of the Right, Rykov, Tomsky, Bukharin, etc. This policy fails to face up to the real difficulties, it's no kind of policy at all. The working class must be told *the truth about the situation*. We must put our trust in the masses, we must take account of the *needs of the masses*, and in our management of their affairs we must identify ourselves with the masses.'[98]

Bukharin then proceeded to make a vigorous attack on the Party's internal organization. 'Here,' he said,

'we have two distinct trends. One of these is concerned with "the need for self-criticism", and stresses the importance of a whole number of principles, including self-criticism, democratic leadership and democratic election, etc. But, in fact, have you ever seen a Party secretary elected in a *guberniya*? There has undoubtedly been an increase in bureaucratic practices in our Party.'[99]

More of Bukharin's speech has been reported by another well-informed source. 'The Party has no share in the solution of these problems. Everything is decided at the top.' At this point, Bukharin was interrupted by cries of 'Where did you get that?—You borrowed it from Trotsky.'[100] Ruthlessly he continued with his indictment of the Central Committee: 'The Central Committee is dismantling the Comintern, and encouraging the growth of bureaucracy within the Party.'[101]

He went on to question the right of an inner enclave within the Politburo to exercise surveillance over other members of the Politburo. 'The attitude of the Politburo towards the opposition can only be explained by the fact that the principle of collective leadership within the Central Committee has been destroyed.' And,

'We are opposed to the practice whereby responsibility for matters of Party administration is left in the hands of one man. We stand by the principle of collective action, and refuse to accept the principle of control by a single individual, no matter how great his authority.'[102]

The text of this part of Bukharin's speech was not published until twenty years later.

Stalin was extremely sensitive to accusations of this nature, and he reacted to this particular charge far more violently than he had ever done to other criticisms which had been directed at him. He described Bukharin's allegations as 'a shameless and hypocritical declaration' by one who was attempting to cover up his own 'treacherous behaviour'.[103] He even resorted to smear tactics, by reminding his audience that, at the time of Brest-Litovsk, Bukharin had made common cause against Lenin with the Left Social Revolutionaries. In an attempt to arouse their suspicions, he threw in some veiled allusions to the effect that it was still not clear what kind of agreement had been reached.[104] Stalin would not tolerate any suggestion of autocratic behaviour on his part, hence his anger on this occasion. It was still important for him at this stage to conceal his ambition for personal power, and the contempt in which he held his supporters. So long as there remained within the Politburo a group of leaders who opposed him, it was still possible that he might be deposed, and accordingly the majority in the Central Committee who supported him must not be antagonized.

Bukharin's speech contained a critical appraisal of the country's most pressing problems, and of the solutions which had been proposed. He argued that the recession in agriculture, if it were allowed to continue, would jeopardize the country's very existence 'For a long time to come, the private farm will continue to be the mainstay of the country's supplies.' The kolkhozes and sovkhozes, he said, were not in a position to act as a substitute for the private sector. 'The kolkhozes and sovkhozes will provide enough grain in five to ten years time; our problem is how to exist in the meantime.'[105] Despite this situation, the Party's decisions on the action which must be taken to stimulate production and increase yields in the private sector had not been implemented.[106]

At this point, Bukharin's indictment became intensely dramatic in tone. He challenged the Politburo's policy on industrialization, which he said was based on false assumptions. The existing rate of growth was already excessive. Socialist industrialization could not be based upon 'tribute' and a total and fatal expenditure of reserves. The only rational basis on which the country could industrialize was to improve the farms of the bednyaks and serednyaks, and raise the level of labour productivity throughout the whole of the national economy. Yet ever since the session of July 1928, the keynote of Party policy had been Stalin's watchword of 'tribute', which implied a *'military/feudal exploitation of the peasantry'*.[107]

Never in the history of the Party had one of its leaders made such accusations during a session of a top-level Party organ. The occasion was not to arise again until Khrushchev's famous 'Secret Speech'.

Moreover, Krushchev's indictment related to past ills, whereas Bukharin, at the time at which he was speaking, was diagnosing the source of these very ills with a clarity that was almost prophetic.

The charge of 'military/feudal exploitation of the peasantry' was the last straw. It provoked such resentment that henceforth the Stalinists used the expression as proof of the 'anti-Party' treachery of the Bukharinists.

The short-term measures which were proposed by the three during the sessions of the Politburo, and also at the Plenum of April 1929 (and which we have reconstructed from references contained in various official documents)[108] were based on the assumption that if an intensive effort were made to pacify the peasants, and to stabilize relations with them, it might then be possible to proceed with the implementation of a rational long-term policy. We shall be discussing the Bukharinists' long-term policy later.

They urged that there should be an end to all coercive measures, and a resumption of normal economic relations in conformity with the principles of NEP. For this purpose, it would be necessary to restore free market and exchange relations, and remove the obstacles to trade and kulak production. Action to restrict the activities of the kulaks should be limited to the use of fiscal measures. It was recommended that control of the market and of peasant production should operate mainly through the medium of taxation and the price mechanism. The three stressed that a serious effort was needed to assist the peasants to increase production, whereas in the matter of kolkhoz and sovkhoz construction the authorities must proceed with the greatest caution, and seek to limit the numbers of such enterprises to those which could reasonably be expected to establish themselves on a sound economic footing and fulfil a sound economic function.

As an interim solution to the problem of procurements and food supplies, Rykov proposed that grain should be imported, Bukharin adding that grain imports were preferable to the emergency measures.[109] In a speech which was not published at the time, Stalin replied that the Politburo were of quite the opposite opinion.[110]

In April 1929 the Bukharinists supplemented these proposals with an alternative draft version of the Five-year Plan in which, among other things, they had made provision for a special Two-year Plan aimed at giving priority to the rehabilitation of the agricultural sector. According to Rykov, it was essential that agriculture should make up the ground it had lost, otherwise proper implementation of the Five-year Plan would be impossible.[111]

Every one of the proposals put forward by the three was automatically rejected, and branded from this time on as 'heresy'.

Meanwhile, the sessions of the Politburo were marked by ever-increasing tension. On February 7th a special committee met to discuss the conversations between Bukharin and Kamenev, and it was suggested to Bukharin that he admit the harmful nature of these conversations, and retract all his accusations against the Party leadership as having been made 'in the heat of the moment' (*sgoryacha*). The three were also instructed to withdraw their resignations. In return, the Politburo undertook not to submit to the Central Committee the indictment which had already been drawn up against the three, and to guarantee them the normal conditions in which to carry on their work.[112]

The three indignantly refused to allow themselves to be humiliated by agreeing to these extraordinary proposals, which they described as 'political chicanery'.[113] They also stood by their resignations, until the time of the April Plenum. Only Rykov subsequently agreed to remain, for reasons which are not clear.[114] Was it infirmity of purpose which led him to yield to the Stalinists efforts to cause a split among the three. Or had the three already agreed on this move, in order to retain at least one position of importance within the Politburo? There are some indications that the latter may have been the case.

Faced with this refusal to capitulate, the majority, at Stalin's instigation, decided to bring matters to a head. In one of his statements made after April 7th, Stalin declared, 'Painful though it may be we have to take account of the formation of a separate group by Bukharin, Rykov and Tomsky'. In order to forestall criticism of the fact that, for over a year, he had concealed the existence of a serious divergence of views among the leadership, he added: 'The Party was unaware of the existence of this group.' The three were then identified according to a pre-arranged formula: 'Bukharin's group is a group of Right-wing deviationist capitulators, whose aim was not to liquidate the capitalist elements in the towns and in the countryside, but to allow them to develop freely.'[115] A long declaration was prepared for the next session of the Central Committee. As soon as this declaration had been read, Stalin delivered a lengthy speech, certain important parts of which were kept secret at the time.[116] He dismissed as slanderous all the allegations which had been made by the Right, and counter-attacked with a formidable list of charges, for which he drew on every available weapon, from accusations of a political and ideological nature to personal abuse. While the debates in the Politburo were still in progress, the press opened fire on the Right-wing deviationists.

However, even these manoeuvres did not bring Stalin complete success. Rykov retained his post. Bukharin and Tomsky were relieved of their respective functions in *Pravda*, the Comintern and the Trades Union leadership, but still continued as members of the Central Committee, despite the grave charges which were piling up against them. It is more than likely that many members of the Central Committee were reluctant to have the three removed from the leadership. This was the first they had heard of the accusations which were being made against them and it is probable that their reactions had something to do with the rather odd decision to relieve Bukharin and his associates of their minor functions only.

The decisions of the Plenum of April 1929 were couched in slightly more moderate terms than Stalin's original denunciation. (These decisions were not published, but merely made known to Party meetings). While the three still stood condemned, they were not referred to as Right-wing deviationists, which was the term Stalin had used, but simply as defenders of the Right-wing deviation, who showed a tendency to embrace Right-wing opinions.[117] However, since Right-wing opinions had been declared to be inconsistent with the general Party line, the three were warned that at the slightest sign of insubordination they would be expelled from the Politburo.

There were still a few preliminaries to be got through before that stage was reached. On July 21st, readers of *Pravda* learned for the first time that Bukharin had been removed from the Comintern. On August 21st, it was announced that it was indeed Bukharin who was the leader of the Right-wing deviationists.

This marked the end of any effective political role which the three might have played. Their resistance was no longer of any importance. Although they still refused to recant, they were now little more than prisoners of the Politburo. They abstained from voting on the Five-year Plan and the grain problem, but even their tactical device of pretending to be in agreement with the general Party line, while expressing reservations on certain issues, was turned against them.[118] Towards the end of 1929 Stalin forced them to make amends. They publicly admitted that they had been entirely mistaken throughout, and that the General Secretary's policy was correct.[119] After this, their expulsion from the Politburo presented no problem. The main threat to Stalin's policies had been definitively overcome.

3. *Bukharin's Alternatives*

Shortly after Krupskaya had attempted to sound a warning note on collectivization by quoting Lenin's views on the subject, Bukharin published in *Pravda*[120] an important public address which he had given in Moscow on the fifth anniversary of Lenin's death. The speech contained a faithful account of Lenin's political testament, but was mainly taken up with a summary of Bukharin's own views on the future course of development in Russia, as he saw it at the time. In this text, in an article published four days earlier, and in his important 'Economist's Notes,' Bukharin set forth his objections to the Politburo's policy.[121] The totality of views expressed in his appraisal of the immediate situation and the long-term prospects, together with his proposed long-term and short-term solutions, amounted in effect to a complete alternative programme to that which was being followed by the régime. Now that the Party bureaucracy was in full control, this was to be the last occasion on which there would be any public statement of views which differed from those of Stalin.

Only those in the inner Party circles, and a few informed observers, were in a position to understand the implications of the problems which had been raised, and the importance of what was at stake. The population as a whole were unaware that Bukharin and his associates were in fact proposing an alternative policy which could, so they believed, preserve the country from many ills.

Bukharin in effect dismissed every one of Stalin's basic theories, including some which had not even been put before the Central Committee, but which Bukharin either knew about, or which, he suspected, Stalin would soon be introducing. His views on the state of capitalism, and on the policy which the Comintern should adopt towards it, were diametrically opposed to those of Stalin. In Bukharin's opinion, capitalism was passing through a period of great technical and scientific progress. No major upsurge of revolutionary activity was therefore to be expected in the capitalist world. At this stage, any significant national and social movements of a revolutionary nature were more likely to take place in the East.[122] As we have seen, there were indications that Bukharin favoured the idea of an alliance between communists and social democrats as a bulwark against the fascist danger, although he had formally accepted the anti-Right line which was being forced upon him.[123]

Stalin, on the other hand, maintained that the days of capitalism were numbered, and that the tide was again turning in favour of revolution. Communists in all countries were being instructed to intensify the struggle against the social democrats, and against the Left-wing social democrats in particular. It was not until Hitler had come to power, and the German Communist Party and the social democrats had been destroyed, that these orders were countermanded.[124]

Bukharin took a calmer view of the situation, and attached much less importance to the danger of encirclement, or the possibility of an attack on the USSR. In his opinion, the surest safeguard against eventual complications on the international front was political stability at home. He believed that the maintenance of good relations with the peasantry was the best possible guarantee of the country's safety in time of peace, and of victory in the event of war.

Bukharin, therefore, was primarily concerned with the conduct of internal affairs, in respect of which he was guided, as Lenin had been, by the following principles: The October Revolution had been the outcome of an exceptional combination of circumstances, and of the interaction of 'specific class forces'. This fruitful combination of a 'peasant war and a proletarian revolution', in Marx's phrase, continued to be the mainstay of the Soviet régime, the foundation on which its policies were based, the guarantee of its continued existence. But since the Revolution, changes had taken place both in the nature of the struggle and in the objectives of the régime.

Initially, the political struggle had been of overriding importance, but with the introduction of NEP, problems of construction and organization had begun to take priority.[125] Here, too, a form of class struggle was involved, but one of a different order. Although the majority of Bukharin's readers were unaware of the fact, this was a direct criticism of Stalin, who had made a speech in July in which he expounded his theory on the progressive intensification of the class struggle. This speech had not been made public, and only the members of the Central Committee had heard it.

Bukharin denied that, in the Soviet context, there was any widening of the gulf between the two principal classes, that is the workers and the peasants, and expressed the view that events were in no way building up towards a 'third revolution'.[126] This was not a false prophecy on Bukharin's part, even though the 'third revolution' was none the less to take place shortly after his speech; indeed it was Bukharin's accurate insight into the probable consequences of Stalin's actions which led him to propose an alternative policy. At this stage, neither Stalin's supporters nor, in a sense, Stalin himself knew where the line which they were following would eventually lead. According to Bukharin, 'the theoretical assumptions underlying our major policy undertaking' should be made within the context of a class struggle of ever-decreasing intensity.[127] Lenin, he recalled, had advocated extreme caution 'in those aspects of policy which touch on relations between the proletarian régime and the peasantry'. The ultimate triumph of the revolution would only be assured 'when the peasants had full confidence in the dictatorship of the proletariat.[128]

This was the basis of Bukharin's approach to the major problems of internal policy, and in particular to the problem of transforming the rural economy and enabling the peasants to progress towards socialism. The ideas he put forward were essentially those he had expressed in 1925, with some alterations to take account of the current situation. As he had done in his treatment of industrialization, he quoted freely from Lenin in support of his argument that there should be no 'impetuous leap forward'.[129]

Bukharin was quite categorical on this point. The workers' organizations in the towns might be mobilized to assist the peasants, but there could be no question of attempting to apply strictly communist principles in the countryside (and Lenin had said as much), for 'So long as the material basis for communism does not exist in the countryside, such a move would be harmful, and the *consequences for the communist cause would be disastrous.*'[130]

Bukharin was obviously convinced that in 1929 no such material basis existed. Accordingly, what he advocated was progress 'in partnership with the peasant masses', and the implementation of the *smychka* on the basis of 'co-operative commodity circulation'. In his view, the only way to lead the peasants towards socialism was to 'give them an incentive', and to find 'the simplest means of appealing to them'. The peasants must advance 'through awareness of what is in their own best interests'.[131]

This being so, it was clear that for a long time to come private farming would continue to be the dominant factor in agricultural production, and the chief mode of existence in the rural areas. Bukharin was convinced that if adequate assistance were given and if, above all, the co-operative movement could be used as a framework for development, the private sector would respond and produce satisfactory economic results. While accepting the need for kolkhozes and sovkhozes, he considered that these were little more than emergency means of dealing with the grain crisis, and would have preferred to invest the money devoted to 'grain factories' in the iron and steel industry.[132] Of the two forms, he preferred the kolkhoz but regarded it as a long-term solution, and by no means the only valid one. Moreover, he considered it important that, in every case, the real advantages of the kolkhoz should be demonstrated.

Bukharin also stressed another of Lenin's ideas, which was that a 'cultural revolution' would have to take place in the countryside long before any attempt could be made to impose new ideas and social structures. Otherwise, such changes could never be understood. He contemptuously dismissed the idea of a 'metal-based *smychka*' which had recently been put forward by Stalin.

Later, when the Right was fighting its rearguard action during the session of April 1929, he described this *smychka* as 'monstrously unilateral'. Tomsky hit out even harder. 'Now you have started to threaten us with new forms of *smychka* which you have discovered. . . . There is nothing new in this idea. What it means is emergency measures plus ration cards.'[133]

Bukharin was well aware that the new forms of *smychka* virtually meant the abolition of NEP, which he regarded as offering the only kind of relationship which was acceptable to the peasants, and the only one which they could understand. He stressed this point, and reminded his audience of Lenin's anxiety to avoid a split with the peasantry. Indeed, the country was threatened with just such a split as a direct result of 'this new invention'. We have already discussed the measures which the three recommended in order to pacify the peasants and preserve the general framework of NEP. Almost all of their proposals were held up to ridicule during the Central Committee session in April 1929. At this session they were faced with a new and different interpretation of NEP, in which the accent was laid on the importance of state intervention[134] and the need to combat the kulaks and capitalist elements.

In Bukharin's eyes, this amounted to a refusal to return to the principles of NEP, which in any case, in his opinion, had ceased to exist. 'What you want is a NEP without Nepmen, merchants or kulaks,' Tomsky had protested at the Central Committee meeting in July 1928, 'but this is impossible.' However, Bukharin now realized that the country was heading towards an economy of just this type.

It would be wrong to suppose that at this time Bukharin's ideas were considered unusual, or that he and his associates were alone in holding the views they expressed. In several important branches of the state administration such as *Gosplan*, the *Narkomzem*, and in *TsIK*, his ideas were widely accepted. In view of what was happening inside the Politburo, some Party officials in these departments no doubt took care to dissociate themselves from 'the Right-wing deviation', but there were certain basic ideas which were shared by everyone. Thus, there was general agreement about the continuation of NEP, the long-term role of the private sector in agriculture and the need to encourage growth in this sector, the importance of market relations and of co-operation in trade. As we shall shortly see, that part of the Five-year Plan which related to agriculture owed much more to Bukharin and Rykov than to Stalin, whose ideas on this aspect of the economy were still extremely fluid.

As the American economist Erlich has pointed out,[135] the year 1927 marked the beginning of an entirely new chapter in Bukharin's development as a theoretician, for it was at this time that he began to outline his theory of industrialization and his ideas on the scientific management of the economy.[136] In view of the great strides which the capitalist countries were making in the fields of science and technology, and of the new disciplines which were being applied in the domain of economic organization, Bukharin had no hesitation in criticizing the 'narrow provincial outlook' which was still so much a feature of the Russian scene, and nowhere more so than in the scientific and technological contexts.[137] He was particularly critical of the obscurantism of the 'bureaucratic breed', who cared more for the 'portfolio and the Party card' than for real knowledge and dedication to the task in hand.

He also castigated the leadership for their narrow-minded nationalism and their lack of any true international culture. Naturally, in so doing he used the indirect approach, which took the form of praise for those of Lenin's qualities in which the present leaders were so sadly lacking. But there was no doubt whom Bukharin had in mind. Lenin's role in the Russian Revolution had been of primary importance because he had been 'in no sense a "Muscovite", but a man with both theoretical and practical ability. He was a revolutionary both in thought and deed; an international communist, and an international revolutionary thinker'.[138]

This sustained praise of Lenin's habit of constant study, his familiarity with the achievements of capitalism, and his knowledge of European languages, can scarcely have gone down very well in the Kremlin. Bukharin was obviously implying that the present leaders were lacking in the qualities which would be required if they were to carry out their complex task, and run the country efficiently.

Bukharin, who was a man of wide reading, referred to recent developments abroad in the mechanization of agriculture, to the contribution which was being made in this sphere by the chemicals industry, and to developments in economic organization in general. He stressed the enormously increased role 'of science in the functioning of the capitalist economy', and declared, '*Victory will either be achieved through scientific management of the economy, or it will not be achieved at all.*'[139]

Bukharin knew that the current mood of the Party did not favour such academic 'deviations' (he had just been elected to the Academy of Sciences), but he did not despair of being able to communicate to the public 'the historical truth of the period of reconstruction'. He therefore advanced the following argument: Under capitalism, errors in the economic policy of enterprises cancel each other out. But the component parts of a planned economy, 'entire sectors of which *are affected by a single decision*', do not achieve equilibrium in this way. Bukharin was alluding to the phenomenon of waste, a characteristic of the Soviet economy which he had clearly observed to be on the increase. He went on to make the point that, in a planned economy, the administration of which is needlessly over-centralized, 'the losses incurred by fully implementing the *wrong* policy may be no less than those engendered by capitalist anarchy'.[140]

Thus, for Bukharin the intellectual, the superiority of socialism was not automatically self-evident. In a planned economy, he emphasized, policy-making must become 'a separate science, with roots in other branches of science, but with its own theory'. If this approach were adopted, a situation in which statistical data could be adapted to suit the wishes of various 'dignitaries' would be intolerable. The government organs which were responsible for the implementation of policies must also be studied in order to discover how economic management could best be organized. The research worker must be freed from the toils of red tape, so that he could work independently and exercise the necessary initiative. Young people should strive after knowledge rather than 'one hundred per cent communism'.[141]

These ideas, which were those of a perceptive intellectual, were virtually ignored at the time at which he advanced them, only to be rediscovered by the Soviet régime at a much later date, when it had already passed through a period of severe trial.

Bukharin's article, from which we have been quoting, was accompanied by another article contributed by Savelev, who had been appointed by the Politburo to supervise Bukharin's activities on the editorial board of *Pravda*, and to counteract his influence. The title of Savelev's article was unequivocal: 'Lenin on the struggle on two fronts, and on the conciliatory attitude.'[142]

In the context of Bukharin's theory of industrialization, his ideas on scientific economic management were reflected in his insistence that the development plan should be implemented 'in conditions of dynamic equilibrium' in the economy.[143] Only if such conditions were assured could the country industrialize with the minimum of crises and upheaval. The difficulties which the country was experiencing were caused by 'relative anarchy' or a 'relative lack of planning'. The balance of the economy was being upset by an incoherent economic policy and 'faulty co-ordination of the factors of reproduction (including the factor of consumption)'. These were pardonable errors, given the constant and unpredictable intervention of market forces. But unless one were to give way before the petty-bourgeois elements, the authorities would require at all costs to create the conditions for proper inter-sector co-ordination, and correct resource allocation, etc.

In Bukharin's view, if there was a simultaneous shortage of bread and raw materials, it was because these conditions were not being taken into account. In such circumstances, he remarked ironically, 'one really needs to be a humorist to insist on a programme of super-industrialization into the bargain'.[144]

Bukharin was opposed to any acceleration of the rate of industrialization. He brought up a question which was to be of crucial importance for the success of industrialization, namely, that of an upper limit on investment in machinery and equipment. In his opinion, this limit had already been reached, hence the total lack of reserves and the endless queues outside the shops. These queues, he said, were 'disorganizing our entire productive activity'. He issued a grave warning to this effect: 'It is little short of foolhardy to embark upon such a policy when there is a chronic shortage of reserves.'

The shortage of building materials, metal and agricultural raw materials was a further indication that demand was overstretched. Bukharin bitterly complained of the absurdity of a situation in which the planners took it for granted that a whole variety of building materials would be in short supply. No construction project could be rationally planned if existing requirements in materials were not taken into account. 'Even Böhm-Bawerk has pointed out that one cannot build present factories with future bricks.'[145]

Although the foregoing points would seem to be fairly obvious, Bukharin's criticisms were in fact dismissed by spokesmen for the official point of view, who took him to task for suggesting that rate of growth should be conditional upon the existence of reserves, and accused him of wishing to obstruct the rapid advance of industrialization by 'siding with those who exaggerate the seriousness of bottle-necks'.[146]

Bukharin warned the authorities that any hopes inspired by an over-stretched growth rate, which reflected an excessive volume of investment, would soon be shattered, for there would be no corresponding increase in the amount of real construction. Instead, other sectors of the economy would be disrupted, poverty would increase, and in the long run development would be slowed down. An analysis of the manner in which Soviet development plans were actually implemented will serve to illustrate the accuracy of Bukharin's forecast. What he was recommending at this time was that the government should hold to the existing annual industrial growth rate of between 18 and 20%, with the appropriate volume of investment, and that action be taken to ensure that this amount of growth in industry was managed as efficiently as possible. As we shall see later, he also recommended a less centralized institutional framework within which the mass of the population could more readily participate in the common effort. It was only in the more relaxed social atmosphere which he hoped these measures would create that continuous, steady growth could be achieved.

These proposals were rejected, and their author was accused of being a 'spokesman for the kulaks'. The authorities were in fact proposing to *double the growth rate*, thereby exacerbating the existing social pressures. No thought was given to measures which could have relieved these pressures, and spared the people much suffering.

The result of the régime's policy was that the actual rate of growth achieved fell below the figure envisaged by Bukharin, and the social and political aftermath was grievous to a degree which exceeded the gloomiest forecasts. One long-term consequence of the rejection of balanced growth, and of the failure to pursue a policy of proportionate development in industry and agriculture, was that the agricultural sector became, and still is, the Achilles heel of the Soviet economy.

Bukharin disapproved of any excessive drainage of resources from the agricultural sector into industry. While admitting that this form of taxation was to some extent inevitable, he considered that it should be linked to the growth of peasant incomes. To base industrialization on a 'military/feudal exploitation of the peasantry' (the expression he had used during the session of the Politburo) would be to discredit the whole idea of 'socialist industrialization', whose aim should be to 'transform' the peasant economy, and 'raise it to a higher level'. A policy of industrialization must include the industrialization of the rural sector, so that the age-old contradiction between town and country might gradually be eliminated. He was well aware that in a backward country accumulation posed a difficult problem, and therefore felt that a 'thoughtful' (vdumchivy) approach was all the more necessary.

He refused to regard the rural sector as the only possible source of accumulation. Attainment of the highest possible rate of growth depended on the countryside itself being given a chance to accumulate, and Bukharin was confident that this could in fact be done. But he hoped to find other important sources of accumulation outside of the agricultural sector. It was, for example, more important to ensure that the economy was rationally and scientifically managed, to improve labour productivity, to make better use of science, to increase efficiency, and to reduce the enormous waste of resources which could have served to ease the strain on the country.

These improvements obviously did not depend on successful planning alone, for they involved many factors which related to the fundamental nature of the country's social structure. We have already noted Bukharin's anxiety that scholars should be given greater freedom in which to pursue their researches. This was not all. In his opinion, over-centralization of the administration was holding back development. He spoke of the need for 'greater freedom of action at local level' and the desirability of enlisting, in Lenin's phrase, 'the real participation of the real masses'.[147]

Another of Lenin's ideas, that of the 'Commune-State', appears several times in Bukharin's writings at this period.[148] The fact that he was drawn in this direction is indicative of his desire to democratize the State, and to mitigate the harshness of its dictatorship; but these ideas ran counter to the existing official tendency, which was to strengthen the State apparatus, and particularly its repressive functions.

New life would have to be breathed into the Party, and a new approach was called for in Party work. This too could be achieved by reducing the number of bureaucratic practices, by drawing upon 'the best and most truly enlightened forces' in the country, and by encouraging a high sense of duty and moral responsibility among the Party activists and, most important of all, among the officials who ran the State's supervisory organs, and who should 'refuse to accept a single word without proof, and refuse to utter a single word which went against their consciences. (Conscience has a part to play in politics, despite what some people seem to believe) [Laughter].' No struggle would prove too much for them. Nor would they be afraid to admit to difficulties.[149] This renaissance within the Party would itself create the conditions for freedom of speech, and the freedom to criticize, because these conditions would be regarded as inherent in its organization, and indispensable to its proper functioning. As we have already shown, the Plenum of April 1929 had its own concept of democracy. Accordingly it greeted these ideas of Bukharin's with derision, and refused outright to entertain them.[150]

Bukharin's deep-seated fear that the revolution might lose its socialist character, and his suspicion that this was most likely to be caused by the growth of bureaucracy, brought him close to the position taken up by Rakovsky. In one of his speeches to the Party he spoke of this fear, which had haunted him since 1922, and which can be detected in everything he wrote during the period of his struggle against Stalin. If the proletarian régime 'took too much upon its own shoulders, it would be forced to set up a huge *administrative apparatus*'. If it decided to take over the economic functions of the small rural producer, an enormous number of administrative and clerical staff would have to be employed, and the apparatus would become even more cumbersome.

'Any attempt to replace these small producers with *chinovniki* (civil servants)—and no matter what you choose to call them, that is what they are—will result in a bureaucratic machine of such complexity that the expenditure necessary to maintain it will be incomparably greater than the losses engendered by the anarchic conditions of small-scale production itself. Far from doing anything to assist in the development of the forces of production, *a bureaucratic apparatus of this order in fact obstructs development*, and the end result is the very opposite of what was intended. For this reason, it is absolutely imperative that the proletariat should destroy this kind of bureaucratic growth. If it fails to do so, other forces will take it upon themselves to destroy the power of the proletariat.'[151]

Bukharin's entire outlook was conditioned by the repugnance he felt at the prospect that the idealistic and socialist character of the revolution might one day be destroyed by the 'bureaucratic Leviathan'. He was now in open opposition to the views of the majority. The bitterness of the struggle against the Bukharinists and their ideas may be attributed, in part, to the leadership's realization that these ideas represented an 'alien' programme, which was essentially that of an entirely different party.

Since Stalin's death, almost every one of Bukharin's major theories has been revived in the communist world which, without admitting it, is making an enormous effort to implement his programme of 1929. Do not the efforts of leaders like Khrushchev, Kosygin and Gomulka recall Bukharin's insistence on the importance of balanced, scientific planning, and of maintaining a prosperous agricultural base during the process of industrialization, as well as his realistic appraisal of capitalism and his informed awareness of its achievements? Or again, there is his determination to destroy bureaucracy, or at least to loosen its grip; this was an aim which was indeed common to all the oppositions, it was also the very essence of Lenin's testament, and it remains one of the major preoccupations of the most progressive elements in Soviet society at the present time.

Bukharin may not have been alone in his concern with the problem of bureaucracy, but there is another important aspect of his development theory, which relates to his desire to find the means whereby the peasantry could participate in socialist construction on a fair and equal social and economic footing. This has remained an ideal, and a guiding light for all progressive movements in countries which have been endeavouring to solve the problem of underdevelopment, and to create new social structures.

The conviction that the peasant should be accepted first of all for what he is, and then guided along the path of self-interest towards better and more evolved social and economic structures, was one of the most seminal of Bukharin's ideas, and the one which has most relevance today. It was a theory to which he had devoted sustained effort and thought since 1925, and in which he had been guided by Lenin's testament.

On this point, as on many others, the Stalinists were opposed to the views expressed in the testament. It was true that their attitude could to some extent be justified by reference to other aspects of Lenin's teaching. They maintained that the peasant possessed a 'dual nature', that although by nature a worker he had capitalist inclinations, and might at any given moment side with the enemy. At this point, however, all legitimate reference to Lenin ceases, and the argument becomes specifically Stalinist. In respecting the peasant's status as an independent producer, NEP had merely fostered his anti-proletarian tendencies. In order to counteract this trend, the Stalinists put forward their idea of a 'new *smychka*' which, in effect, amounted to increased state control and management of the peasant economy and peasant society. The creation of kolkhozes, it was claimed, would enable the State to take a hand in the 'productive aspects' of the rural economy, and suppress its 'commercial aspects'.[152]

A detailed examination of the history of the kolkhozes, and of the problems of Soviet agriculture up until the present day, will enable the reader to judge of the validity of this argument.

NOTES AND REFERENCES

1. Trotsky's theses for the Fifteenth Party Conference of September 1926, quoted from the Trotsky Archives by Daniels, *op. cit.* (see Ch. 2, Note 3), p. 180.

2. The *Platform*, in *Les Bolcheviks contre Staline* (see Ch. 2, Note 34), p. 124.

3. Daniels, *op. cit.*, p. 362.

4. Daniels, *op. cit.*, p. 325, according to documents from the Trotsky Archives; *Sotsialisticheski Vestnik*, July 23, p. 15.

5. Stalin, *Sochineniya*, Vol. XI. p. 13; *Pravda* February 15, 1928.

6. Letter of March 15th from a Russian correspondent published in *Sotsialisticheski Vestnik*, 1928, No. 6.

7. Daniels, *op. cit.*, p. 326.

8. *KPSS v Rezolyutsiyakh*, Vol. II. The resolution is on pp. 492–500, the quotation from p. 497.

9. *ibid*, pp. 494–5.

10. Stalin, *Sochineniya*, Vol. XI, p. 27.

11. *ibid*, pp. 46–7.

12. *ibid*, p. 48.

13. The first to stand up to Stalin was Rykov; Bukharin, shortly after, followed suit.

14. Bukharin, quoted by Astrov, *Pravda*, July 3, 1928.

15. Daniels, *op. cit.*, pp. 328–9.

16. Conversation between Bukharin and Kamenev, *Sotsialisticheski Vestnik*, 1929, No. 6, p. 10.

17. This letter has been partly reconstructed here from excerpts

quoted by Stalin in his reply of June 20, 1928. This reply was published for the first time in *Sochineniya*, Vol. XI, p. 116. A further excerpt is quoted in a speech by Thalman, *Pravda*, August 11, 1929.

18. Stalin, *Sochineniya*, Vol. XI, p. 117.

19. *ibid*, pp. 117–8.

20. *ibid*, p. 123.

21. Thalman, speech delivered at a meeting of the Comintern Executive, *Pravda*, August 11, 1929.

22. Bukharin and Kamenev, *Sotsialisticheski Vestnik*, 1929, No. 9, p. 10.

23. Stalin, *Sochineniya*, Vol. XI, pp. 123–4.

24. Bukharin and Kamenev, *op. cit.*, *loc. cit.*

25. Deutscher, *The Prophet Unarmed*, pp. 409–10, 455–7; the statements made by Bukharin to Kamenev on July 11, *op. cit.*; Ciliga, *op. cit.* (see Ch. 9. Note 64), pp. 38–9.

26. Bukharin and Kamenev, *op. cit.*

27. Stalin, *Sochineniya*, Vol. XI, p. 320. This is a speech to the Politburo in which Stalin mentions this first 'outburst'. The details are given in the conversation between Bukharin and Kamenev, *op. cit.*

28. At this time there were nine members of the Politburo, but in general only seven attended its meetings, the non-participants probably being the two new members, Kuibyshev and Rudzutak.

29. During a previous encounter, Stalin, in an attempt to win Bukharin over, had remarked 'You and I are two Himalayan peaks; the others are nonentities.' *Sotsialisticheski Vestnik*, 1929, No. 9.

30. *Sotsialisticheski Vestnik*, 1929. No. 9.

31. The proceedings of this session have been reconstructed here from the following sources: Daniels, *op. cit.*, pp. 329–32, who quotes an account found in the Trotsky Archives; Sokolnikov and Kamenev, *Sotsialisticheski Vestnik*, 1929, No. 9, pp. 9–11; Stalin, *Sochineniya*, Vol. XI, pp. 157–87; *KPSS v Rezolyutsiyakh*, Vol. II, pp. 511–24.

32. Daniels, *op. cit.*, p. 329 (from the Trotsky Archives).

33. *ibid*, pp. 329–30.

34. Stalin, *Sochineniya*, Vol. XI, pp. 157–87.

35. On this latter point, in his Moscow speech after the session, Stalin stated that there should be no change of leaders, on the contrary the present leadership should be retained, *Sochineniya*, Vol. XI, p. 32.

36. Daniels, *op. cit.*, p. 331.

37. *ibid*. The speech is on p. 331, the final part of the speech on p. 355.

38. Sokolnikov and Kamenev, *Sotsialisticheski Vestnik*, 1929, No. 6.

39. *ibid*.

40. Stalin, *Sochineniya*, Vol. XI, p. 189.

41. Bukharin and Kamenev, *Sotsialisticheski Vestnik*, 1929, No. 6.

42. A reference to the question of the formation of a peasant party, which was sometimes raised by various anti-Bolshevik elements, and which found a response among those better-off peasants who took an interest in politics.

43. Sokolnikov and Kamenev, *Sotsialisticheski Vestnik*, 1929, No. 6, p. 10.

44. This part of Stalin's speech was not reproduced when the speech was officially published twenty years later, but there is no reason to doubt its authenticity. Kaganovich made similar remarks before a restricted audience in October of the same year.

45. Stalin, *Sochineniya*, Vol. XI, pp. 193–4. The speech of July 11th is on pp. 188–196. (Emphasis in the original.)

46. *ibid*, pp. 191–2.

47. It would appear that Stalin was in possession of documents which might be used to compromise recalcitrant colleagues. He might have been able to blackmail Voroshilov by divulging that the latter's patriotic zeal had led him to enlist voluntarily in the Tsarist Army. See Daniels, *op. cit.*, p. 329.

48. Bukharin and Kamenev, *Sotsialisticheski Vestnik*, 1929, No. 9, p. 10.

49. *ibid*.

50. Notes of the conversation with Bukharin were made by Kamenev during and after their meeting. These notes were later published by the Trotskyists; they constitute a unique document, of incontestable authenticity. The excerpts quoted are based upon the text published in *Sotsialisticheski Vestnik*, 1929, No. 6 and No. 9. This excerpt is from No. 6, p. 10.

51. On Trotsky's attitude see Deutscher, *The Prophet Unarmed*, pp. 448–50.

52. Stalin, speech delivered in Leningrad on July 13th, *Sochineniya*, Vol. XI, pp. 204–6. Frumkin delivered a note during the session in which he stated that the *razmychka*, or breach in the alliance, was already a *fait accompli*. See Stalin, *Sochineniya*, Vol. XI, p. 179.

53. *Pravda*, July 15, 1928.

54. Daniels, *op. cit.*, pp. 332–3.

55. In Stalin's speech 'Na khlebnom fronte' in *Pravda*, June 2, 1928, *Sochineniya*, Vol. XI.

56. Rykov, *Pravda*, July 15, 1928.

57. A letter of July 25th from Moscow (some details of which are incorrect) in *Sotsialisticheski Vestnik*, 1928, No. 5; Daniels, *op. cit.*, pp. 332–3. According to material in the Trotsky Archives it would

appear that Trotsky believed victory for the Right to be imminent, since 'Stalin's temporizing tactics had failed'.

58. Daniels, *op. cit.*, p. 332.

59. Speech by Stalin in Moscow, *Pravda*, October 24, 1928, *Sochineniya*, Vol. XI, p. 235.

60. According to Bukharin, Yagoda and Trilisser initially shared his views. Trilisser was to be dismissed from the *OGPU* in October 1929; Yagoda, on the other hand, sided with the more powerful faction.

61. Bukharin on the Moscow Congress, *Pravda*, September 12, 1928. Speeches made by Bukharin at the Congress are contained in *Pravda*, July 19, 22, August 4, 14, 19, September 2, 1928.

62. Personal letter from Bukharin to Humbert-Droz, a Swiss-born representative of the Comintern who was expelled as a member of the Right. Bukharin expresses his regrets to Humbert-Droz for having failed to defend his opinion in public, but explains that he had been forced to act in this way because of the situation within the Bolshevik Party. Quoted by Daniels, *op. cit.*, pp. 335–6.

63. Leontev's article, 'Khozyaistvennoe razvitie i problem ravnoveshchiya', which criticizes the *Zametki* without directly mentioning Bukharin's article, is in *Pravda*, November 4, 1928; Stalin, *Sochineniya*, Vol. XI, p. 260.

64. The details of this struggle are omitted here. See Daniels, *op. cit.*, the chapter devoted to the Right. Tomsky was to be definitively deposed by a decision of the April 1929 session of the Central Committee. Uglanov was dismissed from his post in Moscow in November 1928, and appointed Commissar of Labour, *Pravda*, November 28, 1928.

65. Krumin and Savelev were the *politruki* in question. Bukharin's weak heart could have been used as a pretext.

66. *Bolshevik*, 1928, No. 19, pp. 3–7.

67. Stalin, *Sochineniya*, Vol. XI, p. 224.

68. *ibid*, p. 225.

69. *ibid*, pp. 225–7.

70. *ibid*, pp. 232–3.

71. *Pravda*, editorial, October 20, 1928. (Emphasis supplied.)

72. Stalin, *Sochineniya*, Vol. XI, p. 234.

73. *ibid*, p. 236.

74. *KPSS v Rezolyutsiyakh*, Vol. II, p. 539.

75. *ibid*; also Stalin's speech delivered at the November session, *Sochineniya*, Vol. XI, p. 278.

76. The effects of Stalin's master stroke are still apparent in present-day Soviet attitudes; it would seem that Bukharin has been rehabilitated, but not 'ideologically'.

77. Bukharin related these events in the course of his conversation with Kamenev, which took place between December 1928–January 1929. *Sotsialisticheski Vestnik*, 1929, No. 9, p. 11.

78. The source for this last demand is Ordzhonikidze, *16-ty S'ezd VKP(b)*, stenogramme, p. 236. For the others see *KPSS v Rezolyutsiyakh*, Vol. II, p. 566.

79. Bukharin and Kamenev, *Sotsialisticheski Vestnik*, 1929, No. 9.

80. Stalin, *Sochineniya*, Vol. XI, pp. 269–77.

81. Stalin attempted to omit the subordinate clause, but Frumkin forced him to read the whole sentence. Stalin, *Sochineniya*, Vol. XI, p. 275.

82. *ibid*, p. 260.

83. *ibid*, pp. 286–8. Stalin was to repeat this to the Presidium of the Executive of the Communist International on December 19th, stating that in Russia the members of the Right had never infringed Party discipline. *Sochineniya*, Vol. XI, p. 317. The concessions made to the Right probably included the dismissal of Kostrov of *Komsomolskaya Pravda*; in this organ, Kostrov had violently attacked the Right, accusing it of wishing to restore bourgeois democracy. Rykov, *Pravda*, December 4, 1928.

84. Stalin, *Sochineniya*, Vol. XI, p. 250.

85. *ibid*, p. 307.

86. The *prorabotka* was admitted by the Politburo in one of its resolutions. *KPSS v Rezolyutsiyakh*, Vol. II, pp. 563–4. The term 'civil death' is used, *ibid*.

87. This resignation is mentioned in *KPSS v Rezolyutsiyakh*, Vol. II, p. 557.

88. Deutscher, *The Prophet Unarmed*, pp. 455–7; *Byulleten Oppozitsii*, 1929, No. 1–2, p. 3.

89. Deutscher, *op. cit.*, p. 469.

90. Krupskaya, 'Lenin i kolkhoznoe stroitelstvo', *Pravda*, January 20, 1929.

91. Bukharin on the occasion of Krupskaya's birthday, *Pravda*, February 27, 1929.

92. A peasant version of the word *kommuna*.

93. One remark made by those who sighed after the 'good old days of the revolution', and which originated perhaps with Krupskaya herself, was that if Lenin were to return to the USSR in its present state he would immediately be imprisoned as a deviationist. . . .

94. A copy reached the editors of *Sotsialisticheski Vestnik*. See 1929, No. 9, p. 9.

95. Bukharin and Kamenev, *Sotsialisticheski Vestnik*, 1929, No. 9, p. 11.

96. *Voprosy Istorii KPSS,* 1960, No. 4, pp. 72–3.

97. According to a letter from Moscow, published by the Trotsky-ists and reproduced in *Sotsialisticheski Vestnik,* 1929, No. 9, p. 11. According to the same source, Kamenev was called before Ord-zhonikidze (head of the Central Control Commission and the *RKI*) (*Raboche-Krestyanskaya Inspektsiya*) to whom he confirmed the authenticity of the notes.

98. Bukharin in referring to the regional conferences held in pre-paration for the Party Conference. (Emphasis in the original.)

99. Quoted by Ordzhonikidze, *16-ty S'ezd VKP*(*b*), stenogramme, p. 325.

100. Letter from Moscow, *Sotsialisticheski Vestnik,* 1929, No. 9, p. 11.

101. Ordzhonikidze, *16-ty S'ezd VKP*(*b*), stenogramme, pp. 201–2. The first paragraph may be a condensed rather than a verbatim version.

102. Rudzutak, *16-ty S'ezd VKB*(*b*), Stenogramme, pp. 201–2. The first paragraph may be a condensed rather than a verbatim version.

103. Stalin, *Sochineniya,* Vol. XII, p. 100. This is part of a speech made by Stalin in April 1929 which was not published at the time. The expression in the original is *predatelskaya....*

104. *ibid,* pp. 100–1. The editors of Stalin's 'Works' remind the reader on p. 372 that at that time Bukharin and the Socialist Revolu-tionaries had been plotting together to assassinate Lenin, Stalin and Sverdlov, as was shown at the trial in 1938.

105 Rudzutak, *16-ty S'ezd VKP*(*b*), stenogramme, p. 201. The remark concerning the kolkhozes, made by Yakovlev, is on p. 577.

106. *KPSS v Rezolyutsiyakh,* Vol. II, p. 559.

107. Rudzutak, *16-ty S'ezd VKP*(*b*), stenogramme, p. 201, and the text of the resolution of the Politburo of February 9th in *KPSS v Rezolyutsiyakh,* Vol. II, p. 558. (Emphasis supplied.)

108. Stalin, *Sochineniya,* Vol. XI, pp. 318–25 (a summary of Stalin's contributions to the debates in the Politburo); *Bolshevik,* 1929, No. 23–4, pp. 30–5, 46; *Sochineniya,* Vol. XII, p. 92; *16-taya Konferentsiya VKP*(*b*), stenogramme. (Moscow, 1962), Notes No. 56, 133, 135, 215, 266.

109. From the Central Archives of the Party, *16-taya Konferent-siya VKP*(*b*), stenogramme, p. 780, Note 56.

110. Stalin, *Sochineniya,* Vol. XII, p. 92. Publicly Stalin claimed that such a step could not be taken owing to lack of currency.

111. Report of a debate on the Five-year Plan in the *Sovnarkom. Pravda,* April 6, 1929.

112. The proposals made by this commission are quoted by Ordzhonikidze, *16-ty S'ezd VKP(b)*, stenogramme, pp. 325–6, and in Stalin, *Sochineniya*, Vol. XII, pp. 6–7.

113. Ordzhonikidze, *16-ty S'ezd VKP(b)*, stenogramme, p. 326.

114. Stalin, *Sochineniya*, Vol. XI, p. 323.

115. Stalin, *Sochineniya*, Vol. XI, pp. 318–9; a summary of speeches made to the Politburo in January and February 1928.

116. The declaration of February 9th is in *KPSS v Rezolyutsiyakh*, Vol. II, pp. 550–67, the speech is in *Sochineniya*, Vol. XII, pp. 1–59.

117. Resolution of the Central Committee of April 1929, *KPSS v Rezolyutsiyakh*, Vol. II, p. 555.

118. Stalin, *Sochineniya*, Vol. XII, pp. 8–9; *KPSS v Rezolyutsiyakh*, Vol. II, p. 555.

119. Their 'self-criticism' is contained in *Pravda*, November 26, 1929.

120. Bukharin, 'Politicheskoe zaveshchanie Lenina,' *Pravda*, January 24, 1929.

121. Bukharin, 'Zametki ekonomista', *Pravda*, September 30, 1928, and 'Lenin i zadachi nauki v sotsialisticheskom stroitelstve', *Pravda*, January 20, 1929.

122. According to Bukharin, *op. cit.* (see Note 120), and Stalin, *Bolshevik*, No. 23–4, 1929, p. 20. In *Pravda*, January 20, 1929, Bukharin writes: 'we are living at a time of *resurgence* of the militant forces of capitalism, of its technology, science and economy'.

123. Letter to Humbert-Droz, Daniels, *op. cit.*, pp. 335–6.

124. Stalin, *Bolshevik*, 1929, No. 23–4, p. 20.

125. Bukharin, *op. cit.* (see Note 120). It should be noted that in this speech Bukharin summarizes the contents of five articles which Lenin had dictated in January and February 1923, when he was already ailing. The articles are to be found in Lenin, *Sochineniya* (4th edition), Vol. XXXVI, pp. 541–59. They were rightly regarded by Bukharin as Lenin's last will and testament, and are so considered in the Soviet Union today. See Lenin, *Sochineniya* (4th edition), Vol. XXXVI, Note 661, pp. 541–59. In our discussion of Bukharin's views, we have not always distinguished between those ideas which are his own, and those he quotes from Lenin.

126. Bukharin, *op. cit.* (see Note 120).

127. *ibid.*

128. *ibid.*

129. *ibid.* The Russian is *skoropalitelny*.

130. *ibid.* Emphasis supplied by Bukharin, quoting Lenin, *Sochineniya* (4th edition), Vol. XXXIII, p. 425.

131. *ibid.* Further quotations from articles by Lenin.

132. Bukharin, 'Zametki ekonomista', *Pravda*, September 30, 1928.

133. According to the Central Archives of the Party, cited in *16-taya Konferentsiya VKP(b)*, stenogramme. (Moscow, 1926), p. 803, Note 215.

134. Stalin, *Bolshevik*, 1929, No. 23–4, pp. 29–31.

135. Erlich, *op. cit.* (see Ch. 6, Note 55), pp. 78–89.

136. Bukharin, in both *op. cit.* (see Footnote 121).

137. Bukharin, 'Lenin i zadachi nauki . . .' (see Note 121).

138. *ibid.*

139. *ibid.*

140. *ibid.* (Emphasis in the original.)

141. *ibid.*

142. Savelev, 'Lenin o borbe na dva fronta i o primirenchestve', *Pravda*, January 20, 1929.

143. Bukharin, 'Zametki ekonomista' (see Note 121).

144. *ibid.*

145. *ibid.*

146. For the attack on 'Zametki ekonomista' see Leontev, 'Khozyaistvennoe razvitie i problema ravnoveshchiya', *Pravda*, November 4, 1928, and Kuibyshev, *16-taya Konferentsiya VKP(b)*, stenogramme. (Moscow, 1962), pp. 38–59.

147. Bukharin, *op. cit.* (see Note 120).

148. *ibid.* Also 'Zametki ekonomista' (see Note 121).

149. Bukharin, *op. cit.* (see Note 120).

150. *KPSS v Rezolyutsiyakh*, Vol. II, p. 554.

151. Quoted by Erlich, *op. cit.* (see Ch. 6, Note 54), p. 355. Bukharin here quotes from a speech he himself made to the Fourth Congress of the Comintern.

152. Stalin, *Bolshevik*, 1929, No. 23–4, p. 32.

Chapter 13

THE FIVE-YEAR PLAN:
STALIN LOOKS AHEAD

The task of elaborating the Five-year Plan had been put in hand
with the greatest haste, in response to intense pressure from the
Politburo, who were calling for rapid action and an increasingly
ambitious set of objectives. When the Plan received its official
blessing in April–May 1929, the work of preparation had still not
been completed. Certain aspects of the Plan, such as the problem of
market equilibrium, or the programme for training the cadres who
would be required if the rest of the Plan were to be effectively
implemented, had not yet been worked out by that date.[1] It was
clear that, so far as the Politburo were concerned, the actual announcement and launching of the Plan were more important than
the question of adequate preparation. No doubt the agencies involved in the Plan, and the planners themselves, had other ideas,
but the Politburo, having by this time virtually shaken off the restraining influence of the Right, were in a position to set the pace.

The Plan, as presented to the country in the spring, was conceived
on grandiose lines, both in respect of its objectives, and of the
resources which would have to be deployed if these objectives were
to be attained.

Following on an intensive investment campaign, investments
were to be trebled within the coming five years. Over the national
economy as a whole, investments were to increase 2·5 fold according to the 'minimal version', and 3·2 fold according to 'optimal
version'.[2] In the planned sector of industry, investments were to
increase by 340% (420%), the sum involved being of the order of
19·1 milliard roubles, whereas expenditure in this sector over the
five previous years had been only 4·9 milliards. 80% of the sum in
question was to be devoted to production of the means of production.

Large sums of money were to be spent on communications, and
the production of electricity, and there was to be a rather more
modest expenditure on agriculture, but the total amount of investment in the economy was to be the enormous sum of 47·31 milliard
roubles, with additional expenditures amounting to a minimum of
19·19 milliards for social and cultural needs, and 9·76 milliards for
administration and defence. The total resources required for the

five-year period would amount to 76 milliards (83 milliards in the optimal version).

The following comparison serves to illustrate the extent of the effort involved. According to the plan, the amount invested in the economy was to be four times greater than in the preceding five-year period. Expenditure on social and cultural requirements alone was to be almost three times greater.[3]

In terms of the Plan, the annual growth rate for industry over the five years was to be somewhere between 17·5% and 21·5% (21·5% and 25·2% optimal) which would give a total increase in production of 135% (181% optimal).[4]

As a result of the foregoing deployment of effort and resources, it was estimated that the national income would increase by 81·6% (103%), thereby enabling the country to make a spectacular leap forward in industrial production, and a rather more modest amount of progress in the agricultural sector, while at the same time increasing the real wages of industrial workers by 58% (71%), and the incomes of agricultural workers by 30%.

In affirming that implementation of the Plan would provide the country with a powerful industrial force, particularly in the field of heavy industry, and would at the same time make it possible for the level of individual and social consumption to be raised, despite the enormous burden of investment, the planners showed considerable optimism. The impressive series of figures for the production of iron and steel and electricity, and the machinery which would at last serve to create a new 'metal-based Russia' within the shortest possible time, were greeted with a wave of enthusiasm in some quarters, and with rather less audible murmurs of scepticism, or indeed derision, from certain observers and from the planners themselves. Even the most dedicated of the Party's specialists must have had some doubts about the possibility of achieving such a spectacular increase in investments coupled with a rise in the level of individual consumption. In fact, the more clear-sighted of them, notably Krzhizhanovsky and Strumilin, realized that such assumptions were unrealistic, but they continued to hope that once the most important part of the programme had been carried through, some relief would be afforded to the mass of the population, and a flood of new industrial goods would reach the market.[5]

Despite this underlying weakness in the Plan, the planners, whether communist or otherwise, did their best to ensure that it had some measure of coherence, and that the calculations on which it was based were such as to afford a reasonable chance that the objectives in question might be achieved.

At the outset, *Gosplan* in a body tried to stem the flood of unreasonable demands by openly criticizing the proposals of the *VSNKh* which, under the leadership of Kuibyshev, showed little inclination to be guided by the restraining influences which were then still powerful within *Gosplan*.[6] Resistance from *Gosplan* was not overcome until the Politburo purged it, in the course of 1929, removing not only its 'bourgeois' and non-Party directors and specialists, but a considerable number of communist specialists as well. In the meanwhile, *Gosplan* endeavoured to do its best in the circumstances, and to produce a plan which was based on sound technical and economic calculations.

However, the criteria and the assumptions on which *Gosplan* was working were constantly being distorted by external pressures. There was one thing on which the Politburo insisted, and which in practice took priority over all other considerations; this was the question of 'growth rates'. In their view, the best plan was the 'tightest' one, the one that achieved most in the least time. Any official who attempted to take other factors or criteria into account was obliged to leave *Gosplan*, or even the Party, and laid himself open to the most serious charges. The views of *Gosplan* experts on the practicability of the project on which they were engaged counted for very little. Strumilin, who was the most 'voluntarist' of the *Gosplan* specialists, felt it his duty to defend his subordinates, who were constantly being faced with increasingly ambitious objectives, without the least regard for the practical considerations involved.

In January 1929, Strumilin said: 'Naturally, by bringing sufficient pressure to bear on the specialists who are engaged in drafting the various sections of the Plan, I could have thrown caution to the winds with the greatest of ease'. In answer to the attacks of another Party economist, who had suggested that he was opposed to a rapid rate of industrial growth, Strumilin replied with truly 'Bukharinist' logic that the rate of growth could not outpace the actual availability of resources.

However, the atmosphere at *Gosplan* during this period was such that it would have been an act of 'civic courage' on the part of the planners to insist that there were sectors in which the brake should be applied. Strumilin made this point in the course of the argument we have just quoted. 'Unfortunately it would scarcely be reasonable . . . to put the civic courage of the said specialists to the test in this way.'[7]

The planners were aware of the risks involved in arguing too much, or raising objections on technical or other grounds. In the privacy of their own offices, they remarked that it was better 'to comply with the demand for rapid growth rates than to go to prison for having advocated more moderate ones'.[8]

Despite external interference and pressure, and despite their lack of expertise in a field which was new to them, the 500 specialists of *Gosplan* made a remarkable effort. The three volumes of the Five-year Plan remain an unprecedented achievement. *Gosplan* submitted two versions of its draft Plan, one being the 'minimal' or 'initial' version, the other the 'optimal' version.[9] This was no doubt another device by which the planners hoped to bypass unreasonable demands, or counteract the effects of an over-rigid interpretation of the functional aspects of the Plan. By putting forward alternative versions, they were affording the economic administrators some room for manoeuvre, and some chance of being able to adapt their policies to the dictates of changing cicumstances, while at the same time ensuring that *Gosplan* was given the opportunity to preserve the general framework of the Plan and to see that it was implemented.

Generally speaking, the margin between the objectives in the alternative versions was of the order of 20%. Certain parts of the Plan, which were of a particularly complex or urgent nature, such as the plans for the socialization of agriculture, and for the distribution of the national income, or the plan for the defence industries, were almost identical in both versions.[10]

The 'minimal' version was to be implemented in five years. If external conditions should prove favourable, it was hoped to put the 'optimal' version into effect within the same space of time. But if, on the other hand, conditions proved to be less favourable than had been anticipated, some of the planners hoped that it would be possible to achieve the objectives contained in the 'optimal' version within six years.[11] However, the majority of the officials engaged on the Plan must have been completely convinced that such a favourable combination of circumstances was unlikely to arise. Any attempt to implement the objectives of the 'optimal' version was dependent on the following factors: (1) that there should be five good harvests in a row; (2) that the *TsIK*'s target of a 35% increase in yields should be achieved; (3) that there would be a favourable movement in commercial exchanges on the international market, largely due to the availability of grain for export; and (4) that international relations would be such as to warrant keeping defence commitments at a fairly low level.[12]

Could it really be expected that all of these conditions would be fulfilled at the required moment? At all events, it appeared that the planners were concentrating the bulk of their efforts on the 'minimal' version of the Plan, for the more ambitious alternative was not even ready by the time that the broad general outline of the Plan was put before the public, prior to its ratification by the Sixteenth Party Conference in April 1929.

However, the government, or rather the Politburo, had its own opinions, and its own specific criteria in respect of the Plan and its objectives, and the way in which these should be implemented. Thus it came about that it was the 'optimal' version which was adopted, that is to say the version which depended for its operation on a set of circumstances which were, in the event, *totally unrealistic*.[13] No sensible planner would base his forecasts on the probability of five good harvests in succession. From the very outset, the Plan, in the form in which it was adopted by the authorities, was based on utopian assumptions.

There were at least two further weaknesses, which were apparent both in the 'minimal' and the 'optimal' versions of the Plan. In the first place, the success of the Plan depended upon its being possible to mobilize the resources required for investment. *Gosplan* had based its estimates mainly upon a certain number of so-called 'qualitative indicators' (*kachestvennye pokazateli*) or objectives which it would be essential to achieve. These included such factors as labour productivity, costs, soil fertility, cost of building materials, and economy and maximum utilization of resources in all sectors.

In this connection, the 'optimal' version envisaged an increase of 110% in the productivity of industrial workers, a drop of 35% in industrial production costs, a drop of 30% in fuel consumption, a drop of 50% in building costs, a rise of 35% in soil yields and a rise in real wages of 65% ...[14].

In addition to the foregoing objectives there were many others, such as high standards in the quality of goods, efficient organization and management, etc., which could only be described as pious hopes. None of these objectives were to be realized. If anything, there was a rise in costs, productivity failed to increase rapidly enough, or indeed tended to decrease, and so on. All these hopes were doomed to failure, largely because of the methods which were used to put the plan into execution, and these were beyond *Gosplan*'s control.

As we have said, the whole of the Five-year Plan was based on the assumption that these objectives would be fulfilled. The finance plans, for example, were dependent for their success on the availability of certain sums resulting from the savings which were envisaged in a number of sectors; if the resources in fact failed to materialize, it would be impossible to carry these plans through. The planners were well aware that this whole series of objectives was the foundation on which the Plan rested. As one of the heads of *Gosplan* wrote: 'This is one of the decisive elements, not only for the industrial plan but for the whole of the national economic plan for the coming five years.' [15]

Among the ranks of the planners, even the most enthusiastic communists could see clearly that there was a basic incompatibility between the emphasis being laid on quantitative growth and the objectives relating to the lowering of costs.[16] There were, one need hardly add, other inconsistencies so obvious that an expert of the standing of Bazarov was constrained to observe: 'In this domain, the worst possible results are to be expected, and we may end up with a distribution of productive forces which is so patently irrational that the very idea of industrialization could be discredited.' [17] Bazarov was a man of vision and courage, and he was not a communist. But there were plenty of Party members, not all of them on the Right, whose view of the situation was equally critical.

The forecasts for agriculture revealed yet another weakness, though this was practical, rather than theoretical. Fulfilment of the plans for industrial production and external trade, and of the objectives relating to improvement in the standard of living, depended on there being an increase in agricultural production. The nation's food supply, supplies to light industry, export availabilities or the saving of foreign currency were all factors which were subject to the size of the harvest, and to availability of a given amount of agricultural raw materials.

The heads of *Gosplan* knew that the Plan was being launched in the very middle of a grain crisis. Ratification of the Plan had coincided with a failure in procurements which was even more marked than in the previous year, despite the fact that that year had been the one in which the 'emergency measures' had been introduced. The rationing of bread and other foodstuffs had already started in the towns. One of the leading *Gosplan* officials stated the problem in the most unequivocal terms, and this in a propaganda hand-out which was intended for mass circulation: 'The prospects for production in the agricultural sector in the initial year of the *pyatiletka* (Five-year Plan) give grounds for the gravest anxiety as to the fate of the entire Five-year Plan.' [18]

Rykov was no doubt expressing the general view held both in government circles and inside *Gosplan* when he advocated, along Bukharinist lines, a broadly based movement towards a more peaceful and normal relationship with the peasantry, and a concentrated effort directed at remedying the unhealthy situation in agriculture. His suggestions were put before the *Sovnarkom* and were subsequently embodied in theses on the *pyatiletka* which he submitted to a meeting of the Central Committee in April 1929. The 'optimal version' was virtually rejected by Rykov, since the only figures in this version which he was prepared to accept where those relating to the creation of kolkhozes and sovkhozes, which were the same in both versions, and the targets for a number of products, such as fuel, chemicals, and possibly metals,' which were in particularly short supply. His view was that it would be more practicable for the authorities to proceed with due regard to the exigencies of circumstances, rather than to commit themselves in advance to projects which might prove over-ambitious.[19]

According to Rykov, the essential function of the Five-year Plan was not investment in heavy industry, 'but the problem of achieving a properly balanced development in the various sectors of the national economy'.[20] In voicing this opinion, he had touched upon the real point at issue, so far as majority opinion within the Politburo was concerned. It is clear that what he had in mind was, mainly, the backward state of agriculture. The immediate situation, as he outlined it to the *Sovnarkom*, was a reflection not only of 'adverse factors in the short-term' (this, he might have added, being the view put about by the Politburo) but of more chronic ills 'which could last not for one year, but for several' and which might persist over a long period. He was careful to avoid the word 'crisis', but this is obviously what was in his mind. Rykov predicted that if 'the downward trend' in agriculture went on, these 'difficulties' would continue, and the crisis would therefore grow worse.

The foregoing appraisal served as a basis for his proposed 'two-year plan' (*dvuletka*), the purpose of which was 'rehabilitation of the agricultural sector of the national economy within the shortest possible time'.[21] His suggestion was as follows:

'... would it not be more reasonable to concentrate on those essential elements of the Five-year Plan which would enable us to redress this imbalance, let us say over the next two years, and to devise a plan of action for eliminating the contradiction between the slow growth of agriculture and the needs of the population, thereby creating the conditions in which this part of the Plan could be implemented more effectively?'[22]

His effort to focus greater attention on the problems of the market economy, both in the context of his *dvuletka* and of the national economy in general, reveals an unspoken criticism of the majority view. 'The others,' he was convinced, were already relying too much, or perhaps even exclusively, on the kolkhoz movement, and had ceased to have any faith in the private sector of agriculture. He also pointed out, very sensibly, that 'even if efforts to organize the kolkhoz movement should meet with every success, this would not dispose of the problem of the circulation of goods, since we still have to purchase grain, even if we are purchasing it from the kolkhozes'.[23] He was, therefore, assuming that in all matters relating to production and the conditions in which sales were effected, the reactions of the kolkhozes would be similar to those of the other peasant producers.

Rykov's proposals were immediately branded as 'heresy'. At the Plenum, Stalin rejected the *dvuletka* more or less without benefit of argument. He said that while it seemed like a good idea, it in fact underlined the unrealistic character of the Five-year Plan.[24] Stalin also suggested that Rykov could not see the difference between the kolkhoz and the private peasant who held on to his stocks of grain, and denounced him for what was indeed a very realistic view of the situation . . . on the grounds that his attitude was reminiscent of Frumkin's observations. This may serve as an example of the type of argument employed by Stalin in his speech attacking the Right at the April Plenum.

The targets which *Gosplan* had set for agriculture were more realistic than those envisaged for industry.[25] At this stage, the Politburo were less ambitious in their aims for agriculture than they had been in the industrial sector, but even so they had set their sights high. There was to be an increase of 20% in sown areas, an increase of 17% in harvests,[26] the number of horses was to rise by 19%, and the number of cows by 21%, etc.

A spectacular increase was planned for cotton and flax, and for a number of other raw materials. Sizeable resources were to be made available for the agricultural sector, including some 7–8 milliards of direct investment by the State, in addition to the very large proportion of the people's own resources which likewise figured in the Plan. During the period of the Five-year Plan, according to decrees emanating from the Party and the Supreme Soviet,[27] there were to be produced some 3 milliard roubles' worth of agricultural machinery, including 80,000 tractors, and not counting imports of tractors. (It should be pointed out that when the Plan was launched the total value of existing agricultural machinery was no more than 1 milliard, and the machines in question were either of rudimentary design, or consisted of peasant implements of the simplest kind.)

Under the provisions of the Plan, the Party were hoping to make a significant effort to develop production of chemical fertilizers. At this stage, production of fertilizers was infinitesimal—some 420 thousand tons—but it was estimated that, by the end of the five-year period, production would have risen to 8 million tons, and it would be possible to provide fertilizer for almost all the area given over to industrial crops, and some proportion, though still a small one, of the other sowings.[28] According to the resolutions of the Sixteenth Party Conference, an undertaking was given that, once these objectives had been achieved, by the end of the quinquennium, 'a solution would be found in principle to the grain problem'.[29] This was a promise that was to be made on several occasions.

However, despite the fact that the objectives of the agricultural part of the *pyatiletka*, had, as we have seen, been kept within realistic limits, it was precisely in this sector that the Plan met with one of its worst setbacks.

The agricultural Five-year Plan suffered from a number of weaknesses, which were no doubt as apparent to the economists of the time, as they are to present-day economists. In particular, the assumptions about the amount of financial resources available for agriculture were over-optimistic,[30] and the planners had also been guilty of excessive optimism in their 'qualitative indicators'. However, when the plan not only proved to be impracticable, but in fact suffered a series of disastrous reverses, the failure was not attributable to shortcomings in the economic and technical calculations on which it was based. The projects for the development of agriculture, as envisaged not only by *Gosplan* but also by the *Narkomzem*, the co-operative movement and the *Kolkhoztsentr*, had been conceived within a social framework which nowadays seems remarkable for its moderation. This aspect of the Plan had also proved acceptable to the leaders of the Right-wing, who did not oppose it.

Volf, who was *Gosplan*'s chief spokesman on agricultural affairs,[31] was a man who had never been suspected of 'Right-wing deviations', and who always made some token reference to those 'who failed to understand the importance of the anti-kulak struggle', etc.,[32] but in his writings and in conferences of planning experts, the proposals which he put forward did not in practice comprise any sensational anti-kulak measures. On the contrary, he stressed the need for encouraging the peasant to become better-off. The authorities, as he sought to impress upon senior *Gosplan* officials, should not be so unwise as to suppose that they could afford to discount the productive activities of 'the most commercially active groups among the serednyak farmers'.[33] The speculators must be curbed, and the better-off peasants must be prevented from turning into kulaks, 'but we would be doing our own cause irreparable damage if we failed to distinguish between the peasant who has grown rich on the basis of exploiting others, and the peasant who is improving his condition not by speculation, but by learning what we are trying to teach him, and hoping to teach him, in the way of reconstruction and of improved farming methods'.

Such an attitude, if it had proved acceptable, would have done much to mitigate the ferocity of the anti-kulak campaign. The author of these words, knowing full well that his warning implied a more moderate approach to the kulak question, added: 'Naturally, there is no firm line which separates the rising serednyak from the kulak.' [34]

The Plan, and the programme which it embodied, as presented to the country and endorsed at the highest levels in April–May 1929, still placed considerable long-term emphasis on the private agricultural sector. It was conceived in the genuine hope of affording assistance to this sector, and holding out to it the possibility of continuing to improve its situation within the social framework which was familiar to the peasant.

The 'class nature' of the Plan lay not in its militant anti-kulak aims, but rather in its objective of bypassing the better-off strata of the peasantry, while continuing to collaborate with them, by creating a state and collective sector whose productive force would at least equal that of the upper 10% of the 'better-off peasants and the kulaks'. According to Volf, this stratum were in possession of 40% of the marketable grain, although the figure seems excessive.

As Kuibyshev informed the Sixteenth Party Conference, it was logical to assume that 'the State will have such effective means at its disposal for regulating the flow of goods between the town and the rural areas, that by the end of the five-year period the difficulties which we are now experiencing should be easily overcome'.[35] Volf added the observation that the rich peasants would no longer be able to indulge in speculation, or to withhold their grain, but would be obliged to sell it to the government. If this was indeed the intention, it might well be believed that the official government attitude to the kulak was fundamentally no different from the Bukharinist theory about the 'rooting' (*vrastanie*) of the kulak in socialism, which had been so vigorously attacked. As we shall see, this was in effect what *Gosplan* envisaged.

The role of the state and collective sector, as seen by *Gosplan*, would be two-fold: it was to be an important source of grain supplies, and at the same time it was, by virtue of its demonstrable economic superiority, to serve as an example even to the more prosperous peasant, by helping to win him over and recruit him for the collective sector. (It should be borne in mind that at this stage, this was also the official view within the Party and the government). In a situation in which quality was of overriding importance, it was essential to avoid imposing unduly ambitious objectives, which might prejudice the quality of the work which was required of this sector.

According to *Gosplan*'s estimates, it was expected that by 1932 the kolkhozes and sovkhozes would be responsible for 13% of the sown area (and 17·5% by the following year), which would yield 43% of the marketable grain,[36] that is, 500 million poods of grain from the total estimated harvest.

If this hope had in fact materialized, is it not likely that the Soviet nation would have been spared a disastrous period in its history?

It was estimated that, by the end of the quinquennium, the sovkhoz sector would be of the order of 5 million hectares, and the kolkhoz sector 22 million.[37] The population of the kolkhozes would amount to 20 million persons, or some 4·5 million households, organized mainly in *tozy*.[38]

On this question opinions were divided: the co-operative view was that the *toz* should be the basic form, whereas others advocated 'superior' forms, *arteli* in particular. The Five-year Plan put forward by the co-operative movement proposed that of 4·4 million collectivized households, 3·5 million should be organized in *tozy*.[39]

According to Volf, the greater part of the kolkhoz lands should be organized on the basis of large-scale farms, which would be served by machine tractor stations and columns: these were new forms, which raised high hopes at the time. However, in view of the fact that the 120,000 tractors which were to be allocated to the kolkhozes would not be sufficient to mechanize the entire kolkhoz sector, it was estimated that half of the kolkhozes would still consist of small-scale farms, because of a foreseeable shortage of machines.[40] The bulk of their power was to be provided by horses.

Within the kolkhozes, the main effort at socialization was to be directed towards grain production, while half of the livestock would remain the property of the kolkhoz members.[41] The restraint which the planners had shown in this respect was due to the rather more complex nature of livestock-raising, which made it difficult to organize activities along communal lines, or to find a focus for these activities similar to that which they hoped the tractors would provide in the case of the grain sector.

Gosplan's view was that the contribution of the sovkhozes in the livestock sector would be similarly restricted, and that such activities as they did undertake would be largely experimental in character.

As for the various types of machine tractor stations, whose function was to enable the kolkhozes to operate on a larger scale, the role assigned to them under the Five-year Plan was a very modest one, involving only 2·3 million hectares. Their task was to explore the possibilities of this new form, with the ultimate aim, possibly in ten years' time, of serving some twenty million hectares. . . .[42]

Since the individual peasant would still be the mainspring of agricultural production, there could be no question of neglecting the private sector of the agricultural economy. Therefore, despite the enormous effort which it was felt would be necessary to establish a powerful socialized sector, the bulk of the available credits would continue to be allocated to the peasantry. The dominant role would be played by the co-operative movement, since the planners did not envisage the organization of collective farms otherwise than within the co-operative framework.

A closer link was to be created between the co-operative movement and the peasantry, largely through use of the 'contract system', which would affect the total production of raw materials, and 75% of the sowings.[43] At this time, the government departments concerned, and the Central Committee in particular, attached a great deal of importance to the 'contract system', which was regarded as a major instrument both in the task of collectivization and in the effort to increase production. The contracts, which would be entered into with groups of peasants, or more frequently with whole communities, and which it was hoped would operate over periods of several years, afforded the Central Committee a vision of an agricultural sector which could be fitted into the general framework of the national economic plan as the industrial sector had been.

In August, the Central Committee were to make the following observation:

'By reorganizing the work of the peasant farms on the basis of contracts with the State, thereby ensuring that the State acquires the peasants' marketable surplus, the system of *kontraktatsiya* will bring millions of peasant holdings within the orbit of a single State plan, and by so doing will help to put an end to the chaotic condition of the market.'[44]

It is interesting to note the part which *Gosplan* expected the village communities to play. Through the operation of the contract system, these communities were destined to evolve gradually towards a collectivized system of production by forming themselves into agricultural co-operatives, which in the initial stages would be 'producers' associations' of the simplest type. This process would serve as a stepping-stone for future mass collectivization of the peasantry, which was not envisaged in the present Five-year Plan.

Within the community itself, the farms would remain in private ownership for a long time to come, and class distinctions would continue to exist, but the better-off peasant who entered into a contract in company with the rest of the community would no longer have much scope for disposing of his surplus grain.[45] In this connection, the policy which the plan proposed with regard to the communities and the part they should play in collectivization of the peasantry followed very closely on the lines suggested by Sukhanov, despite the bitter criticism to which his ideas had previously been subjected by the Communist Academy. Unfortunately, like so many other good ideas, this one was not followed up.

One function of the co-operative movement was to bring within its orbit 85% of the peasant households, it having been estimated, according to the most favourable figures, that some 40% of households were already engaged in some form of agricultural co-operation,[46] but in addition to the foregoing task, the co-operative movement was also responsible for assisting farms in the work of production by increasing the use of mechanization and of improved farming methods, and by promoting the growth of all existing forms of agricultural association, including the kolkhozes. Their efforts would be further reinforced by a series of incentives linked with price and fiscal policy, supplies, and a distribution of the national income which would favour the peasants, etc.

The primary purpose of the agricultural Five-year Plan was to find a solution to the basic problem which was plaguing the State, namely, the grain shortage.[47] *Gosplan*'s chief concern was to extricate the country from a situation in which the threat of famine was an ever-present reality, and the planners were therefore reluctant to commit themselves over the coming five years to any programme of social changes or intensified development which might prove excessively ambitious or costly. The plan did not provide for exports of grain until near the end of the quinquennium, when it was estimated that the first five million tons would be available. Until then, it was thought unlikely that there could be any resumption of the Russian grain trade abroad.[48]

Similarly, it was not expected that there would be any improvement in the nation's food supplies before the end of the five-year period. Meanwhile, it was generally understood that the 'grain and fodder budget' would be tight. Now that Rykov's proposals for a *dvuletka* had been turned down, no one in government planning circles had any idea how the country would surmount its difficulties over the next few years, until the new factories and the other developments promised in the Five-year Plan should begin to bear fruit. Meanwhile, the country would need to make a leap in the dark, but the planners were confident that once the hazards of the next few years had been negotiated, it would at last be possible to provide a more solid foundation on which Soviet Russia would build for the future. The programme as they envisaged it embraced plans for the production of agricultural machinery and artificial fertilizers, an increase in the output of tractors,[49] plans based on the expansion of the co-operative movement and the contract system, a powerful state agricultural sector centred on the kolkhozes and sovkhozes, which would be equipped for *industrialized agriculture* with the best scientific techniques, and, in addition to all this, the training of suitably qualified cadres, and the overall effect of the various economic incentives which were to be offered to the small peasant farmer. Once these objectives had been achieved, it would be possible 'to deal a crushing blow at the upper stratum of kulaks in the villages, and usher in a progressive régime in agriculture for the broad mass of bednyak and serednyak farms'.[50] At the same time, this would provide a solution to the problem of food supplies. Here again, it should be emphasized that the phrase 'a crushing blow at the upper stratum of kulaks' was simply a form of words which was 'fashionable' at the time, and which had to be employed in order to safeguard against the danger of provoking the Politburo's displeasure. *So far as the actual programme was concerned, it was unquestionably* vrastanie *which was intended, although the word itself was not mentioned. There was no suggestion of recourse to violence, or to any other methods beyond those of a purely economic nature. Indeed, any such ideas were strongly discouraged.*

The plans for collectivization were bold in conception, as befitted an undertaking which was without precedent in world history at the time, but here too the bounds of prudence had not been overstepped. *The question of mass collectivization affecting the majority of the peasantry was one which had not even arisen.* Even a wholly fantastic and baseless Fifteen-year Plan, the work of the economist Sabsovich at *Gosplan*, did not hold out any prospect for collectivization of the peasantry before the end of the third quinquennium, that is by about 1943.[51]

There was general acceptance of the principle that both large-scale agricultural production and collectivization could only be introduced gradually, as material circumstances permitted. Similarly, the general body of texts and calculations emanating from the various departments of the Central Committee, and from Stalin himself, were unanimous in their assumption that collectivization would not be practicable without an adequate degree of mechanization, and particularly an adequate supply of tractors.

In spirit, the projects and planning documents relating to the social development of the peasantry which were circulating during mid-1929, and even towards the end of that year, were basically very little different from the programme put forward by the Right. Gosplan's *Five-year Plan for agriculture had been put together by a number of specialists drawing on a considerable common fund of expert knowledge and good sense, and it could undoubtedly have served as a basis for shaping the future development of the Soviet rural sector.*

In view of the dramatic turn which events finally took in the Soviet countryside, the question which is often asked is whether another solution could not have been found, and whether an alternative choice of policy existed. The answer is that the Five-year Plan for agriculture, worked out by *Gosplan* in conjunction with the Commissariat for Agriculture and specialists from the co-operative movement, provided just such an alternative, but was not put into effect.

The Central Committee, or rather the Politburo and the Secretariat, had independent departments which were also engaged in the study of agricultural problems, but the lines along which they worked were not always consistent with the general opinion among Party or non-Party experts and officials in the various government departments which were concerned with agricultural questions. Moreover, even Bauman, who was the Moscow *obkom* secretary, and second in command after Molotov in the rural department of the Central Committee, had no notion of what was afoot in the offices of the General Secretary until after the event. In June 1929, Bauman stated: 'We shall not need a hundred years, but we shall certainly need one or two decades; these are the terms in which we must view the growth of collectivization within the Moscow *guberniya*.'[52] In making this statement, he was fully consistent with the spirit of the Five-year Plan and with the general current of opinion within the Party. There is no doubt that his words reflected a sincerely-held belief; at this stage, it was unthinkable that a more rapid rate of development should be imposed in this sector, and the Party would not have accepted such a suggestion. However, one curious and disturbing factor had already emerged, although its significance was not grasped at the time: while the General Secretary was outlawing the theories of the Right, plans for agriculture and for collectivization which had a great deal in common with Right-wing 'heresy' were solemnly being adopted at all the highest levels. This was evidence of the contradiction of which we have been speaking.

2. *The Debate on Kolkhoz Strategy*

How was the rural sector to be collectivized? What methods would be used, and what forms would collectivization take? The subject had been formally discussed by the Fifteenth Party Congress, but a year and a half later there was still no centre for research on kolkhoz questions, nor indeed was any serious research being done on the kolkhoz movement, although the latter had been in existence for at least ten years. Kalinin pointed out that the situation compared very unfavourably with the fact that the *VSNKh* had thirty-six research institutes engaged in studying industrial questions.[53]

At this time, the co-operative production movement took a great number of different forms. *Kommuny, arteli* and *tozy* were all broadly included under the general heading of kolkhoz. As late as the end of 1929, the proportion of *tozy* had been steadily growing, and accounted for over 60% of all existing kolkhoz organizations. These three types of association were regarded as superior forms, but at a lower level a whole range of organizations had developed more or less spontaneously; these were even more numerous than the kolkhozes, though with a lesser degree of socialization, and a number of authors had demanded that they be regarded as forming part of the kolkhoz movement. An official document from the Central Committee had in fact proposed to include them in the local branches of the kolkhoz administrative structure.[54]

These were small-scale associations, often consisting of one large family or a few families at most, who had banded themselves together to buy machines for their communal use, or to consolidate their holdings, which could then be cultivated communally. They occasionally consisted of whole villages (or farming communities) which had formed themselves into a collective for communal work on selected seed growing, or on some particular crop or branch of livestock raising.

Alongside the co-operative enterprises which existed for the processing of agricultural products, and which were regarded by *Gosplan* as an important factor in the task of collectivizing agricultural production, there had been a further new development, in the shape of '*co-operative machine and tractor columns*' and simple stations for the hiring-out of agricultural implements.

Both the press and the government departments concerned were the scene of lively discussion among the various currents of opinion, not only on the relative merits and potentialities of these different forms, but also on questions of principle relating to the nature of the movement as a whole. It was generally agreed, however, that the necessary knowledge and experience in this domain were lacking, and that the properly trained cadres who would be required for an operation of such magnitude did not exist. It was essential, therefore, to proceed slowly, and to begin by encouraging the growth of good model enterprises, which would in turn pave the way for a rapid expansion of the collective movement as a whole. This was the logical course favoured by a number of people, and in particular by Kalinin. In May 1929, he addressed the following observation to some person or persons unknown: 'Anyone who thinks that all this can be achieved without effort, by primitive means and without the aid of engineers and highly qualified specialists, is neither a Marxist nor a communist but merely a petty-bourgeois in outlook, a man with the limited vision of a peasant.'[55] On the same occasion, Rykov voiced similar sentiments when he remarked that collectivization was not only a matter of financial resources, and that in practical terms a far more important factor would be the ability to provide the necessary supplies of tractors, machinery and fertilizers. 'Any attempt to set up a kolkhoz on the basis of the *sokha* would reflect nothing but discredit on the whole task of socialization and would in practice be a certain recipe for failure.'[56]

Rykov, Kalinin and, indeed, the majority of the leadership were all convinced that if they observed this principle, they could safe-guard the kolkhoz movement from the disastrous effects of over-precipitate action, thereby ensuring its ultimate emergence as a superior social and economic force, which was in fact the only justification for the entire undertaking.

But the problem of materials and equipment was not the only one facing the activists and specialists who were engaged in the co-opera-tive and collective movement. Amid the spirited discussions which were taking place, it was already apparent that there were two opposing schools of thought, the 'State' faction and the 'co-operative' faction. The former were more concerned with the immediate interests of the State, while the latter tended to place greater em-phasis on the interests of the peasantry as a whole, and were anxious to ensure that the movement would enjoy the genuine whole-hearted support of the farmers.

If one bears this in mind, the arguments of those who supported the simplest forms of co-operation are more readily understandable. Some people were strongly opposed to the small kolkhozes which at this time made up the greater part of the movement, on the grounds that an organization of this size was scarcely more efficient than a well-run kulak farm. Their aim, therefore, was to prevent the setting-up of these dwarf kolkhozes.[57] However, those who seriously subscribed to the principle that the collective movement should be voluntary in character were well aware that such a proposal could not be implemented without some degree of administrative pressure, nor did they share the enthusiasm of the Politburo and some of the leading *Kolkhoztsentr* officials for outsize structures.[58]

According to Kubyak, *Narkomzem* of the RSFSR, the desire to dis-courage the growth of small collective farms was misguided, in the sense that for a long time to come the collective sector would still have to do without tractors, and would have to use horses or oxen for its work. As long as this situation lasted, small-scale collectives would necessarily be the dominant form.[59]

Other authors were even more outspoken in their denunciation of large-scale organizations, which they described, either openly or in veiled terms, as 'bureaucratic'. They issued warnings about the dangers of making an abrupt transition to excessively large organizations instead of proceeding by gradual stages. In their view, any attempt to disregard these intermediate stages in the process of development would be contrary to the régime's avowed aim of re-educating the peasant and effecting a gradual transformation in the structure of the rural economy. The result might well be regression or indeed a breakdown of the entire process.[60]

For many of these authors, the task of transforming the social and economic structure of the peasant sector was of necessity a many-sided one, which must take into account the whole range of existing co-operative forms, from the most primitive associations, which were none the less worthy of every support, to those which, being more complex, were better equipped and better organized, and had reached a higher degree of socialization.[61] In their view, respect for the voluntary principle made it imperative at this stage to accord a leading role to the *toz*,[62] which in practice had emerged as the dominant collective form.

Kalinin, for his part, had nothing against the setting-up of large-scale farming enterprises, particularly if they were organized within the framework of 'inter-village stations', as they were known at the time. But his views on small collective farms were coloured by Marx's theories on the history of capitalist enterprises, and he saw them as representing the 'manufacturing phase' which would be followed by the industrial phase proper, in which the *MTS* would play the part of the 'factories'. In this context, the kolkhozes should be supported as necessary factors in the process of development which would ultimately pave the way for the future 'inter-village stations'.[63]

In addition to the foregoing ideas, he had an interesting theory on the relations between the collective and the private sector in agriculture, which he put forward at the Party Conference. 'The most Right-wing of the Right-wingers' (as he was described by V. Serge), Kalinin had rallied to the support of Stalin against the Right, though the alliance was a purely tactical one. Kalinin's arguments against the Right were singularly lacking in conviction, for he was unquestionably in favour of a greater emphasis on the private sector, and despite his tactical manoeuvres in the factional struggle his pro-peasant views remained for the moment unchanged. He was profoundly opposed to the use of any kind of force against the peasants, and while his support of Stalin might have committed him to policies of an exactly opposite nature, he no doubt hoped that the steadily worsening crisis might lead Stalin to adopt a more moderate line.

He viewed collectivization not as a process which might prove inimical to the private sector, but rather as a complementary activity which would be of direct benefit to the peasant as an independent farmer.[64] In this sense, he had welcomed the agronomist Markevich's experiment at the 'Shevchenko' sovkhoz near Odessa as a most hopeful development.

This was the first of the *MTS*, and we shall be discussing the experiment which was conducted there later on in these pages. The peasants were encouraged to collectivize their holdings, and the *MTS* carried out the heavy agricultural work for them, thus relieving them of the most burdensome of their tasks, and setting them free to specialize in livestock-raising, horticulture and other branches of production in the non-collectivized sectors of their farms. The sovkhoz reported that numerous orchards, vegetable gardens and vineyards had sprung up around the *MTS*, and that the livestock were better cared for. There was a visible improvement in the condition of many of the peasants.[65]

These reports were over-optimistic and slightly premature, for the 'Station' experiment was still in too early a stage to provide a valid basis for any such conclusions, but in the end they proved sufficiently plausible to convince Kalinin that he had found one possible solution to the problem of reconciling the interests of the private and the collective sector, as he had hoped to do. He was undismayed by the suggestion that the 'Station' was, so to speak, engendering better-off peasants, or potential kulaks, within its orbit; and he emphasized that there were no grounds for supposing this to be so. On the contrary, he was convinced that the development was a favourable one. 'The more collectivization can be seen to benefit the peasant farm. [i.e. the *individual* peasant farm.—M.L.] the more it will capture the enthusiasm of the individual peasant, thereby paving the way for further collectivization'.

Kalinin's theory was that it would be easier to collectivize the whole of agricultural production if the peasant was first allowed to grow more prosperous under a system of partial collectivization. For this reason, he supported Markevich's idea of leaving the livestock sector in the hands of the peasants for the time being. After their successes in the communal cultivation of their fields, thanks to the activities of the 'Station', the next step would be to collectivize livestock production, and this would prove all the easier in that it would have the support of the peasants, now suitably reassured and won over by the favourable outcome of their efforts in grain production.[66]

In the light of what we now know, it is possible to see more clearly what troubles the Soviet Union might have been spared, not least in the domain of livestock production, if such ideas had been adopted.

The problem which aroused most controversy was connected with the 'Machine and Tractor Columns' and the 'Stations' and on this issue the protagonists were clearly split into two opposing camps, the 'State' faction and the 'co-operative' faction.

The first of these experiments, as we have said, had been launched in 1927 in the 'Shevchenko' sovkhoz under the leadership of Markevich.[67] By 1929 it was well under way and was already attracting attention, its activities having aroused great hopes for the future. At this time, the 'Station' had signed contracts with some thirty or so villages, the arrangement being that some or all of the inhabitants were organized as a *toz* or a 'Sowing association' (*posevnoe tovarishchestvo*) and handed over to the Station the responsibility for carrying out heavy work in the fields, which had been grouped for this purpose into large units. Under the terms of the agreement, the 'Station' provided tractors and other essential machinery, together with selected seeds and technicians whose duty it was to instruct the peasants in the use of the machines. All the work, including that done by the tractors, was carried out by the peasants themselves, under the guidance of agronomists and technicians attached to the 'Station'.

All the heavy equipment was owned, at this stage, by the sovkhoz, and simply provided for the peasants under contract, but the association were given the option of purchasing it, if they had the means to do so. All the peasants were obliged to carry out whatever additional work was necessary on the fields, and to exercise the normal care over them, particularly in the matter of hoeing and weeding. Each individual was responsible for his own holding, since the fields were grouped together for communal cultivation only when heavy field work was involved.

The harvest was shared according to the size of the individual holdings, so that the principle of private ownership of the land had in no way been abandoned. In return for its services, the 'Station' received a third or a quarter of the grain harvest. Upon giving suitable notice, any peasant was free to terminate his contract, and he was then allocated a strip of land from the main holding. The group or the community naturally enjoyed similar rights.[68]

At this stage, Markevich was in favour of limiting collectivization to the grain-producing sector, because of the lack of experience, and, above all, of resources. He saw no problem in allowing the peasants to continue farming their individual holdings, which they were in fact improving. But in the long term, Markevich had visions of a 'Station' consisting of a 'power centre' responsible for all the work of cultivation, covering an 'optimum' area of 50,000 hectares and operating from a central *usadba* (farmstead) which would incorporate machinery, workshops, enterprises, etc. . . .[69]

He had no designs on the private plot, nor was he obsessed with speed in the matter of socialization, but in the long run his aim was to set up large-scale farming enterprises along the lines of his 'Station', for in his view this was the collective form par excellence, superior by far to the *kolkhozes*—which term he reserved for the small collective farms, which were too under-powered and ill-equipped ever to be equal to the real work of socialist reconstruction.

As we have seen, he was not opposed in principle to the idea that the peasants' associations might buy back agricultural equipment from the sovkhoz, but in practice he rather tended to discount it, and was generally inclined towards a more 'state-centred' solution. The 'Station' was to be more of a State concern (in the form of a state-co-operative company) managed by directors whose responsibility it would be to appoint additional personnel and to take charge of planning and finance.[70]

Meanwhile another type of enterprise had emerged and was beginning to gain ground. Although slightly different in character, it was at the same time based on the Markevich experiment. This was the 'Machine and tractor column', which was organized mainly by the *Khlebotsentr* in conjunction with the grain co-operatives, and which, suitably equipped with tractors, was operating on a similar basis with the peasants, by signing contracts with the peasant associations.

In 1928, there were only thirteen of the columns, with a total of 442 tractors in all, and they had managed to set up fifty-one of the so-called 'simple producers' associations', covering an area of 68,500 hectares. By November 1929, their number had risen to sixty-two, with a total of over 2,000 tractors, and they had entered into contracts with 400 associations, over an area of more than a million hectares.[71] Each column signed contracts with a number of villages ranging between three and twenty; there was even one instance in which they succeeded in recruiting an entire *raion*, the Volvovski *raion* in the province of Tula, in which all the villages, with some 60,000 inhabitants and over 80,000 hectares, combined to form a region of total (*sploshnaya*) collectivization. (Later on, at the end of 1929 and the beginning of 1930 *sploshnaya kollektivizatsiya* was to become the compulsory watchword throughout almost the entire country.)

In addition to the 'Columns', there were also a score or so of *MTS* operating in Russia and in the Ukraine which were directly managed by the State, but in the middle of the year they were all placed under the control of the *Traktortsentr*, a body which had been set up by government decree in June.[72] However, this decision did not have any bearing on the future of the kolkhoz movement in general, or on the form which these stations should take. These were questions which were provoking much heated discussion at this time.

In those days, the *Sovnarkom* had not yet begun to set itself up against the accumulated expertise of the specialists attached to it. The majority of the departments and officials concerned were agreed that, if the most effective use were to be made of the limited number of tractors available at the time, it would be necessary to concentrate them in the hands of those who were best qualified to operate them. This the small kolkhozes were unable to do.[73]

However, there were several forms which this deployment could take, and this was the issue on which opinions were so sharply divided. Should the 'Stations' be state-operated, or should they be managed by a state-co-operative company? In this case, it was generally agreed, the difference would be a purely formal one. There was, however, the additional possibility that they could be set up and managed by the general co-operative movement, or by the kolkhoz movement in particular.

In addition, there was a considerable body of opinion which favoured direct ownership of tractors by the kolkhozes, but this scarcely seemed practicable since the latter were too small and ill-organized. Moreover, the whole idea of the 'Station' was that it should act as a means of encouraging the peasants to form associations in the first place.

There was a great deal of opposition to the idea of state-managed 'Stations', particularly from officials of the co-operative and kolkhoz movement. As well as reflecting a general concern for the interests of this movement, their arguments were also based on a number of much more important factors. In the first place, there was the simple economic fact that the State did not possess the means to set up a sufficient number of these 'Stations', and that unless a decisive contribution were to be made by the rural population itself, they could not even begin to think in terms of the vast amount of resources which would be required if they were to extend collectivization beyond the grain-producing sector.[74] Only the co-operative movement, by virtue of its ostensible role as a voluntary movement having direct links with the peasants, could mobilize support from the peasants on this scale. The latter would have no vested interest in a state-run institution which might, for all they knew, be dissolved by its organizers at any moment.[75]

This school of thought believed that the co-operative movement alone was capable of carrying out the essential task of collectivist reconstruction in the countryside, whereas it would be a long time before the *MTS* could play any significant part in the movement, irrespective of the basis on which they were organized.[76] They were of the opinion that the dominant role in the movement would continue to be played by kolkhozes of the 'classic' type, that is, small-scale associations.

Lyubchenko, one of the leading co-operative officials, was among those who opposed the suggestion that the columns should be entirely 'state-managed'. At the Sixteenth Party Conference, he put forward a number of arguments, the substance of which was that the State had not the means to create an adequate number of these 'Stations', and that such organizations would not, in any case, provide the necessary stimulus for collectivization. The incentive to form associations was something that arose from the villagers' own need to join forces for the purchase of a tractor. Similarly, Lyubchenko dismissed Markevich's view of the 'Station' as a 'power centre', fulfilling a function akin to that of an electricity generating station. In his opinion, this was a false analogy.[77]

Lyubchenko's criticisms were directed against a growing trend among the Party leadership to place excessive reliance on the tractor, and on mechanization in general, as a means of accomplishing the desired changes in the social structures of the countryside and in the nature of agricultural production. This attitude derived from an over-simplification of Marxist theories about the role of the machine in industry, and its ultimate outcome was to be seen in the utopian projects for 'agro-industrial centres' which created havoc in the Soviet economy for over a year. The Chinese popular communes were to provide a further example, some twenty-five years later.

There were other writers who also sounded a warning note about this deification of the machine, pointing out that mechanization of itself could not bring about the required transformation. Other factors must be taken into account, particularly the role of the human element, in the shape of a spontaneous movement by the peasants themselves. For this reason, it was not for the kolkhoz movement to adapt itself to the 'Stations', but the other way about; the *MTS* would require to be geared to the character and needs of the kolkhozes.[78]

Those who favoured 'co-operative columns',[79] including a number who also advocated that the peasant associations should ultimately become the owners of their material and equipment,[80] advanced their arguments against the *MTS* with some caution. The campaign against Right-wing 'heresies' was at its height, and criticism of excessive State intervention in the peasant sector was a delicate matter. But the views of many of these co-operative supporters were summed up by one writer who put the arguments against state-operated *MTS* in unequivocal terms. He declared himself opposed to any form of 'bureaucratic set-up', since the fundamental weakness of such bodies was their inability, or unwillingness, to take into account either the practical aspects of the problem, or, more important still, the initiative of the broad mass of individuals who were most directly concerned.

According to this author, those who held that state-managed *MTS* should play the major role in the collective movement were

'... advocating something that was more extreme in conception than the columns; they are, so to speak, moving alongside the peasants. They start from the assumption that the means of agricultural production should be concentrated, to the maximum possible extent, in the hands of state-controlled organizations, and that the production of grain should be organized along factory lines; their purpose is to remove the means of production from those who in fact produce the grain—in other words, they are aiming at re-creating urban production relationships in the countryside'.

Those who enthusiastically advocated the 'bureaucratic' solution were reminded of Lenin's injunctions about the need for effecting changes in the structure of rural society solely within the framework of the co-operative movement, and about the importance of progressing 'hand in hand with the mass of the peasantry', rather than on the basis of so-called companies of the German capitalist type [the latter remark being attributable to the author and not to Lenin.—M.L.]. He went on to argue that the economic revolution brought about by the tractor would require to be accompanied by a corresponding revolution in the social system, and that this 'transformation in the traditional forms and patterns of the agricultural economy would only be possible if the task of collectivization were conceived not merely in terms of machines, but rather in terms of machines plus the concerted efforts of the peasants themselves'.[81]

As we know, there was in the Soviet context at this time a preponderance of factors which combined to influence the leadership in a direction diametrically opposed to that recommended by the author whom we quote. Many Party members had misgivings on this score, but the nature of the government apparatus was such as to predispose it strongly in favour of solving its economic difficulties, and tackling the infinitely complex problem of transforming and modernizing the Soviet rural sector, by adopting the 'machines plus State-control' formula, and imposing it upon the peasants without their agreement, or indeed against their will.

At the period of which we are speaking, autocratic tendencies of this kind were still virtually illegal, or it might be more correct to say that they were not officially countenanced. Instances in which such principles had been at work were constantly being denounced, after the event. However, a man like Rykov was fully aware of what he was saying when he declared, at the Fifth Congress of Soviets, 'We have no right to lose sight of the fact that all this [i.e. technology.—M.L.] is meant for the benefit of mankind. Man is not made for the machine, but the machine for man.'[82] In the end, however, as the economic crisis added its own pressures, those tendencies which had always been officially condemned in earlier days were gradually to gain the upper hand with increasing ease, and in the debate on the methods by which social progress might be achieved, it was the cruder counsels which prevailed, for they had the support of the highest authority in the land, the General Secretary himself.

3. *The General Secretary's Solution*

The experts and activists had arrived at certain conclusions which, broadly speaking, found their expression in the text of the Five-year Plan. Meanwhile, the head of the Party apparatus, at a meeting of the Central Committee called in April 1929 for the purpose of ratifying this same plan, had put before the Committee a number of views which were considerably at variance with the spirit of the document produced by *Gosplan*. In one of the longest speeches of his career, Stalin attacked the theories of Bukharin and Rykov, at the same time revealing what his own ideas were.

From the beginning of 1928, these ideas had developed consistently along lines which were partly dictated by the pressures of an economic crisis which was growing graver as time went on. However, his ideas were also profoundly influenced by his manoeuvres in the factional struggle. Stalin was a deadly and vindictive opponent, and the desire to crush his enemies often outweighed all other considerations with him. He was a poor theoretician, and his political approach was largely empirical, so that, as a statesman, he was always liable to be influenced by the ideas of his rivals. Consciously or unconsciously he tended to assimilate those ideas, either by direct borrowing, as he borrowed certain ideas of Trotsky's, or indirectly, as in the case of his struggle with Bukharin, by adopting the very opposite point of view. So it was that his own programme was unfolded before the Central Committee as part of an attack aimed at discrediting, or rather demolishing, an adversary who for all practical purposes had already been silenced. The essence of Stalin's thought and tactics, as they were at the time and as they developed in the future, lies in the speech which he made at that meeting in April 1929.[83]

According to Stalin, Bukharin's gravest error had been his failure to comprehend the principles and the practical implications of the class struggle. In order that his hearers should be left in no doubt about the matter, Stalin painted a grim picture of the danger threatening the country from the forces of capitalism, and especially from the kulaks. In his opinion, these capitalist elements were 'remustering' in order to defend their former positions.[84] He then went on to give an appraisal of the forces in question. A formidable enemy, namely, the saboteur, was at work within the government apparatus. These *Shakhtintsy* were everywhere, for their numbers were recruited from the ranks of specialists and bourgeois intellectuals in general. They were engaged in economic sabotage, one of the most dangerous forms of capitalist opposition. There had been several cases of sabotage which the *GPU* had either uncovered, or fabricated themselves, during the previous year, mainly in the defence industry, in the coal and gold mines, and in various other sectors; these had been conveniently linked with the machinations of international capitalism[85] and now provided Stalin with the proof he needed to convince his audience of the danger which threatened.

The largest of these capitalist forces consisted of the kulaks, whom Stalin described as the régime's most redoubtable enemy; and one whose numbers were growing in the countryside. This enemy, said Stalin, 'never sleeps, is growing ever more powerful, and undermining the Soviet régime'.[86]

Stalin's allegations were no more than exaggerated generalizations, a distorted image of the truth. Not enough is known about the attitude and the struggles of the old intelligentsia towards the end of the twenties. No doubt they were critical of the régime, and even at times violently opposed to it, particularly during the Stalin era, but this general charge of sabotage was pure invention. The régime itself was to refute it later, when the witch-hunt among the specialists was dropped at the point where it threatened to interfere with the drive for industrialization.

As for the kulaks, while they were undoubtedly growing more hostile, their influence was no longer increasing; on the contrary, their importance as an economic force was diminishing. Similarly, the supposed 'attempts to undermine the régime' were not so grave as Stalin had suggested, a point which we shall be discussing more fully at a later stage.

Stalin's famous theory about the intensification of the class struggle with the gradual approach of socialism was no abstract concept, intended for use solely within the context of academic research. It was a political instrument, a weapon which the régime might use to combat opposition, not from the capitalists but from the mass of the peasantry and the discontented workers, and those factions within the Party who were over-susceptible 'to the influence of the petty-bourgeois element'. This latter accusation was aimed at all oppositionists in general, and was broad enough in its application to embrace Bukharin as well as Trotsky.

One of the characteristic features of Stalin's method was his technique of turning *ad hoc* theories into universal truths. His theory about the class struggle, and the tactics he adopted in this connection, were a response to the pressure of internal difficulties, and they were meant for internal use, but they were greatly strengthened by being given universal validity.

This was the origin of the theory concerning the 'third period' in the history of the struggle of the proletariat against the capitalist world, which was developed by the Comintern at this time. At Stalin's instigation, the Comintern announced 'the end of the capitalist *status quo*'—a prophecy which was to be made repeatedly in the years that followed—and declared that this would be accompanied by a renewed upsurge of revolutionary activity in the West. This was followed up by a declaration of war to the death on all non-communist left-wing movements, and on all moderate elements in the world communist movement which were suspected of being capitalist agents.[87]

Thus, having conjured up an all-powerful and all-pervasive class enemy, and situated him within the context of heightened class struggle on a world scale, Stalin was free to discredit Bukharin and *ipso facto* the theory of *vrastanie* which, it should be remembered, had been official Party policy, in principle, since 1925.

He pursued his argument, stating the problem in highly individual terms which were none the less presented as the purest distillation of Marxist thought. In his view, Bukharin's theory of the *vrastanie* was incompatible with the Marxist theory of the class struggle. At this point, he was interrupted by Rozit, who exclaimed: 'But Bukharin's *vrastanie* presupposes the existence of a class struggle, that's the point!' Stalin did not deign to reply, but went on to reason as follows: a choice would have to be made between a process of class liquidation preceded by a bitter struggle, which had been the policy envisaged by Lenin, and Bukharin's policy, which aimed at 'destroying the class system by eliminating the class struggle and bringing about the *vrastanie* of the capitalists within the framework of socialism'.[88]

Under the influence of Stalin's arguments, the Sixteenth Party Conference adopted a resolution which reduced the policy issue to a clear choice between two alternatives: the development of the national economy must be controlled either by the kulaks, or by a socialist State. To present the dilemma in this form was to exclude the possibility of a third solution, and this in turn gave rise to the further proposition that the choice must lie exclusively between the kulaks and the kolkhozes.[89] Here again we have an example of the technique of giving political point (*zaostrit*) to a problem.

The programme, as Stalin envisaged it, called for liquidation of the class system and, of course, the elemination of capitalists and kulaks, within the shortest possible time. The equivocal nature of the term 'liquidation' served his purpose very well. As he said— 'Their days are numbered.' [90]

This was true, to some extent. During 1929 an enormous amount of pressure was put upon the kulaks, and the drive to oust the Nepmen from industry and private enterprise continued. The proportion of industrial production accounted for by the Nepmen fell to 0·6%, and that of retail trade from 24·8% to 16·1%, while in the following year it was less than 6%.[91] The same movement was apparent in wholesale trade, though to a less marked degree. Thousands of traders and entrepreneurs were forced to abandon their business activities as a result of the economic, political and fiscal pressure brought to bear on them. Many were imprisoned or deported on charges of speculation which were sometimes genuine and sometimes not.

The campaign against the private sector was conducted with much publicity, and with the full resources of the propaganda machine and the *GPU*. Its effect on the Soviet economy was serious, for the timing of the operation could not have been more ill-judged. In a scarcity economy in which the machinery of state and co-operative trading was still cumbersome [92] and inefficient, the effect of suppressing private enterprise in one form was simply to encourage its resurgence in another, and more dangerous, guise, and to create the conditions in which speculation and the black market could flourish unchecked.[93] There was a sustained increase in the activities of the black market and the speculators throughout the entire period of the Five-year Plan, and by 1932 these had reached unprecedented heights. Thus the anti-Nepman campaign of 1928–9 could scarcely be said to have resulted in any positive gain for the régime.

The drive against the specialists (*spetsledstvo*) which was an integral part of the same policy, proved equally harmful. At a time when the country was committed to a policy of industrialization, Stalin called upon the authorities to root out the pernicious *Shakhtintsy*, and accordingly the main weight of the régime's attack was directed precisely against those whose contribution was most vital, that is the engineers.

Aside from the immediate damage caused by this policy, the full effects of the Stalin mystique of the class struggle were only to become apparent at a later stage. In the present context, we need only say that *one of the reasons for the turn which Soviet affairs took under Stalin was the régime's failure in the preceding period to pursue a policy aimed at increasing agricultural output among the small peasant farmers by the use of direct aid and co-operative methods, in accordance with the principles of* NEP.

Bukharin and Kalinin, in company with other leading officials and experts, were convinced that the private sector in agriculture, given proper assistance and encouraged to operate within the framework of an efficient co-operative movement, was still capable of expanding and providing the food which the country needed.[94] Stalin too made a number of statements along similar lines, but it was clear that he no longer had faith in the future of small-scale farming, and was pinning his faith on the sovkhozes and kolkhozes, as forms which offered a much wider scope for State control.

He pointed out that the private agricultural sector was lagging behind industry, and behind the country's needs. 'It is clinging to old-fashioned implements and traditional farming methods, to outmoded techniques which are unsuited to the present day, and to a pattern of economic activity which is outdated.' [95] The small strips which went to make up these farms could not produce an adequate marketable surplus of grain, and were not suited for the practice of new farming techniques.

It was clear from such arguments that Stalin had already made up his own mind about the private sector, and had written it off.[96] In his view, the backward state of agriculture was likely to cause a breach between town and country, and he was sincerely persuaded that this constituted a very real danger. The immediate solution which he proposed was to organize the agricultural sector in such a way that it would ultimately achieve a rate of growth comparable to that of the industrial sector. This was an immense undertaking, and one so unrealistic in its assumptions that even today the USSR has still not succeeded in carrying it out.

Stalin claimed that this objective was to be attained 'gradually'; it is not clear, at this stage, what his views were on the time which would be required to complete the task, or indeed if he had any specific period in mind. However, from the way in which he described the gravity of the situation and the dangers which were threatening the régime, and also from his suggestions that the country was now in a sufficiently advanced stage of development to be able to initiate radical changes, it is evident that he was already planning a number of drastic and far-reaching measures to deal with the crisis.

In the event, he made an astonishing statement at the Plenum, to the effect that there had already been a radical change in the peasants' attitude to the kolkhozes. Their earlier atttitude, he said, had been one of contempt, but millions of peasants were now in favour of collectives, having been converted to this point of view by the many kolkhozes and sovkhozes which were helping the peasant farmers and serving as an example to them.[97]

Stalin did not actually name any of these model collectives, for the very good reason that they were still so rare that they could not, in fact, have played any positive role in influencing the mass of the peasantry in the manner suggested.

He went on to argue that the Party itself had now reached a stage where it was ripe for a change in policy, and that it would henceforth be in a better position to act as a bulwark for the Central Committee. This was mainly due to the lessons it had learnt during the procurements crisis at the beginning of 1928.[98] By so arguing, Stalin was placing the responsibility for the delay in adopting new tactics on the Party, the implication being that the Party had up till now been blind to issues of which the Central Committee had been fully aware for some time. The further implication was that the Central Committee, with great forbearance, had been waiting for the Party to draw the correct moral from the sharp lesson which it had received, and to give its full support in future to whatever action was initiated by the leadership. In this way, the Party leadership were automatically absolved from the charge of lack of foresight, which had been levelled at them for some years past, and the responsibility was laid on the shoulders of 'the men on the spot'.

However, Stalin had some further words of reassurance to add. The State, he said, now had at their disposal the resources necessary to undertake a programme of social and economic change in the rural sector. The truth was that such means as they had might have sufficed for a programme of collectivization on a modest scale, along the lines envisaged by *Gosplan,* although *Gosplan* itself was far from confident on this score; in the event, five months after Stalin's statement, Molotov, his second in command, informed those same members of the Central Committee that all the State had available for this project was a few miserable farthings (*groshi*). . . .[99]

In the course of the long speech which Stalin made at the April meeting, and which he devoted mainly to an attack upon Bukharin's theories, he gave a brief outline of the Politburo's programme. This was, broadly, as follows: (1) the reconstruction of industry; (2) a start on the reconstruction of agriculture; (3) the construction of kolkhozes, sovkhozes and *MTS,* and implementation of the system of *kontraktatsiya*; (4) procurements were to be carried out with the help of 'temporary emergency measures reinforced by the support of the broad mass of serednyaks and bednyaks': (5) the private sector in agriculture was to continue to play a leading part for the time being, but would be reinforced by the contribution of the kolkhozes and sovkhozes; and (6) the cornerstone of the entire project would be the rate of industrial growth.[100]

Stalin made no mention of figures or timing. His audience, having been convened for the purpose of adopting the Five-year Plan, saw nothing amiss, for they believed that the Plan in question had been properly elaborated. But if the objectives of the Plan had already been fixed and were soon to be endorsed, what was the purpose of repeated injunctions about the need for ever-increasing rates of growth?

This was no accident. Stalin did not venture any appraisal of the economic or social factors involved in implementation of the plan. The essence of his thinking on the problem of industrialization was contained in *his theory of an ever-increasing rate of growth, and this was to become a dominant feature of the Soviet industrialization effort*. This theory, and the practices to which it gave rise, were in turn largely responsible for a further development, namely the *'administrative approach' to planning and the implementation of plans, which resulted in a rapid increase in the apparatus of a totalitarian bureaucracy*.

During the first few months of 1929, Stalin advanced a number of theories which together went to make up the body of Stalinist doctrine. There was, in the first place, his belief in growth rates as the ultimate criterion of progress, with certain accompanying theories which had acquired the status of myths, as exemplified, in particular, by the linking of the sabotage danger with the class struggle; similarly, there was his belief that progress could automatically be equated with the quantity of productive forces; and his insistence that priority for the needs of heavy industry should be accepted as an article of faith without reference to any other criterion. This body of dogma was presented as Marxism, and finally crystallized, under pressure of the tremendous effort involved in the *pyatiletka* and the methods which were used, into what later became known as 'Stalinism'.

Since the rate of growth was now considered more important than the Plan itself, despite the expert calculations on which the latter had been based, the first thing the government did upon adopting the Plan was to step up its objectives.[101] They not only adopted the 'optimal' version, but at once set about broadening its aims. The targets relating to sown areas, the number of sovkhozes and the production of inorganic fertilizers were all raised, and there was a similar increase in the provisions for production of electricity and fuel; the investment plan for non-ferrous metals was doubled. The plan for cotton cultivation was to be fulfilled within four years. By July it was expected that there would be further increases in the targets fixed for iron and steel, with particular emphasis on agricultural machinery, and also in the plans for certain sectors of light industry.[102] The increases were also reflected in the programmes for kolkhoz construction, and in the plans for the amounts of marketable grain to be supplied by the kolkhozes and sovkhozes.

By September 1929, a new watchword was current: *the Five-year Plan must be fulfilled in four years*.[103] November brought yet more changes in the plans for collectivization, of a far more sweeping nature than any of the revisions or adjustments which had been made in the original plan.

These incessant changes, which were before long to reach truly fantastic proportions, were accompanied by reassuring statements to the effect that the general framework of the Plan remained unchanged, and would be respected. In fact, as Jasny has said,[104] the Plan had become simply another myth, a mere façade; the Politburo was in direct control of the most vital sectors of the country's activities, and was setting overall targets virtually from day to day, so that the routine work of reconstruction was being planned on an *ad hoc*, short-term basis. In order to maintain this degree of control over the country, and to drive it to the superhuman efforts which were often demanded of it, Stalin resorted to tactics which had already been foreshadowed, or indeed suggested in broad outline, in his April speech. He announced that all State and Party organs and institutions must be politically 'activized' in order that they might play a more effective part in the overall task of reconstruction.

Stalin and the Sixteenth Party Conference announced that there would be a wholesale purge of the State apparatus.[105] The purge was accompanied by measures against the specialists, and seriously disrupted the work of all the departments concerned throughout the entire year. It had particularly severe repercussions in the trade unions, where the supporters of Tomsky and those cadres who, it was thought, would be incapable of following the new policy line, were ousted as part of a so-called drive against bureaucracy.

In the event, the unions were obliged to reorganize themselves 'for their role in the production drive', their function being to act as an instrument in the process of industrialization. By insisting that unions and both Party and non-Party intellectuals should fall into line in this way, the authorities were guarding against any danger of disaffection in two sectors which might be liable to oppose the great leap forward, or to withhold their whole-hearted co-operation.

However, the Party itself, as the sole organized political force in the country, also required to be 'activized', since the sources of opposition within its ranks were particularly dangerous. Here, too, the purge was the weapon used to combat both the Right-wing and any other source of actual or potential opposition, and also to ensure discipline, or rather compliance, from the régime's principal arm of power. The campaign against Bukharin provided the opportunity for applying pressure to the members of the Central Committee itself. From this time on, any indiscretion or leakage of information from the Central Committee was to be punished by expulsion from the Committee, and a more stringent press censorship was imposed, so that the newspapers could be relied upon to follow an exclusively Central Committee policy line.[106]

However, the Party still sheltered within its ranks a certain hard core of members who, because of their political past, were unlikely to welcome Stalin's grandiose plans for a monolithic Party and State, and who could be counted upon to resist any attempt to impose this kind of uniformity on them. These were elements from the 'Old Bolshevik' cadres, many of them intellectuals who had grown up with the Party in pre-revolutionary days, and later on in Lenin's time, after the October revolution. They were sceptical, and critical, and it was always possible that from their midst there might arise, at any given moment, potential rivals for Stalin's power.

At the time of which we are speaking, Stalin was making increasing use of one particular method of dealing with opposition; this consisted not only of taking preventive measures against individual opponents, but primarily of striking at whole groups of people who might be capable of offering organized resistance. He had already used this technique in dealing with the bourgeois specialists and the kulaks. Now, some of the Old Bolsheviks within the Party were ousted as part of the drive against the Right, while another group, that of the Left opposition, who had been isolated at an earlier stage, were temporarily called upon to lend their support. At this point, Stalin needed cadres, and he needed support against the Right-wing; he was able to satisfy both these requirements by enlisting the support of numbers of 'reformed' Trotskyists, who were mainly attracted by the promised programme of industrialization.

But Stalin continued to be suspicious of all those former opponents, whether of the Right or the Left, who were now engaged in self-criticism. He distrusted the Old Bolsheviks as a whole, he often showed a deep hatred of them, and from the time of Kirov's assassination he was to set about ruthlessly exterminating them. He had already fired a warning-shot at the old guard in this same crucial speech made in April 1929. An extract which was kept secret at the time, and not published until after the war, contained the following cruel and bitter words: 'Any Old Bolshevik who turns aside from the path of revolution, or fails in his duty or compromises his political reputation, even if he is a hundred years old, has no right to be called an Old Bolshevik, and has forfeited his claim on the Party's respect.'[107] These warning words were ostensibly directed at Bukharin in person, but they appplied equally to those officials who were employed at the time in the central offices of *Gosplan*, in the *VSNKh* and the various commissariats, and who had frequently tried to curb the Politburo's excesses.

Stalin was virtually the sole judge of who had 'failed' or 'sullied his political honour' in this way; and many of the cadres were painfully aware of the fact. Many of those who joined him, even from the ranks of the Left opposition, did so against their better judgement, because they had no alternative. Ivan Smirnov, who was a convinced Trotskyist, finally capitulated like many of his colleagues in October 1929[108] and formally accepted the general Party line, declaring that he was henceforth severing his allegiance to Trotsky. In private, he explained what his motives had been for defecting from his former leader: 'I cannot remain inactive. I must build! The Central Committee is building for the future, barbarous and stupid though its methods may often be. Our ideological differences are relatively unimportant compared with the building of major new industries.'[109] Smirnov was to think differently some two or three years later.

As for Stalin, it will be seen that, from his point of view, his mistrust of the old guard of the revolution was entirely justified.

NOTES AND REFERENCES

1. See Grinko, 'Plan velikikh rabot', *Planovoe Khozyaistvo*, 1929, No. 2; Borisov, *Podgotovka proizvodstvennykh kadrov selskogo khozyaistva SSSR* (Moscow 1960), pp. 48–53 has shown that round about 1930 no one had any idea of overall requirements in cadres, whether for industry or agriculture. For reasons which are easy to understand the authors of the Five-year Plan did not succeed in drawing up a *pyatiletka* for the training of cadres.

2. For details of both versions see Grinko, *op. cit.* The following figures are those of the 'minimal' version, those in parenthesis belong to the 'optimal' version.

3. The target figures are taken from: Grinko, *op. cit., passim*; *Istoriya narodnogo khozyaistva SSSR*. (Moscow 1960), pp. 506–

13. Zaleski, *op. cit.* (see Ch. 7, Note 5), pp. 59–60; *KPSS v Rezolyutsiyakh*, Vol. II, p. 573.

4. These planners' figures were later to be scaled upwards by the government and do not, therefore, always correspond to the final figures.

5. Zaleski, *op. cit.*, pp. 66–7.

6. Daniel, *op. cit.* (see Ch. 2, Note 3), pp. 350–1.

7. Strumilin, 'O tempakh nashego razvitiya', *Planovoe Khoszyaistvo*, 1929, No. 1, p. 109.

8. Strumilin, *op. cit.* The expression is untranslatable. The conclusion arrived at by the planners was that it was better to *stoyat* for accelerated growth rates than *sidet* for the sake of slow growth rates.

9. *Otpravnoi i optimalny variyanty*.

10. Grinko, *op. cit.*, pp. 9–10.

11. *Ibid*, p. 10.

12. *Ibid*, p. 9.

13. Rykov, *16-taya Konferentsiya VKP(b)*, stenogramme, p. 6, and the resolutions of this conference in *KPSS v Rezolyutsiyakh*, Vol. II, p. 573.

14. Grinko, *op. cit.*, p. 65; Kuibyshev, *16-taya Konferentsiya, VKP(b)*, stenogramme, p. 35.

15. Grinko, *op. cit.*, p. 65.

16. *ibid*, p. 66.

17. Quoted from a Soviet source by Daniels, *op. cit.*, p. 358. Bazarov is not referring directly to the problem of 'qualitative indicators', but to the relationships between industry and agriculture in general, and to the problem of rate of growth.

18. Grinko, *op. cit.*, pp. 71–2. For details see later; his 'Plan velikikh rabot' was published as a pamphlet.

19. Rykov's closing speech to the *Sovnarkom*, *Pravda*, April 6, 1929.

20. *Ibid*.

21. Quoted from the Party Archives, *16-taya Konferentsiya, VKP(b)*, stenogramme. (Moscow, 1962), p. 794, note 135. We have already mentioned Rykov's Plan in Ch. 12.

22. Rykov, *Pravda*, April 6, 1929.

23. *ibid*.

24. *Bolshevik*, 1929, No. 23–4, p. 43.

25. A present-day Soviet viewpoint has rejected the *dvuletka* on the grounds that it dealt only with 'secondary matters such as the agricultural tax, prices policy, fertilizer, the agrominimum', and ignored the Party's line on industrialization and socialist recon-

struction of the countryside. See *16-taya Konferentsiya, VKP(b)*, stenogramme. (Moscow, 1962), p. 794, note 135.

26. For these figures see Grinko, *op. cit.*; Volf, *Planovoe Khozyaistvo*, 1929, No. 2, and *NAF*, 1929, No. 4; Resolution of the Fifth Congress of Soviets on the Five-year Plan in *Kollektivizatsiya selskogo khozyaistva*, doc. No. 41; Resolution of the Sixteenth Party Conference in *KPSS v Rezolyutsiyakh*, Vol. II, pp. 570–3.

27. Different texts give different figures, since the government was for ever changing them. Data relative to plan fulfilment are more important.

28. René Dumont, in his recent *Sovkhoz, Kolkhoz, et le Problématique Communisme*. (Paris, 1964), p. 54, reports that in 1940 only 3 million metric tons were produced.

29. *KPSS v Rezolyutsiyakh*, Vol. II, p. 573.

30. For example, the financial plans for agriculture were based to a large extent on the assumption that it would be possible to recoup the loans made to peasants within a reasonable time, although such an assumption was known to be unrealistic. See *NAF*, 1929 No. 6, p. 54.

31. He was to be executed as a saboteur in April 1933.

32. *Planovoe Khozyaistvo*, 1929, No. 2, and *NAF*, 1929, No. 4.

33. *Planovoe Khozyaistvo*, 1929, No. 2, p. 133.

34. *ibid.*

35. *16-taya Konferentsiya, VKP(b)*, stenogramme, p. 34; Volf, *NAF*, 1929, No. 4, p. 6.

36. These figures are those of the resolution of the Sixteenth Party Conference, see *KPSS v Rezolyutsiyakh*, Vol. II, p. 571. *Gosplan* was less ambitious.

37. Volf, *NAF*, 1929, No. 4, p. 6.

38. Veisberg, 'Leninskaya kooperatsiya v pyatiletnem plane', *Planovoe Khozyaistvo*, 1929, No. 3, p. 102.

39. See Kraev's criticism of the plan for Co-operation in 1928–9, 1932–3', *NAF*, 1929, No. 6.

40. Volf, *Planovoe Khozyaistvo*, 1929, No. 2, p. 111.

41. *Ibid*, p. 113.

42. *Ibid*, p. 106.

43. *Ibid*, p. 116; Veisberg, *Planovoe Khozyaistvo*, 1929, No. 3, p. 106.

44. Decision of the Central Committee of August 26, 1929. *Kollektivizatsiya selskogo khozyaistva*, doc. No. 52. In Russian the last expression is *rynochnaya stikhiya*.

45. Volf, *Planovoe Khozyaistvo*, 1929, No. 2, pp. 116–7.

46. Veisberg; *op. cit.*, p. 100; in *KPSS v Rezolyutsiyakh*, Vol. II,

p. 576 it is stated, in April 1929, that 'over a third of the peasants' were taking part in co-operation.

47. Grinko, *op. cit.*, p. 69–71.

48. Volf, *NAF*, 1929, No. 4, pp. 6, 8, passim.

49. Gosplan was fully aware that production of tractors was lagging behind and that the aid granted to the poor peasants and the serednyaks was inadequate. Volf, in *NAF*, 1929, No. 4, p. 6 speaks of an 'inadmissible' shortfall in the production of tractors, etc.

50. Grinko, *op. cit.*, pp. 71–2.

51. Sabsovich, *Planovoe Khozyaistvo*, 1929, No. 1, p. 103.

52. Speech by Bauman to a plenary session of the Moscow Party Committee, *Pravda*, June 16, 1929.

53. Kalinin, *16-taya Konferentsiya, VKP(b)*, stenogramme, p. 143.

54. Decision of the Central Committee of June 27, 1929, *Kollektivizatsiya selskogo khozyaistva*, doc. No. 46.

55. Kalinin, *5 ty S'ezd Sovetov*, stenogramme, bulletin No. 15, p. 39. Would he have said as much in November?

56. *5-ty S'ezd Sovetov*, stenogramme, bulletin No. 7, p. 8, likewise, Volf, *Planovoe Khozyaistvo*, 1929, No. 2, p. 103. Stalin himself said as much in April, *Bolshevik*, 1929, No. 23–4, p. 32.

57. Volf, *NAF*, 1929, No. 4, p. 8.

58. Kaminsky, *16-ty S'ezd, VKP(b)*, stenogramme, p. 187.

59. Kubyak, *16-ty S'ezd, VKP(b)*, stenogramme, pp. 200–1.

60. Bumper, 'Dalneishie vekhi kolkhoznogo stroitelstva', *Bolshevik*, 1929, No. 1, p. 35; Sharikov, *Bolshevik*, 1928, No. 16, pp. 58–60; Anissimov, 'O traktornykh kolonnakh', *Bolshevik*, 1929, No. 1, p. 48.

61. Kulikov, *NAF*, 1959, No. 2, p. 76.

62. Bumper, *op. cit.*, pp. 34–5.

63. Kalinin, *16-taya Konferentsiya, VKP(b)*, stenogramme, p. 142.

64. Kalinin, *16-taya Konferentsiya, VKP(b)*, stenogramme, p. 140, and *5-ty S'ezd Sovetov*, stenogramme, bulletin No. 19, pp. 3–4.

65. Kalinin, *ibid, loc. cit.*

66. Kalinin, *5-ty S'ezd Sovetov*, stenogramme, bulletin No. 19, p. 4. Rykov expressed the very same idea at the *Sixteenth Conference, 16-taya Konferentsiya, VKP(b)*, stenogramme, p. 9. For a contrary opinion see, for example, Tsylko, *NAF*, 1929, No. 11–12, pp. 154–5.

67. Markevich summed up his experiences in his book *Mezhselennye mashino-traktornye stantsii* (unobtainable). We have drawn upon the two speeches by Kalinin already mentioned, the text of the

model contract given in an appendix to the stenogramme of the Sixteenth Conference, the travel-notes of A. L. Strong, *The Soviets Conquer Wheat*. (New York, 1931), and various polemical articles.

68. Text of the model contract, *16-taya Konferentsiya, VKP(b)*, stenogramme, Appendix No. 2.

69. Kulikov, *NAF*, 1929, No. 5, p. 61.

70. *Ibid*, p. 67. By the end of the year Markevich's ideas were to be attacked as 'opportunist', but by then times had changed.

71. *Planovoe Khozyaistvo*, 1929, No. 11, p. 104.

72. A decision of the *STO*, in *Kollektivizatsiya selskogo khozyaistva*, doc. No. 44, p. 179–80.

73. On June 1, 1929 only a quarter of kolkhozes owned or were served by tractors. In or around October 1929 there were only 26,863 tractors in the entire Russian Republic. This figure is given by Danilov, (ed.), *Ocherki po istorii kollektivizatsii selskogo khozyaistva v soyuznykh respublikakh*. (Moscow, 1963), pp. 32, 82.

74. No one even considered at this time that livestock could be collectivized before stables and cow-sheds had been constructed.

75. Kulikov, *NAF*, 1926, No. 6, pp. 67–8; Lyubchenko, *16-taya Konferentsiya, VKP(b)*, stenogramme, p. 182.

76. Kulikov, article on the 'birth of the *MTS*', *NAF*, 1929, No. 2, pp. 73–8.

77. Lyubchenko, *16-taya Konferentsiya VKP(b)*, stenogramme, p. 182.

78. Kulikov, *NAF*, 1929, No. 6, passim.

79. Belenky, *Pravda*, November 15, 1929; Anissimov, *Bolshevik*, 1929, No. 1, p. 53.

80. See Bumper, *Bolshevik*, 1929; No. 1, p. 89; Kulikov, *NAF*, 1929, No. 6; Anissimov, *Bolshevik*, 1929, No. 1.

81. Anissimov, *Bolshevik*, 1929, No. 1, p. 52. What has been translated as 'the concerted efforts of the peasants themselves' is in Russian *obshchestvennost*.

82. Rykov, *5-ty S'ezd Sovetov*, stenogramme, bulletin No. 2, pp. 18–19.

83. This speech was not published until the end of 1929, in *Bolhevik*, 1929, No. 23–24. A further thirty pages, omitted from *Bolshevik*, are given in *Sochineniya*, Vol. XII, 'O pravom uklone v VKP(b)'. The restored passages are pp. 1–10, 49–56, 92–103, 106–7, and pp. 1–2 of the introduction.

84. *Bolshevik*, 1929, No. 23–4, p. 27.

85. *ibid*, p. 17.

86. *ibid*, p. 16.

87. *ibid*, pp. 18–20.

88. *ibid*, pp. 24–5. The speech was interrupted several times by Rozit and others, criticizing Stalin, and supporting Bukharin.

89. *KPSS v Rezolyutsiyakh*, Vol. II, pp. 576–7.

90. *Bolshevik*, 1929, No. 23–4, p. 27.

91. Lyashchenko, *op. cit.* (see Ch. 1, Note 42), Vol. III, p. 259; Trifonov, *op. cit.* (see Ch. 2, Note 9), pp. 131–9; Stalin, *Sochineniya*, Vol. XI, speeches made during the sessions of the Central Committee of July 1928 and April 1929.

92. To this day the functioning of Soviet trade organizations still shows the effects of this ill-advised elimination of the private operator from the various services.

93. Mendelson, *Planovoe Khozyaistvo*, 1929, No. 8, pp. 8–9, 17.

94. See for example, Rykov, *16-taya Konferentsiya, VKP(b)*, stenogramme, p. 18.

95. Stalin, *Bolshevik*, 1929, No. 23–4, p. 32.

96. *ibid*. The resolutions of the *16th Conference*, in enumerating what are considered to be the most important tasks, mention the improvement of agriculture last.

97. *Bolshevik*, 1929, No. 23–4, p. 36.

98. *ibid*.

99. Molotov, *Bolshevik*, 1929, No. 22, pp. 16–17.

100. *ibid*, p. 28.

101. Rykov, *16-taya Konferentsiya, VKP(b)*, stenogramme, pp. 6–7; Kviring, *Planovoe Khozyaistvo*, 1929, No. 7, p. 7.

102. Kaminsky, *Pravda*, June 20, 1929; Mikoyan, *Bolshevik*, 1929, No. 15; Milyutin, *NAF*, 1929, No. 9; Stalin, *Sochineniya*, Vol. XII, pp. 125–6.

103. *Pravda*, September 1 and 4, 1929.

104. Jasny, *op. cit.* (see Ch. 11, Note 48), p. 12.

105. Stalin, *Bolshevik*, 1929, No. 23–4, pp. 16–17.

106. Plenary session of the Central Committee, 1929, *KPSS v Rezolyutsiyakh*, Vol. II, p. 566.

107. Stalin, *Sochineniya*, Vol. XII, p. 2.

108. *Pravda*, November 3, 1929.

109. Serge, *op. cit.* (see Ch. 6, Note 71), p. 274.

Chapter 14

THE CRISIS CONTINUES

According to Mikoyan, and to official observers who studied the situation at the time, the economic year 1928–9 was more difficult than the preceding year, and very much worse than *Gosplan* and the government had anticipated.[1] As we have already seen, in Rykov's opinion the country was experiencing a prolonged economic crisis, and a further year or two must elapse before there could be any hope of improvement.[2] The outstanding feature of the whole situation at this stage was that the crisis and its attendant difficulties were steadily worsening.

Meanwhile, the country had to subsist on the fairly poor harvest of 1928, and on such supplies as had been obtained from the procurements during the winter and the spring of 1929. These had yielded less than in previous years, and the results had declined from the level reached in 1928, the year of the emergency measures. As a consequence of earlier losses of winter wheat in the Ukraine and the North Caucasus, the 1928 harvest in the main grain-producing regions was again a bad one. Owing to the dearth of seed corn, and to the treatment which had been meted out to the peasants by the local authorities, there was a drop in sowings of winter wheat during the autumn of 1928, and this had further serious repercussions not only on the national economy but also on the peasants and the authorities, who were now faced with the additional burden of making up the loss during the spring sowing of 1929. The Party had, in fact, endeavoured to conduct the spring sowing campaign under its own direct supervision along the 'class lines' urged upon it by the Politburo. But despite the claim that this had resulted in an increase in sowings in the farms of the poor and middle peasants, the Party had not succeeded in arresting the downward trend in production among the better-off peasants. In 'class terms', the campaign might have been successful, but this still could not offset the loss to the economy in practical terms; among the least efficient sector of the peasantry, the increase in sowings had allegedly been of the order of 2%, the remainder of the increase being attributable to the socialized sector, but there was little likelihood that this would be reflected in increased availabilities of grain on the market during the coming autumn.[3]

Because of the lack of fodder, and also as a reaction against the abuses to which the peasants had been subjected, there was a drop in livestock holdings, and this was reflected in a temporary abundance of meat supplies, with an accompanying decline in production and sales of butter, milk and eggs, all of which products were becoming increasingly scarce in the countryside.[4]

Since the government were unable to provide grain for the peasants in the non-grain-producing areas, there was growing pressure from the population of these regions on the free market and on the towns, which were usually better supplied. Large quantities of bread began to disappear from the towns,[5] as the *meshochniki* filled their sacks (*meshok*) with loaves, which they then carried off for resale in areas which were short of bread. In an effort to stop this disastrous leakage, the government adopted restrictive measures and tightened up the rationing regulations which had been in force in the towns since December. In February, ration cards were introduced.[6]

The ration per head of the population was small, and the supply system frequently broke down owing to shortage of supplies and the lack of a properly organized distribution network. An industrial worker received 600 grammes of bread per day and 300 grammes for each member of his family. Sugar was rationed to one kilo per month, oil to something between 200 grammes and one litre, and the tea ration was very small and irregular. Towards the end of the year, the standard rations became still smaller.[7]

In view of the inadequacy of the rations, the workers were forced to buy on the free market, which was already subject to considerable pressure from the 'non-working elements' who had no ration cards.

The small non-industrial towns received no supplies from the government either, and for this reason the roads were thronged, summer and winter, with sledges and carts, as peasants and others who had anything to sell set out on the long trek in search of bread, making for the grain-producing regions, and the Volga in particular.[8]

Conditions were ideal for the black marketeers and the speculators. When pressure was put on the entrepreneurs in the town, they speedily reacted by closing down their legitimate businesses, and many of them went over to various forms of illegal trading which, although hazardous, proved very lucrative. Their activities in this field contributed towards the disruption of the supply system and of the national economy.[9]

Prices of food and grain on the free market now began to rise alarmingly. In March 1929, the gap between the official price of wheat and the free market price was of the following order: Ukraine: +282; North Caucasus: +230; Urals: +190; Siberia: +57. Corresponding figures for rye were: +365; +241; +308.[10]

The rise in prices of grain and livestock products brought about a general rise in prices, including those in the state sector, which was unable to withstand the inflationary pressure. In view of its serious financial position, the State increased the monetary flow by some 23%, thus helping to reduce the purchasing power of the rouble still further.[11] As a result, all the government's plans and forecasts relating to prices and financial balances were upset, and despite official denials, real wages began to go down.[12] The drop in the standard of living, together with the increase in production norms in the factories, the uncertainties of the supply system and poor treatment on the part of the authorities all helped to create profound discontent among the workers, who protested against the increased norms and the 'socialist emulation' which the State was urging upon them. There were frequent strikes, particularly in the Donbas and in Smolensk, and no doubt in many other places as well.[13] Complaints began to pour into the arbitration tribunals who were obliged to deal with a great number of labour disputes.

The workers reacted to the decline in their living standards by absenteeism, or by abandoning the factories. The general fluidity of the labour situation, with workers on the move in search of employers who might be able to offer them better supplies, was bad for labour discipline, and inevitably had an adverse effect on productivity and on the quality of production. The government retaliated by strengthening the powers of the administration, and in particular by reinforcing the famous principle of *edinonachalie*, which vested absolute authority in the director of an enterprise and which gave rise to a growing degree of despotism in enterprise management.[14] At the same time, an effort was made to curb absenteeism by introducing increasingly severe legislation to deal with it.

In addition to the serious unrest in the countryside, there was now mounting pressure in the towns, and this was mainly reflected in a worsening of the relations between the régime and the workers. At the same time, the power which the administration exercised over the people, and which the Politburo in turn exercised over the administration, tended to grow more dictatorial as the major construction projects got under way, and the situation on the 'grain front' began to dominate all other considerations.

1. The 'Uralo-Siberian Solution' (the procurements campaign in the winter of 1929)

The Soviet régime was now facing the problem of grain supplies with greater anxiety than ever, for the 'grain front' had proved to be the source of periodic disturbances which shook the entire economy, disrupting plans, disorganizing production and plunging the whole country into chaos.

Meanwhile, the latest procurements campaign was being carried on under mounting difficulties. According to the official figures, the 1928 grain harvest, which would be the source of the current procurements and the country's food supplies for the whole of the coming year, had shown a drop of some 500–600 million poods on the previous year's results. Frost followed by drought in the Ukraine, and to some extent also in the North Caucasus, the Central Black Earth region and the North West, had been the reason for the very bad harvests. Consequently, the result of the procurement campaign in these grain-growing regions had been disastrous. By April 1st of the previous year, the Ukraine had provided 200 million poods of grain; its contribution had now sunk to a meagre 26–7 million poods. The yield from the North Caucasus in the same period was one quarter of the previous year's total, that of the Central Black Earth region one eighth. The figure for the Eastern regions was double that of the previous year, but this was not sufficient to make up for the losses in the chief grain-producing areas.[15]

The official source for these figures attempted to put forward the view that the failure was attributable solely to climatic conditions, but several authors suggested[16] that the poor success of the procurements campaign was also a reflection of social factors, and of the policy which the government were pursuing. Stalin himself admitted that social factors had played an important part in the disaster, and stated that in future a great deal of grain would have to be extracted 'by calculated pressure on the kulaks and the better-off strata of the peasants in the rural areas'.[17]

Figures from the Commissariat of Trade showed that there had been a continuous decrease in deliveries of grain from November 1928[18] and throughout the ensuing months. Alarmed at this turn of events, the Party adopted the coercive measures which were henceforth to bear the stamp of official approval, only this time, it was claimed, the methods used would be different. It was important not to break faith with the peasants, who had been promised[19] that there would be no more emergency measures of the kind employed in 1928. As it happened, very little use was in fact made of article 107, and the body of measures which was adopted during the winter of 1928–9 came to be known as the 'Uralo-Siberian method'. This was defined as 'temporary emergency measures reinforced by support from the bednyak and serednyak elements',[20] as opposed to emergency measures pure and simple. In practice, the distinction was far from clear. According to Stalin, the principle involved was that of 'pressure from below', that is, from the mass of the peasantry, but he also admitted that additional pressure was supplied by the authorities, and reinforced by 'emergency measures directed at the kulaks'. 'And what harm is there in that?' he added, for the benefit of the 'oversensitive' Bukharinists. . . .[21]

We should add that these anti-kulak measures, as Stalin and other sources acknowledged,[22] were aimed at 'the kulaks and the better-off peasants' (or 'strong serednyaks', as it was sometimes put). As was clearly to be expected, the serednyaks, having been included in the kulak category, were at once subjected to numerous *peregiby*[23] on the old familiar lines.

This year, it was laid down that the amount of grain to be provided by each village would be agreed by so-called democratic decision of the village society, so that the quantity finally fixed would be binding on the entire village. However, there being no legal provisions as to what constituted a quorum of the village society, it was sufficient in practice for the local officials and members of the Party cell, together with the local bednyak group if there was one, to act as a representative meeting of the village, and to take whatever decisions were necessary. The available sources tell us nothing about what action was taken by the local authorities in cases where the assembly refused to agree amounts which, as the Central Committee subsequently admitted, were all too often excessive.[24] In such instances one may well ask how the local inhabitants came to agree on delivery figures which were later acknowledged as having been too high, and, as in many other cases too, it is not hard to gauge the extent of the strictly 'official' element in the coercive measures which were adopted.

There were a number of factors which caused the peasants to build up reserves of grain; for one thing, there was the poor harvest and the scarcity of fodder, coupled with shortages in the regions which had suffered climatic reverses, and in the non-grain-producing regions; there was also a general tendency to hold back until the prospects for the coming harvest became clearer. This was a normal reaction in the circumstances. The people in the towns, where supplies were short and rationing was in force, reacted in the same way.[25] As a result, the supply of agricultural produce inevitably decreased.

In view of the disparity between the prices paid by the State and prices on the free market, the peasants' reaction was both predictable and entirely natural.[26] Officially, no action had yet been taken to put an end to the free market. The peasants considered that they were exercising both a traditional and a *de facto* right in selling in the market, and that such action was consistent not only with the provisions of NEP but indeed with the law itself. Naturally, those who had more to sell were more directly concerned than their fellows, but even the bednyak or the serednyak felt himself cheated if he was prevented from selling his grain for the best price he could get. Nor was he unduly troubled if prices should rise so steeply as to smack of speculation. As one author noted disapprovingly, 'in a whole number of regions, other social elements besides those of the better-off peasants were caught up in the rush' and 'even the poor peasants in the villages sometimes acted as henchmen of the kulaks in grain speculation'.[27] In fact, this must have been a widespread phenomenon; through the operation of elementary economic forces, it affected even those peasants who were communists, thus weakening the impact of Party propaganda when it exhorted the peasants to sell their grain exclusively through government channels.[28]

The procurement agencies found that they were obliged to raise the prices being paid to the peasants, to a level far in excess of that authorized by the Centre. The additional expenditure thus incurred (some 150 million roubles) proved yet another burden on the government's finances, which were already seriously overstrained.[29] As it was, prices on the free market had already risen too steeply for this measure to have any effect.

One may well imagine the bitterness and vexation of the Politburo when faced with the incorrigible obstinacy of *homo economicus*, who seemed deliberately bent on frustrating all the régime's most ambitious plans. Meanwhile, the authorities had not failed to profit from the lessons of 1928, and they were now armed for the task in hand with coercive powers which, in their severity and scope, sometimes exceeded the earlier emergency measures.

Pravda mentions at this time the government's increasing efforts to mobilize the financial resources of the peasantry, thereby mopping up their surplus funds and forcing them to sell more grain to the procurements agencies.[30] In fact, the combined effect of various forms of taxation, including local levies, state taxes, contributions to the industrialization loan, subscriptions to the co-operative organizations, etc., was to drain off a markedly greater amount of money from the villages than in the previous year.[31]

Towards the end of 1928, because of the poor success of the procurements campaign in those regions which were normally the most productive, the government stepped up its demands in Siberia,[32] and probably also in other eastern regions such as the Urals and the Volga. The peasants in these areas, having already partly fulfilled their previously agreed quotas for grain deliveries, were greatly angered at the government's lack of good faith, and at the further demands which were now being made upon them. It was in response to this situation that the so-called 'Uralo-Siberian' solution was devised. The Party secretaries for the Lower and Middle Volga, and several other speakers at the Sixteenth Conference, reported that the same method was being tried in their regions, and also in Kazakhstan and a number of other areas. Lominadze incurred some disapproval for referring to 'the method' by the rather simpler term of 'emergency measures'.[33]

Those who were speculating or trafficking in grain now became the object of a whole series of preventive measures. While it was undoubtedly true that the private traders had succeeded in persuading the peasants to part with large quantities of grain, attempts to curb their activities failed to produce any result; indeed, the efforts of the private traders during the winter campaign were rewarded with even more grain than had been obtained by them during the previous spring.

It is probable that the peasants who simply sold grain on the free market were more seriously affected by the anti-speculation measures than the genuine speculators, for the level of free market prices was so high at this time that any peasant was in constant danger of being accused of speculation. There were, too, many other ways in which the authorities could prevent the peasants from using the market.[34]

While all this was going on, the Party was enlisting the support of its rural members in an effort to impose an economic boycot on any peasants who hoarded grain and refused to fulfil the agreed delivery quotas. This action, backed by administrative pressure, caused an unprecedented upheaval in the countryside.

Those who resisted were expelled from the co-operatives, and thereby deprived of supplies of goods at fixed prices. The kulaks and better-off peasants were subject to the punitive *pyatikratka* (a fine payable in grain, the amount of which was five times the quantity in arrears). In principle, this penalty was supposed to be enforced by decision of the village society, but the societies must have failed to display sufficient zeal in the matter to satisfy the local authorities, for in April 1929 the Russian *VTsIK* authorized the *selsovety* to impose the *pyatikratka* on the kulaks on their own initiative.[35]

Thousands of kulaks, or better-off peasants, were brought before the tribunals and sentenced to have their belongings confiscated.[36] Penalties of such draconian severity should have been covered by those articles of the penal code which related to speculation, not necessarily article 107 which was rarely invoked, but certain other articles. However, these provisions were not thought to be sufficiently comprehensive for the purposes of the grain war which the régime was waging, and in June the government of the RSFSR found a more convenient legal foundation for its action by expanding an article of the penal code which covered the non-fulfilment of compulsory services. To this, the following clause was added:

'Refusal to deliver grain in fulfilment of the voluntary undertaking entered into by the village, a joint refusal by a group of rural households, and offering resistance to the implementation of the plan for building up reserves of grain [will be dealt with—M.L.] in accordance with part three of this article.'

Part three of article 61 provided for sentences of up to two years' imprisonment, confiscation of property and the possible deportation of the guilty party.[37] This enactment already formed part of the body of measures which had been prepared in anticipation of the coming campaign for 1929–30, which we shall be discussing later. But, with the possible exception of deportation, all the penalties which we have mentioned were in fact in general operation before the advent of the new clause.

Needless to say, these measures which were ostensibly aimed at exerting 'social pressure' fell hardest, in many cases, on the middle peasants. Sheboldaev, Party Secretary of the Lower Volga, discussing the abuses which had taken place during the 1928–9 procurements campaign, underlined this point when he said that the worst feature of the situation was that 'in some cases it is not the kulak but the serednyak who suffers when, with the government's backing, social pressure is brought to bear.'

This was an old story, and Sheboldaev went on to describe the circumstances in which such things could happen. According to him, the fault lay with the 'Right-wing' supporters, who failed to identify the village kulaks. Faced with government instructions to take a certain quantity of grain from the kulaks, those local officials who had 'Right-wing' sympathies claimed that there were no kulaks in their midst, and transferred the appropriate quotas to the serednyaks, together with the accompanying coercive measures.[38]

Apart from his use of the term 'Right-wing', which is irrelevant in this context, Sheboldaev's statement provides a clear indication of the nature of the administrative procedures involved. He does not even suggest that the village assemblies were responsible for what happened, and indeed it is hard to see how the 'basic mass' of the serednyaks could have chosen, of their own volition, to instigate discriminatory treatment of this kind against themselves. The phrase 'our organizations and our *obshchestvennos*' which Sheboldaev uses, means the Party cell, if there was one, the local officials, and the local bednyak group, or simply a number of bednyaks with no group organization.

During the campaign under discussion, the authorities had tried harder than ever before to enlist the co-operation of the 'bednyak element'. However, despite decrees and exhortations from the Centre, the work of organizing bednyak groups had made no significant progress; groups were formed, and subsequently lapsed through lack of attention on the part of those who were nominally in charge of bednyak activity. In the majority of *selsovety* there were no such groups. Similarly, the co-operative organizations and regional centres which had also been enjoined to form bednyak groups set about the task in a half-hearted manner and were no more successful than the selsovets had been. Indeed, the bednyak organizations were yet another of those near-myths which flourished so frequently on the fringe of the Soviet régime's real preoccupations, a purely administrative exercise which the men on the spot carried out reluctantly and uncomprehendingly, and which had arisen in the first place from an attempt to relate the theory of the class struggle to a rural context in which it did not fit properly.

Such semi-fictions had their origin in fact—the existence of poor peasants, better-off peasants and kulaks, for example. But the attempt to superimpose on these facts a preconceived theory which was ill-adapted to the realities of a complex situation, led to the formulation of concepts and conclusions which were fallacious, thus: 'the bednyak, mainstay of the proletariat, an essential element in the system of dictatorship by the proletariat'; 'the serednyak, wavering between capitalism and the proletariat'; or again: 'the kulak, the rural capitalist, dangerous and implacable enemy of the régime', etc.

The element of unreality and ambiguity in these concepts reached its highest point when they were formulated as part of the body of Stalinist doctrine.

In the context of everyday life, it was inevitable that these ideas should undergo a further distortion when translated into vague and impractical instructions which were then 'wrongly' carried out. They thus became increasingly detached from their true social content, and assumed the quasi-mythical form in which they were used as coercive instruments by 'deviationist' local officials of the traditional *derzhimorda* type.

During the campaign, the authorities had in fact enlisted a certain amount of support from among the bednyaks, but the latter were themselves victims of the procurements policy. Many of them resisted, and in so doing were branded by the authorities as 'henchmen of the kulaks' (*podkulachniki*).[39]

One of the surest methods of bringing pressure to bear on the peasants was the widespread practice among State trading organizations of effecting direct exchanges between supplies of manufactured goods and supplies of grain. Any peasant, whether rich or poor, who failed to hand over his quota of grain was accordingly debarred from obtaining goods which were in short supply. In effect, this amounted to depriving him of necessities like oil for his lamp, matches, nails, cloth, etc.[40] This device, which only a short time before had been officially condemned as extortion, now became a generally accepted method, and before long the Central Committee were to recommend that it be made compulsory.[41]

The combined effect of these economic measures, together with the financial pressure and direct controls applied by the State, was to make life very difficult for any peasant who attempted to evade his obligations, or who was behindhand in fulfilling them. As a result, the social climate in the countryside became charged with tension and bitterness, as one of the delegates to the 5th Congress of Soviets in May 1929 indignantly pointed out.

This peasant delegate was convinced that the methods which were being used were contrary to the régime's intentions (had he not, after all, read numerous articles in the press supporting the drive against the kulaks, but at the same time warning against the abuses to which it gave rise?). He criticized the local authorities who failed to read their newspapers, were ignorant of the law and waged war upon the kulaks by means which overstepped the bounds of what was either lawful or acceptable. As an example, he quoted certain incidents which had taken place in the Novo Ussovski district, in the Tomsk region in Siberia: 'In this district', said the delegate indignantly, 'there have been serious malpractices. In some of the villages, demonstrations were organized; the schoolchildren and some of the more backward elements among the bednyaks were rounded up, and made to parade through the village, stopping in front of the houses of kulaks, and sometimes serednyaks, and shouting when the word was given—"Here lives an enemy of the Soviet régime". Blackboards were nailed on the houses carrying inscriptions to the same effect, and strict orders were given that the boards must not be removed. One peasant was even given a board of this sort which he was forced to carry, although he could not lift it'. Finally, said the delegate, permission had been given to have the board carried on horseback; he was shocked by the fact that such incidents could go on happening when the press were preaching non-violence. He further relates that in Siberia the peasants who had any surplus at all were squeezed 'to the last pood of grain'.[42]

Here was a simple peasant, who called a spade a spade, and had not realized that these coercive measures were part of the official line. He must have received the news that he was a right-wing deviationist with great bitterness and a total lack of comprehension. Neither he nor the great majority of local officials, even as far up as *obkom* level in some cases, had any idea what was meant by this term.[43]

The middle peasants, Party members included, and certain *selsovet* officials, were opposed to the methods which were used to extract grain, and did everything possible to evade the procurements, which were universally hated. Consequently the *selsovety*, the rural Party cells and the district administrations had been undergoing a continuous series of purges since the beginning of 1928, with the result that the composition of these ill-fated organizations was the subject of radical and virtually incessant change.

During the latest elections, there had already been a change in the membership of the village soviets, involving the removal of serednyaks and their replacement by a considerable number of bednyaks, who at this stage formed a majority inside the *selsovety*; similarly, a greater number of the posts of chairman and secretary were now held by Party and *Komsomol* members. These changes were effected while the procurements campaign was under way, but failed to produce the hoped-for stability in *selsovet* structures. After the elections, changes were still taking place, and by March 1930 82% of the *selsovet* chairmen had been replaced: of these, only 16% had gone voluntarily, the rest having been dismissed.

In twenty districts in the Smolensk province, 304 chairmen out of 616 were relieved of their duties during the year 1929: of the 304, 258 were private farmers.[44]

The resistance offered by the broad mass of the peasantry was mainly passive in character, finding its expression in sales of grain on the free market, wherever possible, and in efforts to keep grain from falling into the hands of officials and procurement agents; however, with mounting government pressure, they began to retaliate in other ways as well. Some villages, driven to desperation, withheld supplies in a form of strike action known as the *volynka*. These *volynki*, particularly in Siberia, were summarily repressed, and Syrtsov regarded it as a matter for self-congratulation that they had ended in an increased flow of the grain which had previously been held back from the government's procurement agents.[45]

At the beginning of the year, a more serious peasant uprising broke out in Adzharie, an autonomous mountain region in Georgia, and this was put down with great severity by the military. Another peasant rising in the Pakov region was reported by a Russian correspondent of the *Menshevik* press abroad.[46] Regarded as isolated phenomena, none of these revolts and uprisings were of particular gravity. The authorities must have been more alarmed by the counter-terror with which the peasants and especially, no doubt, the better-off among them, retaliated against local officials, bednyak activists, procurement agents and rural press correspondents.

There was a lot of shooting in the villages, particularly during election and procurements campaigns. Anna Louise Strong, the

American journalist, was informed by official sources that 300 procurement agents had been killed in the period from 1927–9.[47]

We learn from other sources, too, that there was an increase in acts of violence in the countryside during the collectivization and procurements campaigns. During the period from December 1928 to February 1st 1929, when elections and procurements were both under way, the records of the Moscow *prokuror* show 101 cases of terrorism, including killings, woundings, assault and arson. The records for the previous year show only thirteen such cases. For the RSFSR as a whole, *VTsIK* mentions a total of 702 cases during 1928, most of these relating to the months of October and November. The all-Union figure for December was 377. During nine months of 1929, there were 1,002 cases in the RSFSR, including 384 killings, 70 woundings, etc. Records for the Ukraine show 300 cases of violence in October 1928 and February 1929.[48]

Anti-Soviet activity was clearly on the increase, and the counter-terror was to become even more marked in the following winter. The *zagotovki* had ceased to be a normal economic procedure, carried through under relatively calm conditions, as they had been up till 1928; instead, they had developed into an offensive launched by the State, in which the State's agents ran considerable risks. The same was true of collectivization.

The peasants, and particularly the better-off among them, or those who were so classified, were subjected to such pressures that they were frequently driven to abandon their farms. They were persecuted in a number of ways, and incurred severe penalties, ranging from the *pyatikratka* to sentences of imprisonment and confiscation of their property; in such conditions, they sometimes retaliated with acts of violence.

However, care should be taken not to overstress the importance of such acts of terrorism at this stage. Given the size of the USSR, the figures quoted would not support the contention that the problem was as yet a very serious one. Soviet sources have been reluctant to publish any overall figures; if such figures had been disclosed, they might well have cast some doubt on the official presentation of the kulak as a mortal enemy of the régime who was preparing to overthrow it by force of arms.

It should also be said that in a countryside where hundreds of thousands of dwellings went on fire accidentally every year, and where assaults and violence were the not uncommon outcome of the many brawls and disputes which broke out, it was easy in the overheated atmosphere of political strife at the time to connect straightforward accidents, or acts of 'kulak' violence, with terrorist activity. Some of the cases aforementioned must certainly have related to

attacks by kulaks on bednyaks, which were not necessarily a manifestation of the 'class struggle'.[49] Further information which we have
on kulak activities gives, for example, a figure of 1,000 'illegal' kulak
meetings which were supposed to have been uncovered in the RSFSR
during the winter of 1928–9[50] (it should be noted that there were
over 50,000 *selsovety* and over 100,000 villages) but here again there
is nothing to suggest the existence of organized terrorist activities
on a large scale.

Resistance was mainly passive: subterfuges, concealment of grain,
and the like. The peasants had no sense whatsoever of having the
upper hand.

The leadership wholeheartedly congratulated themselves on having
been bold enough to take a firm line, and on having perfected the
'Uralo-Siberian' method which had enabled them to overcome their
problems on the grain front. The laudatory remarks were mainly
addressed to the General Secretary who, as chief architect of the
plan, was likely to be gratified by such expressions of confidence in
his policy.

However, the régime continued to meet with growing difficulties
in all sectors. Despite enthusiastic propaganda for the 'strong arm'
methods which were being employed, there was violent criticism
among the Moscow cadres, who maintained that such techniques
were not only harmful but completely ineffectual.[51] Indeed at this
stage it would have been hard to give the lie to the critics. The
amount of grain brought in by the procurements was 20% less than
in the previous year, a figure which speaks for itself. The poor success
of the procurements campaign, together with the reduction in livestock holdings, were ample indication that 1929 would be a year of
even greater difficulty and growing political tension. The Politburo
were desperately seeking a way out. As we already know, the General
Secretary had his own solutions, and these were different in character
from the views current in the upper echelons of the government departments concerned.

2. *The cost of over-rapid industrialization*

The troubled state of affairs in the agricultural sector had had
serious repercussions on the national economy as a whole, but this
was not the only reason for the advanced state of tension, or rather
the crisis, through which the country had been living since the first
year of the Five-year Plan. A further cause must be sought in the
strain imposed both on the people and the economy by the drive to
industrialize, and the speed at which industrialization was to be
carried out. The results of the first annual plan (for the year 1928–9)
would naturally be a decisive factor in determining the course of the

plans for the coming years, and the policy which should be followed in the light of previous experience.

In addition, the flood of information on the implementation of this annual plan, and the various appraisals of the situation which reached the Politburo during the second half of the economic year, played a key role in the momentous decisions which were subsequently taken in November and December 1929.

Ostensibly, the note sounded in the official reports was one of triumph. The global figures for the volume of investment, the general growth indices for industrial production, the contribution of the state sector to the national economy, and quantitative successes in the domain of collectivization, had all exceeded the objectives laid down in the Five-year Plan. The desired rate and amount of growth had been achieved, and these were regarded as the supreme criteria of success.

The November 1929 Plenum reported that the planned sector of industry had shown an increase of 24% in production, as compared with an initial forecast of 21·4%.[52] However, the fact was that the global figures concealed many weaknesses and cases of non-fulfilment of plans in various sectors; in some instances, there had even been a downward trend in production. Despite the flourish of trumpets with which the government announced their success at the time, recent researchers have expressed the gravest doubts about these successes, and have indeed been led to question the real importance of the role supposedly played by the Plan during those years.[53]

The Plan, as conceived by *Gosplan*, was based mainly on attainment of a number of so-called 'qualitative' objectives, such as, for example, the lowering of costs, increases in labour productivity and in yield per hectare, etc. *All of these factors were human factors, in that they depended for their success on goodwill, devotion to duty, pride in the work in hand, efficient organization and initiative on the part of the population as a whole. In so far as the 'human element' was concerned, the régime suffered a severe setback.*

Failure to achieve the desired reduction in costs, and the hoped-for improvement in yields, must be attributed, firstly, to the excessively rapid growth rates which were demanded, secondly, to lack of proper co-ordination among the various branches of the economy, thirdly, to inefficiency on the part of the administrators, who were overwhelmed by the demands which were made upon them, and ill-equipped for the work which they had to undertake. But above all, this failure must be seen as a general reaction against falling living standards and mounting administrative pressure.[54]

The demand for labour increased, and the resultant drain on the wages fund proved to be greater than had been foreseen (a similar example was quoted earlier on, in connection with the government's additional expenditure on grain) so that the financial plan, which had been insecurely based from the very outset, was thrown out of balance.[55] The government attempted to redress this imbalance by increasing the monetary flow, and by exerting increased fiscal pressure.[56] It also exerted pressure of a more physical kind on the workers, by greatly intensifying the demands made upon them in their work.

The workers, many of whom were recent recruits from the country-side and, as such, unused to factory discipline, and to work norms and rations, sought to escape from these pressures by moving from one factory to another; the resulting instability in the labour situation had a disastrous effect on productivity. The time lost in queuing at the shops only served to make matters worse, and productivity fell still further in consequence.

From the time when the plan was put into operation, another disquieting symptom made its appearance: there was a *deterioration in the quality of manufactured goods.*[57] In the years which followed, the amount of bad workmanship continued to increase, despite the government's efforts to cure this particular ill. As a result, machines frequently broke down, or were put out of action for lack of the necessary spare parts, tools proved unserviceable after a short time, and clothes were dear and wore out quickly. One has only to read a sample of the innumerable complaints which reached the press from consumers, including a considerable number of peasants, about the poor quality of production compared with that of pre-war days, to see what a damaging effect this failure had on the popular image or industrialization, to say nothing of the tremendous loss to the economy which was involved.

From this time on, waste was to become a characteristic feature of Soviet industrialization methods. It reflected the absence of any genuine system of planning in a country where the plan, as presented, had become a fetish. For lack of proper intersector co-ordination, development of one branch of the economy was impeded by another; in this way, for example, lack of the necessary production of non-ferrous metals proved a stumbling-block to progress in the machinery industry,[58] major building projects were halted owing to shortage of building materials, and the endless shortages of fuel, metal, etc., led to innumerable breakdowns and bottlenecks in production.

In the context of economic planning, one outstanding and inexcus-able defect, which was to persist for a whole epoch, involving the country in incalculable losses, was the government's propensity for embarking on large-scale building projects without having made sufficient provision beforehand for training the necessary cadres.

This problem of cadres, although an easily foreseeable one, always took the government unawares.

The reason was always the same, and it lay in the approach which was characteristic of the Stalinist dictatorship: act first and think later. This is one of the factors which must largely be held responsible for the poverty and misery which the population suffered, and for the way in which the dictatorial apparatus tightened its control when faced with an objectively explosive situation which could only be aggravated by such procedures. This was to become particularly obvious in the developments which took place in the countryside at the close of the year.[59]

From this time on, the country was transformed into one vast building site, a fact which in itself was encouraging enough; unfortunately, the projects which were undertaken always swallowed up a greater amount of resources than had been anticipated, they took longer to complete and thereby immobilized too much capital, and contributed still further to the general waste and disorganization. There were times when the whole immense task of reconstruction went forward amid scenes of the utmost confusion, so much so that the government rapidly adopted a solution which was the very antithesis of planning. This consisted of designating priority projects (*udarnye stroiki*) in an effort to salvage the most vital elements of the plan from the chaos in which the Soviet economy was plunged during the first quinquennium.

It was impossible to calculate what the cost of all this waste must have been to a country like the USSR, which was not rich in capital assets. Many examples come to mind, among them the following, reported by Krzhizhanovsky, the Chairman of *Gosplan*, shortly before he was transferred. 'It is a known fact that almost 30% of our consignments of supplies go bad in the distribution channels before they ever reach the consumer'.[60] This was happening in a country which was going through a period of the most acute shortage.

Global figures for increased production cannot be regarded as the main criterion of success. Given economy in the use of resources, and the elimination of waste by more efficient management, combined with a more rational approach to problems of planning and co-ordination, similar or even greater progress could have been achieved within a more humane and democratic social framework, and it may be that these are more valid criteria by which to judge a country's attainments.

The habit of 'tight' planning was largely responsible for the dissipation of material resources and, above all, the terrible wastage of human potential which was also to become a feature of industrialization under Stalin. *The interests of the individual were sacrificed in the name of progress of a kind that was to be assessed exclusively in terms of material criteria.* Plans of this kind, however, were presented as the very acme of wisdom. They also provided a ready-made excuse for the steadily mounting difficulties which beset the régime.

The failures which occurred in the 1928–9 annual plan were the result of over-ambitious objectives and the repercussions which these had on the activities of the industrial and agricultural sectors.

The biggest setbacks were those experienced in agriculture. We have already discussed the procurements problem in some detail. Not only did performance in the agricultural sector fall short of the objectives of the plan, but there was a downward trend in production in the most important branches. It was already apparent that the 1929 harvest would probably be poorer than that of 1928.[61] Understandably enough, in view of the unrest in the countryside and the despair which had seized so many of the peasants, the investments which the plan had counted on from the private sector had not taken place.[62]

There was a very marked drop in the production of industrial crops. The reduction in the sugar beet crop was disastrous, and production of hemp, sunflower and potatoes was also down. There had been a slight upward trend in flax and cotton, but even so the targets fixed by the plan had not been reached.[63]

The new improved prices for grain had contributed in no small measure to the shortfall in industrial crops, and the failure in the latter branch had immediate repercussions in the industrial sector. The food industry failed to fulfil its plan, and in some cases also showed a decline in production. This was likewise true of certain branches of light industry.[64] A number of measures which had been devised in order to improve yields in agriculture were not implemented. The chemical industry had not even fulfilled 70% of its plan. Similarly, the plans for the production and supply of agricultural machinery were not executed, and there were, in addition, constant delays in the delivery of materials and equipment, which often arrived too late in the season to fulfil the purpose for which they had been required.

On a whole series of projects which were of the greatest importance to agriculture, such as the liming of the fields, the organization of stations for the hiring of equipment, the fitting-up of repair depots, work was either at a standstill or had not even been started.[65]

Alongside the shortages in the supply of food and agricultural raw materials, there was now an unexpected increase in those factors which contributed to demand (an increase in the labour force beyond the limits foreseen by the plan, a constant increase in the amount of investment required for industry, as well as additional expenditures for agriculture). A considerable effort also had to be made to expand the state and co-operative supply system, as a result of the contraction of the private sector.[66] The combined effect of these and many other interrelated factors was to act as a brake on industrialization, and to contribute to a further drop in the general standard of living, thus intensifying existing social pressures and adding to the régime's political difficulties.

The steady deterioration in the situation was attributable to certain objective factors, as well as to the social and economic policy which was being pursued by the régime. However, the official interpretation put forward by the Politburo blamed the current setbacks almost exclusively on the private sector in agriculture.[67] This sector, it was explained, was the source of the trouble, a potential obstacle which might jeopardize the entire industrialization effort. It was the agricultural sector which had set off the upward price movement in the free market, thereby causing prices to rise in the state sector and undermining the government's prices policy.

The official analysis thus highlighted one single aspect of the problem, namely, the backwardness of agriculture as opposed to the dynamic forward movement in industry. However, this was no mere propaganda statement. *The Politburo were convinced that it was the only valid explanation.* Their interpretation of the situation was further confirmed by the information made available in August–September by the departments responsible for analysing market trends. The country was short of food both for its own requirements and for export, and the peasants were not producing enough. Livestock holdings were going down instead of increasing, as had been envisaged in the plans, and the result had been a reduction of some 10% in livestock products.[68] Since the climate of opinion within the Politburo was steadily growing more and more anti-*muzhik*, the decline in livestock production was readily interpreted as a deliberate move by the peasants to open a 'second front', in addition to the 'grain front' which had already proved so hazardous. Because of the *muzhik*, the government and its administrations were constantly having to shoulder fresh burdens, each more onerous than the last; they had had to organize the distribution of supplies in a country which was going through an acute food crisis, they had had to use direct intervention to supervise activities in the agricultural sector, particularly with regard to the sowing which, since 1928, was no longer being carried out as a matter of routine, and now they were faced with a problem in the livestock sector.

There was still another factor to be taken into account: Stalin was convinced that the industrial sector was capable of further acceleration in its rate of growth. After all, the annual plan for

1929–30 was aiming at an increase of 32·3% in industrial production, which was an impressive figure; the increase envisaged by the initial plan had been 21%, and in fact the actual achievement in 1928–9 had been 23·7%.[69] An increase of over 30% per annum, if such a rate could be reached and maintained over a number of years, would be a truly fantastic achievement, which could transform the whole country, or even change the course of world history, within a matter of a few years.

At this stage, Stalin seemed genuinely to believe that his dream could come true, but he knew that there was one condition, and that was a sufficiently high level of agricultural production. Should agriculture lag behind, the dramatic forward movement in industry would be checked and the rate of growth would inevitably suffer. The Politburo, with Stalin at their head, desperately cast around for some means of protecting the industrialization front from the dangers of a weakened agricultural sector. If there was not a marked improvement in agricultural production in 1930, industrial growth would be halted by 1931. *The situation therefore called for urgent action on a much broader basis than anything that had hitherto been attempted, and this must be implemented during the coming winter and spring,* if agriculture was not to become an obstacle to the growth of the national economy.[70]

This seems to have been the logic behind the Party leadership's change of policy at the end of 1929, and they were no doubt confirmed in the course which they subsequently adopted by the fact that there had, in the meantime, been spectacular successes in the domain of collectivization, particularly in the period from June to October 1929.

The Central Committee was pleased to note, at its meeting in November 1929, that progress in this sector had been 'more rapid than ever before, and had exceeded even the most favourable expectations'. With regard to the acute problems which had arisen, firstly over grain production, and subsequently over livestock production, the plenum's conclusions were that: 'The real solution to our difficulties [lies in] further acceleration of the process of collectivization and the construction of sovkhozes.'[71]

We must now therefore turn our attention to events in the countryside, with particular reference to the development of collectivization, during the year 1929.

NOTES AND REFERENCES

1. *Pravda,* June 13, 1929; Mendelson, *Planovoe Khozyaistvo,* 1929, No. 5, p. 55.

2. His speech to the *Sovnarkom*, *Pravda*, April 6, 1929.

3. Mikoyan admitted this in August. *Bolshevik*, 1929, No. 15, p. 20; for these figures see Golendo, *NAF*, 1929, No. 10, p. 14.

4. Averbukh and Bryukhanov, *Planovoe Khozyaistvo*, 1929, No. 10, p. 98; Mendelson, *Planovoe Khozyaistvo*, 1929, No. 8, p. 14; Zaleski, *op. cit.* (see Ch. 7, Note 5), p. 86.

5. *Pravda*, January 20, 1929.

6. *Pravda*, February 21, 1929.

7. Figures from the Smolensk Archives, quoted by Fainsod, *Smolensk under Soviet Rule* (Cambridge, Mass., 1958), pp. 314–6. The amount of the ration varied from place to place. See also Serge, 'De Lénine à Staline', *Crapouillot*, January 1937, p. 38. Serge mentions 50 grammes of tea, 500 grammes of vegetable oil, 150 grammes of sugar, and 500 grammes of herring, etc., in November 1929. See also *Sotsialisticheski Vestnik*, 1929, No. 9, p. 15, and 1929, No. 10–11, pp. 20–1; Mendelson, in *Planovoe Khozyaistvo*, 1929, No. 8, p. 18 notes a decrease in consumption per head of population.

8. *Planovoe Khozyaistvo*, 1929, No. 10, pp. 92–4.

9. Mendelson, *Planovoe Khozyaistvo*, 1929, No. 8, pp. 9, 17.

10. *Planovoe Khozyaistvo*, 1929, No. 10, p. 94; further details are given by Mendelson, *Planovoe Khozyaistvo*, 1929, No. 5, pp. 61–5.

11. Mendelson, *Planovoe Khozyaistvo*, 1929, No. 5, p. 65.

12. Zaleski, *op. cit.*, pp. 86–7.

13. Fainsod, *op. cit.*, pp. 303–9, 317–18.

14. A secret letter of February 21st to Party organizations, quoted by Fainsod, *op. cit.*, pp. 309–10; a public directive issued by the Party concerning the principle of *edinonachalie*, *Direktivy KPSS i sovetskogo pravitelstva po khozyaistvennym voprosam* (Moscow 1953), pp. 120–6.

15. Figure from Stalin, *Bolshevik*, 1929, No. 23–4, pp. 45–6.

16. For example, Mendelson, *Planovoe Khozyaistvo*, 1929, No. 5, p. 95; Averbukh and Bryukhanov, *Planovoe Khozyaistvo*, 1929, No. 10, p. 95.

17. Stalin, *Bolshevik*, 1929, No. 23–4, pp. 27, 34, 45–6.

18. *Pravda* editorial, January 3, 1929.

19. Syrtsov, *16-taya Konferentsiya*, *VKP(b)*, stenogramme, p. 154.

20. Stalin, *Bolshevik*, 1929, No. 23–4, p. 34.

21. *ibid*, p. 47.

22. *ibid*, p. 46. Mendelson, *Planovoe Khozyaistvo*, 1929, No. 5, p. 61. According to Syrtsov, in spring only the kulaks and the *verkhushka* of the serednyaks had stocks of grain. *16-taya Konferentsiya*, *VKP(b)*, stenogramme, p. 126.

23. Mendelson, *Planovoe Khozyaistvo*, 1929, No. 5, p. 61; Ryzhi-

kov, *5-ty S'ezd Sovetov*, stenogramme, bulletin, No. 3, p. 6; She-boldaev, *16-taya Konferentsiya, VKP(b)*, stenogramme, pp. 184–5.

24. A decision of July 29th by the Central Committee relative to the procurements campaign. It provides further evidence that the quantities of grain to be supplied were prescribed by the Centre. *Kollektivizatsiya selskogo khozyaistva*, doc. No. 49.

25. *Planovoe Khozyaistvo*, 1929, No. 5, p. 71.

26. Kurbatov, *NAF*, 1929, No. 5, pp. 81–2. The average price of rye flour was 324·4% higher in April 1929 than in April 1928. In non-producing regions there was a 403·6% increase. The prices per 100 kilos of flour in producing and non-producing regions about April 1, 1929, differed by 28 roubles.

27. Kurbatov, *op. cit.*, p. 82.

28. *Derevenski Kommunist*, 1929, No. 20, p. 18.

29. Kurbatov, *op. cit.*, p. 80; Mendelson, *Planovoe Khozyaistvo*, 1929, No. 8, p. 22; Strumilin, in *Planovoe Khozyaistvo*, 1929, No. 9, p. 20, states that pressure from the villages caused procurement prices to be increased by 17·2% instead of by 5·5% as provided for in the plan.

30. *Pravda*, January 5, 1929.

31. Kurbatov reports that 144·9 million roubles were mobilized in this way, and what the peasants had gained from the increase in procurement prices was thus mopped up. This leaves out of account what the peasants gained from sales on the free market. Kurbatov, *op cit.*, pp. 80–5.

32. Syrtsov, *16-taya Konferentsiya VKP(b)*, stenogramme, p. 153.

33. Sheboldaev, *16-taya Konferentsiya VKP(b)*, stenogramme, pp. 184–5; Khloplyankin, *ibid*, p. 84; Lominadze, *ibid*. p. 148.

34. Strong, *op. cit.* (Ch. 13, Note 67), p. 16.

35. For this decree of the Russian *VTsIK* of April 28, 1929, see Mikoyan, *Bolshevik*, 1929, No. 15, p. 22, Syrtsov, *ibid*, p. 152, and Khloplyankin, *16-taya Konferentsiya VKP(b)*, stenogramme, p. 84.

36. A figure of 33,000 for the period spring to autumn 1929 is given in Danilov (ed.), *op. cit.* (see Ch. 13, Note 73), p. 174.

37. *Code Pénal* (Paris, 1935), p. 186.

38. Sheboldaev, *16-taya Konferentsiya VKP(b)*, stenogramme, pp. 184–5.

39. As we have already noted, many bednyaks helped the kulaks or intervened on their behalf. Angarov quotes cases of bednyaks seeking to evade certain privileges, such as tax exemption, on the grounds that these privileges made their life in the village unbearable. We should add that these concessions were in any case of little material benefit to them. Angarov, *op. cit.* (see Ch. 2, Note 39), p. 29. In *Derevenski Kommunist*, 1929, No. 20, pp. 18–19, the de-

fence of the kulaks by batraks and bednyaks is attributed to *administrirovanie* of the peasants during the procurements campaign, and to the poor quality of the assistance given to the *bednota*.

40. Kurbatov, *op. cit.*

41. See the decision of the Central Committee of July 29, 1929, in *Kollektivizatsiya selskogo khozyaistva*, doc. No. 49.

42. Ryzhikov, *5-ty S'ezd Sovetov*, stenogramme, bulletin No. 3, p. 6.

43. On failure to comprehend the 'Party line', and on deviations among local officials even at *obkom* level (with the possible exception of the three to four principal secretaries), see Krylenko, *Pravda*, June 18, 1929, and the reply to the Middle Volga *obkom*, *Pravda*, July 26, 1929.

44. Pashukanis (ed.), *op. cit.* (see Ch. 3, Note 5), p. 476. Fainsod, *op. cit.*, p. 142.

45. Syrtsov, at this time Party secretary in Siberia, and later to become head of the government of the RSFSR, mentioned these *volynki* at the Sixteenth Party Conference, *16-taya Konferentsiya VKP(b)*, stenogramme, p. 155.

46. Stalin, *Sochineniya*, Vol. XII, pp. 97–8 (unpublished at the time); *Sotsialisticheski Vestnik*, 1929, No. 14, a letter from Moscow dated May 9, 1929.

47. Strong, *op. cit.*, p. 16.

48. For these figures see Bauman, *Pravda*, March 7, 1929; *Pravda*, June 14, 1928, under the heading 'Partiinoe Stroitelstvo'; Kukushkin, *op. cit.* (see Ch. 1, Note 28), pp. 31, 65; *Voprosy Istorii KPSS*, 1958, No. 4, p. 80; Danilov (ed.), *op. cit.* (see Ch. 13, Note 73), pp. 38–9, 173.

49. The editorial of *Pravda*, December 14, 1928, calls upon judges to cease treating as minor offences and acts of hooliganism, activities which it regards as manifestly counter-revolutionary.

50. Kukushkin, *op. cit.*, p. 32.

51. Eikhe, *16-taya Konferentsiya VKP(b)*, stenogramme, p. 45.

52. *KPSS v Rezolyutsiyakh*, Vol. II, pp. 36–7.

53. On this problem see the following three important studies: Bobrovsky, *op. cit.* (see Ch. 7, Note 87); Zaleski, *op. cit.* (see Ch. 7, Note 5); Jasny, *op. cit.* (see Ch. 11, Note 48).

54. Officially it was claimed that a reduction in costs of 4·5% had been achieved, instead of the hoped-for reduction of 7·5%.

55. Mendelson, *Planovoe Khozyaistvo*, 1929, No. 5, p. 58, No. 8, pp. 19–22.

56. Mainly through the medium of indirect taxation; Rykov, for example, mentions an increase in the purchase tax on vodka. *16-taya Konferentsiya VKP(b)*, stenogramme, p. 11.

57. Mendelson, *Planovoe Khozyaistvo*, 1929, No. 5, p. 57, No. 8, p. 13; *KPSS v Rezolyutsiyakh*, Vol. II, p. 628.

58. Zaleski, *op. cit.*, p. 85.

59. See the decision on the cadres problem, consequent upon the non-implementation of the previous decision on this problem. *KPSS v Rezolyutsiyakh*, Vol. II, pp. 633–42.

60. Krzhizhanovsky, *Planovoe Khozyaistvo*, 1929, No. 12, p. 13.

61. According to Zaleski, by 2·2%, *op. cit.*, p. 85. The sowing plan had not been fulfilled. See Golendo, *NAF*, 1929, No. 10, p. 11.

62. Zaleski, *op. cit.*, p. 86.

63. Golendo, *Derevenski Kommunist*, 1929, No. 20, p. 7, and *NAF*, 1929, No. 10, p. 37; Rykov, *5-ty S'ezd Sovetov*, stenogramme, bulletin No. 2, p. 13.

64. Zaleski, *op. cit.*, pp. 86–7.

65. Tsylko, *NAF*, 1929, No. 8, pp. 4–9; Mendelson, *Planovoe Khozyaistvo*, 1929, No. 5; Zaleski, *op. cit.*, pp. 86–7.

66. *Planovoe Khozyaistvo*, 1929, No. 8, p. 22.

67. *ibid*, p. 25.

68. Strumilin, 'Konrolnye Tsifry na 1929–30', *Planovoe Khozyaistvo*, 1929, No. 9, pp. 22–3.

69. *ibid*, pp. 19, 22–3.

70. Golendo, *NAF*, 1929, No. 10, pp. 14–15.

71. Resolutions of the session of November 1929. *KPSS v Rezolyutsiyakh*, Vol. II, pp. 620–4.

Chapter 15

THE PEASANTS FACE AN UNKNOWN FUTURE

1. *The New Line*

In June 1929 the government embarked upon a series of policy changes designed to afford them a greater degree of control over the peasantry. The régime had had enough of the kind of struggles which marked the procurements campaigns, and wished to free itself once and for all from its dependence on the rural sector. The way to independence, as the régime was by now convinced, lay through increased collectivization. At the end of June, therefore, the government decided to undertake a radical reorganization of co-operative structures, and to give further weight to the administrative organs which were responsible for the kolkhozes.

Henceforth, the co-operative movement was to be organized as a series of specialized branches, with administrative departments responsible for the individual sectors of agricultural production. Grain, livestock products and the various types of industrial crops would be the responsibility of administrative organs at local and republican level, or indeed at all-Union level.[1] At local level, the branch administration relating to the main crop in a particular area would also assume responsibility for other forms of production which fell within the scope of other branches. However, this local network would require to be linked by contract with other specialized centres, whose sphere of interest in a given area was not sufficiently important for them to be represented in that area. As will be seen, this was an extremely complicated arrangement. Indeed, the whole administrative apparatus which the government were proposing to set up was both complex and cumbersome, as well as being costly and time-consuming, and it was not surprising, therefore, that before long they found it necessary to introduce further changes whose effect, in the long run, was to impair the efficiency of the measures we have been describing.

In the beginning, however, it should be stressed that the main function of this entire co-operative administration was to adapt the structures of the peasant economy to the needs of 'collectivization and co-operative production, and to mobilize the resources of the peasant population itself to the maximum possible extent, in order to advance progress in the co-operative sector'.[2] In this context, the simple producers' associations were called upon to continue increasing the degree of socialization of property and work to which their members were subject; by so doing, they would gradually evolve towards more complex forms, and would thus 'serve as a basis for the setting-up of large-scale kolkhozes'.[3]

It will be apparent, therefore, that the role assigned to the co-operative movement embraced not only the construction of kolkhozes of the usual pattern, but also the creation of new and hitherto unknown forms, in the shape of the 'large-scale kolkhozes' which were now to figure so prominently in the government's ever-changing plans. In furtherance of these objectives, all the means by which the government could exert influence, or provide incentives, in the form of supplies, credits, agro-technical services and various kinds of aid, were concentrated in the hands of the co-operative movement, and channelled almost exclusively to the simple producers' associations, by means of the contract system.

The contracts too were to undergo a complete change of character, and here again it was the Central Committee which laid down, in broad outline, what their new role should be.[4] In the Central Committee's view, the system of *kontraktatsiya* could now serve as a major instrument for ensuring that the peasants' surplus grain reached the government without fail, and that production would be increased and collectivization speeded up. This could be achieved, it was thought, by making supplies of machinery, fertilizers, and credits, etc. to the peasants conditional upon the contracts which they signed, and the manner in which they carried them out.

The signing of the contract was to be a matter for decision by majority vote of the village associations, which decision would then be binding on the entire village, including the kulaks.[5] Under the terms of the contract, the peasants would be invited to join the co-operative movement, and to make numerous contributions, which were listed by the Central Committee as follows: '. . . entrance fee [upon joining the co-operative movement.—M.L.] and share contribution, deposits for specific purposes (a building, or the purchase of a tractor), contributions towards purchase of the means of production, supply of a proportion of the allotted quantity of grain to the State on credit . . .' etc.[6] The Council of Commissars further stipulated that the contracts should cover a number of years and that in this case the signatories must undertake to form themselves into kolkhozes.

The question is, was there equality of rights between the contracting parties?

So far, experience had shown that co-operative or government organizations had been far from satisfactory in the fulfilment of their obligations. The *Sovnarkom* itself had been critical of the way in which *kontraktatsiya* operated. The contracts were signed in great haste, since there was always a delay at the start of the campaign; information about plans and targets [which were, of course, laid down by the central authorities.—M.L.] always arrived too late, there was a corresponding hold-up in the financial and technical resources which had been promised, the authorities amended clauses in already existing contracts.[7] In cases where the official side failed to fulfil its part of the contract, the peasants who were party to the contract had not the right either to revoke it or to appeal to any juridical body charged with the responsibility of supervising the fulfilment of contractual obligations. In fact, no such body existed. *This meant, in effect, that the agreement entered into by the peasants was unilateral in character, and purely an instrument of state coercion.*

Some attempt at face-saving was made by the press, notably by *Bolshevik*, which was the Party's theoretical organ; the local authorities were urged to draw a distinction between those compulsory services which were demanded of the kulaks (that is, the handing over of supplies) and the obligations of the other strata of the peasantry, which were in the nature of 'a voluntary undertaking reflecting the general will of the village community', and which should therefore be implemented purely on the basis of persuasion by the local officials concerned.[8] The latter, as *Bolshevik* pointed out, seemed to be none too clear about this distinction, for they had been allotting to the serednyaks certain 'fixed' (*tverdye*) assignments which were applicable only to the kulaks, and non-fulfilment of which was punished by the *pyatikratka*.

In this, the Party and its organ were playing a rather devious game with the local authorities. Some weeks previously, in an article dealing with the current procurements campaign, Mikoyan, who was commander in chief of the operation, had stated clearly that the contracts made with village societies [i.e. contracts involving entire villages or communities.—M.L.] or with an entire *okrug* 'require that these villages and districts in their entirety should hand over *the whole of their marketable production*'.[9] These were the government's latest instructions.

It was obvious from the start that the peasants would hardly be enthusiastic about signing contracts on these conditions, and that the local officials would never be able to persuade them to sign and honour so drastic an undertaking without using every available means of coercion.

However, the Politburo was undismayed by such inconsistencies, for it believed that it had at its disposal a powerful weapon which would at one and the same time ensure the success of both procurements and collectivization. Furthermore, the government were of the opinion that the contracts system could be used not only as a means of setting-up simple collective farms, but also of enlarging their size. Full of hopes and illusions on this score, they now began to rally support for the task of creating 'giant' kolkhozes.

By August, these giant collectives already extended over a total area of one million hectares, being made up of collective farming enterprises of between two to eight thousand hectares and over. At this stage, the extent of the kolkhoz sector as a whole was already of the order of four to five million hectares (as compared with 1·9 million in the previous year) and the plan for 1930 was to treble this area.[10] In the Urals, the North Caucasus and the Ukraine there was an upsurge in mass collectivization (*sploshnaya kollektivizatsiya*), in which the population of entire *raiony* had joined the collectives.[11]

The press now began to speak of a new stage in development, *the stage of mass collectivization*. From now on, Party members in the rural areas were to be invited to join the kolkhozes under threat of expulsion from the Party.[12]

At this point, the rate of collectivization was still, in theory at least, regulated by the availability of financial and technical resources, since 'mass collectivization is unthinkable without the necessary heavy agricultural equipment'; however, so far as the government were concerned, the superiority of the kolkhozes, especially the large-scale ones, was already beyond question. Like the sovkhozes, they could be required to hand over their entire surplus production.[13] There had already been a considerable number of instances in which kolkhozes had sought to evade their obligations in this respect, thus giving some cause for anxiety,[14] but the government hoped that the problem would be easier to solve than it was in the case of the small farmer.

The kolkhoz unions (*kolkhozsoyuzy*) which had been developing as an administrative body since 1928 (and developing, it was said, rather too slowly) were now given wider powers which would enable them to administer the kolkhozes, and particularly the larger-scale ones, more efficiently.[15] The lower echelon of this organization was the *kust* (group) or *kolkhozsoyuz* of the *raion*, which was responsible to the appropriate departments at *oblast* and republican level, the topmost echelon being represented by the *Kolkhoztsentr* which became, as from October, an all-Union organization. These administrative bodies were to assume responsibility for allocating equipment and credits to the kolkhozes and for handling their products; they were also to be responsible for signing contracts with the kolkhozes in respect of procurements and production. Through *Gosplan*, the *Kolkhoztsentr* was to submit an overall plan for the whole of the kolkhoz sector to the government.

At the same time, the government gave orders for all kolkhoz statutes, and all current kolkhoz legislation, to be revised; in particular, *Gosplan* and the *Kolkhoztsentr* were entrusted with the joint task of drafting regulations concerning kolkhoz funds, the period allowed for this operation being only two weeks.[16]

From this time on, it would seem that the bulk of the credits were channelled exclusively to the collective sector,[17] so that the individual peasant farmer could no longer count on receiving any appreciable assistance, or possibly any assistance at all. This in itself was a very effective means of ensuring increasingly rapid developments in the collective sector along the lines desired by the government.

Due attention was also being given to the needs of the columns and tractor stations, at least in the matter of legislation, for it was now felt that these formations afforded hopeful prospects for the future. In December 1928, the *STO* had ordered that priority in the supply of tractors should be given to the machine tractor stations and columns, and the large kolkhozes and sovkhozes, rather than to the peasant associations. By June 1929, the government had already adopted the view that the Stations would be 'a major factor in transforming the private farms into large-scale collective farms'. As a means of co-ordinating the work of columns and stations (it should be noted that no official distinction was now made between these two forms) they ordered the setting-up of a new administrative body, the *Traktortsentr*. This organization was to be responsible for putting one million hectares under cultivation during 1928–9.[18]

In September, the Central Committee launched a major campaign for the building of new machine tractor stations.[19] The local authorities found themselves faced with yet another onerous task.

However, this was only the beginning, so far as the central authorities were concerned. Meanwhile, at local level, the task of implementing the recent decisions and setting up the new administrative bodies met with innumerable difficulties. In this connection, the wishes of the government were sometimes disregarded, and there was obstruction from the co-operative organizations when attempts were made to set up rival kolkhoz organizations.[20] The government's intentions were not always clear, and were sometimes misunderstood. Indeed, it frequently happened that the demands which were made were not only beyond the comprehension but also beyond the powers of the men on the spot,[21] the more so as the central authorities were too impatient to wait for results and were apt to overburden the local officials with too many fresh assignments at one time.

The Politburo were aware that there were not enough trained cadres in the countryside to undertake organizational work of this scale and complexity. They hoped that the necessary recruits might be forthcoming from the ranks of the workers, a class on whom the Soviet régime had always drawn during the testing time of the revolution and the Civil War, and from whom it had always evoked the desired response. The Central Committee turned therefore to the trade unions. However, on this occasion, they were not so much appealing to them as reproaching them on the rather curious grounds that the activities of the rural unions 'were not always directed to the tasks involved in the collectivization of agriculture. At times there is evidence of a total lack of understanding and awareness of the nature of these tasks'.[22] There was of course no justification for this accusation, which was aimed at the unions as a whole, and not only those which operated in the rural areas. The collectivization of agriculture was something which was quite new, and indeed foreign to the working masses, and to the unions which had been set up for entirely different purposes. In any case, no one had ever instructed them to set about putting the peasants into the kolkhozes. It was clear that the government was acting dishonestly, but it had all the power it needed to enforce the necessary discipline. The unions which had so very recently been called upon to reorganize themselves 'for the production drive' were now faced with a new and, for them, totally unexpected role. Regardless of their feelings in the matter, the General Council for the Trade Unions set up a 'commission for work in the villages',[23] whose duty it would be to ensure that the unions sent more brigades into the rural areas to help in the campaigns in progress (procurements, sowing, or collectivization, for example), and that villages or entire agricultural regions were placed under the 'patronage' of the large factories. The unions were also to require of those of their members who had connections in the villages that they should do propaganda for the cause of collectivization whenever they visited their families.

However, the government was not relying exclusively on the unions: everyone was called upon to participate in the common task —the co-operative movement, the unions, the *Kolkhoztsentr* and its various ramifications, the village soviets, the local bureaux of the *Narkomzem*, the sovkhozes and, of course, the Party. The local Party organizations were severely criticized for having failed in their duty as far as agriculture was concerned, and it was made clear that from now on the value of the individual contribution made by each of the local Party branches would be assessed in terms of the diligence with which they applied themselves to increasing soil fertility by 35% and making propaganda on behalf of the agrominimum and other such tasks, and, of course, to advancing the cause of collectivization. The local Party secretaries were well aware of what this meant.[24]

This feverish activity on the part of the government was no doubt the result of acute anxiety. As we have said, the Central Committee, with its genius for creating administrative apparatus, had just set up a whole number of new organizations, including an extremely complex series of co-operative networks. Furthermore, when it came to projects which were regarded as being of overriding importance, the government tended to delegate responsibility for these to all its departments at the same time. The general effect of this attempt to concentrate all available forces in one priority sector was to create a great deal of administrative confusion. Before long, the Centre was flooded with complaints about the proliferation of authorities whose responsibilities were so ill-defined that they could achieve little or nothing in practical terms. All in all, it was no longer clear who was to be responsible for creating the kolkhozes, or who was to administer them.

However, in the matter of planning the coming procurements campaign the Central Committee showed a great deal more efficiency. In this sector, preparations were being made for a deployment of forces on a greater scale than ever before. In making their dispositions, procurements headquarters were taking due note of the experience gained in the two previous campaigns. They were well aware that unless the resources of both the Party and the régime were fully mobilized it would be impossible to extract the grain either from the kulaks or the serednyaks. Another essential element in their tactics would be the adoption of 'a proper class line', and great care was taken with the preparation of these two aspects of the campaign. By June, the *Sovnarkom* had reorganized the various procurements agencies on more rational lines, so that they would no longer be indulging in the cut-throat competition and mutual obstruction which had marked their activities in the past. The responsibilities of the various agencies were now delineated according to a fairly clear-cut plan. The State procurements organization which was Mikoyan's responsibility—that is, the *Soyuzkhleb*—was to act as a receiving centre for the quantities of grain collected by its own agents and those of two other agencies; the consumers' co-operative (the *Tsentrosoyuz*) was to procure grain from those peasants who were not covered by any other collecting agency, and the agricultural co-operative (the *Khlebotsentr*) was to be responsible for the collection of grain from the producers' associations which had contracts with the government.[25]

The Central Committee issued instructions to the Party organizations to mobilize all their resources for the coming campaign.[26] This year a number of new methods would be introduced, in addition to those which had been employed in previous campaigns. Large stocks of consumers' good were amassed for supply to the rural areas, but this year they would be released only upon due fulfilment of the delivery quotas, an arrangement which applied not only to the individual peasants but also to any given region as a whole. Goods which were in particularly short supply would be reserved for those who made an outstanding contribution.[27]

Instructions were given for the setting-up of 'auxiliary procurements commissions', which were to be attached to the local soviets. The Party, the unions and local administrative organizations were all alerted, and brigades were sent to the villages from the administrative centres and the other towns. Numerous Party representatives (*upolnomochennye*) supervised and guided the activities of the procurements organizations, and the Party leaders were given the task of preparing daily situation reports on the progress of the campaign. The villages were subjected to a full-scale onslaught by propagandists and other Party officials, who organized meetings with the local inhabitants and members of the co-operatives, in order to persuade them to accept the plans for grain delieveries.[28]

In so far as the concept of 'rural democracy' was concerned, the role of the village assemblies now counted for very little. As in previous years, they were called upon to co-operate in bringing pressure to bear on any peasants who were withholding sizeable quantities of grain. This year, however, for the first time they themselves were given notice, well in advance, of the quotas which were to be delivered, and were invited to discuss these, but only for the purpose of agreeing them. As Mikoyan himself said, the plan which had been drawn up at the outset of the campaign for a given village or *raion* 'could not subsequently be altered in any respect'.[29] With the control figure as the focal point of their attention, 'the entire village must be activized. The bednyaks, the *komsomol*, the local Party cell and the village soviet must all be mobilized in a combined effort to exert pressure on the kulaks and the speculators'. The latter must be subjected 'to the full rigours of the revolutionary law',[30] which meant enforcing the *pyatikratka* and even, if necessary, the law of June 1929 which we have already mentioned, and under which any person who failed to fulfil the common obligations which were binding on the village as a whole was liable to sentence of imprisonment, confiscation of property or even deportation.[31]

The Politburo were apparently convinced that the *muzhik* would never be able to hold out against vigorous and concerted action on the part of the authorities. Once they had been cornered and made to feel the full force of the political and economic offensive which was being pressed home relentlessly, and once they had been sufficiently unnerved by the punitive measures which were in principle reserved for the better-off elements in the villages, but which often struck at many of the poorer ones as well, the village communities, being isolated one from the other, would be more readily cowed into submission, and would do as the government ordered.

The government's present aim was to succeed in building up adequate reserves of grain, as a bulwark against the shortages which in the past had hampered progress, and left them little room for manoeuvre in a difficult situation. Despite the fact that the harvest had been far from good, they contemptuously dismissed the estimates and moderate proposals put forward by the committee of experts attached to the *TsSU*[32]—'The bankruptcy of bourgeois statistics' were the words used by Mikoyan—and fixed a procurements target which was 50·7% higher than in the previous year.[33]

The time allowed for the campaign was also shorter than ever before. The main grain-producing regions had until January 1st to fulfil their plan, and the other regions were to have a month longer. Even so, these periods were to be further shortened in the future. One of the reasons for the government's optimism was their belief that they could count not only on the 'socialized sector' in agriculture, including kolkhozes and sovkhozes (whose contribution this year would be a sizeable one), but also on the villages which had signed contracts. Under the new dispensation, these contracts would ensure fulfilment of one quarter of the total plan.[34]

At the beginning of December, Mikoyan announced triumphantly that the plan had been all but completed, that the required reserves had been built up and that kulaks and speculators had been dealt with 'by prompt and concerted action'.[35] In fact, the success had been unprecedented. Although the harvest had been poorer than that of the previous year, the procurements had yielded 982 million poods of grain (sixteen million tons), whereas the previous year's total had only been 10·8 million tons.[36]

This success confirmed the Politburo in its policies, and suggested a further course of action. The time allowed for the procurements was shortened to a minimum, and *with the campaign almost completed by the beginning of December, the rural authorities had a powerful ready-made 'task force' at their disposal, which could be deployed for other purposes.* Fortified by the experience gained in the campaign, and the tactical lessons which had been learned, the régime now turned this force to the task of collectivization, for which the *zagotovki* had in fact prepared the ground.

414

2. A Time of Anxiety for the Peasants

Since the winter of 1928, there had been growing tension between the peasants and the régime. The atmosphere of life in the villages was one of anxiety and uncertainty as to what the future would bring.

The peasants, still fresh from the experiences of the *zagotovki* and their encounter with the brigades and Party representatives who had descended on them from the cities, bringing trouble and injustice in their wake, were now asking themselves what hope there was of maintaining their farming activities at the present level, let alone of expanding them. Partly as a result of climatic reverses and the shortage of feeding-stuffs, many of the peasants and particularly the better-off among them, had shown a tendency to cut down their sowings. It was only by determined action in urging the poor peasants to sow more that the authorities were able to stave off disaster, but this by itself was not enough to compensate for the fall in the supply of marketable grain occasioned by the attitude of the more prosperous peasants, who were the chief source of supply.

Although it could be claimed that government intervention had had some effect in arresting the downward trend in sowing, the efforts of the authorities to exercise a similar control over the livestock sector proved unavailing. The better-off peasants and the serednyaks were, for a variety of reasons, selling off their livestock; in some cases, the cause was lack of feeding-stuffs, or the belief that the 'smaller man' would in the end be less vulnerable; in other cases the recession was simply a reflection of the prevailing mood of uncertainty about the future.[37] The net effect, so far as the State was concerned, was a further aggravation of the food shortage, which in turn had repercussions in the countryside, since it drove the State to put even more pressure on the peasants.

The better-off peasants were the first to suffer. They were singled out for special treatment under a policy which, particularly after the summer of 1929, was to become increasingly harsh. For them, each new procurements campaign became a veritable siege, from which they emerged still further reduced, and always on the losing side. The fact that some officials did, from time to time, turn a blind eye to their attempts at evasion or concealment[38] did little to alter their general predicament. Many of these more prosperous peasants finally fell victim to the law, had their property confiscated, and were sentenced to imprisonment or even deportation.

Apart from their obligations under the procurements system, they were also subject to severe fiscal and other financial pressure, in respect of individual levies[39] and an increasing number of other charges which were made on them, including local taxes, compulsory loan contributions and subscriptions of various kinds. A further source of trouble was the inspectorate responsible for supervising the working conditions of the batraks who were employed on the bigger farms; this body harried the more prosperous peasants incessantly, and made endless demands on them. The *selsovet* further added to their difficulties by placing restrictions on the conditions under which additional land could be rented.[40] Another method of harassing them was to demand repayment of previous loans before the statutory time.[41] Action was frequently taken against the better-off peasants on the grounds of alleged speculation. Given the state of the grain market and the level which prices had already reached by the summer of 1929, any sale of grain other than to the procurements agencies could be described as speculation, if the authorities thought fit. In fact, the bulk of selling activities took place under semi-black market conditions, and in consequence a great many peasants were persecuted for supposed speculation irrespective of their social condition. The local authorities were under orders from the Centre to follow 'a strict class line' on all matters, whether in respect of the contracts system, collectivization, admission to the *MTS*, or taxes and other payments, and they therefore did their best, according to their own lights and with as much zeal as they could muster, to make life difficult for the kulaks and *zazhitochnye*, or any whom they regarded as being in this category. Given the particular combination of circumstances at the time, it was inevitable that any refusal on the part of these peasants to comply with the wishes of the authorities would be construed as 'counter-revolutionary'.[42]

The régime now set about sharpening the class struggle in the countryside, and stirring up class enmities. The poor peasants were urged to lend their support, by boycotting or spying on their more prosperous neighbours. A spirit of class warfare at work in a village which was divided against itself, and in which, as the theorists put it, the progressive elements 'rallied to the support of the Soviet régime against the kulaks', would surely hasten the process of building socialism in the countryside.

However, at this stage, the most tangible results of this policy were all negative. The better-off peasants abandoned production, and reduced the size of their holdings. They sold their stock and equipment to neighbours who were less liable to be persecuted by the authorities, ceased renting land for additional farming activities, and paid off their batrak labourers.[43] Some left for the towns, or moved to other regions, and some turned themselves into serednyaks. Others again carried out a sort of 'auto-dekulakization' (*samoraskulachivanie*) by selling up the greater part of their farms.[44]

There was a significant decline in the economic importance of the better-off strata of the peasantry. It was true that, by selling off their property, they had acquired more ready cash, which they frequently turned to account in illicit trading activities, but this, while being harmful to the economy, did nothing to arrest the general process by which these classes as a whole were gradually being weakened.[45]

As in the past, the punitive measures which in principle were aimed at the kulaks also affected large numbers of serednyaks. The explanation put forward by the central authorities was that such things happened 'in error', through deviation from a Party line which had been 'imperfectly understood'. Occasionally, injustices were put right, but each attack on the kulaks brought fresh repercussions on the peasantry as a whole. To some extent, this was the product of tendencies which were inherent in the nature of the régime and its administrative apparatus, perhaps even more so at the time of which we are speaking than at an earlier stage; it was also the result of the deficiences, or the wrongful application, of a class doctrine which had little relevance in the rural context. Stalin was well aware of the situation, and had in fact said, in the course of his attacks on Bukharin: 'Can you mention one single political measure undertaken by the Party which has not been accompanied by some deviation or other? (*peregiby*).'[46]

As these *peregiby* were a standard occurrence, they had come to be accepted by the peasants as a stable feature of the régime. Even when it could be shown that the government's coercive measures were aimed at a small minority, the individual peasant, although perhaps unaffected personally, could not but be profoundly alarmed. The fate ostensibly reserved for the kulak was constantly being used by the authorities as a weapon for intimidating the peasants in general. Paradoxically, the kulaks used the same argument in their attempts to persuade the peasants to resist the authorities, pointing to themselves and to their fate as a warning. . . .[47]

Undoubtedly the persecution of the kulaks deeply shocked the peasants, particularly as many of them could not understand wherein lay the essential difference between themselves and those whom the régime had singled out for its attacks. As we have seen, the Party intellectuals were none too clear about the definition of a kulak; local officialdom was even more in the dark. Had the local authorities not been severely criticized on numerous occasions for their failures to unmask, or indeed to detect, the kulaks in their midst? For fear of reprisals, the men on the spot were impelled to seek out kulaks everywhere, and in great numbers; in the process serednyaks and even poor peasants were made to suffer, and this contributed still further to the general turmoil and distress in the countryside.

During the summer, when the régime began to press the peasants more urgently on the question of the kolkhozes, this feeling of anxiety became widespread throughout the entire peasant population, particularly in the grain-growing regions.

The villages now became a venue for numbers of political activists who extolled the virtues of socialism and the kolkhozes. In the majority of cases, these were workers' or students' brigades from the towns, Party activists or officials sent by the *raion*, the *okrug* or the *oblast*, people holidaying in the villages or soldiers on leave. Less frequently, they might be local activists or officials, such as members of the young *komsomol* or the local Party cell, or school teachers. The resources of the village as such were not equal to the task of winning over the peasants, or undertaking the work of organizing the kolkhozes; consequently, the majority of the political agitators and organizers came from the towns. The first object of their propaganda was often the local authorities themselves, beginning with the presidium of the *selsovet* and the members of the local cell, since these officials, who could normally be relied upon to perform any other duty which was demanded of them, showed the same negative attitude to the kolkhozes as the rest of the peasants.

The villages were invaded by Party representatives, workers and officials who came armed with strict instructions, and set about the task of persuading an unreceptive peasant audience of the superior virtues of the kolkhoz. The great majority of these activists had never seen a kolkhoz, nor had they any knowledge of agriculture. For the most part, their arguments were based simply on their own faith in the superiority of socialism in general (the impact of such an argument on a peasant audience can well be imagined) and above all in the manifest advantages, in theory at least, of large-scale fully mechanized agriculture, organized and managed by technicians and agronomists on the basis of the latest scientific developments.

Many of these agitators were acting in all good faith when they attempted to convince the peasants of the glowing prospects which lay before them, once they had joined the collectives. More often than not, however, in order to persuade the peasants to join as quickly as possible, they made far too many promises which were totally unrealistic. The prospect of government assistance in the matter of tractors, fertilizers, loans and technicians served very well as an argument or an inducement, but came near to fraud when one considers that the government was in no position to keep such promises.

The stream of eloquence tended to dry up when the peasants began to ask practical questions: how was work to be organized and who would be in control of it, what would be the basis of payment for work done, what prices would the government pay for farm products? The brigades did their best but, being unable to reply, either attempted to evade the issue or to defer giving an answer, and the peasants thereupon became even more suspicious. Their suspicions were only too well-founded. So far, they had heard a great deal, but seen very little. There were rumours everywhere—a tractor column or station in one place, a giant kolkhoz being formed in another, a sovkhoz being set up somewhere else, and so on.

So far as the peasants were concerned, what troubled them most of all was the obvious determination with which the representatives of the régime were going about their present task. In those villages where the prospects for rapid results seemed most promising, they organized innumerable meetings for the purpose of discussing the kolkhoz question or signing delivery contracts, or agreeing proposals for communal work on the land under the new *MTS*. The peasants felt that their way of life was being threatened, and their whole world shaken by so many new ideas—tractors, contracts, promises, anti-religious propaganda and, worst of all, the dreaded, unfamiliar kolkhozes—which had been thrust upon them all at once.

In the village assemblies they argued, jeered and shouted—the women especially—and resisted in every way that was open to them. Predictably, since they were peasants, their first reaction was to postpone taking a decision, protesting that they must have time to think, that they must discuss the matter with their wives, or that they should perhaps send a delegation to see what was being done in other places. As the time for decision approached and tension increased, the opposition grew more violent and more vociferous; meetings broke up in disorder, or were broken up by organized groups, speakers were shouted down by the peasants, there were fights between villagers and the new members of the kolkhozes.[48]

The harder the authorities pressed for a decision, the more the unrest grew. Some of the peasants finally gave in, among them young *komsomol* members, who were more likely to be critical of the backwardness of their elders, and were eager to try a new way of life; there was also some following among the bednyaks, who saw the kolkhoz as the only way out of their wretched condition, particularly since the government had promised to assist those who joined.

On the other hand, there was growing hostility from other sectors of the peasantry, in particular the better-off peasants, for whom the kolkhoz represented a threat. Between those two extremes lay the broad mass of the peasantry, who remained hesitant and noncommittal, suspicious and above all afraid. Such was the determination of the authorities that the peasants were constantly being forced to retract earlier refusals to join the collectives. And in any case, the State was still taking their grain, and had stopped all credits and all assistance to them, whereas the kolkhozes were being given priority in supplies of consumer goods, seed, etc. It might have been easier for them to make up their minds if examples of these ideal kolkhozes had been available; as it was, the more they saw of the changes which were taking place, the more disillusioned they became.

Many official sources are agreed that the general standard of the propaganda work which was carried on in the villages by the volunteer brigades was very low indeed. These activists and organizers had been hastily recruited from the towns, they had little knowledge of the rural areas, and little or nothing in common with village attitudes and the village mentality. Their activities were further handicapped by the inefficiency and the over-bureaucratic approach which characterized the Soviet administrative apparatus in the countryside.[49] However, the major stumbling-block was the excessive demands which the Politburo had made, both in respect of the scale of these operations, and the speed at which they were to be carried out.

The only way of convincing the peasants would have been to offer them tangible proof of the superiority of collective farming. Without this proof, the régime was, in effect, demanding of a group of people who were traditionally conservative and cautious in their outlook that they should abandon their way of life, and make a great leap of faith into the unknown. It would be irrelevant, in any case, to speak of conservatism in this particular instance. Is there any social class or stratum, no matter what its level of education or adaptability, which will give up its way of life and its institutions (and this is, after all, what the Soviet peasants were being asked to do) without fierce internal conflicts and a bitter struggle?

Here we have a peasant community, which was described as 'the last capitalist class' and the most serious obstacle in the way of socialist progress, suddenly being required, at the behest of the Central Committee, or rather of a small enclave within that Committee, to advance at a rate even greater than that which had been expected of the proletariat, who were regarded as the most progressive sector. No one had demanded that the proletariat should change their way of life, or even their methods of production, which were the same as they had been before the revolution. Now, under the leadership of the proletariat, who had never been called upon to make similar sacrifices, the peasants were being urged to pool their property and to organize their production along totally new lines, to make an abrupt transition from a pre-capitalist phase of development to socialism, which was still for them an unknown quantity.

It was unthinkable that the peasants could ever accept such a total disruption of their society of their own free will, unless they could be shown that at least some of their neighbours had tried the experiment and succeeded, particularly when the evidence of their own eyes suggested the very contrary. There was ample proof that the State could not even run its own enterprises in the countryside efficiently, as a good *khozyain* should.

In the first place, the majority of the sovkhozes which, according to the theoreticians, were the 'most advanced form' of socialist enterprise, were in fact running at a loss;[50] they were badly managed and some of them were in a lamentable state. As Vareikis had noted with some alarm [51] 'the sovkhozes are often managed by people who lack even the most elementary experience'. The living standards of sovkhoz workers were notoriously low, their wages being at most a third of the earnings of an industrial worker,[52] while their housing conditions were deplorable. Batraks or bednyaks might seek work there from necessity, but the rest of the peasants could not but be repelled by the sovkhozes. Apart from the question of wages, any peasant casting a farmer's eye over these establishments would see, not without a certain malicious satisfaction on occasion, too many things which were wrong, machinery broken or unprotected from the weather, buildings in a state of disrepair, frequent breakdowns in the tractors, and so on.

The result was inevitable. A report from the Commissariat of Inspection, relating to the results of an enquiry on the state of the sovkhozes in the Ukraine in the summer of 1929, stated that although the population were not actively opposed to the sovkhozes 'it may be said, in general, that the attitude of the peasants remains negative: while there is no note of any overtly hostile reaction, it is equally evident that there is no particular enthusiasm for the sovkhozes, nor interest in their economic development'.[53]

The same could be said of the kolkhozes; neither the old ones nor the new afforded attractive prospects. Indeed there were very few which could serve as a model. The peasants sometimes took a trip to see them, and returned with mixed feelings. There were not enough cadres available to carry out experiments of this nature efficiently on the vast scale which was being attempted. Halfway through the year, the Russian *Narkomzem* estimated that of the 40,000 chairmen who were in charge of kolkhozes, only some 10–15,000 were qualified to fill such posts. The *Kolkhoztsentr* further reported that some 17–20% of these chairmen had gone through an intensive training course (lasting a few weeks at most) but that the others had no training.[54] Many of the senior officials concerned in the central administration were persuaded that, given time and patience and the necessary mobilization of scientific and technical resources, it should be possible to create a highly efficient nucleus of some thousands of collectivized farming enterprises. With this source of cadres and experience to draw on, the collective movement would then be capable of more rapid expansion. This was the course suggested by the authors of the Five-year Plan which had been worked out by *Gosplan*.

However, by the summer of 1929 the Politburo apparently no longer looked on patience as a virtue, despite the many experiences which had shown that progress was not something which could be administered to the countryside in over-powerful doses. The story of the arrival of tractors in the kolkhoz fields provides a striking example. 'The appearance of tractor columns caused a major up-heaval in all sectors of the rural population, and was an event of the greatest significance in the countryside. The tractors were the occasion of a fierce class struggle which broke out between the different social strata of the peasantry.'[55] Kulikov's statement is only partly true, for the struggle took place, in the majority of cases, not among the peasants themselves but between the peasants and the local authorities aided by their supporters.

At the time in question, the Columns and Stations which had been organized in the principal grain-growing regions were extremely inefficient, both from the technical and the agronomic point of view.[56] Tsylko, the future deputy Commissar for Agriculture, reported that as much as 48% of the operational time of the tractors was lost through breakdowns, or through their being used on non-productive activities. Nobody knew how the work should be organized in enterprises of this kind.[57] The score or so of Stations which were operating had no agronomists on their staff, and even the few agronomists who were available had little idea how to go about their task. On the technical side, there was a similar shortage of trained personnel who were capable of seeing that the machines were efficiently used and properly maintained. In such conditions, a column which was supposed to be responsible for working some 3–4 thousand hectares had no chance of being able to discharge its duties satisfactorily. Consequently, the work was done badly, and at too high a cost.[58] Vareikis, who was a member of the Central Committee and Party secretary of the Central Black Earth region, put the point very forcefully at the Party Conference: 'The man in charge of a large tractor column is sometimes a schoolmaster with no experience of agriculture or agronomy.'[59]

A conference of students who had been doing a course of training with the Columns of the *Khlebotsentr* passed a resolution containing the following statement: 'The technical staff of these Columns is so inefficient that it is highly questionable whether the Columns can ever be transformed into *MTS*.' [60] Thus, the appearance of tractors in the fields may have inspired a great deal of curiosity, but from the work point of view they commanded little respect.

Another rather more disturbing fault which the above authors had to find with the Stations was the nature of their administrative and bureaucratic structures. Their organization, and their dealings with the peasantry, were those of an outside body imposed on the local population, who had no say in their management. The producers' associations which had signed contracts with the Stations were occasionally represented on the Station committees, 'but these committees were usually a formality, and had no active say in the running of the tractor station'. Tsylko reported that, as a rule, the two sides were mutually antagonistic in their attitudes: '. . . it frequently happens that the chairmen of the associations find themselves in direct opposition [*protivopostavlyayut sebya*] to the Station directors'.[61] Turned the other way round, Tsylko's statement gives an even more realistic picture of the situation.

The inefficiency of the Stations, and the high-handed attitude of those in charge, who failed to enlist the peasants' co-operation for their work, and did not give them an adequate explanation of what the objectives were, served to heighten the peasants' mistrust and often aroused a deep hostility to the Stations. It often took scores of meetings of the village assemblies before they could be persuaded to sign a contract with the Station. Any form of counter-propaganda, either on the part of the kulaks or the village priests or any other group of peasants, was sure of a credulous audience. Indeed, the role of counter-propagandist was not a difficult one to sustain. There were alarming rumours about the 'famine rations' which would be the lot of those who signed contracts with the Stations, and particularly about imminent action to dispossess the peasants of their lands; having been started, these rumours gained currency and were soon circulating freely.[62] *The credulity of the peasants was a reflection of their deep mistrust of the régime and its intentions, and this was something in which the kulaks had had no hand.*

From the peasants' point of view, the Station was merely another State organization, which was linked with the peasantry by contractual obligations. In this instance, the peasants 'regarded themselves as having handed over their land to be farmed by the State'.[63] The Station was, in other words, *kazennaya* (official, or pertaining to the State),[64] and as such it inspired the kind of profound mistrust which had its roots in Tsarist times. The behaviour of the administration merely confirmed the peasants in their attitude.

Many of them had refused to sign contracts, and registered their disapproval on occasion by outbursts of violence and arson. The men sent their wives to demonstrate against the Stations—an old peasant tactic, based on the knowledge that women involved in a fracas generally ran less risk of reprisals from the authorities. Even when the peasants had finally agreed, willingly or otherwise, to sign a contract with the Station, their attitude to it was strangely detached. Anissimov writes—'The peasants sometimes refused to bring water or fuel for their own land, which was being ploughed by Station tractors, unless they were paid to do so.'[65] The peasants saw the officials with whom they had to deal as outsiders, from whom nothing good was to be expected, and their lack of identification with the Station was in no way lessened by the amount of bureaucratic confusion they saw around them.

The lack of proper co-ordination started with the upper echelons of the administration. On matters relating to the Stations, the centres—that is, the *Kolkhoztsentr*, the *Khlebotsentr* and the *Selskosoyuz*—were at odds with each other, and found it difficult to reach a unanimous decision.[66] This had very serious repercussions at the lower administrative levels, where all those local authorities, such as officials in charge of organizing Stations and kolkhozes, or those responsible for procurements, or the signing of grain delivery contracts, who had to deal directly with the peasants hounded them incessantly from pillar to post. The following is one of many such examples: in connection with the contracts campaign, Kalinin reported: 'There was a great deal of confusion over the allocation of responsibility for contracts. Time after time the assignments were revised and modified, and as a result the local authorities, and in turn the population, were harassed almost beyond belief.'[67]

As well as wrangling with each other, *Narkomzem* and *Narkomtorg* which, in the administrative sense, were two major vested interests, also conducted a steady campaign aimed at limiting the influence and prestige of the co-operative administration, although the latter was, in principle, solely responsible for operations in the contracts field. All of these bodies ruthlessly obstructed each other's efforts, and so bitter were the controversies that arose over each issue that, as one author reports, '*Narkomzem* circulated memoranda to the effect that they would not obey orders from *Narkomtorg*', while the latter expressed the same intentions with regard to their rivals, and announced that they were 'proposing to disregard orders from *Narkomzem*'.[68]

The confusion grew steadily worse at the lower levels of the administration. 'The *okrugi* received dozens of orders of the most contradictory kind, and the *okrug* authorities, in their turn, were not slow to follow the example set by their superiors.' [69] The same source adds that much energy was wasted in this inter-sector rivalry, to which the various branches of the co-operative administration also contributed enthusiastically. No action could be taken without prior consultation with several other departments, and the number of departments involved tended to increase as matters reached the level where direct contact was made with the peasants. Each *okrug* had some five or six departments among whom agreement had to be reached, viz '*Okrtorg, Okrzu, Gosbank,* the credit association and the co-operative administration. Furthermore, since none of these bodies was content to play a passive role, they were all actively engaged in pursuing their own interests.' [70]

As a result, the villages received at least two contracts plans, one from the *Okrzu* (*Narkomzem's* agricultural department in the *okrug*) and the other from the co-operative authorities, the difference between the two being of the order of 200%. According to our source, this kind of 'readjustment' in the plans was happening in Russia as well as in the Ukraine.[71]

The peasants found themselves obliged to sign contracts which they did not always understand, and in which certain clauses gave them grounds for anxiety; the above author quotes one such clause, which he describes as 'badly drafted', and which required them to deliver 'all marketable surpluses, but not less than 150–250% of the sums advanced . . .' [by the State—M.L.].[72] After having signed, the peasants were faced with 'supplementary' demands, and the provisions of their contracts were accordingly altered by the authorities to comply with the latest instructions received from the various local centres.

Lvov also states, giving a further reference to Kalinin, 'in this context, countless instances can be quoted in which additional demands were made while the contracts and sowing campaigns were under way, and they sometimes cost the country very dear'.[73]

This method of working would not have proved practicable unless backed by harsh coercive measures. The contracts which were signed under such conditions had virtually no effect at all in the work of inculcating or introducing improved farming techniques or furthering the cause of collectivization. Moscow regarded the contracts campaign as the spearhead of the socialist advance in the countryside; to the peasants it meant nothing but State interference, which brought confusion and frustration in its wake.

When driven to despair, they often gave vent to their feelings in biting *chastushki*, which sang the praises of a planned régime whose officials were constantly descending on them to countermand one series of orders after another.

The co-operative authorities alone were responsible for many such visitations, since officials from the various branches responsible for grain, credits, meat, milk, a number of industrial crops, consumers' co-operatives, etc., all had direct dealings with the peasants.

'The peasant is being torn asunder by the various branches of the co-operative movement; he is subject to a great many questions and a great deal of form-filling, and has to deal with a considerable number of our co-operative officials. It must be said that the situation is absolutely intolerable.' [74]

The foregoing remark, made by a planning official, tells us much about the nature of the co-operative movement, which had simply become another highly bureaucratized branch of the State administrative apparatus, and was entirely under central control. The situation, as seen through the eyes of the peasant or any other citizen, was full of paradoxes: there was a desperate shortage of trained men for all constructive purposes, but a plethora of *chinovniki*; at the top, the levers of power were in the hands of an ever-narrowing circle of individuals, while at the base there was a proliferation of administrative bodies, each tending to duplicate the work of the other. The régime's failure to set up a simple and efficient administration in the rural areas was but another aspect of its inability to communicate with the peasants in terms which were appropriate to them, as adults and citizens. Indeed, the régime did not look on them in this light.

3. *The Growth of the Kolkhozes in 1929*

During 1929, there was a significant development in the kolkhoz movement. This took place in three successive phases, firstly in the period up until June, subsequently during the period from June to October, and finally during the months from October to December. This latter phase in fact belongs to the new stage in development marked by the radical change in policy which took place during these months.

During winter and spring, the kolkhozes had been developing at a slower rate than in the corresponding period of the previous year. Thousands of new associations had sprung up, but had proved short-lived, and the authorities were worried by the number of false starts, and by the general fluidity of the situation, which was hindering progress or indeed causing a recession in their campaign. [75] The head of the *Kolkhoztsentr* noted this slowing-up in the rate of growth, but considered that it was to some extent offset by the creation of several outsize kolkhozes on a scale much larger than anything that had hitherto been attempted.[76] There are few exact figures available. According to one source, there had been a drop in the number of kolkhozes in several regions in the RSFSR; however, this statement is questioned by several other sources.[77] Be that as it may, the *Kolkhoztsentr* reported that by about June 1st an average of 3·9% of households, over the country as a whole, had joined the kolkhozes, as compared with 2·1% in June 1928. The Ukraine even recorded a figure of 4·3%. One recent source estimates the degree of collectivization for various regions as extending from 0·6% to 3·9%, with a total of 1,008,000 households distributed among 57,035 collective enterprises of all types.[78] The North Caucasus, the two *krai* of the Volga and the steppes of the Ukraine were in the lead with, respectively, 7·3%; 5·3% (Lower Volga); 3·9% (Middle Volga), and 5·3%. For the most part, these kolkhozes were still very small-scale undertakings, the average size being some 10–15 families, with about 50–80 *desyatiny* of land.[79] Despite the relative importance of this development, the authorities were disappointed by these 'dwarf kolkhozes'. Their rate of productivity was low, and their existence precarious, and they frequently amounted to no more than family associations. Some of them were, in fact, pseudo-kolkhozes set up by enterprising peasants as a means of escaping the attentions of procurements agents or tax collectors, or as a convenient front behind which they could qualify for State aid while retaining the bulk of their private property intact.[80] It should, however, be noted that the suspicions which were entertained about these 'pseudo-kolkhozes' were often exaggerated.

The majority of these collectives were *tozy* (62·3%), while the *arteli* and *kommuny* accounted respectively for 30·8% and 6·9% of the total. However, the degree of socialization of property in the *tozy* was very restricted. In the *tozy* of the North Caucasus, for example, 65% of the seed, 71% of the agricultural machinery, 87% of the draught animals and 96·6% of the herd were all in private ownership. A similar situation existed in Siberia and in the Lower Volga. In the Ukraine, the *arteli* had socialized 61% of their means of production, whereas the corresponding figure for the *tozy* was a bare 11%, and 8·8% in the case of horses. The *tozy* were also a less stable form than the others. In Siberia, 25% of the *tozy* had been dissolved, whereas only 10·6% of the *arteli* had ceased to function.[81]

The *toz* was a more simple form of collective association than the others, but it was also more readily accessible to the peasants, being particularly favoured by the serednyaks, who comprised some 20–30% of the membership, while the *arteli* and *kommuny* were made up of bednyaks.[82] Those in charge of the co-operative and collective movement had also demonstrated their preference for the *toz*, which they regarded as an indispensable first stage in the process of development.[83]

Meanwhile, however, the more influential elements within the Politburo and certain members of the Central Committee were turning their attention to a new development which had become apparent at the beginning of the year. In March, the *Kolkhoztsentr* informed the *Sovnarkom* that in Russia and the Ukraine, and more especially in certain regions of the North Caucasus, the Volga and the steppes (Nikolaev, Odessa, Zaporozhe) whole villages had 'adopted a statute', that is, had gone over to collective farming. During the month of March 180 villages in the Ukraine had formed *tozy* (the *Sovnarkom* of the Ukraine sent them practically all the tractors which they had available)[84] At the same time, as we have already mentioned, giant kolkhozes had been set up, which consisted not of one village but of a whole group of villages; these covered thousands of hectares of land, and took the form of *arteli*, *kommuny* or large-scale *tozy*. The decision to organize large collectives on these lines had been taken by the *Kolkhoztsentr* in December 1928, their aim being to cover a total area of 775 thousand hectares with these giant formations. By June, it was reported that 208 kolkhozes of this type had already come into being, including 150 in the RSFSR with between 2,000 and 8,000 hectares of land apiece, and eighteen with 10,000 hectares apiece.[85] At this point, the head of the *Kolkhoztsentr*, with the support of the Politburo, began to suffer from delusions of grandeur. The giant kolkhozes were heralded as the ultimate solution to the problem of expanding the collective sector, and since the government were now placing such enormous faith in them, all the available technical resources which they could muster, and a sizeable proportion of the credits, were to be channelled in this direction, while the rest of the kolkhozes made do with their own horses.

The *Kolkhoztsentr* decided that the area cultivated by these 'giants' should be doubled in the period between June and October.[86] This sector was henceforth to become a movement on its own, receiving priority treatment of its problems directly from the *STO*, and calling its own special conferences; according to the plans as they were envisaged at this stage, it would by 1930 be responsible for 30% of the total area farmed by the kolkhozes.

In the period between June and October there was a spectacular upsurge (in terms of numbers) in the kolkhoz movement. During these four months, 900,000 households joined the kolkhozes, and the percentage of collectivization rose from 3·9% in June to 7·6% in October, which meant almost two million households and 8·8%

of the country's sown areas. In these few months, more kolkhozes were formed than at any other time in the history of the USSR.[87] The same features which had been apparent in the earlier period remained in evidence: the kolkhozes were small in size and of a very limited degree of socialization, and there was a preponderance of *tozy*.

At this point, the membership was essentially bednyak in composition, and the serednyaks were still largely uncommitted.[88] However after October there was some increase in the numbers of serednyaks joining,[89] the net effect being to increase the proportion of *tozy*, since this was the only form which the serednyaks were prepared to accept while they were still free to choose, and were not forced to 'change their statute'.

In the meantime, there was evidence of a new phenomenon, *the emergence of regions with a particularly high degree of collectivization among the population.* For example, the proportion of collectivization in the North Caucasus was now 19% of the population, the corresponding figure for the Lower Volga being 18·3%; the Middle Volga showed 14% of collectivization, and the Ukraine 10% (which rose to 16% in the steppe area). It was this phenomenon which gave rise to the idea of the *raion sploshnoi kollektivizatsii*. At the period under discussion, the term *sploshnaya kollektivizatsiya* had not yet been very clearly defined. According to some authorities, it related to a region—initially a *raion*, but subsequently an entire *okrug*—in which the degree of collectivization was moving towards 50% or more of the population. Other sources suggest that the term was applied to regions which had *in effect* either reached or exceeded this figure, while others again held that it related to regions where the great majority of the households already formed part of the kolkhoz organization.[90]

Whatever the definition may have been, the press announced in November that there were now some twenty-five *raiony* in this category, including the Volovski *raion* (Tula province) and the Tiginski *raion* (Northern *krai*), (forming two enormous *kolkhoz-kombinaty* which included the bulk of their respective populations), and the Khopersk *raion* in the Lower Volga. The movement spread, and soon it was no longer a matter of *raiony* but of entire *okrugi* of mass collectivization, the first of these being Khopersk which we have just mentioned. Every week, new names were added to the list, and before long the Lower Volga announced that it had three such *okrugi*, while the north Caucasus reported two, and the Ukraine six, including the Nikolaev *okrug* in which 50% of all households had been collectivized.[91]

In the period prior to October the increase in the numbers of families joining the collectives was not, in the majority of cases, attributable to direct pressure on the part of the authorities. Such pressure as they brought to bear was mainly indirect, and stemmed largely from the atmosphere of tension which had been built up during the procurements, the coercive measures which had been aimed at the better-off peasants, and the economic aid which was made available to the kolkhozes while being withheld from the individual farmer. It was a situation in which the bednyaks could be won over, while the rest of the peasantry held back. The initiative for setting-up the kolkhozes still rested with the local authorities, in accordance with the plans laid down for them by the central authorities to whom they were responsible. When the number of willing bednyaks was no longer adequate to meet the requirements of the plan, the element of coercion and pressure, which so far had been a secondary factor in the situation, began to play a major role.

The element of 'administrative' pressure was particularly important, from the very outset, in the creation of the giant kolkhozes. Whereas the setting-up of small kolkhozes could be achieved on a voluntary basis, the amalgamation of numbers of these small collectives to form 'giants' could not have been carried out other than by administrative order. In fact, the 'giants' were a purely administrative invention.[92]

From the beginning of the year, there had been fairly widespread evidence of pressure, and of the use of semi-coercive measures, or of coercive methods accompanied by acts of violence against the peasants. One author denounced the semi-coercive techniques to which the authorities had occasionally resorted during the contracts campaign in the spring. The instances in question had arisen when 'it was suggested to them [i.e. the villagers who were signing contracts—M.L.] that they should adopt the statute', that is, form a kolkhoz.[93] The writer does not specify what methods were used to persuade the villagers to agree to this proposal.

Certain other sources, among them Kaminsky, also note with disapproval cases in which pressure was brought to bear on serednyaks, who were first of all required by the authorities to join the kolkhoz, and then obliged to hand over their entire means of production to the common fund. Kaminsky denounced this 'anti-seredynak attitude'[94] as evidence of an 'over-zealous approach' which could only alarm the peasants. Indeed, there were many such cases. No adequate action had been taken to clarify the complex position with regard to kolkhoz funds, particularly that part of the common fund which was not repayable to any member who decided to leave the kolkhoz; in fact, there was no clear provision on the question of resignation from the kolkhoz either, and people did not know where they stood. In June, the *Sovnarkom* instructed *Gosplan* and the *Narkomzem* to prepare draft statutes covering the matter of kolkhoz funds, and to submit them within a few weeks, but it is probable that this order was not implemented.[95]

These were complex and highly controversial issues, but it was a long time before they were finally clarified and resolved. The government's failure to do so earlier was particularly harmful in its effects, since even the best-intentioned of the peasants were reluctant to commit themselves to an undertaking whose implications were not clear, while the kolkhoz organizers, being unable to give a definite answer to these questions, were the more inclined to resort to subterfuge and coercion.

Vareikis uses material emanating from the Commissariat of Inspection as his source for a description of the creation of the Vidonovo kolkhoz in the *okrug* of Tyumen in Siberia. The events described had taken place in March, at a time when such cases were still relatively infrequent. However, the technique which was used at Vidonovo had become much commoner by the autumn, and for this reason Vareikis's report is of interest. 'About March 20th,' he writes, 'a representative from the *Oblispolkom* arrived in Vidonovo to see to the setting-up of the kolkhoz. He issued a directive to the local authorities, about the recruitment of new members. According to his instructions, articles 112, 113 and 114 of the agrarian code were to be brought into operation. These articles stipulated that in agrarian communities where a majority had voted in favour of going over to collective farming, the minority who were opposed to this decision could nevertheless be forced to comply with it.'

'On this basis,' Vareikis goes on,
'the method of recruiting individual members was replaced by a method aimed at compelling the dissentient minority to join, and thereby ensuring total collectivization of the entire peasantry without exception. Furthermore, the so-called minority group were not always in fact in the minority. Thus, for example, in the village of Zhuravlevka, which comprised a total of 77 households, 50 persons attended the village meeting. Of these, 18 voted in favour of joining the kolkhoz, and 14 voted against.'

'At the meeting which was called in Vidonovo there were 110 people present. The matter on the agenda, namely whether the village should join the kolkhoz, was put to the vote in the form of a single question: "Who is against?" *Nobody voted against joining.* A committee of 15 kolkhoz members and 15 individual peasants was elected, and it was proposed that they should recruit members for the kolkhoz. The 15 individual peasants then refused to sit on the committee. They were fined and imprisoned for 36 hours. The same situation arose in other villages in this region.'

At this point, the authorities began to use coercion, threatening the peasants and sending those who resisted to the *selsovet*, where they were sometimes held for twenty-four or thirty-six hours. Local officials found plenty of ways in which the peasants could be intimidated: 'arrest and deportation to the town under escort, like prisoners', 'a fine of up to 300 roubles', 'expulsion from the community', etc.[96]

Vareikis then gives the names of peasants who had been fined, together with the amount of the fines, and goes on to say that as a consequence of the methods used 444 out of 448 households had joined the kolkhoz by April 1st. However, 'anti-Soviet elements', taking advantage of the unrest that this had created among the peasants, organized a sizeable number of illegal meetings, which led to numerous defections. The *okrug* authorities succeeded in arresting the loss in membership (Vareikis does not say how) and 204 households stayed on in the kolkhoz. The author also quotes further examples from the Stalingrad *oblast*, where the chairman of the *selsovet* brought pressure to bear on the bednyaks by informing them that if they did not join the kolkhoz they would receive neither seed nor machinery.[97]

Cases of this kind had been occurring in the period prior to June, but by the second half of the year, the trend had become much more marked. The initiative came from Moscow. We have already discussed the steps which the government took to speed up collectivization from the month of June onward. Every means at their disposal, in the form of *MTS*, credits and kolkhoz and co-operative administrative apparatus, was used to this end. Those peasants who were Party members were now faced, for the first time, with the duty of setting an example to the others by joining the kolkhozes.[98] We shall see later on what the reaction of these rural communists was.

The increased emphasis which the government was placing on the kolkhozes was reflected in the demands which were made on the local authorities in this connection. Present-day Soviet sources now admit that during the latter half of the year there was evidence of 'over-precipitate action' and undesirable developments.[99] One of the examples which they quote was the tendency of the authorities responsible for the backward eastern regions 'to emulate the level of collectivization which had been achieved in the pilot-regions of the USSR'. In the course of one year, the percentage of collectivization in Buryat Mongolia rose from 1·2% to 5·7%: the corresponding figures for Bashkiria were 1·4% to 5·5%, and Kazakhstan 1·8% to 5·3%.[100]

But these were not the only regions so affected. By the end of the summer, collectivization had become a State campaign in which the régime were deploying the full range of resources and administrative action generally associated with such campaigns. In August, the Central Committee announced that October 14th would be 'a day of yield and collectivization'. In preparation for this 'day', the local authorities were canvassed for weeks beforehand in a drive intended to whip up the competitive spirit, and stimulate them to improve their performance and beat all records.[101]

It was inevitable that a 'high-pressure' campaign of this nature, conducted with the maximum publicity throughout the entire country, should be accompanied by a wave of violence and coercive measures.

The campaign was also the occasion for propaganda statements on the *raiony* or *okrugi* which had been announced as regions of *sploshnaya kollektivizatsiya*, and these served the Party cadres as an example of what was expected by Moscow. Yet again, this amounted in practice to an invitation to arbitrary administrative action by those concerned.

It was the Party that decided which regions would be declared areas of mass collectivization. By September, there were already twenty-three *raiony* in this category; a month later, Moscow decided that by the end of the quinquennium, there should be thirty-five to forty *okrugi* with 100% collectivization. This announcement was prompted by the zeal of the local Party organization, or rather the Party Committee. The famous Khopersk *okrug* in the Lower Volga, which had launched the movement for *sploshnaya kollektivizatsiya* of entire *okrugi* and forced the *Kolkhoztsentr* to applaud its initiative was, on the authority of the *Kolkhoztsentr* itself, no different from other regions, either in respect of its degree of collectivization or its economic importance. It was the local Party committee which had decided that the region should figure as a pilot-*okrug* in the collectivization campaign. The same procedure was followed in the case of the other thirty-five to forty *okrugi* which copied the example of Khopersk. This soon came to be known as 'the method of mass collectivization', and was presented by Stalin as an essential precondition 'without which it would be impossible to implement the Five-year Plan for collectivization'.[102]

While the Centre was preparing to speed up the rate of collectivization still further, it was clear from the situation of the kolkhozes, and from the objective conditions in which they were operating and developing, that what was in fact needed was a period of respite.

There was abundant evidence of this, not least in the reactions of the peasant Party members.

The rural communists had been urged to set an example in order to encourage the rest of the peasants. However, they attempted to evade this obligation in every way possible. There were considerable numbers of middle peasants in the local Party cells, in fact the Central Committee had calculated that 20% of their effective membership was made up of better-off peasants [or perhaps peasants who had reached this condition by virtue of being Party members. —M.L.]. The proletarian elements were not sufficiently represented in the local cells, a fact which the Central Committee criticized in its November decision relative to the Party in the Ukraine. Consequently the role of the communists in the kolkhozes was negligible. Out of 4,037 *arteli* and *kommuny* in the Ukraine, only 174 had Party cells.[103]

The fact was that the peasant Party members were reacting in the same way as the rest of the peasants, particularly if they did not come from the bednyak stratum. Many Party cells refused to pass a resolution forcing all their members to join the kolkhozes.[104] *Pravda* reported, 'There is unanimous agreement, from a great number of accounts, that the recruitment of communists to the kolkhozes is not going well'. The paper quoted reactions from the rural communists; some who were serednyaks said that before joining the collective 'you must first become a bednyak'. Others took refuge behind their wives: 'I would go willingly, but my wife won't let me'.[105] This was no mere excuse; there were many instances in which wives had threatened to divorce their husbands, communist or no, if they joined the kolkhoz. Some communists were therefore faced with a dilemma, in which they had to choose between expulsion from the Party and the disruption of their family life.

Despite opposition from certain members of the Central Committee, notably Vareikis,[106] the Party decided to take disciplinary action, this being consistent with the logic of its internal set-up. It did not know how to educate its rural members,[107] who constituted the most neglected sector of its organization. *During the previous years nothing had been done to prepare the Party cadres for the important tasks that lay ahead of them, and all of a sudden they were being called upon to act as pioneers in a revolution which they did not understand and which was not of their choosing.* It was not surprising, therefore, that the Party leadership had to fall back on 'bureaucratic' techniques.

In the course of a purge which was carried out in the summer of 1929, 13% of the rural communists, and in some regions 25%, were expelled from the Party.[108] Despite this action, the situation remained unchanged, and the cells either persisted in their reluctance to join the kolkhozes, or, if they had already joined, maintained a negative attitude to their work, and slowed down the process of socializing the means of production.[109] Nor was this attitude confined to the remoter regions; it was equally apparent in the Moscow *oblast* itself, close to the very seat of power.[110] Faced with the lack of enthusiasm or the opposition which they were encountering from the rural communists on the subject of collectivization, the Central Committee accused them of having been 'corrupted', of having 'fused' (*srashchivanie*) with the kulaks, and being guilty of 'opportunist deviations'.[111]

These difficulties with the Party showed that, by the autumn of 1929, the kolkhoz movement had progressed as far as it could go under the then existing circumstances.

In September, the *Kolkhoztsentr* submitted to the Politburo, who were at that time preparing for the coming session of the Central Committee, a detailed report on the situation of the kolkhozes. This account began by noting the successes which had been achieved, and went on to give an extremely realistic appraisal of the defects from which the movement suffered. In one chapter entitled 'Negative developments and defects in the kolkhoz movement' the authors (probably Kaminsky himself) listed a whole series of shortcomings.[112]

The report informed the Politburo that the intake of peasants into the kolkhozes was not accompanied by a corresponding intake of the means of production, since the peasants, and notably the serednyaks, were selling off their implements and livestock before joining. It was further stated that even in the regions of mass collectivization the numbers of *serednyaks* who joined the collectives were still small.[113]

In themselves, these two symptoms of weakness in the movement should have sufficed to give the leadership cause to think twice before decreeing a further speed-up in the rate of collectivization. The report itself already foreshadowed the means which would be employed to achieve expansion in this field. It specifically mentioned that the authorities were resorting to administrative pressure in their efforts to promote the setting-up of kolkhozes, particularly in the case of the giant kolkhozes. There was one procedure which the *Kolkhoztsentry* had adopted, in certain instances, in dealing with already existing kolkhozes, and which the authors of the report wholeheartedly condemned. This consisted of issuing an administrative order fixing consumption norms for the kolkhoz members, and requiring them to hand over the rest of their production to the State. This, we should add, was the 'rationing scheme' which the peasants particularly dreaded, and which constituted one of their most powerful arguments against the kolkhozes. The press had accused 'kulak propagandists' of spreading these rumours about 'rationing', but it is obvious that they had some basis in fact.

The report then went on to state that there was a tendency for the kolkhozes to sell their grain 'on the side', and that though this was sometimes prompted by ill-will, it was often done in order to improve their poor financial position.

One of the reasons for the very low level of organization within the kolkhozes was the shortage of trained cadres, particularly agronomists. The management was inefficient, and those in charge had no clear idea how to draw up production plans—a defect which was particularly serious in the case of large-scale undertakings—or how to deal with the innumerable problems which arose in connection with the organization of production, particularly the crucial question of renumeration for work on the kolkhoz. Yet another source of weakness was the nature of social life in the kolkhozes. 'The old way of life, with its characteristic outbursts of drunkenness, stealing and violence, is highly prejudicial to the stability of the kolkhoz.'[114]

In fact, the matters raised in the report had been known about for months. In May, Kaminsky had told the Fifth Congress of Soviets that the movement was suffering from a lack of trained personnel, and machinery, and that its administrations were short of officials with the necessary juridical training.[115] The latter defect was quickly remedied, but the September report made it clear that there was still a dangerous divergence between the size of the movement and the weaknesses which were apparent in its cultural and educational services. According to the *Kolkhoztsentr*, the question of illiteracy, the shortage of schools and clubs, the low level of political propaganda and the lack of basic agronomic instruction were all problems which called for urgent solution.

It was clear from these accounts, and from the general body of information on the situation, that what the authorities must do at this stage was to call a halt in the growth of the movement, which would give the kolkhozes and their administrations time to consolidate past gains, and to learn how to function efficiently. However the Politburo, acutely conscious of the country's predicament, and obsessed by the quantitative aspects of kolkhoz expansion, were bent on pursuing a different policy. The only thing which counted for them was figures, figures which showed, for example, that the kolkhozes had already sown over 4 million hectares, and that the sovkhozes had sown almost 2 million, or that they were already producing 1·3 and 0·8 million tons of marketable grain respectively.[116] (This amounted to 11·9% of the country's total marketable grain.) Meanwhile, the private sector in agriculture was at a standstill, or in fact undergoing a recession, and was incapable either of increasing its very small production of grain for the market, or improving the poor yield of its farms. Given these circumstances, the Politburo would appear to have reasoned as follows: everything must be gambled on a spectacular effort to ensure that this figure of 11·9% which the 'socialist sector' had already achieved would be increased to 40%. When this figure was reached, the Politburo would hold the key to the nation's food supplies once and for all. . . .

As we have seen, during the course of the year the difficulties which the country was experiencing over grain were further aggravated by a downward trend in the livestock sector. The reduction in livestock holdings represented a further threat to the nation's already precarious food supplies.

Again, the solution proposed by the Politburo followed the earlier line of reasoning: the rate of collectivization must be speeded up, and livestock sectors must be developed both in the sovkhozes and the kolkhozes, particularly in the 'giants'. It will be remembered that, some four to five months previously, *Gosplan's* original draft for the Five-year Plan had suggested postponing the collectivization of livestock until the next quinquennium. However, in September and October *Pravda* and *Bolshevik* were urging the introduction of collective livestock herds, and had published proposals drafted by the appropriate departments for the socialization, during the coming year, of 80% of livestock in the large kolkhozes, and 50% (including cows) in the others. It was agreed that the State ought to assist the kolkhozes to build up these herds, but that in the absence of adequate resources to finance such purchases, the cost of the operation would have to be borne by the individual kolkhoz members.[117]

This was a radical change in policy, which had been prompted by pressure of immediate difficulties, and its implications can best be judged if it is remembered that, under the terms of the *toz* and kolkhoz statutes which were in operation at that time, socialization of cows was not compulsory.[118] Thus, an even greater burden was being laid on the peasants, in addition to those which they had already been required to shoulder.

These constant changes of objective, which we have already discussed in the context of industrial planning, were also a feature of the government's agricultural plans. As we have seen, by the month of April Stalin had already ceased to hope for anything from the private sector, and was pinning his faith on the collective movement. But the extent and the timing of the collectivization operation, as he envisaged it, were still consistent with the provisions laid down by *Gosplan*. However, since the Five-year Plan had been ratified, every month had brought further changes of objective, which reflected the régime's growing preoccupation with the problems which beset it, and the growing optimism inspired by reports of the numbers of households which had been collectivized, the large kolkhozes which had been created, and the regions which had undergone mass collectivization.

Thus, the Five-year Plan had envisaged a figure of 5 million households in collective farms by the year 1932–3, with a total area of 21–22 million hectares. In June 1929, the *Kolkhoztsentr* was already thinking in terms of 7–8 million peasants in collectives, and 8 million hectares of collectivized land during 1930 alone.[119] From this moment, the initial Five-year Plan for agriculture became meaningless, since the *Kolkhoztsentr* was now aiming at collectivizing half the rural population during the quinquennium, and at trebling the figure for collectivized land which had initially been envisaged by the plan, so that by 1933 the kolkhozes would be providing 10 million tons of marketable grain, which amounted to the nation's total requirements.[120]

One might add that independently of these plans, Bauman had expressed the opinion that collectivization of the entire population would take as much as twenty years, and the Moscow Party Committee were aiming no higher than a figure of 25% for the number of collectivized households in their *oblast* by the end of the quinquennium.[121]

In June, the *Kolkhoztsentr* had declared an objective of 8 million hectares of land under kolkhoz cultivation by 1930. By August, Mikoyan was speaking of 10 million hectares. In September, the target fixed for 1929–30 in *Gosplan*'s control figures was of the order of 13 million hectares, with 10% of the rural population in 89,000 kolkhozes.[122] But these control figures were to be revised during October and November, the new target being 15·2 million hectares, 12% of the population collectivized, and exactly 3·139 million households.[123]

In December, there was a further revision in the plans, though this time it took a new form: The *Sovnarkom* decided to collectivize 30 million hectares of peasant holdings, and to create sovkhozes on 3·7 million hectares of land.[124]

As we have already seen, the objectives relating to the socialization of livestock and to the *MTS* had undergone similar revision. These constant changes of objective reflected the absence of any

stable programme or clearly-defined long-term aims for the agricultural sector in general, and for the collective movement in particular. The Politburo were incessant in their demands, and from
the summer of 1929 onwards, they exerted continuous pressure on
the local organizations of the Party to exceed the targets that had
previously been set for them. The local authorities complied with
these demands, and the resultant reports about over-fulfilment of
earlier plans which reached the Centre from the men on the spot
encouraged the central authorities to set their sights even higher.

About the beginning of December, the Politburo once more
chose to disregard all the existing directives on agriculture, but
this time their demands were not confined to increases in current
plans; what they now required was a veritable 'leap forward',
which had nothing in common with any of their own previous
plans for the agricultural sector.

NOTES AND REFERENCES

1. *Kollektivizatsiya selskogo khozyaistva*, doc. No. 46: decision
of the Central Committee of June 27, 1929.

2. *ibid*, p. 183.

3. *ibid*, p. 184.

4. *ibid*, doc. No. 52: decision of August 26th of the Central
Committee on *kontraktatsiya*.

5. *ibid*, doc. No. 57: decree of October 7, 1929 of *Sovnarkom*.

6. *ibid*, decision of the Central Committee on *kontraktatsiya*.

7. *ibid*, decree of October 7, 1929 of *Sovnarkom*.

8. *Bolshevik*, 1929, No. 19, p. 14.

9. Mikoyan, 'Novaya khlebozagotovitelnaya kampaniya i
zadachi partii', *Bolshevik*, 1929, No. 15, p. 20. (Emphasis supplied.)

10 Kessel, 'Kontraktatsiya i kollektivizatsiya', *Planovoe Khozyaistvo*, 1929, No. 11, p. 100.

11. *Pravda* editorial, August 7, 1929, p. 7.

12. *ibid*.

13. *ibid*.

14. A report by *Kholkhoztsentr* in *Dokumenty po istorii sovetskogo obshchestva* (Moscow 1959), Vol. VIII, pp. 267–70.

15. *Kollektivizatsiya selskogo khozyaistva*, doc. No. 45; decree
of the *TsIK* of *Sovnarkom*, 'O merakh ukrepleniya kolkhoznoi sis-
temy'; *Sobranie Zakonov*, Part One, July 8th, No. 40.

16. *ibid*.

17. The decree says so, but in a rather ambiguous way. However,
the sum total of measures taken with regard to collectivization,

including the use of *Kontraktatsiya* as a means of concentrating resources in the co-operative sector, provide sufficient proof that this was the case. Towards the end of the year, the decision to this effect was explicit.

18. For these decrees see *Kollektivizatsiya selskogo khozyaistva,* doc. No. 21, 44.

19. *ibid,* No. 48–59.

20. *Dokumenty po istorii sovetskogo obshchestva,* Vol. VII, pp. 267–70.

21. See the criticism made by the Central Committee at the end of June, relative to bad management of agricultural affairs, methods of *administrirovanie,* and inefficiency in the context of aid for the kolkhozes. *Kollektivizatsiya selskogo khozyaistva,* doc. No. 50, p. 193.

22. For the pronouncement of the Central Committee of May 27th concerning the tasks of these rural trade unions see *Kollektivizatsiya selskogo khozyaistva,* doc. No. 42, p. 173–4.

23. In the 'circular' of *Pravda,* June 23, 1929.

24. An appeal of the Central Committee concerning the autumn sowing campaign. *Kollektivizatsiya selskogo khozyaistva,* doc. No. 50.

25. Decree of *Sovnarkom* of June 21, 1929. *Istoriya kolkhoznogo prava* (see Ch. 5, Note 7), Vol. I, pp. 106, 142.

26. Pronouncement of the Central Committee of July 29, 1929, on Party work in preparation for the procurements campaign. *Kollektivizatsiya selkogo khozyaistva,* doc. No. 49.

27. *ibid.*

28. *ibid.*

29. Mikoyan, *Bolshevik,* 1929, No. 15, p. 23.

30. *ibid,* p. 29.

31. *ibid,* and *Code Pénal* (Paris, 1935), p. 186, on the penalty *pyatikratka.*

32. Mikoyan, 'Liniya partii pobedila', *Pravda,* December 7, 1929. Groman was a member of this commission; he was to be violently criticized, and removed from his post. See the reply to his letter in *Pravda,* November 10, 1929.

33. This figure is in *Bolshevik,* 1929, No. 19, p. 9.

34. Mikoyan, *Bolshevik,* 1929, No. 15, p. 16.

35. Mikoyan, 'Liniya partii pobedila', *Pravda,* December 7, 1929.

36. The figure is quoted from the archives by Moshchkov in an article in *Istoriya SSSR,* 1960, No. 4; *Planovoe Khozyaistvo,* 1932, No. 4, p. 77.

37. Details have already been given. The state of affairs in the

sphere of stockbreeding alone provides ample proof of the correctness of Frumkin's observation on the absence of any will to produce.

38. The régime reacted to this widespread connivance by carrying out purges. See, for example, Angarov, *op. cit.* (see Ch. 2, Note 39), pp. 76–8, on the phenomenon of *srashchivanie*.

39. It was intended that 4–5% of the peasants should pay 30–45% of all taxes. In 1929 the 2·9% considered to be the richest peasants, paid 22·8% of the entire agricultural tax.

40. Under the law relative to wage-labour employed in kulak farms (*Kollektivizatsiya selskogo khozyaistva,* doc. No. 27), and legislation governing the renting of land.

41. Sheboldaev, *Bolshevik,* 1930, No. 11–12, pp. 57.

42. In August the Central Committee organ for rural cadres wrote in connection with the industrial loan that 'there must be no standing on ceremony with the kulak over this question, any more than there is over procurements. Kulak agitation against the loan must be combatted, in the same way as one would combat counter-revolutionary activities.' *Derevenski Kommunist,* 1929, No. 18, p. 18. The seriousness of such a directive is underlined by the fact that it was issued in connection with subscriptions to a loan, a measure which by definition implies voluntary contribution.

43. Mendelson *Planovoe Khozyaistvo,* 1929, No. 8, p. 19. See also Kurbatov, *NAF,* 1929, No. 5; Sheboldaev, *Bolshevik,* 1929, No. 11–12, pp. 53–4 (for the years 1927–9). A detailed account is contained in *Postroenie fundamenta sotsialisticheskoi ekonomiki v SSSR* (see Ch. 1, Note 30), p. 272.

44. *Bolshevik,* 1929, No. 12, p. 41.

45. Gaister, speech to the Conference of Agrarian-Marxists, *NAF,* 1930, No. I, pp. 96–7. Gaister mentions a 'relative and absolute decrease in the number of kulaks'.

46. Stalin, *Bolshevik,* 1929, No. 23–4, p. 47.

47. Angarov, *op. cit.,* pp. 45–6.

48. For an account of the strained relations which existed between the kolkhozes and the rest (that is the majority) of the population, see, for example, Vareikis, member of the Central Committee and secretary of the Central Black Earth Region, in *NAF,* 1929, No. 18, p. 79–80.

49. According to Yakovleva, a delegate to the Sixteenth Party Conference, the millions which the State was spending and investing in the countryside were being squandered owing to the illiteracy of rural cadres. It was her opinion that more should be done in the first place to raise standards of education and culture. *16-taya*

Konferentsiya VKP(b) stenogramme, p. 93. See also Pashukanis, *op. cit.* (see Ch. 3, Note 5), p. 472.

50. Golendo stated in October 1929 that the majority of sovkhozes were making a loss. *NAF*, 1929, No. 10, pp. 92–3.

51. Vareikis, *16-taya Konferentsiya, VKP(b)*, stenogramme, p. 161.

52. Agaev gives the following figures: the average salary of a worker in a sovkhoz administered by the *Sovkhoztsentr* was, in 1928–9, 33·9 roubles per month. A worker in the urban food industry earned 86·8 roubles, in the leather industry 89·6 roubles, while a metal worker earned 89·9 roubles. *NAF*, 1929, No. 3, pp. 79–80.

53. *Dokumenty po istorii sovetskogo obshchestva* (see Note 14), Vol. VIII, doc. No. 5, p. 295.

54. According to Soviet archives, quoted by Borisov, *op. cit.* (see Ch. 13, Note 1), p. 20.

55. Kulikov, *NAF*, 1929, No. 2, p. 73.

56. For a description of the state of the 'columns' and the MTS see Anissimov, *Bolshevik*, 1929, No. 1. Tsylko, *NAF*, 1929, No. 11–12. Tsylko's account is particularly depressing: the stations had been set up in haste, personnel had not been prepared in advance, there were no operational or construction plans, etc.

57. Tsylko, *op. cit.*, pp. 149–51.

58. Tsylko, *op. cit.*, Anissimov, *op. cit.*, pp. 49–51.

59. Vareikis, *16-taya Konferentsiya VKP(b)*, stenogramme, pp. 161.

60. Borisov, *op. cit.*, p. 21.

61. Tsylko, *op. cit.*, p. 149; Anissimov, *op. cit.*, p. 50.

62. Kulikov, *NAF*, 1929, No. 2, p. 73. Kalinin argued that the main cause of the peasants' reluctance to join the kolkhozes was their fear of losing their land. *5-ty S'ezd Sovetov*, stenogramme, bulletin No. 19, p. 3.

63. Tsylko, *op. cit.*, p. 148.

64. Kulikov, *op. cit.*, p. 73.

65. Anissimov, *op. cit.*, p. 50.

66. Anissimov, *op. cit.*, The *Traktortsentr* was set up precisely vith the object of rationalizing this situation.

67. *16-taya Konferentsiya VKP(b)*, stenogramme, p. 26.

68. Lvov, *NAF*, 1929, No. 7, p. 34.

69. *ibid*, p. 34.

70. *ibid*, p. 33.

71. *ibid*, p. 34.

72. *ibid*, p. 40. We have already quoted Mikoyan as stating that all surpluses' was indeed what was meant.

73. *ibid*, p. 41.

74. Veisberg, 'Leninskaya kooperatsiya v pyatiletnem plane', *Planovoe Khozyaistvo*, 1929, No. 3, p. 105.

75. Kotov, *NAF*, 1929, No. 10, p. 101.

76. Kaminsky, *16-taya Konferentsiya VKP(b)*, stenogramme, p. 186; Kotov, *op. cit.*, p. 97.

77. Kotov, *op. cit.*, p. 101; these figures relating to the Central Black Earth Region are given the lie in an article on the kolkhozes of that region by Voronov, *NAF*, 1929, No. 10.

78. A report of the *Kolkhozsentr* in *Dokumenty po istorii sovetskogo obshchestva*, Vol. VII, p. 299; *Postroenie fundamenta sotsialisticheskoi ekonomiki v SSR*, p. 299; Danilov (ed.), *op. cit.* (see Ch. 13, Note 74), p. 29.

79. Danilov, *op. cit.*, p. 31.

80. *Dokumenty po istorii sovetskogo obshchestva*, Vol. VII, pp. 267–70.

81. According to the Central Archives of the October Revolution quoted in *Voprosy Istorii KPSS*, 1958, No. 4, p. 78. Slightly different figures in respect of the forms of kolkhozes are given in *Postroenie fundamenta sotsialisticheskoi ekonomiki v SSSR*, p. 291.

		1925	1927	1928	1929
Kommuny	%	10.6	7.3	5.4	6.2
Arteli		63·3	46·0	38·4	33·6
Tozy		24·1	46·7	59·8	60·2

82. *Dokumenty po istorii sovetskogo obshchestva*, Vol. VII, pp. 239–40.

83. In *Postroenie fundamenta sotsialisticheskoi ekonomiki v SSSR*, pp. 345–6 this tendency of the *Soyuz Soyuzov* and of the All-Soviet Council of Kolkhozes is described as 'mistaken'.

84. *Voprosy Istorii KPSS*, 1958, No. 4, pp. 74–5; Danilov (ed.), *op. cit.*, pp. 174–5.

85. *Dokumenty po istorii sovetskogo obshchestva*, Vol. VII, p. 222; *Kaminsky, 5-ty S'ezd Sovetov*, stenogramme, bulletin No. 18, pp. 29–30; Ratner, *NAF*, 1929, No. 10, p. 48.

86. Kaminsky, *16-taya Konferentsiya, VKP(b)*, stenogramme, p. 187; Golendo, *NAF*, 1929, No. 10, p. 18; this target in the 'control figures' for 1929–30 was officially confirmed by the *Sovnarkom*. See *Dokumenty po istorii sovetskogo obshchestva*, Vol. VII, pp. 220–1.

87. Danilov (ed), *op. cit.*, pp. 32–3, 174–5; Lyashchenko, *op. cit.* (see Ch. 1, Note 42), Vol. III, pp. 362–5; *Voprosy Istorii KPSS*, 1958, No. 4, p. 79.

88. Kukushkin, *op. cit.* (see Ch. 1, Note 28), p. 41; on p. 291 of *Postroenie fundamenta sotsialisticheskoi ekonomiki v SSSR* it is stated that the bednyaks, who represented 35% of the rural population, comprised 78% of the members of the *kommuny*, 67% of the members of *arteli*, and 60% of the members of the *tozy*.

89. Kukushkin, *op. cit.*, p. 41; Danilov (ed), *op. cit.*, p. 32.

90. Ratner, *NAF*, 1929, No. 10, pp. 52–3.

91. Borisov, *op. cit.* (see Note 54), pp. 43, 84; Danilov (ed.), *op. cit.*, p. 179; Kukushkin, *op. cit.*, p. 51.

92. Naumov, in Gaister's pamphlet, *op. cit.* (see Ch. 11, Note 15), pp. 81–2; *Dokumenty po istorii sovetskogo obshchestva*, Vol. VIII, pp. 276–80. See also Kaminsky's statement that large kolkhozes cannot be formed spontaneously. *16-taya Konferentsiya VKP(b)*, stenogramme, p. 187.

93. Lvov, *NAF*, 1929, No. 7, p. 39.

94. Kaminsky at the Council of Kolkhozes, *Pravda*, June 20, 1929.

95. Decree of the *TsIK* of *Sovnarkom* of June 21, 1929, *Kollektivizatsiya selskogo khozyaistva*, doc. No. 45.

96. Vareikis, 'O partiinom rukovodstve kolkhoza', *NAF*, 1929, No. 8, pp. 64–5.

97. *ibid*.

98. See *Pravda*, June 7, 1929. The decision whereby a communist who owned a farm would be required to be the first to join the kolkhoz was taken in November 1929; in the Central Committee declaration concerning work in the Ukraine, see *KPSS v Rezolyutsiyakh*, Vol. II, p. 662. At local level decisions of this kind had been taken before this date. See Vareikis, *NAF*, 1929, No. 8, p. 67.

99. Danilov (ed.), *op. cit.*, pp. 29–43.

100. *ibid*, p. 29.

101. For the decision of the Central Committee concerning this particular 'day' see *Kollektivizatsiya selskogo khozyaistva*, doc. No. 51. On the increased wave of collectivization resulting from this campaign see Kukushkin, *op. cit.*, p. 51–5.

102 *NAF*, 1930, No. 7–8 in which is quoted part of Stalin's speech to the Sixteenth Party Congress.

103. *KPSS v Rezolyutsiyakh*, Vol. II, pp. 661–2. The figure of 20%, quoted by Vareikis, is an estimate by the Department for Rural Affairs of the Central Committee. *NAF*, 1929, No. 8, p. 62.

104. Vareikis, *NAF*, 1929, No. 8, p. 67.

105. 'Partiinoe Stroitelstvo', *Pravda*, June 7, 1929.

106. Vareikis, *op. cit.*, pp. 68–70.

107. *ibid*, p. 81.

108. Yaroslavsky, 'O kommunistakh v derevne', *Pravda*, August 25, 1929.

109. Paikin, 'Kommunisty krestyane Belorusskoi derevni', *Bolshevik*, 1929, No. 17, pp. 74–5.

110. In *Derevenski Kommunist*, 1929, No. 18, p. 2, it is stated that only 18·3% of communists in rural areas had joined kolkhozes.

111. *ibid*, p. 4.

112. This report was published for the first time in *Dokumenty po istorii sovetskogo obshchestva*, Vol. VII, pp. 211–70. For the chapter devoted to the weaknesses of the movement see pp. 267–70.

113. Emphasis supplied.

114. *ibid*, p. 269.

115. Kaminsky, *5-ty S'ezd Sovetov*, stenogramme, bulletin, No. 18, pp. 29–30.

116. Stalin, *Sochineniya*, Vol. XII, pp. 125–6; Milyutin, *NAF*, 1929, No. 9.

117. *Pravda*, October 8, 1929; *Bolshevik*, 1929, No. 21, pp. 64–5; Golendo, *NAF*, 1929, No. 10, pp. 19; another article in the same issue of *NAF*, pp. 64–5.

118. Noted by Kotov, *NAF*, 1929, No. 10, p. 100.

119. Kaminsky, *Pravda*, June 20, 1929.

120. Ratner, *NAF*, 1929, No. 10, p. 57.

121. Bauman, *Pravda*, June 16, 1929; Ukhanov during the session of the Moscow Committee, *Pravda*, August 31, 1929.

122. Reported by Milyutin, *NAF*, 1929, No. 9.

123. *Bolshevik*, 1929, No. 21, p. 61. The Five-year Plan envisaged an investment of 1,084,000 roubles in the socialist sector of agriculture in 1929–30. In the 'control figures' this figure was raised to 1,740,000. The initial intention was that the sown area in the sovkhozes should increase by 25%, and in the kolkhozes by 82%. The new measures called for increases of 108% and 182% respectively. Strumilin, *Planovoe Khozyaistvo*, 1929, No. 9, pp. 35–40; Krzhizhanovsky, *ibid*. p. 9.

124. On this last decision of the *Sovnarkom* see *Pravda*, December 4, 1929.

PART 3

THE GREAT TURN

Chapter 16

THE SIGNAL FOR THE ATTACK
(November—December 1929)

1. *The Birth of the Cult*

The countryside was now subjected to an all-out attack by the most powerful task-force that had yet been mobilized on the procurements front, and the campaign was yielding grain on an unprecedented scale. Meanwhile, the leadership had taken up action stations, and were making their final preparations to lead the Party into battle, in an atmosphere which recalled that of the Civil War days.

It was probably during the month of September that the triumvirate in power, Stalin, Molotov and Kaganovich, decided to go far beyond the limits of even the boldest ideas and perspectives that the Party had yet conceived of, and launched themselves on an enterprise which was audacious to the point of madness. Stalin was moved by a number of considerations, among them the successes and failures in the domain of industrial construction, the recession in agricultural production and the upward movement in collectivization, the dynamic of the industrialization drive and enthusiasm for the socialist offensive. As he saw it, to retreat at this stage would bring the whole edifice crashing, whereas there was everything to be gained by a decisive and concerted assault on all fronts. He therefore carried out the most spectacular and the most daring change of policy in his entire career, and in the history of the USSR: the 'great turn' of the end of 1929.

Tension throughout the country was mounting to an alarming degree, bread was rationed and meat was scarce. A certain section of the workers, mainly among the younger generation, were full of enthusiasm for the task of construction, but the majority remained either indifferent or, at times, hostile. Subjected to the rigours of an increasingly tyrannous *edinonachalie*, large numbers of them were constantly on the move from one factory to another in search of better living conditions. As work norms were stepped up and the requirements of factory discipline grew ever more stringent, so productivity and working conditions continued to deteriorate.

The workers reacted adversely to the despotic behaviour of factory managements, who were strongly backed up by the trades union officials, and whose efforts were now exclusively concentrated on the priority objective of increasing productivity. Meanwhile, additional pressure was being brought to bear on the labour force by a new managerial stratum, which was largely composed of recently promoted elements from the working class itself.

In the agricultural sector production was declining, the setback having been particularly severe in the case of industrial crops. At the same time, there was an absolute drop of 3·5% in the number of cattle, and 15% in the number of pigs, while the upward trend in the numbers of draught animals and sheep had been checked.[1] There was growing discontent in the villages. In despair, the better-off farmers had considerably cut down their production; in the RSFSR, for example, their sowings had been reduced by 42·4%, and their grain production by 42·7%, during the year 1928–9.[2] There had been some progress in other branches of agricultural production, but despite official affirmations to the contrary, this had not been sufficient to offset the losses at this stage.

The broad mass of the middle peasantry were no less confused and anxious, easily falling prey to the wildest rumours. They were being harassed as never before by the procurements agents, while pressure was also being exerted on them by the many ruthless and determined Party representatives (*upolnomochennye*) who had been sent to drive them into the kolkhozes by a mixture of threats and promises.

Party circles were now thoroughly alarmed by the evidence of social unrest and mass discontent, and by the explosive nature of the situation. There were rumours that even the *OGPU* were feeling uneasy on this score, and that the *OGPU* chiefs, including Yagoda, had sent a joint report to the Politburo, calling attention to the dangers of compulsory collectivization.[3]

The reaction among the activists was to rally more closely to the support of the leadership, and this was true even of those who were most hostile to Stalin, but who nevertheless were dedicated to the cause of the revolutionary régime. This explains the flood of capitulations from the ranks of the Left opposition, and sheds some light on the state of mind of those 'repentants' who promptly resumed responsible employment in industry or the diplomatic service. 'He does the job badly,' they said of Stalin, 'but he does it.' One witness who took part in these events sums up the attitude of the most intelligent of the Party cadres in this way:

'Stalin's iron hand is hard to bear. His narrow outlook and his despotic methods are costing the country dear. . . . But . . . thanks to this man's indomitable will, Russia is being modernized. Despite his shortcomings, a few more years of this terrible, almost superhuman effort will bring an all-round increase in prosperity and happiness.'[4]

The same sentiments were voiced by Ivan Smirnov, who had previously been a diehard of the Left. He justified his decision to go over to the Stalinist camp in the following terms: 'I cannot bear inaction. I must build! Stupid and barbarous though their methods often are, the Central Committee are building for the future. Our ideological differences are of little consequence compared with the task of constructing powerful new industries.'[5]

Another member of the Left, the economist Smilga, who had been one of the founders of *Gosplan*, explained his point of view to Victor Serge. 'You must realize, what is at stake in this struggle is the agony of a nation of 160 million people.' Drawing a comparison with the French Revolution, Smilga went on: 'I have come back from Minussinsk [where he had been deported—M.L.]. . . . What does it matter if a few of us were deported? Should we not now be walking about with our heads underneath our arms. . . .?' 'If we now win this victory —i.e. collectivization—over the age-old peasantry without exhausting the proletariat, it will be magnificent. . . .'[6] Serge adds that Smilga was in fact doubtful if this could be done.

Even those who were prepared to let themselves be carried away by the watchword about 'catching up and overtaking', and who were filled with enthusiasm at the grandiose prospect of turning the entire country into one gigantic construction site, were constantly beset by doubts. And when in doubt, many of the former October revolutionaries had only one answer: blind devotion. However, there was a minority who saw things differently, and for whom it was important to know not only what was being done, but also how it was being done and by whom, and what methods were being employed. One such man was Rakovsky, who did not come into line until 1934. In a letter signed by 500 of the opposition, and written in protest against the capitulation of Smilga, Radek and Preobrazhensky, Rakovsky accused the leadership of having 'brought the methodology of command and coercion to a fine point of perfection such as history has seldom seen',[7] and of having elevated these same methods to the rank of dogma.

Trotsky was by this time in exile in Turkey. His reaction to the capitulation of the three leaders was the following prophetic statement: 'By capitulating, Radek is asking for his name to be deleted from the list of the living. He is now one of that category headed by Zinovev, those that are half-hanged and half-forgiven.'[8]

At all events, many of the activists believed that all criticism and differences of opinion should be set aside while the régime was in danger, and this attitude greatly assisted the Party leadership in transforming the Party into a rigidly disciplined corps who would blindly obey any order from above.

Isolated pockets of resistance still remained, particularly in circles connected with the *Komsomol* leadership, where some of the younger elements, including students and other members, did not take kindly to the Centre's insistence on blind obedience. Shatskin, who was a member of the Central Control Commission and of the *Komsomol* administration, and had been a Bolshevik since 1917, joined with several other *Komsomol* leaders, including Sten and Kostrov, the editors of the *Young Guard*, in an attack on the prevailing spirit of unquestioning obedience in the Party. (They were later to deny, when making their self-criticisms, that they had collaborated in this way.) The anti-Stalinist point was clearly made. Sten called upon young Party members to consider 'and examine all questions seriously, in the light of their experience, and thus to convince themselves of the correctness of the Party line'.[9]

Prior to this, in an article in *Komsomolskaya Pravda* entitled 'Down with the petty-bourgeois spirit in the Party', Shatskin had already put forward a view of the 'Party Philistines' which was different from that held by the leadership. So far as the leadership were concerned, the 'Philistines' were the Right. Shatskin, while agreeing with this conception, suggested that there was yet another petty bourgeois element in the Party, consisting of officials who acted purely as functionaries, and who, although faithful in the execution of their duties, carried these out in an uncritical and uncomprehending manner. In Shatskin's view, this type of official was the kind of man who perhaps neither smokes nor drinks and remains 'pure' all his life, who has a resplendent revolutionary record of undercover activity and deportation, who is genuinely dedicated to the proletariat and the Party, but who 'can, and often does, develop into a petty-bourgeois Party Philistine (*partiiny obyvatel*) . . . if he should become infected by the germ of ideological cowardice. For when one eliminates the element of caricature from this portrait of the Party Philistine, the essential feature which remains is the absence of ideas, the total lack of principles.'[10]

Shatskin also made a plea for the very human right 'to have doubts, and to make mistakes'.[11] However, the leadership were well aware that what really worried Shatskin was not the existence of a Right-wing, but the fact that the Party was becoming ossified under the influence of those mindless officials whom the Politburo preferred. Moreover, the right 'to have doubts and to make mistakes' reflected a spirit which was directly opposed to that which the Politburo were engaged in inculcating in the Party. Accordingly, there was a violent attack on 'decadent liberalism', and this was followed by the inevitable purges in the *Komsomol* leadership. The *Komsomol* Central Committee issued a statement condemning Shatskin and Sten, and their associates, and denouncing the appeal to the Party youth to reflect, and to express their doubts, as 'disguised propaganda aimed at inspiring mistrust of the general Bolshevik line', and as 'an echo of the Right-wing deviationist theory concerning the freedom to deviate from the general Bolshevik line'.[12] But this rebellion, which marked the last occasion on which there was to be public criticism of the Party, came to nothing; Shatskin, Sten, Kostrov and the others withdrew from their position.

At this point, in December 1929, the Party leadership undertook an important manoeuvre designed, at one and the same time, to strengthen their disciplinary grip on the Party and to provide the people with a new source of faith. On the occasion of Stalin's fiftieth birthday, the Politburo for the first time provided the Party and the nation with a very different criterion for assessing the correctness of the 'general line'. It was precisely at the beginning of the 'great leap forward', or just immediately beforehand, that the propaganda campaign for the glorification of Stalin and the creation of the Stalin cult was launched.

The editorial which *Bolshevik* devoted to Stalin already contains all the characteristics which were to become associated with the systematic 'beatification' of the Party leader. Party history was falsified as and when necessary, in order to show that, even before the revolution, Stalin had played a dominant role alongside Lenin; this made it possible to transfer the already-perfected Lenin cult 'to the most outstanding disciple and comrade-in-arms' of the dead leader. Since this cult, like all cults, did not rely for its effectiveness either on logical proof or historical accuracy, it provided a convenient cover for whatever excesses might be involved in the process of glorification, especially when the facts did not fit the desired interpretation. We learn from the afore-mentioned editorial (the text of which was edited, or may possibly have been almost entirely written, by Stalin himself, since it concerned the interpretation of history, which he regarded as his personal prerogative) that Stalin had passed in glorious fashion all the tests for leadership, after Lenin's death 'as well as during the lifetime of Lenin', with whom he had marched towards the October Revolution. 'As far back as the period when the foundations of the October Revolution were being laid, Stalin stressed and defended the Leninist principle of the possibility of building socialism in one single, backward country.'

Thus Stalin awarded himself the victor's crown which no one had thought of bestowing on him. He was the 'only theoretician' after Lenin, combining a profound knowledge of dialectics and the principles of organization with an enormous wealth of experience. In short, he was 'the greatest strategist of the Leninist school'. Since it was also important that the leader should be endowed with a knowledge of military strategy, the Party organ produced a singular proof of this by referring the readers exclusively to one note which Stalin had written in connection with the southern front during the Civil War. (The history of the southern front, then relatively little known, obviously has no bearing on the present context.) However, since these 'strategical writings' were scarcely adequate for the purpose, the editorial went on to explain the source of Stalin's greatness as a military strategist. As 'a political strategist of such a high order', who 'had reached such a profound understanding of Leninist principles, and had perfected the art of applying them to such a high degree', he was 'capable of employing them in a sphere which was allied to that of politics, namely the art of war'. In conclusion, Stalin was hailed as 'the perfect prototype' of the man who 'combines Russian revolutionary fervour with American efficiency'.[13]

One of the reasons for the cult was Stalin's fear of rivals, and a necessary precondition for its survival and its efficacity was a steady stream of self-immolating sacrificial victims from the ranks of those who opposed him. Some weeks earlier, after a powerful preliminary 'build-up' at the November Plenum, Bukharin, Rykov and Tomsky had signed an unconditional surrender, by declaring that they had been mistaken, and that the Party line was correct.[14] This kind of guarantee was also part of the cult operation.

It is significant that the fullest statement of this basic principle of personal loyalty to Stalin should have come from Pyatakov, who was a 'repentant' oppositionist; Pyatakov was to be one of the pillars of industrialization during the Five-year Plan, and one of Stalin's future victims. 'It is now absolutely clear,' Pyatakov stated in *Pravda*, 'that one cannot be for the Party and *against* the present leadership, and that one cannot be for the Central Committee *and* against Stalin.'[15] He was obviously wrestling both with the oppositionists of his acquaintance, and with his own conscience. The exiled Rakovsky spoke up, saying that it was important to know how things were done. Pyatakov on the other hand looked at the problem from the opposite angle: 'It is absolutely essential to take into account not only *what* is done, but *by whom* it is done. . . .' Thus loyalty to the leader took priority over all other considerations. 'We must reject the profoundly corrupt attitude which refuses to link the problem of policy with that of the leadership.' And again: 'Only hopelessly vulgar minds, which are blinded by hatred of the Party, are capable of arguing that the problem is one of whom to obey.' The words 'whom to obey' were those which Pyatakov himself had spoken to Kamenev, less than a year before.

Thus it was that the principle of personal loyalty came to take the place of programme, criteria and analysis, and that a Marxist, rationalist, revolutionary Party ended up, by a peculiar twist, with a personality cult. This was largely made possible by the conditions of social and economic development, and particularly by the crisis which set in during the winter of 1927–8. In so far as Stalin and his immediate associates were concerned, it was a calculated political manoeuvre.

The part played by the 'cult' is readily understandable, given the nature of the political and social situation in the country at the end of 1929. The peasants were by this time in a state of deep distress, in which they might be driven to desperate action; the 'personality cult' gave them an image, which had much in common with the icon of their orthodox religious faith, and with the father-figure of the *Tsarbatyushka*, who was too far removed to know what was going on, but who, if only he knew the truth, would never allow his evil lieutenants to act as they did. . . .

Similarly, it provided the Party activists with a new source of faith, at a time when they were beset by doubts about the future of the revolution, and were seeking something to sustain and strengthen them in their beliefs. At the same time, another myth, that of industrialization, was to provide an outlet for their energies.

The secretaries and officials who ran the Party bureaucratic machine had acquired a supreme authority, in the shape of an infallible leader, who would henceforth relieve them of the responsibility for thinking, since obedience was the only quality which he required of them.

As for the leaders, and Stalin in particular, now that they were engaged in an undertaking whose consequences they could not foresee, and for which they had no pre-conceived programme, the 'personality cult' provided them with an alibi, since the object of the cult could be elevated *au dessus de la mêlée*, safely out of reach of criticism when the crisis, which they could feel building up, should eventually burst upon them.

Stalin was a source of strength and a rallying-point for the bureaucracy, and likewise for all those revolutionaries who believed that the régime was in danger. At the same time, however, as an individual, he was the most vulnerable point in the entire system, and he was well aware of this fact. In the event of criticism, the first target would be the individual who, ever since the beginning of 1928, had been the symbol of all that the régime stood for, and who would inevitably be associated with whatever excesses or failures might be attributable to the régime in the future.

The purpose of the 'personality cult' was therefore to consolidate Stalin's position, by making it both invulnerable and impregnable, irrespective of what might happen to the people, and regardless of the true qualities of their leader. The operation succeeded admirably. Stalin certainly had need of a powerful protective armour against criticism, for by the end of the year his plans had gone beyond the limits of anything which might be acceptable to the experts or to the public, who at this stage were more free to express their opinions than was subsequently the case. Although the economy was showing unmistakable signs of being overstrained, the Politburo were proposing to increase the target figure for the growth in industrial production from the original 22·5% to 32·5%. Investments for the year 1929–30 were to exceed by three milliard roubles the sum which had been envisaged in the Five-year Plan. It was proposed to increase the country's overall production by 21% (whereas the figure laid down in the original plan had been only 16%), and this despite the fact that the actual growth achieved over the past year had been a mere 12·3%. Plans were also afoot for building almost twice the number of factories envisaged by the Plan.[16] In addition to all this, the costs of production were to go down by 11%, and productivity was to rise by 25%.

There was not the slightest chance that these figures would be reached. As one specialist in the history of the *pyatiletka*, E. Zaleski, has pointed out, the plans for the year had got off to a bad start, and were compromised in advance as a result of under-fulfilment of the previous year's objectives.[17] The statistics relative to plan fulfilment at the end of 1930 show how unrealistic the plans were: the figures indicate that industrial production had increased by 22% instead of by 35%, productivity had increased by 12·2% instead of 25%, and costs of production had fallen by 7%, instead of 11%.[18]

In fact, when freed from any control on the part of the planners, the government took a highly specific view of the functions of the plan, although this was never admitted. As Zaleski has further pointed out, 'The government's whole attitude to the plan underwent a change.'[19] The only purpose of the figures was to spur the country on to ever-increasing efforts, and each individual figure served purely as an indication of the limit which was to be exceeded. In this sense, the plan became merely a body of figures which were constantly being scaled upwards,[20] and this was its sole function. All those considerations which assumed a scientific approach to the question of planning—equilibrium, proper inter-sector co-ordination, the entire problem of inner coherence in the plan—were disregarded, and this great undertaking was reduced to a level of muddle and confusion so great that the authorities were only able to extricate themselves at the cost of superhuman efforts and continual emergency operations. As for other aspects of planning, such as the problem of mass initiative, and the role of research, scientific analysis and public opinion, these things had no meaning for a régime which dealt with all problems by methods which were demonstrably bureaucratic in character, and which regarded itself as the supreme arbiter and the sole repository of political leadership and initiative.

However, the régime's plans for the agricultural sector went far beyond the limits of anything that might have been suggested or imagined even in the most ambitious of the earlier plans. What they were proposing in this context amounted, in effect, to a 'new October revolution in the countryside'.[21]

2. Had the Serednyak turned towards the Kolkhoz?

By the end of October, the Politburo had already decided to embark on its new 'line', without waiting for the decisions of the Central Committee, which was due to meet on November 10th. The session was to be faced with the existence of a new policy as a *fait accompli*, without having any knowledge of the methods by which it was being put into practice. On October 31st *Pravda* published an important editorial, which was probably written by some top-ranking political personality, and which announced a new departure in policy. The article referred to the current procurements campaign, which was now approaching its climax, and went on to say that all the forces which had been deployed on this campaign '*must be used for an equally intensive effort on a second front, namely the front of collectivization and assistance for bednyak and serednyak farms*, in order to reconstruct and rehabilitate the economy'. However, the forces which had been mustered on the procurements front would not be adequate for this new undertaking. *Pravda* announced 'a mass mobilization of all forces at the disposal of Party and soviet organizations, in order to speed up the rate of growth and hasten the process of socialist reconstruction of the agricultural sector'.

This was a task which had been the subject of frequent discussion in the past, but never before had the problem been presented in terms of the 'mobilization of all available forces', nor had it ever been linked in such a direct manner with the procurements campaign, with the intensive nature of that campaign and, most important of all, with the methods used in the campaign. On this latter point, *Pravda* was quite unequivocal. Since it was assumed that the kulaks were counter-attacking, instructions on the line to be taken were repeated with unwonted harshness: 'We must strike at the kulak in every sector of his counter-offensive, using the full organizational resources of the proletarian dictatorship.' This was to be a battle in which 'the appeasers, the traitors and the uncommitted' must not be tolerated. Chairmen of kolkhozes and sovkhozes which concealed their grain surpluses would be put on trial. Persons who failed to fulfil their contracts would be treated 'with great severity' and 'very severe measures' would be taken against 'those better-off elements who might attempt to follow the example of the kulaks'.

Here, then, was a whole series of recommendations to violent action. There was mention of harsh treatment, measures of great severity, striking with the full force of dictatorial power, but no specific statement on the practical methods which were to be employed.

On the following day, a member of the Ukrainian *Sovnarkom*, who was conversant with the Politburo's plans, supplied further information. This made it clear that there had been a radical change of attitude. In the past it had been regarded as axiomatic that the role of the socialized sector of agriculture should be that of an auxiliary to the private sector, and this was the basis on which the Five-year Plan had been ratified some five or six months earlier. It was now proposed to reverse the roles, so that the position would be one of 'the private sector playing a secondary part to that of the socialized sector'.[22] It must be understood, the author went on to say, that 'what is taking place in the domain of agriculture is not a reform but a revolution'.

What change had taken place in the country over the past six months which could both necessitate and justify a 'revolution'? Stalin himself supplied the answer, in an article entitled 'The great turn'.[23] The article contained an appraisal of the country's achievements during the past year, that is 1928–9, and was designed to show that this year had marked a turning-point. Stalin listed the three basic factors which had contributed to success (1) there had been a decisive improvement in labour productivity in the industrial sector; (2) there had been successes in the field of industrial construction which would set the country firmly on the road to becoming a 'metal-based Russia'. This second argument was based on the 1928–9 figures and on the *estimates* for 1930, and in fact leaned more heavily on the latter: production was to increase by 32%, and heavy industry by 46%, and the 'optimal' version of the Five-year Plan was already being treated as a 'minimal' Plan.

However, Stalin's third and main argument in support of the alleged 'turning-point' was based on the régime's success in the domain of collectivization, in which 'we have managed to bring about a radical change of attitude within the peasantry itself'.[24] In this sector, he said, a rate of progress had been attained 'which surpassed even the achievements of our great socialist industry'.[25] This success, in his opinion, was 'the most important and the most decisive of all our victories during the past few years'.

In Stalin's opinion, this new and sensational development which, more than anything else, illustrated the radical change which had come over the peasantry, consisted of the fact that 'the serednyak has moved towards the kolkhozes . . .'.[26] Stalin triumphantly presented this move as his own personal achievement, a feat which had never been managed either in Lenin's time, or under any other government. In Stalin's view, this development had played a decisive part in transforming the Five-year Plan into a 'Five-year Plan for the construction of a socialist society', and, secondly, in enabling the government to reach the stage where 'we are now overcoming, or have already overcome, the grain crisis'.[27]

This article unquestionably reflects the state of mind of Stalin and his immediate associates at the time. If the kolkhoz and sovkhoz movements continued to develop at a rapid rate 'our country will, in some three years time, have become one of the richest granaries, if not the richest, in the whole world'.[28]

This was a promise intended to spur the population on to greater efforts, as well as being a sincerely held belief. Thanks to the existing trends in social and economic development, which had been fostered by his policy and in accordance with his theories, success of the most spectacular kind was within the country's grasp. All that was needed was to maintain steady progress in the same direction, and the result would be 'a second October', perhaps even more significant and more securely based than the first. At this point, Stalin begins daydreaming:

'We are forging full speed ahead along the road of industrialization which leads to socialism, we are leaving behind us our age-old backward "Russian" past . . . and when we motorize the USSR and put the *muzhik* on a tractor, then let them try to catch us up, those respectable capitalists with their much-vaunted civilization. We shall see then which is the backward country, and which the developed.'[29]

The perspectives, as outlined by Stalin, were certainly impressive. However, he was arguing from false premises, and the year had not, in fact, marked a 'great turning-point' in the sense in which he meant it to be understood. There was no improvement in labour productivity, indeed this was the very weakness which had impaired implementation of the government's plans. The country was embarking on its construction project, but was still not 'metal-based'. The increase of 32% or 46% in industrial production was merely another pious and unfulfilled hope. Above all, there were no grounds for suggesting that there had been a change of attitude among the mass of the peasantry with regard to the kolkhozes. The supposed change was a product of Stalin's peculiar form of reasoning which consisted of taking the wish for the deed. It followed that the peasants were being won over because, this spring, *there would be* sixty thousand tractors in the fields, and in a year's time, there would be over a hundred thousand, and in two years, two hundred and fifty thousand.[30]

Present-day Soviet writers reject the view that 'the serednyak moved towards the kolkhozes' at the end of 1929.

'The change which took place in the principal grain-producing regions was taken by J. V. Stalin as an indication of general agreement among the serednyaks that they should go over to collective farming. In reality, no such fundamental change in the attitude of the middle peasantry had as yet taken place.'

As far back as mid-1964, the general opinion was that this change in outlook had developed towards the end of 1930 and the beginning of 1931, but at this time the trend 'was only just beginning to emerge in the pilot grain-growing regions'.[31] The author here quoted makes reference to a decision of the Party Committee of the Kuban *okrug* on January 3rd 1930, which he has taken from the records: 'The broad mass of the peasantry, including those strata which are most sympathetic towards us, have no understanding of the fundamental implications of collectivization. . . .' 'And yet,' the author observes, 'this was the *okrug* which was considered to be in the most advanced state of readiness for mass collectivization'.[32] He concludes: 'Stalin's over-optimistic view of the actual situation in this respect led to widespread and erroneous anti-serednyak action by a great many organizations.'

In Danilov's *Ocherki po istorii kollektivizatsii* . . . (Notes on the history of collectivization . . .) Abramov states clearly that, at the beginning of the autumn, in a whole series of *okrugi* in the Volga and Central Black Earth regions, in Siberia and the North Caucasus 'and in other regions, the kolkhoz movement was artificially forced, by the use of coercive methods of a bureaucratic nature against the peasants'.[33]

Stalin's method consisted of presenting his plans and his wishes as accomplished fact, so as to encourage Party organizations and the other sectors of the administration to come into line with the 'actual situation' as it allegedly existed 'everywhere else'. The purpose of his article, therefore, was to influence the coming Plenum of the Central

Committee in a particular direction, and to suggest the form which he wished its decisions to take. The Soviet author of the *Ocherki* . . . of 1963 states that Stalin's article

'brought pressure to bear on the Party cadres, and even influenced the course of the discussion on the kolkhoz movement which took place at the November Plenum of the Central Committee. In their appraisals of the collective movement and its rate of growth, an overwhelming majority of the speakers who took part in these discussions followed the line taken by this article.'[34]

So it was that the members of the Central Committee and the *obkom* secretaries of the time found out what was going on in their own regions by reading the leader's articles. In his speech, the chairman of the *oblispolkom* of the Central Black Earth region claimed that there had been a mass influx of serednyaks in his region into the kolkhozes, whereas the facts showed that only 60,000 out of a total serednyak population of 1,300,000 in the *oblast* had joined. As recently as September of that year, Kaminsky, the chairman of the *Kolkhoztsentr*, had stated, in a report to the Central Committee which we have already quoted, that the number of serednyaks joining the collective movement was very small. He now yielded to pressure from the officials representing the Asiatic and non-cereal regions, and approved 'the transition to mass (*sploshnaya*) collectivization in the non-cereal regions, while at the same time moving towards the view which favoured the creation of giant kolkhozes, and a speeding up of the rate of collectivization'.[35]

These 'unhealthy tendencies' were directly attributable to pressure from the summit, as was the reaction of the officials responsible for the more backward regions, the majority of whom had pressed for an even more rapid rate of change, although their regions were least advanced on the road to collectivization.

Molotov, the Politburo's principal spokesman during this plenary session, openly appealed for an intensive effort aimed at effecting a radical change in peasant structures during the next few months. All his arguments were designed to create within the Party the feeling that the régime would have a unique opportunity, during the coming spring, of disposing once and for all of the private agricultural sector, and that this opportunity was 'not to be missed' on any account. 'Since our imperialist friends are not quite ready for a direct attack on us, we must take immediate advantage of the situation by making a decisive move in the matter of the economic rehabilitation and collectivization of millions of peasant households. If we are not to miss our chance, we must use every moment of the days, the weeks and the months that lie ahead. . . .'[36]

According to the logic of this argument, since the forces of imperialism would attack the day after tomorrow, the régime's task must be completed by tomorrow. Before the sowing compaign was due to begin, the procurements campaign would have been concluded, and the countryside would be ready manned with the largest task force it had ever known. Molotov made no secret of the fact that, during the coming spring, he was counting on having solved 'the problem of collectivization in a number of the major agricultural regions; from then on, the problem of the collectivization of the USSR as a whole will have assumed an entirely new aspect'.[37]

A present-day Soviet writer expresses indignation at the following passage from this fateful speech, which he quotes from the Party archives: 'We have good reason for asserting—and I personally have no doubts about the matter—that by the summer of 1930 we shall, in all essentials, have completed the collectivization of the North Caucasus.'

In saying this, Stalin and Molotov were setting aside the decisions taken by the *kraikom* which was farthest advanced on the road to collectivization, and whose secretary, Andreev, had announced that it was the committee's intention to complete collectivization in the summer of 1931. We have already quoted the statement from one of the pilot-*okrugi* of this region, the Kuban, to the effect that even the peasants who were most favourably disposed towards the régime had no understanding of the problems of collectivization. But even although the feeling in this, the most advanced of all the regions, was that the rate of collectivization was already extremely rapid, the process was still further speeded up at the behest of the Politburo, and the time allowed for completion was reduced to a few months. Nor was the North Caucasus the only region involved. Molotov's words were not specific, but the implications were fairly clear: 'This coming autumn, we shall already be in a position to say definitely that, for all essential purposes, collectivization has been completed, not just in one *oblast*, and not only in the North Caucasus.'[38]

In so saying, Molotov was clearly proposing to open the floodgates. At the same time, he made light of the government planning departments which were engaged in drawing up Five-year Plans for agriculture. These, he said, were 'useless'. Instead of talking about five-year plans, people would be better advised to turn their attention to practical matters. 'As for the main agricultural regions, irrespective of the differences in their rate of collectivization, we must stop thinking in terms of the *pyatiletka* and think in terms of next year.'[39]

In this way, the very idea of planning any aspect of collectivization, of slowing the movement down, or even of giving it a proper, centrally-based leadership, was disregarded. It was made clear to the authorities responsible that they would have a free hand, provided that the coming months produced the desired 'revolution'. The fact that there were not enough trained cadres for implementing the proposed changes should not weigh too heavily on them, nor were they to be deterred by lack of equipment and experience. The Politburo were well aware of the difficulties, and were prepared to take 'all the sins' of the officials concerned on their own consciences; this was, presumably, good enough for the men on the spot. 'It must be freely admitted that, given the amount of illiteracy among the broad mass of the peasantry, it would be mere wishful thinking to count on the availability of large numbers of trained cadres and kolkhoz organizers.' [40]

There was also a frank avowal of a further drawback, the shortage of State funds: 'The amount of material assistance (from the State) cannot be very great, in view of our strained resources.' 'When all is said and done, all that the State can give, despite its efforts, is a very small sum.' [41]

However, since consciences must be salved and hope revived, the strategists in the Politburo came up with a new theory. It was now suggested that the collective movement would be financed out of the peasants' own resources. Over the years, the activists had grown accustomed to the idea that the socialist transformation of the country, and *ipso facto* the proof of the superiority of socialist change over other forms, would be wrought on the basis of new techniques, without which the creation of large-scale farming enterprises would be unthinkable. In a single day, this doctrine was changed. The peasants' resources, that is, their implements, farm buildings, etc. . . . were 'poor, sometimes downright wretched, but when pooled together, they make an imposing sum'. [42]

So far, the idea that 'millions of *sokhi* (wooden ploughs) all added together would make an imposing sum' had been treated as a joke: now it had seriously been put forward at a session of the senior Party organ, and was endorsed as official doctrine.

Neither the shortage of cadres and resources, nor even the internal defects and 'the weaknesses which are evident in kolkhoz construction at the present stage' [43] were to be regarded as an excuse for slowing down the growth of the movement. 'To attempt to do so would be ridiculous'—though Molotov did not endeavour to explain why.

According to a modern Soviet source, numerous Central Committee members were alarmed at these tendencies within the Politburo; however, the author in question quotes practicaly no names, or extracts from the speeches (although he had access to the minutes of the Plenum). Kubyak, *Narkomzem* of the RSFSR, was probably the one who had the most serious misgivings; he expressed his disapproval of the proposal to embark on a policy of immediate and wholesale collectivization. It would appear that Sheboldaev, Party secretary of the Lower Volga, also suggested that the Party was not yet ready for such a move.[44] Nevertheless, although a considerable number of Central Committee members were doubtless uneasy, there was no overt opposition of any kind at the meeting. This was the same Plenum which had excommunicated the Right-wing tendency, and expelled Bukharin from the Politburo; many of Bukharin's supporters had capitulated either during the course of the session, or shortly afterwards. The Central Committee was thus sufficiently under control to endorse any of the Politburo's decisions without question. The only form in which objections to the proposed policy, and suggestions for slowing down the rate of collectivization, might be said to have found their expression, was in the many complaints which were made about the disparity between the growth of the movement and its technical base, and about the very unsatisfactory internal organization of the kolkhozes, their low rate of productivity and labour discipline.[45] If anyone had been prepared to take account of all these complaints, he would have been forced to the obvious conclusion that it was time to apply the brake.

In fact, there must have been some backstage opposition, some expression of doubt or uncertainty, some fairly determined effort to slacken the pace. No *obkom* secretary, however willing he might be to comply with the wishes of the Politburo, could have been wholeheartedly in agreement with the rate of growth which the latter were proposing to adopt, in order to fulfil their avowed aim of completing the process of *sploshnaya kollektivizatsiya* by the spring of 1930.[46] Sheboldaev's suggestion that a permanent commission be set up under the auspices of the Central Committee, in order to deal with problems relating to the collective movement, was probably made in the hope that such a body, if created, might be able to exert some restraining influence. A commission was in fact set up on December 5th,[47] and made an effort to curb the over-rapid pace of collectivization, but, as we shall see later, the Politburo had no intention of letting its plans be sabotaged in this way.

The November Plenum ended with the adoption of resolutions which were in conformity with the line taken by Molotov's speeches, and with Stalin's wishes.[48] The control figure for industrial development during 1929–30, embodying Stalin's unrealistic objectives, were duly ratified, and endorsed with the watchword: 'catch up and overtake in the shortest time ever known'. The main theme of the resolutions seems to be the possibility of solving all the régime's problems, and fulfilling all its hopes, with great speed, and speed was to be the dominant note in the government's subsequent policy and propaganda. The previous year's successes were interpreted as proof *'that the construction of socialism in a country governed by dictatorship of the proletariat can be carried out with a speed never before known in history'*.[49] (In so saying, the authorities were basing themselves mainly on the influx of peasants into the kolkhozes, and on the progress which had been made in eliminating capitalist elements.) As an answer to current difficulties, or rather to the crisis through which the country was passing, the government's sovereign remedy and its salvation was to be 'continued acceleration of the process of collectivization and sovkhoz construction' and 'increasingly rapid industrial development'.[50]

The document reflects an obsessive preoccupation with the large-scale, and those responsible for implementing its recommendations were accordingly encouraged to 'think big'. It was claimed, for example, that 'the record of achievement in the domain of collectivist construction shows the gigantic potentialities for improvement of the productive forces of agriculture which are implicit in the nature of the Soviet régime'.[51]

For some time past, the idea of potentialities 'inherent in the nature of the Soviet régime' had been treated as axiomatic, in order to impose on reluctant planners, and on the country as a whole, objectives and efforts which were excessive.

The Politburo believed that they had found the way to speedy fulfilment of their grandiose promises and their hopes: the solution lay in giant sovkhozes and giant kolkhozes. The Central Committee resolution lays great emphasis on the creation of enormous 'grain factories', and of factories for the processing of livestock products, and directs the attention of the local authorities to

'. . . the setting-up, whenever possible, under the general management of these enterprises [in the context, industrial enterprises in the rural areas.—M.L.] and of the sovkhozes, of combined sovkhoz–kolkhoz associations with a co-ordinated economic plan, a common technical base . . . and common enterprises for the processing of agricultural produce'.[52]

What the Central Committee were announcing was a 'great leap forward' from the *muzhik*'s tiny family holding straight to these fairy-tale 'sovkhoz–kolkhoz combines', and this giant stride, it should be remembered, was to be taken in the time remaining before the coming spring, and during the spring sowing campaign.[53]

While waiting for the advent of these agricultural factories, which were to play a preponderant role in agricultural production, the Central Committee made preparations to run them by the same management methods as those used in industry. The Plenum took the decision to set up a vast new administrative body, an all-Union *Narkomzem*, which would act as a sort of *VSNKh* for agriculture; in so doing, it chose to disregard fairly vigorous opposition from the republics, which had up till now enjoyed a considerable degree of autonomy in the matter of agricultural administration.[54]

A further decision of the Plenum related to the building of two new tractor factories at Kharkov and Chelyabinsk, two factories for the production of combine harvesters at Rostov and Novorossiisk, factories for agricultural equipment and chemical products, and 102 *MTS*. In fact, the Plenum had begun the process of revising the government's previous plans. Henceforth, the Five-year Plan had no further part to play, save as a smoke-screen for propaganda purposes, whereas the decisions taken on agriculture amounted to an entirely new programme.[55]

The Central Committee should have been giving instructions on the complex and intractable problem of organizing production in the new kolkhoz structures. There was a total lack of any coherent policy on this matter, but the Central Committee said very little about it, beyond affirming its belief in the possibility of applying the experience gained in industry to the context of agriculture. Since, according to the prevailing official theory, agriculture was due to be industrialized in the coming months, it was indicated that solutions to its organizational problems should be sought along industrial lines. The document accordingly suggests that kolkhoz production be organized on the basis of piecework, norms and output bonuses. *Bolshevik* put forward a further suggestion on the same general principles, to the effect that kolkhoz members' earnings should be determined with reference to the scales in operation in the sovkhozes.[56]

The Party decided to mobilize 25,000 industrial workers as shock troops to assist in the tremendous transformation which was to take place in the rural areas in the spring; from a doctrinal point of view, only the proletariat were regarded as sufficiently dedicated and sufficiently experienced to be able to guide the peasantry in bringing about the kolkhoz revolution. Their task was to be the application, in the rural context, of those methods which they had already learned from their experience in industry. In order to overcome the difficulties which had arisen as a result of the reduction in livestock holdings, they were also to be instructed, by directive of the Plenum of the Central Committee, to speed up the socialization of other branches of agriculture as well as the grain-growing sector. It was further proposed to use rapid collectivization as a means of settling the nomadic and semi-nomadic farmers in Central Asia, the Caucasus and other regions, and to consolidate the kolkhozes by the speedy establishment of indivisible and other kolkhoz funds.[57] This latter issue was a particularly controversial one, for it related to a field in which the Central Committee had very little experience, despite the forcefulness and lavishness with which it was now issuing recommendations and directives. The peasants were already generally known to be selling off their livestock and equipment before joining the kolkhozes, a fact which caused the authorities considerable anxiety. It was felt that this tendency might eventually produce the kind of situation which Rykov had so feared. Speaking at the Congress of Soviets in May, he had said: 'We cannot construct either sovkhozes or kolkhozes or a socialist industry if this is accompanied by pauperization of huge masses of the population.'[58]

The Central Committee had similar fears, and called for an effort to combat the *razbazarivanie* (selling off) of stock by the peasants, which deprived the kolkhozes of the necessary minimum of resources without which they could not operate. The Central Committee issued a warning to the effect that State aid would only be granted to the kolkhozes 'on condition that there is an increase in the amount of investment by the peasants themselves, and above all on condition that the provisions in kolkhoz statutes and contracts relative to the accumulation of kolkhoz funds are duly observed'.[59] The text also indicated that the same proviso would operate in the case of those clauses in kolkhoz agreements which related to 'the compulsory supply, by kolkhozes, of marketable grain within the time, and in the quantities stipulated by the contract . . .'.

Scarcely had they come into being, therefore, when the kolkhozes proved the occasion of a fresh onslaught by the Party, who now found it necessary to combat the tendency on the part of the collectives to sell their grain to whichever buyer would give them the best price for it. From the outset of the procurements campaign, the press had been complaining of 'instances of a scandalous attitude on the part of the kolkhozes' in that they were selling grain to private traders. In its issues of September 8th, 14th and 15th, *Pravda* carried reports from its correspondents in various parts of the country, under alarming headings: 'The kolkhozes are going in for grain speculation,' 'The kolkhozes are holding up procurements,' or again, 'Put a stop to the commercial attitude of the kolkhozes.' *Pravda* was forthright in its injunctions as to the spirit in which this offensive was to be conducted. As it explained, the kulaks who were operating under cover in the kolkhozes, and were responsible for these dealings, must be brought to justice. The entire press was up in arms, and clamouring for simultaneous action on all fronts. The Plenum had taken care to stress the fact that the attack on the kulaks must be intensified. Although he had not given any specific instructions,

Molotov had let it be clearly understood that this time it would be necessary 'to assume in dealing with the kulak the attitude which should properly be assumed towards the worst of our enemies whom we have not yet liquidated'.[60]

People could interpret this as they chose. The most dangerous enemy who still remained to be liquidated must be liquidated, but no one said when or how this was to be done. Such indications as had been given at the Plenum, or gathered by the activists either from Molotov's statements or the article in *Bolshevik*, were of the vaguest possible nature, consisting as they did entirely of allusions which were both clear and obscure at one and the same time. Nothing was said about the way in which the kulaks were to be treated, about the time-limits within which collectivization should be carried out, which items of property should be socialized and which should remain the private property of the peasants, what should be done, for example, about the cows, particularly in cases where the family owned only one, or whether poultry should be socialized or not.

Meantime, while there were still no answers to these questions, the authorities went ahead with the work of collectivization, and also took some action in the matter of dekulakization. On November 15th, Molotov informed the Plenum that 'the countryside is in the process of being turned upside down, it has become a veritable maelstrom'.[61] Nevertheless, the Politburo still delayed laying down any clear line for the collective movement. They were obviously bent on producing a major upheaval, and in this sense Molotov was justified in his assertion that any talk of planning in the context of collectivization was 'pointless', since there were only a few weeks and days available for the operation.

3. *The Central Committee and Politburo Commissions*

After the Central Committee session, the Politburo took three weeks to set up and convene the commission which was to deal with the problems of collectivization, and to decide on the timing of the operation.[62] The chairman of the commission was the new all-Union Commissar for Agriculture, Yakovlev, and its membership consisted of the Party secretaries of the principal grain regions and heads of the appropriate departments, including Kaminsky and Sheboldaev (Lower Volga), Ivanov (North Caucasus), S. Kosior (Ukraine), Khataevich (Middle Volga) and Vareikis (Central Black Earth Region), together with representatives from the Nizhgorod *krai* and from pilot-*okrugi* such as Khopersk.[63]

At its first meeting on December 8th, the commission appointed eight sub-committees; one of these, under the chairmanship of Kaminsky, was to deal with the question of the rate of collectivization, while the others were to study, respectively, the various forms of collective farming, organization, the allocation of resources, the question of cadres, the mobilization of peasant resources, political and cultural services, and the kulak question. On December 16th–17th, the commission met in full session, with representatives of the government departments concerned, to hear the proposals which had been worked out by the sub-committees. However, the commission's efforts were handicapped by lack of data on the state of collectivization throughout the country. Accordingly, the *okrugi* were urged to furnish the necessary information; the figures which were finally laid before the commission covered 2,373 *raiony*, and revealed the following situation.

In 124 of these *raiony*, over 70% of households had been collectivized; in 117 *raiony*, there was 50 to 70% of collectivization; in 266, from 30 to 50%; there were 461 *raiony* with from 15 to 30% of collectivization, and 1,405 where the proportion was 15% or under.[64] The figures had undoubtedly been inflated to some extent, having been provided by *okruzhkom* secretaries who were already caught up in the rush to establish impressive percentage results, but what they chiefly revealed was the results that had already been obtained by 'bureaucratic methods', that is, by various forms of pressure. *Raiony*, *okruzhkomy* and *obkomy* were all seized with an access of competitive zeal—in which they were duly encouraged by the Politburo before, during and after the Plenum—and even as early as the autumn the movement was being considerably distorted by the use of coercive methods. The journal *Voprosy istorii KPSS* makes this point, and quotes the following evidence of what it describes as 'the unwarranted forcing of the pace of collectivization' in certain regions: in fifty-one *raiony* of the Lower Volga (a *krai* consisting of ninety-six *raiony*) there were in August 1929 only 14% of households in the kolkhozes, whereas by December 15th the figure had already exceeded 70% (60% for the *krai* as a whole). In the autumn of that year, in the famous Khopersk *okrug*, 13% of households had joined the kolkhozes; by December 15th the figure was 80%! The journal states that there had been rapid increases of this order in a whole number of regions.[65]

Everyone was aware of this at the time, and it was mentioned both at the Plenum (Kaminsky, Kosior) and in the Commission. The Politburo were fully informed of what was happening from the letters and memoranda which they received; as from the month of December they were in receipt of regular reports every seven to ten days on the progress of the collectivization campaign. This fact is underlined by the above-mentioned periodical[66] and by other present-day Soviet sources, who accuse Stalin, Molotov and Kaganovich of not having taken action to put a stop to these abuses. They are held to account for having ignored a letter from Baranov, the *Kolkhoztsentr* instructor at Khopersk, which reached the Politburo before the Plenum. In this letter, Baranov wrote: 'The watchword of the entire operation was "Who will go one better?" At local level, directives from the *okrug* were sometimes reduced to the simple formula "Anyone who does not join the kolkhoz is an enemy of the Soviet régime." . . . In some instances, there were promises of tractors and credits on a very large scale. "We will give you everything. Join the kolkhozes!" ' [67] There is evidence from many sources that these methods, particularly the use of misleading promises, were widespread throughout the country. [68] Baranov goes on to make the following comments:

'So far, the net effect of these factors has been to give a formal figure of 60% collectivization, which may possibly have risen to 70% as this letter is being written. No thought has been given to the qualitative aspect of the kolkhozes. . . . A serious imbalance is therefore developing between the quantitative growth of these large-scale farming enterprises and their qualitative organization. *If action is not taken at once to consolidate these kolkhozes, the whole campaign may be jeopardized. The kolkhozes will disintegrate.* It must also be borne in mind that livestock is being sold off in the *okrug*. . . . All this places us in a very difficult position.'

In the Kursk *okrug*, the campaign was being carried on in the same spirit; the keynote of the operations—'It is better to do too much than not enough' [69]—was worthy of a bureaucrat who was in touch with inner Party circles, and knew what the prevailing mood was in these quarters. The Russian words *peregnut* and *nedognut* are untranslatable, but their political overtones were perfectly clear to the activists.

The prevailing mood within the Politburo was responsible for a drastic shortening of deadlines and an increase in pressure which yielded ever more impressive results in terms of percentages, and these in turn generated even greater enthusiasm and fervour within the Politburo. During the months of October, November and December, 2·4 million households joined the kolkhozes, at a rate of 30 thousand per day. [70] This was already a direct reflection of the pressure being exerted by the authorities. However, some of these figures had no basis in fact. Kosior, the Ukrainian Party secretary, told the Plenum: 'Throughout the region, we had total collectivization of dozens of villages, but it was subsequently shown that these results were artificially inflated, and that the population is not in fact taking part in this movement and knows nothing about it.' [71]

By December, the population 'had learned', for the kolkhozes were enough of a reality to have caused an upheaval in the lives of the peasants, although it could not be said that they had as yet truly established themselves on a firm footing.

It was on the basis of such information that the commission worked out its first set of proposals, which it submitted to the Politburo on December 22nd. With regard to the timing of the collectivization operation, the commission suggested that the main grain-producing regions should be collectivized within two to three years, and that this period might even be reduced in the case of certain *okrugi*. As for the other regions, especially the 'consumer' ones, the period suggested by the commission was three to four years.

Stalin, however, rejected these proposals and demanded that the time be shortened. The commission was therefore obliged to redraft its proposals in a form which would prove more acceptable to the General Secretary. A new draft was submitted on January 3rd 1930, and this formed the basis of a public statement, entitled 'On the timing of collectivization and the government's measures to assist kolkhoz construction'.[72]

Under the new proposal, collectivization in the North Caucasus and the two Volga *krai* was to be completed by the autumn of 1930, or the spring of 1931 at the latest. The other grain-producing regions were to have finished the process of collectivization by autumn 1931, or spring 1932 at the latest. The public statement gave no further details, since the Politburo had turned down the commission's proposed 'time-table' under which, for example, Belorussia, the Trans-caucasian regions, Central Asia, the Far Eastern regions, the North and the North-West, etc., would not complete the process of collecti-vization until the autumn of 1933.[73]

The commission was also forced to pronounce in favour of the *artel* as the only acceptable form of collective enterprise, although it is probable that no such statement had figured in the original pro-posals. However, while agreeing to give exclusive support to the *artel*, the commission endeavoured to make the point that the house-holds belonging to the *artel* should be allowed to retain in private ownership some implements, small livestock and their milk cows, in cases where these were required in order to feed the family. Danilov, the author of the most recent Soviet work to reach us on this subject (1963), states that Stalin struck out the clauses relating to the degree of socialization of property, and also rejected other suggestions which the commission had put forward with regard to methods of estab-lishing the kolkhoz indivisible fund, a matter on which the local authorities had sent repeated urgent letters asking for guidance. Stalin argued that provisions of this kind should properly be covered by the model-statute. The model-statute did not make its appearance until February 6th, but even when it was finally drawn up, it contained no detailed instructions on these pressing problems. Nothing was said about the amount of property which was to remain in the possession of individual members, or about the problem of those peasants who had only one cow, etc.[74]. Stalin did not amend the document. He was obviously unwilling to introduce any element which might contribute to a slackening of the pressure which he had built up, not without difficulty at times. Since the aim was to carry out the bulk of the work of collectivization in a few months (that is, by the coming spring and during the spring sowing campaign), it was a question of using the accelerator rather than the brake. Any kind of restrictive provision in the statute might provide an escape clause for 'unco-operative' peasants, thereby hindering the work of those who were 'collectivizing' them. Stalin was anxious not to leave the peasants any loophole, indeed he took pains to remove as many obstacles to action as possible, and on December 27th, in his speech at the conference of agrarian Marxists, he announced the most significant move in his rural strategy, the 'liquidation of the kulaks as a class'.[75]

Throughout the year, the kulak question had been the subject of considerable controversy among Party members; the matter had been argued out publicly in the press, particularly in *Selskokhozyaist-vennaya Gazeta* and in *Komsomolskaya Pravda*, and also in speeches from the platform at the Sixteenth Party Conference, as well as being discussed by all organizations which were directly concerned with the problem.

At the April Conference, many of the speakers had discussed the kulak question in connection with the decisions which were being taken on the kolkhoz movement, the contracts system, and the tractor 'columns' and 'stations'. Although the matter on the agenda was kolkhoz construction, in the end the discussion centred mainly on the kulaks, since this was an issue on which feelings became heated and on which the participants felt impelled to speak their mind. By this time, the Stalinist faction were already firmly entrenched, since the Right had, for all practical purposes, been eliminated and formally denounced by the previous Plenum. However, such was the nature of the kulak question, and the problems pertaining to it, that this seemingly united faction once more split into a 'right' and a 'left' tendency, and while the debate was going on the two tendencies found themselves involved in a controversy of considerable bitterness.

Opinions were divided on the kulak problem. The question was whether or not the kulaks should be admitted to the kolkhozes. At the April Conference, the majority view was that the kulaks should not be allowed to join the small kolkhozes, except in specific cases where the individual concerned consented to undergo a process of 'dekulakization', or in other words to contribute his property to the common kolkhoz fund. However, even in this instance opinions varied, for some speakers, or authors of articles on the subject, held that this kind of 'dekulakization' could not be genuine, while others quoted examples in which kulaks had already been 'dekulakized' in this way. However, the main part of the discussion revolved round the policy which was to be followed in cases where the 'columns' had signed contracts with entire communities.

Kalinin took a firm stand in favour of admitting kulaks to the tractor 'Stations', his arguments being based on the fact that it had, for some considerable time, been the practice to allow kulaks in the co-operative movement, while debarring them from ful-filling any managerial function. In support of his view, he also cited the experience of the 'Shevchenko' Station in the Ukraine, which signed contracts with all the peasants.[76] In Kalinin's opinion, the kulak was not a source of danger within the 'Station', particularly if the régime's own forces were properly organized there.[77] At the April Conference, Kalinin was vigorously attacked by the left tendency, whose two principal adherents were Shatskin and Lominadze; in turn, he decried the 'r-r-revolutionaries' and defended his own view-point, stressing that the matter should be decided in the light of prac-tical experience, on the basis of local conditions and after due consideration of the personal attitude of the kulak in question.[78]

Kalinin was convinced that the kulak could be re-educated, pro-vided he was properly organized within the correct institutional framework. This view was closely akin to that held by Bukharin, which was now branded as heretical. As far back as 1925, Bukharin had expressed the opinion that the extent and the nature of kulak opposition was determined by the quality of the Soviet administration at local level.

'Radicals' like Shatskin and Lominadze were against allowing the kulaks to function even within the large 'Stations'. There was also a difference of opinion on the measures which should be adopted for dealing with kulaks who were excluded from membership of large kolkhozes, to which the rest of the peasant population had been re-cruited en masse. It was suggested in some quarters that they should be isolated in *otruba* or *khutora*. Shatskin proposed that they be settled separately 'on the edge of the rotation fields'; others again thought that they should be kept apart in small strictly kulak villages (*poselki*), etc. One author strenuously opposed these suggestions, on the grounds that their effect would be to strengthen the kulaks instead of weakening them, a view in which he was joined by Belenky; in an article in *Bolshevik*, in which he described the proposals to exclude the kulaks from the large kolkhozes as 'anti-Leninist', he stated: 'However, we have not heard it suggested that the kulak should be chased off the land, or that he should be forced to move to the remote wastelands, or to some desert island.'[79]

The Conference left the matter in abeyance, without coming to any decision, for the commission which was responsible for putting forward a solution, and on which Stalin had been sitting, in company with Kalinin, Ordzhonikidze, Syrtsov and others, was unable to reach agreement, and referred the matter back for decision by the Politburo.[80]

No one at this time was thinking in terms of 'dekulakization', that is, of expropriating the kulaks; still less was there any thought of mass deportations.

As late as June 2nd, *Pravda* carried an article under the heading 'Neither terror nor dekulakization (*raskulachivanie*) but a socialist offensive on NEP lines'. The article was protesting against the murder of two kulaks by a bednyak who had claimed that the kulaks were hindering the work of socialist construction. *Pravda* advanced an interesting argument against the use of such methods, and likewise against expropriation: '. . . by taking such an "easy" way out, we shall only be adding to the ranks of the kulak supporters among the serednyaks (whose farms will inevitably be affected during the process of dekulakization . . .)'.

However, other articles appeared in *Pravda* which were symptomatic of the tendencies at work in the editorial board and, above all, in the Central Committee. These articles were couched in extremely violent terms, and denounced the 'blindness' of those who failed to realize 'that the kulak is not sleeping, he is growing, he is undermining the policy of the Soviet régime. . . .'[81] This was a quotation from Stalin, although no names were mentioned. The local activists, faced with such vague and contradictory instructions, were at a loss as to how they should conduct an offensive 'along NEP lines' against an enemy who was 'preparing to undermine the régime'. As a result, towards the end of the year, there were the beginnings of a 'spontaneous' dekulakization movement in the regions of the *sploshnaya*, which probably set in some time in October.

Nevertheless, few people at the Centre believed that this 'undermining' was going on. The kulak was often violent in his resistance, and was liable on occasion to arm himself with an axe or a gun; this was true of other peasants too. As the régime intensified its punitive measures and tightened its stranglehold on the kulaks, so their resistance became fiercer. But the kulaks, as a social stratum, never constituted a serious political force within the Soviet context, in the sense that they were not capable of organizing themselves on a wider scale than that of the village. Even at a later stage, when they had been driven to take up a much more embattled position, their political thinking and their organization did not extend beyond the context of the *raion*. With the exception of certain regions in the North Caucasus, for example, where there was a tradition of resistance to the 'reds', the kulaks had neither the ability nor indeed the desire to organize themselves as a vast anti-Soviet ideological force.

One member of the Communist Academy wrote, 'Generally speaking, the theme of the opposition between town and country figures very little in his political agitation. The kulak is mainly concerned with his own village affairs. These are more than enough for him. The main source of pressure on him is from the organizations of the *bednota*'.[82]

In the villages where such organizations existed, their activities were primarily directed against the better-off elements in the village, and this explains the hatred felt by the more prosperous peasants for the bednyaks and their groups, but the kulak's position was mainly a defensive one. The author of the above article states that the kulaks were clearly acting in self-defence. 'It is not correct to interpret the class struggle in terms of an attack by the kulaks on the *bednota*. The kulak only attacks sporadically, but in general he is the one who is attacked.'[83]

Speaking from his experience in Siberia, where the degree of social tension was particularly acute, Syrtsov stated at the April 1929 Conference that the kulak was showing signs of wishing to free himself from existing Soviet structures, but that 'he does not possess the necessary organizing ability, he has no nation-wide organization, he lacks a programme which, within the context of the Soviet constitution, could give legal expression to such a movement on an all-Union scale, and there are within the ranks of the kulaks no personalities with sufficient authority to support him in his aspirations'.[84]

Subsequent events merely served to confirm the political weakness of this stratum, which had been accused by the official propagandists of harbouring detailed plans, of working out its tactics with painstaking thoroughness and, in short, of scheming with diabolical ingenuity to 'undermine' the régime.

In September, the *Kolkhoztsentr* submitted a report to the Politburo in which it spoke of the bitterness of the class struggle in the regions of mass collectivization, and of the kulaks' resistance to the kolkhozes.[85] The examples quoted in the document related to only two regions. In the Chapaev *raion* in the Lower Volga, the kulaks who had been admitted to the kolkhozes were agitating to be allowed to leave, and those who remained outside the kolkhozes were engaging in anti-kolkhoz propaganda. However, when they realized that they would not succeed, they themselves had begun joining the collectives, and some of them had even agreed to hand over their property 100% to the kolkhozes. The report stated that they had acted in this way from fear of being isolated from the village with a plot of land situated somewhere on the edge of the sown area. There was also hanging over their heads the threat that they might even be deported from the *raion*. Nevertheless, the report went on, kulak resistance for the most part took the form of indirect action, such as propaganda directed at the womenfolk, the spreading of anti-kolkhoz rumours, and so on.[86]

In the Irbitski *okrug* in the Urals, three *raiony* were in the process of setting-up a giant kolkhoz covering an area of 135,000 (!) hectares. This was the famous Urals *Gigant*. According to the report, kulak resistance in this region was particularly fierce. However, the only example of this resistance quoted by the authors of the report was a letter from one village which again mentioned rumours (about 'the end of the world being near' and 'Antichrist having come down to earth') but also spoke of fires and the 'poisoning' of fields.[87]

Thus, in September 1929 the situation was far from being as grave as the press, inspired by the Politburo, were trying to make out. A very anti-kulak article appearing in *Na Agrarnom Fronte* discussed the kulaks 'counter-offensives', and listed the following acts of anti-kolkhoz violence: during 1929, the kolkhoz movement had recorded 311 cases of kulak terrorism, of which 171 were fires; the rest were cases of assault, attempted murder and murder. The number of murders was not however specified.[88]

Such figures for the USSR as a whole would still not warrant the assumption that the situation was unduly serious. The *Kolkhoztsentr*, which was aware of these figures, and had not made a full statement on the matter but confined itself, as we have seen, to two rather inconclusive examples, put forward the following proposals: no kulaks should be allowed in the kolkhozes; those who were already members should be removed; a law should be passed laying down severe penalties for any kulaks who committed acts of terrorism; public trials should be organized in respect of such persons.[89]

It is abundantly clear that the idea of dekulakization was slow to take root in the minds of the Central Committee. At the November Plenum the matter was in fact raised, but was left unresolved. The only record of this Plenum available to us is a relatively small number of extracts, or reports based on the account of the Plenum, which have been produced by present-day Soviet authors who have had access to the Party Archives. Kaminsky repeated the proposals he had put forward in September for expelling the kulaks from the kolkhozes, and strengthening the legislative measures which could be used against them. Mikoyan suggested that the problem of kulak membership of the kolkhozes should be decided not in the abstract, but with reference to the class struggle, that is, presumably, taking local conditions into consideration. The source from whom we quote [90] does not specify whether these speakers suggested dekulakization. Stalin also contributed to the discussion, and stressed that the emergency measures were the product of a mass offensive of the bednyaks and serednyaks against the kulaks, [91] an interpretation which reveals very clearly the direction in which Stalin's thoughts were turning.

Andreev, Party Secretary of the North Caucasus *krai* which was setting the pace in the collectivization drive, announced that his *krai* would be able to complete its task 'in essence' by the summer of 1931, and he expressed the hope that the peasantry would support the Party in this decision. At this point, he was interrupted by Petrovsky, who asked: 'And what about the kulak?' Andreev—'I think that, for the moment, the kulak should be isolated (*vydelit*) so as not to complicate our task during this first phase.' A voice from the audience: 'Why "for the moment"?' Andreev—'I said "for the moment" because I believe that when we have consolidated our position, when we are assured of positive gains in our kolkhoz movement, when we have duly expropriated the kulaks (it being understood that we have no intention of liquidating them physically), once we have done all that, there will no longer be any risk involved in allowing this sector of the population to play a part within our social economy, but we must first of all score a decisive victory, strengthen our leadership, and dekulakize this element.' [92]

Thus, it will be seen that Andreev was in favour of expropriating the kulaks, but saw no danger in allowing them to remain *in situ*, since he was merely proposing to 'isolate' them, and was hoping to be able to integrate them in the kolkhozes at a later stage. It should be borne in mind that his *krai*, with its Cossack population, had been reported as being the most rebellious region of all. Could it then be that he too was smitten by 'blindness'?

Andreev's relatively 'light-hearted' approach was probably shared by the majority of the *obkom* secretaries, whose duty it would be to attend the Politburo commission and reach decisions on the progress of collectivization and the treatment which was to be meted out to the kulaks. They had no desire to go to such lengths as the Politburo, which via its spokesman Molotov was talking in terms of 'the enemy who has still not been liquidated', and which even at this stage must have been meditating a much more extreme course of action. However, in the regional centres and the *obkom* leadership, even among the Stalinists, the 'Old Bolshevik' influence still prevailed. Rykov was still official head of the *Sovnarkom*, and he was backed up even in his most tentative objections by some *obkom* secretaries who could not possibly have been said to have any leanings towards the 'Right' or to be involved in any kind of opposition.

Nevertheless, the Politburo had original methods for forcing its own members to accept a policy line with which they were not in agreement. It had, for example, bypassed the *obkom* and *kraikom* (which was not common practice within the Party) by establishing direct contact, at the beginning of December, with the *okrugi*, and in particular with thirty *okrugi* of its own choosing, which were probably those designated as regions of *sploshnaya kollektivizatsia*.[93] This step, which was ostensibly taken in order to improve the flow of information, enabled the Politburo to urge upon the most important *okrugi* a different policy from that favoured by the *obkomy*, thus forcing the latter's hand and obliging them to consent to a more rapid rate of collectivization or to measures of a more extreme character, by facing them with *a fait accompli* and with the threat of 'being swamped by the movement'. Naturally, the Politburo had other methods as well,[94] but the job of overcoming all these objections still took time.

While some dekulakization, of a partial and unsystematic kind, had already taken place in the regions of mass collectivization, in those *okrugi* which the Central Committee had taken directly 'under its wing',[95] the sub-committee on the kulak question was preparing the proposals which it was to submit to the Politburo. According to Ivnitsky in an article written in 1962, the committee took into consideration the hostility of the kulaks but also recognized 'the possibility that some elements among the kulaks might, through the power of the proletarian dictatorship, be induced to adopt a submissive and loyal attitude towards socialist construction in the countryside'.[96]

The sub-committee placed the kulaks in three categories. The first of these, comprising active enemies of the régime who had been guilty of hostile acts, should be sentenced to imprisonment, or deportation to distant regions. It is not clear, in this version of the text, what was to be the fate of the families of the kulaks in question. The second category, subject to decision by the village assembly, was to be removed outwith the *oblast*, but not deported to Siberia. Here again, it is not clear whether the sub-committee was proposing to allow the kulaks concerned to retain some part of their property. As for kulaks in the third category, they were to be left *in situ* and were to be subject only to partial expropriation, so that they might settle on the plots of land which would be allocated to them, and begin farming there. The sub-committee was of the opinion that this latter category could be 're-educated'. For this reason, they were to be permitted to enter the kolkhozes as workers without voting rights for a period of three to five years, with the proviso that they might subsequently be admitted to membership as of right. In this way, the sub-committee was hoping to turn to advantage the labour force represented by the kulak families, which it estimated at about five to six million persons.[97]

Another source[98] specifies that over the major part of the RSFSR there were 52,000 kulaks in the first category and 112,000 in the second category (these being unquestionably heads of households). In this second category were included kulaks who were 'less actively anti-Soviet' but were opposed to the kolkhozes. The author states that the third category comprised three-quarters of all the kulaks.[99] This gives a figure of some 650,000 households for the Russian republic alone, a figure which it is important to bear in mind.

It is evident, therefore, that the sub-committee of the Central Committee commission was prepared, on certain conditions, to admit to the kolkhozes some three-quarters of these alleged 'fierce enemies', whom it did not in fact regard as such. The committee was further proposing that they be allowed to retain some part of their property. Deportation to Siberia was not envisaged except for those kulaks who were accused by the tribunals of having committed counter-revolutionary acts.

At this stage, we still do not know in what form the initial set of proposals was submitted to the Politburo on December 22nd, or what form it took after the Politburo had, as we know, insisted that the entire body of proposals put forward by the commission should be reformulated. In so far as the kulak question was concerned, the Politburo finally rejected the suggestions and dispensed with the services of the sub-committee.

The Politburo thereupon appointed another commission, in January 1930, to study the kulak problem.[100] On this issue, opposition to Stalin's ideas was more vigorous and more determined than it was in other contexts. However, the new commission proved to be more amenable, and its activities led to the production on January 30th and at the beginning of February, of directives (which were naturally kept secret at the time), relating to anti-kulak measures. These were very different from the proposals put forward by the previous sub-committee of the commission of the Central Committee.

In his speech on December 27th, Stalin announced the new policy of 'liquidating the kulaks as a class', and removed the prohibition on expropriation since, as he said, expropriation was at present being effected by the mass of the peasantry on the basis of *sploshnaya kollektivizatsiya*. This could not be done earlier, he explained, but now, thanks to the kolkhozes and sovkhozes, the State had the wherewithal to replace the kulaks' contribution to agricultural production. Moreover,

476

'Now dekulakization in the areas of complete collectivization [the official view being at this point that dekulakization was taking place only in these regions.—M.L.] is no longer just an administrative measure. Now, it is an integral part of the formation and development of the collective farms. Consequently it is now ridiculous and foolish to discourse at length on dekulakization. When the head is off, one does not mourn for the hair.' [101]

Crowned with the laurels which the press had newly bestowed on him as the leading theoretician of Leninism, Stalin read a lengthy statement, in the form of a lesson on theory, to the Marxist agrarian theoreticians, who were assembled for a conference. Essentially, what he told them, in fairly blunt terms, was that they had very little grasp of the most pressing problems. In this context, even Engels underwent some drastic revision, for his statement that socialism would give the peasant all the time that he needed 'to think things over on his small holding', a statement which was universally known, and to which Lenin had subscribed, was dismissed by Stalin as invalid. Engels, he declared, was thinking of the Western peasantry, who were accustomed to the institution of private property. 'Can it be said that a similar situation exists here in the USSR? No, it cannot. It cannot be said because here we have no private ownership of land chaining the peasant to his individual farm.' [102]

Since private ownership of the land had been abolished, the Russian peasant—so Stalin's theory went—willingly joined the kolkhoz, because he was not attached to his private property. Accordingly, Engels' principle was now declared invalid. Henceforth, the Russian peasant was to have no time to think things over.

NOTES AND REFERENCES

1. Danilov (ed.), *op. cit.* (see Ch. 13, Note 73), p. 106. Information from the Archives of the National Economy.

2. *ibid*, pp. 88–9.

3. Nikolaevsky, 'Stalin i ubiistvo Kirova', *Sotsialisticheski Vestnik*, December 1956, Footnote to p. 24.

4. Barmin, *One Who Survived*. (New York, 1945).

5. Serge, *op. cit.* (see Ch. 6, Note 71), p. 74.

6. *ibid*, pp. 279–80.

7. Letter signed by Rakovsky, Kosior, and Okudzhava and dated August 22, 1929, *Byulleten Oppozitsii*, 1929, No. 7, p. 14.

8. *Byulleten Oppozitsii*, 1929, No. 1–2, p. 14.

9. Quoted in the criticism of Shatskin and Sten by the *Komsomol* in *Pravda*, August 8, 1929.

10. Quoted in *Bolshevik*, 1929. No. 16 (August), pp. 51–5.

11. Ezhev, Mekhlis, Pospelov, 'Pravy uklon v prakiticheskoi rabote i partiinoe boloto', *Bolshevik*, 1929, No. 16, p. 51.

12. *Pravda*, August 9, 1929.

13. *Bolshevik*, 1929, No. 23–4.

14. Bukharin was expelled from the Politburo, his two collegues remained, but dissemination of Right-wing ideas was declared incompatible with Party membership. The decisons relating to the Right are in *KPSS v Rezolyutsiyakh*, Vol. II, pp. 662–3, the capitulation of the 'trio' in *Pravda*, November 20, 1929.

15. Pyatakov, 'Za rukovodstvo', *Pravda*, December 23, 1929.

16. Figures in *Planovoe Khozyaistvo*, 1929, No. 9, pp. 23–7.

17. Zaleski, *op. cit.* (see Ch. 7, Note 5), p. 102.

18. Strumilin (ed) *Ekonomicheskaya Zhizn SSSR.* (Moscow 1961), p. 244; Kviring, *Planovoe Khozyaistvo*, 1930, No. 9.

19. Zaleski, *op. cit.*, p. 93.

20. See for example a remark made by Stalin at the 17th Party Conference, *17-taya Konferentsiya VKP(b)*, stenogramme, p. 233.

21. Phrase coined by Krzhizhanovsky, *Planovoe Khozyaistvo*, 1929, No. 12, p. 12.

22. Shlikhter, 'Kak perestroit pyatiletku', *Pravda*, November 1, 1929.

23. Stalin, *Sochineniya*, Vol. XII, pp. 118–35; *Pravda*, November 7, 1929.

24. *ibid*, p. 125.

25. *ibid*, p. 126.

26. *ibid*, pp. 129, 132.

27. *ibid*, pp. 132–3.

28. *ibid*, p. 132.

29. *ibid*, p. 135.

30. *ibid*, pp. 132–59. Note that by January 1, 1933, there were 148,481 tractors in the USSR whereas the target for 1932 had been 260,000. See *Itogi vypolneniya pyatiletnego plana.* (Moscow 1933.)

31. Article by Abramov in Danilov (ed.) *op. cit.*, pp. 95–6.

32. *ibid*, p. 96. The claim that by the end of 1929 the attitude of the serednyaks had changed is also challenged by Ivnitsky in *Voprosy Istorii KPSS*, 1962, No. 4, p. 71.

33. Abramov, article in Danilov (ed.), *op. cit.*, p. 96. In support of his argument, Abramov reports that by December 15th, in 59% of the 1,416 *raiony* of the RSFSR only from 1% to 5% of the households had been collectivized.

34. *ibid*, pp. 96–7.

35. *ibid*, p. 97.

36. Molotov's speech to the Plenum was published 'with cuts' in

Bolshevik, 1929, No. 22, pp. 10–23. The quotation is from p. 13.

37. *ibid*, p. 14.

38. *Voprosy Istorii KPSS*, 1962, No. 4, p 65. Molotov's speech was made on November 15th. On November 14th Andreev declared that the aim of the North Caucasus was to have completed collectivization by the summer of 1931. See his speech in *Voprosy Istorii KPSS*, 1958, No. 4, p. 79. A criticism of Molotov's speech is contained in Danilov (ed.), *op. cit.*, and that part of Molotov's speech is reproduced in which he claimed that during 1930 entire Republics would be fully collectivized.

39. Molotov, *Bolshevik*, 1929, No. 22, p. 12.

40. *ibid*, pp. 15, 16–17.

41. *ibid*, pp. 15, 17.

42. *ibid*, p. 16.

43. *ibid*, p. 19.

44. Abramov, in Danilov (ed.) *op. cit.*, pp. 97–8, and his article in *Voprosy Istorii KPSS*, 1964, No. 1, p. 33.

45. See *Voprosy Istorii KPSS*, 1962, No. 4, p. 69.

46. Abramov, in Danilov (ed.), *op. cit.*, p. 107, states that this was indeed the Politburo's intention.

47. On Sheboldaev's proposal see Abramov, in Danilov (ed.), *op. cit.*, p. 98, and *Voprosy Istorii KPSS*, 1964, No. 1, *loc. cit.*

48. For the decisions of the November Plenum see *KPSS v Rezolyutsiyakh*, Vol. II, pp. 620–3.

49. *ibid*, p. 630. (Emphasis in the original.)

50. *ibid*, p. 645.

51. *ibid*, p. 645.

52. *ibid*, p. 651. See also pp. 642–4.

53. *ibid*, p. 653. This resolution mentions, in the same vague terms as those employed by Molotov, the decisive victories in the sphere of collectivization, which must be won during the coming spring.

54. *ibid*, pp. 653–6: the decision concerning the setting up of *Narkomzem*, in conformity with proposals made by Molotov. The corresponding decree of the *TsIK* is in *Kollektivizatsiya selskogo khozyaistva*, doc. No. 65.

55. See *KPSS v Rezolyutsiyakh*, Vol. II, p. 645, and *Kollektivizatsiya selskogo khozyaistva*, doc. No. 66. On the complete revision of plan targets resulting from the new policy for the countryside see, for example, *Pravda*, November 18, 1929, and Zaleski, *op. cit.*, pp. 88–9, 96–9.

56. *KPSS v Rezolyutsiyakh*, Vol. II, p. 647; Terletsky, 'Na novom pod'eme', *Bolshevik*, 1929, No. 21 (November), p. 67.

57. Decisions of the plenum, *KPSS v Rezolyutsiyakh*, Vol. II, pp. 649–50, 651.

58. Rykov, *5-ty S'ezd Sovetov*, stenogramme, bulletin No. 7, p. 17.

59. Decisions of the plenum, *KPSS v. Rezolyutsiyakh*, Vol. II, p. 649.

60. Molotov, *Bolshevik*, 1929, No. 22, p. 19.

61. *ibid*, p. 12.

62. Ivnitsky, 'O nachalnom etape sploshnoi kollektivizatsii', *Voprosy Istorii KPSS*, 1962, No. 4.

63. For details concerning the work of this commission see Ivnitsky, *op. cit.*, and Danilov (ed.), *op. cit.*, pp. 35–6.

64. Ivnitsky, *op. cit.*, p. 62.

65. *ibid*, pp. 62–3. On the *peregiby* of that autumn see *ibid*, p. 64 and Abramov in Danilov (ed.), *op. cit.*, p. 95.

66. Ivnitsky, *op. cit.*, p. 62.

67. *ibid*, pp. 64–5. The data in this article are taken from the Central Archives of the Party, and from the Central Archives of the National Economy. The letter is from the Party Archives.

68. On the promises made by activists, in their anxiety to report back as quickly as possible with impressive percentages, see also Ulashevich, *op. cit.* (see Ch. 1, Note 8), p. 5.

69. Abramov, in Danilov (ed.), *op. cit.*, p. 95.

70. *Postroenie fundamenta sotsialisticheskoi ekonomiki v SSSR* (see Ch. 1, Note 30), pp. 316–7.

71. Quoted in Danilov (ed.), *op. cit.*, p. 96.

72. On Stalin's alterations to the first draft see Danilov (ed.), *op. cit.*, pp. 35–6. It has not yet been admitted, even by Ivnitsky in 1962, that the commission proposed different time limits. For the decisions of the Central Committee see *KPSS v Rezolyutsiyakh*, Vol. II, pp. pp. 664–7.

73. Ivnitsky, *op. cit.* (see Note 62), p. 62; Danilov (ed.); *op. cit.*, p. 37.

74. On the problem of the *artel* and the degree of socialization see Danilov (ed.), *op. cit.*, p. 36. The abortive model statute produced by *Narkomzem* is in *Pravda*, February 6, 1930. It recommends, among other things, that, circumstances permitting, 'all productive livestock' (which includes cattle), be placed under collective ownership.

75. The speech 'K voprosam agrarnoi politiki SSSR' is in *Pravda*, December 29, 1929, *Sochineniya*, Vol. XII, and *NAF*, 1930, No. 1. It is this last version which is quoted here.

76. Kalinin, *16-taya Konferentsiya*, stenogramme, pp. 132–42, and his closing speech, p. 208. On the treatment of the kulaks by the Shevchenko *MTS* see *Bolshevik*, 1929, No. 13, p. 50, where it is stated that the station charged them increased rates for its services and did not grant them credit. This practice was general throughout the Southern Ukraine.

77. Kalinin, *ibid*, p. 142.

78. Kalinin, *ibid*, p. 208; Shatskin, *ibid*, pp. 57–8; Lominadze, *ibid*, pp. 148–53; Kaminsky, *ibid*, pp. 189–90. Fifteen speakers took part in the discussion on this question.

79. Karpinsky, 'O kolkhozakh i kulake', *Bolshevik*, 1929, No. 11, p. 34.

80. *Voprosy Istorii KPSS* 1959, No. 4, p. 77. The chairman of the commission was S. Kosior.

81. *Pravda*, June 14, 1929.

82. Angarov, *op. cit.* (see Ch. 2, Footnote 39), p. 31.

83. *ibid*.

84. Syrtsov, *16-taya Konferentsiya VKP(b)*, stenogramme, p. 154.

85. *Dokumenty po istorii sovetskogo obshchestva*, Vol. VII, pp. 241–6.

86. *ibid*, pp. 241–3.

87. *ibid*, pp. 244–5.

88. Karavaev, *NAF*, 1929, No. 10, p. 70.

89. The report by the *Kolkhoztsentr* in *Dokumenty po istorii sovetskogo obshchestva*, Vol. VII, pp. 245–6.

90. Ivnitsky, *Voprosy Istorii KPSS*, 1962, No. 4, p. 67.

91. *ibid*.

92. Quoted from the Party Archives in an article by Semerkin, 'O likvidatsii kulachestva kak klassa', *Voprosy Istorii*, 1958, No. 4, p. 79. 'Dekulakize' here means 'expropriate'.

93. *Pravda*, December 7, 1929.

94. It will be recalled that Molotov in effect overruled Andreev, for the following day he spoke of much shorter time limits for collectivization in Andreev's territory. He was thus inciting the *okrugi* to outstrip their *obkomy*.

95. Ivnitsky, in *Voprosy Istorii KPSS*, 1962, No. 4, pp. 68–70, sometimes states that collectivization began 'in autumn', at other times that it began 'towards the end of the year'.

96. *ibid*, p. 68.

97. *ibid*, p. 68–9.

98. Abramov, in Danilov (ed.), *op. cit.*, pp. 104–5.

99. *ibid*, p. 104.

100. Ivnitsky, *op. cit.*, pp. 68–9. According to Bogdenko, writing in *Voprosy Istorii*, 1963, No. 5, p. 31, the following were members of this commission: Y. D. Kabanov, N. V. Krylenko, Ya. A. Yakovlev, S. S. Odintsov. Others who took part in its activities were: S. Kosior, M. Khataevich, B. Sheboldaev, Y. Vareikis.

101. Quoted in *NAF*, 1930, No. 1, p. 15.

102. *ibid*, p. 8.

Chapter 17

DEKULAKIZATION

The Politburo's strategy, in the months which followed, was dictated exclusively by the objective it had in mind, and the time in which this objective was to be achieved. The task it had set itself was immense: the entire social structure of the countryside was to be radically altered, and control of the greater part of the country's marketable grain was to be wrested from the private sector. There was no historical precedent for a transformation of this magnitude, and even the most ambitious of the Bolshviks had reckoned that it would take some ten to fifteen years of revolutionary changes to complete. But abruptly the Stalinist leadership decided otherwise. An official deadline of three years was set for the country as a whole, and one of one to two years for the principal grain-producing regions. However, as we have seen, the Party had vague intentions of completing 'the bulk of the work'[1] (the very expression betrays uncertainty as to what this involved) 'in the months, weeks, and days ahead'.[2] The 'months, weeks, and days ahead' were to be spent preparing the sowing campaign. Molotov had explicitly stated that only 'November, December, January, February and March'[3] remained for this purpose, and that during these few months a sufficient number of kolkhozes would have to be set up to ensure 'the first Bolshevik spring'. In other words, the collectivized sector would require to be sufficiently powerful to obviate any danger of sabotage either in the sowing campaign or, subsequently, in the procurement campaign.

If such an ambitious aim were to be achieved—and this, in effect, meant disposing of Soviet Russia's most intractable problems with a single wave of the dictatorship's magic wand—the methods employed would have to be adequate to the task in hand.

This could only mean one thing—solving the problem of collectivization by a 'swift, decisive blow' similar to that aimed at the peasants during the current procurements campaign. To this end, the methods, the slogans and the whole atmosphere of the Civil War would have to be re-created, and all the forces of the Party and the régime would have to be mobilized for one tremendous onslaught aimed at driving the *muzhik* into the kolkhoz.

In Soviet conditions, a return to the methods of the Civil War presented no difficulty, for the practice of such methods was deeply ingrained not only among the cadres who ran the Soviet bureaucratic machine, but even more so among the Party cadres. During the NEP period, these methods had been regarded as no better than 'semi-legal' but, owing to the way in which the régime had evolved, particularly under pressure from the series of difficulties which set in at the beginning of 1928, they had gradually come to gain increasing acceptance. The process continued, until eventually the Politburo were to begin resorting freely to such methods, with the addition of new and characteristic variations of their own. Trotsky has provided the following explanation of one of the characteristic features of the Soviet bureaucracy:

'The demobilization of the Red Army of five million played no small role in the formation of the bureaucracy. The victorious commanders assumed leading posts in the local Soviets, in economy, in education, and they persistently introduced everywhere that régime which had ensured success in the Civil War.'[4]

This explains the ease with which the leadership could, if they wished (and indeed they saw no alternative) plunge the country back into the same atmosphere simply by giving the ubiquitous 'commanders' the signal to go ahead and behave as they had been accustomed to behaving during the Civil War. There was another element too, which had always been latent in the Soviet governmental apparatus, particularly in the rural areas; this was the typical Russian *derzhimorda*, brutal, ignorant and rapacious. These two types of bureaucrat, both widely represented in the government apparatus, were virtually given a free hand to bring about what was officially described as 'the destruction of the last class of exploiters in the USSR'.

Dekulakization was the key-weapon in the strategy of collectivization. Even today, the official apologists still maintain that without dekulakization, collectivization would have been impossible. This is perfectly true, but those who advance this argument seem to be unaware that it invalidates another official tenet, concerning the preparedness of the peasants for collectivization, and their willingness to accept it.

The rigours to which the better-off peasants had been subjected during the procurements campaigns had already crippled their activities as producers. Many of them had been ruined. One present-day author has observed that 'even before the summer of 1929, whole groups of kulaks were unable to resist, and were ruined'.[5]

The State had it in its power to ruin the kulaks, or to *restrict* them in their activities, to reduce them to the condition of simple serednyaks, or even lower. The strategy of lightning collectivization called for their 'liquidation as a class'. One of the reasons given was the kulaks' increasingly fierce resistance to the measures adopted by the government. In reality, this was the desperate resistance of a stratum which realized that it was doomed.

The kulaks were not so isolated in the countryside as was officially claimed. They were strongly represented in the *selsovety* and the co-operative organizations, they were even represented in the Party cells, either directly or through serednyaks, or even bednyak sympathizers. The press, and official documents, often complained that the Soviet administrations at *raion* level, and sometimes at *okrug* level, were 'riddled with alien elements'. The Smolensk archives mention the existence of a pronounced 'right-wing deviation' among People's judges and members of tribunals, which would suggest that the latter adhered to the 'NEP' concept of the village. In many cases, judges dealt leniently with kulaks accused of speculation.[6] In this way, the kulaks were sometimes able to evade prosecution or taxation, or even straightforward census-taking. What is more, they were occasionally in a position to bribe officials, bednyaks and in particular batraks who worked for them, by the simple process of offering them a meal, or some vodka. The practice of getting a number of bednyaks drunk, in order to persuade them to vote against certain government measures, was no doubt fairly widespread.

However, although the better-off peasants unquestionably wielded some influence in the countryside, the extent of their influence should not be exaggerated. Such power as they had was largely due to the inferiority, and at times the rank inefficiency of the official organs, and the numerical weakness of the Party cells and of the rural administrations in general.[7] Their influence merely enabled them to take flight, or to take cover, a fact which is demonstrated by the ways in which they reacted, and the forms in which their undoubtedly growing resistance manifested itself. Some fled the countryside to settle in the towns; others moved from their own villages to different ones where they were not known. Whenever they were allowed to do so, a great many joined the kolkhozes. Others still set up a kolkhoz on their own. In order to gain admittance to a kolkhoz, some agreed to contribute their property to the indivisible fund. Others, by selling off their belongings, 'dekulakized' themselves, so that they might join as bednyaks, or serednyaks.[8]

According to official propaganda these were 'premeditated tactics' aimed at the destruction of the kolkhozes, but it is quite clear that no such predetermined plan existed. The persecuted, better-off peasants were simply using every means in their power to ward off the blows which the régime was inflicting on them. The better-off peasant who voluntarily surrendered all his property to a kolkhoz, so that he might become a member, was not an inveterate agent of capitalism, but a frightened, desperate creature.

However, the peasant who joined a kolkhoz did not automatically turn 'socialist'. This was even less likely in the case of the dispossessed kulak. When, upon arrival in the kolkhozes, the kulaks found a defective organization, or a lack of cadres who were sufficiently dedicated to the régime, or even capable of managing kolkhoz affairs, they could easily, by reason of their experience and their literacy, take over the management of the kolkhoz, and then endeavour, as many other peasants did, to postpone the transition from the status of *toz*, and to block any further socialization of property. There was, therefore, a risk that some kolkhozes might become mere façades, concealing not only private cultivation of the land, but even wage-labour and exploitation. The authorities fought against this kind of 'pseudo-collectivization' by purging, or liquidating many 'kulak-kolkhozes'.[9] A law published in 1929 laid down severe penalties for officials found guilty of connivance in, or toleration of 'pseudo-cooperation'.[10]

As we have seen, the problem of admitting kulaks to the kolkhoz was debated by the Party during 1929, and many prominent Party officials, including some members of the Politburo, were in favour of allowing them to join the larger collectives and the *MTS*. The Sixteenth Party Conference had failed to reach a decision on this matter; consequently, the regional organizations were issuing conflicting instructions. In the Lower Volga, for example, kulak membership of the kolkhozes was permitted. This decision was not declared invalid until September 30, 1929.[11]

However, even after the apparently final decision of the November 1929 session of the Central Committee, prohibiting kulak membership of the kolkhozes, there still remained the problem of whether or not to admit 'dekulakized' peasants. The Politburo commission had proposed that some four-fifths of the kulaks be admitted to the kolkhozes, but that they be deprived of the right to vote and of access to managerial posts, and that they be allowed to enjoy full membership only after a trial period. While obviously in possession of the facts, and aware that acts of terrorism were frequently committed against kolkhoz members and bednyak activists, the commission had nevertheless no misgivings about the presence of expropriated peasants in the kolkhozes.[12]

Most Party leaders at the time would probably have been amazed if they could have read some of the allegations subsequently made by writers who were anxious, at all costs, to justify the treatment meted out to the kulaks. One modern writer, for example, has said: 'We must take into account the fact that the kulaks were aiming to provoke civil war, at a time when military intervention by the most powerful imperialist states was imminent'.[13]

485

Even in its most extreme manifestations, kulak resistance took the form of individual acts of terrorism, the murder or attempted murder of activists, arson (particularly in the case of kolkhoz buildings or the houses of bednyak activists) and assault. To this day, no full account of these activities can be found in Soviet sources, which provide only partial and incomplete data. Thus, we learn that there were 1,002 acts of terrorism, including 384 murders, over a period of nine months in the Russian Republic in 1929 [14] and this is the most important piece of statistical information available to us. Such figures certainly afford an indication of social pressures, and of active hostility to the régime itself. From the autumn of 1929 onwards, when the government declared total war on the kulaks, and the drive for collectivization was fully underway, the incidence of terroristic activity must have increased. However, no complete data are available for this period, and one has to rely on scattered indications. Thus, one present-day writer, who has had access to the archives, states that in the Leningrad *oblast* in October 1929, more acts of terrorism were committed than in the whole of 1928. In the Ukraine, it would appear that four times as many acts of terrorism were committed in 1929 as in 1927.[15] An article on the Ukraine, in the collection from which the above figures were taken, mentions a recrudescence of kulak terror, but gives figures which in themselves reveal little. During the first half of 1928, 117 acts of terrorism were recorded, and from October 1928 to February 1929, there is a record of 300 offences of various kinds, including murder, arson, and assault and battery.[16] It is difficult to deduce from this, as the authors of the article have done, that some overriding necessity drove the régime to dispose of the 'kulak menace' once and for all.

These acts of terrorism, although indicative of the kulaks' hatred of the régime, must, in the final analysis, be interpreted as a sign of weakness. As one Soviet author has put it, the kulaks were no longer strong enough to go in for organized banditry, as they had done in 1920–1. Consequently, they turned to individual terrorism.[17] Until the advent of dekulakization, the scale of these activities did not constitute a serious threat. Kulak resistance did not become more dangerous until about the spring of 1930, for reasons which can more appropriately be discussed in connection with the events of that period.

Meanwhile, a greater source of danger than murder or arson was oral propaganda, the spreading of countless rumours, often of the most fantastic kind, which were mainly directed against the kolkhozes, and which found a receptive audience among the peasants. In this respect, the village priests played a not inconsiderable part; numerous cases were reported of priests addressing 'epistles' to their flock, organizing processions and other religious ceremonies and preaching against the kolkhozes in the churches.[18]

The extreme efficacy of this propaganda was due, not to the strength of the kulaks, but to the weakness of official propaganda, and above all to the distrust which the peasants felt, and were so frequently justified in feeling, for the government during the collectivization campaign and more especially during the autumn and winter of 1929–30.

About the autumn of 1929, when the authorities were setting-up large kolkhozes composed of entire villages, they had begun amalgamating the kulaks' holdings with the kolkhoz lands, and allocating plots for the kulaks themselves on the outskirts of the village. This was the prelude to expulsion of the kulaks from the villages, an event which was dreaded by the better-off peasants, who had already seen it happening on numerous occasions. Those who had been dealt with in this way were recalcitrant kulaks, who had been accused of obstructing the procurements; their property had been confiscated, and they had been deported.[19]

It was in December that mass dekulakization began in the regions of *sploshnaya kollektivizats'ya*. It began 'spontaneously', that is to say by decision of the *okrug* and *raion* authorities. Treatment of the dekulakized peasants varied; sometimes they were detained pending enquiries, sometimes they were sent to regional centres and handed over to the *OGPU*. So far, the Centre had not issued any definite instructions in the matter, for the Politburo commission whose responsibility it was to put forward proposals for the solution of the 'kulak problem' was still sitting during the month of December, and another commission had subsequently been appointed, and had begun working on the problem in January. No doubt, vigorous opposition to the solutions envisaged by Stalin, Mototov and Kaganovich had led to delay in the promulgation of the appropriate laws and directives, despite the fact that instructions in the matter of dekulakization had now become urgently necessary.[20]

Stalin now decided to dispose of any lingering doubts in the Central Committee by facing them with a *fait accompli*. Before the commission had drawn up the necessary instructions, he waived the prohibition on dekulakization, and in a public statement on December 27th, 1929, he announced the policy of 'liquidation of the kulaks as a class'.

Stalin's announcement had the desired effect. In the absence of any instructions which might have curbed their excesses, the local activists, wherever they were so inclined, set about the process of dekulakization in a manner that was chaotic, brutal and cruel. There was, in any case, a strong tendency among the activists to fall upon the enemy with the utmost ferocity, in order to have done with him as quickly as possible. 'There proved to be a widespread, and very pronounced tendency to "naked" (*goloe*) dekulakization not only among local and *raion* officials, but among officials at *okrug* level also.'[21] This observation was made by the Party secretary of the Middle Volga *krai*, and it is borne out by one modern Soviet writer, who suggests that it was valid for the country as a whole. He writes: '... the officials of the Party and the local Soviets concentrated their efforts primarily on the liquidation of the kulaks'.[22]

The Soviet term 'naked dekulakization' is used to designate a form of dekulakization which was regarded as being of negative value, that is to say, expropriation carried out for its own sake, without regard to the interests of the kolkhoz and its level of development. This was considered a serious infringement of the official principle that dekulakization was only to be carried out in regions of mass collectivization, and that it should be related to the ripening of the kolkhoz movement.[23]

In practice, officials who were impatient to set about their task often acted in a manner which was in direct contradiction to official theory:

'In their anxiety to proceed as quickly as possible to dekulakization, they [the local authorities] began to force the pace of the kolkhoz movement as far as possible, and did not hesitate to exert pressure on the serednyaks in cases where the latter were not yet ready to enter the kolkhoz.'[24]

This writer accuses Stalin of having encouraged dekulakization in the so-called 'non-sploshnaya' regions in order to prevent the kulaks from 'squandering' their property, while waiting their turn to be expropriated. This tendency for dekulakization to take priority over collectivization, rather than the reverse, was the most significant feature of the events of the winter of 1929–30.

In order to understand this process of wholesale dekulakization, it is also essential to bear in mind the misery in which millions of bednyaks lived. All too often they went hungry; they had neither shoes nor shirts, nor any other 'luxury items'. The tension which had built up in the countryside, and the eagerness to dispossess the kulaks, were in large measure contributed to by the wretchedness of the bednyaks' condition, and the hatred which they were capable of feeling on occasion for their more fortunate neighbours, who exploited them pitilessly whenever they had the chance to do so.

The Centre, for its part, did everything in its power to turn dekulakization into a series of acts of pillage. Following on Stalin's speech to the Agrarian Marxists, who were no doubt dumbfounded at what they had heard, 'a million households suddenly found themselves reduced to the state of outcasts, deprived of all their rights and not knowing which way to turn'.

The above description is provided by Anna Louise Strong, an American journalist of pro-Soviet sympathies, who was in the USSR at the time.[25] Events now took a predictable turn, and for five weeks dekulakization and expulsion proceeded apace, in conditions of complete chaos, spreading fear and consternation and reducing the villages to a state of shock.

At this stage, however, there was still no legal basis for action against the kulaks. The first law authorizing expropriation of the kulaks was a decree issued by the *TsIK* and the *Sovnarkom* relative to the 'struggle against barbarous slaughter of livestock'.[26] This mass slaughtering of livestock had by now become a real menace, in a country in which food was rationed, and which was traditionally weak in livestock production. Under the new decree, therefore, the authorities were required to expropriate kulaks who were either guilty of this offence, or of inciting others to commit it, and to prosecute them, and punish them by loss of liberty, with or without deportation. The press now took up the battle cry: 'We are liquidating the kulaks as a class!' 'Not one kulak, priest or Nepman left by next spring!' and so on.[27] *Pravda* of January 18th 1930, called for a firm stand against 'doubts or vacillation of any kind' which, as it accurately foresaw, were to become more pronounced as the process of dekulakization continued. On January 26th, the paper carried a contemptuous reference apparently aimed at those who asked for instructions: 'There is no need for a statute of a hundred paragraphs,' it declared, and the activists were accordingly advised to make do with the general guidance they had been given. The main points were outlined by *Pravda*: they were to '. . . take over (the kulaks') means of production and transfer them to the kolkhozes'. The most troublesome elements among the kulaks 'should be deported'. People who waited for instructions would simply allow the kulaks to escape, for the latter would sell up and disappear 'into the blue'. Activists were enjoined to display 'a spirit of revolutionary initiative and steadfast resolution'. *Bolshevik*, the Party's theoretical organ, took up these slogans in more general terms: 'Class against class, in an overt, cruel and merciless struggle, a battle to the death of one of the two classes'. And again: 'The death-knell of the rural exploiters has sounded; the *bednota* has the right to demand that the property of these exploiters and oppressors should be used in the interests of the socialist reconstruction of agriculture'.[28]

Having been thus incited to open 'class warfare', the activists and the local authorities hurled themselves upon the kulaks from all sides, in a positive orgy of violence which was later referred to as 'excesses'. But an action whose guiding principle might be summed up in the phrase 'shoot first and ask questions afterwards' could not but turn into one long series of 'excesses'. When instructions for the conduct of the operation were provided, they did nothing to change its arbitrary nature, their effect merely being to ensure that it was carried out in a somewhat more systematic manner, and to make the executants feel that they were acting within a framework of 'legality'. The indiscriminate nature of the dekulakization operation, and the fact that it turned into a series of violent reprisals against whole sectors of the broad mass of the peasantry, were an inevitable consequence of the vagueness attaching to the term 'kulak'. (In following up our sources we have been obliged, for the purposes of our account, to make constant use of this term, but would remind the reader of the reservations expressed in this connection in the earlier chapter on class stratification, where the status of the 'kulak' is examined in greater detail). Furthermore, the deliberate policy of giving priority to the anti-kulak operation over the collectivization campaign meant that violent measures could be taken against anyone who opposed collectivization.

Obviously, before the government could issue instructions about the expropriation of the kulak, it had to be able to identify him. The definition in force during the winter of 1929–30 was the one provided in March 1929 by *Narkomfin*, for purposes of the individual levy to which the richest peasants were subject. In May, this definition was adopted by the *Sovnarkom*, and adjusted in such a way as to widen its scope.[29] *Sovnarkom* now suggested the following features by which a kulak farm might be identified:

1. A farm which regularly hires wage-labour for employment in agriculture or artisanal industry.
2. A farm possessing an 'industrial undertaking', viz. a mill, a butter-making establishment, a pearling and hulling mill, a wool-combing installation (*sherstobitka*) or plant for the pulping of sugar-beet (*terochnoe zavedenie*) or for dehydrating potatoes, vegetables or fruit—wherever these were powered by motor, or even by windmill or water-mill.
3. A farm which hires out, on a permanent basis, complex, power-driven agricultural machinery.
4. A farm which hires out, on a seasonal or permanent basis, premises intended for use as a dwelling-house, or by an enterprise.
5. A farm whose members are involved in commercial activities, or in usury, or who have other income not deriving from work. This category includes the priesthood.

Thus, a peasant who could be identified according to any one of these definitions could be classified as a kulak. The law did not specify what number of wage-labourers entitled an employer to be so classed; it would seem that one was sufficient. The expressions 'industrial undertaking' and 'artisanal industry' are obviously also capable of extension; the employment of one or two wage-earners would suffice to put the owner in the 'rural capitalist' class.

Several of the definitions were disquietingly vague, notably 'commercial activities', 'usury', and above all 'other income not deriving from work'. Even a fairly scrupulous investigator would have had difficulty in finding any peasant, let alone a slightly better-off peasant, whose activities were not classifiable under this particular heading, and who was not, therefore, liable to expropriation.

Given the context of this chaotic attack on an enemy whom it was well-nigh impossible to identify with any accuracy, given especially the effects of a frenetic propaganda campaign which constantly exaggerated the enemy's cunning, treachery and skill in concealing himself, it was possible for zealous and 'vigilant' executants to find kulaks wherever they chose to look.

Under the terms of this same law, republican, *krai* and *oblast* authorities were given the right to modify the above definitions to suit local conditions, a provision which increased the arbitrary nature of this whole system of classification to an even more dangerous degree.

It was no accident that the picture of the kulak provided by the Politburo was somewhat blurred round the edges; this is borne out by a retrospective description, not of the kulak, but of the *zazhitochny*, which Stalin gave in 1933, when this stratum had already ceased to exist. 'A peasant could only become prosperous (*zazhitochny*) at the expense of his neighbours, by hiring a few batraks and duly exploiting them until such times as, having improved his position, he was able to join the ranks of the kulaks.'[30]

The category of peasants described here would obviously come under one of the aforementioned headings by which kulak status was defined. The constant use by Stalin, and the press, of the term *zazhitochny* in conjunction with the term 'kulak' was not, therefore, fortuitous.

What this meant in practical terms can readily be imagined. Syrtsov, who was at this time head of the government of the RSFSR, has given the following description of the period immediately preceding dekulakization: 'In certain localities, the argument goes as follows: "Every self-respecting economic region ought to have what it is supposed to have, according to the rules. Consequently, if we have no kulaks, we shall have to acquire some by nomination." And so, in the absence of kulaks, the *zazhitochnye* are appointed as temporary acting kulaks.'[31]

It is interesting to examine some of the arguments put forward to justify dekulakization. The Politburo commission which agreed this solution in principle in December 1929, although the proposals it submitted were apparently rejected as being too soft, advanced three arguments in support of its conclusion that conditions were now ripe for 'practical consideration of the problem of liquidating the kulaks as a class'.[32]

FIRST ARGUMENT: The serednyak had now turned towards the kolkhozes, an obvious indication (in the commission's view) that the kulak was isolated, and that the broadest masses of the peasantry had rallied to the Party.

SECOND ARGUMENT: The material pre-conditions for liquidation now existed; the kolkhozes had already delivered 130 million poods of grain (the quantity the kulaks were estimated to have delivered in 1927) and would deliver 400 million poods in 1930.

THIRD ARGUMENT: Kulak resistance was in fact on the increase, as witness the figures which showed a recrudescence of terroristic acts. Resolute action was therefore essential.[33]

It should be noted that the commission's text, which was not intended for publication (in fact, it has still not been published) contains nothing relative to the international situation, or to the 'kulak plot to start a civil war', or to any of the other allegations of this nature which were made for propaganda purposes after the event, and which are still being repeated today in an increasingly awkward attempt to justify dekulakization.

As it happens, none of the above arguments stands up to criticism. The most important of the commission's arguments, which relates to the changed attitude of the serednyaks as a result of their supposed move in favour of the kolkhozes, is vigorously contested by modern Soviet writers, at least insofar as it relates to the winter of 1929–30. But if this argument is not supported by the facts, these same authors' attempts at justification are automatically invalidated by the same token.

The claim that the kulaks, at this period, were more isolated than ever, and that the broad mass of the peasantry had rallied to the Party, is equally worthless. The lack of foundation for this particular argument is amply shown by examination of the events of the following two months, when the country stood on the brink of a terrible civil war.

Even more astonishing is the argument that the amount of grain the kolkhozes and sovkhozes had delivered, and would deliver in the future, was such as to justify replacement of the kulaks' share in production by production from the socialized sector. The country was suffering from a chronic grain shortage, bread and food in general were rationed, the population were becoming increasingly impoverished. In these circumstances, the claim that this so-called 'abundance' of kolkhoz production was such as to justify liquidation of the country's best producers shows an extraordinary lack of any sense of reality, to say the very least.

As for the argument relating to the increase in kulak violence, this is no more soundly based than the others. Here again, the historical review which quotes the commission's report gives only a few incomplete data: thus, 290 acts of terrorism were committed in the Ukraine between the end of 1928 and the beginning of 1929. During September and October 1929, 183 such acts were committed in the Middle Volga *krai*. There were seventeen murders in one region of the same *krai* in the course of eighteen months. Finally, the most impressive figure of the lot reveals that 4,000 'kulak elements' were active in clandestine anti-Soviet organizations in the North Caucasus in 1929.[34]

Can it be that the commission based its appraisal of the 'kulak danger' on such meagre information as this? At present we have no means of knowing, but it can be assumed that the author of the article quoted, having had access to the minutes of the commission's proceedings, would have given fuller data, had such information been available to the commission itself.

Soviet sources, both contemporary and present-day, advance from time to time other, more realistic assessments of the role of dekulakization in the government's rural policy.

The fate reserved for the kulak was intended primarily to 'convince' the peasants that all roads, save those that led to the kolkhoz, were henceforth barred to them. As one writer observed in 1930, 'The rout of the kulaks simultaneously puts paid to the hopes of those among the serednyaks who aspired to better themselves by developing their private farms. . . . There is no question but that the liquidation of the kulaks helped the serednyaks in the kolkhozes to overcome their doubts. . . .'[35]

Another author, writing in 1963, puts forward an equally frank, if somewhat more subtle, explanation: 'The resolute offensive against the kulaks in 1928 and 1929 demonstrated to the middle Russian peasantry that there was, in practice, no future in the pursuit of capitalism.'[36]

Indeed from the very outset of the anti-kulak campaign, an attempt was made to subdue the serednyaks, and to coerce them into 'overcoming their doubts', by branding as 'kulak' any sign of opposition to collectivization, or to any other aspect of the government's rural policy. One present-day writer makes the following realistic appraisal:

'From the autumn of 1929 onward, the problem of the peasant's attitude to the kolkhozes became the focal point of the class struggle in the countryside. The alignment of class forces was based on the attitude adopted towards collectivization. Support for the kolkhozes meant support for the dictatorship of the proletariat . . . and a resolute struggle against the kulaks. Any kind of resistance to collectivization was equated with support for the kulaks and rejection of the alliance between the proletariat and the peasantry.'[37]

As applied to the realities of the situation in 1930, the above statement admits the use of terror, in that the question of joining the kolkhoz was put to the peasants in the form of an ultimatum: 'Whoever is not for the kolkhoz is a friend of the kulaks and an enemy of the régime.' In March 1930, this approach was criticized as a deviation from the 'general line'. . . . In fact, it was the very essence of the line which was being followed. Soon, therefore, the term 'kulak', which had always been imprecise, ceased to have any real meaning or social content, and instead was used for the purpose of denouncing real or alleged opposition, the kulak having become a kind of bogy whose presence served to explain or justify any failure or disorder. One author, writing in a publication of the Communist Academy, described various defects in the kolkhoz movement, in villages where not one kulak was left, as being due to 'kulak agitation'. He was constrained to observe that 'By "kulak", we mean the carrier of certain political tendencies which are most frequently discernible in the *podkulachnik*, male or female.'[38]

The concept of the *podkulachnik*, or 'henchman of the kulak', which is devoid of any sociological significance, proved to be a most formidable weapon in extending the horrors of the anti-kulak offensive, and was universally employed by the government in pursuit of its objectives.

One who witnessed the events of 1930, and who may possibly have taken part in them, has provided the following example of the part played by dekulakization in the collectivization of an important region in the Urals: '. . . rural organizations on the spot found, in dekulakization, a powerful lever for encouraging the peasants to join the kolkhozes, and for transforming certain kolkhozes into *kommuny*. The use of intimidation and other coercive methods was often accompanied by threats of dekulakization in the case of those who refused to be so "encouraged".'[39]

Dekulakization also played an economic role in the process of collectivization, a fact which had likewise been taken into consideration by the policy-makers of the Politburo.[40] Property confiscated from the kulaks was to be used to start up the kolkhozes, since the State had not the resources to make any appreciable contribution to an undertaking of this magnitude, and was relying much more on contributions from the peasants themselves. In practice, however, the burden of this contribution could only fall on the serednyaks, for the bednyaks arrived in the kolkhozes almost empty-handed. The property of the kulaks was to serve as the bednyaks' 'entrance fee' and their contribution to the kolkhoz indivisible fund. In addition, part of the kulaks' goods (their food supplies, clothing, etc.) was to be used for immediate relief among the bednyaks, so that their entry into the kolkhozes should be marked straightaway by an improvement in their circumstances. In this way, it was hoped that the bednyaks' enthusiasm at their improved prospects could be turned to account by further strengthening the régime's hand and affording it an additional lever for recruiting peasants who had so far refused to join the kolkhozes, or were showing reluctance to do so.

This, then, was the purpose of dekulakization, which began, according to Khataevich, 'in several localities', in the form of 'a spontaneous, freelance operation, in which bednyak and batrak elements participated actively without waiting for authorization from the *raion* or *okrug* officials'.[41]

It was not until the beginning of February that the long-awaited instructions arrived from the Centre. On January 30th, the Politburo issued a sort of formal injunction to the local authorities,[42] and on February 1st a decree of *TsIK* and *Sovnarkom* was promulgated; this was published in the press on February 2nd. This tersely worded document abolished the right to rent farmland and to hire wage-labour in the regions of mass collectivization, while simultaneously empowering the republican, *krai* and *oblast* authorities 'to adopt, in these regions, all such measures as are required in order to combat the kulaks, including confiscation of their entire property and deportation outside the boundaries of the *raion* or *krai*'. When the kulak's debts to the State had been deducted, the property confiscated was to be added to the indivisible funds of the kolkhozes 'as entrance fee for the batraks and bednyaks joining the kolkhozes'. Republican governments were ordered to issue detailed instructions concerning the implementation of this decree to their subordinates.[43]

On the same day, the government took a decision prohibiting kulaks from changing their place of residence or selling their property without authorization; this decision was not published in the press, but local authorities were probably instructed accordingly. A kulak who attempted 'auto-dekulakization' in this way, or tried to take refuge in the towns, was liable to have his property confiscated, and to be prosecuted, and this in itself amounted to dekulakization in practice.[44]

The obvious consequence of a decree of this nature was to extend the scope of the anti-kulak measures so that they were given nation-wide application, despite the official theory about confining dekulakization to the regions of mass collectivization. In effect, the decree authorized universal dekulakization, for it was to be expected that a great many of the better-off peasants would do their utmost to forestall its consequences, and would not wait for confiscation and deportation to take place.

Once this rather terse decree had been published, the *TsIK* and *Sovnarkom* followed it up with a more detailed directive concerning the initial stages of the anti-kulak operation. The directive in question was kept secret, and was never published.[45] It divided the kulaks into three categories, the first of which comprised the richest peasants, and those who were considered to be most actively and directly involved in counter-revolutionary activities. Their property was to be confiscated and they were to be prosecuted, following on which they were to be sentenced either to imprisonment or to internment in a concentration camp. Their families were to be deported to the outlying Northern or Eastern regions, mostly to Siberia. There may possibly have been some provision in the text for sentencing certain of the kulaks in this category to death.[46]

After this *verkhushka* (upper stratum) came the second category, consisting of 'economically strong' kulaks, who had been guilty of 'pitiless exploitation of their neighbours'. Their property was to be confiscated, and they were to be deported to the North. For the RSFSR as a whole, this category numbered over twice as many persons as the preceding one, and according to a recent source, the kulaks in this category were not accused of any direct 'anti-Soviet activities'.[47] It is not clear what instructions were given with regard to the families of the kulaks in this second category. According to one source, the Politburo authorized them to remain in the locality if they wished, and if the *ispolkomy* were prepared to allow them to do so.[48] In fact, in most cases the entire family was deported.

The kulaks in the third category were subject only to partial dekulakization, and could either be left in the locality or moved, but only within the confines of the *oblast*. They were allocated plots of 'poor land', and allowed to keep a small part of their belongings with which to carry on, so that they might set up a new farm on the land allotted to them. The instructions did not specify how these people were to be housed once their own homes had been confiscated. Some writers claim that there were practically no facilities on the lands allocated, and that the dispossessed families were obliged to build huts.

The Politburo also ordered that 15,000 horses be set aside for the deportees, and that they be granted loans and given a few tools to enable them to set themselves up in their place of exile.[49] An effort was also made to provide them with food and warm clothing. These measures, which in the event proved to be relatively ineffective, were prompted by the fact that, in the chaos of deportation prior to the issuing of instructions, totally destitute peasant families had been packed into wagons and sent to Siberia, without any provision having been made for their survival en route.[50]

The government also made another concession, by ruling that families who had a son in the army should not be expropriated. Provision was also made for more lenient treatment in the case of families which included a teacher or an industrial worker.

The Smolensk Archives, on which Merle Fainsod has drawn for his book, provide a specific example of the way in which dekulakization was organized in the Velikie Luki *okrug* in the Western *oblast*.[51] In this *okrug*, the Party committee took the decision to proceed with expropriation and dekulakization on January 21st, that is, before the *TsIK* had issued its instructions. Two *GPU* officers had drawn up a plan of campaign. The *GPU* apparatus was reinforced, and eleven men were called up from the reserve. The local militia was exempted from all other tasks, so that it might concentrate exclusively on the matter in hand. All those who were to take part in the operation were issued with arms. It was decided to postpone the intended closure of churches and the removal of church bells, in order to avoid antagonizing the peasants during the 'delicate' operation of dekulakization. In the *okrug* and in each of its *raiony* 'committees of three'—the traditional 'special purpose' *troiki*—were set up and placed in general charge of the operation. These *troiki* consisted of the most important officials in the *raion*, the *raikom* secretary, the secretary of the *raiispolkom* and the chief of the local *GPU*. The *okrug* put a force of twenty-six men at the disposal of the *raiony*.

On February 12th, by which time the instructions from the centre would have been received, a secret letter to the *troiki* ordered them to draw up, in collaboration with the *selsovety*, and with the help of the trade unions, lists of kulaks, and to divide these into three categories, according to how dangerous they were supposed to be. The first category was to be arrested by the *GPU*, the second deported, and the kulaks in the third were to remain in the *okrug*, where plots were to be allocated to them on land which was suffering from soil-erosion, or which required improvement (e.g. marsh-land or forest-land).

The property of the 'dangerous' kulaks was to be handed over directly and forthwith to already existing kolkhozes, or to those which were in process of being set up; in the absence of either, the property was to be delivered to the nearest available kolkhoz. The property of kulaks in the second category was to be confiscated progressively, as the deportations continued. Families remaining in the locality pending deportation were to be allowed to keep one cow, and a minimum of provisions. Deportees were to receive 500 roubles per family to enable them to set themselves up in Siberia. The remainder of their property was to be confiscated.

The *okrug* supplied figures for the proportions of kulaks in the various categories. We learn from the report made on January 28th to the *oblast* secretary that, in the *okrug*, a total of 3,551 households were classified as kulak. The first category comprised 947 households, the second 1,307; the third category, comprising those kulaks who were to be allowed to remain, included only 1,297 households.[52]

This is a far cry from the mere 'fifth' of deportees (a 'seventh' in the RSFSR) which had figured in the proposals put forward by the Politburo's December commission. In December, this same commission had also discussed the question of allowing 'dekulakized' kulaks who had not been deported to enter the kolkhozes, on a trial basis at first, and subsequently as full members. In the *okrug* which concerns us at present, the kulaks in this minority category remained *in situ*, and were permitted to keep some of their property, but were relegated from the very outset to the bottom of the social scale, and deprived of civil rights. The letter of February 12th to the *troiki* stipulated that persons in this category must undertake hard labour in the forests, and on road-building, and that, upon the slightest failure to meet compulsory procurements from their new farms, their property was to be confiscated, and they were to be prosecuted.

The letter also criticized and forbade the further use of practices which up till then had been countenanced by the Party emissaries (the *upolnomochennye* sent to supervise the work of dekulakization). The practices in question related to the expropriation of bednyaks and serednyaks by subjecting them to what the letter referred to as 'ideological dekulakization'—a significant description of a phenomenon which was to become even more widespread—and amounted in effect to the persecution of anyone who refused to obey instructions from the aforementioned emissaries.[53] The *troiki* were also reminded that dekulakization of the families of serving soldiers, which had been taking place regularly, was in fact prohibited.

The letter further noted that in several localities expropriation and deportation had been carried out 'without even the vestige of a plan', and stated that no action was to be taken in this matter without authorization from the *troika* in the okrug. Detailed preparations must be made; a dossier should be compiled for every kulak household, and an exact inventory made in respect of all property confiscated; there should also be a campaign for explaining dekulakization to the bednyaks, and emphasis should be laid on the official nature of the operation. All of these requirements were clearly laid down in the letter from the *okrug* centre.

However, the instructions emanating both from the local centre, and from Moscow, and the warnings against inadequate organization in the implementation of the dekulakization policy, were not translated into action. Few people believed that these recommendations could in fact be implemented. Indeed, the events of this period were marked by a wave of disorder, violence, looting, brutality and debauchery which swept the whole country, and reached even more alarming proportions after these instructions had been issued.

The dekulakization operation spilled over into regions where collectivization had only just got under way. While it is true that, a few weeks later, almost every region in the country was declaring itself to be a region of mass collectivization, this had no bearing on the actual degree of preparedness for dekulakization which these regions might be alleged to have reached. The combined effect of accelerated collectivization on the one hand and premature dekulakization on the other was to provoke, during the winter of 1930, an outburst of mass violence the like of which had not been experienced since the horrors of the Civil War.

One official report states: 'In several places, dekulakization was carried out without any regard to collectivization. Many officials neglected the work of collectivization and the task of consolidating the kolkhozes, and set about liquidating the kulaks "in a conspiratorial manner", without the co-operation of the masses. Naturally, the result was a number of "scandalous cases", such as the "dekulakization" of former Red partisans who had been the original organizers and champions of the Soviet régime in the locality, and similar treatment of people who were widely known to be bednyaks or batraks.'[54]

As in the case of the Velikie Luki *okrug*, which we have been discussing (and which was likewise not one of the regions of *sploshnaya*), the administrative organs which had been set up all over the country took as their watchword the slogan 'Dekulakize first, and collectivize later!'[55] According to Milyutin, it was in these so-called 'unripe' regions that most of the excesses occurred. On the other hand, the claim that dekulakization took place 'normally' in regions that were 'ripe' for mass collectivization, and 'abnormally' in those regions that were 'less ripe', is not supported by the facts. The 'scandalous cases' mentioned above occurred in the Middle Volga region, a typical *sploshnaya* region administered by Khataevich.

The operation itself was carried out by specially constituted detachments, usually led by a representative of the *raion* or *okrug troika*, and assisted by several bednyak members of the local Party or *Komsomol* organization, some of whom were armed. The detachments also included members of the militia or the *GPU*, particularly when 'kulaks of the first category' were being dealt with. It would seem that in some cases units of the armed forces were also involved.[56] By the month of February, when tension in the countryside had reached its height, the army no doubt played a particularly important part.

Reinforcements sent by the trade unions also played a major role. These included the famous 25,000 workers who had been mobilized from the towns to carry out the work of collectivization in the countryside, and some tens of thousands of brigade members sent by the towns to the rural areas for a limited period, but who were probably all armed. One anonymous witness claims that the 25,000 were given special training by the *GPU*, which is very likely.[57]

As for the role of the rural population in general, this amounted to the active participation of some of the bednyaks and the less active participation of *selsovet* members, who were themselves often bednyaks or Party members. The charge that the rural assemblies insisted upon dekulakization, and that they drew up and ratified lists of victims, is refuted by evidence from many Soviet sources.

In an attempt to demonstrate the 'democratic nature' of dekulakization, and to prove that it was truly an expression of the will of the people, one author has described a typical instance of 'mass initiative' in a village in the North Caucasus: 'Having heard Comrade Merkulov's report, and an accompanying report by Comrade Pimlenko on the liquidation of the kulaks as a class, the general assembly of the *bednota* [consisting] of thirty to forty [persons] note that the rapid growth of the kolkhoz movement, and the implementation of mass collectivization, present them with the urgent problem of isolating the kulaks, in order to put a stop to the acts of sabotage which they have already committed against the bednyaks; they have concluded that the line being followed by the Party and the government is correct, and have accordingly decided that the kulaks should be liquidated forthwith, and deported from the North Caucasus *krai*.'[58]

We do not know exactly which village was involved. What is clear, however, is that several dozen bednyaks 'decided' upon dekulakization, whereas in reality, as we know, this decision had already been taken, and the operation planned in detail, elsewhere; the wishes of the bednyaks in question had very little to do with the matter. The instructions from the Velikie Luki *okrug*, which we mentioned earlier on, clearly authorized assemblies of batraks and bednyaks to add, if they wished, to the lists of persons to be expropriated.[59] The Party secretary of the Middle Volga, writing in *Pravda* about the progress of collectivization and dekulakization in his *krai*, also states that the decisions on dekulakization were taken by assemblies of bednyaks, batraks and kolkhoz members; it is clear therefore that it was not the village assemblies which were involved.[60] The broad mass of the so-called serednyaks were not even called on to give their assent, even though, as we have seen in the case of the bednyaks, this would have been a mere formality.

The detachments or brigades which had been formed to carry out the task often reported to their superiors in a style which was wholly appropriate to an administrative and quasi-military operation: 'During the night of such and such a date, the kulaks as a class were liquidated; this will be done in the other *raiony* as soon as possible.' This example was given by the head of the government of the Russian Republic; speaking before a restricted audience of Party intellectuals, he both deplored and condemned this type of report.[61] He also quoted a 'battle-report' from another *raion*, which was couched in similar language: 'During the period from 5 p.m. to 7 a.m., the kulaks as a class were liquidated.'

With time pressing, and feelings running high, there were thousands of cases in which, owing to the ignorance of the 'men on the spot', the decision to classify an individual as a kulak was taken on the most absurd grounds, though the problem was one which might well have baffled a sociologist. Frequently, the presence of a servant in the house, the employment of a paid worker for a few days (or even some similar arrangement made one or two years previously), the fact that a family owned a rudimentary 'four-wheeler' or some other 'status symbol', were taken as 'signs' that they belonged in the kulak category. Later, when the 'excesses' had been stopped, the Soviet press was full of such details. Rumyantsev mentions cases where the decision to add a name to the lists of kulaks had been taken on mere hearsay.[62] One writer, describing events in an important region in the Urals, where the then famous *Gigant* kolkhoz was situated, affirms that what took place was not 'the liquidation of the kulaks as a class, and the transfer of their property to the kolkhoz' but 'the confiscation of the property of certain individuals (down to the removal of bottles containing a few drops of iodoform) and the sale of this property to kolkhozes, institutions, and private persons who, in most cases, were bednyaks and officials'.

The same author reports instances in which dekulakization simply provided an excuse for settling old scores, and others where it was sufficient for a man to be considered by the authorities as a 'harmful element' to have his name added to the fatal lists. In such cases, the attitude behind the entire operation would seem to have been 'Enough! You've had a good coat on your back. Now it's our turn to wear it! ' [63] Since the expropriated kulak was all too often regarded simply as 'this harmful element who must at all costs be rendered harmless', and since, in the words of the local official quoted above, he was also 'a source of boots, shirts, warm coats, etc.', dekulakization turned into a positive 'goldrush' after confiscated property, which went on throughout the entire country, with everyone making the most of whatever opportunity arose. This large-scale 'share-out' (*delezhka*) aroused the indignation of the peasants, and was viewed with both embarrassment and anxiety in Party circles.

Pravda angrily protested at the way in which dekulakization was turning into 'nothing but a division of spoils', and Stalin himself expressed disapproval, albeit rather discreetly,[64] while Syrtsov, alarmed and possibly ashamed at this development, quoted 'one significant example, which is unfortunately far from being an isolated instance' of the extraordinary way in which kulak property was sometimes 'auctioned'. In a *stanitsa* in the North Caucasus, the house of one kulak went for 60 kopecks, a cow and a calf for 15 kopecks, geese for a kopeck apiece, the 'buyers being, without exception, members of the *selsovet*'.[65]

What Syrtsov indignantly described as 'the most shameful travesty of Soviet power' had in fact become common practice. At times, the men on the spot seem to have behaved like a gang of ordinary ruffians.[66] According to a report by the Smolensk *GPU*, the victims were stripped of their shoes and warm clothing. Another source states that they were left 'in their underclothes, for everything was confiscated, including old rubber boots (Kazanka village), women's drawers (same village), 50 kopeck's worth of tea (Kremmevka village), pokers, wash-tubs, etc. . . . Kulak families with small children (who were sometimes young 'Pioneers') were left without any means of feeding themselves'.

The loot, according to the same source, went to the bednyaks, usually those who had in fact carried out the confiscations.[67] The *GPU* report quoted above states that the 'brigands', in the process of despoiling the kulaks, ate, drank, and held drunken orgies, and that their motto was 'Eat up, drink up, it's all ours! '

Drunken soldiers and *Komsomol* members roamed the villages, 'arbitrarily closing churches, destroying icons, threatening the peasants' and brutally ill-treating them.[68] A report from the Smolensk *GPU*, dated February 23rd, states that poor peasants and serednyaks were being arrested by anyone at all who had duties connected with collectivization. People were being thrown into prison by the militia with not the slightest proof of guilt.[69]

Throughout the country, it was the peasantry as a whole which bore the brunt of this onslaught. In the earlier stages of the anti-kulak offensive, the non-militant bednyaks, and the serednyaks had lived under permanent threat of suffering the fate officially reserved for the 'last class of exploiters'. But by the time that the kulaks 'as a class' were finally being liquidated, the entire peasantry felt that it was under attack, and that none could escape the hammer-blows of the anti-kulak campaign.

Peasant reactions to the brutal facts of dekulakization were reported by GPU informers. 'If all this is sanctioned from above, then we are doomed; there is no one left for us to complain to.' On witnessing the expropriation and deportation of former bednyaks who had managed to buy a horse or a cow during the NEP period, the peasants came to the despairing conclusion that 'the same fate awaits us all. It would be better if war broke out, otherwise we'll never be able to set up a home. . .'.[70]

It was well known that this was the attitude among the peasants. An author writing at this time in Na Agrarnom Fronte, a scientific monthly published by the Communist Academy, observed that the abuses which were going on were discrediting the whole idea of mass collectivization. 'The peasant is beginning to associate this idea [sploshnaya kollektivizatsiya] with the possibility that he too might find himself in the position of being dekulakized some day, thereby ending up in the same camp as the enemies of the Soviet régime.' [71]

The very thought of this was enough to make the peasant tremble. He had seen enough, often from his own personal experience, to know how disastrous the consequences could be.

There is abundant evidence on this point. Of the 1,200 households dekulakized in the raion of the Gigant kolkhoz, 400 had belonged to serednyaks, who were subsequently reinstated, and had their property restored to them, during the period of rehabilitation.[72] In the villages of Plovitsy in the Ukraine, 66 out of 78 households listed were serednyak.[73] According to a writer in Bolshevik, one selsovet in the Baturinski raion of Smolensk listed 34 households for dekulakization, of which 3 were kulak. The same source quotes specific examples, as illustrative of what had become widespread practice: the Gertsenski selsovet of the Sverdlovsk oblast, which was particularly hostile in its attitude to the serednyaks, decided to dekulakize according to the following criteria: sale of grain surpluses in the market; purchase of a plot of land (attached to the house), sale of a cow within the last two years; sale of soles for boots; sale of hay to the co-operative in . . . 1927, etc. Shepherds were expropriated, one for having brought up an orphan nephew, another because his grandfather had been a kulak, and so on. . . .[74]

The same article in *Bolshevik* recounts the following anecdote: while one peasant was being expropriated another, wishing to defend him, argued that if his friend were to be dekulakized, he himself would have to be dekulakized too, since his farm was exactly the same size. The bednyak members of the *selsovet* asked him to draw up a declaration to this effect, which they thereupon endorsed with the following resolution: 'Dekulakization to be carried out at the request of the applicant.' [75]

The archives of the Ukraine record yet another incident, which must have been typical of many such. While one serednyak, as a member of an expropriation commission, was taking part in the seizure of kulak property at one end of the village, a second commission at the other end was busy taking over his own property.[76]

According to the authors of a recent study, expropriation and dekulakization of serednyaks took place in many *okrugi*, both in the Ukraine and elsewhere.[77] *Istoriya KPSS* states that in certain regions of the USSR up to 15% of households, many of them bednyak, were dekulakized.[78]

Seizure of property, imprisonment and deportation were mainly carried out under the ample coverage provided by certain stringent articles of the penal code, notably article 61 which dealt with failure to meet procurements, article 79, directed at persons who slaughtered livestock unlawfully, and the redoubtable article 58 relating to cases of counter-revolutionary agitation. In June 1930 Krylenko, the Republican *Prokuror*, told the Sixteenth Party Congress that 'the blow inflicted on the seredynaks' had been the result of erroneous interpretation of these articles. In connection with the drive against the slaughter of livestock, serednyaks were punished without even being given the benefit of the cautionary *pyatikratka*—a fine five times the value of the damage done; a peasant could be prosecuted in February for having sold a calf the previous autumn, and people were harried under article 58 'sometimes for mere loose talk'. Local *prokurory* who occasionally tried to protest against illegal proceedings of this kind were accused of 'right-wing deviationism' and removed from office.[79] According to the Republican *Prokuror*, such practices were illegal because the articles in question were intended to apply only to kulak households. The texts 'presupposed the existence of a kulak household, before the rigorous counter-measures authorized by the law could be invoked'.[80] It was intended that the seredynak and the bednyak should be treated much more leniently.

Krylenko says nothing about the vagueness of the term 'kulak'. Although it was supposed to have a precise meaning, it was in fact so elastic that any provision in the penal code which was based on this concept was bound to lead to excesses. This was all the more true in the context of an administrative operation directed against a sector of the population which was regarded as hostile to the régime. Dekulakization was aimed at a category of people; there was no provision for enquiry into individual cases, or for detailed checking of the lists of condemned people. Any bednyak was at liberty, and was indeed in duty bound, to 'discover' additional cases where kulak status had not hitherto been suspected.[81] The arbitrary nature of these procedures, and of the whole system of classification, particularly the categories employed for the purposes of dekulakization, is self-evident. As a result, the 'legality' of the entire operation was compromised in advance, even in cases where the policy was implemented in a relatively orderly manner, as it may well have been on fairly frequent occasions. Many of the *prokurory* certainly tried to ensure that dekulakization was carried out within a framework of legality, by attempting to put a stop to flagrant abuses and all kinds of nonsense. But even in this task, which was bound to prove a thankless one, the organs of the judiciary, and notably those of the *prokuratura*, whose duty it was to see that the rules were observed in what was essentially an arbitrary operation, were themselves overruled by the organs responsible for implementing the Party's orders.

Krylenko notes this fact with some bitterness, observing that the judiciary, of which he was the head, functioned 'at times as an adjunct to the administrative apparatus'. Further on in his remarks, he drops the qualifying words 'at times'.[82] But what he complains of is a characteristic more or less common to all dictatorships, and one which was more marked in the case of Stalin's régime. In such a context, legality is purely mythical.

Dekulakization—a term which embraced both expropriation and, sooner or later, the inevitable deportations—was a drama of epic proportions, composed of a series of events each of which in turn was more tragic than the last. Syrtsov alludes somewhat euphemistically to a 'series of dramatic episodes'.[83] But a *GPU* report from the Smolensk archives speaks of a wave of suicides among the better-off peasants.[84] Another source mentions mass suicides of whole families.[85] Peasants under threat of dekulakization strove desperately to ward off the attack. Some abandoned their property and went into hiding; others used divorce as a means of saving at least some part of their belongings from confiscation. When heads of households were imprisoned, their dependents dispersed throughout the countryside and into the towns, forming a veritable army of beggars and vagabond children (*besprizornye*).

The deportations were the most harrowing feature of the operation, for the railways were not equipped to deal with a mass exodus on this scale. Once the confiscations had been carried out, the local authorities were anxious to get rid of the dispossessed peasants as quickly as possible; the latter were by now desperate or vengeful, and either way they could only prove an embarrassment, particularly to those who had profited personally from the expropriations, or who had 'dekulakized' recklessly or indiscriminately. The railways, however, had not enough wagons. Pressure on the authorities to deport as many persons as possible was creating 'a burden too great for the State's resources', as Syrtsov announced, in an attempt to curb the zeal of the enthusiasts.[86]

The Politburo was obliged to intervene, by allocating transport facilities to each region on a quota basis[87] which in turn led to the restriction and staggering of departures. Whereas expropriation of a proportion of the kulak population had taken only a few weeks, the task of deporting them probably dragged on until the autumn. Many of the people in the villages were deeply shocked at the sight of the 'candidates', stripped of their belongings and kept under guard while waiting to be deported. The mere sight of the trainloads of deportees, frequently referred to as 'death trains', produced a shattering effect. Anna Louise Strong writes: 'Several times, during the spring and summer, standing by the railway lines, I have seen these trains on the move: a painful sight, men, women and children uprooted.'[88]

This was a time of scarcity. The workers in the sovkhozes and on the main construction sites were themselves short of food and supplies, and it was hardly to be expected that any would be forthcoming to alleviate the distress of the deportees. Crammed into goods wagons, the peasants died of cold, hunger and disease. An eyewitness has given the following description of these trains, and of certain other aspects of dekulakization:

'Trainloads of deported peasants left for the icy North, the forests, the steppes, the deserts. These were whole populations, denuded of everything; the old folk starved to death in mid-journey, new born babies were buried on the banks of the roadside, and each wilderness had its crop of little crosses of boughs or white wood. Other populations dragging all their mean possessions on wagons, rushed towards the frontiers of Poland, Rumania and China, and crossed them—by no means intact, to be sure—in spite of the machine-guns.'[89]

It is impossible at present to say how many households were expropriated, how many families or persons were deported, or how many perished during this exodus. As for the cost of dekulakization, and collectivization as a whole, in terms of human lives, a detailed study of this problem can only be made after an examination of events up to the middle of 1933. In the present context, we shall there-fore confine ourselves to a brief preliminary analysis.

The first wave of the anti-kulak measures began in the winter of 1929–30, and continued until the autumn of 1930. The second wave began at the beginning of 1931, and the third at the end of 1932. The whole operation was spread over three years, and affected a large number of peasants in each of its phases; only at the end of this period were the kulaks finally 'liquidated as a class'.

The number of expropriations must certainly have exceeded the figure of 1·3–1·5 million households, or 6–7 million souls, which Molotov gave as the size of the kulak population when addressing the session of the Executive of the Communist International.[90] Up till now, the official figure quoted has been 240,757 families, or approximately 1,200,000 persons, but this figure cannot be taken as definitive, since it has been made clear that it relates only to the regions of *sploshnaya kollektivizatsiya*, and to the period from 1930 to the end of 1932.[91] However, an examination of the most recent Soviet sources enables us to revise this estimate quite considerably. Abramov, author of an important article on collectivization in the RSFSR, which appeared in a collection published in 1963, discusses the way in which the kulaks were classified under three categories, and says of the third that 'the kulaks in this category were initially reinstated within the boundaries of their *oblast* or *krai*, on land out-with the kolkhozes. It had been decided that if they did not offer any resistance to the kolkhozes, they might be admitted at the end of a period of three to five years. But since this category likewise opposed the kolkhozes, it became necessary to move them too, to more distant regions'.[92]

According to Abramov, four-fifths of all kulaks belonged to this category. There were 164,000 households, including kulaks who were imprisoned or deported, in the first two categories. The total number of deportees in the RSFSR alone would therefore seem to have been in the region of 820,000 families, or some 4 million souls.

The latest available figures for the Ukraine suggest that 200,000 households were expropriated in 1930, almost half of whom, accord-ing to another source, were deported.[93] However, in the Ukraine, as in other regions of the USSR, the operation of dekulakization took place in several phases, and during these successive waves of deku-lakization, fresh numbers of expropriated peasants were added to the above total, while the remainder of the 200,000 households had prob-ably also been deported, as had occurred in the RSFSR. Thus, the number of deportees more or less admitted so far by Soviet sources already exceeds one million households, or 5 million souls. To this figure must be added kulaks from other republics, representing tens of thousands of households, including 40,000 in Uzbekistan.[94] Even so, this is by no means the sum total. The events of 1930–33 were no less grave than those of the winter and spring of 1929–30. 'Ideological dekulakization' and persecution of the *podkulachnik* added huge numbers of peasants to the ranks of the deportees. In the absence of adequate data, it is impossible to arrive at an exact figure; what is certain is that several million households, to a total of 10 million persons, or more, must have been deported, of whom a great many must have perished.

In the final analysis dekulakization was not, as the official historians made out, a revolutionary process arising out of the class struggle in the countryside, whose object was the hated kulak, and whose instruments were the mass of the bednyaks and the serednyaks. Modern Soviet authors, while still formally subscribing to this theory, have in practice rejected it, though as yet the admission is implicit rather than explicit. For some years now, most writers have stressed that Stalin was grossly mistaken in his estimate of the extent to which the peasants were ready for collectivization by the end of 1929; this view is particularly in evidence in a recently published collection of studies on the history of collectivization in the Russian republics. Even if one subscribed to what has now become official dogma, and accepted the proposition that, once the peasants had reached this state of preparedness, dekulakization was bound to ensue as part of a natural and justifiable process, it still could not be said that the Soviet authorities were right in undertaking dekulakization in 1930. By admitting that the broad mass of the peasantry were not ready for collectivization, present-day Soviet writers are now calling in question the entire basis of justification for the terrible events that the Soviet peasantry were forced to experience from 1930 onwards.

Dekulakization was not a mass movement initiated by the peasant population. The masses were never consulted at any stage of the operation, either when the decision was taken, when the policy was elaborated, or when the time came to put it into effect. Many sources confirm that the majority of the peasants not only disapproved of the measures which were adopted, but also opposed them on frequent occasions.[95] Popular disapproval, according to these same sources, manifested itself in a variety of ways, ranging from pity and compassion for the victims to active resistance. In the Smolensk archives, there is mention of the assistance frequently rendered to the persecuted kulaks by *selsovet* chairmen, Party members and numerous peasants; and also of petitions on behalf of the kulaks signed by bednyaks and batraks. Soviet writers of the period report instances both of passive and active resistance by the peasants to the policy of dekulakization, and record many cases in which peasants listed as kulaks were either warned, or hidden, or helped in other ways. One author, writing in 1930, revealed the significant fact that, in the regions not officially recognized as regions of *sploshnaya kollektivizatsiya* (i.e. the majority of regions in 1930) the authorities were experiencing difficulty in recruiting activists to carry out the work of dekulakization.[96]

Such reactions were only natural. Primarily, the broad mass of the peasantry were victims of the policy of dekulakization, and it was in this light that they saw themselves. The allegedly 'revolutionary process carried out by the masses' was in fact a purely administrative operation, conceived and executed on a vast scale by the leadership, and appallingly mismanaged at that. Dekulakization was a major strategic manoeuvre in the leadership's campaign to collectivize the peasants.

NOTES AND REFERENCES

1. The expression used by Molotov: *reshayushchi sdvig.*
2. Speech of November 1929, *Bolshevik*, 1929, No. 22, p. 13.
3. *ibid.*
4. Trotsky, *The Revolution Betrayed.*
5. Trifonov, *op. cit.* (see Ch. 2, Note 9), p. 209; on cutting back in production by the kulaks, and their liquidation of their own homesteads from 1928 onwards see Danilov (ed.), *op. cit.* (see Ch. 13, Note 73), p. 90. Other sources have been mentioned earlier.
6. Fainsod, *op. cit.* (see Ch. 14, Note 7), p. 179.
7. We should remind the reader of the despairing cry uttered by Vareikis at the Sixteenth Party Conference in a speech already quoted: 'but you know perfectly well what the rural cells are worth!'
8. There are many accounts of such reactions on the part of the kulaks. See Trifonov, *op. cit.*, pp. 231–2; Karavaev, *NAF*, 1929, No. 10, p. 74; Katsenelenbogen, *Bolshevik*, 1929, No. 19, pp. 58–60; Azizyan, *Bolshevik*, 1929, pp. 51–9; Syrtsov, *Bolshevik*, 1930, No. 5, p. 53.
9. Karavaev, *op. cit.* (the other sources mentioned in Note 8), and *Bolshevik*, 1929, No. 22, p. 63.
10. The *Sovnarkom* decree of December 28, 1928, against 'pseudo-cooperation', reissued with certain amendments in November 1930. *Kollektivizatsiya selskogo khozyaistya*, doc. No. 22, p. 107.
11. Semernin, *Voprosy Istorii KPSS*, 1958, No. 4, p. 77.
12. It should be remembered that this was also the opinion of Andreev.
13. Kulkushkin, *op. cit.* (see Ch. 1, Note 28), p. 66. In his lengthy speech on December 27, 1929, in which he announced the

policy of liquidating the kulaks, Stalin did not advance any such 'international' arguments.

14. Data of the *VTsIK* RSFSR in Kukushkin, *op. cit.*, p. 65.

15. Danilov (ed.) *op. cit.*, p. 38.

16. *ibid*, p. 173.

17. Trifonov, *op. cit.*, p. 205.

18. Karavaev, *NAF*, 1929, No. 10, p. 71.

19. Aver'ev, in *NAF*, 1930, No. 6, reports this 'erroneous' dekulakization during the procurements campaign, a practice totally unrelated to the process of collectivization, and which occurred particularly in Siberia, in the Central Black Earth region, and elsewhere.

20. Strong, *op. cit.* (see Ch. 13, Note 67), pp. 81–2.

21. Khataevich, *Pravda*, February 16, 1930.

22. Abramov, in Danilov (ed.), *op. cit.*, p. 108.

23. Stalin had referred only to the regions of *sploshnaya*. See *Sochineniya*, Vol. XII, p. 182. He had said the same thing on December 27, 1929.

24. Abramov, in Danilov (ed.), *op. cit.*, p. 108.

25. Strong, *op. cit.*, p. 81.

26. *Pravda*, January 17, 1930. Under this law, non-kulak peasants who had slaughtered their livestock before entering the kolkhozes were to be expelled or refused admittance.

27. Various issues of *Pravda*, January 1930.

28. Editorial of *Bolshevik*, 1929, No. 2, p. 5.

29. The definition employed by *Narkomfin* is contained in *Sobranie Zakonov*, Part One, 1929, No. 12, Par. 103; for the decision of *Sovnarkom* 'O priznakakh kulatskikh khozyaestv v kotorykh dolzhen primenyatsa zakon o trude', see *Kollektivizatsiya selskogo khozyaistva*, doc. No. 38.

30. Stalin, *Sochineniya*, Vol. XIII, p. 248.

31. Tal, *NAF*, 1930, No. 11–12, p. XII.

32. Quoted in *Voprosy Istorii KPSS*, 1958, No. 4, p. 80.

33. *ibid*.

34. *ibid*. Andreev, secretary of the North Caucasus, was in possession of the facts on terrorism and on the illegal organizations operating in his region, but, as we know, he did not recommend mass deportations.

35. Kurbatov, *Planovoe Khozyaistvo*, 1930, No. 2, p. 69.

36. Abramov, in Danilov (ed..) *op. cit.*, p. 90.

37. Trifonov, *op. cit.*, pp. 227–8.

38. Article by Leikin in Ulashevich (ed.), *op. cit.* (see Ch. I, Note 8), p. 28.

39. *NAF*, 1930, No. 7–8, p. 94. The region in question is that of the giant kolkhoz *Gigant*.

40. Kurbatov, *Planovoe Khozyaistvo*, 1930, No. 2, pp. 68–9.

41. Khataevich, *Pravda*, February 16, 1930.

42. On this decision of the Politburo and on the directive of February 4th see *Voprosy Istorii KPSS*, 1962, No. 4, p. 68–9.

43. For the text of this decree see *Pravda*, February 2, 1930, and *Kollektivizatsiya selskogo khozyaistva*, doc. No. 78.

44. Trifonov. *op. cit.*, p. 238. On April 26th this decree was given a juridical basis by the Supreme Court. See *Code Pénal* (Paris, 1935), p. 201.

45. This directive was never published and is reconstructed here from: Danilov (ed.), *op. cit.*, pp. 104–5; Trifonov, *op. cit.*, p. 237, Kukushkin, *op. cit.*, pp. 67–8; *Voprosy Istorii KPSS*, 1958, No. 4, p. 81.

46. Letter from Russia dated February 1st in *Sotsialisticheski Vestnik*, 1930, No. 4.

47. Kukushkin, *op. cit.*, p. 68.

48. *Voprosy Istorii* 1962, No. 4, pp. 68–9.

49. *ibid*.

50. Strong, *op. cit.*, p. 88; a letter from Moscow dated March 13th in *Sotsialisticheski Vestnik*, 1930, No. 6–7.

51. Fainsod, *op. cit.*, pp. 242–4, 259.

52. *ibid*, p. 245.

53. *ibid*, pp. 243–4.

54. Pashukanis (ed.), *op. cit.* (see Ch. 3, Note 5), p. 474. One should not be misled by such extenuatory formulae as 'in a number of localities', 'certain officials', etc.; these were undeniably widespread occurrences. See also Aver'ev, *NAF*, 1930, No. 6, p. 89; Angarov, *Bolshevik*, 1930, No. 6, p. 19, and various other sources which testify that dekulakization was a country-wide phenomenon.

55. Quoted by Milyutin, *Bolshevik*, 1930, No. 6, p. 16.

56. A secret letter by Rumyantsev, secretary of the Western *oblast* (Smolensk) which includes among the 'excesses' the use of the armed forces. Fainsod, *op. cit.*, p. 247.

57. Letter from Russia dated March 13, 1930, *Sotsialisticheski Vestnik*, 1930, No. 6–7, p. 18.

58. Aver'ev, *NAF*, 1930, No. 6: from the report of a delegation of the Communist Academy sent to the North Caucasus. (Emphasis supplied.)

59. Fainsod, *op. cit.*, p. 243.

60. Khataevich, *Pravda*, February 16, 1930. It will be recalled that in Sholokhov's Virgin Soil Upturned, published in the USSR in 1931, three communist activists (one of them an urban worker sent out by the Party), decided upon dekulakization, and directed the operation with the help of several bednyaks.

61. Syrtsov, *Bolshevik*, 1930, No. 5, p. 41.

62. Letter from Rumyantsev, secretary of the Smolensk *obkom* to *okrug* officials, dated January 20, 1930, Fainsod, *op. cit.*, p. 247.

63. *NAF*, 1930, No. 7–8, p. 94.

64. *Pravda* editorial, February 1, 1930. Stalin, *Pravda*, February 10, 1930; same article by Stalin in *Sochineniya*, Vol. XII, p. 188.

65. Syrtsov, *Bolshevik*, 1930. No. 5, p. 55.

66. Angarov, *Bolshevik*, 1930, No. 6, p. 21, tells of a group of 'five' appointed in one village to carry out dekulakization. The 'five' 'prowled about at night', entered the peasants' houses, carried off icons and burned them. They also burned stools and blankets, etc., explaining that these would not be needed in the kolkhoz.

67. A *GPU* report of February 27, 1930, Fainsod, *op. cit.*, p. 245. The quotation is from an article by Kazansky dealing with events in the Russian villages of Kazakhstan. *NAF*, 1930, No. 6, p. 134.

68. Letter by Rumyantsev, *obkom* secretary, dated February 20, and another dated May 2, 1930. Fainsod, *op. cit.*, p. 247.

69. *ibid*, p. 246.

70. *ibid*, pp. 244–5. This is the report of February 20th.

71. Aver'ev, *NAF*, 1930, No. 6, p. 20.

72. *NAF*, 1930, No. 7–8, pp. 89–93. The text is not clear: it may have been 400 serednyak households out of a total of 855 dekulakized households.

73. Danilov (ed.), *op. cit.*, p. 155.

74. Angarov, 'Selsovety i likvidatsiya kulachestva kak klassa', *Bolshevik*, 1930, No. 8, p. 20.

75. *ibid*, p. 20.

76. Ganzha, Slinko, Shostak, 'Ukrainskoe selo na puti k sotsializmu', Danilov (ed.), *op. cit.*, p. 185.

77. *ibid*. The authors mention six *okrugi* and add ' . . . and elsewhere'.

78. *Istoriya KPSS*. (Moscow 1962), p. 446; Trifonov, *op. cit.*, also quotes numerous cases of 'dekulakization' of bednyaks and serednyaks: in the Stalingrad *okrug* a third of those 'dekulakized' were serednyaks. By May 25th, in 24 *raiony* of the Moscow *okrug*, 18,000 people had been deprived of the right to vote, but in the case of 12,500 this had been done 'illegally' (i.e. they were not kulaks).

79. Krylenko, *16-ty S'ezd VKP(b)*, stenogramme, p. 352.

80. *ibid*.

81. An article entitled 'The *bednota* exposes the kulaks' in *NAF*, 1930, No. 6, pp. 71–2, mentions approvingly the work of a group of bednyaks in the village of Staro-Shcherbinovka in the Yeisk *raion* of the North Caucasus. During the procurements campaign of that summer the group had helped the authorities to exert pressure upon

the better-off peasants. In the winter of 1930 they 'exposed' an additional sixteen kulak households previously regarded as *trudovye*. From these were taken twenty-two horses, thirty cows, nineteen sheep and a 'considerable' quantity of agricultural implements. On average, therefore, each household possessed 1·4 horses, 1·8 cows, and 1·2 sheep. No reason is given for the classification of these households as kulak.

82. Krylenko, *16-ty S'ezd VKP(b)*, stenogramme, pp. 352, 353.

83. Syrtsov, *Bolshevik*, 1930, No. 5, p. 46.

84. Fainsod, *op. cit.*, p. 246.

85. Letter dated February 17th in *Sotsialisticheski Vestnik*, 1930, No. 4.

86. Syrtsov, *Bolshevik*, 1930, No. 5, p. 54.

87. Letter dated March 13th, *Sotsialisticheski Vestnik*, 1930, No. 6–7, p. 19.

88. Strong, *op. cit.*, p. 88; Aver'ev, in *NAF*, 1930, No. 6, p. 86, states that these trains often contained families separated from the head of the household, who had been arrested for counter-revolutionary activities.

89. Serge, *op. cit.* (see Ch. 6, Note 71), pp. 267–8. In Danilov (ed.), *op. cit.*, instances are also mentioned of inhabitants taking their herds and crossing over into Kirghizia and Turkmenistan, pp. 408 and 481 (respectively).

90. Molotov, *Bolshevik*, 1930, No. 5, p. 11.

91. *Istoriya KPSS*. (Moscow 1962), p. 143.

92. Abramov, in Danilov (ed.), *op. cit.*, p. 105.

93. Ganzha, Slinko, Shostak, in Danilov (ed.), *op. cit.*, p. 183; Trifonov, *op. cit.*, p. 249. The latter source, the less recent of the two, having been published in 1960, states that in the Ukraine 160,000 households had been expropriated by 1931. He adds that 'less than half' of these were deported.

94. In Uzbekistan 40,000 households were dekulakized between 1930 and 1933. It is not stated how many were deported. In Kazakhstan 3,123 households were deported in 1930. See Danilov (ed.), *op. cit.*, pp. 252–78.

95. Fainsod, *op. cit.*, p. 246; Syrtsov, *Bolshevik*, 1930, No. 5, p. 54; *NAF*, 1930, No. 6, pp. 89, 134; *NAF*, 1930, No. 4, pp. 130–1; *NAF*, 1930, No. 7–8 p. 90.

96. Aver'ev *NAF*, 1930, No. 6, p. 89. At the beginning of 1930 the officially recognized regions of *sploshnaya* were: North Caucasus, Middle and Lower Volga, and the regions of the Ukrainian steppe.

CONCLUSION

In the months from October to December 1929, the speed-up in the rate of collectivization had resulted in the recruitment of over two million households to the kolkhozes; by the beginning of 1930, the movement had become frenetic in its intensity. In the shadow of dekulakization, with the régime exerting constant pressure by every means in its power, a veritable storm broke over the Soviet countryside. The events of this period cannot properly be discussed within the context of the present work, but will, it is hoped, form the basis for a subsequent study; meanwhile, they may be sketched in broad outline.

At the end of September 1929, the percentage of households collectivized was 7·4%; in the three months which followed, this figure doubled, 2·4 million new households having joined the kolkhozes during this period. But the months of January and February brought a positive landslide, for the number of households in the kolkhozes rose from some 15% at the end of December to 59·3% by about the 1st March, that is, roughly 15 million households.[1] This means that in the space of two months, some 11 million households joined the collectives.

In some regions, the upsurge was fantastic. In the Moscow region, for example, the proportion of collectivized households in October 1929 had been a mere 3·2%; by the end of January 1930, this region could boast a total of 36·5%, and by the end of February the figure had already risen to 73%. Comparable figures for the Urals showed a rise from 6·3% to 47·4%, and thereafter to 68·8%. The Tatar Republic, one of the most backward regions in the matter of collectivization, with a bare 2·4% of collectivized households in October 1929, had increased this figure to 42·2% by the end of January, and to 77·3% one month later. The Central Black Earth Region (Tambov-Voronezh *oblast*) did even better: from a total of 8·3% of households collectivized in October 1929, it had moved from a figure of 50% by the end of January to occupy top place in the 'league tables' with a total of 81·8% by March 1st.[2] The same thing happened in many other regions which were no less backward than the Tambov province.

Behind these figures there lay a record of violence such as the peasants had not experienced since the days of the Civil War. The rush to join the kolkhozes was inspired by fear and by despair, and

514

it was accompanied by mass destruction of livestock and equipment. In the beginning, the peasants themselves had destroyed their stock, their motto being that join the kolkhoz they must, since there was no other way out, but that they would join empty-handed;[3] the destruction continued through the fault of the authorities, who succeeded in creating chaos that wrought more havoc than an earthquake. The cost of this upheaval in terms of human lives, livestock and equipment was immense.

But the storms which had been unleashed on the countryside did not rage unchecked. It was clear that the mass of the peasantry, seething with anger and driven to the point of despair, were nearing the end of their tether, and that at any moment their wrath might be expected to explode into violence. It was at this point that Stalin applied the brake, in his 'Dizzy with success' article, which appeared in *Pravda*, on March 2nd, 1930. This manoeuvre enabled him to save the régime and his own power by smearing the Party cadres. In the villages, editions of the newspaper were passed eagerly from hand to hand. Processions of peasants paraded copies of Stalin's article on banners, while the local officials dared not show their faces in the villages. . . .

In the space of a few weeks, the fantastic figure of 59·3% collectivization dwindled to 23%; nine million households left the kolkhozes, and the downward trend continued until the autumn.

The rash undertaking of the winter of 1929–30 cost the country very dearly. It was to be many a long year before the USSR recovered from the mass slaughter of its livestock. Indeed, it is true to say that to this day Soviet agriculture has still not fully recovered from the damaging effects of that winter.

The offensive against the peasants which was suddenly decreed at the end of 1929 caught not only public opinion, but also the State administrative apparatus unprepared. The State caused an upheaval in the countryside without having prepared its administrative organs to take the strain. This is why collectivization was carried out not by the normal machinery of village administration, but by *ad hoc* bodies hastily mobilized for the purpose. The majority of the *selsovety* had to be re-elected. The entire local co-operative structure, built up after many years of effort, was destroyed and had to be reconstituted afresh. The kolkhoz administrations which had newly been set up to guide the movement were outpaced by events, and were largely dismantled.

Thus, the cost of these policies in terms of the losses suffered was enormous; seldom was any government to wreak such havoc in its own country.

Having no alternative programme or position upon which to fall back, the government neither could nor would see any way out, other than to exert further pressure, and to carry on with collectivization. In effect, the pressure was renewed in the autumn of 1930, and from this time on the situation developed into a trial of strength with the peasantry, which was to continue for nearly four years, and was to prove much more arduous than Stalin and his general staff had foreseen. Stalin himself admitted this to Churchill in 1942. The following is quoted from Churchill's note of their conversation:

'Tell me,' I asked, 'have the stresses of this war been as bad to you personally as carrying through the policy of the Collective Farms?'

This subject immediately roused the Marshal.

'Oh, no,' he said, 'the Collective Farm policy was a terrible struggle.'

'I thought you would have found it bad,' said I, 'because you were not dealing with a few score thousands of aristocrats or big landowners, but with millions of small men.'

'Ten millions,' he said, holding up his hands. 'It was fearful. Four years it lasted.'[4]

How, and for what reasons, did the Soviet régime and its leader come to embark on this course? The purpose of the present work has been to put forward an explanation for these events.

The spectacular 'great turn' at the end of 1929, and the well-nigh incredible venture of the winter of 1929–30, were the culmination of a chain-reaction which had been set off by the 'procurement crisis' of 1928. This crisis, in its turn, had stemmed from the interaction of three major factors: the overthrow of NEP, the structure of the Soviet State and the personality of its leader.

The Communist Party proved unable to maintain and to manage a mixed economy consisting of a state sector and, especially in the countryside, a private sector as well. The Bukharinists were not alone in believing that NEP could still be made to work; even the Trotskyists, who had never looked upon NEP as a permament fixture, were still in favour of preserving the framework of a mixed economy in 1928.

However, an economy of this type could not function 'on its own'. The market mechanism of NEP, which had worked wonders at the start simply by following its natural course, had in the end led the régime into an impasse, from which the Party, being preoccupied with its own internal conflicts, was unable to devise any effective or timely means of rescuing it. In addition, the régime failed to learn, during the years of NEP, how best to reach an understanding with the peasants, how to consolidate its position in the countryside, how to build up a powerful, non-State co-operative movement, or to devise efficient collective structures. Thus, the régime wasted time, and failed to give sufficient attention to the preparation of effective instruments of government which, before long, were to be sorely needed.

When the difficulties materialized, the Soviet régime, which was essentially urban in character, and was to a great extent regarded in the villages as an alien force, emerged as a highly centralized hierarchy, within which the major decisions were taken by one body consisting of a few individuals, that is, the Politburo.

The bureaucracy was dominated by one man, who showed a greater aptitude than his colleagues for creating bureaucratic structures, and for manoeuvring within the institutional framework thus created. His personality, therefore, came to play a predominant role in the final choice of solutions and methods.

While the élite of the 'Old Bolsheviks' clung to their ideals, and saw, in the régime which the revolution had brought to power, features which did not in fact exist, or no longer existed, Stalin was less burdened with either moral or theoretical scruples, and took an altogether more realistic view of the realities of power.

He knew that the only existing political force within the country was the Party, and the Party's real strength lay in its discipline, firmly backed by the Party secretarial machine, which he himself had largely been responsible for creating. This was Stalin's greatest talent: he was a master-builder of bureaucratic structures, and this it was that determined his conceptions and his methods.

In his view, the peasantry was a hostile force with which no alliance would be possible unless it were duly brought within the orbit of State control, and forced to deliver up the required amount of production.

When faced with a dangerous 'procurements crisis' he reacted, as was to be expected, by using the lever whose use he best understood; he resorted to force, with the appropriate controls, as a means of extricating the country from its predicament and setting it on the road to greatness—as he conceived it—while at the same time consolidating his own personal power. Within a few years, the end-result of his policy was to be the Stalinist totalitarian dictatorship. When he manipulated this particular lever in January 1928, Stalin did not know where the process set in motion by his 'emergency measures' would ultimately lead him. The crisis had caught him unawares, it was for this reason that his reaction had been so violent. However, the emergency measures only made matters worse. It was at this point that Stalin turned his attention to the kolkhozes and sovkhozes, in the first instance primarily as a means of solving the grain problem. At this stage, however, the kolkhozes and sovkhozes still represented no more than a hoped-for solution. For a year and a half, very little action was taken in this direction. The régime was still groping for a way out of its growing difficulties, and meanwhile the Party leadership was engaged in a bitter struggle with the Right.

The month of May 1929 was to see the launching of the Five-year Plan, a grandiose project which inspired tremendous hopes among the leadership, but at the same time created new pressures. Problems arose over the implementation of the Plan for the year 1928–9, and these were still further complicated by difficulties over procurements; this was the Gordian knot which Stalin was to sever abruptly by his sudden change of policy at the end of the year.

The industrial growth rates achieved during this year were very high, so high as to persuade Stalin that they might be even further accelerated. But the successes in this sector were expressed in global figures which masked a great many failures, and these merely added to the troubles already besetting the régime.

Stalin hoped to find a solution to these problems precisely by a further acceleration of growth rates. As he saw it, a forced rate of growth, achieved at the cost of exhaustive efforts over a limited period, was the sovereign remedy which would change the whole face of the country and extricate it from the crisis which had overtaken it.

However, at this point, he found himself up against another obstacle: the downward trend in agriculture was now threatening to wreck everything. Harvests were poor, the livesock sector was declining, and procurements were presenting a growing problem.

But Stalin drew from the procurements campaigns the moral which best suited him. The conclusion he arrived at was that the peasantry was weaker than had been supposed, and that it yielded under pressure, if the pressure was properly applied. Stalin's version of the 'class attitude', a method which consisted of carrying on 'class warfare against the kulak and the *zazhitochny*', seemed to him to pay off handsomely. And indeed, the new procurements campaign, which was launched in July 1929, yielded grain on an unprecedented scale.

Meanwhile, under increasing pressure from the authorities, the drive to set up the kolkhozes had also got under way that summer, and was going forward at a rapid rate. Kolkhoz membership had doubled between the months of July and October, and was to treble in October, November and December.

However, it was the bednyaks who had been mainly responsible for this influx. Since the government's available resources were being swallowed up in the industrialization drive, these kolkhozes would be too under-powered to survive for long, or at best would stagnate on the verge of insolvency, in a condition which could not but discourage the rest of the peasants from joining them. The only means of effecting a material improvement in the state of the kolkhozes would be to persuade the serednyaks to join them en masse.

These then were the simple facts of the situation, as the Politburo saw it: without the serednyak, the kolkhozes would disintegrate: without the kolkhozes, the industrialization programme *would be a failure by 1931*!

Towards the end of the economic year, i.e. the period between September and the beginning of October, the many reports reaching the Politburo left them in no doubt about the position. These weeks were spent in a desperate search for some solution which would save the situation. The solution finally suggested was prompted by overall consideration of the various factors which we have already discussed. It was decided that a radical change must be effected in the agricultural sector during the course of 1930, if the rates of industrial growth were to remain unimpaired. However, as from the start of the spring sowing season, the peasants would be fully occupied on their farms. Collectivization must therefore be speeded up, so that as many collectives as possible could be set up before the sowing commenced. This was what Molotov said at the November 1929 session of the Central Committee.

The decision to embark on wholesale collectivization was probably taken by the Politburo round about the end of October. The leadership did not know how many kolkhozes it would be possible to create. The recruitment figures for November and December merely whetted their appetite. Stalin, dazzled by the figures, now lived in a fever of anticipation. He genuinely believed that the required transformation could be brought about in the space of a few months, if only a sufficiently powerful and compelling means could be devised for driving the mass of the peasantry to join the kolkhozes. This he found in dekulakization.

It is clear that when they launched this winter offensive, the leadership had no idea of the scale on which their mass collectivization drive was to take place. They were not thinking in terms of engulfing fifteen million households in the kolkhozes. On the other hand, they wished to recruit as many as possible, and the results seemed to be encouraging.

By the end of March, the bubble had burst. Nevertheless, a fifth of the households were to stay on in the kolkhozes, and after a period of recession in the autumn of 1930, collectivization was to be resumed.

NOTES AND REFERENCES

1. Cf. *Pravda*, February 20, 1930; Molotov in *Bolshevik*, No. 5, 1930, p. 10; Kraev, *Planovoe Khozyaistvo*, No. 5, 1930, p. 78.

2. Figures for all regions in Tsylko, *NAF*, No. 5, 1930, p. 26.

3. The peasants used to say: let us join the kolkhoz 'naked as the falcon' (*gol kak sokol*).

4. Churchill, W. S., *The Second World War: The Hinge of Fate*. (London, Cassell, 1951), p. 447.

Churchill is, possibly, mistaken. Stalin probably said 100 million.

BIBLIOGRAPHY

I. OFFICIAL DOCUMENTS

(a) *Party Congresses and Conferences*

15-TY S'EZD VKP(B), *stenograficheski otchet* (Moscow-Leningrad, 1928).

15-TAYA KONFERENTSIYA, *stenograficheski otchet* (Moscow/Leningrad, 1929). The edition of the minutes of this conference published in Moscow in 1962 is more complete and contains some very valuable annotations.

5-TY S'EZD SOVETOV, *stenotchet* (Moscow, published by the *TsIK*, 1929).

16-TY S'EZD VKP (B), *stenotchet* (Moscow/Leningrad, 1930).

6-OI S'EZD SOVETOV, *stenotchet* (Moscow, published by the *TsIK*, 1930).

17-TAYA KONFERENTSIYA, *stenotchet* (Moscow, 1932).

17-TY S'EZD VKP(B), *stenotchet* (Moscow, 1934).

(b) *Collections of Documents*

CODE PÉNAL DE LA RSFSR. Official text, with appendices, including amendments up to October 1, 1933. Translated by Jules Patouillet (Librairie générale de droit et de jurisprudence, Paris, 1935).

DIREKTIVY KPSS I SOVETSKOGO PRAVITELSTVA PO KHOZYAISTVENNYM VOPROSAM (Moscow, *Gos. Izd. Polit. Lit.*, 1953. Vol. I: 1917–28, Vol. II: 1929–45).

DOKUMENTY PO ISTORII SOVETSKOGO OBSHCHESTVA, in *Materialy po Istorii SSSR*. Volumes I and VII (Academy of Sciences, 1955 and 1959).

ISTORIYA KOLKHOZNOGO PRAVA (ed. Prof. Kazantsev). Vol. I, 1927–36 (Moscow, *Gos. Izd. Yurid. Lit.*, 1959).

ITOGI VYPOLNENIYA PYATILETNEGO PLANA NARODNOGO KHOZYAISTVA (Moscow, *Gosplan*, 1933).

KOLLEKTIVIZATSIYA SELSKOGO KHOZYAISTVA (*vazhneishie postanovleniya po kolkhoznomu stroitelstvu*) (Moscow, Academy of Sciences, 1957).

KPSS V REZOLYUTSIYAKH, Volumes II and III, 7th edition (Moscow, 1957).

ORGANIZATSIYA TRUDA V KOLKHOZAKH (*Sbornik dokumentov*) (Tbilisi, *Kolkhoztsentr* of Transcaucasia, 1931).

SOBRANIE ZAKONOV I RASPORYAZHENII RABOCHE-KREST'YANSKOGO PRAVITELSTVA SSSR, the official journal published by *Sovnarkom* and the *STO*, Parts I and II, 1928–33.

SPRAVOCHNIK PARTIINOGO RABOTNIKA, vypusk 8-oi (Moscow, *Partizdat*, 1934).

SPRAVOCHNIK SOVETSKOGO RABOTNIKA (Moscow, 1937).

ZAKONY O ZEMLE (ZEMELNY KODEKS RSFSR), introduction by D. I. Gomberg (Moscow, *Narkomyust* RSFSR, 1927).

II. SOVIET AUTHORS

(a) LENIN (V. I.), *Sochineniya* (4th edition), particularly Volumes XXXIII and XXXVI (Moscow, 1942–50).

(b) *Works written during the period*

ANGAROV (A.), *Klassovaya borba v sovetskoi derevne* (Moscow, Communist Academy, 1929).

BOLSHAKOV (A.), *Derevnya 1917–27*, preface by Kalinin and Oldenburg (*Rabochee Prosveshchenie*, 1927).

BOLSHAKOV (A.), *Kommuna Kudrovo* (Leningrad, *Priboi*, 1930.)

BUKHARIN (N.), *Put k sotsializmu i raboche-krest'yanski soyuz* (Moscow/Leningrad, *Gos. Izdat.*, 3rd edition, 1926.)

GAISTER (A.), *Dostizheniya i trudnosti kolkhoznogo stroitelstva* (Communist Academy, 1929).

PASHUKANIS (E.) (ed.), *15 let sovetskogo stroitelstva, 1917–32* (*Ogiz*, 1932).

PROEKT PLATFORMY BOLSHEVIKOV-LENINTSEV (OPPOZITSII) K 15-OMU S'EZDU VKP(B), illegal, cyclostyled publication (Moscow, 1927). The French translation of this *Platform* of the opposition is in LES BOLCHEVIKS CONTRE STALINE (Paris, 1957).

PREOBRAZHENSKY (E.), *Novaya Ekonomika* (Moscow, Communist Academy, 1926). (Published in English as *The New Economics*, translated by B. Pearce, with a preface by A. Nove, Oxford, Clarendon Press, 1965.)

PREOBRAZHENSKY (E.), *Ot NEPa k sotzializmu* (Moscow, *Moskovski Rabochi*, 1922).

RATNER (G.), Agricultural Co-operation in the Soviet Union (translated from the Russian), (London, Routledge and Sons, 1929.)

REZUNOV (M.), *Selskie sovety i zemelnye obshchestva* (Moscow, Communist Academy, 1928).

SHOLOKHOV (M.), *Podnyataya Tselina* (Virgin Soil Upturned), Volumes I and II (Moscow, 1962). (The first volume, which concerns us here, was published in 1931.)

STALIN (I. V.), *Sochineniya*, Volumes VIII to XIII (Moscow, 1949–50).

ULASHEVICH (V.), *Zhenshchina v kolkhoze* (Moscow, Communist Academy, 1930).

VAREIKIS (Y.), *Usloviya uspekha i organizatsii sotsialisticheskogo stroya v derevne*, 2nd edition (Voronezh, *Kommuna*, 1935).

(c) *Soviet Authors of the post-Stalin period*

BORBA KPSS ZA SOTSIALISTICHESKOE SELSKOE KHOZYAISTVO (*sbornik*) (University of Moscow, 1961).

BORISOV (Yu. S.), *Podgotovka proizvodstvennykh kadrov selskogo khozyaistva SSSR v rekonstruktivny period* (Moscow, Academy of Sciences, 1960).

DANILOV (V. P.) (ed.), *Ocherki istorii kollektivizatsii selskogo khozyaistva v soyuznykh respublikakh* (Moscow, Gos. Izd. Polit. Lit., 1963).

DANILOV (V. P.), 'Izuchenie istorii sovetskogo krest'yanstva', in *Sovetskaya istoricheskaya nauka ot 20-ogo do 22-ogo S'ezda KPSS* (Moscow, Academy of Sciences, 1962).

ISTORIA KPSS, 2nd edition (Moscow, *Gos. Izd, olit. Lit.*, 1926).

ISTORIYA NARODNOGO KHOZYAISTVA SSSR (*Tsikl lektsii*), (Moscow, 1960).

ISTORIYA SOVETSKOGO KREST'YANSTVA I KOLKHOZNOGO STROIT-ELSTVA V SSSR. (Study Session held at the Academy of Sciences in April 1961.) (Moscow, Academy of Sciences, 1963.)

KONYUKHOV (G. A.), *KPSS v borbe s khlebnymi zatrudneniyami v strane 1928–9* (Moscow, *Sotsegiz*, 1960).

KUKUSHKIN (Yu.), *Rol selskikh sovetov v sotsialisticheskom preobrazovanii derevni* (Moscow University, 1962).

LYASHCHENKO (P.), *Istoriya narodnogo khozyaistva SSSR*, Volume III: *Sotsializm* (Moscow, Gos. Izd. Polit. Lit., 1956). This posthumous edition was edited during the Stalinist era, and is therefore 'Stalinist' in conception.

MOSKOVSKIE KOMMUNISTY V BORBE ZA POBEDU KOLKHOZNOGO STROYA (Moscow, *Institut Istorii Partii*, 1960).

PARTIYA V PERIOD NASTUPLENIYA PO VSEMU FRONTU, *Sozdanie kolkhoznogo stroya, 1929–32* (*Gos. Polit. Izd.*, 1961).

POSTROENIE FUNDAMENTA SOTSIALISTICHESKOI EKONOMIKI V SSSR, 1926–32 (Moscow, Academy of Sciences, 1960).

SELUNSKAYA (V. M.), *Borba KPSS za sotsialisticheskoe preobrazovanie selskogo khozyaistva* (Moscow, *Vysshaya Shkola*, 1961).

STRUMILIN (S.) (ed.), *Ekonomicheskaya zhizn SSSR, Khronika sobytii i faktov* (Moscow, *Sovetskaya Entsiklopediya*, 1961).

TRIFONOV, *Ocherki klassovoi borby v gody NEPa 1927–37* (Moscow, *Gos. Izd. Polit. Lit.*, 1960).

YAKOVTSEVSKY (A.), *Agrarnye otnosheniya v SSSR v period stroitelstva sotsializma* (Moscow, *Nauka*, 1967).

III. JOURNALS AND PERIODICALS

The titles of the most important articles quoted or referred to are given in the notes.

BOLSHEVIK: theoretical organ of the Central Committee, bi-monthly, complete set.

BYULLETEN OPPOZITSII: monthly journal of the Trotskyist opposition, edited by Trotsky himself, and published from 1929 in Berlin and Paris. The B.D.I.C. holds a complete set.

DEREVENSKI KOMMUNIST: journal published bi-monthly by the Central Committee for rural cadres. Individual numbers only available in the B.D.I.C.

KOLLEKTIVIST: journal of the Turki (Lower Volga) *raikom* which appeared twice weekly; the issues for May 1932 are available.

KOLLEKTIVIST: Kolkhoz journal of *Narkomzem* and the *Kolkhoztsentr*; separate issues only are available.

NA AGRARNOM FRONTE: monthly review of the Agrarian Section of the Communist Academy; there exists a complete set for the years 1925–31, and a few issues for 1932.

NA FRONTE KOLLEKTIVIZATSII: bi-monthly of the agricultural cooperatives and of the Kolkhozsentr; individual issues only available.

PARTIINOE STROITELSTVO: journal of the Central Committee; individual issues.

PLANOVOE KHOZYAISTVO: journal of *Gosplan*; complete set 1928–33.

PRAVDA: organ of the Central Committee, published daily; complete set 1928–33.

SELSKOE KHOZYAISTVO RSFSR: published thrice monthly by the *Narkomzem* of the RSFSR; separate issues.

SOTSIALISTICHESKI VESTNIK: Menshevik journal published first in Berlin, later in Paris, and finally in the USA; complete set 1928–59.

SOTSIALISTICHESKAYA REKONSTRUKTSIYA SELSKOGO KHOZYAISTVA: theoretical journal of *Narkomzem*, and of the 'Timiryazev' and 'Lenin' Academies; separate issues.

SOTSIALISTICHESKOE SELSKOE KHOZYAISTVO: bi-monthly journal of the *oblispolkom* and of the Agrarian Department of Moscow *obkom*; separate issues.

ZA VYSOKI UROZHAI: journal of the Turki (Lower Volga) MTS; which appeared twice weekly; issues for May 1932.

ZA KOLLEKTIVIZATSIYU: daily publication of the Moscow *obkom* and *oblispolkom*; separate issues.

(The dates given above refer to those years of the set which have been used; incomplete sets and separate issues all fall within the years 1928–33.)

Articles based upon archive material and containing much new information have appeared in historical journals in the post-Stalin era; they are listed separately below, in the order in which they appeared in these reviews.

Istoriya SSSR.

MEDVEDEV (V. K.), *Likvidatsiya kulachestva v Nizhne-Volzhskom krae*, 1958, No. 6, pp. 9–29.
BUTYLKIN (P. A.), *Organizatsiya i deyatelnost kollektivnykh khozyaistv v pervye gody sovetskoi vlasti*, 1959, No. 5, pp. 80–97.
MOSHCHKOV (Yu. A.), *Politika gosudarstvennykh zagotovok v gody sotsialisticheskoi rekonstruktsii selskogo khozyaistva—1930–34*, No. 4, 1960, pp. 101–111.
ZELENIN (I. E.), *Kolkhoznoe stroitelstvo v SSSR v 1931–2 gody (Itogi sploshnoi kollektivizatsii selskogo khozyaistva)*, 1960, No. 6, pp. 19–39.
BOGDENKO (M. L.), ZELENIN (I. E.), *Istoriya kollektivizatsii selskogo khozyaistva v sovremennoi sovetskoi istoriko-ekonomicheskoi literature*, 1962, No. 9, pp. 131–33.

Voprosy Istorii KPSS.

TRAPEZNIKOV (S. P.), *Istoricheskaya Rol MTS v sozdanii i ukreplenii kolkhoznogo stroya*, 1958, No. 3, pp. 50–67.
SEMERNIN (P. V.), *O likvidatsii kulachestva kak klassa*, 1959, No. 4, pp. 72–85.
VALANOV (F. M.), *Razgrom pravogo uklona v VKP(b) (1928–30)*, 1960, No. 4, pp. 62–80.
MARKOV (S. F.), *Ukreplenie selskikh partiinykh organizatsii v period podgotovki massovogo kolkhoznogo dvizheniya*, 1962, No. 3, pp. 113–22.
IVNITSKY (N. A.), *O nachalnom etape sploshnoi kollektivizatsii*, 1962, No. 4, pp. 55–71.
ABRAMOV (B. A.), *O rabote komissii Politbyuro TsK VKP(b) po voprosam sploshnoi kollektivizatsii*, 1964, No. 1, pp. 32–43.

Voprosy Istorii.

BOGDENKO (M. L.), *K istorii nachalnogo etapa sploshnoi kollektivizatsii selskogo khozyaistva*, 1963, No. 5, pp. 19–35.

IV. NON-SOVIET AUTHORS

ABRAMOVITCH (R.), The Soviet Revolution 1917–39 (N.Y. Int. Univ. Press, 1962).

ARGENTON, Les doctrines agraires du marxisme (thesis), (Paris, 1934).

ASTIER (E. D'.), Sur Staline (Paris Plon, 1963).

BARMIN (A.), One Who Survived (N.Y., 1945).

BARRINGTON MOORE (Jr.), Terreur et progrès en URSS (Paris, Vitiano, 1955).

BELOV (F.), The History of a Soviet Collective Farm (N.Y. Praeger, 1955).

BERDYAEV (N.), The Origin of Russian Communism (London, 1937).

BOBROVSKY (Cz.), La Yougoslavie socialiste (Paris, Armand Colin, 1956).

BOBROVSKY, Formation du systéme soviétique de planification (Paris / The Hague, Mouton & Co., 1956).

LES BOLCHEVIKS CONTRE STALINE (Paris, Publications de la 4e Internationale, 1957).

BROUÉ (P.), Le Parti Bolchevique (Paris, éd.de Minuit, 1963).

CARR (E. H.), A History of Soviet Russia; The Bolshevik Revolution, Volumes I–III (London, Macmillan 1950–53).

CARR (E. H.), A History of Soviet Russia; The Interregnum 1923–24 (London, Macmillan, 1954).

CARR (E. H.), A History of Soviet Russia; Socialism in one Country, Volume I (London, Macmillan, 1958).

CARR (E. H.), 'The Russian Revolution and the Peasant,' The Listener, May, 1963.

CHAMBERLIN (W. H.), Russia's Iron Age (London, 1935).

CHAMBRE (H.), Le Marxisme en Union soviétique. Idéologie et Institutions (Paris, Le Seuil, 1955).

CHOMBART DE LAUWE (J.), Le Paysan soviétique (Paris, Le Seuil, 1961).

CILIGA (A.), Au pays du grand mensonge (Paris, Gallimard, 1938).

CILIGA (A.), Sibérie, terre de l'exil et de l'industrialisation (Paris, Plon, 1960).

COLLECTIVIZED AGRICULTURE IN THE SOVIET UNION (School of Slavonic Studies, University of London, August 1934).

COLLECTIVISATION DU VILLAGE (Association financière, industrielle et commerciale russe, Paris, 1930).

COLLECTIVISATION DE L'AGRICULTURE SOVIÉTIQUE ET LE RÉGIME DES KOLKHOZES (La documentation française, April 11, 1952, No. 1602).

DALLIN (D.) NIKOLAEVSKY (B.), Forced Labour in Soviet Russia (London, 1949).

DANIELS (V.), The Conscience of the Revolution (Harvard University Press, 1960).

DEUTSCHER (I.), Stalin (London, Oxford University Press, 1949).

DEUTSCHER (I.), Russia after Stalin (London 1953).

DEUTSCHER (I.), The Prophet Armed (London, Cumberlage, 1954).

DEUTSCHER (I.), The Prophet Unarmed (N.Y., Toronto, Oxford University Press, 1959).

DEUTSCHER (I.), Heretics and Renegades (London, Macmillan, 1951).

DUMONT (R.), Sovkhoz, kolkhoz et le problématique communisme (Paris, Le Seuil, 1964).

ELLISON (H.), 'The Decision to Collectivize Agriculture,' American, Slavic and East European Review, April 1961.

ERLICH (A.), The Soviet Industrialization Debate (Cambridge, Mass., Harvard University Press, 1960).

FAINSOD (M.), Smolensk under Soviet Rule (Cambridge, Harvard University Press, 1958).

FAINSOD (M.), How Russia is ruled (Cambridge, Harvard University Press, 1953).

GEORGE (P.), Economie de l'URSS, collection 'Que Sais-je' (Paris, P.U.F., 1961).

GORKY (M.), 'Lénine' et 'Le Paysan Russe' (Paris, 1925).

HUBBARD (L. E.), The Economics of Soviet Agriculture (London, Macmillan, 1939).

JASNY (N.), Soviet Industrialization 1928–52 (Chicago 1961).

JASNY (N.), 'The Plight of the Soviet Collective Farms,' The Journal of Farm Economics, May 1948, No. 2.

JASNY (N.), Kolkhozy, the Achilles Heel of the Soviet Régime (Oxford, Blackwell, 1951).

JASNY (N.), The Soviet Socialized Agriculture of the USSR (Stanford University Press, 1949).

KARDEL (E.), Les problèmes de la politique socialiste dans les campagnes (Paris, La Nef de Paris, 1960).

MALEVSKY-MALEVICH, Russia–USSR: a complete handbook (N.Y., 1933).

MALEVSKY-MALEVICH, The Soviet Union Today (supplement to Russia–USSR) (N.Y., 1937).

MARCUSE (H.), Soviet Marxism: A critical analysis (N.Y. Columbia University Press, 1958.)

MASLOV (S.), Kolkhoznaya Rossiya (Berlin, *Krest'yanskaya Rossiya*, 1937) (in Russian).

MAYNARD (J.), Russia in Flux (London, Macmillan, 1943).

MIGLIOLI (G.), La Collectivization des campagnes soviétiques (Paris, Reider, 1934).

MUSHKELY AND YEDRYKA (S.), Le gouvernement de L'URSS (Paris, P.U.F., 1961).

NEUMANN (F.), The Democratic and the Authoritarian State (N.Y., The Free Press, 1957).

NOVE (A.), The Soviet Economy (London, George Allen and Unwin, 1961).

PAVLOVSKY (G.), Agricultural Russia on the Eve of Revolution (London, 1933).

PERROUX (F.), La révolution agraire en Russie soviétique (Paris, Reider, 1934).

PHAM-VAN-BACH, Le marxisme agraire et l'expérience russe (thesis).

PORTAL (R.) (ed.), Le Statut des paysans libérés du servage (Paris/ The Hague, Mouton & Co., 1963).

PROKOPOVICH (S. N.), Histoire économique de l'URSS (Paris, Flammarion, 1952).

RESWIK (W.), I Dreamt Revolution (Chicago, Regnary, 1952).

SERGE (V.), Le tournant obscur (Paris, Les Iles d'Or, 1951).

SERGE (V.), Destin d'une revolution, URSS 1917–37 (Paris, Grasset, 1937).

SERGE (V.), 'De Lénine, Staline', Crapouillot, January 1937.

SERGE (V.), Mémoires d'un révolutionnaire (Paris, Le Seuil, 1951).

SCHILLER (O.), Die Landwirtschaft des Soviet Union 1917–53 (Tubingen, 1954).

SCHLESINGER (R.), Marx, his Time and Ours (London, Routledge, Kegan Paul, 1950).

SHAPIRO (L.), The Communist Party of the Soviet Union (London, Eyre and Spottiswoode, 1960).

STRONG (A. L.), The Soviets Conquer Wheat (N.Y., Holt, 1931).

TROTSKY (L.), 'What Now?' The Third International after Lenin (N.Y., Pioneer Publications, 1957).

TROTSKY (L.), History of the Russian Revolution (London, 1932, 1933).

TROTSKY (L.), La Révolution trahie (Paris, 1937).

TROTSKY (L.), Staline (Paris, 1948).

VAKAR (N.), The Taproot of Soviet Society (N.Y., Harper and Brothers, 1961).

WESSON (R. G.), Soviet Communes (New Brunswick, New Jersey, Rutgers University Press, 1963).

YUGOV (A.), Pyatiletka (Berlin, Sotsialisticheski Vestnik Publication, 1932) (in Russian).

ZALESKI (E.), Planification de la croissance et fluctuations économiques en URSS, Vol. I (1918–32) (Paris, SEDES, 1962).

GLOSSARY

In a study of this kind the use of Russian expressions is often unavoidable. Such expressions may belong to political or scientific terminology, refer to institutions, or be very firmly anchored in popular speech; in most cases they are untranslatable. Certain Russian words often help in portraying the social climate, or in depicting a characteristic of, say, the peasantry, or certain politicians; they are indispensable in a work of research describing conditions in a linguistic region which is both distant and little known.

Russian words, when first encountered, are generally explained in the text or in a footnote; in order to facilitate reading, however, the following glossary is provided.

ADMINISTRIROVANIE—government by administrative order, irrespective of the opinion and interests of the masses.

ARTEL—a producers' collective, formed by artisans or peasants; in particular a form of agricultural production later to be called the kolkhoz. See: TOZ, KOMMUNA.

BARSHCHINA—the system of forced labour or service to the landowner which had obtained in the Russian countryside until 1861, and which was definitively abolished by the October Revolution.

BATRAK—an agricultural wage labourer employed by private peasants or by their communities. During NEP, the agricultural wage labourer employed throughout the year by the sovkhozes or by other state enterprises was no longer a *batrak* but an 'agricultural worker'.

BEDNYAK—a poor peasant.

BEDNOTA—the poor peasantry.

CHASTNIK—merchant or private entrepreneur of the NEP period. See also NEPMAN.

CHASTUSHKI—popular songs, improvised in quatrains, in which the Russian peasant commented on events or expressed his feelings.

CHEKIST—member of the *Cheka* (*Chrezvychainaya Kommissiya*), the political police formed by the Soviet government after the Revolution. The *Cheka* later became the GPU, and later still the OGPU.

CHINOVNIK—Tsarist Russian official; the word has become synonymous with bureaucracy.

DERZHIMORDA—literally, 'he who holds by the snout'. The word was popularly used to describe Tsarist police officers and was synony-mous with brutal treatment of the population.

DVOEVLASTIE—dual power or power which is simultaneously held by two different forces.

DVOR—the peasant household; both a social and an economic unit.

GENSEK—*Generalny Sekretar*: General Secretary. After Stalin, the occupant of this post was known as the 'First Secretary'; the title 'General Secretary' was recently revived, and the post is currently held by Brezhnev.

GPU—*Glavnoe Politicheskoe Upravlenie*: the political police which replaced the *Cheka* and which was later to become the OGPU ('O' for *obedinnennoe*: 'united'). Even after the change some official docu-ments continued to use the initials GPU.

GUBERNIYA—the largest administrative unit of Tsarist Russia; in the USSR the *guberniya* has been replaced by the *oblast*.

ISPOLKOM—*Ispolnitelny komitet*: the Executive Committee of the Soviet of an administrative unit: thus *raiispolkom*, *oblispolkom* in the *raion* and *oblast*. See also: *TsIK*, *VTsIK*, *VIK*.

KAZENNY—provided out of official funds; belonging to the State.

KHOZYAIN—head of the *dvor* and generally the father of the family. *Khozyain* may also mean 'farmer', 'good farmer' frequently being implied. Plural: *khozyaeva*.

KHUTOR—a farm which does not belong to the agrarian community but is situated around a *dvor* outside the village. The Stolypin re-form strongly encouraged peasants with initiative to leave the com-munity and found *khutora*. See also: OTRUB.

KKOV—peasants' mutual aid association.

KOLKHOZ—*Kollektivnoe khozyaistvo*: a collective farm. Before coming, in 1930, to refer to the only form of collective existing in agriculture, the word *kolkhoz* referred to any one of three forms: *toz*, *artel*, or *kommuna*.

KOLKHOZTSENTR—centre in charge of the administration of the coun-try's kolkhozes.

KOMMUNA—a community, and in particular an agricultural com-munity or type of collective in which production is collectively organ-ized and all property collectively owned. Families live in communal dwellings and eat in refectories; children are brought up in nurseries and communal schools; work is not rewarded by wages or by any other form of distributed income, since, in theory, the community undertakes to provide for all the needs of its members.

KOMNEZAMY—*Komitety nezamozhnykh selyan*: Poor Peasants' Committees in the Ukraine.

KONTRAKTATSIYA—a campaign designed to achieve the signing by peasants and procurement agencies of contracts whereby the peasants would be obliged to deliver to the State at pre-arranged prices part of their produce, while the State undertook to give advance payments, provide agronomic aid, seed grain, tools, credit, etc.

KRAI—literally, 'country'; a very large administrative unit existing in certain regions only, and most often in those of a 'national' character. Thus for a long time the North Caucasus was a *krai*.

KULAK—literally 'fist'; a rich peasant exploiting the labour of batraks; merchant or money lender.

MALOMOSHCHNY—'weak'; refers to a 'middle', but economically weak peasant whose condition is close to that of the bednyak.

MIR—the government of the peasant community; widely used to refer to the community itself.

MTS—*Mashino-traktornaya stantsiya*: Machine and Tractor Station.

MUZHIK—a slightly pejorative name for the Russian peasant.

NACHALNIK—head of any administrative unit, director, 'boss'.

NADEL—a very imprecise term for the plot of land to which the peasant was legally entitled during NEP as his *trudovoi nadel*, that is the plot which he and the members of his family cultivated without the help of wage labour.

NARKOMFIN—People's Commissariat of Finance.

NARKOMZEM—People's Commissariat of Agriculture.

NEP—*Novaya Ekonomicheskaya Politika*: the New Economic Policy inaugurated by Lenin in 1921.

NEPMAN—private entrepreneur, industrial or commercial, of the type that appeared on the scene as a result of NEP.

OBKOM—*Oblastnoi komitet* (Partii): the highest Party committee at *oblast* level. The committees of other administrative units are the *volkom*, the *ukom*, the *raikom*, the *okruzhkom*, and the *gubkom* in the *volost*, *uezd*, *raion*, *okrug* and *guberniya* respectively.

OBLAST—the largest administrative unit outside the regions organized as *krai*. Within the *oblast* there are the *okrug* (abolished in 1930), the *raion*, and the *selsovet*. This structure was introduced in 1929; the previous administrative structure had comprised the *guberniya*, *okrug*, *volost*, and *selsovet*.

OBRASTANIE—the process whereby a poor peasant, generally a party member, became more prosperous, and turned into a kulak.

OBSHCHINA—the agrarian community. See ZEMOBSHCHESTVO, SELS-KOE OBSHCHESTVO.

OGPU—see GPU.

OKRUG—see OBLAST.

OSEREDNYACHIVANIE—the levelling of peasant fortunes and attenuation of social differences brought about by the agrarian reform.

OTRUB—another means, in addition to the *khutor* arrangement, whereby the peasant could separate himself from the agrarian community: he continued to live in the village, but had land allocated to him for private exploitation, the land not being subject thereafter to reallocation.

OTTESNENIE—eviction; in particular the ousting of middle peasants from their positions in the *selsovety*.

PEREGIBY—excesses or deviations from the policy line laid down by the 'Centre'.

PEREKACHKA—pumping action; describes the extraction from the peasant sector of the resources required for industrialization.

PEREROZHDENIE—degeneration.

POMESHCHIK—landowner, landed gentleman.

POZHIRANIE—act of devouring (used by Preobrazhensky to describe the devouring of the private sector by the nationalized sector).

PRODRAZVERSTKA—imposition of tax in kind in quantities prescribed by the authorities. This procedure, employed in the countryside during the Civil War, and carried out by armed detachments of workers sent to obtain provisions for the starving towns, was hated by the peasants as it amounted to outright confiscation.

PROKURATURA—office of the Procurator, responsible for the observance of legality in the functioning of the security organs and tribunals.

PRORABOTKA—'intensive preliminary preparation'.

RAION—see OBLAST.

RAZLOZHENIE—disintegration; close in meaning to PEREROZHDENIE.

RAZMYCHKA—breach; political term for the breaking up of an alliance. See SMYCHKA.

RAZVERSTKA—the allocation by administrative order of quantities of produce to be delivered by households, irrespective of the views of the latter. See PRODRAZVERSTKA.

SAMODEYATELNOST—the activity of the masses themselves, as opposed to activity urged on them or enforced from above.

SAMOGON—spirit illegally distilled by the peasants, 'moonshine'.

SAMOTEK—purposeless, unguided activity; drift.

SELSKOE OBSHCHESTVO—juridical term designating the rural community in legislation after the reform of 1861.

SELSOVET—*Selski sovet*: the rural soviet, and first link in the administrative chain.

SEREDNYAK—middle peasant.

SKHOD—rural assembly.

SKIDKI I NAKIDKI—the addition and subtraction of surplus land which takes place during the reallocation of land carried out by the assembly of the rural community.

SMYCHKA—refers to the alliance between workers and peasants. See RAZMYCHKA.

SNK—abbreviation of SOVNARKOM.

SOKHA—wooden plough.

SOVKHOZ—*Sovetskoe khozyaistvo*: State Farm.

SOVNARKOM—Council of People's Commissars. See SNK.

SOYUZ SOYUZOV—Supreme Council for the administration of all branches of co-operation.

SRASHCHIVANIE—the fusion of parts of the state (or Party) apparatus with strata of the bourgeoisie or petty bourgeoisie.

SROKOVOI (pl. SROKOVYE)—batrak or worker hired for a fixed period, as opposed to the day labourer or seasonal worker.

STANITSA—large village in the regions inhabited by the Cossacks.

STIKHIYA—spontaneous force; refers most often to the influence exerted on the proletariat or Party by the petty-bourgeois masses.

STO—*Sovet Truda i Oborony*: Council of Labour and Defence. A committee attached to the Council of People's Commissars, whose main function after the Civil War was the co-ordination of the administration of the national economy.

TORGASH—Shopkeeper, trader, sometimes used familiarly as 'shark'.

TOVARISHCHESTVO—association.

TOVARNOST—'marketability': alternatively, capacity to produce for the market.

TOZ—*Tovarishchestvo po obshchestvennoi obrabotki zemli*: an association for the common cultivation of land. In this, the simplest form of kolkhoz, only the land and heavy implements were held in common. Livestock, dwellings, much of the equipment, and even part of the land continued to be privately cultivated. The *artel* was collectivized to a greater degree, though less so than the *kommuna*.

TROIKA—committee of three, usually formed to deal with an emergency.

TSEKIST—familiar title for a member of the Central Committee.

TSIK—*Tsentralny Ispolnitelny Komitet*: the Central Executive Committee elected by the Congress of Soviets. Its role was similar to that of the Presidium of the Supreme Soviet today. See *VTsIK*.

TSKK—*Tsentralnaya Kommissiya Kontrolya*: the Central Control Commission, a Party organ elected by the Party Congress.

TSSU—*Tsentralnoe Statisticheskoe Upravlenie*: The Central Statistical Administration.

URYADNIK—village policeman.

VERKHUSHKA—the summit; the upper stratum of a social group.

VERSTA—old measure of distance; 1·06 kilometres.

VIK—the *ispolkom* of the *volost*.

VOLOST—see OBLAST.

VSNKh—*Vysshi Sovet Narodnogo Khozyaistva*: Supreme Council of the National Economy; a sort of super-ministry which managed all of industry until 1932, when the industrial commissariats were formed, and it was abolished.

VTSIK—The *TsIK* of the Russian Republic (RSFSR).

VYROZHDENIE—see PEREROZHDENIE.

VYSELOK—hamlet.

ZAGOTOVITEL—person in charge of ZAGOTOVKI, procurements official.

ZAGOTOVKI—agricultural procurements carried out by the State.

ZASORENNOST—a state of infiltration by 'foreign elements'.

ZAZHITOCHNY—better off (peasant).

ZEMOBSHCHESTVO—*Zemelnoe Obshchestvo*: Soviet juridical term for the rural community.

ZEMORGANY—local administrations of NARKOMZEM.

INDEX OF NAMES AND SUBJECTS

(excluding names of authors)

Administrirovanie, 83, 125, 181

Agrominimum, 179, 411

Andreev, 222, 299, 302, 459; and dekulakization, 474

Associations, simple producers', 100–1, 269, 276

Associations, 'wild' so-called, 100–1

Astrov (editor of *Pravda*, Bukharinist), 229, 271, 301–2, 304

Baranov, 467

Batrak, 42, 49–52, 158, 285, 416, 501; in the Party, 121

Bauman (Moscow Secretary), 93, 227, 229, 240–1, 276, 438; on collectivization, 358

Bazarov (economist), 349; on the kulak, 74

Bednyak (*bednota*), 28, 30–1, 36, 42, 44–5, 52–60, 113, 115, 137, 158–9, 226–7, 271, 284–5, 387–8, 484–5, 488, 489

Bubnov, 24

Budenny (Marshal), 34–5

Bukharin, 12–15, 259, 260, 294–336, 368, 370; the watchword 'Get rich', 42, 165; on the kulak, 1925, 74; on co-operation, 1925, 94–5; on the kolkhoz, 1925, 116; his views in 1925–6, 135–142; attack on Preobrazhensky, 148–52; initial differences with Stalin, 298; relieved of his functions, 325; his theories in 1929, 325–36. *See also* Right

Bureaucracy (bureaucratization of the régime), 156, 188–91, 334–5

Campbell, 306

Chastnik (Nepman), 192, 200; the ousting of, 280, 370–1. *See also* Trade (private)

Churchill, 516

Columns, tractor, 364, 366, 410, 419, 422–3

Collectivization, 107, 108, 109–10, 401, 409, 414, 429–36, 454–69, 514–19; opinions of the Left on, 156; Stalin's views prior to 1927, 163; at the 15th Congress, 198, 206–9; under the Five-Year Plan, 357–8; *sploshnaya*, 429, 433, 458–9, 475; kolkhoz strategy, 358–68; views of *Gosplan*, 357–8. *See also* Kolkhoz

Commission of the Politburo on collectivization, 461, 465–6; sub-committee on dekulakization, 475–6, 487, 492

Communists, rural, 84, 119–26, 434

Conciliatory attitude, 312–13, 331

Contract system (*kontraktatsiya*), 207, 268–9, 270–1, 278, 355, 373, 407, 408

Co-operation, 93–102, 198, 256, 354–8, 406–7, 426, 515; Bukharin's views on, 136–8; Preobrazhensky's views on, 155

Dekulakization, 228, 281, 299–300, 371, 389, 469, 474–6, 482–509; decisions of the Politburo commission, 475–6; 1929–30, 482–509

Dubrovsky, 73

Dvor, 25–6, 92

Frumkin (deputy-commissar of Finance), 48, 174, 299, 300, 301, 309, 316

Gaister, 49, 53
Gorky, 22, 25
G.P.U. (OGPU), 203, 205, 241, 310, 315, 371, 447, 487, 497, 500, 502, 503, 505

Industrialization: Bukharin's views in 1925, 139–40; Trotsky's views on, 142–3; and the Left in 1927, 165; Preobrazhensky's view on, 148–55; views of Stalin prior to 1927, 163; at the 15th Congress, 201–2; Stalin's views at the end of 1928, 288; criticized by Bukharin, 331–3; Stalin in 1929, 374–5; cost of over-rapid industrialization, 395–401; situation at the end of 1929, 453–4
Instruction (provided for the peasants): 24–5

Kaganovich, 25, 302–3, 312, 446; on the *serednyak*, 285–6
Kalinin, 35, 37, 70, 76, 77, 164, 181, 204, 276, 295, 299, 306, 372, 424; and the kulak in 1929, 470
Kalmanovich (head of the sovkhoz administration), 277
Kamenev, 157, 162, 166, 260, 307, 308, 320, 324
Kaminsky (chairman of *Kolkhoztsentr*), 98, 183, 430, 435, 436, 458, 465, 466, 473.
Khataevich (Central Committee, Secretary of Middle Volga), 465, 495, 501
Khrushchev, 322, 335
Khutor (and *Otrub*), 85, 230, 470
Kolkhoz, 107–19, 163, 255, 306, 322, 406–11, 454–7; definition of collective forms: commune (*Kommuna*), 110; *artel* 110–11; *toz* 111; Stalin changes course,

250; situation at the beginning of 1928, 269–70, 271–2; plans for 1929, 273; Bukharin's views, 138, 322; Five-Year Plan objectives, 350–1; giant kolkhozes, 407, 409, 427, 473; growth in 1929, 426–39; situation at the end of 1929, 455–6; situation from 1930, 518–19. *See also* Collectivization
Kolkhoztsentr, 274, 352, 360, 409, 421, 424, 426–7, 433, 435, 436, 438, 467, 472–3
Kolkhozsoyuzy (kolkhoz unions), 409–10
Kolkhozkombinaty, 429, 462
Kombedy, 54, 81, 133, 219
Komarov, 305
Kosior (S.), 88, 217, 466, 467
Kostrov, 449
Kritsman, 47, 51, 72–3; on the kulak, 75; on the dual nature of the revolution, 133
Krupskaya, 24, 318–19, 325
Krylenko (Republican *Prokuror*), 504–5
Krzhizhanovsky (Chairman of *Gosplan*), 209, 345, 398
Kubyak (*Narkomzem*), 230, 275, 276, 300, 360, 460
Kuibyshev, 279, 346, 353
Kulak, 71–8, 182, 186–7, 204–5, 210, 218–19, 221, 222, 227, 235, 254, 260, 435, 455; Bukharin's views on, 43, 138–9; in the *mir*, 91–2; the kulak's market production, 175; restrictive measures against them in 1928, 281–3; individual levy, 282; *samoraskulachivanie*, 286; weakening of their position in 1928 and 1929, 415–16; provisions of the Five-Year Plan, 352–3, 357; terrorist activity, 393–4, 473, 486; discussion in the Party, mid-1929, 470–1; at the November 1929 Plenum, 473; as a political force, 471–2;

defined by the government, 490–1; repressive measures in 1929, 389–90. *See also* Dekulakization

Kviring, 276

Larin, 26, 72

Latsis, 276

Left (the), 13–14, 51, 142–59, 188, 190–1; and collectivization, 154–6; 157–8; and bureaucratization, 188–90. *See also* Trotsky, Preobrazhensky

Lenin, 23, 41, 318–19, 327, 329, 330, 333, 335; on the cultural revolution, 23–4; on the definition of the *serednyak*, 65–6; on co-operation, 94; on the definition of the revolution, 133; and Stalin, 165–6

Lominadze, 388, 470

Lyashchenko, 50–1, 55–6, 107

Lyubchenko, 366

Markevich, 362, 363, 366

Meshochniki, 384

Mikoyan, 210, 217, 221, 225, 231, 236, 276, 302, 408, 412, 413, 473

Milyutin, 72, 101

Mir, 26–7, 85–93, 355

Molotov, 52, 54–5, 68, 72, 115, 116, 121, 164, 187, 200, 203, 205, 206, 207, 300, 302, 304, 305, 315, 446, 458–9, 465

M.T.S., 359, 361–4, 365, 366, 410, 422

N.E.P., 133–5, 142, 148, 150, 172, 177, 186, 200, 203, 204, 207, 226, 235, 236–7, 516; as seen by the peasants, 27; shifts in Party policy with regard to the peasants, 66; in its second phase (Neo-NEP), 41–2, 69, 135, 177–8; and the position of the *bednyak*, 69; Bukharin's views in 1929, 327–9

Osinsky, 302

Ordzhonikidze, 306, 316, 471

Perekachka: Preobrazhensky on, 151–2; Rykov on, 202–3, 309. *See also* Tribute

Plan, Five-Year, 276–7, 344–9, 374–5; at the 15th Congress, 201–2; for agriculture, 351–358. *See also* Industrialization

Podkulachnik, 260, 391, 494, 508

Preobrazhensky, 14, 145, 448; on co-operation, 95, 155; theory of primitive accumulation, 148–54

Prices, agricultural, 182–5, 242, 287, 296, 303, 384–5, 388

Production, agricultural, in 1925–7, 172–5; in 1928–9, 383–4, 399–400, 447

Pyatakov, 298, 320, 451

Radek, 448

Rakovsky, 189–90, 448, 451

Religion (among the peasants), 22–3

Right (the); 294–336. *See also* Bukharin, 'Three'

R.K.I., 58, 85, 109, 112, 118

Rozit, 370

Rykov, 162, 164–5, 202, 209, 214, 230, 240, 294, 295, 309–10, 315–16, 323, 324, 360; changed attitude on industrialization, 202–3; his proposed *dvuletka*, 350–1. *See also* 'Three'

Savelev, 331

Selsovet, 26, 81–4, 222, 223, 267, 392–3, 411, 413, 416, 418; and the *mir*, 89; the *mir* brought under control of, 284

Serednyak, 43, 45, 46, 55, 56, 65–71, 77, 221, 224, 229, 231, 232, 235, 251–2, 261, 387, 390, 417, 429, 434, 454–7; attitude to the poor peasants, 28; shifts in policy with regard to, 66–7; in

the *mir*, 91–2; dekulakization of, 504–5
Shakhty affair, 261–2
Shatskin, 449–50, 470
Sheboldaev (Secretary of Lower Volga), 388, 461, 465
Shvernik, 217, 312
Slepkov (Bukharinist), 298
Smilga, 448
Smirnov, A.P. (*Narkomzem*), 230; view of the kulak, 74; on the *mir*, 92
Smirnov, Ivan (Trotskyist), 377, 448
Smychka (alliance), 69–71, 132, 135, 242, 251–2, 302, 303–4, 327–8, 336; Trotsky's view of, 143–44; Preobrazhensky's view of, 152–4; Stalin's view of, 251–2; the Stalinist version of, 286; 'metal-based', 258, 328, 336
'Socialism in one country', 148
Sokolnikov, 202, 302, 304, 306, 308, 320
Sosnovsky (Trotskyist), 224–5
Sovkhoz, 255–6, 277–8, 306, 328, 362–4, 421, 436–7; under the Five-Year Plan, 353–7; 'Shevchenko', 276
Stalin, 12–15, 142–3, 157, 159–66, 182, 205, 206–7, 217–18, 234, 235, 237, 238, 239, 240, 275, 279, 287–8, 398, 455–7, 466, 468, 476–7, 491, 515, 516–18; on the better-off peasant, 49; on the kulak, 72, 205, 237–8; defence of Bukharin, 164; procurements campaign of 1928, 217–18; the 'turn' of 1928; 250–65; tactics against the Right, 295–6, 300–1, 303, 307–9, 311–15, 316, 322, 324–5, 368–70; his theories during 1929, 374–7; the 'cult', 450–3
Stetsky, 302, 304, 305
Sten, 449–50
Strong, A. L., 393–4, 488–9, 506

Strumilin, 45, 48, 53, 75, 184, 345–6
Sukhanov, 73, 88, 93, 356
Svi'dersky, 230
'Sympathizers', 314–15. *See also* Conciliatory attitude

Teodorovich, 230
'Three' (*troika*: Bukharin, Rykov, Tomsky), 278, 300, 307–8, 315, 317, 320, 323–4, 325; capitulation of, 451
Tomsky, 164, 230, 295, 298, 306, 312, 317, 324, 328, 329. *See also* 'Three'
Tovarnost, 175–8,, 183–4, 257
Trade, private, 186–8, 280, 389. *See also* Chastnik
Traktortsentr, 410
Tribute (*dan*), 258, 303, 305, 322. *See also* Perekachka
Trotsky, 13–15, 41, 142–6, 147, 148, 163, 166, 237, 264, 318, 448–9; and collectivization, 155; influence on Stalin, 254–5; and bureaucratization, 190–1; his view of tendencies within the C.C., 294; attitude to Bukharin in 1928, 308; expulsion from the
Tsylko, 272, 422–3

USSR, 318
Uglanov, 157, 298, 302, 312

Valentinov (Volsky), 204
Vareikis (Secretary, Central Black Earth Region), 422, 431–2, 434, 465
Vodka, 32
Volf (agricultural division of *Gosplan*), 173, 352–3, 354
Voroshilov, 299, 303, 306, 309
Vserabotzemles, 52

Yagoda (head of *GPU*), 447
Yakovlev (deputy-commissar of R.K.I., Commissar of Agriculture), 113, 209, 270, 276

Yaroslavsky (presidium of the Central Control Commission), 120, 124

Zagotovki (agricultural procurements), 54, 177–8, 184–7, 210, 216–17, 230–1, 239, 240, 281, 296–8, 406; procurements crisis of 1928, 214–44; situation at the end of 1928, 286–7; the winter of 1929, 385–95; campaign at the end of 1929, 412–14; and collectivization, 454

Zazhitochny, 43, 48–9, 66, 69, 77, 228–9, 255, 261, 281, 387, 389, 394, 483, 487, 491

Zemleustroistvo, 29, 87, 114, 179, 271, 283

Zhdanov, 217

Zinovev, 42, 143–4, 157, 159, 449

NORTON BOOKS IN RUSSIAN AND SOVIET HISTORY

Paul Avrich *Kronstadt 1921* • *Russian Rebels, 1600-1800*
M. M. Bober *Karl Marx's Interpretation of History*
Emile Capouya and Keitha Tompkins, eds. *The Essential Kropotkin*
Edward Hallett Carr *The Bolshevik Revolution, 1917–1923*, Vol. I • *The Bolshevik Revolution, 1917–1923*, Vol. II • *The Bolshevik Revolution, 1917–1923*, Vol. III
Harvey Firestone *Soviet Psychoprisons*
John G. Gurley *Challengers to Capitalism: Marx, Lenin, Stalin, Mao*
John Keep *The Russian Revolution*
George F. Kennan *The Decision to Intervene* (Soviet-American Relations, 1917–1920, I) • *Russia Leaves the War* (Soviet-American Relations, 1917–1920, Vol. II)
Alexandra Kollontai *A Great Love* • *Selected Writings*
Thomas B. Larson *Soviet-American Rivalry*
Moshe Lewin *Russian Peasants and Soviet Power: A Study of Collectivization*
Roy A. Medvedev *Nikolai Bukharin* • *On Socialist Democracy*
Roy A. Medvedev and Zhores A. Medvedev *Khrushchev: The Years in Power*
Roy A. Medvedev, ed. *An End to Silence: Uncensored Opinion in the Soviet Union, from* Political Diary • *The Samizdat Register*
Zhores A. Medvedev *Andropov* • *Nuclear Disaster in the Urals* • *Soviet Science*
Zhores A. Medvedev and Roy A. Medvedev *A Question of Madness: Repression by Psychiatry in the Soviet Union*
Alexander Nekritch *The Punished Peoples: The Deportation and Fate of Soviet Minorities at the End of the Second World War*
Alexander Rabinowitch *The Bolsheviks Come to Power: The Revolution of 1917 in Petrograd*
Varlam Shalamov *Graphite* • *Kolyma Tales*
Robert C. Tucker *The Marxian Revolutionary Idea* • *Stalin as Revolutionary, 1879-1929*
Robert C. Tucker, ed. *The Lenin Anthology* • *The Marx-Engels Reader* • *Stalinism*